Mathematical Theory of Production Planning

Alain BENSOUSSAN

University Paris-Dauphine
Paris, France
and
INRIA - Domaine de Voluceau
Rocquencourt, Le Chesnay, France

Michel CROUHY

CESA (HEC-ISA-CFC)
Jouy-en-Josas
France

and

Jean-Marie PROTH

INRIA - Domaine de Voluceau
Rocquencourt, Le Chesnay
France

N·H
P C

1983

NORTH-HOLLAND
AMSTERDAM · NEW YORK · OXFORD

ISBN: 0 444 86740 6

Publishers:

ELSEVIER SCIENCE PUBLISHERS B.V.
P.O. Box 1991
1000 BZ Amsterdam
The Netherlands

Sole distributors for the U.S.A. and Canada:

ELSEVIER SCIENCE PUBLISHING COMPANY, INC.
52 Vanderbilt Avenue
New York, N.Y. 10017
U.S.A.

Library of Congress Cataloging in Publication Data

Bensoussan, Alain.
Mathematical theory of production planning.

(Advanced series in management ; v. 3)
Bibliography: p.
1. Production planning--Mathematical models.
I. Crouhy, Michel, 1944- . II. Proth, Jean-Marie, 1938- . III. Title. IV. Series.
TS176.B46 1983 658.5'03'0724 83-13295
ISBN 0-444-86740-6 (U.S.)

PRINTED IN THE NETHERLANDS

MATHEMATICAL THEORY OF PRODUCTION PLANNING

Advanced Series in Management

Volume 3

Series Editors

A. BENSOUSSAN

University Paris-Dauphine
and INRIA
Paris, France

and

P. A. NAERT

European Institute for
Advanced Studies in Management
Brussels, Belgium

NORTH-HOLLAND
AMSTERDAM · NEW YORK · OXFORD

EXTENSIVE DESCRIPTION OF THE BOOK

This book proposes a unified mathematical treatment of production planning and production smoothing problems, in the framework of optimal control theory. General concave and convex cost models which relate most closely to real life applications are considered. Planning horizon results are always central to the discussion and developments. They allow to consider only finite horizon problems, and guarantee that the production plan implemented over the first periods is optimal with regard to any demand pattern beyond the planning horizon. Algorithms are proposed to compute the optimal production policy, together with the corresponding softwares designed to be implemented on any microcomputer.

The book is organized in seven chapters and one mathematical appendix. The following topics are covered.

Demand is deterministic in the first three chapters and stochastic in chapter 4. The formulation is in discrete time except in chapter 3 where time is continuous. In chapter I we consider production planning with concave production and inventory costs. Chapter II considers the case of convex cost production planning and production smoothing models. In chapter III we extend the models developed in chapters I and II to a continuous time formulation. Two alternative techniques are used : continuous control and impulse control. In chapter IV we address the problem of production planning and production smoothing in a stochastic environment. In chapters V to VII we propose different softwares corresponding to the previous theoretical developments.

Finally a mathematical appendix provides the reader with all the necessary background in order to make the book self-content.

The last section of the first four chapters comments our results, and relates them to the relevant literature. They can be read as an initial motivation, independently of the mathematical derivations.

CONTENTS

INTRODUCTION

PRODUCTION PLANNING IN PERSPECTIVE

Production planning is primarily concerned with the adaptation, or more exactly the tuning of the firm's industrial resources, in order to meet demand for its final products. The production manager has the responsibility to implement the production plan, once it has been agreed upon by the "planning committee". The production manager must then take all decisions to make sure that the necessary capacity and qualified workforce, the required materials and components will be available in right quantity, at the right place, at the right time ; the objective is to fulfil a marketing plan at minimum overall cost.

Production planning becomes a challenging problem for at least three important reasons :

1 - Demand and costs vary over time, usually according to a seasonal pattern. This calls for some adjustment in the production capacity and the use of it. Moreover, it is difficult to precisely forecast demand at the most detailed level of the end products. At regular intervals the marketing plan must be revised, and as a consequence the production plan also.

2 - There is in the firm less and less flexibility to modify the operating conditions. Rigidities are at a peak with regard to labor management. At least in some countries, any change in the size of the labor force, resort to overtime and temporary manpower must be negociated with the unions, and the (regional bureau of the) labor department. Moreover, too many frequent changes in operating conditions may deteriorate the workers' morale and affect productivity.

3 - There are long and uncertain technical delays in obtaining industrial resources. These are : delays to install new machines, to train new workers, to negociate subcontracting capacity, to deliver materials and components from suppliers. These long delays are often the consequence of the rigidities borne by the other firms. In addition, suppliers are ready to allow clients substantial rebates if they are able to sign yearly blanket orders with some indication of demand distribution, for some families of products. Usually, detailed supply schedules are only notified on short notice. A longer forecast horizon gives the suppliers the opportunity to plan more efficiently their production, and to pass on their clients part of the cost reduction so obtained.

There is therefore an apparent contradiction between :

- the need for more flexibility and the necessity to quickly adjust the production plan with respect to changes which have occured in the commercial objectives,

- and, the relatively fixed production capacity available in the short run, with strong pressure for long term commitments concerning material procurement, work force and subcontracting.

The solution to overcome this conflict is more planning with an adequate planning horizon which, in any rate, must be greater than the seasonal cycle and the production lead time. This medium range horizon is usually one year, but may be longer up to two years for heavy industries where the production lead time is in the order of one year. However, it is practically impossible on this medium range horizon to forecast demand at the most detailed level, neither to plan precisely the industrial resources.

As a consequence, firms must adopt a two stage production planning process : production planning is first conducted at the aggregate level over the medium range horizon,and mainly concerns capacity and procurement planning in the aggregate ; then, in the short run detailed plans, named production schedules, are released. Only these detailed plans can be implemented. They are derived from short run forecasts and must satisfy the constraints imposed by the aggregate plans. We shall elaborate on the production planning process in the first section.

Obviously, in a steady state environment where not only demand, but also the cost structure would not change with time, the aggregate planning stage could be entirely bypassed . Capacity and procurement planning would be made once for all, and the only problem left to the production manager would be the implementation of the detailed production schedules, and short run capacity adjustments due to day to day operational aleas like machine break-downs, late deliveries of materials, absenteeism , ... Real life industrial environments are unfortunately more intricate than this ideal situation.

Over the medium range horizon,capital resources like expensive machines, which determine the base plant size, are assumed to be fixed. The delay in installing new pieces of equipment is generally longer than this horizon. Paradoxically this does not imply that production capacity is fixed. There is still the possibility to regulate, or smooth, capacity through the combined change of flexible resources which are complementary to capital equipments. In practice the capacity slack is quite important and production planning encompasses a wide range of decisions. The following represents the main alternatives opened to a production manager to smooth capacity (see Buffa and Taubert [1972]) :

- change the size of the work force through hiring and firing of workers ;

- use overtime in peak demand periods and idle time when demand is low, to vary the production rate while maintaining the work force level constant ;

- absorb excess demand through outside subcontracting ;

- build seasonal inventories during periods of slack activity in anticipation of higher demand in a near future ;

- resort either to planned backlogs in peak demand periods whenever customers are willing to accept a longer delivery lead time, or to lost sales otherwise.

The next two decisions are still relevant to production smoothing but relate to a higher level of management :

- adopt a pricing policy combined with advertising campains in order to induce customers to shift their buying decision from peak to off season ;

- adopt a mix of product lines which use the same resources (machines and labor skills) but with counter seasonal demand cycles.

However, internal and environmental constraints may limit, or even forbid the use of some of these practices. For a more elaborate discussion of these smoothing techniques and examples, see Crouhy [1983].

The optimal combination of these smoothing techniques involves the search for the minimum cost tradeoff inside the following cost structure :

- Regular time costs associated with operations under normal conditions and which include direct and overhead costs. We can further split direct costs into fixed (set-up costs for example) and variable costs.

- Overtime and undertime penalty costs which consists of a wage rate premium for overtime work, and costs associated with maintaining an idle work force in the other case.

- Subcontracting costs which correspond to a premium over production costs in regular time, the expenses associated with monitoring subcontracted production, and the cost of duplicating some tools.

- Costs of changing the production rate which are associated with hiring, training or laying off workers. There are also costs of reorganizing production in the workshops like new line balancing of assembly lines, machine set-up, ... and the opportunity losses during the transition period due to quality problems and adjustment to new operating conditions.

- Inventory costs which include :

  . holding costs : financing, storage, insurance, depreciation,...
  . shortage costs due to backlogged demand and lost sales, which include extra cost of expediting late orders, loss of consumer goodwill, lost profits, ...

A detailed discussion of the nature and the structure of these costs may be found in McGarrah [1963] ; see also Holt et al. [1960, Chapters 2 and 3] for quadratic approximations of these cost elements.

I - THE PRODUCTION PLANNING PROCESS

From our introductory comments, it is now clear that a production plan cannot be implemented efficiently with a short sight view. It forces the production manager to plan ahead of time simply because manufacturing resources are not fully flexible, and there is an incompressible procurement and manufacturing lead time.

Moreover, the optimal economic tradeoff among the smoothing techniques can only be reached over a minimum length period, given the seasonal demand pattern for the final products. It is called the medium range planning horizon, and as we mentioned ealier it varies between one and two years. Usually it is one year which corresponds to the budget cycle. Since the plans are reviewed periodically, say monthly on a rolling horizon basis, it is important to avoid discountinuities in the planned production decisions for the last months of the horizon, at each update. Therefore demand is forecasted over a forecast horizon, longer than the planning horizon, usually 1.5 times the length of the planning horizon.

Over this forecast horizon it is practically impossible to forecast demand at the level of the detailed end product references, which may vary from one another just by the size, color, packaging, or some optional accessories.

For this basic reason a production plan can only be elaborated at the <u>aggregate</u>

level of product families, where a family is a group of items which share common manufacturing resources (machines and labor skills). Each item corresponds to the most detailed end product reference. Moreover demand forecasted at the family level should be a good approximation of the sum of the ex-post realized demands at the item level. Experience shows that aggregate forecasts are rather accurate.

Only a small number of aggregate plans need to be made for a wide range of items. In some industries like hosiery,farming equipments, electronic ... the aggregation ratio is in the order of one family for one hundred items.

With a medium range view of the firm's activity,not only item demand must be aggregated in family demand, but also machines in load centers, labor skills in manpower classes, materials and components in procurement groups, and so on. The aggregation process may differ from one industry to another and should always be ad hoc to the precise environment of the firm.

Hax and Meal [1975] consider a third level of product aggregation which they call "type",where each type includes families of items which have the same seasonal demand pattern and the same production rate. In such instance aggregate plans are developed at the type level. However, in most industrial cases two levels of aggregation are enough to solve the aggregate planning problem.

Detailed production plans at the item level are provided only in the short run,up to an horizon of one to six months, for which detailed forecasts are made possible. Detailed schedules may proceed from individual forecasts at the item level but they must fit in the aggregate constraints which concern production rates, workforce levels, overtime and idle time, supply of componentsand materials. Rationing or inventory building may occur depending whether the sum of the detailed requirements is higher or smaller than the aggregate forecast. Figure 1 summarizes the articulation between both planning levels (see also Meal [1978]).

Both aggregate and detailed plans are revised on a rolling horizon basis, monthly for the first ones, weakly for the second ones, from updated information on demand, capacity, costs,suppliers lead time, ... Because of the uncertainties on these data,only the first periods (frozen horizon) of the plans are implemented. The length of the frozen horizon is dictated by the procurement and manufacturing lead time.

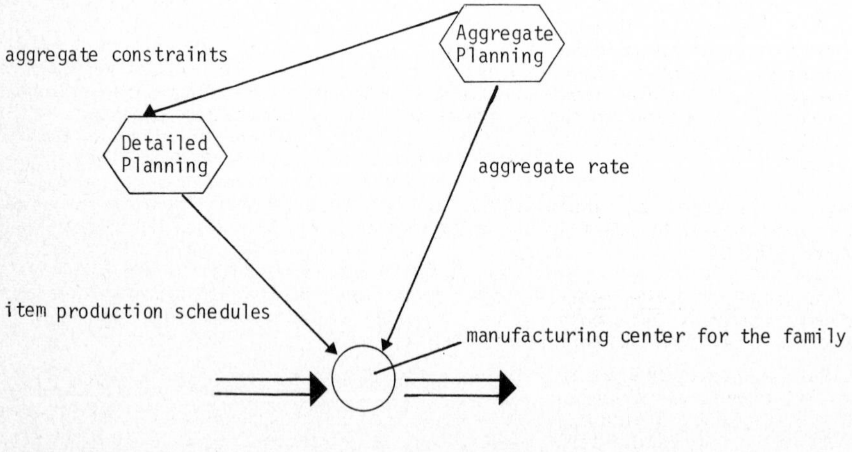

FIGURE 1 : Consistency between aggregate and detailed planning

To sum up, aggregate planning must be viewed as capacity and procurement planning in the aggregate. Total capacity is allocated among all the product families. Smoothing techniques are used to find the minimum total production cost at the aggregate level. Aggregate plans determine for each product family and each month over the entire planning horizon :

- the production rates,
- the work force levels,
- the number of worked hours (idle time and overtime),
- seasonal inventories and stockouts,
- the quantities to be delivered of materials and components by supply groups.

On the other hand, these aggregate outputs are aggregate constraints which must be satisfied by the short run detailed production schedules.

In addition, aggregate planning corresponds to the operational phase of the budgeting process, which deals with physical quantities. Budgets are obtained simply by direct valuation of aggregate plans.

II - MAIN SCOPE OF THE BOOK

There is an extensive literature on aggregate production planning models which starts in the mid-1950's with the pioneering works of Holt, Modigliani, Muth and Simon (HMMS) [1960].

Roughly there are two broad classes of models depending on the nature of the cost structure involved :

1 - Production planning models which include only two cost elements : a production cost $c_t(v_t)$ where v_t denotes the production level in period t, and an inventory cost $f_t(y_t)$ where y_t denotes the inventory level at the beginning of period t ; $f_t(y_t)$ refers to a holding cost or a shortage cost whether y_t is positive or negative. Obviously production planning models are just lot sizing models considered in a production instead of a distribution (or procurement) environment.

Analytical techniques and properties of the optimal production policy differ whether the cost structure is concave or convex, i.e. describes a production process with economies or diseconomies of scale. Concave cost functions allow for set-up costs which are ubiquitous in production, and constitute key elements in the short run production scheduling decision ; however,they are often neglected at the aggregate planning level when we deal with product families. The concave cost litterature relates to the seminal work by Wagner and Within [1959] , while the convext cost literature follows the initial contribution of Modigliani and Hohn [1955].

Surveys of the major contributions and expositions of the techniques in inventory theory are proposed by Scarf [1963] and Veinott [1966]. See also Johnson and Montgomery [1974].

2 - Production smoothing models which in addition to production and inventory costs consider adjustment (or smoothing) costs usually associated with a change in the production level from one period to the next : $g_t(v_{t-1},v_t)$. They may possibly be directly related to changes in the work force level,when the number of workers is an explicit decision variable in the model formulation. These adjustment costs are mostly hiring and training expenses, set-up charges for additional equipment when production is increased ; firing costs, and overheads for equipments used below normal capacity, when production is reduced.

General reviews of the contributions in this area are due to Silver [1967], Buffa and Taubert [1972], Johnson and Montgomery [1974], Peterson and Silver [1979] and Hax [1979], the latter being the most comprehensive.

Table 1 drawn from Kleindorfer et al. [1975] sketches the major classes of assumptions and the most common alternatives incorporated in production planning and production smoothing models. Mutually exclusive alternatives are bracketed within each class.

The purpose of this book is to extend the single product models, and to consider the most general versions workable in the framework of optimal control theory. Only general concave and convex cost models, which relate most closely to real life applications, are analyzed. Ad hoc formulations which, for computational purpose, have adopted linear costs or even quadratic costs will not be discussed. They are simply special cases of more general formulations for which we are able to propose algorithms to compute the optimal production policy. We also provide the reader with the corresponding softwares which are easy to implement on any minicomputer.

Planning horizon results will be always central to our discussion and developments. Roughly H is said to be a "planning horizon" if for any problem horizon greater than H, the period 1 to H portion of the optimal production plan stays unaffected. Rigorous definitions will be given in Chapter I, section III.4. These results are of great value for practical purpose, since they allow to consider only finite horizon problems and guarantee the production manager, that the production plan implemented over the first periods (frozen horizon) is optimal with regard to any demand pattern beyond the planning horizon.

Since we are mainly interested in analytical techniques, we shall not comment on the various heuristic decision rules which have proliferated in the literature.

The book is organized in seven chapters and one mathematical appendix. The following topics are covered.

Demand is deterministic in the first three chapters and stochastic in chapter IV. The formulation is in discrete time except in chapter III where time is continuous. In chapter I we consider production planning with concave production and inventory costs. Chapter II considers the case of convex cost production planning and production smoothing models. In chapter III we extend the models developed in chapter I and II to a continuous time formulation. Two alternative techniques will be used : continuous control and impulse control. In chapter IV we address the problem of production planning and production smoothing in a stochastic environment. In chapters V to VII we propose different softwares corresponding to the previous theoretical developments. Finally a mathematical appendix provides the reader with all the necessary background in order to make the book self-content.

The last section of the first four chapters comments our results and relates them to the relevant literature. They can be read as an initial motivation, independently of the mathematical derivations.

Table 1 : General classification of production planning and production smoothing model assumptions

Products	Demand	Problem Horizon	Cost Elements	Cost Functions	Constraints
Single Multiple	Deterministic Known Cumulative Convex Concave Monotone Increasing Decreasing Stochastic Stationary Non-stationary	Finite Infinite	Direct production Output units Work force Payroll Overtime Inventory Lost sales Back orders Smoothing Production rate Work force level Both Revenues Price-independent demand Demand function	Continuous Discrete Both Convex Concave Linear (piecewise linear) Set-up plus - Marginal Costs Increasing Decreasing Monotone Intertemporal Discounting Stationary Non-stationary Non-decreasing marginals	Stock-flow identity (inventory balance) Non-negative inventory Backlogging Lost sales Initial/Terminal Conditions Decision variables State variables Capacities Production Work force hours Inventories

III - CRITICAL ISSUES WHICH ARE NOT ADDRESSED IN THIS BOOK

There are at least two critical issues related to production planning which are not addressed in this book.

The first one concerns the disaggregation of the aggregate plan into detailed production schedules, for the items which compose the product family.

The second issue relates to the need for coordinated multi-echelon production planning when the production process (more generally the logistics system) must be decomposed into several levels which broadly correspond to materials and parts, sub-assemblies, assemblies and possibly distribution, with decoupling inventories between each echelon.

III - 1. DISAGGREGATION OF THE AGGREGATE PRODUCTION PLAN

One way to address this problem would be to develop simultaneously the aggregate plan for the product family and the detailed schedules for the items. Our earlier comments made it clear that this approach is not practical simply because demand at the item level can be forecasted accurately only in the very short run.

However, there has been numerous attemps to solve the overall multi-item production planning problem, with a monolithic formulation which relies on mixed-integer mathematical programming. Hax [1979, pp. 144-151] and Johnson and Montgomery [1974, pp. 242-258] provide detailed discussions of this approach, and excellent review of the basic contributions.

Solving these models present enormous technical difficulties because of the large number of variables, part of them being integer associated with set-up costs. Indeed you may easily end up with several hundred products to schedule over 12 to 18 months, which make several thousand variables. Then, the programs must be run each month on a rolling horizon basis with updated information . Most of the contributions thus develop ad hoc decomposition heuristics to circumvent the dimensionality problem.

A much more powerful and relevant approach to coordinate aggregate planning and detailed scheduling, consists in developing a hierarchical planning system with two levels of decision. The aggregate level decision imposes constraints on the lower level corresponding to scheduling ; then, the bottom level decision sends the necessary feedback to the higher level for updating and corrective action. This alternative approach has been developed by Hax and Meal [1975] and further extended by Bitran and Hax [1977]. Hax and Golovin [1978-1] report on these works and related contributions. See also Peterson and Silver [1979, chapter 18].

At the higher decision level an aggregate capacity planning technique must be adopted and implemented for each product family on the medium range horizon. The aggregate plan determines the monthly production rates which constrain the sum of the production rates for the set of items belonging to the family. This will assure the consistency between the aggregate and detailed plans. In more general formulations however, additional consistency constraints should be added regarding labor skills, material and part supplies.

Detailed schedules are only developed for the first period (s), and the consistency should be achieved at the minimum short run cost, usually the sum of set-up and shortage costs.

There are several disaggregation methods proposed in the literature , which are reviewed by Hax and Golovin [1978-1]. They all consist in heuristics with compute the batch quantities for each item, which achieve minimum total set-up cost for the family, while equilizing the runout times for all the items of the family.

Hax and Golovin [1978-2] have developed a general software for the Hax and Meal's hierarchical planning systems.

III - 2. COORDINATION OF MULTI-ECHELON PRODUCTION SYSTEMS

So far we have implicitly assumed that production of goods can be performed in just one stage, and consequently planned entirely at the end product level. This can be the case for very simple processes which consist in the assembly of a few components or in the direct transformation of inputs.

Unfortunately most manufacturing contexts are much more complex. A product is usually elaborated in several steps from the transformation of the raw materials to the final assembly line. The technology, the required machines and labor skills, usually necessitate to distinguish between distinct semi-autonomous work centers, disconnected from each others by decoupling inventories. A typical manufacturing organization thus involves four level of inventories : raw materials, parts, sub-assemblies, and assemblies. There are also in process inventories at each transformation stage, the volume of which depends on the manufacturing lead time at this echelon.

The more complex is the product structure, the more intermediate manufacturing steps, and the more inventory points. The product structure is described by the bill of materials (figure 2). A bill of materials is much more than a part list in the sense that it shows,precisely,how the product is actually put together from raw materials and parts into sub-assemblies, and then into final assemblies. Each element of the bill of materials corresponds both to a production step with its own lead time (either the supply of materials or parts, the manufacturing of a part, a sub-assembly level or the final assembly), and also to an inventory point. The bills of materials also reflect the firm's policy to reduce the number of its inventory points by increasing the modularity of its products.

Consequently several work centers must be planned in coordination,in order to fulfil a marketing plan. The aggregate plan can only concern one of the final steps of the production process, for which aggregate forecasting makes sense. It is usually the assembly line, but in some instances it can be a former step (like the molding stage in the toy industry). In all cases the aggregate planning phase concern the production stage where all the most expensive equipments and toolings, the strategic know-how of the firm are concentrated, and for which capacity planning is essential. Here subcontracting would simply imply losing some market share in favor of the competing firms in the industry. The production plan at this stage is often called the master plan when it is considered at the aggregate level, or the master schedule at the detailed level.

Since all production stages are disconnected by decoupling inventories, production planning becomes a problem of inventory replenishment coordination.

However traditional stock replenishment techniques, i.e. "order point-order quantity" systems are not adapted to a manufacturing environment. As a matter of fact they have been developed to support the procurement function in a distribution context. Order point-order quantity systems require the individual item demands to be independent of each other,and of statistical nature. Demand must originate from a large number of independent sources which allow the use of statistical forecasting techniques to anticipate demand, and the resort to safety stocks for stockout protection.

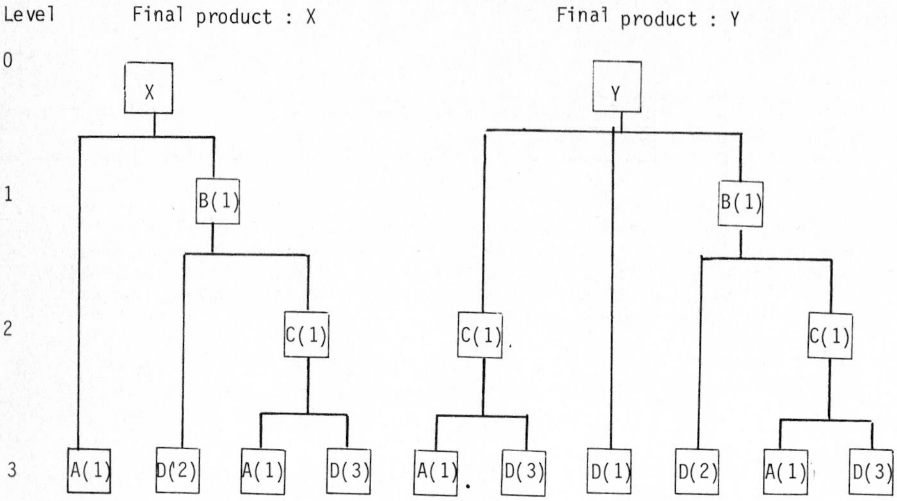

FIGURE 2 : Two examples of bills of materials.
In brackets is noted the number of components or parts required in the lower sub-assembly level (also called the "parent").

The weaknesses of these techniques when applied in a manufacturing environment are obvious. Demands for materials, parts and sub-assemblies are dependent and deterministic. They follow by simple arithmetic from the master plans (schedules), and the bills of materials which establish the link structure between individual demands. As a consequence demand fluctuations which may be of wide magnitude,have nothing to do with forecasting errors ; safety stocks are thus required to play a role for which they are not suited. Because production is run in batches, it is not unusual for a component to notice several periods of large demand followed by periods of inactivity (figure 3). In such instances safety stocks computed on the basis of historical demand fluctuations are either too large and yield unnecessary high inventory immobilisations, or are to small and provoke abnormal stockouts. Moreover,if at a parent level n components are required, then if they are managed independently the probability at the parent level to realize the assembly is $(1-\varepsilon)^n$, where ε is the allowed stockout percentage. For example, with a service level of 0.9 ($\varepsilon = 0.1$) at the individual level, the chance to find 10 different parts simultaneously is only 0.35. It is therefore not surprising when you visit a factory where inventories are managed with order point-order quantity systems, to notice there are often more products standing on the side of the assembly line because of missing parts, than being actually mounted, although you are told by the production manager that the factory is plagued with excess inventories. Crouhy [1980] provides an elaborate discussion on this matter. See also Peterson and Silver [1979, Chapter 12].

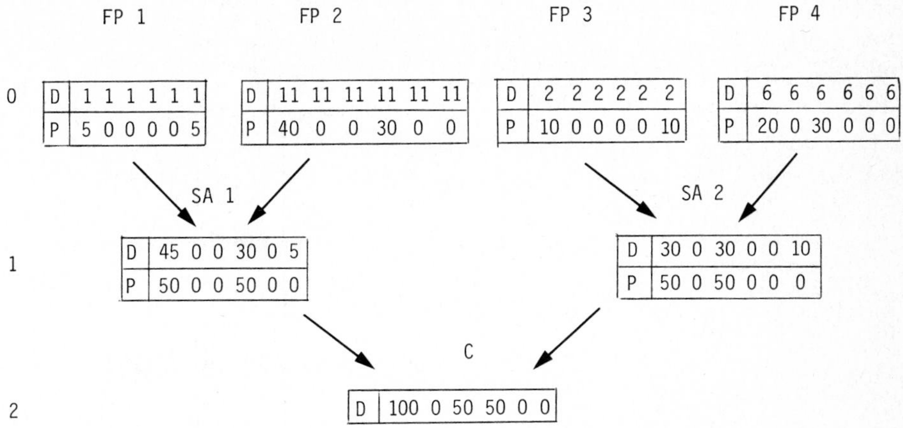

FIGURE 3 : Illustration of erratic demand patterns in production due to batch manufacturing

FP : final product
SA : sub-assembly
C : component
The arrows correspond to the link of the bills of materials, and the requirements are one unit for one unit of parent with zero lead time.

Clark and Scarf [1960] propose a decentralized procedure which fits well the organizational set up previously described, where production is conducted in semi-autonomous work centers. Their model considers an n echelon serial system with manufacturing lead time at each echelon :

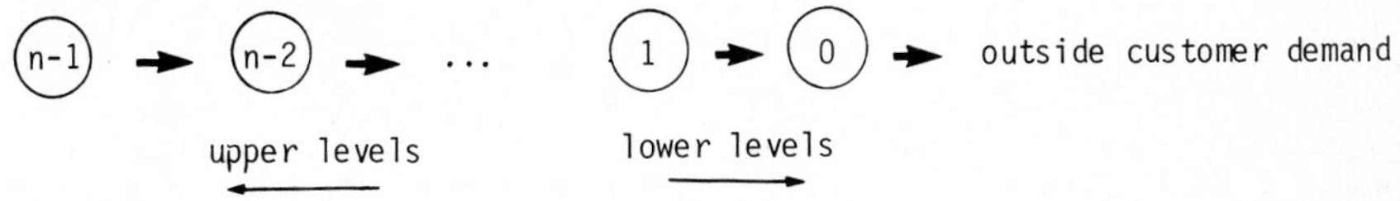

There is only one product for which exogeneous demand is stochastic and dynamic. In this model the inventory system is interpreted as a nested set of echelons where y_0 is the final product inventory, y_1 denotes the sum of y_0, in-transit inventory between echelons 1 and 0, and inventory at echelon 1, and so on for $y_2, \ldots, y_{n-1}$. Replenishment decisions are made independently starting with echelon 0, and the system is reviewed periodically. Optimal coordination is obtained through a penalty function passed on from one level (k) to the next upper level (k+1). It simply corresponds to the shortage cost due to the fact that facility k may be rationed if level (k+1) does not carry enough inventory. Production or procurement costs are linear except for facility n-1 where a set-up reorder cost is allowed.

Clark and Scarf [1962] further generalize their model by incorporating a set-up cost in production at the intermediate facilities 1 to n-2. See also Bensoussan and Crouhy [1980] for an optimal control formulation of this problem.

However, Clark and Scarf decentralization procedure has not been generalized to more complex bills of materials.

The most promizing approach to multi-echelon production planning is offered by Graves [1981]. He proposes a "multi-pass" heuristic procedure which consists in three iterative steps. In a first step single-echelon Wagner-Within problems for level 0 are solved independently. The solutions determine the demand for the higher level echelon when considering the bills of materials. In step 2 the Wagner-Within problems are solved for level 1 with demand generated by step 1. Demand is then generated for the next higher echelon and the procedure is repeated until the last echelon. Step 3 is identical to step 1 except that the production costs are revised by adding to the variable production cost at level 0, the marginal cost incurred at all higher levels.

The procedure then iterates until convergence is reached.

Still this procedure and its convergence properties are limited to simple multi-echelon assembly systems.

For other analytical approaches to the multi-echelon production planning problem consult the survey conducted by Clark [1972] which covers the literature until 1971. See also Johnson and Montgomery [1974], Crowston et al. [1973], Williams [1974], and Blackburn and Millen [1982].

Given the limitations of the analytical approaches, a sub-optimal method called Material Requirements Planning (MRP) has, over the years, forced itself among practionners. Now, good computer softwares are available which have helped the wide-spread diffusion of this technique. The best known apostles of MRP are Orlicky [1975] and Wight [1974]. The American Production and Inventory Control Society (APICS) has also been very active through its publications, in the promotion of MRP.

The basic concepts of MRP are very intuitive. However, the practicability of this method is only recent and owes a great deal to the advent of the new computer generations. Table 2 gives a quick and synthetic illustration of the MRP logic applied to an example based on the bills of materials given in figure 2.

For further discussion of MRP consult Crouhy [1983] and Peterson and Silver [1979].

Level	Item		0	1	2	3	4	5	6
0	X	Gross requirements		60	35	95	115	20	130
		On hand	(20)	60	25	135	20	0	0
		Scheduled and planned receipts		140	0	205	0	0	130
		Planned order release		205			130		
	Y	Gross requirements		10	40	50	40	30	50
		On hand	30	20	60	30	30	0	0
		Scheduled and planned receipts			80	20	40	0	50
		Planned order release			40		50		
1	B	Gross requirements		205	40		50 130		
		On hand	100	45	5		0	0	0
		Scheduled and planned receipts		150			175		
		Planned order release				175			
2	C	Gross requirements			40	175	50		
		On hand	50		310	135	85	85	85
		Scheduled and planned receipts			300				
		Planned order release		300					
3	A	Gross requirements		300 205			130		
		On hand	310	5	5	5	75	75	75
		Scheduled and planned receipts		200			200		
		Planned order release		200					
	D	Gross requirements		900	40	350	50		
		On hand	1000	100	60	710	660	660	660
		Scheduled and planned receipts				1000			
		Planned order release			1000				

TABLE 2 : Illustration of the MRP logic

IV - THE PRODUCTION PLANNING SYSTEM

The general structure of a production planning and control system is described in figure 4, which summarizes all the considerations made in the course of this introductory chapter.

Production planning is a hierarchical process which starts with the generation of a master plan for each product family. This master plan establishes the best allocation of capacity resources in the aggregate, usually at the final assembly level. Capacity planning for the intermediate work centers then proceeds using macro-MRP based on macro-bills of materials and macro-routings. Aggregate production planning allows to plan,at a broad level, procurement and basic capacity resources like work force level, overtime, subcontracting.

In the short run detailed master schedules are released,together with the associated production plan for parts and sub-assemblies, and detailed procurement schedules. Detailed programs are generated by micro-MRP on the basis of the master schedules and the micro-bills of materials and routings. They are constrained by the aggregate production rates.

Once the detailed production plans have been released, the management of physical flows of orders through the work centers and the manufacturing units really starts. The control system aims at smoothing the traffic of the production orders through the manufacturing units, while satisfying operational objectives like : respect of due dates, minimization of in-process inventories, smoothing of bottlenecks, etc... The scheduling function in this regard is essential since it provides the work centers with queue discipline. It consists of priority rules for selecting in the queue the next job to be processed,once the machine becomes available. See Buffa and Taubert [1972] for a detailed presentation of the scheduling function and analysis of scheduling priority rules.

An extensive analysis of the planning and control procedures in the framework of figure 4 can be found in Crouhy [1983].

Wagner [1974], [1980] , Meal [1978] and Peterson and Silver [1979] discuss the structure of the total logistics system (procurement, production, distribution) from a broad perspective.

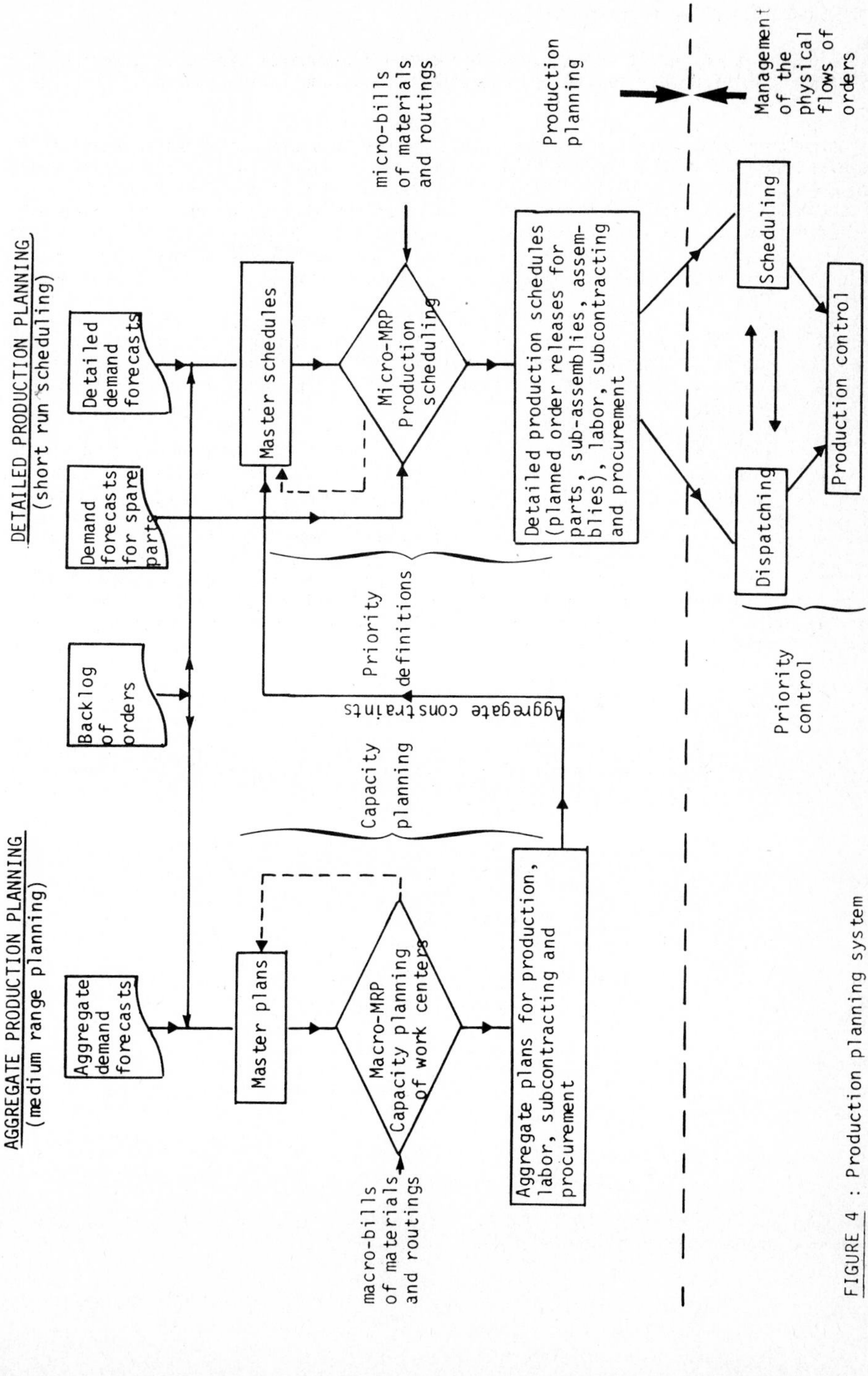

FIGURE 4 : Production planning system

REFERENCES

BITRAN G.R. - HAX A.C., [1977] , On the design of hierarchical production planning systems, Decision Sciences, 7(1), pp. 28-57.

BENSOUSSAN A. - CROUHY M., [1980] , Multi-level control systems for inventory management, in D.G.Laïniotis and N.S. Tzannes, eds., Applications of Information and Control Systems, Reidel Publishing Company.

BLACKBURN J.D. - MILLEN R.A., [1982] , Improved heuristics for multi-stage requirements planning systems, Management Science, 28(1), pp. 44-56.

BUFFA E.S. - TAUBERT W.H., [1972] , Production-Inventory systems : Planning and control, Irwin.

CLARK A.K., [1972] , An informal survey of multi-echelon inventory theory, Naval Research Logistics Quarterly, 14(4), pp. 621-650.

CLARK A. - SCARF H., [1960] , Optimal policies for a multi-echelon inventory problem, Management Science, 6(4), pp. 475-490.

CLARK A.K - SCARF H., [1962] , Approximate solutions to a simple multi-echelon inventory problem, in K.J. Arrow, S. Karlin, and H. Scarf, eds., Studies in applied probability and management science, Chapter 5, Stanford University Press.

CROUHY M., [1980] , Stocks de distribution ou stocks de fabrication : nécessité d'une gestion différentiée, Revue Française de Gestion, 25, pp. 55-68.

CROUHY M., [1983] , Gestion informatique de la production industrielle, Editions de l'Usine Nouvelle.

CROWSTON W.B. - WAGNER M. - WILLIAMS J., [1973] , Economic lot size determination in multi-stage assembly systems, Management Science, 19(5), pp. 517-527.

GRAVES S.C., [1981] , Multi stage lot sizing : an iterative approach, in L.B. Schwarz ed., Multi-level production/inventory control systems : Theory and practice chapter 4, TIMS Studies in the Management Sciences, 16, pp. 95-110.

HAX A.C., [1979] , Aggregate production planning, in J. Moder and S.E. Elmaghraby eds., Handbook of Operations Research, Vol. I, Van Nostrand Reinhold, pp. 127-172.

HAX A.C. - GOLOVIN J.J.,[1978-1], Hierarchical production planning systems, in A.C. Hax, ed., Studies in Operations Management, Chapter 4, North Holland, pp. 400-428.

HAX A.C. - GOLOVIN J.J.,[1978-2] Computer based operations management system (COMS), in A.C. Hax,ed., Studies in Operations Management, Chapter 16, North Holland.

HAX A.C. - MEAL H.C., [1975] , Hierarchical integration of production planning and scheduling, in M.A. Geisler, ed., Studies in the Management Sciences, Vol. I, Logistics, North Holland, pp. 53-69.

HOLT C.C. - MODIGLIANI F. - MUTH J.F. - SIMON H.A., [1960] , Planning production, inventories, and work force, Prentice Hall.

JOHNSON L.A. - MONTGOMERY D.C., [1974] , Operations research in production planning scheduling and inventory control, Wiley.

KLEINDORFER P.R. - KRIEBEL C.H. - THOMPSON G.L. - KLEINDORFER G.B., [1975] , Discrete optimal control of production plans, Management Science, 22(3), pp. 261-273.

McGARRAH R.E., [1963] , Production and logistics management, Wiley.

MEAL H.C., [1978] , A study of multi-stage production planning, in A.C. Hax, ed., Studies in Operations Management, Chapter 9, North Holland, pp. 253-285.

MODIGLIANI F. - HOHN F.E., [1955] , Production planning over time and the nature of the expectation and planning horizon, Econometrica, 23(1), pp. 46-66.

ORLICKY J., [1975] , Material requirements planning : The new way of life in production and inventory management, Mc Graw-Hill.

PETERSON R. - SILVER E.A., [1979] , Decision systems for inventory management and production planning, Wiley.

SCARF H.E., [1963] . A survey of analytic techniques in inventory theory, in H.E. Scarf, D.M. Gilford and M.W. Shelly, eds. Multistage inventory models and techniques Chapter 7, Stanford University Press, pp. 185-225.

SILVER E.A., [1967] , A tutorial on production smoothing and work force balancing, Operations Research, 15(6), pp. 985-1010.

VEINOTT A.F.Jr, [1966] , The status of mathematical inventory theory, Management Science , 12(11), pp. 745-777.

WILLIAMS J.F., [1974] , Multi-echelon production scheduling when demand is stochastic, Management Science , 20(9), pp. 1253-1263.

WAGNER H.M., [1974] , The desing of production and inventory systems for multi-facility and multi-warehouse companies, Operations Research, 22, pp. 278-291.

WAGNER H.M., [1980] , Research portfolio for inventory management and production planning systems, Operations Research, 28(3), Part I, pp. 445-475.

WAGNER H.M. - WITHIN T.M., [1959] , A dynamic version of the economic lot size model, Management Science, 5(1), pp. 89-96.

WIGHT O., [1974] , Production and inventory management in the computer age, CBI Publishing Company.

CHAPTER I

PRODUCTION PLANNING MODELS FOR CONCAVE COSTS AND DETERMINISTIC DEMAND

DISCRETE TIME FORMULATION

INTRODUCTION

In this chapter we consider the problem of Production Planning in a deterministic environment, assuming that all cost functions are concave which corresponds to the case of increasing returns to scale. The model is formulated as a discrete time optimal control problem. The solution is obtained using Dynamic Programming. Concavity leads to simplified equations, and to a useful property of the optimal control in the case of no backlogging and no disposal (known as Wagner-Within's theorem), namely that an order is placed only when the inventory level at the start of the period is zero. An efficient algorithm to compute the optimal policy is also derived. We then proceed with the Planning Horizon problem. Indexing the optimal cost function with the horizon, we let the horizon vary. An horizon N is called a "planning horizon" if the corresponding optimal control remains unchanged for the first N periods of an N'-period problem, with N' > N. This property has important technical and managerial implications since it makes the optimal control robust, at least for a few periods, with respect to the demands which are posterior to the planning horizon. The initial problem can thus be decomposed into smaller problems that can be treated independently. The various sufficient conditions which lead to planning horizons are presented in detail. We then allow for backlogging and derive analogous results. Planning horizon theorems are however much more difficult to obtain, and several weaker forms are given.

The Infinite Horizon problem is finally treated. A last section relates to the existing literature relevant to this chapter and comments the main results.

I - NOTATION, ASSUMPTIONS AND PROBLEM DEFINITION

I - 1. NOTATION AND ASSUMPTIONS

N is the problem horizon which is divided into N periods, where 0,1,...,N-1 are the decision instants. A demand function for a single product is defined by the sequence

$$\xi_1, \ldots, \xi_N$$

with

$$\xi_i \geq 0.$$

The demand ξ_i is assumed to occur at time i, and must be satisfied instantaneously. $y_0, y_1, \ldots, y_N$ denote the inventory levels at times 0, 1, ..., N just after the demand has been met. The production levels or quantities ordered, are denoted by

$$v_0, \ldots, v_{N-1}$$

A single lot $v_i \geq 0$ may be launched in any period i at time i, and inventory is replenished at time i + 1 : there is a one period lead time in production or delivery of the product. Negative production which would correspond to disposal, is not allowed. The inventory balance equations are

$$(1.1) \qquad y_{i+1} = y_i + v_i - \xi_{i+1}, \ \forall\ i = 0,\dots,N-1$$

No shortages are permitted until Section VI, which implies for the moment the constraint

$$(1.2) \qquad y_i \geq 0 \quad \forall i = 0,\dots,N \ \text{ or } v_i \geq (\xi_{i+1} - y_i)^+, \ \forall i = 0, \dots, N-1$$

We denote

$$V = (v_0, \dots, v_{N-1})$$

a control, in this case a production or a reordering policy. Let

$$(1.3) \qquad c_i(v),\ f_i(x),\ \forall i = 0, \dots, N-1$$

be functions defined on R^+, which are non decreasing, concave and positive, where $c_i(v)$ denotes the cost of producing, or purchasing, the lot $v > 0$ at time i, and $f_i(x)$ is the cost of holding in stock a quantity x at time i for one period until (i+1). Note there are no upper bounds on quantities.

In addition we allow $c_i(0)$ and $f_i(0)$ to be different from zero. As a matter of fact, there may be an irreducible cost to maintain production and storage facilities even though they do not operate. The set up costs are then $c_i(0)^+ - c_i(0) \geq 0$ and $f_i(0)^+ - f_i(0) \geq 0$.

I - 2. THE CONTROL PROBLEM

The control problem on the interval [n,N] is defined as :

$$(1.4) \qquad y_n = x$$

$$(1.5) \qquad y_{i+1} = y_i + v_i - \xi_{i+1}, \quad i = n, \dots, N-1$$

$$(1.6) \qquad J_n(x;V) = \sum_{i=n}^{N-1} [c_i(v_i) + f_i(y_i)]$$

The objective is to minimize the cost function $J_n(x;V)$ subject to the constraints on V :

$$(1.7) \qquad v_i \geq (\xi_{i+1} - y_i)^+, \quad i = n, \dots, N-1$$

In the sequel the emphasis will be given on the following dynamic programming equations :

$$(1.8) \qquad \begin{cases} u_N(x) = 0 \text{ , and for } n = N-1, \dots, 0 \\ u_n(x) = f_n(x) + \inf\limits_{v \geq (\xi_{n+1}-x)^+} \{c_n(v) + u_{n+1}(x + v - \xi_{n+1})\} \end{cases}$$

The function $u_n(x)$ is connected to (1.6) by the formula

(1.9) $u_n(x) = \underset{V}{\text{Min}}\ J_n(x;V)$

and must be interpreted as the minimum cost production policy on the interval $[n,N]$ when the initial inventory is x.

II - STUDY OF THE DYNAMIC PROGRAMMING EQUATIONS

II - 1. ANALYTICAL RESULTS

In order to simplify the exposition, the cumulative demand is denoted

(2.1) $$\begin{cases} \sigma_i^j = \sum_{k=i}^{j} \xi_k & \text{for } 1 \le i \le j \le N \\ \sigma_i^j = 0 & \text{for } j < i \end{cases}$$

Recall : $c_i(v)$ and $f_i(x)$ being concave, non decreasing functions on R^+, are necessarily continuous or $R^+ - \{0\}$ and have a right limit at 0.

Theorem 2.1

Under the assumptions (1.3) and for n = 0, ..., N-1

a) If $0 \le x < \xi_{n+1} = \sigma_{n+1}^{n+1}$, then :

$$u_n(x) = f_n(x) + \underset{r=n+1,\ldots,N}{\text{Min}} \{c_n(\sigma_{n+1}^r - x) + u_{n+1}(\sigma_{n+2}^r)\}$$

b) If $\sigma_{n+1}^s \le x < \sigma_{n+1}^{s+1}$ (s = n+1, ..., N-1, n = 0, ..., N-2), then :

$$u_n(x) = f_n(x) + \text{Min}[c_n(0) + u_{n+1}(x-\xi_{n+1}), \underset{r=s+1,\ldots,N}{\text{Min}} (c_n(\sigma_{n+1}^r-x)+ u_{n+1}(\sigma_{n+2}^r))]$$

c) If $x \ge \sigma_{n+1}^N$, then

$$u_n(x) = f_n(x) + c_n(0) + u_{n+1}(x - \xi_{n+1}).$$

Moreover $u_n(x)$ is concave on $[0, \xi_{n+1}[$, on each of the intervals $[\sigma_{n+1}^s, \sigma_{n+1}^{s+1}[$, $n + 1 \le s \le N-1$, (for $n \le N-2$), and on $[\sigma_{n+1}^N, \infty[$. The function u_n is increasing on $[\sigma_{n+1}^N, \infty[$. If $\sigma_{n+1}^N > 0$, then the function $u_n(x)$ is continuous except at point σ_{n+1}^s, s = n+1,...,N where it has left and right limits. It is continuous on $[\sigma_{n+1}^N, \infty[$ and

$$u_n(\sigma_{n+1}^s) \le u_n(\sigma_{n+1}^{s-}) \text{ for } s = n + 1, \ldots, N$$

$$u_n(\sigma_{n+1}^s) \le u_n(\sigma_{n+1}^{s+}) \text{ for } s = n, \ldots, N - 1$$

A statement on $[a,a[$ is void. If $\sigma_{n+1}^N = 0$, then 0 is the only discontinuity point and $u_n(0) \le u_n(0^+)$.

The following graphs thus obtain.

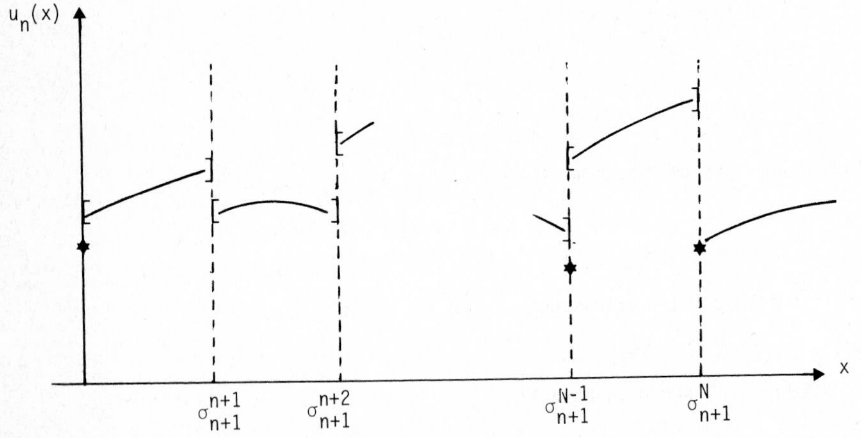

Figure 1.1 : Graph of $u_n(x)$ for $n \leq N-2$

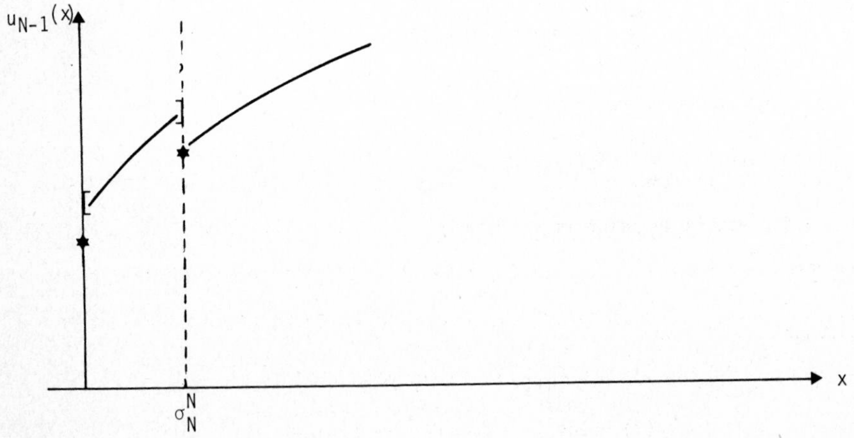

Figure 1.2 : Graph of $u_{N-1}(x)$

Proof :

Function $u_{N-1}(x)$. Assume first that $\xi_N > 0$.

For $n = N - 1$, (1.8) becomes

$$u_{N-1}(x) = f_{N-1}(x) + \operatorname*{Inf}_{v \geq (\xi_N - x)^+} c_{N-1}(v).$$

For $0 \leq x < \xi_N$ since c_{N-1} is increasing, we thus have

$$u_{N-1}(x) = f_{N-1}(x) + c_{N-1}(\xi_N - x) \;;$$

and, for $x \geq \xi_N$

$$u_{N-1}(x) = f_{N-1}(x) + c_{N-1}(0).$$

All the properties of the graph of $u_{N-1}(x)$ are then easily deduced.

If $\xi_N = 0$, thus

$$u_{N-1}(x) = f_{N-1}(x) + c_{N-1}(0)$$

and 0 is the only point of discontinuity.

Induction argument

The statement is assumed to hold for $u_{n+1}, \ldots, u_{N-1}$, and is proved for u_n.

(i) case $\sigma_{n+1}^N = 0$. Clearly $\xi_{n+1}, \ldots, \xi_N = 0$ and

$$u_n(x) = f_n(x) + \operatorname*{Inf}_{v \geq 0} \{c_n(v) + u_{n+1}(x+v)\}$$

Since $\sigma_{n+2}^N = 0$, by induction :

$$u_{n+1}(x) = \sum_{k=n+1}^{N-1} (f_k(x) + c_k(0))$$

which is increasing, hence

$$u_n(x) = \sum_{k=n}^{N-1} (f_k(x) + c_k(0))$$

The only discontinuity point is $x = 0$.

(ii) case $\sigma_{n+1}^N > 0$.

Proof of a)

Assuming $\xi_{n+1} > 0$ and $0 \leq x < \xi_{n+1}$, (1.8) becomes :

$$u_n(x) = f_n(x) + \operatorname*{Inf}_{v \geq \xi_{n+1} - x} \{c_n(v) + u_{n+1}(x+v-\xi_{n+1})\}. \tag{2.2}$$

By the induction argument the discontinuity points of $u_{n+1}(x)$ are σ_{n+2}^r, $r = n + 1, \ldots, N$, hence the discontinuity points of $v \to u_{n+1}(x+v-\xi_{n+1})$ on

$[\xi_{n+1} - x, +\infty[$ are $\sigma^r_{n+1} - x$, $r = n+1, \ldots, N$.

Define

$$\phi_n(v) = c_n(v) + u_{n+1}(x+v-\xi_{n+1}).$$

Since $\xi_{n+1} - x > 0$ on $[\xi_{n+1} - x, \infty[$, $c_n(v)$ is continuous, increasing and concave. For $v \in [\sigma^r_{n+1} - x, \sigma^{r+1}_{n+1} - x[$, $n+1 \le r \le N-1$, $x + v - \xi_{n+1} \in [\sigma^r_{n+2}, \sigma^{r+1}_{n+2}[$, hence $v \to u_{n+1}(x+v-\xi_{n+1})$ is concave on $[\sigma^r_{n+1} - x, \sigma^{r+1}_{n+1} - x[$, is continuous on the open interval and has limits at the end points. It follows that $\phi_n(v)$ is concave on $[\sigma^r_{n+1} - x, \sigma^{r+1}_{n+1} - x[$, is continuous on the open interval and has limits at the end points. Therefore :

$$\phi_n(v) \ge \text{Min } [\phi_n(\sigma^r_{n+1} - x), \phi_n(\sigma^{r+1}_{n+1} - x - 0)], \text{ for } v \in [\sigma^r_{n+1} - x, \sigma^{r+1}_{n+1} - x[.$$

In the meanwhile :

$$\begin{aligned}\phi_n(\sigma^{r+1}_{n+1} - x - 0) &= c_n(\sigma^{r+1}_{n+1} - x) + u_{n+1}(\sigma^{r+1}_{n+2} - 0)\\ &\ge c_n(\sigma^{r+1}_{n+1} - x) + u_{n+1}(\sigma^{r+1}_{n+2})\end{aligned}$$

which gives :

$$\phi_n(v) \ge \text{Min } [c_n(\sigma^r_{n+1} - x) + u_{n+1}(\sigma^r_{n+2}), c_n(\sigma^{r+1}_{n+1} - x) + u_{n+1}(\sigma^{r+1}_{n+2})] \tag{2.3}$$

for $v \in [\sigma^r_{n+1} - x, \sigma^{r+1}_{n+1} - x[$, $n+1 \le r \le N-1$.

Moreover when $v \in [\sigma^N_{n+1} - x, \infty[$, $x + v - \xi_{n+1} \in [\sigma^N_{n+2}, \infty[$ and, therefore :

$$\phi_n(v) \ge c_n(\sigma^N_{n+1} - x) + u_{n+1}(\sigma^N_{n+2}) \text{ for } v \ge \sigma^N_{n+1} - x. \tag{2.4}$$

a) follows from (2.3) and (2.4) since,as it can be easily verified, u_n is less or equal to the right hand side of a).

<u>Proof of b)</u>

Assume here that $\sigma^s_{n+1} \le x < \sigma^{s+1}_{n+1}$, $s = n+1, \ldots, N-1$, then from (1.8) it follows :

$$u_n(x) = f_n(x) + \underset{v \ge 0}{\text{Inf}} \{c_n(v) + u_{n+1}(x+v-\xi_{n+1})\}. \tag{2.5}$$

Consider the function $\phi_n(v)$ on $[0, +\infty[$, the discontinuity points are now 0 and $\sigma^r_{n+1} - x$, with $r = s+1, \ldots, N$.

For $v \in [0, \sigma^{s+1}_{n+1} - x[$, $x + v - \xi_{n+1} \in [x - \xi_{n+1}, \sigma^{s+1}_{n+2}[\subset [\sigma^s_{n+2}, \sigma^{s+1}_{n+2}[$, hence $\phi_n(v)$ is concave on the interval $[0, \sigma^{s+1}_{n+1} - x[$, is continuous on the open interval and has limits at both ends.

Therefore

$$\phi_n(v) \geq \text{Min}\ [c_n(0^+) + u_{n+1}(x - \xi_{n+1} + 0),\ c_n(\sigma_{n+1}^{s+1} - x) + u_{n+1}(\sigma_{n+2}^{s+1} - 0)]$$

$$\text{for } v \in]0,\ \sigma_{n+1}^{s+1} - x[$$

Since $c_n(0^+) \geq c_n(0)$,

$$u_{n+1}(x - \xi_{n+1} + 0) \geq u_{n+1}(x - \xi_{n+1}),\ u_{n+1}(\sigma_{n+2}^{s+1} - 0) \geq u_{n+1}(\sigma_{n+2}^{s+1})$$

It follows :

$$(2.6)\qquad \begin{cases} \phi_n(v) \geq \text{Min}\ [c_n(0) + u_{n+1}(x - \xi_{n+1}),\ c_n(\sigma_{n+1}^{s+1} - x) + u_{n+1}(\sigma_{n+2}^{s+1})] \\ \text{for } v \in [0,\ \sigma_{n+1}^{s+1} - x[. \end{cases}$$

Consider next an interval $[\sigma_{n+1}^{r} - x,\ \sigma_{n+1}^{r+1} - x[$, with $r = s + 1, \ldots, N$. An inequality similar to (2.3) is then derived. A similar argument on the inverval $[\sigma_{n+1}^{N} - x, +\infty[$ leads to (2.4). This completes the proof of b).

Proof of c)

If $x \geq \sigma_{n+1}^{N}$, $x - \xi_{n+1} \geq \sigma_{n+2}^{N}$ and therefore by induction

$$u_{n+1}(x + v - \xi_{n+1}) \geq u_{n+1}(x - \xi_{n+1})$$

c) follows immediately from (2.5). The properties of $u_n(x)$ are easily derived from formulas a), b), c).

By induction, one easily checks that u_n is increasing on $[\sigma_{n+1}^{N}, \infty[$. If $\sigma_{n+1}^{N} > 0$, from the induction argument and formulas a), b), c), it is easily shown that the only possible discontinuity points of $u_n(x)$ are σ_{n+1}^{s}, $s = n, \ldots, N$. It is also obvious that $u_n(x)$ has left and right limits at these points (except for $s = n$ where only a right limit exists). Then, as a consequence of formula a) :

$$u_n(0) = f_n(0) + \underset{r=n+1,\ldots,N}{\text{Min}} \{c_n(\sigma_{n+1}^{r}) + u_{n+1}(\sigma_{n+2}^{r})\}$$

$$u_n(0^+) = f_n(0^+) + \underset{r=n+1,\ldots,N}{\text{Min}} \{c_n(\sigma_{n+1}^{r}) + u_{n+1}(\sigma_{n+2}^{r})\} \geq u_n(0).$$

$$u_n(\sigma_{n+1}^{n+1} - 0) = f_n(\sigma_{n+1}^{n+1}) + \underset{r=n+1,\ldots,N}{\text{Min}} \{c_n(\sigma_{n+2}^{r} + 0) + u_{n+1}(\sigma_{n+2}^{r})\}$$

$$= f_n(\sigma_{n+1}^{n+1}) + \text{Min}\ \{c_n(0^+) + u_{n+1}(0),\ \underset{r=n+2,\ldots,N}{\text{Min}} (c_n(\sigma_{n+2}^{r}) + u_{n+1}(\sigma_{n+2}^{r}))\}$$

and

$$u_n(\sigma_{n+1}^{n+1}) = f_n(\sigma_{n+1}^{n+1}) + \text{Min}\ [c_n(0) + u_{n+1}(0),\ \underset{r=n+2,\ldots,N}{\text{Min}} \{c_n(\sigma_{n+2}^{r}) + u_{n+1}(\sigma_{n+2}^{r})\}]$$

$$\leq u_n(\sigma_{n+1}^{n+1} - 0)$$

$$u_n(\sigma^{n+1}_{n+1}+0) = f_n(\sigma^{n+1}_{n+1}) + \mathrm{Min}[c_n(0)+u_{n+1}(0^+), \mathop{\mathrm{Min}}_{r=n+2,\ldots,N} \{c_n(\sigma^r_{n+2}-0)+u_{n+1}(\sigma^r_{n+2})\}].$$

From formula b) with $s = n + 1$, necessarily $\sigma^{n+1}_{n+1} < \sigma^{n+2}_{n+1}$, which implies $\xi_{n+2} > 0$, therefore $c_n(\sigma^r_{n+2} - 0) = c_n(\sigma^r_{n+2})$ for $r = n + 2, \ldots, N$, and $u_n(\sigma^{n+1}_{n+1}+0) \geq u_n(\sigma^{n+1}_{n+1})$.

The other majorations are proved in a similar way.

Remark 2.1

Suppose that $\sigma^{s+1}_{n+1} = \sigma^s_{n+1}$ (i.e. $\xi_{s+1} = 0$), $s \geq n + 1$ and $\sigma^s_{n+1} = \sigma^{s+1}_{n+1} \leq x < \sigma^{s+2}_{n+1}$ $(s + 2 \leq N)$. Then, of course b) must be applied with $s + 1$ instead of s.

II - 2. INTERPRETATION OF THE SOLUTION OF THE DYNAMIC PROGRAMMING EQUATIONS

The objective is now to prove result (1.9) and to exhibit an optimal control.

A function $\hat{v}_n(x)$, called a feedback, is defined as follows

(2.7) $\hat{v}_n(x) =$

- If $x < \xi_{n+1}$: $\sigma^{\hat{r}}_{n+1} - x$, where $\hat{r}$ is the index (depending on x) realizing the minimum in a).
- If $\sigma^s_{n+1} \leq x < \sigma^{s+1}_{n+2}$, $s \in [n+1, N-1]$: 0 or $\sigma^{\hat{r}}_{n+1} - x$, depending on which term realizes the minimum in b).
- If $x \geq \sigma^N_{n+1}$: 0

This definition implies :

$$(2.8) \quad \begin{cases} u_n(x) = f_n(x) + c_n(\hat{v}_n(x)) + u_{n+1}(x+\hat{v}_n(x) - \xi_{n+1}), \\ \qquad \forall x \; ; \; n = 0 \ldots N-1 \\ u_N(x) = 0. \end{cases}$$

Next define :

$$(2.9) \quad \begin{cases} \hat{v}_i = \hat{v}_i(\hat{y}_i) \\ \hat{y}_{i+1} = \hat{y}_i + \hat{v}_i - \xi_{i+1}, \quad i = n, \ldots, N-1 \\ \hat{y}_n = x \end{cases}$$

and set

(2.10) $\hat{V}_n = (\hat{v}_n, \ldots, \hat{v}_{N-1}).$

Theorem 2.2

Under assumptions (1.3), we have

(2.11) $u_n(x) = \underset{V}{\mathrm{Min}}\, J_n(x;V) = J_n(x;\hat{V}_n)$

Proof

From (2.9) and (2.8) for i = n, ..., N-1, we have :

$$u_i(\hat{y}_i) = f_i(\hat{y}_i) + c_i(\hat{v}_i) + u_{i+1}(\hat{y}_{i+1})$$

Summing up for i = n, ..., N - 1, yields :

$$u_n(x) = J_n(x;\hat{V}_n).$$

Let V be an arbitrary control. From (1.8) and equations (1.5) (taking (1.7) into account),it follows :

$$u_i(y_i) \leq f_i(y_i) + c_i(v_i) + u_{i+1}(y_{i+1}).$$

Summing up for i from n to N - 1, yields :

$$u_n(x) \leq J_n(x;V)$$

which completes the proof of (2.11). □

A direct proof of :

(2.12) $u_n(x) = \underset{V}{\mathrm{Inf}}\, J_n(x;V)$

may be also given. Define $u_n(x)$ by (2.12), then the sequence u_n satisfies the relations (1.8).

Indeed by definition :

(2.13) $$\left\{ u_n(x) = \underset{\substack{v_n,\ldots,v_{N-1} \\ y_{n+1},\ldots,y_N}}{\mathrm{Inf}} \sum_{i=n}^{N-1} [c_i(v_i) + f_i(y_i)] \right.$$

and satisfies (1.5), (1.7).

Clearly in (2.13), v_n can be chosen arbitrarily with the only restriction $v_n \geq (\xi_{n+1} - x)^+$. Therefore assuming $n \leq N - 2$

$$u_n(x) = f_n(x) + \underset{v_n \geq (\xi_{n+1}-x)^+}{\mathrm{Inf}} [c_n(v_n) + \underset{\substack{v_{n+1},\ldots,v_{N-1} \\ y_{n+2},\ldots,y_N}}{\mathrm{Inf}} \sum_{i=n+1}^{N-1} (c_i(v_i) + f_i(y_i))]$$

and satisfies (1.5), (1.7),

from which (1.8) can be easily derived.

III - THE SIMPLIFIED EQUATIONS OF DYNAMIC PROGRAMMING

The dynamic programming equations are very useful to derive an optimal control. As it is illustrated in §II.2, Theorem 2.1 shows that a simplified version of the initial equations (1.8) can be obtained in the form a), b), c). From this, it was possible to show that an optimal decision at time n, with inventory on hand equal to x, is either 0 or such that $x + \hat{v}_n(x)$ equals the sum of some future demands. Moreover, from (2.7) :

$$(3.1) \qquad \hat{v}_n(x) = (\sigma_{n+1}^{\hat{r}(x)} - x)^+, \ \hat{r}(x) \in [n,N].$$

However , some a priori information exists on $\hat{r}(x)$, namely

$$(3.2) \qquad \begin{cases} \hat{r}(x) = n & \text{if } x \geq \sigma_{n+1}^N \\ \hat{r}(x) \geq n+1 & \text{if } x < \xi_{n+1} = \sigma_{n+1}^{n+1} \\ \hat{r}(x) = n \text{ or } \geq s+1 & \text{if } \sigma_{n+1}^s \leq x < \sigma_{n+1}^{s+1}, \quad (s \in [n+1, N-1]) \end{cases}$$

In this section, it is shown that the equations of dynamic programming can be further simplified to obtain additional information on the optimal control.

III - 1. THE CASE OF PRODUCTION (PURCHASING) COSTS WHICH DECREASE WITH TIME

Theorem 3.1

Assuming (1.3), and $\forall n, n = 0, \ldots, N-2$

$$(3.3) \qquad \begin{cases} c_n(v) \geq c_{n+1}(v) \\ c_n(0) = c_{n+1}(0) \end{cases}$$

then the functions $u_n(x)$ satisfy the relations (n=0, ..., N-1) :

$$(3.4) \qquad \begin{cases} \underline{\text{If } 0 \leq x < \xi_{n+1}} \\ u_n(x) = f_n(x) + \underset{r=n+1,\ldots,N}{\text{Min}} \{c_n(\sigma_{n+1}^r - x) + u_{n+1}(\sigma_{n+2}^r)\} \end{cases}$$

$$(3.5) \qquad \begin{cases} \underline{\text{If } x \geq \xi_{n+1}} \\ u_n(x) = f_n(x) + c_n(0) + u_{n+1}(x - \xi_{n+1}) \end{cases}$$

Proof

Property (3.4) was already proven. Thus, assume that $x \geq \xi_{n+1}$. From part c) it follows that (3.5) holds for $n = N - 1$. Assuming that (3.5) holds for $n + 1 \leq N - 1$ the property is shown to hold for n. The situation is identical to case b) with $s \in [n + 1, N - 1]$ and

$$\sigma_{n+1}^s \leq x < \sigma_{n+1}^{s+1}$$

The statement to be proven is :

$$(3.6)\quad \begin{cases} u_{n+1}(x - \xi_{n+1}) + c_n(0) \le c_n(\sigma^r_{n+1} - x) + u_{n+1}(\sigma^r_{n+2}) \\ \qquad\qquad \forall r = s + 1, \ldots, N. \end{cases}$$

But,

$$\sigma^r_{n+2} \ge \sigma^{s+1}_{n+2} \ge \sigma^{n+2}_{n+2}$$

hence, from the induction assumption

$$(3.7)\quad \begin{cases} u_{n+1}(\sigma^r_{n+2}) = f_{n+1}(\sigma^r_{n+2}) + c_{n+1}(0) + u_{n+2}(\sigma^r_{n+3}), & \text{if } n + 3 \le N \\ \qquad = f_n(\sigma^r_{n+2}) + c_{n+1}(0), & \text{if } n = N - 2. \end{cases}$$

When $n = N - 2$, $s = N - 1$, $r = N$, then (3.6) amounts to

$$(3.8)\quad \begin{cases} u_{N-1}(x - \xi_{N-1}) + c_{N-2}(0) \le c_{N-2}(\sigma^N_{N-1} - x) + u_{N-1}(\sigma^N_N) \\ \qquad = c_{N-2}(\sigma^N_{N-1} - x) + f_{N-1}(\sigma^N_N) + c_{N-1}(0) \end{cases}$$

But recalling that $\xi_{N-1} \le x \le \sigma^N_{N-1}$, leads to

$$u_{N-1}(x - \xi_{N-1}) = f_{N-1}(x - \xi_{N-1}) + c_{N-1}(\sigma^N_{N-1} - x).$$

Therefore,

$$(3.9)\quad \begin{cases} f_{N-1}(x - \xi_{N-1}) + c_{N-1}(\sigma^N_{N-1} - x) + c_{N-2}(0) \\ \qquad \le c_{N-2}(\sigma^N_{N-1} - x) + f_{N-1}(\sigma^N_N) + c_{N-1}(0) \end{cases}$$

But

$$f_{N-1}(x - \xi_{N-1}) \le f_{N-1}(\sigma^N_N) \text{ since } x - \xi_{N-1} \le \sigma^N_N$$

and assuming

$$c_{N-1}(\sigma^N_{N-1} - x) \le c_{N-2}(\sigma^N_N - x)$$

$$c_{N-2}(0) = c_{N-1}(0)$$

yield (3.9), and hence (3.8) and (3.6) when $n = N-2$. If it is now assumed that $n \le N - 3$, the first part of (3.7) can be derived. We know that $s \ge n + 1$.

First, assume that $s \ge n + 2$, hence $x - \xi_{n+1} \ge \sigma^s_{n+2} \ge \xi_{n+2}$ and $u_{n+1}(x - \xi_{n+1})$ is computed using formula b) :

$$u_{n+1}(x-\xi_{n+1}) = f_{n+1}(x-\xi_{n+1}) + \text{Min}\,[c_{n+1}(0) + u_{n+2}(x-\sigma^{n+2}_{n+1}),$$

$$\underset{r=s'+1,\ldots,N}{\text{Min}} \{c_{n+1}(\sigma^r_{n+2} - x) + u_{n+2}(\sigma^r_{n+3})\}],\ s' \in [n + 2, N - 1]$$

$$\le f_{n+1}(x-\xi_{n+1}) + c_{n+1}(\sigma^r_{n+2}-x) + u_{n+2}(\sigma^r_{n+3}),\ \forall r = n+3,\ldots,N$$

$$\leq f_{n+1}(x-\xi_{n+1}) + c_{n+1}(\sigma^r_{n+1}-x) + u_{n+2}(\sigma^r_{n+3}),$$

and from $x - \xi_{n+1} < \sigma^{s+1}_{n+2} \leq \sigma^r_{n+2}$:

$$\leq f_{n+1}(\sigma^r_{n+2}) + c_{n+1}(\sigma^r_{n+1} - x) + u_{n+2}(\sigma^r_{n+3})$$

From the assumption on c) :

$$c_{n+1}(\sigma^r_{n+1} - x) \leq c_n(\sigma^r_{n+1} - x)$$

$$c_n(0) = c_{n+1}(0),$$

it follows

$$u_{n+1}(x - \xi_{n+1}) + c_n(0) = u_{n+1}(x - \xi_{n+1}) + c_{n+1}(0)$$

$$\leq f_{n+1}(\sigma^r_{n+2}) + c_n(\sigma^r_{n+1} - x) + c_{n+1}(0) + u_{n+2}(\sigma^r_{n+3})$$

which is (3.6), by virtue of (3.7).

Second, consider the case where s = n + 1. Then $x - \xi_{n+1} < \sigma^{n+2}_{n+2} = \xi_{n+2}$, and formula a) applies, which gives

$$u_{n+1}(x-\xi_{n+1}) = f_{n+1}(x-\xi_{n+1}) + \underset{r=n+2,\dots,N}{\text{Min}} [c_{n+1}(\sigma^r_{n+2}-x) + u_{n+2}(\sigma^r_{n+3})]$$

$$\leq f_{n+1}(x-\xi_{n+1}) + c_{n+1}(\sigma^r_{n+2}-x) + u_{n+2}(\sigma^r_{n+3}), \forall r = n+2,..,N$$

$$\leq f_{n+1}(\sigma^r_{n+2}) + c_{n+1}(\sigma^r_{n+1}-x) + u_{n+2}(\sigma^r_{n+3})$$

$$\leq f_{n+1}(\sigma^r_{n+2}) + c_n(\sigma^r_{n+1}-x) + u_{n+2}(\sigma^r_{n+3})$$

This completes the proof of Theorem 3.1.

Remark 3.1

The interpretation of Theorem 3.1 is of special interest. When the production, or purchasing costs decrease with time, it is not economical to produce ahead of time when the initial inventory is high enough to cover the current demand.

Corollary 3.1

Under the assumptions of Theorem 3.1, the index $\hat{r}(x)$ defined in (3.1) and (3.2) satisfies

$$(3.10) \quad \begin{cases} \hat{r}(x) \geq n + 1 & \text{if } x < \xi_{n+1} \\ \hat{r}(x) = n & \text{if } x \geq \xi_{n+1} \end{cases}$$

Proof

Immediate

III - 2. GENERAL CASE

We leave out the hypothesis (3.3) and turn back to the general assumptions (1.3).

Theorem 3.2

Assuming (1.3), then the equations of dynamic programming reduce to

(3.11)
$$\begin{cases} \underline{\text{If } 0 \le x < \xi_{n+1} :} \\ u_n(x) = f_n(x) + \underset{r=n+1,\dots,N}{\text{Min}} \{c_n({}^{r}_{n+1} - x) \\ \quad + \sum\limits_{k=n+1}^{r-1} (f_k(\sigma^r_{k+1}) + c_k(0)) + u_r(0)\} \quad (^1) \end{cases}$$

(3.12)
$$\begin{cases} \underline{\text{If } \sigma^s_{n+1} \le x < \sigma^{s+1}_{n+1} \ (s = n+1, \dots, N-1):} \\ u_n(x) = f_n(x) + \text{Min} \{c_n(0) + u_{n+1}(x - \xi_{n+1}), \\ \underset{r=s+1,\dots,N}{\text{Min}} (c_n(\sigma^r_{n+1} - x) + \sum\limits_{k=n+1}^{r-1} [f_n(\sigma^r_{k+1}) + c_k(0)] + u_r(0))\} \end{cases}$$

(3.13)
$$\begin{cases} \underline{\text{If } x \ge \sigma^N_{n+1} :} \\ u_n(x) = \sum\limits_{k=n}^{N-1} [f_k(x - \sigma^k_{n+1}) + c_k(0)] \end{cases}$$

Remark 3.2

We can provide an interpretation of (3.11), (3.12), (3.13) not only in terms of the feedback, but also in terms of the whole control policy.

Clearly (3.13) means that if the initial stock is sufficiently large to satisfy all demands till the horizon, the optimal policy is to produce nothing. However, if the initial inventory is strictly inferior to the next demand as for (3.11), one should produce an amount such that total supply meets exactly a fixed number of forthcoming demands. There will be no further ordering decision until the inventory is zero.

Lastly, if the initial inventory is high enough to satisfy some forthcoming demands, it may yet be economical to produce immediatly a positive amount. Again this amount should be such that total supply meets exactly a fixed number of forthcoming demands, and no further ordering decision is made before the inventory vanishes.

Proof of Theorem 3.2.

Starting with (3.13), the proof is conducted by induction from c) of Theorem 2.1. In the following it is assumed that $0 \le x < \xi_{n+1}$.

---

(1) $\sum\limits_{n+1}^{n} = 0$

(i) $u_n(x)$ is first shown to be less or equal to the right hand side of (3.11). Let r be fixed in [n + 1, ..., N]. Consider a control policy

$$\tilde{V}_n = (\tilde{v}_n, \ldots, \tilde{v}_{N-1})$$

with

$$\tilde{v}_n = \sigma^r_{n+1} - x$$

$$\tilde{v}_{n+1} = 0$$

$$\tilde{v}_{r-1} = 0 \qquad \text{(if } r-1 \geq n+1\text{, otherwise void)}$$

$$\tilde{v}_r = \tilde{v}_r(0)$$

$$\vdots$$

$$\tilde{v}_{N-1} = \tilde{v}_{N-1}(\tilde{y}_{N-1})$$

$$\tilde{y}_{i+1} = \tilde{y}_i + \tilde{v}_i - \xi_{i+1}, \qquad i = n, \ldots, N-1$$

$$\tilde{y}_n = x$$

Clearly $\tilde{y}_r = \sigma^r_{r+1} = 0$ (if r = N, $\tilde{v}_r$ ... disappears from the above formulation).

$J_n(x;\tilde{V}_n)$ is then computed:

$$J_n(x;\tilde{V}_n) = c_n(\sigma^r_{n+1}-x) + f_n(x) + \sum_{k=n+1}^{r-1} (f_k(\sigma^r_{k+1}) + c_k(0)) + u_r(0).$$

From Theorem 2.2 and the definition of $\tilde{V}_n$, it implies that $u_r(0)$ equals the cost from the period r till N - 1. We may assert that

$$u_n(x) \leq J_n(x;\tilde{V}_n).$$

Since r is arbitrary, denoting the right hand side of (3.11) by $w_n(x)$, it follows :

(3.14) $$u_n(x) \leq w_n(x).$$

(ii) The reverse inequality is now demonstrated. Consider the optimal control $\hat{v}_n, \ldots, \hat{v}_{N-1}$ as defined by formulas (2.9). From definition (2.7) we have

$$\hat{v}_n = \sigma^{\hat{r}}_{n+1} - x$$

If $\hat{r} = n + 1$, from a) of Theorem 2.1, it follows :

$$u_n(x) = f_n(x) + c_n(\sigma^{n+1}_{n+1} - x) + u_{n+1}(0)$$

$$\geq w_n(x) \quad \text{(from the definition of } w_n\text{).}$$

We may thus assume that $\hat{r} \geq n + 2$.

If $\hat{v}_{n+1} = \dots = \hat{v}_{\hat{r}-1} = 0$, then one easily checks that

$$w_n(x) = J_n(\hat{V}_n) = u_n(x).$$

Assume now that there exists indices h with $h \in [n+1, \hat{r}-1]$ such that $\hat{v}_h > 0$. Let h be the first such index, we have therefore the following structure for the optimal policy

$$\hat{v}_{n+1} = 0, \dots , \hat{v}_{h-1} = 0 , \hat{v}_h > 0 , \hat{v}_{h+1} \dots \hat{v}_{N-1} \geq 0.$$

and the sequence of optimal states is then

$$\hat{y}_n = x, \quad \hat{y}_{n+1} = \sigma^{\hat{r}}_{n+2}, \dots, \hat{y}_h = \sigma^{\hat{r}}_{h+1}.$$

Note that

$$\sigma^{\hat{r}}_{n+1} - x \geq \sigma^{\hat{r}}_{h+1} = \hat{y}_h \tag{3.15}$$

or $\qquad x \leq \sigma^{h}_{n+1}$ (which is true since $x < \xi_{n+1}$).

Define

$$\Delta = \text{Min}\ (\hat{y}_h, \hat{v}_h),$$

if $\hat{y}_h = 0$, then

$$J_n(\hat{V}_n) = c_n(\sigma^{\hat{r}}_{n+1} - x) + f_n(x) + \sum_{k=n+1}^{h-1} + (f_n(\sigma^{\hat{r}}_{k+1}) + c_k(0)) + u_h(0)$$

and again

$$u_n(x) = J_n(\hat{V}_n) \geq w_n(x).$$

Assume now that $\Delta > 0$, and consider two new control policies $V^a_n = (v^a_n, \dots, v^a_{N-1})$, $V^b_n = (v^b_n, \dots, v^b_{N-1})$ which are deduced from $\hat{V}_n$ by the following transformations :

$$v^a_n = \hat{v}_n - \Delta,\ v^a_{n+1} = 0, \dots, v^a_{h-1} = 0,\ v^a_h = \hat{v}_h + \Delta,\ v^a_{h+1} = \hat{v}_{h+1}, \dots, v^a_{N-1} = \hat{v}_{N-1},$$

and

$$v^b_{h+1} = \hat{v}_n + \Delta,\ v^b_{n+1} = 0, \dots, v^b_{h-1} = 0,\ v^b_h = \hat{v}_h - \Delta,\ v^b_{h+1} = \hat{v}_{h+1}, \dots, v^b_{N-1} = \hat{v}_{N-1}.$$

From (3.15) $\hat{v}_n \geq \Delta$, and therefore the components of V^a_n, V^b_n are positive numbers. Consider the corresponding trajectories

$$y^a_n = x,\ y^a_{n+1} = \hat{y}_{n+1} - \Delta, \dots, y^a_h = \hat{y}_h - \Delta,\ y^a_{h+1} = \hat{y}_{h+1}, \dots, y^a_N = \hat{y}_N$$

$$y^b_n = x,\ y^b_{n+1} = \hat{y}_{n+1} + \Delta, \dots, y^b_j = \hat{y}_h + \Delta,\ y^b_{h+1} = \hat{y}_{h+1}, \dots, y^b_N = \hat{y}_N.$$

Δ being positive it follows that $y^a_i \geq 0$, $i = n, \dots, N$, hence V^a_n, V^b_n are admissible controls.

Then, we want to show that :

$$u_n(x) = J_n(\hat{V}_n) = J_n(V_n^a) = J_n(V_n^b) \tag{3.16}$$

First indeed

$$\begin{cases} J_n(V_n^a) - J_n(\hat{V}_n) = c_n(\hat{v}_n - \Delta) - c_n(\hat{v}_n) + c_h(\hat{v}_h + \Delta) - c_h(\hat{v}_h) + \\ \qquad + \sum_{i=n+1}^{h} [f_i(\hat{y}_i - \Delta) - f_i(\hat{y}_i)]. \end{cases} \tag{3.17}$$

$$\begin{cases} J_n(V_n^b) - J_n(\hat{V}_n) = c_n(\hat{v}_n + \Delta) - c_n(\hat{v}_n) + c_h(\hat{v}_h - \Delta) - c_h(\hat{v}_h) + \\ \qquad + \sum_{i=n+1}^{h} [f_i(\hat{y}_i + \Delta) - f_i(\hat{y}_i)]. \end{cases} \tag{3.18}$$

Adding up, yields

$$J_n(V_n^a) + J_n(V_n^b) - 2J_n(\hat{V}_n)$$

$$= c_n(\hat{v}_n + \Delta) - c_n(\hat{v}_n) - [c_n(\hat{v}_n) - c_n(\hat{v}_n - \Delta)]$$

$$+ c_h(\hat{v}_h + \Delta) - c_h(\hat{v}_h) - [c_h(\hat{v}_h) - c_h(\hat{v}_h - \Delta)]$$

$$+ \sum_{i=n+1}^{h} \{f_i(\hat{y}_i + \Delta) - f_i(\hat{y}_i) - [f_i(\hat{y}_i) - f_i(\hat{y}_i - \Delta)]\}$$

which, by concavity of the functions involved, is ≤ 0.

Second, $\hat{V}_n$ being optimal

$$J_n(V_n^a) \geq J_n(\hat{V}_n)$$

$$J_n(V_n^b) \geq J_n(\hat{V}_n)$$

which proves (3.16).

To proceed we need to consider the two following cases for Δ.

a) $\Delta = \hat{y}_h$

In this case

$$v_n^a = \sigma_{n+1}^{\hat{r}} - x - \sigma_{h+1}^{\hat{r}} = \sigma_{n+1}^{h} - x$$

$$v_{n+1}^a = \dots = v_{h-1}^a = 0, \; y_h^a = 0$$

and consequently

$$J_n(V_n^a) = c_n(\sigma_{n+1}^h - x) + f_n(x) + \sum_{k=n+1}^{h-1} [c_k(0) + f_k(\sigma_{k+1}^h)]$$

$$+ \sum_{k=h}^{N-1} [c_k(v_k^a) + f_k(y_k^a)]$$

Since $y_h^a = 0$, then

$$J_n(V_n^a) \geq c_n(\sigma_{n+1}^h - x) + f_n(x) + \sum_{k=n+1}^{h-1} [c_k(0) + f_k(\sigma_{k+1}^h)] + u_h(0)$$

$$\geq w_n(x).$$

Hence again $u_n(x) \geq w_n(x)$.

b) $\Delta = \hat{v}_h$

In this case :

$$J_n(V_n^b) = c_n(\hat{v}_n + \Delta) + \sum_{k=n+1}^{h} c_k(0) + f_n(x) + \sum_{k=n+1}^{h} f_k(\hat{y}_k + \Delta) +$$

$$+ \sum_{k=h+1}^{N-1} [f_k(\hat{y}_k) + c_k(\hat{v}_k)]$$

However

$$\hat{v}_h = \hat{v}_h(\hat{y}_h) = \hat{v}_h(\sigma_{h+1}^{\hat{r}}), \quad \hat{r} \geq h + 1.$$

Hence from b) of Theorem 2.1 and $\hat{v}_n$ being positive, we have :

$$\hat{v}_h = \sigma_{h+1}^{r_1} - \sigma_{h+1}^{\hat{r}}, \text{ with } r_1 \in [\hat{r}+1, \ldots, N]$$

$$= \sigma_{\hat{r}+1}^{r_1}$$

hence

$$v_n^b = \hat{v}_n + \Delta = \sigma_{n+1}^{r_1} - x$$

$$v_{n+1}^b = \ldots = v_h^b = 0.$$

Considering V_n^b instead of $\hat{V}_n$, we still have

$$u_n(x) = J_n(x, V_n^b).$$

V_n^b has the same structure as $\hat{V}_n$ with index $r_1 \geq \hat{r}+1$ instead of $\hat{r}$, and the number of components which vanish after $n + 1$ is increased by 1. The same procedure as above is applied to V_n^b.

Note that for $i \geq h + 1$, v_i^b is still given by the optimal feedback. After a finite number of steps, we necessarily end up with a situation where it can be asserted that $u_n(x) \geq w_n(x)$.

This completes the proof of (3.11).

The proof of (3.12) is similar and left to the reader.

Remark 3.3

Theorem 3.2. is due to Bensoussan and Proth [1982]. More details may be found in Proth [1982-1].

Remark 3.4

Our approach to the dynamic programming equations (1.8) consists,when possible,in deriving results by purely analytic techniques, without relying on the control interpretation. This is more natural from the mathematical point of view,since the functions $u_n(x)$ are defined inductively.

This objective is fulfilled in Theorem 2.1, but not in Theorem 3.2 where the control interpretation of $u_n(x)$ is used.

It would be very interesting to derive Theorem 3.2 by purely inductive arguments. Probably the main difficulty stems from the fact that the relations of Theorem 3.2 do not involve just two subsequent functions u_n and u_{n+1}, but rather u_n and several u_r, $r > n$.

Remark 3.5

Note that the proof of Theorem 3.2 relies on the results of Theorem 2.1. Therefore we need to consider two stages in deriving the most simplified form of the dynamic programming relations. In addition as already mentioned, the methods of proof are different.

III - 3. A WAGNER-WITHIN TYPE THEOREM

Some interesting features of the optimal control can be derived from Theorem 3.2.

Theorem 3.3

Assume (1.3). Consider the control problem (1.4), (1.5), (1.6), (1.7) assuming that $\sigma_{n+1}^N > x$. Denote by $n_o \in [n, N-1]$ the first time $i \in [n,N-1]$ for which $\hat{v}_i > 0$. Then,there exists an optimal control $\hat{V}_n = (\hat{v}_n, \ldots, \hat{v}_{N-1})$ such that :

(3.19) $\hat{v}_i \hat{y}_i = 0, \forall i \in [n, N-1], i \neq n_o$

(3.20) $\hat{y}_N = 0$

Proof

By definition of n_o, (3.19) holds when $n \leq i < n_o$. Assume $i \in [n_o+1, N-1]$, then from formulas (3.11), (3.12) :

(i) we can define a sequence $n_o < n_1 < n_2 < \ldots < N-1$, such that

$$\hat{v}_i = 0 \quad i \neq n_o, n_1, \ldots$$

$$\hat{y}_i = 0 \quad i = n_1, n_2, \ldots$$

so that (3.19) holds for $i \in [n_0+1, N-1]$.

(ii) moreover,

$$(3.21) \qquad \hat{v}_{n_k} + \hat{y}_{n_k} = \sigma^{s_k}_{n_k+1}, \qquad n_k+1 \le s_k \le N.$$

Let l be the largest value of $n_k \le N-1$; from (3.21) we have

$$\hat{y}_{l+1} = \sigma^s_{l+1}, \quad \hat{y}_{l+2} = \sigma^s_{l+3}, \ldots, \hat{y}_{N-1} = \sigma^s_N$$

for some $s \in [l + 1, N]$ (assuming $l + 1 \le N - 1$). The positivity constraint on $\hat{y}_N$ implies $s \ge N$; therefore $s = N$ and $\hat{y}_N = 0$. If $l = N-1$, then

$$\hat{v}_l + \hat{y}_l = \sigma^N_N$$

and again $\hat{y}_N = 0$.

III - 4. EFFICIENT ALGORITHM TO COMPUTE AN OPTIMAL CONTROL

From Theorem 3.2 Proth [1982-1] derived an efficient algorithm to compute an optimal control for $J_0(x;V)$, which is presented in this section.

It is much faster than the usual dynamic programming solution procedures.

The first step consists in computing the numbers :

$$(3.22) \qquad z^m = u_m(0), \quad m = 0, \ldots, N$$

which are connected by the following induction

$$(3.23) \qquad \begin{cases} z^m = f_m(0) + \underset{r=m+1,\ldots,N}{\text{Min}} \{c_m(\sigma^r_{m+1}) + \sum_{k=m+1}^{r-1} [f_k(\sigma^r_{k+1}) + c_k(0)] + z^r\} \\ z^N = 0. \end{cases}$$

Define for $n \le m$

$$(3.24) \qquad \begin{cases} z^m_n = \sum_{k=n}^{m-1} [f_k(\sigma^m_{k+1} + c_k(0)] + z^m \\ z^m_m = z^m \end{cases}$$

From (3.23) and (3.24), it follows

$$(3.25) \qquad z^m_n = f_n(\sigma^m_{n+1}) + c_n(0) + z^m_{n+1}, \qquad n < m$$

$$(3.26) \qquad z^m = f_n(0) + \underset{r=m+1,\ldots,N}{\text{Min}} \{c_m(\sigma^r_{m+1}) + z^r_{m+1}\}$$

Starting with $z^N = 0$, all the functions z^m_n, $n \le m$ can be computed by induction.

When z^m is computed, the integer $\hat{r}_m \in [m+1, \ldots, N]$ which realizes the minimum in (3.26) is kept in memory. The optimal control is now defined :

(i) Consider first the case $x < \xi_1$. From (3.11), it follows

$$u_0(x) = f_0(x) + \underset{r=1,\ldots,N}{\text{Min}} \{c_0(\sigma_1^r - x) + z_1^r\}. \tag{3.27}$$

The numbers z_1^r being known, we can deduce from (3.27) the value of $\hat{r}(x)$. Then, the sequence

$$\hat{r}(x),\ \hat{r}_1(x) = \hat{r}_{\hat{r}(x)},\ \hat{r}_2(x) = \hat{r}_{\hat{r}_1(x)},\ \ldots$$

represents the sequence of instants where an order is placed. Moreover, the sizes of orders are given by

$$\sigma_1^{\hat{r}(x)} - x,\ \ldots,\ \sigma_{\hat{r}_k+1}^{\hat{r}_{k+1}},\ \ldots$$

(ii) Consider next the case when $\sigma_1^s \le x < \sigma_1^{s+1}$, with $s \in [1, \ldots, N-1]$. We need the values of z_n^m for $m \in [s+1, \ldots, N]$ and $n \in [1, \ldots, s+1]$. Compute

$$u_s(x-\sigma_1^s) = f_s(x-\sigma_1^s) + \underset{r=s+1,\ldots,N}{\text{Min}} \{c_s(\sigma_1^r - x) + z_{s+1}^r\}$$

$$u_{s-1}(x-\sigma_1^{s-1}) = f_{s-1}(x-\sigma_1^{s-1}) + \text{Min}\{c_{s-1}(0) + u_s(x-\sigma_1^s),\ \underset{r=s+1,\ldots,N}{\text{Min}} [c_{s-1}(\sigma_1^r - x) + z_s^r]\}$$

$$u_1(x-\sigma_1^1) = f_1(x-\sigma_1^1) + \text{Min}\{c_1(0) + u_2(x-\sigma_1^2),\ \underset{r=s+1,\ldots,N}{\text{Min}} [c_1(\sigma_1^r - x) + z_2^r]\}$$

$$u_0(x) = f_0(x) + \text{Min}\{c_0(0) + u_1(x-\sigma_1^1),\ \underset{r=s+1,\ldots,N}{\text{Min}} [c_0(\sigma_1^r - x) + z_1^r]\}$$

We then proceed forward to define the first instant to place an order, and its corresponding size. Next we use the indices $\hat{r}_m$ as above.

Remark 3.6

Suppose for instance that $x = 0$ and $\xi_1 = 0$, $\xi_2 > 0$, then we compute :

$$u_1(0) = f_1(0) + \underset{r=2,\ldots,N}{\text{Min}} \{c_1(\sigma_1^r) + z_2^r\}$$

$$u_0(0) = f_o(0) + \text{Min}\ \{c_0(0) + u_1(0),\ \underset{r=2,\ldots,N}{\text{Min}} [c_0(\sigma_1^r - x) + z_1^r]\}$$

IV - FORWARD DYNAMIC PROGRAMMING AND PLANNING HORIZON RESULTS

IV - 1. NOTATION AND DEFINITIONS

When defining a control V, the number of components will not be restricted. Let $J_n^N(x;V)$ be the functional defined in (1.6) and previously denoted $J_n(x,V)$. The relevant components of V are clearly $(v_n, \ldots, v_{N-1})$. Also write

(4.1) $$J_n^N(0;V) = J_n^N(V)$$

(4.2) $$J^N(V) = J_o^N(V).$$

Let V be any control, i is said to be a <u>set up point</u> if $v_i > 0$. We say that i is a <u>regeneration point</u> if $y_i = 0$ (where y is the trajectory computed from V).

As we mentioned in previous sections an optimal control $\hat{V}$ can be characterized simply by its sequence of set-up points (see §III.4). From Wagner - Within Theorem (see § III 3) we can assert that for this optimal control, set-up points are necessarily regeneration points, except may be for the first one.

IV - 2. FORWARD DYNAMIC PROGRAMMING UNDER THE ASSUMPTION OF NO INITIAL INVENTORY

To obtain an optimal control for $J^N(V)$ we can use the sequence of z^n defined by (3.25), (3.26). The set-up points are easily deduced from z^n by the integers $\hat{r}_n$ (cf. §III.4). If the first demand is 0, we start to operate as in Remark 3.5, but we may have to wait before placing an order. The recursion defining z^n is backward.

We now specify a forward recursion which allows some savings in the computation. It also leads more easily to the concept of planning horizon. Define

(4.3) $$\lambda^N = \operatorname*{Inf}_V J^N(V), \quad N \geq 1, \quad \lambda^0 = 0.$$

The next lemma applies the optimality principle of dynamic programming, to the optimal control V_{op}^N.

<u>Lemma 4.1</u>

Let V_{op}^N be an optimal policy for $J^N(V)$, i.e.

$$J^N(V_{op}^N) = \lambda^N$$

Let s be a regeneration point of V_{op}^N with $1 \leq s \leq N$, then

(4.4) $$\lambda^s = J^s(V_{op}^N).$$

<u>Proof</u>

There is nothing to prove if s = N.

By definition of $J_n^N(x;V)$, it follows

(4.5) $$\lambda^N = J^N(V_{op}^N) = J^s(V_{op}^N) + J_s^N(V_{op}^N)$$

and therefore

(4.6) $$\lambda^N \geq \lambda^s + J_s^N(V_{op}^N).$$

Let now $\hat{V}^s$ be the optimal control for $J^s(V)$, as defined in (4.2) :

$$(4.7) \qquad \lambda^s = J^s(\hat{V}^s).$$

Consider a control $\tilde{V}$ defined as follows

$$\tilde{v}^k = \begin{cases} \hat{v}^s_k & \text{if} \quad k < s \\ v^N_{op,k} & \text{if} \quad k \geq s \end{cases}$$

Denote by $\tilde{y}$ the corresponding state. By (3.20) and the choice of $\hat{v}^s_k$ we have $\tilde{y}_s = 0$. Since s is a regeneration point for V^N_{op}, clearly

$$J^N_s(V^N_{op}) = J^N_s(\tilde{V}).$$

But

$$J^N(\tilde{V}) = J^s(\tilde{V}) + J^N_s(\tilde{V})$$

$$= J^s(\hat{V}^s) + J^N_s(V^N_{op}) \geq \lambda^N$$

or

$$\lambda^s + J^N_s(V^N_{op}) \geq \lambda^N$$

which, compared with (4.6) implies

$$(4.8) \qquad \lambda^N = \lambda^s + J^N_s(V^N_{op}).$$

Comparing (4.8) to (4.5), we deduce (4.4).

The statement can now be made :

Theorem 4.1

Assuming (1.3). Then for N ≥ 1, we have

$$(4.9) \qquad \begin{cases} \lambda^N = \underset{s=0,\dots,N-1}{\text{Min}} \{c_s(\sigma^N_{s+1}) + f_s(0) + \sum_{k=s+1}^{N-1} [f_k(\sigma^N_{k+1}) + c_k(0)] + \lambda^s\} \\ \text{and } \lambda^0 = 0 \end{cases}$$

Proof

In (4.9) we use the convention that for s = N-1, $\sum_{N}^{N-1} = 0$.

If $\sigma^N_1 = 0$, then for s ≤ N,

$$\lambda^s = \sum_{k=0}^{s-1} [f_k(0) + c_k(0)]$$

hence for s ≤ N-1

$$\lambda^N = \lambda^s + c_s(0) + f_s(0) + \sum_{k=s+1}^{N-1} [f_k(0) + c_k(0)]$$

which implies (4.9).

Now assume $\sigma_1^N > 0$. If N = 1, then

$$\lambda^1 = c_0(\sigma_1^1) + f_0(0)$$

and (4.9) is satisfied with the above convention.

Suppose next $N \geq 2$ and $0 \leq s \leq N-1$.

Consider a control defined by

$$(4.10) \quad \begin{cases} \tilde{v}_k = \hat{v}_k^s & \text{if } k < s \\ \tilde{v}_s = \sigma_{s+1}^N & \\ \tilde{v}_k = 0 & \text{for } s < k \leq N-1 \end{cases}$$

where we have used the notation of Lemma 4.1, denoting by $\hat{V}^s$ the optimal control for $J^s(V)$ $(s \geq 1)$. Then

$$\tilde{y}_s = 0 \text{ and } \tilde{y}_k = \sigma_{k+1}^N \text{ for } k = s+1, \ldots, N-1.$$

Hence :

$$J^N(\tilde{V}) = J^s(\hat{V}^s) + c_s(\sigma_{s+1}^N) + f_s(0) + \sum_{k=s+1}^{N-1} [f_k(\sigma_{k+1}^N) + c_k(0)]$$

and since $\lambda^s = J^s(\hat{V}^s)$, $\lambda^N \leq J^N(\tilde{V})$, it follows that $\lambda^N \leq$ right hand side of (4.9).

Now consider $\hat{V}^N$; there is a last set-up point strictly prior to N, namely $0 \leq \hat{s} \leq N-1$.

Then

$$\hat{v}_{\hat{s}}^N = \sigma_{\hat{s}+1}^N$$

and

$$\hat{v}_k^N = 0 \quad k = \hat{s}+1, \ldots, N-1.$$

Moreover $\hat{y}_{\hat{s}} = 0$. From Lemma 4.1, we can assert that

$$\lambda^{\hat{s}} = J^{\hat{s}}(\hat{V}^N)$$

and

$$\lambda^N = \lambda^{\hat{s}} + c_{\hat{s}}(\sigma_{\hat{s}+1}^N) + f_{\hat{s}}(0) + \sum_{k=\hat{s}+1}^{N-1} [f_k(\sigma_{k+1}^N) + c_k(0)].$$

This,and the inequality already proven,imply (4.9).

<u>Remark 4.1</u>

It is easy to deduce the set-up points of $\hat{V}^N$ from relations (4.9). In this case they are obtained following a backward procedure. This is actually the policy denoted by $\hat{V}^N$ in the sequel.

IV - 3. SOME SIMPLIFICATIONS

If $\sigma_1^N > 0$, then $\hat{V}^N$ has a last set-up which is prior to N-1. Denote by l(N) this integer, then

$$\sigma_{l(N)+1}^N > 0$$

and l(N) realizes the minimum in (4.9).

This leads to the following definition

$$(4.11) \qquad l(N) = \begin{cases} N-1 & \text{if } \sigma_1^N = 0 \\ \text{last set-up of } \hat{V}^N & \text{if } \sigma_1^N > 0 \end{cases}$$

and we have

$$(4.12) \qquad \lambda^N = \mu(l(N),N) = \inf_{s=0,\dots,N-1} \mu(s,N)$$

where

$$(4.13) \qquad \mu(s,N) = \lambda^s + c_s(\sigma_{s+1}^N) + f_s(0) + \sum_{k=s+1}^{N-1} [f_k(\sigma_{k+1}^N) + c_k(0)].$$

Note that

$$(4.14) \qquad \begin{cases} \text{if } \sigma_1^N > 0,\ l(N) \text{ is the largest integer } p \in [0,N-1], \text{ for which the infimum is achieved in (4.12) and such that } \sigma_{p+1}^N > 0 \text{ ; } l(N) \text{ is always} \\ \text{a regeneration point of } \hat{V}^N \text{ ; moreover it is the last one before N and} \\ \hat{y}_{l(N)}^N = 0. \end{cases}$$

Note that

$$(4.15) \qquad \begin{cases} \underline{\text{if } 0 \le s_1,s_2 \le N-1 \le M-1, \text{ then}}\ (^1) \\ \mu(s_1,M) - \mu(s_1,N) - [\mu(s_2,M) - \mu(s_2,N)] = \\ = c_{s_1}(\sigma_{s_1+1}^M) - c_{s_1}(\sigma_{s_1+1}^N) - [c_{s_2}(\sigma_{s_2+1}^M) - c_{s_2}(\sigma_{s_2+1}^N)] \\ + \sum_{k=N}^{M-1} [f_k(\sigma_{k+1}^M) + c_k(0)] + \sum_{k=s_1+1}^{s_1 \vee s_2} [f_k(\sigma_{k+1}^M) - f_k(\sigma_{k+1}^N)] \\ - \sum_{k=s_2+1}^{s_1 \vee s_2} [f_k(\sigma_{k+1}^M) - f_k(\sigma_{k+1}^N)] = \phi(s_1,s_2,N,M). \end{cases}$$

We may then assert

(¹) $s_1 \vee s_2 = \text{Max}(s_1,s_2)$

Lemma 4.2

Assume (1.3) and

(4.16) $$c_s(v) = K_s \chi_{v>0} + d_s v$$

with

(4.17) $$d_{s_1} \le d_{s_2} \text{ if } s_1 \ge s_2.$$

Then, if $s_1 \le s_2$ and $\sigma^N_{s_2+1} > 0$, we have

(4.18) $$\phi(s_1,s_2,N,M) \ge 0.$$

Proof

When (4.16) holds, we have :

(4.19) $$\begin{cases} \phi = \chi_{\sigma^M_{N+1} > 0} (K_{s_1} \chi_{\sigma^N_{s_1+1} = 0} - K_{s_2} \chi_{\sigma^N_{s_2+1} = 0}) \\ + (d_{s_1} - d_{s_2}) \sigma^M_{N+1} + \sum_{k=N}^{M-1} f_k(\sigma^M_{N+1}) + \sum_{k=s_1+1}^{s_1 v s_2} [f_k(\sigma^M_{k+1}) - f_k(\sigma^N_{k+1})] \\ - \sum_{k=s_2+1}^{s_1 v s_2} [f_k(\sigma^M_{k+1}) - f_k(\sigma^N_{k+1})]. \end{cases}$$

and if $s_1 \ge s_2$ and $\sigma^N_{s_2+1} > 0$ (hence $\sigma^N_{s_1+1} > 0$), then

$$\phi \ge (d_{s_1} - d_{s_2}) \sigma^M_{N+1}, \text{ since } f_k(\sigma^M_{k+1}) \ge f_k(\sigma^N_{k+1}).$$

Thus, when (4.17) holds (4.18) obtains. □

The following situation is now considered. Assume that $f_s(x)$ and $c_s(v)$ satisfy the following properties, besides (1.3) :

(4.20) $$\begin{cases} c_s \text{ has a right derivative for } v > 0 \text{ denoted by } c'_s , \\ f_s \text{ has a right derivative for } x > 0 \text{ denoted by } f'_s , \\ c'_s(v) \downarrow \bar{c}'_s \text{ as } v \to \infty , \\ f'_s(x) \downarrow \bar{f}'_s \text{ as } x \to \infty , \\ \text{where } \bar{c}'_s > 0,\ \bar{f}'_s > 0. \end{cases}$$

Lemma 4.3

Assume (1.3) and (4.20). Then, if $s_1 < s_2$ and $\sigma^N_{s_2+1} > 0$, and

$$\bar{c}'_{s_1} + \sum_{k=s_1+1}^{s_2} \bar{f}'_k - c'_{s_2}(\sigma^N_{s_2+1}) \geq 0 , \tag{4.21}$$

we have

$$\phi(s_1,s_2,N,M) \geq 0 \quad \forall M \geq N. \tag{4.22}$$

If $s_2 < s_1 \leq N-1 \leq M-1$, $\sigma^N_{s_2+1} > 0$ and

$$\bar{c}'_{s_1} - c'_{s_2}(\sigma^N_{s_2+1}) - \sum_{k=s_2+1}^{s_1} f'_k(\sigma^N_{k+1}) > 0 , \tag{4.23}$$

then (4.22) still holds.

Proof

First consider the case $s_1 < s_2$. From the concavity of the involved functions and formula (4.15), since $\sigma^N_{s_2+1} > 0$ (hence $\sigma^M_{s_1+1} > 0$), it follows :

$$\phi \geq [c'_{s_1}(\sigma^M_{s_1+1}) - c'_{s_2}(\sigma^N_{s_2+1})]\ \sigma^M_{N+1} + \sum_{k=s_1+1}^{s_2} f'_k(\sigma^M_{k+1})\ \sigma^M_{N+1}$$

$$\geq [\bar{c}'_{s_1} - c'_{s_2}(\sigma^N_{s_2+1}) + \sum_{k=s_1+1}^{s_2} \bar{f}'_k]\ \sigma^M_{N+1}$$

≥ 0 by (4.21).

Consider next the second case $s_2 < s_1$. Note first that if $\sigma^M_{N+1} = 0$, $\sigma^M_{s_1+1} = \sigma^N_{s_1+1}$, $\sigma^M_{s_2+1} = \sigma^N_{s_2+1}$, then (4.22) is automatically satisfied. Assume $\sigma^M_{N+1} > 0$, hence $\sigma^M_{s_1+1} > 0$.

Therefore :

$$\phi \geq [c'_{s_1}(\sigma^M_{s_1+1}) - c'_{s_2}(\sigma^N_{s_2+1})]\ \sigma^M_{N+1} - \sum_{k=s_2+1}^{s_1} f'_k(\sigma^N_{k+1})\ \sigma^M_{N+1}$$

$$\geq [\bar{c}'_{s_1} - c'_{s_2}(\sigma^N_{s_2+1}) - \sum_{k=s_2+1}^{s_1} f'_k(\sigma^N_{k+1})]\ \sigma^M_{N+1} \geq 0$$

from assumption (4.23).

Example

Assume that c_s is given by (4.16) (without assuming (4.17)), and

$$f_s(x) = f_s x \tag{4.24}$$

In addition denote :

(4.25) $$a(s,N) = d_s + \sum_{k=s+1}^{N-1} f_k$$

then, conditions (4.21) and (4.23) coincide with

(4.26) $$a(s_1,N) - a(s_2,N) \geq 0.$$

Hence, if we assume (4.16) and (4.24), for

$$0 \leq s_1, s_2 \leq N-1 \leq M-1 \text{ and } \sigma_{s_2+1}^N > 0$$

then (4.26) implies (4.22).

We can then state the following result.

Theorem 4.2

Assume (1.3) and (4.16), (4.17). Let $N \geq 1$ such that $\sigma_1^N \geq 0$, then

(4.27) $$\mu(s,M) \geq \mu(l(N),M), \ \forall s \leq l(N), \ N \leq M.$$

Assume now (1.3) and (4.20). In addition suppose for $N \geq 1$ and $\sigma_1^N > 0$, that

(4.28) $$\begin{cases} \bar{c}'_s + \sum_{k=s+1}^{l(N)} \bar{f}'_k - c'_{l(N)} (\sigma_{l(N)+1}^N) \geq 0 \\ \forall s < l(N) \end{cases}$$

Then (4.27) holds $\forall M \geq N$.

Finally assume (1.3), (4.20). In addition assume (4.28) for $N \geq 1$ and $\sigma_1^N > 0$, and

(4.29) $$\begin{cases} \bar{c}'_s - c'_{l(N)} (\sigma_{l(N)+1}^N) - \sum_{k=l(N)+1}^{s} f'_k(\sigma_{k+1}^N) \geq 0 \\ \forall s \text{ with } l(N) < s \leq N-1. \end{cases}$$

Then we have

(4.30) $$\mu(s,M) \geq \mu(l(N),M), \ \forall s \leq N-1, \ \forall M \geq N.$$

Proof

Recall that

$$\mu(s,N) \geq \mu(l(N),N) \quad \forall s \leq N-1, \text{ then}$$

the following property is deduced from (4.15) :

(4.31) $$\begin{cases} \mu(s,M) \geq \mu(l(N),M) + \phi(s,l(N),N,M) \\ \forall s \leq N-1, \ M \geq N. \end{cases}$$

From (4.31) and Lemmas 4.2, 4.3, we complete the proof if we note that

$\sigma^N_{l(N)+1} > 0$ since $\sigma^N_1 > 0$ (cf. (4.11)).

Corollary 4.1

If (4.27) holds then

$$\lambda(M) = \inf_{s=l(N),\dots,M-1} \mu(s,M) \quad \forall M \geq N \tag{4.32}$$

If (4.30) holds then

$$\lambda(M) = \text{Min}\,[\mu(l(N),M), \min_{s=N,\dots,M-1} \mu(s,M)] \tag{4.33}$$

Proof

Immediate from the definitions.

Remark 4.2

Clearly when we can assert (4.32) or (4.33), the number of necessary computations is decreased for the M-horizon problem. Theorem 4.2 gives criteria for which such simplifications occur.

Corollary 4.2

Assume (1.3), (4.16), (4.17) and suppose K_s is decreasing with time. Then

$$l(N) \leq l(M) \text{ if } N \leq M. \tag{4.34}$$

If we assume (1.3), (4.20), (4.28), $\sigma^N_1 > 0$ then (4.34) also holds.

Proof

If $\sigma^M_1 = 0$ then $l(M) = M-1$ and (4.34) clearly holds.

Assume $\sigma^N_1 = 0$ and $\sigma^M_{N+1} > 0$, then $l(N) = N-1$, and

$$\lambda^s = \sum_{k=0}^{s-1} [f_k(0) + c_k(0)] \text{ , } \forall s \leq N. \tag{4.35}$$

Therefore, for $s \leq N-1$

$$\mu(s,M) = c_1(\sigma^M_{N+1}) + f_s(0) + \sum_{k=s+1}^{N-1} [f_k(\sigma^M_{N+1}) + c_k(0)] + \lambda^s +$$

$$+ \sum_{k=N}^{M-1} [f_k(\sigma^M_{k+1}) + c_k(0)]$$

and from (4.35) we get :

$$\left\{\begin{array}{l}\mu(s,M) - \mu(N-1,M) = c_s(\sigma^M_{N-1}) - c_{N-1}(\sigma^M_{N-1}) + f_s(0) - f_{N-1}(0) + \\ + \displaystyle\sum_{k=s+1}^{N-1} [f_k(\sigma^M_{N-1}) + c_k(0)] + \lambda^s - \lambda^{N-1}\end{array}\right. \tag{4.36}$$

$$= c_s(\sigma^M_{N-1}) - c_{N-1}(\sigma^M_{N+1}) + f_s(0) - f_{N-1}(0) + \sum_{k=s+1}^{N-1} [f_k(\sigma^M_{N+1} + c_k(0)]$$

$$- \sum_{k=s+1}^{N-2} [f_k(0) + c_k(0)] - f_s(0) - c_s(0)$$

$$\geq c_s(\sigma^M_{N+1}) - c_{N-1}(\sigma^M_{N+1}) + c_{N-1}(0) - c_s(0).$$

and, from (4.16) and the fact that K_s is decreasing,

$$\geq (d_s - d_{N-1})\ \sigma^M_{N+1} \geq 0.$$

Hence

$$\lambda^M = \inf_{s=N-1,\dots,M-1} \mu(s,M).$$

Since $\sigma^M_N > 0$, by (4.14) and (4.36), $l(M)$ cannot be strictly less than N-1, hence (4.34) holds.

It remains to consider the case $\sigma^N_1 > 0$. But from Theorem 4.2, (4.27) holds, and $\sigma^N_{l(N)+1} > 0$.

Therefore $l(M)$ cannot be strictly less than $l(N)$, hence (4.34).

Remark 4.3

In Corollary 4.2, the assumptions K_s decreasing in s is not necessary when the demands are strictly positive.

Corollary 4.3.

Assume (1.3), (4.16), (4.17). Suppose that

$$l(N) + 1 \leq l(N-1).$$

Then the optimal policy $\hat{V}^{N+1}$ of J^{N+1} has the property

$$\hat{v}^{n+1}_k = 0 \quad \forall k \in [l(N) + 1, \dots, l(N+1) - 1]$$

Proof

Since

$$l(N) = [l(N) + 1] - 1 \leq l(N-1) - 2$$

$$\leq N - 2,$$

necessarily $\sigma^N_1 > 0$.

Assume that there exists $k \in [l(N) + 1, \dots, l(N+1) - 1]$ such that $\hat{v}^{N+1}_k > 0$, we next prove that

(4.37) $\qquad l(N+1) < N.$

We can always set k to be the largest possible integer.

If (4.37) is not satisfied, then we have

$$l(N+1) = N.$$

Hence N is a regeneration point of $\hat{V}^{N+1}$ and the N-1 first components of $\bar{V}^{N+1}$ constitute an optimal policy for $J^N(V)$. Since $\hat{v}_j^{N+1} = 0$ for $j = k+1, \ldots, N-1$, by definition of k, and $\hat{y}_N^{N+1} = \hat{y}_k^{N+1} = 0$, we have $\hat{v}_k^{N+1} = \sigma_{k+1}^N > 0$, and

$$J^N(\hat{V}^{N+1}) = \lambda^N = \lambda^k + c_k(\sigma_{k+1}^N) + f_k(0) + \sum_{j=k+1}^{N-1}[f_j(\sigma_{j+1}^N) + c_j(0)].$$

By definition of $l(N)$, it follows that $k \le l(N)$, which yields a contradiction.

We now prove that

$$l(N+1) < N-1.$$

Otherwise we have $l(N+1) = N-1$.

Hence N-1 is a regeneration point of $\hat{V}^{N+1}$ and the N-2 first components of $\hat{V}^{N+1}$ constitute an optimal policy for $J^{N-1}(V)$. We have $\hat{v}_j^{N+1} = 0$ for $j = k+1, \ldots, N-2$, and $\hat{y}_{N-1}^{N+1} = \hat{y}_k^{N+1} = 0$, hence $\hat{v}_k^{N+1} = \sigma_{k+1}^{N-1} > 0$. Therefore as above we conclude that $k \le l(N-1)$, and from Corollary 4.2, $k \le l(N)$, which again yields a contradiction.

IV - 4. PLANNING HORIZONS

Definitions :

(i) N is said to be a planning horizon if for $K \ge N$, there exists an optimal policy for $J^K(V)$ which is obtained by extending adequately an optimal policy for $J^N(V)$ on N, N+1, ..., K-1. In other words, N is a planning horizon if for any K-period problem, $K \ge N$, decisions at times 0 through N-1 may be considered by themselves and independently of demand in subsequent periods.

(ii) More generally, N is said to be a planning horizon for the forecast horizon M, $M \ge N$, if for any $K \ge M$ an optimal policy for $J^K(V)$ may be obtained by chosing an optimal policy for $J^N(V)$ and extending it adequately on N, N+1, ..., K-1. In other words, N is a planning horizon for a forecast horizon $M \ge N$ if for any K-period problem, $K \ge M$ decisions at times 0 through N-1 may be considered by themselves and independently of demand beyond the forecast horizon M.

It follows immediately from both definitions that if N is a planning horizon, then N is a planning horizon for the forecast horizon N.

A third definition concerns the concept of forecast horizon per se. While it is useful only in chapter II, it is beneficial at this stage to connect this new notion with the previous ones.

(iii) M is said to be a forecast horizon, if for any K, $K \ge M \ge 1$, there exists $s = s(K)$ with $s(K) \le M$ such that an optimal policy for $J^K(V)$ may be obtained by taking an optimal policy for $J^s(V)$ and extending it adequately on s, s+1, ..., K-1.

We note that if s were independent of K, then s would be a planning horizon for the forecast horizon M, exactly in the sense of (ii).

In this chapter, we derive sufficient conditions for "a planning horizon", or a "planning horizon for a forecast horizon" to obtain. In the next chapter devoted to the convex cost models (still in a deterministic environment) only "forecast horizon" results will be produced, except for very special cases.

Two complementary notions must be also introduced, although they are not crucial in this chapter : strong versus weak planning (forecast) horizons.

Any production planning problem must be envisaged with an infinite decision horizon. But any planning or forecast horizon result will be useful in practive, if only limited (possibly little) information about future demand and cost structure, is needed to compute them. Thus, an horizon is said to be strong if no further information about demand beyond that horizon is needed to compute it. Otherwise it is said to be a weak horizon, with eventually the need to know precisely demand up to infinity in order to recognize a planning or a forecast horizon.

In this chapter only strong planning horizon results are derived. In the next chapter mainly weak forecast horizon results will obtain.

Lemma 4.4

If N is a regeneration point for an optimal policy of $J^K(V)$ for any K such that $K \geq M \geq N$ (or for any K, $K \geq N$), then N is a planning horizon for the forecast horizon M (or a planning horizon).

Proof

Indeed, from the proof of Lemma 4.1

$$\lambda^K = \lambda^N + J_N^K(V_{op}^K) \quad \forall K$$

from which it follows that we can construct an optimal policy for λ^K, by choosing an optimal policy of $J^N(V)$ for the N-1 first components, and completing it adequately on N, ..., K-1. □

Define next

(4.38) $E(N) = \{j = 0, \ldots, N-1 \mid \exists\, M \geq N \text{ such that } l(M) = j\}$

It then follows :

Lemma 4.5

$l(N) \in E(N)$. There exists for any $M \geq N$, an optimal policy for $J^M(V)$ which has a regeneration point in E(N).

Proof

$l(N) \in E(N)$ follows from the definition of E(N).

Let $M \geq N$ and consider $l(M)$. It is a regeneration point for $\hat{V}^M$, hence if $l(M) \leq N-1$, the desired result is proved since then $l(M) \in E(N)$.

Otherwise we have $l(M) \geq N$, then $l(l(M))$ is a regeneration point for an optimal policy of $J^{l(M)}(V)$. Since $\hat{y}_{l(M)}^M = 0$, the optimal policy for $J^{l(M)}(V)$ can be kept as a part of an optimal policy of $J^M(V)$, and $l(l(M)) \leq l(M)-1 \leq M-2$. If $l(l(M)) \leq N-1$, then $l(l(M)) \in E(N)$ and the desired result is proved. Otherwise we proceed as above. After a finite number of steps, the desired result follows.

Theorem 4.3

Assume (1.3). Let $N \leq M-1$ and assume that $\forall P \in E(M)$, there exists an optimal policy for $J^P(V)$, which admits N as a regeneration point. Then N is a planning horizon for the forecast horizon M.

Proof

Let $P \in E(M)$ and V_{op}^P such that

$$\lambda^P = J^P(V_{op}^P),$$

and N is a regeneration point of V_{op}^P. Then from Lemma 4.1, we have

$$\lambda^P = \lambda^N + J_N^P(V_{op}^P) \tag{4.39}$$

Take $K \geq M$. From Lemma 4.5, there exists $P \in E(M)$ which is a regeneration point of an optimal policy for $J^K(V)$, hence

$$\lambda^K = \lambda^P + J_P^K\,(V_{op}^K). \tag{4.40}$$

From (4.39) and (4.40) it follows that

$$\lambda^K = \lambda^N + J_N^P(V_{op}^P) + J_P^K(V_{op}^K)$$
$$= \lambda^N + J_N^K(V^*)$$

which proves that N is a regeneration point of an optimal policy for $J^K(V)$, $\forall K \geq M$, hence the desired result from Lemma 4.4

Corollary 4.4

Assume that $E(N+1) = N$, then N is a planning horizon.

Proof

From Lemma 4.5, $\forall M \geq N+1$, there exists an optimal policy for $J^M(V)$ which admits N as a regeneration point, hence from Lemma 4.4, N is a planning horizon. □

Practically, the construction of the sets E(N), defined in (4.38), is not an easy task, if not impossible. Therefore the above results are not useful to show the existence of planning horizons and produce any of them. In the following we turn to more constructive criteria based on the results derived in §IV.3. However, these sufficient conditions only obtain under restrictions on the cost functions. Namely conditions (4.16), (4.17) used in Theorems 4.4, 4.5 and 9.3 ; conditions (4.20) and (4.28) used in Theorem 4.6 ; and condition (5.14) in the case of linear costs. All of these imply some kind of decrease in production costs overtime. These conditions, nevertheless, are quite reasonable if such elements like technological progress or a discount factor are formally taken into account.

Theorem 4.4

Assume (1.3), (4.16), (4.17), then if

(4.41) $\quad l(N+1) = N$

N is a planning horizon.

Proof

Let us verify the following property, of importance by itself :

(4.42) $\quad \forall M \geq N+1$, there exists an optimal policy for $J^M(V)$ which posesses a regeneration point between $l(N+1)$ and N.

As we have seen in the proof of Lemma 4.5, indeed $l(M)$, $l(l(M))$ ... are regeneration points for an optimal policy of $J^M(V)$. Now by Corollary 4.2, $M-1 \geq l(M) \geq l(N+1)$.

If $l(M) \leq N$, the desired result is proved. Otherwise $l(M) \geq N+1$, hence $l(l(M)) \geq l(N+1)$, and $l(l(M)) \leq M-2$. After a finite number of steps, (4.42) is necessarily obtained.

Therefore, if (4.41) is satisfied, N is a regeneration point for an optimal policy of $J^M(V)$, $\forall M \geq N$, and hence it is a planning horizon.

Theorem 4.5

Assume (1.3), (4.16), (4.17). Let N,M be integers such that $N \leq l(M)$. Suppose that $\forall P \in [l(M), M-1]$, N is a regeneration point for an optimal policy of $J^P(V)$. Then N is a planning horizon for the forecast horizon $l(M)$.

Proof

Provided the above assumptions, we have

(4.43) $$\lambda^P = \lambda^N + J_N^P(V_{op}^P), \ \forall P \in [l(M), M-1].$$

But $\forall K \geq M$, from (4.42) it follows that there exists an optimal policy for $J^K(V)$ which has a regeneration point in the interval $[l(M), M-1]$. Therefore, there exists $P \in [l(M), M-1]$ such that

(4.44) $$\lambda^K = \lambda^P + J_P^K(V_{op}^K).$$

From (4.43), (4.44) we deduce

$$\lambda^K = \lambda^N + J_N^P(V_{op}^P) + J_P^K(V_{op}^K)$$

hence the desired result.

Remark 4.3

There is a clear analogy between Theorem 4.4 and Corollary 4.4, and between Theorem 4.5 and Theorem 4.3.

The role of the set E(N) is played by the interval $[l(N), N-1]$. This reduction is possible by virtue of assumptions (4.16), (4.17).

Theorem 4.6

Assume (1.3) and (4.20). Assume (4.28) and (4.29) for $N \geq 1$ and $\sigma_1^N > 0$. Then $l(N)$ is a planning horizon for the forecast horizon N.

Proof

From Theorem 4.2 and Corollary 4.1, we can assert that (4.33) holds. Take $M = N+1$, then

$$\lambda(N+1) = \text{Min}\,[\mu(l(N), N+1), \mu(N, N+1)]$$

But

$$\begin{aligned}\mu(N, N+1) &= \lambda^N + c_N(\sigma_{N+1}^{N+1}) + f_N(0) \\ &= \lambda^{l(N)} + c_{l(N)}(\sigma_{l(N)+1}^{N}) + f_{l(N)}(0) \\ &+ \sum_{k=l(N)+1}^{N-1} [f_k(\sigma_{k+1}^{N}) + c_k(0)] + c_N(\sigma_{N+1}^{N+1}) + f_N(0)\end{aligned}$$

$$\begin{aligned}\mu(l(N), N+1) &= \lambda^{l(N)} + c_{l(N)}(\sigma_{l(N)+1}^{N+1}) + f_{l(N)}(0) \\ &+ \sum_{k=l(N)+1}^{N} [f_k(\sigma_{k+1}^{N+1}) + c_k(0)].\end{aligned}$$

Therefore we can write

$$\lambda(N+1) = \lambda(l(N)) + J_{l(N)}^{N+1}(\tilde{V})$$

where $\tilde{V}$ is some control.

By induction, using (4.33) it can be inferred that

$$\lambda(M) = \lambda(l(N)) + J_{l(N)}^{M}(\tilde{V})$$

where $\tilde{V}$ is some control.

This proves that $l(N)$ is a regeneration point for an optimal policy of $J^M(V)$ $\forall M \geq N$, which is the desired result.

Remark 4.4

In Theorem 4.4, condition (4.28) for any N is an alternative to assumptions (4.16) and (4.17).

IV - 5. NETWORK REPRESENTATION

Consider the problem $J^N(V)$. We know that an optimal control will have the property that $\hat{y}_N = 0$. We can then, without loss of generality, pose the following problem which is equivalent to minimizing $J^N(V)$, namely

$$(4.45)\quad \begin{cases} \text{Min} \sum_{i=0}^{N-1} c_i(v_i) + \sum_{i=1}^{N-1} f_i(v_i) \\ v_i + y_i - y_{i+1} = \xi_{i+1},\ i = 0, \ldots, N-1 \\ y_0 = y_N = 0,\ y_i \geq 0,\ v_i \geq 0. \end{cases}$$

The set of constraints can be interpreted as a trans-shipment network (Orden [1956], Zangwill [1968]) with N destinations, where the amount of material required is ξ_{i+1} at destination i+1, $i = 0, \ldots, N-1$. There is one source and the quantity to be shipped is $\sum_{i=0}^{N-1} \xi_{i+1}$.

A figure for N = 5 is shown next.

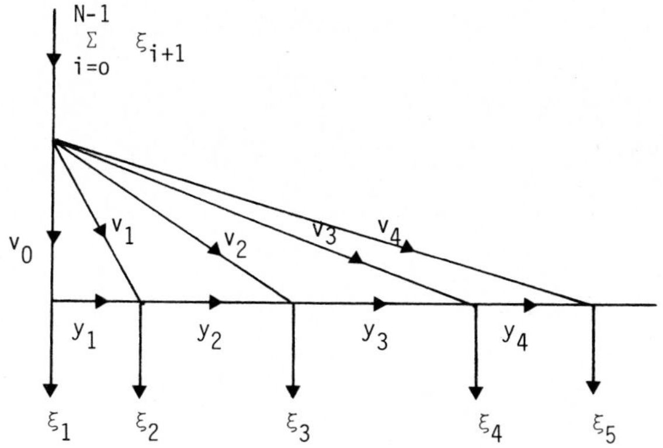

Figure 1.3 : Network representation of problem (4.45).

An optimal control for $J^N(V)$ can thus be interpreted as a transhipment which minimizes the cost functional (4.45). The Wagner-Within Theorem tells that there exists an optimal transhipment such that any node has at most one positive input. This result can also be recovered from properties of concave networks with one source.

Remark 4.5

The existence of an optimal solution in the network formulation follows from network theory

V - PLANNING HORIZONS FOR A POSITIVE INITIAL INVENTORY

In this section the general problem $J_o^N(x;V)$ is considered where x is not necessarily zero.

V - 1. SPECIAL CASE OF LINEAR HOLDING COSTS

However, this case can be easily reduced to the previous situation we considered where x = 0, when we assume

(5.1) $f_s(x) = f_s x,$

(cf. Zabel [1964]).

Consider indeed the problem corresponding to $J_n^N(x;V)$ with

$$\sigma_{n+1}^s \le x < \sigma_{n+1}^{s+1}, \ s \in [n, \ldots, N].$$

We define a new control problem as follows

$$\tilde{y}_n = 0, \ \tilde{y}_{i+1} = \tilde{y}_i + v_i - \tilde{\xi}_{i+1}, \ i = n, \ldots, N-1$$

where

$$\tilde{\xi}_i = 0 \text{ for } i = n, \ldots, s \quad (\text{if } \max(n,s) \ge 1)$$

$$\tilde{\xi}_{s+1} = \sigma_{n+1}^{s+1} - x$$

$$\tilde{\xi}_i = \xi_i \text{ for } i > s+1.$$

Then, consider $\tilde{J}_n^N(0;V) = \tilde{J}_n^N(V)$ where the $\sim$ refers to the problem with demands $\tilde{\xi}_i$ instead of ξ_i. It is easy to check that the constraints on the control V for both problems are identical, since they reduce to

$$v_n \ge 0 \ \ldots \qquad v_n + \ldots + v_{s-1} \ge 0$$

$$v_n + \ldots + v_s \ge \sigma_{n+1}^{s+1} - x = \tilde{\xi}_{s+1}$$

$$v_n + \ldots + v_{s+1} \ge \sigma_{n+1}^{s+2} - x = \tilde{\xi}_{s+1} + \tilde{\xi}_{s+2} \ .$$

---------- ---

But then

$$y_n = \tilde{y}_n + x$$

$$y_s = \tilde{y}_s + x - \sigma_{n+1}^s$$

$$y_i = \tilde{y}_i \qquad i \ge s+1 \ ,$$

which implies

$$J_n^N(x;V) - \tilde{J}_n^N(V) = \sum_{i=n}^{s} f_i(x - \sigma_{n+1}^i)$$

and therefore

$$u_n(x) = \tilde{u}_n(0) + \sum_{i=n}^{s} f_i(x - \sigma_{n+1}^i)$$

V - 2. PLANNING HORIZONS

Consider $J_o^N(x;V)$. It will be convenient to write explicitly the demand as an argument of J_o^N, hence

(5.2) $$J_o^N(x;V) \equiv J_o^N(x;V;\xi_1, \ldots, \xi_N)$$

Recall :

N is said to be a planning horizon if $\forall K \geq N$, an optimal policy for $J_o^K(x;V;\xi_1, \ldots, \xi_K)$ can be obtained by chosing an optimal policy for $J_o^N(x;V;\xi_1, \ldots, \xi_N)$ and extending it adequately on N, ..., K-1. If this property holds only for $K \geq M \geq N$, then we say that N is a planning horizon for the forecast horizon M (see definitions § IV.4). We start with a general sufficient criterion, which will play the role of Lemma 4.4.

Lemma 5.1

Assume (1.3) and $x \leq \sigma_1^N$. Assume that N is a regeneration point for an optimal policy of $J_o^{N+1}(x;V,\xi_1, \ldots, \xi_N, \eta)$ where $\eta \geq 0$ can vary arbitrary. Then N is a planning horizon.

Remark 5 1

Comparing Lemmas 4.4 and 5.1, it appears that we have replaced the arbitrariness of K (the horizon) by the arbitrariness of η for the (N+1)-th demand.

Proof of Lemma 5.1

Consider the problem of minimizing $J_o^N(x;V;\xi_1, \ldots, \xi_N)$, where the additional constraint $y_N = h$, is imposed with h a given positive value. Let

$J_o^N(x;V;\xi_1, \ldots, \xi_N;h)$ be this new functional.

Denote

(5.3) $$F(0,N;x,h;\xi_1, \ldots, \xi_N) = \inf_V J_o^N(x;V;\xi_1, \ldots, \xi_N,h).$$

Note that for $M \geq N$, since $x \leq \sigma_1^N$

(5.4) $$F(0,M;x,0;\xi_1, \ldots, \xi_M) = \inf_V J_o^M(x;V).$$

Indeed the value $\hat{y}_M = 0$ will be attained by the optimal control, even if we do not impose it a priori, (cf. Theorem 3.3).

We next notice that for $M > N$

(5.5) $$\begin{cases} F(0,M;x,0;\xi_1, \ldots, \xi_M) = \underset{h\geq 0}{\text{Min}} \{F(0,N+1;x,h;\xi_1, \ldots, \xi_{N+1}) \\ \qquad + F(N+1,M;h,0;\xi_{N+2}, \ldots,\xi_M)\}. \end{cases}$$

But it is easy to check that

$$F(0,N+1;x,h;\xi_1, \ldots, \xi_{N+1}) = F(0,N+1;x,0;\xi_1, \ldots, \xi_N, h + \xi_{N+1}) \tag{5.6}$$

and, by the sufficient condition already stated

$$= F(0,N;x,0;\xi_1,\ldots,\xi_N) + f_N(0) + c_N(h+\xi_{N+1}).$$

Therefore, we deduce from (5.5) that

$$\begin{cases} F(0,M;x,0;\xi_1, \ldots, \xi_M) = F(0,N;x,0;\xi_1, \ldots, \xi_N) + f_N(0) + \\ + \underset{h\geq 0}{\text{Min}} \{c_N(h + \xi_{N+1}) + F(N+1,m;h,0;\xi_{N+2}, \ldots, \xi_M)\} \end{cases} \tag{5.7}$$

hence

$$\inf J_0^M(x;V) = \inf J_0^N(x;V) + \inf J_N^M(0;V) \tag{5.8}$$

which proves that N is a planning horizon. □

We next give a result which is the analogue of Theorem 4.3.

Theorem 5.1

Assume (1.3) and $x \leq \sigma_1^N$. Suppose that $M \geq N+1$, and

$$\begin{cases} N \text{ is a regeneration point for an optimal control of} \\ J_0^l(x;V;\xi_1, \ldots, \xi_l),\ \forall l = N+1, \ldots, M \end{cases} \tag{5.9}$$

$$\begin{cases} \forall \eta \geq 0, \text{ there exists an optimal control of } J_0^{M+1}(x;V;\xi_1, \ldots, \xi_M, \eta\ ) \\ \text{which posesses a regeneration point between } N+1 \text{ and } M. \end{cases} \tag{5.10}$$

Then N is a planning horizon for the forecast horizon M.

Proof

From (5.9) it follows that the optimal control of $J_0^N(x;V)$ can be kept as a part of an optimal control of $J_0^M(x;V)$. Take now $K > M+1$. We have as for (5.5)

$$F(0,K;x,0;\xi_1, \ldots, \xi_K) = \underset{h\geq 0}{\text{Min}} \{F(0,M+1;x,h,\xi_1, \ldots, \xi_{M+1})$$
$$+ F(M+1,K;h,0;\xi_{M+2}, \ldots, \xi_K)\}$$

and

$$F(0,M+1,x,h;\xi_1, \ldots, \xi_{M+1}) = F(0,M+1;x,0;\xi_1, \ldots, \xi_M, \xi_{M+1} + h)$$

and by (5.10)

$$= F(0,k;x,0;\xi_1, \ldots, \xi_k) + F(k,M+1,0,0:\xi_{k+1}, \ldots, \xi_{M+1} + h)$$

where $k \in \{N+1, \ldots, M\}$. Using now (5.9), we obtain

$$F(0,k;x,0;\xi_1, \ldots, \xi_k) = F(0,N;x,0;\xi_1, \ldots, \xi_N) + F(N,k;0,0;\xi_{N+1}, \ldots, \xi_k).$$

Therefore, collecting results we obtain

$$F(0,K,x,0,\xi_1, \ldots, \xi_K) = F(0,N;x,0;\xi_1, \ldots, \xi_N) + \underset{h\geq 0}{\text{Min}} \{F(N,k;0,0;\xi_{N+1}, \ldots, \xi_k)$$
$$+ F(k,M+1;0,0;\xi_{k+1}, \ldots, \xi_{M+1} + h)$$
$$+ F(M+1,K;h,0;\xi_{M+2}, \ldots, \xi_K)\}$$

from which one easily deduces that we can keep an optimal control for $J_o^N(x;V)$ as a part of an optimal control for $J_o^K(x;V)$. Hence the desired result. □

We can now state a sufficient condition for (5.10) to hold

Lemma 5.2

Assume that

$$(5.11)\qquad \begin{cases} \forall\eta \geq 0, \text{ there exists } j \in [N+1, M] \text{ such that} \\ c_j(0) - c_j(\sigma_{j+1}^M + \eta) + \sum_{k=N}^{j} [f_k(\sigma_{k+1}^M + \eta) - f_k(\sigma_{k+1}^j)] \geq 0 \end{cases}$$

then (5.10) is satisfied

Proof

Consider $J_o^{M+1}(x;V;\xi_1, \ldots, \xi_M, \eta)$ and the optimal policy $\hat{V}^{M+1}$. If (5.10) is not satisfied, there exists $\eta \geq 0$ for which the corresponding $\hat{V}^{M+1}$ has no regeneration point in $[N+1, M]$. Since the stock at N+1 is positive and since $x \leq \sigma_1^N$, there has been a set-up before N. From Theorem 3.3 it follows that $\hat{v}_k^{M+1} = 0$ for $k = N+1, \ldots, M$. Therefore

$$\hat{y}_N^{M+1} = \sigma_{N+1}^M + \eta.$$

It follows that

$$(5.12)\qquad \begin{cases} F(0,M+1;x,0;\xi_1, \ldots, \xi_M, \eta) = F(0,N;x,\sigma_{N+1}^M + \eta;\xi_1, \ldots, \xi_N) \\ \qquad + \sum_{k=N}^{M} [c_k(0) + f_k(\sigma_{k+1}^M + \eta)]. \end{cases}$$

Since (5.11) is satisfied and noting that

$$F(0,N;x;\sigma_{N+1}^M+\eta;\xi_1,\ldots,\xi_N) \geq F(0,N;x;\sigma_{N+1}^j;\xi_1, \ldots, \xi_N)$$

we deduce

$$F(0,M+1;x,0;\xi_1, \ldots, \xi_M, \eta) \geq F(0,N;x;\sigma^j_{N+1};\xi_1, \ldots, \xi_N)$$

$$+ \sum_{k=j+1}^{M} [c_k(0) + f_k(\sigma^M_{k+1} + \eta)] + \sum_{k=N}^{j-1} [f_k(\sigma^j_{k+1}) + c_k(0)] + f_j(0) + c_j(\sigma^M_{j+1} + \eta).$$

But the right hand side of this expression corresponds to the cost of an admissible control which possesses a regeneration point at j. This control is necessarily optimal, which is a contradiction since (5.10) is not satisfied. Hence the desired result.

Example

Consider the situation

$$(5.13) \qquad \begin{cases} c_j(v) = K_j \, \chi_{v>0} + d_j \, v \\ f_j(x) = f_j \, x \end{cases}$$

Then (5.11) is satisfied if there exists $j \in [N+1, \ldots, M]$ such that

$$(5.14) \qquad \begin{cases} K_j + d_j \, \sigma^M_{j+1} \leq \left(\sum_{k=N}^{j} f_k\right) \sigma^M_{j+1} \\ d_j \leq \sum_{k=N}^{j} f_k \end{cases}$$

Remark 5.2

The results of this section are due to Proth [1982-1].

VI - OPTIMAL CONTROL IN THE CASE OF BACKLOGGING

VI - 1. SETTING OF THE PROBLEM

Basically, the problem is the same as in § I.1, I.2, except that now shortages are allowed and backordered, so that the inventory position y_i may assume negative values. The demand is still

$$\xi_1, \ldots, \xi_N, \; \xi_i \geq 0$$

Let y_i be the inventory level at time i, then the inventory balance equations are still :

$$(6.1) \qquad y_{i+1} = y_i + v_i - \xi_{i+1}$$

where

$$(6.2) \qquad V = (v_0, \ldots, v_{N-1}), \; v_i \geq 0$$

is the control. In this case there is no constraint on the sign of the state variable y_i. In order to define the objective function, we need to introduce the following production and inventory cost functions :

$$(6.3) \qquad c_i(v), \; f_i(x)$$

where $c_i = R^+ \to R^+$ is concave, non decreasing and $f_i : R \to R^+$, is concave for $x \leq 0$ and $x \geq 0$, non decreasing for $x \geq 0$ and non increasing for $x \leq 0$.

Remark 6.1

The inventory cost function $f_i(x)$ is not necessarily concave. It is continuous on $]-\infty,0[$ and $]0,+\infty[$ and $f_i(0^-)$, $f_i(0^+)$ exist and are larger thant $f_i(0)$.

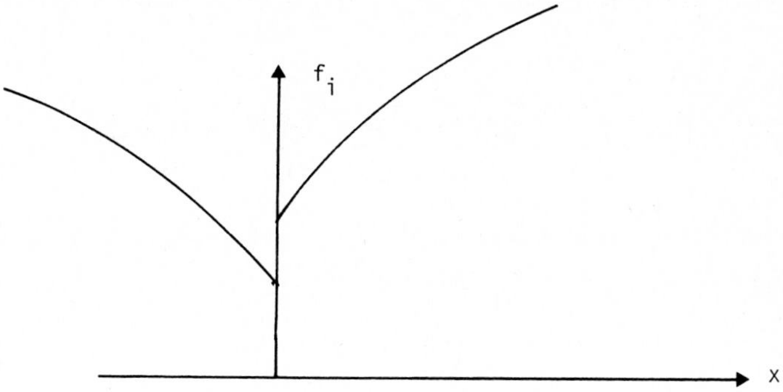

Figure 1.4 : Graph of the inventory cost function

We set the following control problem

$$(6.4)\qquad \begin{cases} y_{i+1} = y_i + v_i - \xi_{i+1},\ v_i \geq 0,\ i = n, \ldots, N-1 \\ y_n = x \end{cases}$$

$$(6.5)\qquad J_n(x;V) = \sum_{i=n}^{N-1} [c_i(v_i) + f_i(y_i)].$$

where it is always possible to introduce a final cost.

Dynamic Programming leads to the following recursion

$$(6.6)\qquad \begin{cases} u_N(x) = 0 \text{ , and for } n = N-1, \ldots, 0 \\ u_n(x) = f_n(x) + \operatorname*{Inf}_{v\geq 0} \{c_n(v) + u_{n+1}(x + v - \xi_{n+1})\} \end{cases}$$

and we have

$$(6.7)\qquad u_n(x) = \operatorname*{Inf}_{V} J_n(x;V)$$

VI - 2. DYNAMIC PROGRAMMING EQUATIONS

Theorem 6.1

Assume (6.3). Then we have

$$u_{N-1}(x) = f_{N-1}(x) + c_{N-1}(0). \tag{6.8}$$

For $n \leq N-2$, the following relations hold

$$\left\{\begin{array}{l} \underline{\text{If } x < \sigma_{n+1}^{n+1}} \\ u_n(x) = f_n(x) + \text{Min}\,[c_n(0) + u_{n+1}(x - \xi_{n+1}), \\ \qquad \underset{r=n+1,\dots,N-1}{\text{Min}} \{c_n(\sigma_{n+1}^r - x) + u_{n+1}(\sigma_{n+2}^r)\}] \end{array}\right. \tag{6.9}$$

$$\left\{\begin{array}{l} \underline{\text{If } \sigma_{n+1}^s \leq x < \sigma_{n+1}^{s+1} \quad (s=n+1, \dots, N-2)} \\ u_n(x) = f_n(x) + \text{Min}\,[c_n(0) + u_{n+1}(x - \xi_{n+1}), \\ \qquad \underset{r=s+1,\dots,N-1}{\text{Min}} \{c_n(\sigma_{n+1}^r - x) + u_{n+1}(\sigma_{n+2}^r)\}] \end{array}\right. \tag{6.10}$$

$$\left\{\begin{array}{l} \underline{\text{If } x \geq \sigma_{n+1}^{N-1}} \\ u_n(x) = f_n(x) + c_n(0) + u_{n+1}(x - \xi_{n+1}). \end{array}\right. \tag{6.11}$$

Moreover u_n is concave on intervals $[\sigma_{n+1}^s, \sigma_{n+1}^{s+1}[$, $n \leq s \leq N-2$, and on $]-\infty,0[$, $[\sigma_{n+1}^N,\infty[$.

The only possible discontinuity points are σ_{n+1}^s, $s = n, \dots, N-1$, for which u_n has left and right limits, such that

$$\left\{\begin{array}{l} u_n(\sigma_{n+1}^s) \leq u_n(\sigma_{n+1}^s - 0) \\ u_n(\sigma_{n+1}^s) \leq u_n(\sigma_{n+1}^s + 0). \end{array}\right. \tag{6.12}$$

In addition u_n is non increasing on $]-\infty,0[$ and non decreasing on $]\sigma_{n+1}^{N-1},\infty[$. We must interpret a statement on an interval $[a,a[$ as void. □

The following picture can thus be drawn :

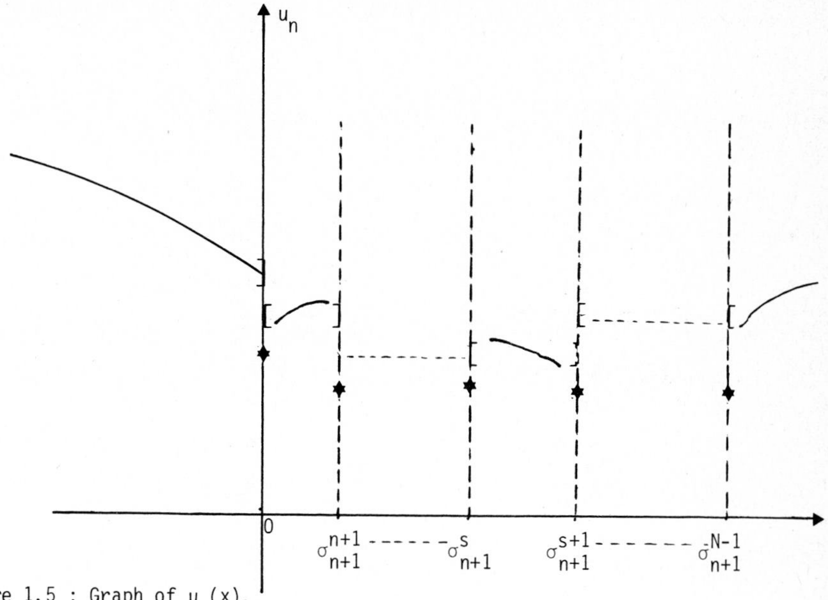

Figure 1.5 : Graph of $u_n(x)$.

Proof of Theorem 6.1

Property (6.8) is straightforward. Take n = N-2, then

$$u_{N-2}(x) = f_{N-2}(x) + \inf_{v\geq 0} \{c_{N-2}(v) + u_{N-1}(x + v - \xi_{N-1})\}.$$

Note in that case that (6.10) is void.

Assume first that $x < \xi_{N-1}$. Then we need to consider two intervals for v, $]0,\xi_{N-1}-x[$ and $]\xi_{N-1}-x,+\infty[$. On each of them the function

$$\psi_{N-2}(v) = c_{N-2}(v) + u_{N-1}(x + v - \xi_{N-1})$$

is concave. Therefore it is easy to deduce that the possible values of v, where $\psi_{N-2}(v)$ can reach its minimum, are 0 and $\xi_{N-2} - x$, hence

$$(6.13) \qquad \begin{cases} u_{N-2}(x) = f_{N-2}(x) + \text{Min}\,[c_{N-2}(0) + u_{N-1}(x - \xi_{N-1}), \\ \qquad\qquad c_{N-2}(\xi_{N-1} - x) + u_{N-1}(0)] \quad \text{for } x < \xi_{N-1} \end{cases}$$

which proves (6.9).

Let next $x \geq \xi_{N-1}$, then $\psi_{N-2}(v)$ is increasing from which it follows that (6.10) is satisfied.

Take now $n \leq N-3$ and assume that (6.9), (6.10), (6.11) hold for N-2, ..., n+1. We want to prove these three realtions hold for n. Define

$$\psi_n(v) = c_n(v) + u_{n+1}(x + v - \xi_{n+1})$$

Assume first $x < \xi_{n+1} = \sigma_{n+1}^{n+1}$ and consider the intervals for v :

$]0, \xi_{n+1} - x[, \ldots,]\sigma_{n+1}^{s} - x, \sigma_{n+1}^{s+1} - x[\ldots]\sigma_{n+1}^{N-1} - x, \infty[$ for $s=n+1,\ldots,N-2$. (if $\xi_{s+1} = 0$, the corresponding interval is omitted). In each of them, $\psi_n(v)$ is concave. From this and (6.12) it easily follows that (6.9) holds.

Assume next $\sigma_{n+1}^{s} \leq x < \sigma_{n+1}^{s+1}$, and consider the following intervals for v,

$]0, \sigma_{n+1}^{s+1} - x[,]\sigma_{n+1}^{s+1} - x, \sigma_{n+1}^{s+2} - x[\ldots, \ldots]\sigma_{n+1}^{N-1}, +\infty[$. In each of them, ψ_n is concave, and using (6.12) we deduce (6.10). Finally if $x \geq \sigma_{n+1}^{N-1}$, then $x - \xi_{n+1} \geq \sigma_{n+2}^{N-1}$, and $\psi_n(v)$ is increasing, from which (6.11) obtains.

Concavity of u_n follows by induction from relations (6.9),(6.10), (6.11). Consider the interval $x \in]-\infty, 0[$, then $x - \xi_{n+1} < 0$. Assuming that u_{n+1} is non increasing on $]-\infty, 0[$, and since this is also true for $f_n(x)$ on this interval, it follows from (6.9) that u_n is non increasing on $]-\infty, 0[$. A similar argument leads to the property that u_n is non decreasing on $]\sigma_{n+1}^{N-1}, \infty[$.

Properties (6.12) are also easily deduced from formulas (6.9), (6.10), (6.11). This completes the proof of Theorem 6.1. □

From Theorem 6.1, the optimal feedback can be derived :

$$(6.14) \quad \begin{cases} \hat{v}_n(x) = \begin{cases} \underline{\text{If } x < \sigma_{n+1}^{n+1} :} \\ 0 \text{ or } \sigma_{n+1}^{\hat{r}(x)} - x, \ \hat{r} \in [n+1, \ldots, N-1] \\ \\ \underline{\text{If } \sigma_{n+1}^{s} \leq x < \sigma_{n+1}^{s+1}, \ s = n+1, \ldots, N-2 :} \\ 0 \text{ or } \sigma_{n+1}^{\hat{r}(x)} - x, \ \hat{r} \in [s+1, \ldots, N-1] \\ \\ \underline{\text{If } x \geq \sigma_{n+1}^{N-1} :} \\ 0 \end{cases} \\ \hat{v}_{N-1}(x) = 0 \end{cases}$$

VII - SIMPLIFIED DYNAMIC PROGRAMMING EQUATIONS IN THE BACKLOGGING CASE

VII - 1. THE CASE OF COST FUNCTIONS WHICH DECREASE WITH TIME

Theorem 7.1

Assume (6.3) and

$$(7.1) \qquad \begin{cases} c_n(v) \geq c_{n+1}(v) \\ c_n(0) = c_{n+1}(0). \end{cases}$$

Then the functions u_n satisfy (6.9) and

$$(7.2) \qquad \begin{cases} u_n(x) = f_n(x) + c_n(0) + u_{n+1}(x - \xi_{n+1}) \\ \text{if } x \geq \xi_{n+1} \end{cases}$$

Proof

For n = N-2, (7.2) follows immediatly from (6.11).

Assume now that $n \leq N-3$, and (7.2) holds for $u_{N-2}, \ldots, u_{n+1}$. We wish to prove (7.2) for n.

Take $\sigma_{n+1}^{s} \leq x < \sigma_{n+1}^{s+1}$, $s = n+1, \ldots, N-2$.

We have to show that

$$(7.3) \qquad \begin{cases} c_n(0) + u_{n+1}(x - \xi_{n+1}) \leq c_n(\sigma_{n+1}^{r} - x) + u_{n+1}(\sigma_{n+2}^{r}) \\ \forall r = s+1, \ldots, N-1. \end{cases}$$

If $s \geq n+2$ (which implies $n \leq N-4$), then $x - \xi_{n+1} \geq \sigma_{n+2}^{s} \geq \xi_{n+2}$. We can then assert by the induction argument that

$$(7.4) \qquad \begin{cases} u_{n+1}(x - \xi_{n+1}) = f_{n+1}(x - \xi_{n+1}) + c_{n+1}(0) + u_{n+2}(x - \sigma_{n+1}^{n+2}) \\ \qquad \leq f_{n+1}(x - \xi_{n+1}) + c_{n+1}(\sigma_{n+1}^{r} - x) + u_{n+2}(\sigma_{n+3}^{r}) \\ \qquad \forall r = n+3, \ldots, N-1. \end{cases}$$

But

$$x - \xi_{n+1} < \sigma_{n+2}^{s+1}$$

therefore, if $r = s+1, \ldots, N-1$

$$x - \xi_{n+1} < \sigma_{n+2}^{r}$$

hence

$$u_{n+1}(x - \xi_{n+1}) \leq f_{n+1}(\sigma_{n+2}^{r}) + c_{n+1}(\sigma_{n+1}^{r} - x) + u_{n+2}(\sigma_{n+3}^{r})$$

and from (7.1)

$$u_{n+1}(x - \xi_{n+1}) + c_n(0) \le f_{n+1}(\sigma^r_{n+2}) + c_{n+1}(0) + c_n(\sigma^r_{n+1} - x) +$$
$$+ u_{n+2}(\sigma^r_{n+3}) = c_n(\sigma^r_{n+1} - x) + u_{n+1}(\sigma^r_{n+2})$$

which is (7.3) .

If $s = n+1$, then $0 \le x - \xi_{n+1} < \xi_{n+2}$, and we have

$$u_{n+1}(x - \xi_{n+1}) \le f_{n+1}(x - \xi_{n+1}) + c_{n+1}(\sigma^r_{n+1} - x) + u_{n+2}(\sigma^r_{n+3})$$
$$\forall r = n+2, \ldots, N-1$$
$$\le f_{n+1}(\sigma^r_{n+2}) + c_n(\sigma^r_{n+1} - x) + u_{n+2}(\sigma^r_{n+3})$$

hence again the desired result.

VII - 2. THE GENERAL CASE

Theorem 7.2

Assume (6.3). Let $n \le N-2$, then the following relations hold

$$(7.5) \quad \begin{cases} \text{If } x < \sigma^{n+1}_{n+1}: \\ u_n(x) = f_n(x) + \text{Min}\,\{c_n(0) + u_{n+1}(x - \xi_{n+1}), \\ \underset{r=n+1,\ldots,N-1}{\text{Min}} [c_n(\sigma^r_{n+1} - x) + \sum_{k=n+1}^{r-1} [f_k(\sigma^r_{k+1}) + c_k(0)] + u_r(0)]\} \end{cases}$$

$$(7.6) \quad \begin{cases} \text{If } \sigma^s_{n+1} \le x < \sigma^{s+1}_{n+1} \quad (s=n+1, \ldots, N-2): \\ u_n(x) = f_n(x) + \text{Min}\,\{c_n(0) + u_{n+1}(x - \xi_{n+1}), \\ \underset{r=s+1,\ldots,N-1}{\text{Min}} [c_n(\sigma^r_{n+1} - x) + \sum_{k=n+1}^{r-1} [f_k(\sigma^r_{k+1}) + c_k(0)] + u_r(0)]\} \end{cases}$$

$$(7.7) \quad \begin{cases} \text{If } x \ge \sigma^{N-1}_{n+1}: \\ u_n(x) = \sum_{k=n}^{N-1} [f_k(x - \sigma^k_{n+1}) + c_k(0)] \end{cases}$$

Proof

The proof of (7.7) follows from (6.11). Take next $x < \sigma^{n+1}_{n+1}$. Let $w_n(x)$ be the right hand side of (7.5). As in the proof of Theorem 3.2, we can assert that

$$(7.8) \qquad u_n(x) \le w_n(x).$$

We wish now to prove the reverse inequality. Consider the optimal feedback, defined by (6.14). If $\hat{v}_n(x) = 0$ or $\hat{v}_n(x) = \sigma^{n+1}_{n+1} - x$, then $u_n \ge w_n$ as a consequence of (6.9).

We may thus assume that $\hat{r}(x) \geq n+2$. The rest of the proof is quite similar to the proof of Theorem 3.2. Details are left to the reader.

VII - 3. WAGNER-WITHIN THEOREM FOR THE BACKLOGGING CASE

We wish now to prove a result similar to Theorem 3.3.

Theorem 7.3

Assume (6.3). Consider the control problem $J_n^N(x;V)$ with $\sigma_{n+1}^{N-1} \geq x$ $(n \leq N-2)$, and the optimal control $\hat{V}_n^N = (\hat{v}_n, \ldots, \hat{v}_{N-1})$ defined using the feedback rule (6.14). Let $\hat{y}_n, \ldots, \hat{y}_N$ be the corresponding optimal state. Assume that some components $\hat{v}_i$ are > 0, and let $n_0 \in [n, N-1]$ be the first time $i \in [n, N-1]$ for which $\hat{v}_i > 0$, then we have :

$$(7.9)\quad \begin{cases} \hat{y}_i^+ \hat{v}_i = 0 & \forall i \neq n_o \\ \hat{y}_{i+1}^- \hat{v}_i = 0 & \forall i \\ \hat{y}_i^+ \hat{y}_{i+1}^- = 0 & \text{for } i > n_0 \end{cases}$$

$$(7.10)\quad \hat{y}_{N-1} \leq 0, \qquad \hat{v}_{N-1} = 0$$

If $\hat{v}_i = 0$, $\forall i = n, \ldots, N-1$ then (7.10) holds.

Proof

For $i < n_0$, $\hat{v}_i = 0$ and the two first relations (7.9) are satisfied.

Assume $i > n_0$. Then from (7.5), (7.6) it follows that we can define a sequence of set-up points

$$n_0 < n_1 < n_2 \quad \ldots \leq N-1$$

Moreover, no order should be placed before the stock has become negative or zero. Therefore there exists a second sequence

$$m_0 < m_1 < m_2 \quad \ldots \leq N-1$$

with

$$n_0 \leq m_0 \leq n_1$$

$$n_1 \leq m_1 \leq n_2$$

where $m_0, m_1, \ldots$ are regeneration points (points where the stock vanishes). We choose $m_0, m_1, \ldots$ to be the closest to $n_0, n_1, \ldots$. For $i > n_0$, if $\hat{y}_i > 0$ then $\hat{v}_i = 0$. If $\hat{v}_i > 0$, then $\hat{y}_{i+1} \geq 0$, and if $\hat{y}_i > 0$, then $\hat{y}_{i+1} \geq 0$, which proves (7.9). At times $n_0, n_1, \ldots$ the amounts ordered are successively

$$\sigma_1^{m_o} - x, \quad \sigma_{m_o+1}^{m_1}, \ \ldots$$

The fact that $\hat{v}_{N-1} = 0$ follows from the feedback $\hat{v}_{N-1}(x) = 0$ (cf. (6.14)). Consider the last set-up point $l(N) \leq N-1$. Then from (7.5) or (7.6) we will order an amount $\sigma_{l(N)+1}^{r} - \hat{y}_{l(N)}$, for some $r \geq l(N)+1$ and $r \leq N-1$. Therefore $\hat{y}_r = 0$ and $\hat{y}_{N-1} \leq 0$. If there is no set-up point in the interval then (7.10) follows from the assumption $\sigma_{n+1}^{N-1} \geq x$.

Remark 7.1

When $x = 0$, the two first relations (7.9) hold $\forall i$. Indeed $y_{n_o} \leq 0$ hence the first relation holds also for $i = n_o$.

VII - 4. NETWORK REPRESENTATION

In this paragraph, we assume besides (6.3) that

$$f_i(0) = 0 \tag{7.11}$$

Hence we can write

$$f_i(x) = f_i(x^+) + f_i(-x^-)$$

which will be denoted

$$f_i(x) = f_i^+(x^+) + f_i^-(x^-) \tag{7.12}$$

where

$$f_i^+, \ f_i^- : R^+ \to R^+ \text{ are concave, non decreasing, and } f_i^+(0)=0, \ f_i^-(0)=0. \tag{7.13}$$

We pose the following optimization problem. Find

$$\begin{cases} v_0, \ \ldots, \ v_{N-1} \\ y_0^+, \ y_0^-, \ \ldots, \ y_i^+, \ y_i^-, \ \ldots, \ y_N^+, \ y_N^- \\ v_i + y_i^+ + y_{i+1}^- - y_i^- - y_{i+1}^+ = \xi_{i+1}, \qquad i = 0, \ldots, N-1 \\ y_0^+ = y_0^- = y_N^+ = y_N^- = 0 \\ v_i \geq 0, \quad i = 0, \ldots, N-1 \\ y_i^+, \ y_i^- \geq 0 \qquad i = 0, \ldots, N \\ \text{Min} \sum_{i=o}^{N-1} c_i(v_i) + \sum_{i=o}^{N-1} f_i^+(y_i^+) + \sum_{i=o}^{N-1} f_i^-(y_i^-) \end{cases} \tag{7.14}$$

Problem (7.14) is not identical to (6.4), (6.5), since the constraint $y_N = 0$ is imposed. Moreover, we do not a priori impose the constraint

(7.15) $y_i^+ \, y_i^- = 0$

where y_i^+ and y_i^- represent respectively the positive part and the negative part of y_i.

We make the following network representation of problem (7.14) for N = 3.

Figure 1.6 : Network representation of problem (7.14), for N = 3

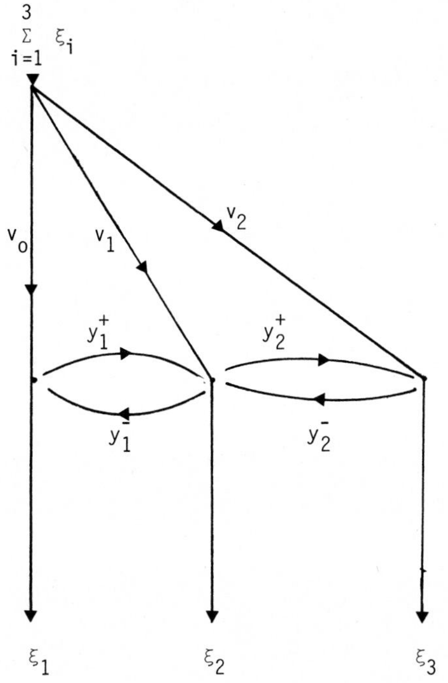

Again we obtain a single source network with concave costs. The theory of concave cost networks shows that it is wasteful to have both y_i^+ and $y_i^- > 0$, hence (7.15) is naturally verified.

In addition, there is at most one positive input at any node for the optimal flow, which implies immediately that relations (7.9) hold, and

(7.16) $v_{N-1} \, y_{N-1}^+ = 0$

which replaces (7.10).

VII - 5. EFFICIENT ALGORITHM

Define again

(7.17) $$\begin{cases} z^n = u_n(0), & n = 0, \dots, N-1 \\ z^{N-1} = f_{N-1}(0) + c_{N-1}(0) \end{cases}$$

and for $0 \le m \le n \le N-2$

(7.18) $$z_m^n = f_n(-\sigma_{m+1}^n) + \underset{r=n+1,\dots,N-1}{\text{Min}} [c_n(\sigma_{m+1}^r) + \sum_{k=n+1}^{r-1} f_k(\sigma_{k+1}^r) + z^r]$$

Then, we obtain :

(7.19) $$z^n = \text{Min} [\sum_{j=n}^{N-1} f_j(-\sigma_{n+1}^j), \underset{s=n,\dots,N-2}{\text{Min}} (\sum_{j=n}^{s-1} f_j(-\sigma_{n+1}^j) + z_n^s)].$$

Indeed the following interpretation can be made :

(7.20) $$\begin{cases} z_m^n = \text{optimal cost starting at time n with backlog } \sigma_{m+1}^n, \\ \text{knowing that n is a set-up point,} \end{cases}$$

and (7.19) expresses the fact that z^n is the minimum value of the cost of ordering nothing, and the cost of ordering at time s when s varies between n and N-2, s being the ordering point after n.

More generally we define for $0 \le m \le n \le N-2$

(7.21) $$\begin{cases} z_m^n(x) = f_n(x - \sigma_{m+1}^n) + \underset{r=n+1,\dots,N-1}{\text{Min}} [c_n(\sigma_{m+1}^r - x) \\ \quad + \sum_{k=n+1}^{r-1} f_k(\sigma_{k+1}^r) + z^r] \end{cases}$$

then we have

(7.22) $$u_n(x) = \text{Min} \{ \sum_{j=n}^{N-1} f_j(x - \sigma_{n+1}^j), \underset{s=m,\dots,N-2}{\text{Min}} [\sum_{j=n}^{s-1} f_j(x-\sigma_{n+1}^j)+ z(x)]\}.$$

Define

$$\hat{s}_n = +\infty \quad \text{if } z^n = \sum_{j=n}^{N-1} f_j(-\sigma_{n+1}^j)$$

$\hat{s}_n$ = smallest index s between n and N-2, realizing the minimum at the right hand side of (7.19), if $z^n < \sum_{j=n}^{N-1} f_j(-\sigma_{n+1}^j)$.

Define also for $0 \le m \le n \le N-2$:

$\hat{r}(m,n)$ = smallest index realizing the minimum at the right hand side of (7.18), $\hat{r} \in [n+1, \dots, N-1]$.

Then for a problem starting at n with 0 initial inventory, there is no order if $\hat{s}_n = +\infty$; there is an order at $\hat{s}_n$ if $\hat{s}_n < \infty$. The size of the order is $\sigma_{n+1}^{\hat{r}(n,\hat{s}_n)}$, and $\hat{r}_n = \hat{r}(n, \hat{s}_n)$ is the first regeneration point after the set up $\hat{s}_n$.

We keep in memory the indices $\hat{s}_n$, $\hat{r}_n$ ($\hat{s}_n+1 \le \hat{r}_n \le N-1$, $\hat{s}_n = +\infty$ or $n \le \hat{s}_n \le N-2$).

Now from (7.22) it follows :

$$u_0(x) = \text{Min}\{ \sum_{j=0}^{N-1} f_j(x - \sigma_1^j), \text{Min}_{s=0,\dots,N-2} [\sum_{j=0}^{s-1} f_j(x - \sigma_1^j) + z_0^s(x)]\}.$$

$$z_0^s(x) = f_0(x - \sigma_1^s) + \text{Min}_{r=s+1,\dots,N-1} [c_s(\sigma_1^r - x) + \sum_{k=s+1}^{r-1} f_k(\sigma_{k+1}^r) + z^r]$$

We define $\hat{s}(x)$ and $\hat{r}(x) \geq \hat{s}(x) + 1$, $\hat{r}(x) \leq N-1$, in a similar way as s_n, r_n.

The optimal policy is obtained as follows

$$\begin{cases} \hat{s}(x),\ \hat{r}(x)\ ;\quad \hat{s}_1(x) = \hat{s}_{\hat{r}(x)},\quad \hat{r}_1(x) = \hat{r}_{\hat{r}(x)}\ ; \\ \hat{s}_2(x) = \hat{s}_{\hat{r}_1(x)},\ \hat{r}_2(x) = \hat{r}_{\hat{r}_1(x)};\ \dots \end{cases}$$

If one of the $\hat{s}_i(x) = +\infty$, then there is no order after the preceding regeneration point $\hat{r}_{i-1}(x)$.

VIII - STUDY OF THE LINEAR VARIABLE COST CASE

We cannot develop a study similar to §IV and V, because the value of $\hat{y}_{N-1}$ is only ≤ 0, but not 0. Hence regeneration points play here a "less" important role than in the non backlogging case. However, some simplifications of equations (7.18), (7.19) can still be obtained.

VIII - 1. A SYSTEM OF RECURSION EQUATIONS

Assume here that

$$c_n(v) = K_n \chi_{v>0} + d_n v \tag{8.1}$$

Then, if $\sigma_{m+1}^{n+1} > 0$ we have from (7.18)

$$\begin{cases} z_m^n = f_n(-\sigma_{m+1}^n) + K_n + d_n \sigma_{m+1}^n \\ \quad + \text{Min}_{r=n+1,\dots,N-1} [d_n \sigma_{n+1}^r + \sum_{k=n+1}^{r-1} f_k(\sigma_{k+1}^r) + z^r] . \end{cases} \tag{8.2}$$

Set

$$\alpha_n = \text{Min}_{r=n+1,\dots,N-1} [d_n \sigma_{n+1}^r + \sum_{k=n+1}^{r-1} f_k(\sigma_{k+1}^r) + z^r] , \tag{8.3}$$

hence

$$z_m^n = f_n(-\sigma_{n+1}^n) + K_n + d_n \sigma_{m+1}^n + \alpha_n. \tag{8.4}$$

From (7.19), if $\sigma_{n+1}^{n+1} > 0$, we also have

(8.5)
$$\begin{cases} z^n = \mathrm{Min}\,\{ \sum_{j=n}^{N-1} f_j(-\sigma_{n+1}^j),\ \underset{s=n,\dots,N-2}{\mathrm{Min}} [\sum_{j=n}^{s-1} f_j(-\sigma_{n+1}^j) \\ \quad + f_s(-\sigma_{n+1}^s) + K_s + d_s\,\sigma_{n+1}^s + \alpha_s]\}. \end{cases}$$

Define

(8.6)
$$\beta_n = \underset{s=n,\dots,N-2}{\mathrm{Min}} [K_s + d_s\,\sigma_{n+1}^s + \sum_{j=n}^{s} f_j(-\sigma_{n+1}^j) + \alpha_s]$$

then (8.5) reads

(8.7)
$$z^n = \mathrm{Min}(\sum_{j=n}^{N-1} f_j(-\sigma_{n+1}^j),\ \beta_n).$$

Define the quantities

(8.8)
$$\begin{cases} \phi(n,r) = d_n\,\sigma_{n+1}^r + \sum_{k=n+1}^{r-1} f_k(\sigma_{k+1}^r) + z^r \\ \text{for } r = n+1, \dots, N-1 \end{cases}$$

(8.9)
$$\begin{cases} \psi(n,s) = K_s + d_s\,\sigma_{n+1}^s + \sum_{j=n}^{s} f_j(-\sigma_{n+1}^j) + \alpha_s \\ \text{for } s = n, \dots, N-2 \end{cases}$$

hence

(8.10)
$$\beta_n = \underset{s=n+1,\dots,N-2}{\mathrm{Min}} \psi(n,s)$$

(8.11)
$$\alpha_n = \underset{r=n+1,\dots,N-1}{\mathrm{Min}} \phi(n,r).$$

VIII - 2. SOME SIMPLIFICATIONS

Set

$r(n)$ = smallest integer between $n+1$ and $N-1$,

such that

$$\alpha_n = \phi(n,r(n))$$

and

$s(n)$ = smallest integer between n and $N-2$, such that $\beta_n = \psi(n,s(n))$.

Take

$$0 \le m+1 \le n+1 \le r_1, r_2 \le N-1$$

then

$$(8.12)\quad \begin{cases} \phi(n,r_1) - \phi(m,r_1) - (\phi(n,r_2) - \phi(m,r_2)) \\ = d_n(\sigma_{n+1}^{r_1} - \sigma_{n+1}^{r_2}) - d_m(\sigma_{m+1}^{r_1} - \sigma_{m+1}^{r_2}) - \sum_{k=m+1}^{n} [f_k(\sigma_{k+1}^{r_1}) - f_k(\sigma_{k+1}^{r_2})]. \end{cases}$$

Next, let $0 \le m \le n \le s_1, s_2 \le N-2$, then we have

$$(8.13)\quad \begin{cases} \psi(n,s_1) - \psi(m,s_1) - (\psi(n,s_2) - \psi(m,s_2)) \\ = \sigma_{m+1}^{n}(d_{s_2} - d_{s_1}) + \sum_{k=n}^{s_1} f_k(-\sigma_{n+1}^{k}) - \sum_{k=m}^{s_1} f_k(-\sigma_{m+1}^{k}) \\ - \sum_{k=n}^{s_2} f_k(-\sigma_{n+1}^{k}) + \sum_{k=m}^{s_2} f_k(-\sigma_{m+1}^{k}). \end{cases}$$

In particular if $r_1 \le r_2$ we obtain

$$(8.14)\quad \begin{cases} \phi(n,r_1) - \phi(m,r_1) - (\phi(n,r_2) - \phi(n,r_2)) \\ = - (d_n - d_m)\, \sigma_{r_1+1}^{r_2} - \sum_{k=n+1}^{m} [f_k(\sigma_{k+1}^{r_1}) - f_k(\sigma_{k+1}^{r_2})] \end{cases}$$

and if $s_1 \ge s_2$

$$(8.15)\quad \begin{cases} \psi(n,s_1) - \psi(m,s_1) - (\psi(n,s_2) - \psi(m,s_2)) \\ = \sigma_{m+1}^{n}\,(d_{s_2} - d_{s_1}) + \sum_{k=s_2+1}^{s_1} [f_k(-\sigma_{n+1}^{k}) - f_k(-\sigma_{m+1}^{k})] \end{cases}$$

Lemma 8.1

Assume that d_n decreases with n, then $r(n)$ increases with n.

Proof

Take $r_1 = r(n)$, and $r_2 = r$ in (8.14), with $r \ge r(n) \ge n+1 \ge m+1$.

Then

$$\phi(n,r(n)) - \phi(n,r) \le 0.$$

Since the right hand side of (8.14) is positive, it follows that

$$\phi(m,r(n)) - \phi(m,r) \le 0$$

which implies $r(m) \le r(n)$.

Lemma 8.2.

Assume that d_n increases with n, then $s(n)$ increases with n.

Proof

Take $s_1 = s$, and $s_2 = s(n)$ in (8.15). As a consequence of the monotonicity assumption on d, $d_{s_2} \le d_{s_1}$.

Now

$$0 \geq -\sigma^k_{n+1} \geq -\sigma^k_{m+1}$$

and since $f_k(x)$ decreases for $x \leq 0$, it follows that

$$f_k(-\sigma^k_{n+1}) \leq f_k(-\sigma^k_{m+1})$$

hence the right hand side of (8.15) is less or equal to 0. Since

$$\psi(n,s) - \psi(n,s(n)) \geq 0$$

we deduce

$$\psi(m,s) - \psi(m,s(m)) \geq 0 \quad \forall s \geq s(n)$$

hence

$$s(m) \leq s(n). \quad \square$$

When

$$d_n = d \tag{8.16}$$

then both Lemmas 8.1 and 8.2 apply. Hence for $0 \leq m \leq n$

$$\left\{\begin{aligned} \alpha_m &= \operatorname*{Min}_{r=m+1,\dots,r(n)} \phi(m,r) \\ \beta_m &= \operatorname*{Min}_{s=m,\dots,s(n)} \psi(m,s) \end{aligned}\right. \tag{8.17}$$

Assuming all demands to be positive, then it is easy to check that $s(n)$ represents the first set up after n, provided there is a set-up, i.e. $\hat{s}_n = s(n)$.

The first regeneration point after n is then

$$\hat{r}_n = r(s(n)).$$

Therefore for $m \leq n$, the first set up for $J_m(V)$ takes place in $[m,\hat{s}_m]$.

IX - BACKLOGGING WITH POSITIVE FINAL INVENTORY

IX - 1. SETTING OF THE PROBLEM

Consider problem (6.4), (6.5) with the additional constraint

$$y_N \geq 0. \tag{9.1}$$

The Dynamic Programming equations are

$$\left\{\begin{aligned} u_N(x) &= 0 \text{ for } x \geq 0 \\ u_{N-1}(x) &= f_{N-1}(x) + \operatorname*{Inf}_{v \geq (\xi_N - x)^+} \{c_{N-1}(v)\} \end{aligned}\right. \tag{9.2}$$

hence

$$(9.3) \qquad u_{N-1}(x) = \begin{cases} f_{N-1}(x) + c_{N-1}(\xi_N - x) & \text{if } x < \xi_N \\ f_{N-1}(x) + c_{N-1}(0) & \text{if } x \geq \xi_N \end{cases}$$

and

$$(9.4) \qquad \begin{cases} u_n(x) = f_n(x) + \underset{v \geq 0}{\text{Inf}} \{c_n(v) + u_{n+1}(x + v - \xi_{n+1})\} \\ \text{for } n \leq N-2 \end{cases}$$

The drawing of $u_n(x)$ simply follows, where the only difference with the situation of Theorem 6.1 is that an additional discontinuity point occurs at σ_{n+1}^N

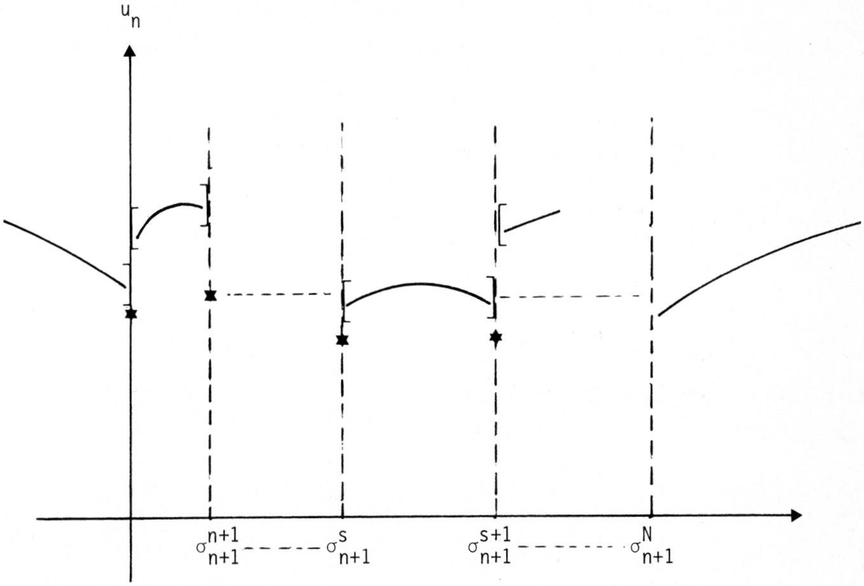

Figure 1.7 : Graph of $u_n(x)$

For $0 \leq n \leq N-2$, we have

If $x < \sigma_{n+1}^{n+1}$

$$(9.5) \qquad u_n(x) = f_n(x) + \text{Min} \{c_n(0) + u_{n+1}(x - \xi_{n+1}), \underset{r=n+1,\dots,N}{\text{Min}} [c_n(\sigma_{n+1}^r - x) + u_{n+1}(\sigma_{n+2}^r)]\}$$

$$(9.6)\quad \begin{cases} \underline{\text{If } \sigma_{n+1}^{s} \le x < \sigma_{n+1}^{s+1}, \quad s = n+1, \ldots, N-1} \\ u_n(x) = f_n(x) + \mathrm{Min}\,\{c_n(0) + u_{n+1}(x - \xi_{n+1}), \\ \qquad \underset{r=s+1,\ldots,N}{\mathrm{Min}} [c_n(\sigma_{n+1}^{r} - x) + u_{n+1}(\sigma_{n+2}^{r})]\} \end{cases}$$

$$(9.7)\quad \begin{cases} \underline{\text{If } x \ge \sigma_{n+1}^{N}} \\ u_n(x) = f_n(x) + c_n(0) + u_{n+1}(x - \xi_{n+1}). \end{cases}$$

The optimal feedback is then

$$(9.8)\quad \begin{cases} \hat{v}_n(x) = \begin{cases} \underline{\text{If } x < \sigma_{n+1}^{n+1}} \\ 0 \text{ or } \sigma_{n+1}^{\hat{r}(x)} - x, \ \hat{r} \in [n+1, \ldots, N] \\ \underline{\text{If } \sigma_{n+1}^{s} \le x < \sigma_{n+1}^{s+1}} \\ 0 \text{ or } \sigma_{n+1}^{\hat{r}(x)} - x, \ \hat{r} \in [s+1, \ldots, N] \\ \underline{\text{If } x \ge \sigma_{n+1}^{N}} \\ 0 \end{cases} \\ \hat{v}_{N-1}(x) = \begin{cases} 0 \text{ if } x \ge \sigma_N^N \\ \xi_N - x \text{ if } x < \xi_N \end{cases} \end{cases}$$

These relations simplify as follows

$$(9.9)\quad \begin{cases} \underline{\text{If } x < \sigma_{n+1}^{n+1}} \\ u_n(x) = f_n(x) + \mathrm{Min}\,\{c_n(0) + u_{n+1}(x - \xi_{n+1}), \\ \underset{r=n+1,\ldots,N}{\mathrm{Min}} [c_n(\sigma_{n+1}^{r} - x) + \sum_{k=n+1}^{r-1} (f_k(\sigma_{k+1}^{r}) + c_k(0)) + u_r(0)]\} \end{cases}$$

$$(9.10)\quad \begin{cases} \underline{\text{If } \sigma_{n+1}^{s} \le x < \sigma_{n+1}^{s+1}, \ s = n+1, \ldots, N-1} \\ u_n(x) = f_n(x) + \mathrm{Min}\,\{c_n(0) + u_{n+1}(x - \xi_{n+1}), \\ \underset{r=s+1,\ldots,N}{\mathrm{Min}} [c_n(\sigma_{n+1}^{r} - x) + \sum_{k=n+1}^{r-1} (f_k(\sigma_{k+1}^{r}) + c_k(0)) + u_r(0)]\} \end{cases}$$

$$(9.11)\qquad \begin{cases} \dfrac{\text{If } x \geq \sigma_{n+1}^{N}}{} \\ u_n(x) = \sum_{k=n}^{N-1} [f_k(x - \sigma_{n+1}^{k}) + c_k(0)]. \end{cases}$$

Then the analogue of Theorem 7.3 obtains.

Theorem 9.1

Assume (6.3) and $x < \sigma_{n+1}^{N}$.

Let n_o be the 1st time ($n \leq n_o \leq N-1$) for which $\hat{v}_i > 0$, then we have

$$(9.12)\qquad \begin{cases} \hat{y}_i^+ \hat{v}_i = 0 & \forall i \neq n_o \\ \hat{y}_{i+1}^- \hat{v}_i = 0 & \forall i \\ \hat{y}_i^+ \hat{y}_{i+1}^- = 0 & \text{for } i > n_o \end{cases}$$

$$(9.13)\qquad \hat{y}_N = 0. \quad \square$$

The proof is left to the reader.

IX - 2. FORWARD DYNAMIC PROGRAMMING

By virtue of (9.13) Lemma 4.1 still holds. We then introduce

$$(9.14)\qquad \lambda^N = \operatorname*{Inf}_{V} J^N(V), \ \lambda^0 = 0$$

Let us define also for $0 \leq r \leq s \leq N-1$

$$(9.15)\qquad \begin{cases} \mu(r,s;N) = c_s(\sigma_{r+1}^{N}) + \sum_{k=r}^{s} f_k(-\sigma_{r+1}^{k}) + \sum_{k=s+1}^{N-1} (f_k(\sigma_{k+1}^{N}) \\ \qquad + \sum_{k=r}^{s-1} c_k(0)) + \sum_{k=s+1}^{N-1} c_k(0) + \lambda^r \end{cases}$$

Then it follows

Theorem 9.2

Asssume (6.3). Then for $N \geq 1$, we have

$$(9.16)\qquad \lambda^N = \operatorname*{Min}_{0 \leq r \leq s \leq N-1} \mu(r,s;N)$$

Proof

If $\sigma_1^N = 0$, then

$$\mu(r,s;N) = \sum_{k=r}^{N-1} [c_k(0) + f_k(0)] + \lambda^r$$

$$= \lambda^N \qquad \forall 0 \leq r \leq s \leq N-1$$

hence (9.16) holds

Assume $\sigma_1^N > 0$, then

$$\lambda^N \leq \mu(r,s;N), \ \forall 0 \leq r \leq s \leq N-1$$

If N = 1,

$$\mu(0, 0, 1) = c_0(\sigma_1^1) + f_0(0)$$
$$= \lambda^1.$$

We may then assume $N \geq 2$. Consider the optimal control $\hat{V}^N$. There is a last set-up strictly prior to N, namely $0 \leq \hat{s} \leq N-1$. From the first relation (9.12) (which holds $\forall i$ since x = 0), we deduce

$$\hat{y}_{\hat{s}}^+ = 0$$

hence $\hat{y}_{\hat{s}} \leq 0$. There is a last regeneration point before $\hat{s}$, namely $\hat{r} \leq \hat{s}$ and $\hat{y}_{\hat{r}} = 0$, and there is no set up between $\hat{r}+1$ and $\hat{s}$ (if $\hat{r} < \hat{s}$). From Lemma 4.1, we have

$$\lambda^{\hat{r}} = J^{\hat{r}}(\hat{V}^N)$$

and

$$\lambda^N = \mu(\hat{r},\hat{s};N)$$

which implies the desired result.

Set next for $s \leq N-1$

$$\tilde{\mu}(s;N) = \underset{0 \leq r \leq s}{\text{Min}} \ [c_s(\sigma_{r+1}^N) + \sum_{k=r}^{s} (f_k(-\sigma_{r+1}^k) + \sum_{k=r}^{s-1} c_k(0)) + \lambda^r] \quad (9.17)$$

then

$$\lambda^N = \underset{0 \leq s \leq N-1}{\text{Min}} \ [\tilde{\mu}(s;N) + \sum_{k=s+1}^{N-1} f_k(\sigma_{k+1}^N) + \sum_{k=s+1}^{N-1} c_k(0)]. \quad (9.18)$$

Then define for $s \leq N-1$

(9.19) $\rho(s;N)$ = largest integer realizing the minimum in (9.17)

Note that

(9.20) If $\sigma_1^N = 0$, then $\rho(s;N) = s$ since $\lambda^r = \sum_{k=0}^{r-1} [f_k(0) + c_k(0)]$.

We set

$$s(N) = N-1 \quad \text{if } \sigma_1^N = 0$$

then

$$r(N) = \rho(s(N);N) = N-1.$$

If $\sigma_1^N > 0$ then there exists $\hat{s}$ and $\hat{r}$ such that $\hat{r} \leq \hat{s} \leq N-1$

and

$$\lambda^N = \mu(\hat{r},\hat{s};N)$$

from which it is easy to check that $\hat{s}$ realizes the minimum of $\mu(s;N)$, and $\hat{r}$ realizes the minimum in r of $\mu(r,\hat{s};N)$. Moreover

$$\hat{r} = \rho(\hat{s};N)$$

since $\hat{r}$ is the last regeneration point before $\hat{s}$.

Because $\hat{s}$ is a set-up, we also have $\sigma_{\hat{r}+1}^{\hat{s}} > 0$.

This motivates the following definition. Define

$$(9.21)\quad \begin{cases} \phi(r;s;N) = c_s(\sigma_{r+1}^N) + \sum_{k=r}^{s} f_k(-\sigma_{r+1}^k) + \sum_{k=r}^{s-1} c_k(0) + \lambda^r \\ \text{for } r \le s \le N-1 \end{cases}$$

$$(9.22)\quad \begin{cases} \psi(s;N) = \tilde{\mu}(s;N) + \sum_{k=s+1}^{N-1} f_k(\sigma_{k+1}^N) + \sum_{k=s+1}^{N-1} c_k(0) \\ \text{for } s \le N-1 \end{cases}$$

Then, we set

$$(9.23)\quad \begin{cases} \underline{\text{If } \sigma_1^N > 0,} \\ s(N) = \text{largest integer} \le N-1, \text{ such that} \\ \lambda^N = \psi(s(N);N) \\ \text{and } \sigma_{\rho(s(N);N)+1}^N > 0; \\ r(N) = \rho(s(N);N). \end{cases}$$

The optimal control $\hat{V}^N$ is then defined backwards as follows :

If $\sigma_1^N = 0$, no set up ; if $\sigma_1^N > 0$ take s(N) as last set-up, and r(N) as last regeneration point (less or equal to N-1). If $\sigma_1^{r(N)} = 0$, no more set-up.

If $\sigma_1^{r(N)} > 0$, then s(r(N)) and r(N) are the one before last set-up and regeneration points, respectively. And so on ...

Let

$$r_1 \le s_1,\ r_2 \le s_2,\ s_1,s_2 \le N-1 \le M-1$$

then we have

$$(9.24)\quad \begin{cases} \mu(r_1,s_1;M) - \mu(r_1,s_1;N) - [\mu(r_2,s_2;M) - \mu(r_2,s_2;N)] \\ = c_{s_1}(\sigma^M_{r_1+1}) - c_{s_1}(\sigma^N_{r_1+1}) - [c_{s_2}(\sigma^M_{r_2+1}) - c_{s_2}(\sigma^N_{r_2+1})] \\ + \sum_{k=N}^{M-1} [f_k(\sigma^M_{k+1}) + c_k(0)] + \sum_{k=s_1+1}^{N-1} [f_k(\sigma^M_{k+1}) - f_k(\sigma^N_{k+1})] \\ - \sum_{k=s_2+1}^{N-1} [f_k(\sigma^M_{k+1}) - f_k(\sigma^N_{k+1})] \\ = \Phi(r_1,s_1 \, ; \, r_2,s_2 \, ; \, N,M) \end{cases}$$

Lemma 9.1

Assume (6.3) and (4.16), (4.17). Let $N \geq 1$, such that $\sigma^N_1 > 0$, then for $M \geq N$

$$(9.25)\quad \begin{cases} \mu(r,s;M) \geq \mu(r,N \, , \, s(N);M) \\ \forall r \leq s \leq s(N), \text{ such that } \sigma^M_{r+1} > 0 \end{cases}$$

Proof

If $s_1 \leq s_2$ and $\sigma^M_{r_1+1}, \sigma^N_{r_2+1} > 0$, then

$$\Phi(r_1,s_1 \, ; \, r_2,s_2 \, ; \, N,M) \geq (d_{s_1} - d_{s_2})\, \sigma^M_{N+1} + \sum_{k=s_1+1}^{N-1} [f_k(\sigma^M_{k+1}) - f_k(\sigma^N_{k+1})] - \sum_{k=s_2+1}^{N-1} [f_k(\sigma^M_{k+1}) - f_k(\sigma^N_{k+1})].$$

If moreover $s_1 \leq s_2$, we have $\Phi \geq 0$.

Take now $r_1 = r$ such that $\sigma^M_{r+1} > 0$ and $s_2 = s(N)$, $r_2 = r(N)$, $s_1 = s$ with $r \leq s \leq s(N)$, then since $\sigma^N_1 > 0$, we have $\sigma^N_{r(N)+1} > 0$, therefore we can assert that

$$(9.26)\quad \mu(r,s;M) - \mu(r(N), s(N);M) \geq 0,$$

which completes the proof.

Theorem 9.3

Assume (6.3) and (4.16), (4.17). Then we have

$$(9.27)\quad s(N) \leq s(M), \text{ if } N \leq M.$$

In addition, if $d_s = d$, then

$$(9.28)\quad r(N) \leq r(M), \text{ if } N \leq M$$

Proof

If $\sigma^M_1 = 0$, then $s(M) = r(M) = M-1$ and (9.27) and (9.28) are straightforward.

Assume $\sigma_1^N = 0$, and $\sigma_{N+1}^M > 0$. Then $s(N) = r(N) = N-1$.

For $r \le s \le N-1$, we have

$$\mu(r,s;M) - \mu(N-1,N-1;M) = c_s(\sigma_{N+1}^M) - c_{N-1}(\sigma_{N+1}^M)$$
$$+ \sum_{k=r}^{s-1} [f_k(0) + c_k(0)] + \sum_{k=s+1}^{N-1} [f_k(\sigma_{N+1}^M) + c_k(0)]$$
$$+ f_s(0) - f_{N-1}(0) + \lambda^r - \lambda^{N-1} = (d_s - d_{N-1})\,\sigma_{N-1}^M + \sum_{k=r}^{s-1} f_k(0)$$
$$+ \sum_{k=s+1}^{N-1} f_k(\sigma_{N+1}^M) + f_s(0) - \sum_{k=r}^{N-2} f_k(0)$$
$$\ge (d_s - d_{N-1})\,\sigma_{N+1}^M \ge 0.$$

Taking $r = \rho(s;M)$, we obtain

$$\psi(s;M) - \psi(N-1;M) \ge 0$$
$$\forall s \le N-1.$$

Since for $s \le N-1$, $\sigma_{s+1}^M > 0$, hence also $\sigma_{\rho(s;M)+1}^M > 0$, and it follows that $s(M) \ge N-1$.

Take now $r \le N-1$, $s \ge N-1$, then

$$\mu(r,s;M) - \mu(N-1,\, s;M) = c_s(\sigma_{r+1}^M) - c_s(\sigma_N^M)$$
$$+ \sum_{k=r}^{s} f_k(-\sigma_{r+1}^k) - \sum_{k=N-1}^{s} f_k(-\sigma_N^k)$$
$$+ \sum_{k=r}^{s-1} c_k(0) - \sum_{k=N-1}^{s-1} c_k(0) + \lambda^r - \lambda^{N-1}$$
$$= \sum_{k=r}^{N-2} f_k(0) + \lambda^r - \lambda^{N-1} = 0$$

hence $\rho(s;M) \ge N-1$, which implies $r(M) \ge N-1$.

Take finally $\sigma_1^N > 0$. Then (9.25) holds. Let $r = \rho(s;M)$ such that $\sigma_{\rho(s;M)+1}^M > 0$; if this condition is satisfied for some $s < s(N)$, then we obtain

(9.29) $\qquad \psi(s;M) \ge \psi(s(N);M).$

However, from (9.21) we see that for $r \le s \le N-1 \le M-1$

$$\phi(r,s;N) = \phi(r,s;M) \text{ if } \sigma_{N+1}^M = 0$$

hence

(9.30) $\qquad \rho(s;M) = \rho(s;N)$ if $\sigma_{N+1}^M = 0.$

When $\sigma_{N+1}^M > 0$ then (9.21) implies

$$\phi(r,s;M) = K_s + d_s\, \sigma^N_{s+1} + d_s\, \sigma^M_{N+1} + \chi(r,s)$$

where

(9.31) $$\chi(r,s) = d_s\, \sigma^s_{r+1} + \sum_{k=r}^{s} f_k(-\sigma^k_{r+1}) + \lambda^r.$$

Denoting by $\tilde{\rho}(s)$ the largest index $r \le s$ which minimizes $\chi(r,s)$ we see that

(9.32) $$\rho(s;M) = \tilde{\rho}(s) \text{ if } \sigma^M_{N+1} > 0,\ s \le N-1.$$

Now if $\sigma^N_{\rho(s;N)+1} > 0$ then $\rho(s,N) = \tilde{\rho}(s)$, therefore from this and (9.30), (9.31) we can assert that

(9.33) $$\begin{cases} \rho(s;M) = \rho(s;N) \text{ if } \sigma^M_{N+1} = 0, \text{ or } \sigma^M_{N+1} > 0 \text{ and } \sigma^N_{\rho(s;N)+1} > 0 \\ \forall s \le N-1 \le M-1. \end{cases}$$

In particular taking $s = s(N)$, we have

$$\rho(s(N);N) = r(N) \text{ and } \sigma^N_{r(N)+1} > 0$$

which implies from (9.33)

$$\rho(s(N);M) = r(N).$$

But then

(9.34) $$\begin{cases} \sigma^M_{\rho(s(N);M)+1} \ge \sigma^N_{r(N)+1} > 0, \text{ which with (9.29) proves that} \\ s(M) \ge s(N). \end{cases}$$

It remains to prove (9.28), assuming $d_s = d$ in the case $\sigma^N_1 > 0$. Let indeed

$$r_1 \le r_2 \le s_2 \le s_1$$

$$s_2 \le N-1,\ s_1 \le M-1$$

such that $\sigma^N_{r_2+1} > 0$

then

(9.35) $$\begin{cases} \mu(r_1, s_1, M) - \mu(r_2, s_1, M) - [\mu(r_1, s_2, N) - \mu(r_2, s_2, N)] \\ = d_{s_1}\, \sigma^{r_2}_{r_1+1} + \sum_{k=r_1}^{s_1} f_k(-\sigma^k_{r_1}) - \sum_{k=r_2}^{s_1} f_k(-\sigma^k_{r_2+1}) \\ - d_{s_2}\, \sigma^{r_2}_{r_1+1} - \sum_{k=r_1}^{s_2} f_k(-\sigma^k_{r_1+1}) + \sum_{k=r_2}^{s_2} f_k(-\sigma^k_{r_2+1}) \\ = \sum_{k=s_2+1}^{s_1} [f_k(-\sigma^k_{r_1+1}) - f_k(-\sigma^k_{r_2+1})] \ge 0. \end{cases}$$

Indeed

$$0 \ge -\sigma^k_{r_2+1} \ge -\sigma^k_{r_1+1}$$

hence since f_k decreases when the argument is negative

$$f_k(-\sigma^k_{r_2+1}) \le f_k(-\sigma^k_{r_1+1})$$

which proves (9.35).

We now apply (9.53) for

$$r_1 = r,\ r_2 = r(N),\ s_1 = s(M),\ s_2 = s(N) \text{ and } r \le r(N),$$

using also

$$\mu(r,s(N),N) \ge \mu(r(N),\ s(N),\ N).$$

We then deduce

$$(9.36) \qquad \begin{cases} \mu(r,s(M),M) \ge \mu(r(N),\ s(M),M) \\ \forall r \le r(N) \end{cases}$$

which implies $r(M) \ge r(N)$.

This completes the proof of Theorem 9.3.

IX - 3. A PLANNING HORIZON RESULT

We can now give the analogue of Theorem 4.4, namely

Theorem 9.4.

Under the hypotheses of Theorem 9.3, if

$$(9.37) \qquad r(N+1) = N$$

then N is a planning horizon.

Proof

We wish to prove that N is a regeneration point for an optimal policy of $J^M(V)$, $\forall M \ge N$. But we have

(9.38) $\left\{ \begin{array}{l} \forall M \ge N+1, \text{ there exists an optimal policy for } J^M(V) \text{ which possesses a re-} \\ \text{generation point between } r(N+1) \text{ and } N. \end{array} \right.$

Indeed $r(M)$, $r(r(M))$ ... are regeneration points for an optimal policy of $J^M(V)$. Now by Theorem 9.3,

$$M-1 \ge r(M) \ge r(N+1).$$

If $r(M) \le N$ the desired result is proved. Otherwise $r(M) \ge N+1$, hence $r(r(M)) \ge r(N+1)$, and $r(r(M)) \le M-2$. After a finite number of steps we obtain (9.38), from which it follows that, when (9.37) is satisfied, then N is a planning horizon.

Remark 9.1

Other results similar to those obtained in the no-backlogging case can also be given. We leave details to the reader.

X - INFINITE HORIZON PROBLEM

X - 1. SETTING OF THE PROBLEM

Consider now an infinite sequence of positive numbers :

$$\xi_1, \ldots, \xi_k, \ldots$$

A control is also defined by

$$V = (v_0, v_1, \ldots, v_k, \ldots).$$

The inventory balance equations are

$$y_{i+1} = y_i + v_i - \xi_{i+1}, \quad i = 0, 1, \ldots \tag{10.1}$$

with the restriction that

$$y_i \geq 0. \tag{10.2}$$

Consider next the production and inventory cost functions

$$c_i(v), \ f_i(x), \ i = 0, 1, \ldots \tag{10.3}$$

defined on R^+, non decreasing, concave and positive.

Set

$$J_n(x,V) = \sum_{i=n}^{\infty} \alpha^{i-n} [c_i(v_i) + f_i(v_i)] \tag{10.4}$$

where

$$y_n = x, \ x > 0 \tag{10.5}$$

and $\alpha < 1$, is interpreted as the discount factor. The function $J_n(x;V)$ is well defined provided we allow for the value $+\infty$. The additional assumption is made

$$\sum_{i=n}^{\infty} \alpha^{i-n} [c_i(\xi_{i+1}) + f_i(x)] \leq \bar{u}_0(x), \ \forall n,x \tag{10.6}$$

where $\bar{u}_0(x) < \infty$.

It implies that the control

$$\bar{V} = (\xi_1, \xi_2, \ldots, \xi_k, \ldots)$$

is admissible. The corresponding state is constant

$$\bar{y}_i = x$$

and

$$J_n(x;\bar{V}) = \sum_{i=n}^{\infty} \alpha^{i-n} [c_i(\xi_{i+1}) + f_i(x)] \leq \bar{u}_0(x)$$

hence

$$u_n(x) = \operatorname*{Inf}_V J_n(x;V) \leq \bar{u}_0(x). \tag{10.7}$$

Assumption (10.6) implies that the possible growth in i is limited. For instance when

$$c_i(\xi_{i+1}) \le \lambda c_1(\xi_1) \ \forall i$$

$$f_i(x) \le \mu\, f_1(x)$$

then

$$\sum_{i=n}^{\infty} \alpha^{i-n} [c_i(\xi_{i+1}) + f_i(x)] \le \frac{\lambda c_1(\xi_1) + \mu f_1(x)}{1 - \alpha} = \bar{u}_0(x).$$

X - 2. DYNAMIC PROGRAMMING EQUATIONS

The Dynamic Programming equations are the following

$$u_n(x) = f_n(x) + \operatorname*{Inf}_{v \ge (\xi_{n+1} - x)^+} \{c_n(v) + \alpha u_{n+1}(x + v - \xi_{n+1})\} \tag{10.8}$$

Theorem 10.1

Assume (10.3) and (10.6). Then the functions $u_n(x)$ defined by (10.7) are solutions of (10.8).

Proof

By (10.6) $u_n(x) < \infty$, $\forall x$.

Also we have

$$0 \le u_n(x) \le \bar{u}_0(x) \tag{10.9}$$

Next we have from (10.4)

$$J_n(x;V) = f_n(x) + c_n(v_n) + \alpha \sum_{i=n+1}^{\infty} \alpha^{i-(n+1)} [c_i(v_i) + f_i(y_i)].$$

The variable v_n must satisfy the constraint

$$v_n \ge (\xi_{n+1} - x)^+.$$

Moreover

$$\sum_{i=n+1} \alpha^{i-(n+1)} [c_i(v_i) + f_i(y_i)] = J_{n+1}(x + v_n - \xi_{n+1} ; V).$$

Writing

$$\operatorname*{Inf}_V J_n(x;V) = \operatorname*{Inf}_{v_n} \operatorname*{Inf}_{v_{n+1},\dots} J_n(x;V)$$

and using the definition of $u_n(x)$, the recursion (10.8) is easily obtained.

Remark 10.1

As opposed to the finite horizon problem, there is no final condition. However, we can replace it by adding the conditions (10.9).

Let us prove an approximation result. Define

$$J_n^N(x;V) = \sum_{i=n}^{N-1} \alpha^{i-n} [c_i(v_i) + f_i(y_i)] \tag{10.10}$$

and set

$$(10.11) \qquad u_n^N(x) = \underset{V}{\mathrm{Inf}}\ J_n^N(x;V)$$

Theorem 10.2

Under the hypotheses of Theorem 10.1, let s(x) be such that

$$x \le \sigma_{n+1}^s, \quad s = n, \ldots$$

Take $N \ge s(x)$. Then we have

$$(10.12) \qquad |u_n(x) - u_n^N(x)| \le \alpha^{N-n}\ \bar{u}_0(0).$$

Proof

We may assume $s \ge n+1$. Indeed if $s = n$ and $N \ge n+1$, then we can take $s = n+1$ instead of $s = n$. If $N = n$, then $u_n^N = 0$ and (10.12) is satisfied. Assume now $s \ge n+1$.

Let $z \ge 0$. There exists controls such that

$$y_N = z$$

Indeed take

$$v_n = z + \sigma_{n+1}^s - x$$

$$v_{n+1} = \ldots = v_{s-1} = 0$$

$$v_i = \xi_{i+1}, \quad i = s, \ldots$$

this second part disappearing when $s = n+1$. Then $y_k = z$ for $k \ge s$. Define

$$\mathcal{V}_z^N = \{V \mid y_N = z\}, \quad \tilde{\mathcal{V}}_z^N = \{V \mid y_N \ge z\}$$

Clearly

$$\begin{aligned}\tilde{\mathcal{V}}_z^N = \{v_n \ge \xi_{n+1} - x,\ v_n + v_{n+1} \ge \xi_{n+1} + \xi_{n+2} - x \\ \ldots\ v_n + \ldots + v_{N-2} \ge \xi_{n+1} + \ldots + \xi_{N-1} - x, \\ v_n + \ldots + v_{N-1} \ge \xi_{n+1} + \ldots + \xi_N + z - x\}\end{aligned}$$

These controls depend also on n and x but we have omitted this dependence in the notation (n and x are fixed). We also remark that

$$\mathcal{V}_z^N \subset \tilde{\mathcal{V}}_0^N.$$

As in the proof of Theorem 10.1, we can check the relation

$$(10.13) \qquad u_n(x) = \underset{z \ge 0}{\mathrm{Inf}}\ \underset{V \in \mathcal{V}_z^N}{\mathrm{Inf}} \{J_n^N(x;V) + \alpha^{N-n}\, u_N(z)\}$$

Indeed let $w_n(x)$ denote the right hand side of (10.13), then

$$\begin{aligned}J_n(x;V) &= J_n^N(x;V) + J_N(y_N;V)\ \alpha^{N-n} \\ &\ge J_n^N(x;V) + u_N(y_N)\ \alpha^{N-n}\end{aligned}$$

Since clearly $V \in \mathcal{V}^N_{y_N}$, we deduce

$$J_n(x;V) \geq \operatorname*{Inf}_{V\in\mathcal{V}^N_{y_N}} \{J^N_n(x;V) + \alpha^{N-n}\, u_N(y_N)\}$$

and since $y_N \geq 0$, it follows $u_n(x) \geq w_n(x)$.

On the other hand for fixed ε, there exists z_ε and $V_\varepsilon \in \mathcal{V}^N_{z_\varepsilon}$ such that

$$J^N_n(x;V_\varepsilon) + \alpha^{N-n}\, u_N(z_\varepsilon) \leq w_n(x) + \varepsilon.$$

Define $\tilde{V}_\varepsilon$ such that

$$J_N(z_\varepsilon;\, \tilde{V}_\varepsilon) \leq u_n(z_\varepsilon) + \varepsilon$$

we get

$$J^N_n(x;V_\varepsilon) + \alpha^{N-n}\, J_N(z_\varepsilon;\tilde{V}_\varepsilon) \leq w_n(x) + \varepsilon + \varepsilon\alpha^{N-n}$$

and we can define $\tilde{\tilde{V}}_\varepsilon$ such that

$$J_n(x;\tilde{\tilde{V}}_\varepsilon) = J^N_n(x;V_\varepsilon) + \alpha^{N-n}\, J_N(z_\varepsilon;\tilde{\tilde{V}}_\varepsilon)$$

hence

$$u_n(x) \leq w_n(x) + \varepsilon(1 + \alpha^{N-n})$$

and since ε is arbitrary we obtain $u_n \leq w_n$.

This completes the proof of (10.13). It follows that

$$u_n(x) \leq \operatorname*{Inf}_{z\geq 0}\ \operatorname*{Inf}_{V\in\mathcal{V}^N_z} \{J^N(x;V) + \alpha^{N-n}\ \bar{u}_0(z)\}$$

$$\leq \operatorname*{Inf}_{V\in\mathcal{V}^N_o} J^N_n(x;V) + \alpha^{N-n}\, \bar{u}_0(0).$$

Since $s \leq \sigma^N_{n+1}$, we obtain from Wagner-Whitin theorem that :

$$\operatorname*{Inf}_{V\in\mathcal{V}^N_o} J^N_n(x;V) = u^N_n(x) = \operatorname*{Inf}_{V\in\tilde{\mathcal{V}}^N_o} J^N_n(x;V)$$

hence

(10.14) $$u_n(x) \leq u^N_n(x) + \alpha^{N-n}\, \bar{u}_0(0).$$

Moreover from (10.13) we deduce (since $u_N \geq 0$)

$$u_n(x) \geq \operatorname*{Inf}_{z\geq 0}\ \operatorname*{Inf}_{V\in\mathcal{V}^N_z} J^N_n(x;V)$$

and since $\mathcal{V}_z^N \subset \tilde{\mathcal{V}}_0^N$

$$u_n(x) \geq \underset{z\geq 0}{\text{Inf}} \underset{V\in\tilde{\mathcal{V}}_0^N}{\text{Inf}} J_n^N(x;V)$$

$$= \underset{z\geq 0}{\text{Inf}} \; u_n^N(x) = u_n^N(x).$$

Therefore we have proved that if $N \geq s(x)$

$$(10.15) \qquad u_n^N(x) \leq u_n(x) \leq u_n^N(x) + \alpha^{N-n}\, \bar{u}_0(0).$$

X - 3. SIMPLIFICATIONS OF THE DYNAMIC PROGRAMMING EQUATIONS

Theorem 10.3

Under the hypotheses of Theorem 10.1 :

$$(10.16) \quad \begin{cases} \text{If } 0 \leq x < \xi_{n+1} = \sigma_{n+1}^{n+1}, \text{ then} \\ u_n(x) = f_n(x) + \underset{r=n+1,\ldots}{\text{Inf}} \{c_n(\sigma_{n+1}^r - x) + \alpha u_{n+1}(\sigma_{n+2}^r)\} \end{cases}$$

$$(10.17) \quad \begin{cases} \text{If } \sigma_{n+1}^s \leq x < \sigma_{n+1}^{s+1} \quad (s = n+1, \ldots), \text{then} \\ u_n(x) = f_n(x) + \text{Min}\, \{c_n(0) + \alpha u_{n+1}(x - \xi_{n+1}), \\ \underset{r=s+1,\ldots}{\text{Inf}} [c_n(\sigma_{n+1}^r - x) + \alpha u_{n+1}(\sigma_{n+2}^r)]\} \end{cases}$$

$$(10.18) \quad \begin{cases} \text{If } \sigma_{n+1}^\infty < \infty \text{ and } x \geq \sigma_{n+1}^\infty, \text{ then} \\ u_n(x) = f_n(x) + c_n(0) + \alpha u_{n+1}(x - \xi_{n+1}) \end{cases}$$

Moreover $u_n(x)$ is concave on each of the intervals $[\sigma_{n+1}^s, \sigma_{n+1}^{s+1}[$, $s \geq n+1$, when such intervals are not empty. If $\sigma_{n+1}^\infty > 0$, the fonction $u_n(x)$ is continuous except at points σ_{n+1}^s where it has left and right limits, and

$$u_n(\sigma_{n+1}^s) \leq u_n(\sigma_{n+1}^{s-}) \text{ for } s = n+1, \ldots$$

$$u_n(\sigma_{n+1}^s) \leq u_n(\sigma_{n+1}^{s+}) \text{ for } s = n, \ldots$$

If $\sigma_{n+1}^\infty = 0$, then 0 is the only discontinuity point and $u_n(0) \leq u_n(0^+)$. □

Therefore $u_n(x)$ admits the following graph

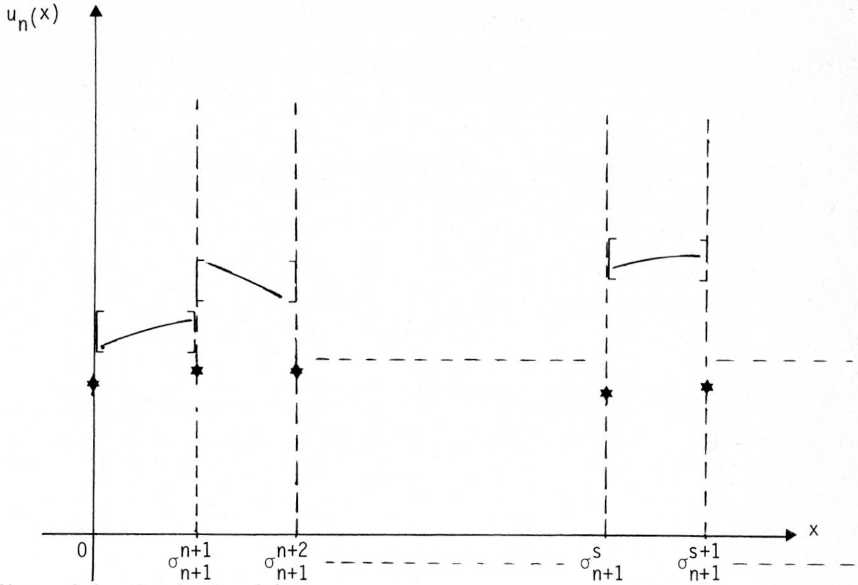

Figure 1.8 : Graph of $u_n(x)$

Proof of Theorem 10.3

If $\sigma_{n+1}^{\infty} = 0$, it is clear that the optimal control is 0, and

$$u_n(x) = \sum_{i=n}^{\infty} \alpha^{i-n} [c_i(0) + f_i(x)].$$

For $x > 0$, $u_n(x)$ is continuous.

Assume now $\sigma_{n+1}^{\infty} > 0$. Take $0 \le x < \xi_{n+1}$, and $N \ge n+1$.

From Theorem 2.1, we have

$$u_n^N(x) = f_n(x) + \underset{r=n+1,\dots,N}{\text{Min}} \{c_n(\sigma_{n+1}^r - x) + \alpha u_{n+1}^N(\sigma_{n+2}^r)\}.$$

From Theorem 10.2, we have

$$|u_n(x) - u_n^N(x)| \le \alpha^{N-n}\, \bar{u}_0(0)$$

and

$$|u_{n+1}(\sigma_{n+2}^r) - u_{n+1}^N(\sigma_{n+2}^r)| \le \alpha^{N-(n+1)}\, \bar{u}_0(0)$$

$$\forall r = n+1, \dots, N$$

therefore we deduce

$$\Big| \operatorname*{Min}_{r=n+1,\dots,N} \{c_n(\sigma^r_{n+1} - x) + \alpha u^N_{n+1}(\sigma^r_{n+2})\}$$

$$- \operatorname*{Min}_{r=n+1,\dots,N} \{c_n(\sigma^r_{n+1} - x) + \alpha u_{n+1}(\sigma^r_{n+2})\}\Big|$$

$$\leq \alpha^{N-n}\, \bar{u}_0(0)$$

hence

$$|u_n(x) - f_n(x) - \operatorname*{Min}_{r=n+1,\dots,N} \{c_n(\sigma^r_{n+1} - x) + \alpha u_{n+1}(\sigma^r_{n+2})\}|$$

$$\leq 2\, \alpha^{N-n}\, \bar{u}_0(0)$$

therefore

$$u_n(x) \geq f_n(x) + \operatorname*{Inf}_{r=n+1,\dots} \{c_n(\sigma^r_{n+1} - x) + \alpha u_{n+1}(\sigma^r_{n+2})\}.$$

But from (10.8) the reverse inequality also holds, hence (10.16). A similar reasoning shows that (10.17) holds.

From (10.16) it follows that $u_n(x)$ is concave hence continuous on $]0, \xi_{n+1}[$. When $x \downarrow 0$ it has a right limit since $f_n(x)$ decreases and

$$\operatorname*{Inf}_{r=n+1,\dots} \{c_n(\sigma^r_{n+1} - x) + \alpha u_{n+1}(\sigma^r_{n+2})\}$$

is an increasing function as $x \downarrow 0$. Let us show that

(10.19) $\qquad u_n(0^+) \geq u_n(0)$

which will also prove concavity on $[0, \xi_{n+1}[$. But for $x \leq \xi_{n+1}$

$$u_n(x) - u_n(0) = u_n(x) - u^N_n(x) + u^N_n(x) - u^N_n(0) + u^N_n(0) - u_n(0)$$

$$\geq u^N_n(x) - u^N_n(0) - 2\alpha^{N-n}\, \bar{u}_0(0)$$

Letting $x \downarrow o$, it follows

$$u_n(0^+) - u_n(0) \geq u^N_n(0^+) - u^N_n(0) - 2\alpha^{N-n}\, \bar{u}_0(0)$$

$$\geq 2\alpha^{N-n}\, \bar{u}_0(0)$$

since $u^N_n(0^+) \geq u^N_n(0)$. Letting N tend to $+\infty$ we deduce (10.19).

Assume now $\xi_{n+2} > 0$ and $\xi_{n+1} \leq x < \xi_{n+1} + \xi_{n+2}$. Then $0 \leq x - \xi_{n+1} < \xi_{n+2}$, and $x \to u_{n+1}(x - \xi_{n+1})$ is concave on $[\sigma^{n+1}_{n+1}, \sigma^{n+2}_{n+1}[$. Functions $c_n(\sigma^r_{n+1} - x) + \alpha u_{n+1}(\sigma^r_{n+2})$ for $r = n+2, \dots$ are concave continuous on $[\sigma^{n+1}_{n+1}, \sigma^{n+2}_{n+1}[$, hence from (9.17) $u_n(x)$ is concave on $[\sigma^{n+1}_{n+1}, \sigma^{n+2}_{n+1}[$. Taking $N \geq n+2$ and $x \in]\sigma^{n+1}_{n+1}, \sigma^{n+2}_{n+1}[$ we have

$$|u_n(x) - u^N_n(x)| \leq \alpha^{N-n}\, \bar{u}_0(0).$$

Using

$$u_n^N(\sigma_{n+1}^{n+1} + 0) \geq u_n^N(\sigma_{n+1}^{n+1})$$

we show, as for (10.19)

$$u_n(\sigma_{n+1}^{n+1} + 0) \geq u_n(\sigma_{n+1}^{n+1}).$$

If now $x \uparrow \xi_{n+1}$:

$$\operatorname*{Inf}_{r=n+1,\dots} \{c_n(\sigma_{n+1}^r - x) + \alpha u_{n+1}(\sigma_{n+2}^r)\} \downarrow \operatorname*{Inf}_{r=n+1,\dots} \{c_n(\sigma_{n+2}^r + 0) + \alpha u_{n+1}(\sigma_{n+2}^r)\}$$

from which it easily follows that $u_n(\xi_{n+1} - 0)$ exists and

$$u_n(\xi_{n+1} - 0) \geq u_n(\xi_{n+1}).$$

A similar argument holds on intervals $[\sigma_{n+1}^s, \sigma_{n+1}^{s+1}[$ provided that $\xi_{s+1} > 0$.

If $\xi_{n+1} = 0$ we start directly with (10.17). This completes the proof.

Theorem 10.4.

Under the hypotheses of Theorem 10.1, the equations of Dynamic Programming reduce to

$$(10.20)\quad \begin{cases} \underline{\text{If } 0 \leq x < \xi_{n+1},} \\ u_n(x) = f_n(x) + \operatorname*{Inf}_{r=n+1,\dots} \{c_n(\sigma_{n+1}^r - x) \\ \qquad + \sum_{k=n+1}^{r-1} \alpha^{k-n} [f_k(\sigma_{k+1}^r) + c_k(0)] + \alpha^{r-n} u_r(0)\} \end{cases}$$

$$(10.21)\quad \begin{cases} \underline{\text{If } \sigma_{n+1}^s \leq x < \sigma_{n+1}^{s+1} \quad (s = n+1, \dots),} \\ u_n(x) = f_n(x) + \operatorname{Min} \{c_n(0) + \alpha u_{n+1}(x - \xi_{n+1}), \\ \operatorname*{Inf}_{r=s+1,\dots} [c_n(\sigma_{n+1}^r - x) + \sum_{k=n+1}^{r-1} \alpha^{k-r} [f_k(\sigma_{k+1}^r) + c_k(0)] + \alpha^{r-n} u_n(0)]\} \end{cases}$$

$$(10.22)\quad \begin{cases} \underline{\text{If } \sigma_{n+1}^\infty < \infty \text{ and } x \geq \sigma_{n+1}^\infty,} \\ u_n(x) = \sum_{k=n}^{\infty} \alpha^{k-n} [f_k(x - \sigma_{n+1}^k) + c_k(0)] \end{cases}$$

Proof

The proof of (10.22) follows from the fact that if $x \geq \sigma_{n+1}^\infty$ the control (0,0...) is optimal.

Take now $0 \leq x < \xi_{n+1}$, then for $N \geq n+1$, we have by Theorem 3.2

$$u_n^N(x) = f_n(x) + \operatorname*{Min}_{r=n+1,\dots,N} \{c_n(\sigma_{n+1}^r - x) + \sum_{k=n+1}^{r-1} \alpha^{k-n} [f_k(\sigma_{k+1}^r) + c_k(0)] + \alpha^{r-n} u_r^N(0)\}$$

But for $r \leq N$, by Theorem 10.2

$$|u_r^N(0) - u_r(0)| \leq \alpha^{N-r} \bar{u}_0(0)$$

hence

$$|\alpha^{r-n} u_r^N(0) - \alpha^{r-n} u_r(0)| \leq \alpha^{N-n} \bar{u}_o(0). \tag{10.23}$$

Therefore we deduce

$$\begin{cases} |\underset{r=n+1,\ldots,N}{\text{Min}} \{c_n(\sigma_{n+1}^r - x) + \sum_{k=n+1}^{r-1} \alpha^{k-n} [f_k(\sigma_{k+1}^r) + c_k(0)] + \alpha^{r-n} u_r^N(0)\} \\ - \underset{r=n+1,\ldots,N}{\text{Min}} \{c_n(\sigma_{n+1}^r - x) + \sum_{k=n+1}^{r-1} \alpha^{k-n} [f_k(\sigma_{k+1}^r) + c_k(0)] + \alpha^{r-n} u_r(0)\}| \\ \leq \alpha^{N-n} \bar{u}_0(0). \end{cases} \tag{10.24}$$

and

$$\begin{cases} |u_n(x) - f_n(x) - \underset{r=n+1,\ldots,N}{\text{Min}} \{c_n(\sigma_{n+1}^r - x) + \sum_{k=n+1}^{r-1} \alpha^{k-n} [f_k(\sigma_{k+1}^r) \\ + c_k(0)] + \alpha^{r-n} u_r(0)\} | \leq 2\alpha^{N-n} \bar{u}_0(0). \end{cases} \tag{10.25}$$

It follows that

$$u_n(x) \geq f_n(x) + \underset{r=n+1,\ldots}{\text{Inf}} \{c_n(\sigma_{n+1}^r - x) + \sum_{k=n+1}^{r-1} \alpha^{k-n} [f_k(\sigma_{k+1}^r) + c_k(0)] + \alpha^{r-n} u_r(0)\}.$$

But from (10.16) and (10.17) the reverse inequality also holds, hence (10.20).

A similar reasoning shows that (10.21) holds. □

We can now prove the existence of an optimal feedback and obtain a Wagner-Whitin type Theorem.

<u>Theorem 10.5</u>

Under the hypotheses of Theorem 10.1 and assuming

$$c_n(v) \uparrow +\infty \text{ as } v \uparrow \infty \ ; \ \sigma_1^\infty = \infty. \tag{10.26}$$

there exists an optimal feedback $\hat{v}_n(x)$ given by

$$\begin{cases} \underline{\text{If } x < \xi_{n+1}} \\ \hat{v}_n(x) = \sigma_{n+1}^{\hat{r}(x)} - x, \ \hat{r}(x) = n+1, \ldots \\ \underline{\text{If } \sigma_{n+1}^s \leq x < \sigma_{n+1}^{s+1}, \ s = n+1, \ldots} \\ \hat{v}_n(x) = \text{or} \begin{cases} 0 \\ \sigma_{n+1}^{\hat{r}(x)} - x \text{ with } s+1 \leq \hat{r}(x) \end{cases} \end{cases} \tag{10.27}$$

Problem (10.4) admits an optimal control $\hat{V}_n = (\hat{v}_n, \hat{v}_{n+1}, \ldots)$ such that, if we denote by n_0 the first time $i \geq n$ for which $\hat{v}_i > 0$, we have

$$(10.28) \qquad \hat{v}_i \, \hat{y}_i = 0 \quad \forall i \geq n, \; i \neq n_0$$

Proof

Assume $x < \xi_{n+1}$. Set for $r \geq n+1$

$$A_r^n(x) = c_n(\sigma_{n+1}^r - x) + \sum_{k=n+1}^{r-1} \alpha^{k-n} \left[f_k(\sigma_{k+1}^r) + c_k(0)\right]$$

which is an increasing function of r.

By (10.26) we have $A_r^n(x) \uparrow +\infty$ as $r \uparrow +\infty$.

Therefore there exists $\hat{r}(x) \geq n+1$, such that in (10.20) the infimum is attained for $r = \hat{r}(x)$. Hence we deduce the first part of (10.27). The second part is proved in a similar way.

Clearly this feedback is such that

$$(10.29) \qquad \begin{cases} u_n(x) = f_n(x) + c_n(\hat{v}_n(x)) + \alpha u_{n+1}(x + \hat{v}_n(x) - \xi_{n+1}), \\ \forall x, \; \forall n \geq 0 \end{cases}$$

Define successively

$$\hat{v}_0 = \hat{v}_0(x) \qquad \hat{y}_1 = x + \hat{v}_0(x) - \xi_1$$

$$\hat{v}_1 = \hat{v}_1(\hat{y}_1) \qquad \hat{y}_2 = \hat{y}_1 + \hat{v}_1 - \xi_2$$

$$\hat{v}_i = \hat{v}_i(\hat{y}_i) \qquad \hat{y}_{i+1} = \hat{y}_i + \hat{v}_i - \xi_{i+1}$$

and

$$\hat{V} = (\hat{v}_0, \hat{v}_1, \ldots, \hat{v}_i, \ldots)$$

Taking $x = \hat{y}_n$ in (10.29) we obtain (after multiplication by α^n)

$$\alpha^n \, u_n(\hat{y}_n) = \alpha^n \left[f_n(\hat{y}_n) + c_n(\hat{v}_n)\right] + \alpha^{n+1}(\hat{y}_{n+1}).$$

Summing up these relations when n runs from 0 to N-1, we get

$$u_0(x) = \sum_{n=0}^{N-1} \alpha^n \left[f_n(\hat{y}_n) + c_n(\hat{v}_n)\right] + \alpha^N \, u_N(\hat{y}_N)$$

and since $u_N \geq 0$

$$u_0(x) \geq \sum_{n=0}^{N-1} \alpha^n \left[f_n(\hat{y}_n) + c_n(\hat{v}_n)\right]$$

Letting $N \to \infty$, we deduce

$$u_0(x) \geq J_0(x;\hat{V})$$

and since $\hat{V}$ is admissible and $u_0(x)$ is the infimum

$$u_o(x) = J_o(x;\hat{V}) = \operatorname*{Inf}_V J_o(x;V).$$

A similar proof shows that problem (10.4) has an optimal control. The proof of (10.28) follows from (10.20), (10.21) as in Wagner-Within theorem for the finite horizon case.

X - 4. PLANNING HORIZONS AND THE INFINITE HORIZON PROBLEM

It is natural to expect a relation between planning horizons and the solution of the infinite horizon problem. We can state the following.

Theorem 10.6

Under the assumptions of Theorem 10.1, let N be a planning horizon (cf. §IV.4) then considering an optimal policy for $J^N(V)$ and completing it adequately on N, N+1, ... we can obtain controls realizing the infimum of the infinite horizon problem starting in period 0 with inventory 0.

If (10.26) is satisfied, then we can complete it adequately to achieve the infimum of the infinite horizon problem.

Proof

Note that with the notation of Section IV.4,

$$\lambda^N = u_o^N(0) \qquad (^1)$$

If N is a planning horizon we have

$$u_o^K(0) = u_o^N(0) + \alpha^N u_N^K(0), \quad \forall K \geq N.$$

But from Theorem 10.2. it follows that

$$u_o^K(0) \to u_o(0)$$

$$u_N^K(0) \to u_N(0) \text{ as } K \to \infty$$

Therefore we obtain

$$u_o(0) = u_o^N(0) + \alpha^N u_N(0). \tag{10.30}$$

For any ε there exists a control V_N^ε such that

$$J_N(0;V_N^\varepsilon) \leq u_N(0) + \frac{\varepsilon}{\alpha^N}$$

Let $\hat{V}^N$ be the optimal control for $J_o^N(0,V)$ constructed as usual with a sequence of regeneration points. We have $\tilde{y}_N^N = 0$. We can complete $\hat{V}^N$ by using V_N^ε for components larger or equal to N. Let $\tilde{V}$ be the corresponding control. We have

(^{1}) Implicitly we have replaced $c_i(v)$ by $\alpha^i c_i(v)$ and $f_i(x)$ by $\alpha^i f_i(x)$.

$$J_0(0;V) = J_0^N(0;\hat{V}^N) + \alpha^N J_N(0;V_N^\varepsilon)$$
$$\leq u_0^N(0) + \alpha^N u_N(0) + \varepsilon$$
$$= u_0(0) + \varepsilon.$$

Since

$$J_0(0;\tilde{V}) \geq u_0(0)$$

then the desired result is proven. When (10.26) is satisfied, we can use the optimal feedback defined in Theorem 10.5 after time N and prove the second part of the statement.

Remark 10.2

Regeneration points of an optimal policy for the infinite horizon problem are not necessarily planning horizons

X - 5. STATIONARY CASE

In this paragraph we consider problem (10.1), (10.2), (10.4), (10.5) in a stationary context. Namely we assume that

$$\xi_k = \xi > 0 \tag{10.31}$$

$$\begin{cases} c_i(v) = c(v) \\ f_i(x) = f(x) \end{cases} \tag{10.32}$$

hence

$$\begin{cases} y_{i+1} = y_i + v_i - \xi \\ y_n = x \end{cases} \tag{10.33}$$

$$J_n(x;V) = \sum_{i=n}^{\infty} \alpha^{i-n} [c(v_i) + f(y_i)] \tag{10.34}$$

Assumption (10.6) becomes

$$\sum_{i=n}^{\infty} \alpha^{i-n} [c(\xi) + f(x)] = \frac{c(\xi) + f(x)}{1 - \alpha} \leq \bar{u}_0(x)$$

and therefore holds automatically.

Lemma 10.1

The function

$$u_n(x) = \operatorname*{Inf}_V J_n(x;V)$$

does not depend on n.

Proof

From (10.33) we obtain

(10.35) $y_i = x + v_n + v_{n+1} + \dots + v_{i-1} - (i-n)\xi$ for $i \geq n+1$

Define next

$$\tilde{y}_0 = x \qquad \tilde{v}_0 = v_n$$

$$\tilde{y}_i = y_{i+n} \qquad \tilde{v}_i = v_{n+i}$$

then

$$\tilde{y}_i = x + \tilde{v}_0 + \dots + \dots + \tilde{v}_{i-1} - i\,\xi$$

and

$$J_n(x;V) = \sum_{i=0}^{\infty} \alpha^i \, [c(v_{i+n}) + f(y_{i+n})]$$

$$= \sum_{i=0}^{\infty} \alpha^i \, [c(\tilde{v}_i) + f(\tilde{y}_i)]$$

$$= J_0(x;\tilde{V}).$$

Since we can associate by a shift operator to any V a $\tilde{V}$ and vice versa, it easily follows that

$$u_n(x) = u_0(x) = u(x). \quad \square$$

Consequently we can assert that the function u(x) is solution of the functional equation

(10.36) $$u(x) = f(x) + \operatorname*{Inf}_{v \geq (\xi - x)^+} \{c(v) + u(x + v - \xi)\}.$$

Moreover it satisfies the approximation inequality :

(10.37) $$|u(x) - u_0^N(x)| \leq \alpha^N \; \bar{u}_0(0), \quad \forall N \geq \frac{x}{\xi}$$

From application of Theorem 10.4, it follows that the function u(x) satisfies

(10.37)
$$\begin{cases} \underline{\text{If } 0 \leq x \leq \xi, \text{ then :}} \\ u(x) = f(x) + \operatorname*{Inf}_{r=1,2,\dots} \{c(r\xi - x) \\ \qquad + \sum_{k=1}^{r-1} \alpha^k \, [f(r-k)\xi) + c(0)] + \alpha^r \, u(0)\} \\ \underline{\text{If } x \geq \xi, \text{ then}} \\ u(x) = f(x) + c(0) + \alpha u(x-\xi). \end{cases}$$

Assuming that

(10.38) $c(v) \uparrow +\infty$ as $v \uparrow \infty$

then one defines an optimal feedback as follows

$$(10.39)\quad \begin{cases} \hat{v}(x) = \hat{r}(x)\xi - x & \text{if } x < \xi \text{ where } \hat{r}(x) \text{ realizes the infimum in (10.37)} \\ \hat{v}(x) = 0 & \text{if } x \geq \xi. \end{cases}$$

Consider the algebraic equation (in λ)

$$(10.40)\quad \lambda = f(0) + \operatorname*{Inf}_{r=1,2,\ldots} \{c(r\xi) + \sum_{k=1}^{r-1} \alpha^k [f((r-k)\xi) + c(0)] + \alpha^r \lambda\}$$

then we obtain the following result.

Lemma 10.2

Equation (10.40) has a unique solution.

Proof

Let λ, μ be two solutions. Then

$$\lambda - \mu = \operatorname*{Inf}_{r\geq 1} \{c(r\xi) + \sum_{k=1}^{r-1} \alpha^k [f((r-k)\xi) + c(0)] + \alpha^r \lambda\}$$
$$- \operatorname*{Inf}_{r\geq 1} \{c(r\xi) + \sum_{k=1}^{r-1} \alpha^k [f((r-k)\xi) + c(0)] + \alpha^r \mu\}$$

hence

$$|\lambda - \mu| \leq \alpha|\lambda - \mu|$$

which implies $\lambda = \mu$

Example

Consider

$$c(v) = K\,\chi_{v>0} + dv$$
$$f(x) = f\,x$$

then (10.40) becomes

$$\lambda = \operatorname*{Inf}_{r\geq 1} \{K + rd\,\xi + \sum_{k=1}^{r-1} \alpha^k f(r-k)\xi + \alpha^r \lambda\}$$
$$= K + \operatorname*{Inf}_{r\geq 1} \{r\,d\,\xi + f\,r\,\xi \frac{\alpha - \alpha^r}{1-\alpha} - f\xi \frac{\alpha - r\alpha^r + (r-1)\alpha^{r+1}}{(1-\alpha)^2} + \alpha^r \lambda\}$$
$$= K - \frac{f\xi\alpha}{(1-\alpha)^2} + \operatorname*{Inf}_{r\geq 1} \{r\,d\,\xi + \frac{rf\xi\alpha}{1-\alpha} + \frac{f\xi\alpha^{r+1}}{(1-\alpha)^2} + \alpha^r \lambda\}$$
$$= K - \frac{f\xi\alpha}{(1-\alpha)^2} + \operatorname*{Inf}_{r\geq 1} \{r\,\xi(d + \frac{f\alpha}{1-\alpha}) + \alpha^r [\lambda + \frac{f\xi\alpha}{(1-\alpha)^2}]\}$$

Define

$$(10.41)\quad \lambda(r) = \frac{K - \frac{f\xi\alpha}{(1-\alpha)^2} + r\xi(d + \frac{f\alpha}{1-\alpha}) + \frac{f\xi\alpha^{r+1}}{(1-\alpha)^2}}{1 - \alpha^r}$$

then we have

$$(10.42)\quad \lambda = \operatorname*{Inf}_{r\geq 1} \lambda(r).$$

Indeed clearly

$$\lambda \leq \lambda(r) \quad \forall r$$

and

$$\lambda = \lambda(r^*)$$

where r^* is the optimal value for r. We next compute $\lambda(r)$ for α close to 1, but first note that

$$\alpha^r \sim 1 - r \,\mathrm{Log}\, \frac{1}{\alpha} + \frac{r^2}{2} (\mathrm{Log}\, \frac{1}{\alpha})^2 \sim 1 - r\,[1 - \alpha - (\frac{1-\alpha}{2})^2] + \frac{r^2}{2} (1-\alpha)^2.$$

Hence

$$\lambda(r) \sim \frac{K - \dfrac{f\xi}{(1-\alpha)^2} + r\xi d + f\xi[\dfrac{r}{1-\alpha} + \dfrac{1}{(1-\alpha)^2} - \dfrac{r}{1-\alpha} + \dfrac{r}{2} + \dfrac{r^2}{2}]}{r(1 - \alpha)}$$

$$\lambda(r) \sim \frac{K + r\xi(d + \frac{f}{2}) + f\xi\frac{r^2}{2}}{r(1 - \alpha)}$$

hence r^* minimizes $\frac{K}{r} + f\xi\frac{r}{2}$

i.e.

$$r^* = \sqrt{\frac{2K}{f\xi}}$$

This corresponds to the well known Wilson economic order quantity, $v^* = \sqrt{\frac{2K\xi}{f}}$ where $v^* = r^*.\xi$.

Remark 10.3

The above example for linear cost functions brings out how it would be interesting to review the results of section 10 when α is close to 1. This is the ergodic problem. It would be also interesting to derive the asymptotic expansion of r^*_α in terms of $1 - \alpha$. This is left to the reader as an exercice.

XI - SURVEY OF RESEARCH AND RESULTS INTERPRETATION

This chapter generalizes the seminal work published by Wagner and Whitin [1958]
Their fondamental contribution is a planning horizon theorem, and a forward algorithm much more efficient than traditional dynamic programming solution techniques.

The results of this chapter are not genuinely new, except in Section X for the infinite horizon case. However, they are presented and analyzed in a unified setting based on optimal control theory. This framework presents the net advantage over other techniques to allow complete generalization of previous works.

The key preliminary property which characterizes an optimal policy is that production may take place in a period only when entering inventory in that period is zero. This Wagner-Whitin theorem is the foundation of their forward algorithm, and was also proved independently by Manne [1958]. For an alternative approach see Klein [1957].

The Wagner-Within planning horizon theorem is directly related to the monotonicity of the last set-up point l(N), in the length of the problem horizon, N. Following our notation :

$$\text{if } N_1 \leq N_2 \text{ then } l(N_1) \leq l(N_2)$$

Furthermore, if l(N+1) = N then N is a regeneration point for any problem of horizon $N_1 \geq N$. N is a planning horizon i.e. decisions at time 0 to N-1 may be considered by themselves, and independently of demand in subsequent periods.

Zabel [1964] proves a stronger planning horizon theorem for the same model. In addition to the above property, he obtains :

(i) For any $M \geq N+1$, there exists an optimal ordering policy with a regeneration point in some $\bar{N}$, such that

$$l(N+1) \leq \bar{N} \leq M$$

(note that the Wagner-Within theorem follows as a special case, and that $\bar{N}$ is not necessarily the last set-up for the M-period problem).

(ii) If $N = l(M) \leq M-1$ and $\forall P \in [l(M), M-1]$, N is a regeneration point for an optimal policy of $J^P(V)$, and then N is a planning horizon (cf. Corrolaries 4.2 and 4.3, as well as theorem 4.5).

Wagner and Within contribution, however, is limited to the simplest finite horizon model where production and holding costs are linear, except for a set-up cost concerning the decision to produce. It is further assumed : a unit production (ordering) cost independent of the amount produced in each period, and constant throughout all time periods (stationary marginal cost) ; zero initial inventory ; and no backlogging. Thus, for any period j, j = 0, ..., N :

$$c_j(v) = K_j \, \chi_{v>0} + dv$$

$$f_j(x) = f_j \, x \text{ for } x \geq 0$$

with K_j,d and f_j being parameters.

The model developed in this chapter is the most general, as far as concave production and holding costs, initial inventory, and the length of the horizon are concerned. It completes the long list of extensions in the literature of the initial Wagner-Within forward algorithm and planning horizon theorem, for less restrictive qualifications.

Wagner [1960] himself already suggested that the forward algorithm is also applicable when the production cost functions differ from period to period, but have non increasing marginal costs with respect to output, thus allowing for quantity discounts. However, this assumption is too weak to prove the planning horizon theorem and examples can be constructed which show that the proposition is violated.

Indeed, Wagner-Within theorem is much more general than initially stated. As demonstrated by Veinott [1969], Manne and Veinott [1967] and Zangwill [1968], [1969] the regeneration set-up rule is valid for any problem which can be formulated as a single-source single -destination network with concave costs, and initial and terminal inventory levels equal to zero (cf. Sections IV.5 and VII.4). Complete generalization is possible but necessitates transformations of the cost data which are not quite intuitive (cf. Veinott [1969] and Blackburn and Eppen [1973]). On the contrary, our theorems 3.3, 7.3 and 10.5 provide full direct generalization of this property, and as a consequence warrant in all cases an efficient forward algorithm.

Our approach leads directly to the existence of an optimal control, just by exhibiting it. Moreover, we do not need to rely on results for transportation networks, which require additional background on graph theory.

On the other hand, extensions of the planning horizon theorem are much more intricate. Eppen, Gould and Pashigian [1969] just remove the stationarity assumption on unit production costs, and thus allow them to vary with time (but not with quantity). They are only able to establish a planning horizon theorem, after a long development, which requires additional conditions on the structure of marginal production costs and holding costs (conditions for no speculative motive of producing in any period $j \neq t$ to satisfy demand in period t). Roughly, a planning horizon theorem is proved only for periods where it is especially advantageous to produce. Eppen et al. introduce two important notions : the forward extrapolation from period N_1 to N_2 ($N_1 \leq N_2$) defined as :

$$a_{N_1,N_2} = d_{N_1} + \sum_{i=N_1}^{N_2} f_i,$$

and the violated set defined as :

$$m(N_1,N_2) = \{N \in \{1, \ldots, N_2\} / a_{N,N_2} < a_{N_1,N_2}\}$$

Following Eppen et al., $l(N-1)$ is a planning horizon if $m(l(N),N-1) = \emptyset$.

Our theorem 4.6 (together with theorem 4.2) generalizes the result of Eppen et al. for general concave production and holding costs, but with no initial inventory and no backlogging. Condition (4.28) is similar to the one imposed by Eppen et al. The additional condition (4.29) is quite restrictive. For example it is violated under conditions (4.16) and (4.17). It requires a significiant drop in the production cost at time $l(N)$.

Blackburn and Kunreuther [1974] extend the above analysis to the backlogging case where holding and penalty costs are concave.

Thomas [1970] includes to the Eppen et al. model a demand function for each period, where in addition to the production decision there is also a price decision to make. The same planning horizon theorem obtains.

In brief, all previous models start with selecting a problem horizon, say N, and then propose a forward algorithm to find planning horizons. The general model (concave production, holding and backlogging cost functions) was also addressed by Manne and Veinott [1967] and Zangwill [1969]. But they developed backward algorithms based on the regeneration point property ; Zangwill's algorithm is rather efficient in the case of a constant marginal cost of production (which may differ in each period).

In practice, there is no guarantee that such horizons exist. As a matter of fact, an extensive empirical investigation conducted by Lundin and Morton [1975] for the linear stationary cost case, show surprisingly that Wager-Within planning horizons occur only for a rather small set of cost parameters and demand patterns. Therefore for many practical situations the methods based on forward algorithms is plagued with the usual problem of knowing how sensitive is the initial part of the production (reordering) policy to the problem horizon N. As noted by Lundin and Morton, this drawback is incompatible with the need of production managers facing incomplete information about their environment. An alternative approach is thus proposed by Lundin and Morton. They provide a forward algorithm that can efficiently solve longer and longer finite horizon problems with a good stopping-rule. They develop new planning horizon and near planning horizon procedures building on Zabel's work.

They define E(N) to be smallest set of decision instants, no posterior to N-1, that have to be considered as potential last set-up times for an optimal policy of every N^*-horizon problem, where N^* is greater that N, i.e. :

$$\text{for any } N^* \geq N \text{ then } l(N^*) \in E(N)$$

E(N), in our notation, is also a regeneration set, i.e. for any $N_1 \geq N^u$, where N^u is the maximum element of E(N), there is at least one optimal solution to the N_1-period sub-problem with a regeneration point belonging to E(N). Then, they show that construction of the regeneration set E(N), is the fundamental issue in finding planning horizons for optimal policies, and near-planning horizons in the sense of determining policies which are guaranteed to cost within an epsilon of optimal. They also show how to find conditions under which a planning horizon procedure can be "protective", that is capable of finding any horizon that actually exists within some finite forecast horizon.

Their theory applies to the general case of concave production and holding cost functions. The no-backlogging and backlogging cases are separately examined (backlogging costs when they are relevant are also assumed to be concave). They show how previous work relate to their results as special cases. For the backlogging case the procedure is quite different, and relies on the Blackburn and Kunreuther cost transformation. From extensive computational tests the Lundin-Morton protective procedures seem to be much more powerful than previous methods, for recognizing planning horizons ; Zabel algorithm appears as a second best, still much more effective than the Wagner-Within technique . Morton [1975], [1978] has extended these protective procedures to general dynamic and linear programming problems. In a recent interesting article, Bean and Smith [1981] have considered a new approach to planning horizons relying on the infinite horizon discounted problem, but, for the time being, is limited to integer valued controls. Our Section X generalizes all previous results for the infinite horizon problems. In the stationary case, the fact that stationary policies are optimal against possibly non stationary ones is intuitive, although it has not been rigorously stated in the literature.

Our Theorems 4.3 and 4.6 constitute alternative proof of Lundin and Morton's main results. Extension to the backlogging case is conducted in Section IX.3.

Other extensions and applications may be reported. The introduction of bound constraints on production and inventory makes the problem difficult to solve, to the extent that efficient algorithm are concerned. In particular, it is difficult to characterize the structure of the optimal solution. See Florian and Klein [1971] and further extensions by Jagannathan and Rao [1973], Love [1973], Swoveland [1975] and Louveaux [1975]. See also Florian and Robillard [1971]. The multi-product, multi-facility problem is addressed by Zangwill [1969]. See also Dzielinski et al. [1963]and Dzielinski and Gomory [1965] for computational aspects. A production cost function with multiple set-up costs is considered by Lippman [1969]. No forward algorithms or planning horizon theorems of any sort have been found for these cases.

Application to the deterministic cash balance problem in finance is due to Blackburn and Eppen [1973]. Extending the network approach they derive an efficient forward algorithm where demand and production are allowed to be negative. Combining the insights of Blackburn-Eppen and Lundin-Morton, Mensching, Gaistka and Morton [1978] provide complete planning horizon procedures for the general cash balance problem.

On the other hand Sethi and Chand [1979] developed efficient forward algorithms and planning horizon procedures for machine replacement problems under an improving technological environment over time.
Optimal capacity expansion for a plant is an other application area explored by Manne and Veinott [1967].

REFERENCES

BEAN J.C. - SMITH R.L. [1981] , Conditions for the existence of planning horizons, Technical Report 81-8, Department of Industrial and Operational Engineering, University of Michigan, Ann Arbor.

BENSOUSSAN A. - PROTH J.M. [1981] , Gestion de stocks avec coûts concaves, RAIRO, Automatique/Systèmes Analysis and Control, Vol. 15, n° 3, pp. 201 - 220.

BLACKBURN J.D. - EPPEN G. [1973] , A two asset deterministic cash balance problem, Research paper 133, Stanford University.

BLACKBURN J.D. - KUNREUTHER H. [1974] , Planning horizons for the dynamic lot size model with backlogging, Management Science, 21(3), pp. 251-255.

DZIELINSKI B. - BAKER C. - MANNE A. [1963] , Simulation tests of lot size programming, Management Science, 9(2), pp. 229-258.

DZIELINSKI B. - GOMORY R. [1965] , Optimal programming of lot sizes, inventories and labor allocations, Management Science, 11(9), pp. 874-890.

EPPEN G. - GOULD F. - PASHIGAN B.P. [1969] , Extensions of the planning horizon theorem in the dynamic lot size model, Management Science, 15(5), pp. 268-277.

FLORIAN M. - KLEIN M. [1971] , Deterministic production planning with concave costs and capacity constraints, Management Science, 18(1), pp. 12-20 ; Erratum : Management Science, 18(11), p. 721.

FLORIAN M. - ROBILLARD P. [1971] , An implicit enumeration algorithm for the concave cost network flow problem, Management Science, 18(3), pp. 184-193.

JAGANNATHAN R. - RAO M.R. [1973] , A class of deterministic production planning problems, Management Science, 19(11), pp. 1295-1300.

KLEIN M. [1957] , Some production planning problems, Naval Research Logistics Quaterly, 4(4), pp. 269-286.

LIPPMAN S. [1969] , Optimal inventory policy with multiple set-up costs, Management Science, 16(1), pp. 118-138.

LOVE S.F. [1973] , Bounded production and inventory models with piecewise concave costs, Management Science, 20(3), pp. 313-318.

LOUVEAUX F.V. [1975] , Extensions of the deterministic production planning model with concave cost and equal capacity constraints, CORE Discussion paper 7522.

LUNDIN R.A. - MORTON T.E. [1975] , Planning horizons for the dynamic lot size model: Zabel vs. Protective procedures and computational results, Operations Research, 23(4), pp. 711-734.

MANNE A.S. [1958] , Programming of economic lot sizes, Management Science, 4(2), pp. 115-135.

MANNE A.S. - VEINOTT Jr. A.F. [1967] , Optimal plant size with arbitrary increasing time paths of demand, in : A.S. Manne, ed. Investments for capacity expansion : Size, location and time phasing, (M.I.T. Press, Cambridge, Mass.), Chapter 11.

MENSCHING J. - GARSTKA S. - MORTON T. [1978] , Protective planning horizon procedures for a deterministic cash balance problem, Operations Research, 26(4), pp. 637-652.

MORTON T.E. [1978] , The non-stationary infinite horizon inventory problem, Management Science, 24(4), pp. 1474-1482.

MORTON T.E. [1975] , Forward algorithms and planning horizons for dynamic and linear programming, Management Science Research Report, Carnegie-Mellon University.

ORDEN A. [1956] , The transhipment problem, Management Science, 2(3), pp. 276-285.

PROTH J.M. [1982-1] , Optimisation des décisions dans les problèmes de production à couts concaves,Thesis, University of Paris IX-Dauphine.

PROTH J.M. [1982-2] , Gestion de stocks avec coûts concaves. Notion d'horizon de planification, Science de gestion, n° 2.

SETHI S. - CHAND S. [1979] , Planning horizon procedures for machine replacement models, Management Science, 25(2), pp. 140-151.

SWOVELAND C. [1975] , A deterministic multi-period production planning model with piecewise concave production and holding-backorder costs, Management Science, 21(9), pp. 1007-1013.

THOMAS J. [1970] , Price-production decisions with deterministic demand, Management Science, 16(11), pp. 747-750.

VEINOTT A.F. Jr. [1969] , Minimum concave cost solution of Leontief substitution models of multi-facility inventory systems, Operations Research, 17(2), pp. 262-291.

WAGNER H.M. [1960] , A postcript to "dynamic problems in the theory of the firm", Naval Research Logistics Quarterly, 7(1), pp. 7-12.

ZABEL E. [1964] , Some generalizations of an inventory planning horizon theorem, Management Science, 10(3), pp. 465-471.

ZANGWILL W.I. [1966] , A deterministic multi-period production scheduling model with backlogging, Management Science, 13(1), pp. 105-119.

ZANGWILL W.I. [1968] , Minimum concave cost flows in certain networks, Management Science, 14(7), pp. 429-450.

ZANGWILL W.I. [1969] , A backlogging model and a multi-echelon model of a dynamic economic lot size production system. A network approach, Management Science, 15(9), pp. 506-527.

CHAPTER II

PRODUCTION PLANNING AND PRODUCTION SMOOTHING MODELS FOR CONVEX COSTS AND DETERMINISTIC DEMAND

DISCRETE TIME FORMULATION

INTRODUCTION

In this chapter the theory of production planning, and the related theory of production smoothing are developed for convex cost functionals where demand is deterministic. The issues are quite similar to those addressed in Chapter I, but the methods and results are much different.

The adopted formulation reduces to a convex optimization problem for which standard techniques exist as far as existence of optimal solutions and necessary conditions for optimality are concerned.

The first four sections are devoted to the production planning model. In Section I the restriction of no backlogging is imposed ; we prove the existence of an optimal policy and derive necessary conditions for optimality. These conditions are then used in Section II to obtain monotonicity properties of the optimal control. Forecast and planning horizon results are proposed in Section III. In Section IV we extend the model to allow backlogging.

The next two sections V and VI investigate the problem of production smoothing where in addition to production and holding costs we consider explicitly the costs of changing the production level from one period to the next. Such costs are called adjustment or smoothing costs, and for the most part consist of hiring and lay off expenses. We discuss both the cases of zero and positive initial inventory, and produce results concerning the existence of an optimal policy, necessary conditions for optimality and planning horizons. Finding planning horizons is a much harder task than before. Conditions are more difficult to derive, mainly because we deal here with a two dimensional state control problem, and thus it is no more sufficient to find regeneration points which are stable with respect to the horizon.

In Section VI we discuss the maximum principle in discrete time, and its relation with the problem of production smoothing.

A final Section VII presents a survey of the literature, the main results and how they relate to our own work.

In this chapter we do not resort on Dynamic Programming, and postpone the use of it until Chapter IV where we shall consider a more general formulation with K-convex cost functions and stochastic demand . We concentrate only on the use of necessary conditions ; these can be stated independently of convexity, but of course the monotonicity properties crucially depend on convexity.

Only a very limited mathematical background is required for this chapter, mostly some familiarity with the theory of convex optimization. Basic elements of the theory are recalled in the mathematical appendix.

I - THE CONVEX PRODUCTION PLANNING MODEL

I - 1. NOTATION AND PROBLEM DEFINITION

The problem of determining a minimum cost production schedule (optimal control) over an N period horizon was investigated in chapter I for concave costs. It is now reexamined when costs are convex instead.

The control problem formulation follows the notation already introduced in Section I of the previous chapter.

The state equations are :

(1.1) $$y_{i+1} = y_i + v_i - \xi_{i+1}, \qquad i = 0, \ldots, N-1$$

where demand is non negative.

In the next two sections we assume that demand must be satisfied with no backlogging, hence :

(1.2) $$y_i \geq 0, \qquad i = 0, \ldots, N$$

The control variables satisfy the no disposal constraint :

(1.3) $$v_i \geq 0.$$

(1.2) and (1.3) lead to :

$$v_i \geq (\xi_{i+1} - y_i)^+, \qquad i = 0, 1, \ldots, N$$

Define

$$V = (v_0, \ldots, v_{N-1})$$

and let

(1.4) $$c_i(v), \; f_i(x), \qquad i = 0, \ldots, N-1$$

be the production and holding cost functions from $R^+ \to R^+$, which are non decreasing and convex, and not reduced to a constant.

The control problem on the interval $[n,N]$ is now defined, setting

(1.5) $$y_n = x$$

(1.6) $$J_n(x;V) = \sum_{i=n}^{N-1} [c_i(v_i) + f_i(y_i)]$$

I - 2. SOME PROPERTIES OF THE COST FUNCTIONS

A convex non decreasing function h from R^+ into R^+ is necessarily continuous on $[0,\infty)$ and tends to $+\infty$ as the argument tends to $+\infty$ (unless it is a constant). In each point it admits a right and left derivative denoted by $h'^+(x)$, $h'^-(x)$ with the properties

(1.7) $$h'^-(x) \leq h'^+(x).$$

Moreover one has

(1.8) $\forall x_1 < x_2$ then $h'^{+}(x_1) \le h'^{-}(x_2)$,

with a strict inequality if h is strictly convex.

I - 3. EXISTENCE OF AN OPTIMAL CONTROL

For simplicity take n = 0 in (1.5) and (1.6). It then follows :

Theorem 1.1

Under assumptions (1.4) there exists an optimal control. It is unique if functions c_i are strictly convex.

Proof

Write J(V) for $J_0(x;V)$. It is convenient to eliminate the y_i's in the expression of J(V) by noting that :

$$y_i = x + v_0 + \dots + v_{i-1} - \xi_1 - \xi_2 - \dots - \xi_i, \qquad i = 1, \dots, N$$

The problem amounts to minimizing

$$J(V) = \sum_{i=0}^{N-1} [c_i(v_i) + f_i(x + v_0 + \dots + v_{i-1} - \xi_1 - \dots - \xi_i)] \tag{1.9}$$

under the constraints

$$\begin{cases} v_i \ge 0 \\ x + v_0 + \dots + v_{i-1} \ge \xi_1 + \dots + \xi_i, \qquad i = 1, \dots, N \end{cases} \tag{1.10}$$

where (1.10) defines a convex set.

The function J(V) being convex, continuous on $(R^N)^+$ (V is an element of R^N), and $J(V) \to +\infty$ as $v_0 + \dots + v_{N-1} \to +\infty$, then J(V) attains its minimum.

When functions c_i are strictly convex, J(V) is clearly strictly convex and the minimum is unique. □

Without strict convexity the optimal control may not be unique. It will be convenient to select a particular solution according to the following :

Theorem 1.2

Under assumptions (1.4) the set of optimal controls is a non empty convex closed set of R^N. There is one optimal control for which the Euclidean norm $|V| = (v_0^2 + \dots + v_{N-1}^2)^{1/2}$ is minimum.

Proof

Let V_{ad} be the set of admissible controls defined by (1.10). Let $\hat{V}^1$ and $\hat{V}^2$ be two optimal controls, then since V_{ad} is convex $\theta\hat{V}^1 + (1-\theta)\hat{V}^2$ belongs to V_{ad} ($\theta \in [0,1]$).

Moreover $$J(\theta\hat{V}^1 + (1-\theta)\hat{V}^2) \le \theta\, J(\hat{V}^1) + (1-\theta)\, J(\hat{V}^2)$$
$$= \inf J(V)$$

hence $\theta\hat{V}^1 + (1-\theta)\hat{V}^2$ is also a minimum. Therefore the set of optimal controls is convex. It is closed since, considering a sequence $\hat{V}^n$ of optimal controls which converges to $\hat{V}$ in R^N :

$$J(\hat{V}^n) \to J(\hat{V})$$

which follows from the continuity of J.

Hence $\hat{V}$ is also an optimal control.

Since $|V|$ is a norm, there is an element which has a minimum norm. This element is unique. Consider next the functional

$$(1.11) \qquad J_\varepsilon(V) = J(V) + \varepsilon(\sum_{i=0}^{N-1} v_i^2)$$

which is strictly convex on V_{ad}. Let $\hat{V}^\varepsilon$ be the optimal control for $J_\varepsilon(V)$ then we have

$$(1.12) \qquad \hat{V}^\varepsilon \to \hat{V} \text{ the optimal control with minimum norm as } \varepsilon \to 0.$$

Indeed $\hat{V}^\varepsilon$ remains bounded as $\varepsilon \to 0$ (since $J(V) \to \varepsilon$ as $|V| \to \infty$). Pick a subsequence, still denoted by $\hat{V}^\varepsilon$, which converges to $\hat{V}$ in R^N. Clearly $\hat{V} \in V_{ad}$. Moreover

$$(1.13) \qquad J(\hat{V}^\varepsilon) + \varepsilon\, |\hat{V}^\varepsilon|^2 \le J(V) + \varepsilon|V|^2 \qquad \forall V \in V_{ad}$$

By the continuity of J(V) we deduce

$$J(\hat{V}) \le J(V)$$

hence $\hat{V}$ is an optimal control.

Let $\hat{V}'$ be any optimal control, then

$$J(\hat{V}') \le J(\hat{V}^\varepsilon)$$

hence from (1.13)

$$J(\hat{V}') + \varepsilon|\hat{V}^\varepsilon|^2 \le J(\hat{V}') + \varepsilon|\hat{V}'|^2$$

therefore

$$|\hat{V}^\varepsilon| \le |\hat{V}'|$$

and as $\varepsilon \to 0$, we obtain

$$|\hat{V}| \le |\hat{V}'|$$

which completes the proof of (1.12). □

Definition

In case of non uniqueness, "the optimal control" is the one which minimizes the Euclidean norm $|V|$.

I - 4. NECESSARY CONDITIONS FOR OPTIMALITY

Let $\hat{V} = (\hat{v}_0, \ldots, \hat{v}_{N-1})$ be an optimal control and let $\hat{y}_0, \hat{y}_1, \ldots, \hat{y}_N$ be the corresponding optimal state.

Theorem 1.3

Assume (1.4). An optimal pair $(\hat{v}_0, \ldots, \hat{v}_{N-1}), (\hat{y}_0, \hat{y}_1, \ldots, \hat{y}_N)$ for problem $J_0(x;V)$ satisfies the following conditions

(1.14) $$\begin{cases} \text{If } \hat{v}_k > 0, \hat{y}_{k+1} > 0, \ldots, \hat{y}_\ell > 0 \text{ for } 0 \le k < \ell < N, \text{ then} \\ \sum_{j=k+1}^{\ell} f_j'^-(\hat{y}_j) + c_k'^-(\hat{v}_k) - c_\ell'^+(\hat{v}_\ell) \le 0 \end{cases}$$

(1.15) $$\begin{cases} \text{If } \hat{v}_k > 0 \text{ for } k < N, \text{ and } \hat{y}_{k+1} > 0, \ldots, \hat{y}_N > 0, \text{ then} \\ \sum_{j=k+1}^{N-1} f_j'^-(\hat{y}_j) + c_k'^-(\hat{v}_k) = 0 \quad \left(\sum_{j=k+1}^{N-1} = 0 \text{ if } k = N-1\right) \end{cases}$$

(1.16) $$\begin{cases} \text{If } \hat{v}_\ell > 0 \text{ for } 1 \le \ell \le N-1, \text{ then } \forall k < \ell \text{ one has} \\ \sum_{j=k+1}^{\ell} f_j'^+(\hat{y}_j) + c_k'^+(\hat{v}_k) - c_\ell'^-(\hat{v}_\ell) \ge 0 \end{cases}$$

(1.17) $$\begin{cases} \hat{v}_k \ge 0, \quad \hat{y}_k \ge 0, \quad \hat{y}_{k+1} = \hat{y}_k + \hat{v}_k - \xi_{k+1}, \hat{y}_0 = x \\ \hat{y}_0 = x \end{cases}$$

Proof

(i) Consider first the case where $\hat{v}_k > 0, \hat{y}_{k+1}, \ldots, \hat{y}_\ell > 0$ for $0 \le k < \ell < N$. Define a new control $\tilde{V}$ by the following transformation of $\hat{V}$:

- all components except k and ℓ are the same,
- $\hat{v}_k$ is changed into $\hat{v}_k - \theta$, and
- $\hat{v}_\ell$ is changed into $\hat{v} + \theta$.

Notice immediately that $\hat{y}_{k+1}$ becomes $\hat{y}_{k+1} - \theta, \ldots, \hat{y}_\ell$ becomes $\hat{y}_\ell - \theta$, the other components of $\hat{y}$ being unchanged. For θ sufficiently small, $\tilde{V}$ is an admissible control, hence

$$\sum_{j=k+1}^{\ell} [f_j(\hat{y}_j - \theta) - f_j(\hat{y}_j)] + c_k(\hat{v}_k - \theta) - c_k(\hat{v}_k) + c_\ell(\hat{v}_\ell + \theta) - c_\ell(\hat{v}_\ell) \ge 0.$$

Dividing by θ and letting θ tend to 0, we obtain (1.14).

ii) Consider next the situation

$$\hat{v}_k > 0,\ \hat{y}_{k+1} > 0,\ \ldots,\ \hat{y}_N > 0 \text{ for } k < N.$$

Then, changing just $\hat{v}_k$ into $\hat{v}_k - \theta$, with θ sufficiently small, we obtain a new admissible control, hence

$$\sum_{j=k+1}^{N-1} [f_j(\hat{y}_j - \theta) - f_j(\hat{y}_j)] + c_k(\hat{v}_k - \theta) - c_k(\hat{v}_k) \geq 0$$

(with $\sum_{j=k+1}^{N-1} = 0$, if $k = N-1$). Since all terms are negative by the monotonicity property of the functions, we obtain equality to 0. Dividing by θ and letting θ tend to 0, we obtain (1.15).

iii) Next (1.16) is derived by modifying $\hat{V}$ as follows :

$\hat{v}_k$ is changed into $\hat{v}_k + \theta$ and $\hat{v}_\ell$ into $\hat{v}_\ell - \theta$, with θ sufficiently small. Proceeding as above we obtain (1.16).

iv) (1.17) follows immediatly from the problem definition.

This completes the proof of theorem 1.3. □

Conditions (1.14) to (1.16) are familiar in intertemporal resource allocation problems.

(1.14) stipulates that if it is optimal to produce in period k whereas optimal inventory positions for periods k+1 to ℓ are positive, then it is more economical to produce an extra unit in period k and store it until period ℓ than to produce it in period ℓ.

(1.15) is very peculiar since it corresponds to the extreme optimal case where production would occur in a period k, the quantity produced $\hat{v}_k$ securing positive inventory positions in all subsequent periods. This situation can obviously be optimal only if it would save (cost) nothing to decrease (increase) production in period k by one unit and to destock (carry) it until the last period.

(1.16) means that if it is optimal to produce in period ℓ, the quantity $\hat{v}_\ell$ is such that at the margin it is more economical to satisfy an extra unit of demand in period ℓ from production in that period, than from production from any previous period.

II - PROPERTIES OF THE OPTIMAL CONTROL

II - 1. MONOTONICITY PROPERTIES WITH RESPECT TO DEMAND

Define cumulative requirements and cumulative production levels as follows :

$$(2.1) \quad \begin{cases} \underline{\xi}_k = \xi_1 + \ldots + \xi_k, & k = 1, \ldots, N \\ \underline{v}_k = v_0 + \ldots + v_k, & k = 0, \ldots, N-1 \end{cases}$$

Note that using chapter I's notation $\underline{\xi}_k$ would be denoted σ_1^k.

Lemma 2.1.

Let $\hat{V}$ be the optimal control associated with the demand $\xi_1, \dots, \xi_N$, and $\hat{V}^*$ be the one corresponding to $\xi_1^*, \dots, \xi_N^*$. Then we have :

(2.2) $\xi_j^* \geq \xi_j \ \forall j = 1, \dots, N$ implies $\hat{v}_i^* \geq \hat{v}_i$, $\forall i = 0, \dots, N-1$

Similarly we have

(2.3) $\underline{\xi}_j^* \geq \underline{\xi}_j$,$\forall j = 1, \dots, N$, implies $\hat{v}_i^* \geq \hat{v}_i$, $\forall i = 0, \dots, N-1$

Before proving lemma 2.1, we claim the two following statements :

1° Without loss of generality we may assume that

(2.4) $c_i(v)$ is strictly convex.

Indeed, replacing $c_i(v)$ by $c_i(v) + \varepsilon v^2$ which is strictly convex, we obtain the problem $J_\varepsilon(V)$.

We showed in Theorem 1.2. that $\hat{V}^\varepsilon \to \hat{V}$ (in R^N). Therefore if we prove (2.2) and (2.3) for $\hat{V}^\varepsilon$, then we recover the same properties for $\hat{V}$, by letting ε tend to 0. Therefore it is sufficient to consider the case (2.4).

As an immediate consequence of (2.4) a situation like (1.15) is ruled out. Indeed since f_j and c_j are non decreasing functions (hence $f_j'^-$, $c_k'^- \geq 0$), all terms in (1.15) must be equal to zero. In particular $c_k'^-(\hat{v}_k) = 0$. Since $\hat{v}_k > 0$, by strict convexity $c_k'^-(\hat{v}_k) > c_k'^+(0) \geq 0$, hence a contradiction .

2° As an additional consequence of strict convexity of $c_i(v)$:

(2.5) If one of the $\hat{v}_k$ is strictly positive, then $\hat{y}_N = 0$.

Indeed let $0 \leq k_0 \leq N-1$ be the last index such that $\hat{v}_{k_0} > 0$. Then one has

$$\hat{v}_{k_0+1} = \dots = \hat{v}_{N-1} = 0$$

Therefore if $\hat{y}_N > 0$, necessarily $\hat{y}_{N-1} > 0, \dots, \hat{y}_{k_0+1} > 0$. This is a situation similar to (1.15) which cannot occur.

Proof of Lemma 2.1

I - We start with the proof of (2.2) which is obtained by the following induction.

(i) First we prove that

(2.6) $\hat{v}_0^* \geq \hat{v}_0$

There is nothing to prove when $\hat{v}_0 = 0$. Hence, let us consider $\hat{v}_0 > 0$, in which case by (2.5) we have $\hat{y}_N = 0$. Since

$$(2.7) \quad \begin{cases} x + \hat{v}_0 + \dots + \hat{v}_{N-1} = \xi_1 + \dots + \xi_N \\ x + \hat{v}_0^* + \dots + \hat{v}_{N-1}^* = \hat{y}_N^* + \xi_1^* + \dots + \xi_N^* \end{cases}$$

we get

(2.8) $\hat{v}_0^* + \ldots + \hat{v}_{N-1}^* \geq \hat{v}_0 + \ldots + \hat{v}_{N-1}$

Assume that (2.6) is not true, i.e. $\hat{v}_0^* < \hat{v}_0$. We then show that in this case

(2.9) $\hat{v}_0^* < \hat{v}_0,\ \hat{v}_1^* \leq \hat{v}_1,\ \ldots,\ \hat{v}_{N-1}^* \leq \hat{v}_{N-1}$

which yields a contradiction with (2.8).

Since $\hat{v}_0^* < \hat{v}_0$, we also have $\hat{y}_1^* < \hat{y}_1$ with $\hat{y}_1 > 0$. From condition (1.14) written for $k = 0$, $\ell = 1$, we deduce

(2.10) $f_1'^-(\hat{y}_1) + c_0'^-(\hat{v}_0) - c_1'^+(\hat{v}_1) \leq 0$

Hence using

$$f_1'^+(\hat{y}_1^*) \leq f_1'^-(\hat{y}_1),\quad c_0'^+(\hat{v}_0^*) < c_0'^-(\hat{v}_0)$$

it follows

(2.11) $f_1'^+(\hat{y}_1^*) + c_0'^+(\hat{v}_0^*) < c_1'^+(\hat{v}_1)$

Let us now prove as an intermediate step that

(2.12) $\hat{v}_1^* \leq \hat{v}_1$

There is nothing to prove when $\hat{v}_1^* = 0$. If $\hat{v}_1^* > 0$, then we can deduce from (1.16) that

$$f_1'^+(\hat{y}_1^*) + c_0'^+(\hat{v}_0^*) \geq c_1'^-(\hat{v}_1^*)$$

Combined with (2.11) it implies

$$c_1'^-(\hat{v}_1^*) < c_1'^+(\hat{v}_1)$$

and therefore (2.12) (otherwise $\hat{v}_1^* > \hat{v}^1$ would imply $c_1'^-(\hat{v}_1^*) > c_1'^+(\hat{v}_1)$).

Given $\hat{v}_0^* < \hat{v}_0$ and (2.12) ($\hat{v}_1^* \leq \hat{v}_1$), we have $\hat{y}_2^* < \hat{y}_2$ with $\hat{y}_2 > 0$. But then we have

$$\hat{v}_0 > 0,\ \hat{y}_1 > 0,\ \hat{y}_2 > 0,$$

hence from (1.14) we deduce

$$f_1'^-(\hat{y}_1) + f_2'^-(\hat{y}_2) + c_0'^-(\hat{v}_0) - c_2'^+(\hat{v}_2) \leq 0,$$

and using

$$f_1'^+(\hat{y}_1^*) < f_1'^-(\hat{y}_1),\ f_2'^+(\hat{y}_2^*) < f_2'^-(\hat{y}_2),$$

$$c_0'^+(\hat{v}_0^*) < c_0'^-(\hat{v}_0)$$

we obtain

(2.13) $f_1'^+(\hat{y}_1^*) + f_2'^+(\hat{y}_2^*) + c_0'^+(\hat{v}_0^*) < c_2'^+(\hat{v}_2)$.

We then prove as a next step that

(2.14) $\hat{v}_2^* \leq \hat{v}_2$.

There is nothing to prove when $\hat{v}_2^* = 0$. If $\hat{v}_2^* > 0$, then by applying (1.16) again we obtain :

$$f_1'^+(\hat{y}_1^*) + f_2'^+(\hat{y}_2^*) + c_0'^+(\hat{v}_0^*) \geq c_2'^-(\hat{v}_2^*)$$

In conjunction with (2.13) it implies (2.14).

By induction, it is easily proved that (2.9) holds, hence a contradiction. This completes the proof of (2.6)

(ii) Assume now that

$$(2.15) \qquad \hat{v}_0^* \geq \hat{v}_0, \ \ldots, \ \hat{v}_{k-1}^* \geq \hat{v}_{k-1}, \qquad 1 \leq k \leq N-1.$$

We want to prove that

$$(2.16) \qquad \hat{v}_k^* \geq \hat{v}_k$$

There is nothing to prove if $\hat{v}_k = 0$. We may thus assume that $\hat{v}_k > 0$. Two situations must be considered : either $\hat{y}_k^* > \hat{y}_k$, or $\hat{y}_k^* \leq \hat{y}_k$.

a) Consider first that

$$(2.17) \qquad \hat{y}_k^* > \hat{y}_k$$

Then the following case is ruled out :

$$(2.18) \qquad \hat{v}_0^* = \hat{v}_0, \ \ldots, \ \hat{v}_{k-1}^* = \hat{v}_{k-1}$$

otherwise $\hat{y}_k^* \leq \hat{y}_k$ which would contradict (2.17). Therefore there is an index k_0 such that

$$(2.19) \qquad \hat{v}_{k_0}^* > \hat{v}_{k_0}, \quad 0 \leq k_0 \leq k-1$$

and we may assume that k_0 is the largest index such that a strict inequality holds. Hence

$$(2.20) \qquad \begin{cases} \text{If } k_0 < k-1, \ \hat{v}_{k_0+1}^* = \hat{v}_{k_0+1}, \ \ldots, \ \hat{v}_{k-1}^* = \hat{v}_{k-1}, \\ \hat{y}_{k_0+1}^* > \hat{y}_{k_0+1}, \ \ldots, \ \hat{y}_{k-1}^* > \hat{y}_{k-1}. \end{cases}$$

In particular we have

$$\hat{v}_{k_0}^* > 0, \ \hat{y}_{k_0+1}^* > 0, \ \ldots, \ \hat{y}_k^* > 0$$

hence from (1.14)

$$\sum_{j=k_0+1}^{k} f_j'^-(\hat{y}_j^*) + c_{k_0}'^-(\hat{v}_{k_0}^*) - c_k'^+(\hat{v}_k^*) \leq 0$$

and also

$$(2.21) \qquad \sum_{j=k_0+1}^{k} f_j'^+(\hat{y}_j) + c_{k_0}'^+(\hat{v}_{k_0}) - c_k'^+(\hat{v}_k^*) \leq 0.$$

Since $\hat{v}_k > 0$, it follows from (1.16) that

$$\sum_{j=k_0+1}^{k} f_j'^+(\hat{y}_j) + c_{k_0}'^+(\hat{v}_{k_0}) - c_k'^-(\hat{v}_k) \geq 0$$

in conjunction with (2.21) it implies

$$c_k'^-(\hat{v}_k) \leq c_k'^+(\hat{v}_k^*)$$

hence (2.16).

b) Consider now the alternative case where, instead of (2.17)

$$\hat{y}_k^* \leq \hat{y}_k \tag{2.22}$$

We first note that, since $\hat{v}_k > 0$, according to (2.5) we have $\hat{y}_N = 0$. But then we have

$$\hat{y}_k + \hat{v}_k + \hat{v}_{k+1} + \ldots + \hat{v}_{N-1} = \xi_1 + \ldots + \xi_N$$

$$\hat{y}_k^* + \hat{v}_k^* + \hat{v}_{k+1}^* + \ldots + \hat{v}_{N-1}^* = \hat{y}_N^* + \xi_1^* + \ldots + \xi_N^*$$

hence necessarily

$$\hat{v}_k^* + \hat{v}_{k+1}^* + \ldots + \hat{v}_{N-1}^* \geq \hat{v}_k + \hat{v}_{k+1} + \ldots + \hat{v}_{N-1} \tag{2.23}$$

Assume that (2.16) is not satisfied, then

$$\hat{v}_k^* < \hat{v}_k \tag{2.24}$$

We next prove that

$$\hat{v}_{k+1}^* \leq \hat{v}_{k+1}^*, \ldots, \hat{v}_{N-1}^* \leq \hat{v}_{N-1} \tag{2.25}$$

which together with (2.24) would imply a contradiction with (2.23). Since $\hat{y}_k^* \leq \hat{y}_k$ and $\hat{v}_k^* < \hat{v}_k$, we have $\hat{y}_{k+1}^* < \hat{y}_{k+1}$ with $\hat{y}_{k+1} > 0$. Hence from (1.14)

$$f_{k+1}'^-(\hat{y}_{k+1}) + c_k'^-(\hat{v}_k) - c_{k+1}'^+(\hat{v}_{k+1}) \leq 0$$

and also

$$f_{k+1}'^+(\hat{y}_{k+1}^*) + c_k'^+(\hat{v}_k^*) - c_{k+1}'^+(\hat{v}_{k+1}) \leq 0 \tag{2.26}$$

If $\hat{v}_{k+1}^* > 0$ (otherwise the first inequality (2.25) is proved) then from (1.16) it follows that

$$f_{k+1}'^+(\hat{y}_{k+1}^*) + c_k'^+(\hat{v}_k^*) - c_{k+1}'^-(\hat{v}_{k+1}^*) \geq 0$$

which in connection with (2.26), implies

$$c_{k+1}'^-(\hat{v}_{k+1}^*) \leq c_{k+1}'^+(\hat{v}_{k+1})$$

hence the first inequality of (2.25). By induction, we complete the proof of (2.25). Hence a contradiction and the desired result (2.16).

II - We turn now to the proof of (2.3) by just showing that

(2.27) $\qquad \underline{\hat{v}}_0^* = \hat{v}_0^* \geq \underline{\hat{v}}_0 = \hat{v}_0$

Actually we can exactly follow the proof of (2.7) where the assumption $\xi_j^* \geq \xi_j$ is replaced by $\underline{\xi}_j^* \geq \underline{\xi}_j$.

Let us prove that

(2.28) $\qquad \underline{\hat{v}_0^*} \geq \underline{\hat{v}_0}, \ \ldots, \ \underline{\hat{v}_{N-1}^*} \geq \underline{\hat{v}_{N-1}}$

If it were not the case, because of (2.27) there would exist k_0, $1 \leq k_0 \leq N-1$, such that

(2.29) $\qquad \underline{\hat{v}_{k_0}^*} < \underline{\hat{v}_{k_0}}, \ \underline{\hat{v}_0^*} \geq \underline{\hat{v}_0}, \ \ldots, \ \underline{\hat{v}_{k_0+1}^*} \geq \underline{\hat{v}_{k_0+1}}$

Therefore, the following would also obtain

(2.30) $\qquad \hat{v}_{k_0}^* < \hat{v}_{k_0}, \ \hat{y}_{k_0+1}^* < \hat{y}_{k_0+1}$

From (2.5) since $\hat{v}_{k_0} > 0$, we would have $\hat{y}_N = 0$.

There is already a contradiction if $k_0 = N-1$.

So we may assume $k_0 < N-1$. Therefore we have

$$\hat{y}_{k_0+1} + \hat{v}_{k_0+1} + \ldots + \hat{v}_{N-1} = \xi_1 + \ldots + \xi_N$$

$$\hat{y}_{k_0+1}^* + \hat{v}_{k_0+1}^* + \ldots + \hat{v}_{N-1}^* = \xi_1^* + \ldots + \xi_N^* + \hat{y}_N^*$$

hence

(2.31) $\qquad \hat{v}_{k_0+1}^* + \ldots + \hat{v}_{N-1}^* > \hat{v}_{k_0+1} + \ldots + \hat{v}_{N-1}.$

But we are going to prove that

(2.32) $\qquad \hat{v}_{k_0+1}^* \leq \hat{v}_{k_0+1}, \ \ldots, \ \hat{v}_{N-1}^* \leq \hat{v}_{N-1}$

which just contradicts (2.31).

Indeed from (2.30) and since, in particular, $\hat{v}_{k_0} > 0$, $\hat{y}_{k_0+1} > 0$, it follows that

$$f'^{-}_{k_0+1}(\hat{y}_{k_0+1}) + c'^{-}_{k_0}(\hat{v}_{k_0}) - c'^{+}_{k_0+1}(\hat{v}_{k_0+1}) \leq 0$$

hence

(2.33) $\qquad f'^{+}_{k_0+1}(\hat{y}_{k_0+1}^*) + c'^{+}_{k_0}(\hat{v}_{k_0}^*) - c'^{+}_{k_0+1}(\hat{v}_{k_0+1}) \leq 0.$

To prove the first inequality in (2.32), it is sufficient to assume $\hat{v}_{k_0+1}^* > 0$ (otherwise it is obviously satisfied). Then from (1.16) we deduce

$$f'^{+}_{k_0+1}(\hat{y}_{k_0+1}^*) + c'^{+}_{k_0}(\hat{v}_{k_0}^*) - c'^{-}_{k_0+1}(\hat{v}_{k_0+1}^*) \geq 0$$

which with (2.33) implies

$$c'^{-}_{k_0+1}(\hat{v}_{k_0+1}^*) \leq c'^{+}_{k_0+1}(\hat{v}_{k_0+1})$$

and the first inequality (2.32) is proven. It follows that

$$\underline{\hat{v}^*_{k_0+1}} < \underline{\hat{v}_{k_0+1}}\ \text{, hence } \hat{y}^*_{k_0+2} < \hat{y}_{k_0+2}$$

But then from (1.14) we have

$$f'^{-}_{k_0+1}(\hat{y}_{k_0+1}) + f'^{-}_{k_0+2}(\hat{y}_{k_0+2}) + c'^{-}_{k_0}(\hat{v}_{k_0}) - c'^{+}_{k_0+2}(\hat{v}_{k_0+2}) \le 0$$

hence also

$$f'^{+}_{k_0+1}(\hat{y}^*_{k_0+1}) + f'^{+}_{k_0+2}(\hat{y}^*_{k_0+2}) + c'^{+}_{k_0}(\hat{v}^*_{k_0}) - c'^{+}_{k_0+2}(\hat{v}_{k_0+2}) \le 0$$

Assuming $\hat{v}^*_{k_0+2} > 0$ (otherwise the second inequality (2.32) is trivial) we get

$$f'^{+}_{k_0+1}(\hat{y}^*_{k_0+1}) + f'^{+}_{k_0+2}(\hat{y}^*_{k_0+2}) + c'^{+}_{k_0}(\hat{v}^*_{k_0}) - c'^{-}_{k_0+2}(\hat{v}^*_{k_0+2}) \ge 0$$

hence

$$c'^{-}_{k_0+2}(\hat{v}^*_{k_0+2}) \le c'^{+}_{k_0+2}(\hat{v}_{k_0+2})$$

which proves the second inequality (2.32). By induction we prove the rest of (2.32). This completes the proof of the lemma. □

II - 2. MONOTONICITY PROPERTIES WITH RESPECT TO COST

Consider in this paragraph a modification of the cost $c_{k_0}(v)$ for any k_0, $0 \le k_0 \le N-1$, such that $\forall v > 0$.

$$(2.34)\quad \begin{cases} c_{k_0}(v) \text{ is changed in } \bar{c}_{k_0}(v)\text{, convex, non decreasing} \\ \bar{c}_{k_0}(v) \ge c_{k_0}(v) \\ \bar{c}'^{-}_{k_0}(v) \ge c'^{-}_{k_0}(v) \end{cases}$$

Denote by $\hat{v}^*_k$, $k = 0, \dots, N-1$ the optimal control corresponding to the modified cost structure. We have

Lemma 2.2.

Under condition (2.34) the following property holds

$$(2.35)\quad \begin{cases} \hat{v}^*_{k_0} \le \hat{v}_{k_0} \\ \hat{v}^*_k \ge \hat{v}_k \quad , \quad \forall k \ne k_0 \end{cases}$$

Proof

As in Lemma 2.1, we may assume without loss of generality that all production costs are strictly convex, i.e. that (2.4) holds. If all $\hat{v}_k = 0$, then obviously all $\hat{v}^*_k$ are also zero. Hence (2.35) is trivially satisfied.

Similarly if all $\hat{v}^*_k$ are zero, then the $\hat{v}_k$ must also be equal to zero.

Therefore it is sufficient to consider a situation where both controls $(\hat{v}_0, \ldots, \hat{v}_{N-1})$ and $(\hat{v}_0^*, \ldots, \hat{v}_{N-1}^*)$ are not identically zero. Then it follows from (2.5) that

$$\hat{v}_0 + \ldots + \hat{v}_{N-1} = \hat{v}_0^* + \ldots + \hat{v}_{N-1}^* \tag{2.36}$$

Consider k_0, $1 \le k_0 \le N-1$.

(i) Let us show that

$$\hat{v}_0^* \ge \hat{v}_0 \tag{2.37}$$

Otherwise we have

$$\hat{v}_0 > \hat{v}_0^*, \; \hat{y}_1 > \hat{y}_1^* \tag{2.38}$$

and as a consequence we prove next

$$\hat{v}_1 \ge \hat{v}_1^*, \ldots, \hat{v}_{N-1} \ge \hat{v}_{N-1}^* \tag{2.39}$$

Thus (2.38), (2.39) will contradict (2.36).

By (2.38), since $\hat{v}_0 > 0$, $\hat{y}_1 > 0$ and (1.14) it follows that

$$f_1'^{-}(\hat{y}_1) + c_0'^{-}(\hat{v}_0) - c_1'^{+}(\hat{v}_1) \le 0 \tag{2.40}$$

Assume $\hat{v}_1^* > 0$, otherwise the first inequality (2.39) is trivially satisfied. Then from (1.16) we get

$$f_1'^{+}(\hat{y}_1^*) + c_0'^{+}(\hat{v}_0^*) - c_1'^{-}(\hat{v}_1^*) \ge 0$$

and from (2.38) and (2.40) we deduce

$$c_1'^{-}(\hat{v}_1^*) \le c_1'^{+}(\hat{v}_1)$$

hence $\hat{v}_1^* \le \hat{v}_1$. Assume $\hat{v}_i^* \le \hat{v}_i$, $i = 1, \ldots, k_0-1$, then $\hat{y}_2 > \hat{y}_1^*, \ldots, \hat{y}_{k_0} > \hat{y}_{k_0}^*$ and from (1.14) we have

$$\sum_{j=1}^{k_0} f_j'^{-}(\hat{y}_j) + c_0'^{-}(\hat{v}_0) - c_{k_0}'^{+}(\hat{v}_{k_0}) \le 0$$

hence

$$\sum_{j=1}^{k_0} f_j'^{+}(\hat{y}_j^*) + c_0'^{+}(\hat{v}_0^*) - c_{k_0}'^{+}(\hat{v}_{k_0}) \le 0 \tag{2.41}$$

Assume $\hat{v}_{k_0}^* > 0$ (otherwise $\hat{v}_{k_0}^* \le \hat{v}_{k_0}$ is trivially satisfied), then from (1.16)

$$\sum_{j=1}^{k_0} f_j'^{+}(\hat{y}_j^*) + c_0'^{+}(\hat{v}_0^*) - \bar{c}_{k_0}'^{-}(\hat{v}_{k_0}^*) \ge 0$$

hence

$$\bar{c}_{k_0}'^{-}(\hat{v}_{k_0}^*) \le c_{k_0}'^{+}(\hat{v}_{k_0})$$

and by (2.34)

$$c'^{-}_{k_0}(\hat{v}^*_{k_0}) \le c'^{+}_{k_0}(\hat{v}_{k_0})$$

which implies $\hat{v}^*_{k_0} \le \hat{v}_{k_0}$. By induction we obtain (2.39), which completes the proof of (2.37).

(ii) By an induction similar to the one of lemma 2.1, we further show that

(2.42) $$\hat{v}^*_0 \ge \hat{v}_0, \dots, \hat{v}^*_{k_0-1} \ge \hat{v}_{k_0-1}$$

a) If $\hat{v}^*_{k_0} \ge \hat{v}_{k_0}$, then we can proceed and obtain $\hat{v}^*_k \ge \hat{v}_k$, $\forall k$. From (2.36) it then follows that $\hat{v}^*_k = \hat{v}_k$, $\forall k$ and (2.35) holds.

b) Assume now that

(2.43) $$\hat{v}^*_{k_0} < \hat{v}_{k_0}$$

as a consequence

(2.44) $$\hat{y}^*_{k_0} \ge \hat{y}_{k_0}$$

Then, we are going to prove that

(2.45) $$\hat{v}^*_{k_0+1} \ge \hat{v}_{k_0+1}$$

If it were not true then we would have

(2.46) $$\hat{v}^*_{k_0+1} < \hat{v}_{k_0+1}$$

Assume first that

(2.47) $$\hat{y}^*_{k_0+1} > \hat{y}_{k_0+1}$$

then there exists an index $i_0 < k_0$ such that

(2.48) $$\hat{v}^*_{i_0} > \hat{v}_{i_0}$$

otherwise from (2.42) we would get $\hat{y}^*_{k_0} = \hat{y}_{k_0}$ and from (2.43) $\hat{y}^*_{k_0+1} < \hat{y}_{k_0+1}$, which would contradict (2.47). We can assume that i_0 is the largest such index, hence

(2.49) $$\begin{cases} \hat{v}^*_{i_0} > \hat{v}_{i_0}, \ \hat{v}^*_i = \hat{v}_i, \quad i = i_0+1, \dots, k_0-1 \\ \hat{y}^*_{i_0+1} > \hat{y}_{i_0+1}, \dots, \hat{y}^*_{k_0} > \hat{y}_{k_0} \end{cases}$$

Therefore from (1.14)

$$\sum_{j=i_0+1}^{k_0+1} f'^{-}_j(\hat{y}^*_j) + c'^{-}_{i_0}(\hat{v}^*_{i_0}) - c'^{+}_{k_0+1}(\hat{v}^*_{k_0+1}) \le 0$$

hence also

$$(2.50) \qquad \sum_{j=i_0+1}^{k_0+1} f_j'^{+}(\hat{y}_j) + c_{i_0}'^{+}(\hat{v}_{i_0}) - c_{k_0+1}'^{+}(\hat{v}_{k_0+1}^{*}) \leq 0$$

But assuming (2.46) which implies $\hat{v}_{k_0+1} > 0$, we get also

$$\sum_{j=i_0+1}^{k_0+1} f_j'^{+}(\hat{y}_j) + c_{i_0}'^{+}(\hat{v}_{i_0}) - c_{k_0+1}'^{-}(\hat{v}_{k_0+1}) \geq 0$$

hence $\hat{v}_{k_0+1} \leq \hat{v}_{k_0+1}^{*}$, which contradicts (2.46).

Therefore when (2.46) holds we have

$$(2.51) \qquad \hat{y}_{k_0+1}^{*} \leq \hat{y}_{k_0+1}$$

This and (2.46) imply $\hat{y}_{k_0+2}^{*} < \hat{y}_{k_0+2}$

We note also that

$$(2.52) \qquad \hat{v}_{k_0+1}^{*} + \dots + \hat{v}_{N-1}^{*} \geq \hat{v}_{k_0+1} + \dots + \hat{v}_{N-1}$$

Reasoning as for (2.39) we prove that

$$\hat{v}_{k_0+2} \geq \hat{v}_{k_0+2}^{*}, \; \dots, \; \hat{v}_{N-1} \geq \hat{v}_{N-1}^{*}$$

which with (2.46) yields a contradiction with (2.52). Hence (2.45) is proven.

(iii) In a similar manner we prove that $\hat{v}_k^{*} \geq \hat{v}_k$. $\forall k \geq k_0+1$. □

We now consider the following modification of the holding costs at period k_0, with k_0 between 1 and N-1 : $\forall x > 0$

$$(2.53) \qquad \begin{cases} \bar{f}_{k_0}(x) \geq f_{k_0}(x) \\ \bar{f}_{k_0}'^{-}(x) \geq f_{k_0}'^{-}(x) \end{cases},$$

We denote by $\hat{v}_k^{*}$, k = 0, ..., N-1, the corresponding optimal control. Then we have

<u>Lemma 2.3</u>

Under condition (2.53) the following property holds

$$(2.54) \qquad \begin{cases} \hat{v}_k^{*} \leq \hat{v}_k, & k = 0, \dots, k_0-1 \\ \hat{v}_k^{*} \geq \hat{v}_k, & k = k_0, \dots, N-1 \end{cases}$$

<u>Proof</u>

We assume that production costs are strictly convex.

We can also consider as in Lemma 2.2 that at least one of the components of both controls is strictly positive. Therefore we still have (2.36).

(i) Let us show that

(2.55) $\hat{v}_0^* \leq \hat{v}_0$

Otherwise we would have

(2.56) $\hat{v}_0^* > \hat{v}_0$

and as a consequence we next prove that

(2.57) $\hat{v}_1^* \geq \hat{v}_1, \ldots, \hat{v}_{N-1}^* \geq \hat{v}_{N-1}$

which would contradict (2.36).

As a matter of fact, $\hat{v}_1^* \geq \hat{v}_1$ implies $\hat{y}_1^* > \hat{y}_1$ and we may assume $\hat{v}_1 > 0$, hence

$$f_1'^-(\hat{y}_1^*) + c_0'^-(\hat{v}_0^*) - c_1'^+(\hat{v}_1^*) \leq 0$$

$$f_1'^+(\hat{y}_1) + c_0'^+(\hat{v}_0) - c_1'^+(\hat{v}_1) \leq 0$$

$$f_1'^+(\hat{y}_1) + c_0'^+(\hat{v}_0) - c_1'^-(\hat{v}_1) \geq 0$$

which permits to demonstrate the first inequality of (2.57).

We have implicitly assumed that $k_0 > 1$. We proceed up to $k = k_0-1$, therefore $\hat{y}_1^* > \hat{y}_1, \ldots, \hat{y}_{k_0}^* > \hat{y}_{k_0}$, hence

$$\sum_{j=1}^{k_0-1} f_j'^-(\hat{y}_j^*) + f_{k_0}'^-(\hat{y}_{k_0}^*) + c_0'^-(\hat{v}_0^*) - c_{k_0}'^+(\hat{v}_{k_0}^*) \leq 0$$

and from assumption (2.53) we deduce

$$\sum_{j=1}^{k_0} f_j'^+(\hat{y}_j) + c_0'^+(\hat{v}_0) - c_{k_0}'^+(\hat{v}_{k_0}^*) \leq 0$$

Assuming $\hat{v}_{k_0} > 0$, we deduce an inequality involving $\hat{v}_{k_0}$, from which we obtain $\hat{v}_{k_0} \leq \hat{v}_{k_0}^*$.

We can proceed to obtain (2.57). Hence (2.55). We then have $\hat{y}_1^* \leq \hat{y}_1$.

We analyze separately both cases $\hat{y}_1^* < \hat{y}_1$, and $\hat{y}_1^* = \hat{y}_1$, in a way similar to that of Lemma 2.1.

By induction we prove the first part of (2.54). Assume now that

(2.58) $\hat{v}_{k_0}^* < \hat{v}_{k_0}$

then necessarily $\hat{y}_{k_0+1}^* < \hat{y}_{k_0+1}$, hence

$$f_{k_0+1}'^-(\hat{y}_{k_0+1}) + c_{k_0}'^-(\hat{v}_{k_0}) - c_{k_0+1}'^+(\hat{v}_{k_0+1}) \leq 0$$

$$f_{k_0+1}'^+(\hat{y}_{k_0+1}^*) + c_{k_0}'^+(\hat{v}_{k_0}^*) - c_{k_0+1}'^+(\hat{v}_{k_0+1}) \leq 0$$

and if $\hat{v}^*_{k_0+1} > 0$, we deduce $\hat{v}^*_{k_0+1} \leq \hat{v}_{k_0+1}$.

We can proceed to obtain $\hat{v}^*_{N-1} \leq \hat{v}_{N-1}$.

This implies a contradiction with (2.36). Therefore we have

$$\hat{v}^*_{k_0} \geq \hat{v}_{k_0} \tag{2.59}$$

We then proceed by induction as in the proof of Lemma 2.2, to obtain the second part of (2.54). □

Remark 2.1

As a consequence of the proof of Lemma 2.1, we can assert that if the production costs are strictly convex, then the solution of (1.14), (1.16), (1.17), (2.5) is unique. Indeed the proof of Lemma 2.1 shows in the "strictly convex" case that (2.2) holds with $\hat{v}_i$, $\hat{v}^*_i$ being any solution of (1.14), (1.16), (1.17), (2.5) corresponding to $\xi_1, \ldots, \xi_N$ and $\xi^*_1, \ldots, \xi^*_N$ respectively. Taking in particular $\xi^*_i = \xi_i$ we obtain the desired result. We know of course that in the case of strict convexity, the optimal control is unique. □

II - 3. THE JONHSON'S ALGORITHM

The monotonicity result (2.2) of Lemma 2.1 leads to an efficient algorithm to obtain an optimal control for piecewise linear cost functions. This algorithm was first due to Johnson [1957] (cf. Section VII of this chapter).

More precisely assume that :

(2.59) all costs are piecewise linear and the discontinuity points of the derivatives occur only for integer values of the arguments, and the slopes of production costs are strictly positive.

(2.60) all demands are integer

(2.61) $x = 0$.

We then show that there exists an optimal control which contains only integer values and which can be easily obtained.

Actually we are looking for optimal controls which are integer valued, but these may not correspond to the optimal control in the sense used in Lemma 2.1 (the one with minimum norm).

The monotonicity property is used as follows. Consider an optimal control for $J^N(V)$ with demands $\xi_1, \ldots, \xi_N$, and the same problem with demands $\xi_1, \ldots, \xi_{N-1}, \xi_N + 1$.

Denote by $\hat{v}_0, \ldots, \hat{v}_{N-1}$ the optimal control in the first case and by $\hat{v}^*_0, .., \hat{v}^*_{N-1}$ the optimal control in the second case.

Because of the last part of (2.59) a situation like (1.15) cannot occur, hence we have

$$\hat{v}^*_0 - \hat{v}_0 + \ldots + \hat{v}^*_{N-1} - \hat{v}_{N-1} = 1. \tag{2.62}$$

We claim that the monotonicity result holds, namely

(2.63) $\hat{v}_0^* \geq \hat{v}_0, \ldots, \hat{v}_{N-1}^* \geq \hat{v}_{N-1}.$

Actually we first notice that we cannot have the reverse inequalities with a drop in one of the component of $\hat{v}^*$ larger than 1, say $\hat{v}_0^* \leq \hat{v}_0 - 1$. Indeed strict inequalities hold between marginal costs, and for such a case we can adapt the proof of Lemma 2.1, to get a contradiction. For drops of size less than 1, $\hat{v}_0 - 1 \leq v_0^* < \hat{v}_0$, then the incremental costs are linear. Using (1.14) one can easily check, that a realization of (2.62) involving such drops will be more costly than a realization satisfying (2.63). Since then $0 \leq \hat{v}_i^* - \hat{v}_i \leq 1$, the additional cost between the second case and the first one is thus

$$\sum_{i=0}^{N-1} (v_i^* - v_i) \; [c'^{+}_i(\hat{v}_i) + \sum_{j=i+1}^{N-1} f'^{+}_j(\hat{y}_j)]$$

and it is therefore obvious that it is optimum to choose :

$$\hat{v}_i^* - \hat{v}_i = \begin{cases} 1 \, , & i = i_0 \\ 0 \, , & i \neq i_0 \end{cases}$$

where i_0 is the index which minimizes over $i = 0, \ldots, N-1$ the incremental cost,

(2.64) $$\phi_i(\hat{V}) = c'^{+}_i(\hat{v}_i) + \sum_{j=i+1}^{N-1} f'^{+}_j(\hat{y}_j).$$

In case of ties, take for instance the largest i (the optimal control with minimum norm will be in such a case not integer valued).

Thus the following simple forward algorithm leads to the optimal solution. First solve the one period problem with demand ξ_1. Clearly $\hat{v}_0 = \xi_1$.

Consider next the two period problem with demands ξ_1, 0. The optimal solution is clearly $(\xi_1, 0)$. Then consider the same problem with demand $(\xi_1, 1)$. We deduce the corresponding optimal control as explained above : the first unit of demand in period 2 is produced by the cheapest way, either at time 1 or at time 2 and stored for one period. The same procedure applies to the next unit of demand to serve etc ... Suppose the optimal control for $J^N(V)$, corresponding to $\xi_1, \ldots, \xi_N$, is known. Then consider $J^{N+1}(V)$ with demands $(\xi_1, \ldots, \xi_N, 0)$. The optimal control is just the preceding one, with the addition $\hat{v}_N = 0$. Then consider $J^{N+1}(V)$ with demands $(\xi_1, \ldots, \xi_N, 1)$. Find the index i_0 (production source), which minimizes (2.64) and add one unit to the control $\hat{v}_{i_0}$ computed at the previous stage, to obtain the updated optimal control for $(\xi_1, \ldots, \xi_N, 1)$. And so on.

III - PLANNING HORIZONS

In this section we make the following assumptions.

III - 1. ASSUMPTIONS

(3.1) $x = 0$

(3.2) $f'^{+}_j(0) > 0 \, , \; \forall j$

Although we do no not assume strict convexity, we still have the analogue ot (2.5), namely

$$(3.3) \qquad \hat{y}_N = 0$$

This is clear when $\xi_1 + \ldots + \xi_N = 0$. Let us prove it when $\xi_1 + \ldots + \xi_N > 0$. Indeed there is a k such that $\hat{v}_k > 0$, therefore reasoning as in Lemma 2.1, we obtain a situation like in (1.15). But since $\hat{y}_j > 0$, we have

$$f_j'^-(\hat{y}_j) \geq f_j'^+(0) > 0$$

hence (1.15) is ruled out.

III - 2. REGENERATION POINTS

The same terminology of regeneration points and set-up points as introduced in Chapter I, §IV.1 is used in this section, together with the notation $J_n^N(x;V)$ which reduces to $J^N(V)$ in the present situation where we assume no initial inventory.

We note

$$(3.4) \qquad \lambda^N = \inf_V J^N(V)$$

By virtue of (3.3), we still get the analogue of Lemma 4.1 of Chapter I.

Namely if V_{op}^N (not necessarily $\hat{V}^N$, the optimal control with minimum norm) is an optimal control for $J^N(V)$, and if s is a regeneration point of V_{op}^N $(1 \leq s \leq N)$, then

$$(3.5) \qquad \lambda^s = J^s(V_{op}^N)$$

Considering the definition of planning horizons given in §IV.4 of Chapter I, we still obtain Lemma 4.4 of Chapter I.

Therefore,the problem of finding planning horizons amounts to searching regeneration points, which do not depend on the number of periods of the particular problem.

The data $c_k(v)$ and $f_k(x)$ are of course defined for any k, since the horizon will vary.

III - 3. FORECAST HORIZONS

First,notice that since $c_k'(v)$ is increasing in v, we can define $c_k'^-(\infty)$, which may be $+\infty$. In the following we assume

$$(3.6) \qquad c_k'^-(\infty) \leq B$$

where B is a constant independent of k.

Definition

For any $k \geq 0$, let H(k) be the integer defined as follows

$$(3.7)\quad \begin{cases} \text{If } f'^{+}_{k+1}(0) + c'^{+}_{k}(\xi_{k+1}) > B \text{ then } H(k) = k \text{ ; otherwise } H(k) \text{ is the} \\ \text{largest integer strictly bigger than } k \text{ such that} \\ \sum_{j=k+1}^{H(k)} f'^{+}_{j}(0) + c'^{+}_{k}(\xi_{k+1}) \leq B \qquad (^1) \end{cases}$$

Given : - the time period k,
- the constant B,
- the production plan $\hat{v}_0 = \xi_1, \ldots, \hat{v}_{N-1} = \xi_N$,

H(k) is the time period such that, satisfying demand beyond the time period H(k) from production between time k and time H(k), has a marginal cost greater than B.

Lemma 3.1

For a problem $J^N(V)$ consider an index k (if it exists) such that $H(k) \leq N-1$, and such that k is also a regeneration point of an optimal control for $J^N(V)$. Then, there exists an additional regeneration point between k+1 and H(k)+1

Proof

There is nothing to prove if N = H(k)+1. Assume then N > H(k)+1. If the statement were not true, then we would have

$$\hat{y}_{k+1}, \ldots, \hat{y}_{\ell} > 0 \text{ with } \ell = H(k) + 1.$$

Since $\hat{y}_k = 0$, necessarily $\hat{v}_k > \xi_{k+1}$. Therefore we may apply condition (1.14). Since $\hat{y}_j > 0$, $\hat{v}_k > \xi_{k+1}$ we have

$$f'^{-}_{j}(\hat{y}_j) \geq f'^{+}_{j}(0)$$

$$c'^{-}_{k}(\hat{v}_k) \geq c'^{+}_{k}(\xi_{k+1}),\ c'^{+}_{\ell}(\hat{v}_{\ell}) \leq c'^{-}_{\ell}(\infty)$$

hence

$$\sum_{j=k+1}^{\ell} f'^{+}_{j}(0) + c'^{+}_{k}(\xi_{k+1}) \leq c'^{+}_{\ell}(\hat{v}_{\ell}) \leq B$$

which contradicts the definition of H(k). □

Theorem 3.1

We assume (1.4), (3.2), (3.6). Let H = H(0) in (3.7). Then H+1 is a Forecast Horizon in the sense already defined in Chapter I, §IV.4. That is, ∀K ≥ H+1 there exists s = s(K) with $1 \leq s \leq H+1$ such that an optimal policy for $J^K(V)$ can be obtained by chosing an optimal policy for J^s and completing it adequately on s, ..., K-1 (if K > H+1).

Proof

We may apply Lemma 3.1 for k = 0. Then we know that for any problem $J^K(V)$, with $K \geq H+1$, there will be an optimal control admitting a regeneration point at some s = s(K), with $1 \leq s \leq H+1$. Therefore, there exists an optimal control consisting of an optimal control for $J^s(V)$, completed adequately at times s, ..., K-1. □

(¹) We do not exclude the case H(k) = +∞, but the Lemma is of course void in such a case

Remark 3.1

Notice that if in Theorem 3.1, $s(K) = s$ independent of K then s would be a planning horizon for the forecast horizon H+1 (cf. Chapter I, §IV.4).

The result of Theorem 3.1 is thus weak. However, it is reasonable to keep the terminology of forecast horizon, since the optimal policies up to time H+1 are the only ones relevant even for problems involving a larger number of periods. In particular $\forall K \geq H+1$, the optimal control $\hat{v}_0$ depends only on the demands $\xi_1,\ldots,\xi_{H+1}$ and not on further demands.

III - 4. WEAK PLANNING HORIZONS

We now assume (3.2), and that the marginal costs of production do not increase with time, namely

$$(3.8) \qquad c_k'^{+}(v) \geq c_{k+1}'^{+}(v) \ , \ \forall v$$

Let us denote by $\bar{\xi}_j$ the mean of demands up to j,

$$(3.9) \qquad \bar{\xi}_j = \frac{\xi_1 + \ldots + \xi_j}{j} \qquad j = 1, 2, \ldots$$

We assume that

$$(3.10) \qquad \bar{\xi}_L = \max_{j=1,2,\ldots} \bar{\xi}_j$$

Theorem 3.2

Assume (1.4), (3.2), (3.8), (3.10). Then L is a (weak) planning horizon.

Proof

In order that L be a planning horizon we have to prove that L is a regeneration point for any optimal control of $J^K(V)$, $\forall K \geq L$.

Consider an optimal control for $J^K(V)$, $K > L$, then we first prove that there exists $1 \leq s_0 \leq L$ which is a regeneration point. Otherwise we would have

$$\hat{y}_1 > 0, \ \ldots, \ \hat{y}_L > 0 \ , \qquad \hat{v}_0 > 0$$

and by (1.14)

$$\begin{aligned} c_1'^{+}(\hat{v}_1) &\geq c_0'^{-}(\hat{v}_0) + f_1'^{-}(\hat{y}_1) \\ &\geq c_0'^{-}(\hat{v}_0) + f_1'^{+}(0) \\ &> c_0'^{-}(\hat{v}_0) \qquad \text{by (3.2).} \end{aligned}$$

Using (3.8) we get

$$c_0'^{+}(\hat{v}_1) > c_0'^{-}(\hat{v}_0)$$

hence $\hat{v}_1 \geq \hat{v}_0$. Therefore also $\hat{v}_1 > 0$. By induction we check that we have

$$\hat{v}_0 \leq \hat{v}_1 \leq \ldots \leq \hat{v}_{L-1}$$

But, also since $\hat{y}_L > 0$,

$$\hat{v}_0 + \hat{v}_1 + \ldots + \hat{v}_{L-1} > \xi_1 + \ldots + \xi_L$$

hence

$$L\,\hat{v}_{L-1} > \xi_1 + \ldots + \xi_L$$

which yields

$$\hat{v}_{L-1} > \bar{\xi}_L \tag{3.11}$$

Let r be the first regeneration point ($r \geq 1$) of the optimal control of $J^K(V)$. Suppose that $r > L (r \leq K)$. Reasonning as above we see that

$$\bar{\xi}_L < \hat{v}_{L-1} \leq \hat{v}_L \leq \ldots \leq \hat{v}_{r-1}$$

hence

$$\begin{aligned} \hat{y}_r &= \hat{y}_L + \hat{v}_L + \ldots + \hat{v}_{r-1} - \xi_{L+1} - \ldots - \xi_r \\ &> L\,\bar{\xi}_L + (r - L)\,\bar{\xi}_L - (\xi_1 + \ldots + \xi_r) \\ &= r(\bar{\xi}_L - \bar{\xi}_r) \geq 0 \end{aligned}$$

which contradicts the fact that r is a regeneration point. We can make the same reasoning , with s_0 instead of 0, if $s_0 < L$. We obtain $s_1 \geq s_0+1$, $s_1 \leq L$ which is a regeneration point of an optimal control of $J^K(V)$. Necessarily L is a regeneration point. □

Remark 3.2

Theorem 3.2 is an extension of the basic result of Modigliani and Hohn [1955]. The proof is due to Morton [1978]. The integer L is a planning horizon in the usual sense. However to compute its value, one should know all demands (up to infinity). This feature justifies the terminology of weak planning horizon in contrast with a strong planning horizon which does not necessitate the knowledge of subsequent demands (cf. Chapter I, §IV.4).

III - 5. CASE OF SMOOTH COST FUNCTIONS AND DEMAND

We assume here that

$$f'_j(x),\ c'_k(v) \text{ exist and are continuous} \tag{3.12}$$

$$f'_j(0) > 0 \tag{3.13}$$

$$c'_{k+1}(v) \leq c'_k(v)\ ,\ \forall v \tag{3.14}$$

$$\xi_1, \ldots, \xi_k, \ldots \text{ are strictly positive.} \tag{3.15}$$

We start with a property which does not require the above regularity assumptions.

Lemma 3.2

If (3.2), (3.8) and (3.15) hold,then for $N \geq 1$, an optimal control of $J^N(V)$ is only made of set-up points.

Proof

We thus want to prove that

(3.16) $\quad \hat{v}_0, \ldots, \hat{v}_{N-1} > 0$

For $\hat{v}_0$ the property follows directly from (3.15) :

$$\hat{v}_0 \geq \xi_1 > 0$$

The rest of the proof is based on the fact that

(3.17) $\quad$ if $\hat{v}_\ell = 0$ then $\hat{v}_{\ell-1} = 0$.

Indeed if $\hat{v}_\ell = 0$, then

$$\hat{y}_\ell \geq \xi_{\ell+1} > 0$$

and if $\hat{v}_{\ell-1} > 0$, then by (1.14) we have

$$f_\ell'^-(\hat{y}_\ell) + c_{\ell-1}'^-(\hat{v}_{\ell-1}) - c_\ell'^+(0) \leq 0.$$

By (3.2) it follows

$$c_{\ell-1}'^-(\hat{v}_{\ell-1}) < c_\ell'^+(0)$$

and by (3.8)

$$c_{\ell-1}'^-(\hat{v}_{\ell-1}) < c_{\ell-1}'^+(0)$$

which implies $\hat{v}_{\ell-1} = 0$.

Since $\hat{v}_0 > 0$, we necessarily have (3.16). □

When (3.12), (3.13), (3.14), (3.15) hold we can write the necessary conditions (1.14), (1.15), (1.16) as follows

$$(3.18) \quad \begin{cases} \text{If } \hat{y}_{k+1} > 0, \ldots, \hat{y}_\ell > 0 \text{ for } 0 \leq k < \ell \leq N-1, \text{ then} \\ \displaystyle\sum_{j=k+1}^{\ell} f_j'(\hat{y}_j) + c_k'(\hat{v}_k) - c_\ell'(\hat{v}_\ell) \leq 0 \end{cases}$$

(3.19) $\quad \hat{y}_N = 0$

$$(3.20) \quad \begin{cases} \forall 0 \leq k < \ell \leq N-1, \\ \displaystyle\sum_{j=k+1}^{\ell} f_j'(\hat{y}_j) + c_k'(\hat{v}_k) - c_\ell'(\hat{v}_\ell) \geq 0. \end{cases}$$

In connection with (3.20), (3.18) is rewritten as follows :

$$(3.21) \quad \begin{cases} \text{If } \hat{y}_{k+1} > 0, \ldots, \hat{y}_\ell > 0 \text{ for } 0 \leq k < \ell \leq N-1, \text{ then} \\ \displaystyle\sum_{j=k+1}^{\ell} f_j'(\hat{y}_j) + c_k'(\hat{v}_k) - c_\ell'(\hat{v}_\ell) = 0 \end{cases}$$

This condition (3.21) reads like a classical first order condition in micro-economics : at the optimum it is indifferent to shift production from source k to ℓ, or vice versa.

Define for $k = 1, \ldots, N-1$

(3.22) $\mu_k = c'_{k-1}(\hat{v}_{k-1}) - c'_k(\hat{v}_k) + f'_k(\hat{y}_k)$

then by (3.20) with $k = k-1$, $\ell = k$, we see that

(3.23) $\mu_k \geq 0$

Applying (3.21) with $k = k-1$, $\ell = k$ we see that if $\hat{y}_k > 0$, then $\mu_k = 0$, hence

(3.24) $\mu_k \hat{y}_k = 0$

Therefore the set of necessary conditions for optimality of problem $J^N(V)$ reduces to

$$(3.25) \quad \begin{cases} \mu_k = c'_{k-1}(\hat{v}_{k-1}) - c'_k(\hat{v}_k) + f'_k(\hat{y}_k), \quad k = 1, \ldots, N-1 \\ \mu_k \geq 0, \ \mu_k \hat{y}_k = 0, \ \hat{y}_k \geq 0 \\ \hat{y}_0 = \hat{y}_N = 0 \\ \hat{y}_{k+1} = \hat{y}_k + \hat{v}_k - \xi_{k+1}, \ k = 0, \ldots, N-1 \end{cases}$$

Lemma 3.3

The system of relations (3.25) with unknowns $\hat{y}_1, \ldots, \hat{y}_{N-1}, \hat{v}_0, \ldots, \hat{v}_{N-1}$ constitutes a set of sufficient optimality conditions for $J^N(V)$.

Proof

Let us consider any solution of (3.25). We first check that

(3.26) $\hat{v}_0 > 0, \ldots, \hat{v}_{N-1} > 0$

For $\hat{v}_0$ it follows from the last relation. In fact

$$\hat{v}_0 \geq \xi_1$$

If $\hat{v}_0 > \xi_1$ then $\hat{y}_1 > 0$ and $\mu_1 = 0$. Hence

$$c'_0(\hat{v}_0) + f'_1(\hat{y}_1) = c'_1(\hat{v}_1)$$

Therefore

$$c'_1(\hat{v}_1) > c'_0(\hat{v}_0) \geq 0.$$

hence $\hat{v}_1 > 0$.

If $\hat{v}_0 = \xi_1$ then $\hat{y}_1 = 0$ and $\hat{v}_1 \geq \xi_2 > 0$.

If $\hat{y}_2 > 0$ then $\mu_2 = 0$ and

$$c'_2(\hat{v}_2) = c'_1(\hat{v}_1) + f'_2(\hat{y}_2) > 0$$

hence $\hat{v}_2 > 0$. If $\hat{y}_2 = 0$ then $\hat{v}_2 \geq \xi_3 > 0$.

By induction we obtain (3.26). Therefore the quantities $\hat{v}_0, \ldots, \hat{v}_{N-1}, \hat{y}_1, \ldots, \hat{y}_{N-1}$ are admissible. Take now any values $v_0, \ldots, v_{N-1}, y_1, \ldots, y_N$ which are non negative and satisfy

$$y_{k+1} = y_k + v_k - \xi_{k+1}, \quad y_0 = 0.$$

Convexity (with obvious notation) implies :

$$(3.27)\quad \begin{cases} J^N(V) - J^N(\hat{V}) = \sum_{j=1}^{N-1} [f_j(y_j) - f_j(\hat{y}_j)] + \sum_{j=0}^{N-1} [c_j(v_j) - c_j(\hat{v}_j)] \\ \geq \sum_{j=1}^{N-1} f_j'(\hat{y}_j)(y_j - \hat{y}_j) + \sum_{j=0}^{N-1} c_j'(\hat{v}_j)(v_j - \hat{v}_j) \\ = \sum_{j=0}^{N-2} [c_j'(\hat{v}_j) + \sum_{h=j+1}^{N-1} f_h'(\hat{y}_h)](v_j - \hat{v}_j) \\ + c_{N-1}'(\hat{v}_{N-1})(v_{N-1} - \hat{v}_{N-1}). \end{cases}$$

Now from (3.25) we have

$$\sum_{k=j+1}^{N-1} \mu_k = \sum_{k=j+1}^{N-1} f_k'(\hat{y}_k) + c_j'(\hat{v}_j) - c_{N-1}'(\hat{v}_{N-1})$$

hence from (3.27)

$$\begin{aligned} J^N(V) - J^N(\hat{V}) &\geq c_{N-1}'(\hat{v}_{N-1}) \sum_{j=0}^{N-1} (v_j - \hat{v}_j) \\ &+ \sum_{j=0}^{N-2} (v_j - \hat{v}_j) \sum_{h=j+1}^{N-1} \mu_h \\ &\geq \sum_{j=1}^{N-1} \mu_j (y_j - \hat{y}_j) \geq 0. \end{aligned}$$

given the fact that $\sum_{j=0}^{N-1} (v_j - \hat{v}_j) = y_N - \hat{y}_N = y_N \geq 0.$ □

Remark 3.3

Assumptions (3.12), (3.13), (3.15) were used in the proof of Lemma 3.3, but not assumption (3.14). This last hypothesis was important in the proof of Lemma 3.2 to show that (3.25) are a set of necessary conditions and thus have a solution. □

Theorem 3.3

Assume (1.4), (3.12), (3.13), (3.15) and

$$(3.28)\qquad c_{k-1}'(\xi_k) - c_k'(\xi_{k+1}) + f_k'(0) \geq 0, \; k = 1, \ldots, N-1$$

then $\hat{v}_0 = \xi_1, \ldots, \hat{v}_{N-1} = \xi_N$ is an optimal control for $J^N(V)$

Note

Given the production plan $\hat{v}_0 = \xi_1, \ldots, \hat{v}_{N-1} = \xi_N$ condition (3.28) says it is not economical to shift production, at the margin, from time k to k-1.

Proof

Under the above assumptions, we can assert (see Remark 3.3) that (3.25) form a set of sufficient conditions for optimality. It is thus enough to check that

$$\hat{v}_0 = \xi_1, \ldots, \hat{v}_{N-1} = \xi_N$$

$$\hat{y}_1 = \ldots = \hat{y}_{N-1} = 0$$

satisfy these relations. This is clearly a consequence of (3.28). □

Let us show now how we can use the relations (3.25) to obtain a planning horizon theorem. Consider the problem $J^K(V)$ with $K \geq N+1$. We write the corresponding set of relations (3.25) as follows (splitting them in three parts) :

$$(3.29) \quad \begin{cases} \mu_k = c'_{k-1}(\hat{v}_{k-1}) - c'_k(\hat{v}_k) + f'_k(\hat{y}_k) \\ \mu_k \geq 0,\ \mu_k\, \hat{y}_k = 0,\ \hat{y}_k \geq 0,\ k = 1, \ldots, N-1 \\ \hat{y}_0 = 0,\ \hat{y}_{k+1} = \hat{y}_k + \hat{v}_k - \xi_{k+1},\ k = 0, \ldots, N-1 \end{cases}$$

$$(3.30) \quad \begin{cases} \mu_N = c'_{N-1}(\hat{v}_{N-1}) - c'_N(\hat{v}_N) + f'_N(\hat{y}_N) \\ \mu_N \geq 0,\ \mu_N\, \hat{y}_N = 0,\ \hat{y}_N \geq 0 \end{cases}$$

$$(3.31) \quad \begin{cases} \mu_k = c'_{k-1}(\hat{v}_{k-1}) - c'_k(\hat{v}_k) + f'_k(\hat{y}_k) \\ \mu_k \geq 0,\ \mu_k\, \hat{y}_k = 0,\ \hat{y}_k \geq 0,\ k = N+1, \ldots, K-1 \\ \hat{y}_k = 0,\ \hat{y}_{k+1} = \hat{y}_k + \hat{v}_k - \xi_{k+1},\ k = N, \ldots, K-1. \end{cases}$$

In (3.29) the unknowns are $\hat{v}_0, \ldots, \hat{v}_{N-1}, \hat{y}_1, \ldots, \hat{y}_N, \mu_1, \ldots, \mu_{N-1}$, and in (3.31) the unknowns are $\hat{v}_N, \ldots, \hat{v}_{K-1}, \hat{y}_N, \ldots, \hat{y}_{K-1}, \mu_{N+1}, \ldots, \mu_{K-1}$. Note that there are 3N-1 unknowns in (3.29) for only 3N-2 relations. There are also 3(K-N)-2 relations in (3.31) for 3(K-N)-1 unknowns. Actually we may consider that $\hat{y}_N$, the only common variable to both subsystems (3.29) and (3.31), is a parameter.

All other variables are then defined in terms of $\hat{y}_N$. In particular we get $\hat{v}_{N-1}$ from (3.29) and $\hat{v}_N$ from (3.31). Then (3.30) is a set of two relations for the unknowns $\hat{y}_N$ and μ_N. In particular, this permits to obtain the right value of $\hat{y}_N$.

These considerations are of course informal but help to understand how the necessary and sufficient conditions are solved.

If we want N to be a planning horizon, this means that we impose the additional condition $\hat{y}_N = 0$. This is acceptable provided the compatibility condition (3.30) is satisfied, namely :

$$(3.32) \qquad c'_{N-1}(\hat{v}_{N-1}) - c'_N(\hat{v}_N) + f'_N(0) \geq 0$$

In (3.32) K enters only through $\hat{v}_N$. Therefore (3.32) should be satisfied independently of $\hat{v}_N$.

A sufficient condition is :

(3.33) $c'_{N-1}(\hat{v}_{N-1}) + f'_N(0) \geq c'_N(\infty)$.

To weaken slightly (3.33) we can try to obtain some information on $\hat{v}_N$ which does not depend on K.

We already know that $\hat{v}_N \geq \xi_{N+1}$, but this does not help. However, we can find a situation where $\hat{v}_N = \xi_{N+1}$, whatever is K. We can use (3.7) and lemma 3.1 to assert that if

(3.34) $f'_{N+1}(0) + c'_N(\xi_{N+1}) > c'_{N+1}(\infty)$

then $\hat{v}_N = \xi_{N+1}$. Therefore we can replace (3.33) by the conditions

(3.35) $$\begin{cases} c'_{N-1}(\hat{v}_{N-1}) + f'_N(0) \geq c'_N(\xi_{N+1}) \\ f'_{N+1}(0) + c'_N(\xi_{N+1}) > c'_{N+1}(\infty) \end{cases}$$

Theorem 3.4

Assume (1.4), (3.12), (3.13), (3.14), (3.15). Let N be an integer such that either (3.33) or (3.35) hold, with $\hat{v}_{N-1}$ being the last value of an optimal control for $J^N(V)$. Then N is a strong planning horizon.

Proof

We prove that (3.29), (3.30), (3.31) has a solution such that N is a regeneration point, whatever is K. When we impose $\hat{y}_N = 0$, then we can solve (3.29) and (3.31) independently, since a solution of (3.29) is an optimal control of $J^N(V)$, and a solution of (3.31) is an optimal control of $J_N^K(V)$. It remains to check the compatibility conditions (3.30). From the above discussion, we can assert that (3.33) or (3.35) imply $\mu_N \geq 0$, whatever is the value of $\hat{v}_N$. Hence the result. □

IV - MODEL WITH BACKLOGGING

IV - 1. ASSUMPTIONS

The control problem is the same as in § 1.1, namely

(4.1) $$\begin{cases} y_{i+1} = y_i + v_i - \xi_{i+1} \\ y_0 = x \end{cases}$$

(4.2) $v_i \geq 0$

(4.3) $$J_0(x;V) = \sum_{i=0}^{N-1} [c_i(v_i) + f_i(y_i)]$$

where

(4.4) $c_i(v) : R^+ \to R^+$ is non decreasing and convex, and not a constant

(4.5) $f_i(x) : R \to R^+$ is convex and achieves its minimum at 0

For reasons similar to those of Theorem 1.1, there exists an optimal control (not necessarily unique).

We can select the control with minimum norm, as explained in Theorem 1.2.

IV - 2. NECESSARY CONDITIONS

We now state the analogue of Theorem 1.3, but we omit the proof.

Theorem 4.1

Assume (4.4), (4.5). An optimal pair $(\hat{v}_0, \ldots, \hat{v}_{N-1}), (\hat{y}_0, \hat{y}_1, \ldots, \hat{y}_N)$ for problem $J_0(x;V)$ satisfies the following conditions :

(4.6)
$$\begin{cases} \text{Let } 0 \le k < \ell <\text{-}N \; ; \\ \underline{\text{if } \hat{v}_k > 0 \text{ then}} \\ \displaystyle\sum_{j=k+1}^{\ell} f_j'^{-}(\hat{y}_j) + c_k'^{-}(\hat{v}_k) \le c_\ell'^{+}(\hat{v}_\ell) \\ \underline{\text{if } \hat{v}_\ell > 0 \text{ then}} \\ \displaystyle\sum_{j=k+1}^{\ell} f_j'^{+}(\hat{y}_j) + c_k'^{+}(\hat{v}_k) \ge c_\ell'^{-}(\hat{v}_\ell) \end{cases}$$

(4.7)
$$\begin{cases} \underline{\text{if } \hat{v}_k > 0,\ 0 \le k \le N-2, \text{ then}} \\ \displaystyle\sum_{j=k+1}^{N-1} f_j'^{-}(\hat{y}_j) + c_k'^{-}(\hat{v}_k) \le 0, \\ \underline{\forall k \ge 0,\ k \le N-2} \\ \displaystyle\sum_{j=k+1}^{N-1} f_j'^{+}(\hat{y}_j) + c_k'^{+}(\hat{v}_k) \ge 0 \\ \hat{v}_{N-1}\, c_{N-1}'^{-}(\hat{v}_{N-1}) = 0 \end{cases}$$

In the case of continuous derivatives then we have

Theorem 4.2

Assume (4.4), (4.5) and $c_i(v)$, $f_i(x)$ continuously differentiable. Then for $(\hat{v}_0, \ldots, \hat{v}_{N-1}),(\hat{y}_0, \hat{y}_1, \ldots, \hat{y}_N)$ to be an optimal solution, it is necessary and sufficient that the following conditions hold :

(4.8)
$$\begin{cases} c_k'(\hat{v}_k) + \displaystyle\sum_{j=k+1}^{N-1} f_j'(\hat{y}_j) \ge 0 \\ \hat{v}_k \ge 0 , \qquad \hat{v}_k \,[c_k'(\hat{v}_k) + \displaystyle\sum_{j=k+1}^{N-1} f_j'(\hat{y}_j)] = 0, \\ \qquad \text{for } k = 0, \ldots, N-2 \end{cases}$$

(4.9)
$$c_{N-1}'(\hat{v}_{N-1})\, \hat{v}_{N-1} = 0, \quad \hat{v}_{N-1} \ge 0.$$

Proof

Similar to that of Lemma 3.3 Details are omitted. □

IV - 3. FORECAST HORIZON

Planning horizon results in the backlogging case are much more difficult to obtain than in the no backlogging case. This is due to the fact that the final state $\hat{y}_N$ is not in general 0. We already noticed this fact in Chapter I, section VIII.

Definition (Recall from Chapter I, §IV.4)

N is said to be a forecast horizon if $\forall K \geq N \geq 1$ there exists $s = s(K)$ with $s(K) \leq N$ such that an optimal policy for $J^K(V)$ can be obtained by chosing an optimal control for J^s and completing it adequately on s, ..., K-1 (cf. Remark 3.1).

First several Lemmas present interesting optimal control properties.

We assume

(4.10) $x = 0$ [1]

(4.11) $f_j'^+(0) > 0, \; f_j'^-(0) < 0$

(4.12) $c_j'^+(0) > 0, \; c_j'^+(0) + f_{j+1}'^-(0) \leq 0$

Lemma 4.1

Under the assumptions of Theorem 4.1 and (4.10), (4.11), (4.12), we have

(4.13) $\hat{v}_{N-1} = 0$

(4.14) $\hat{y}_N \leq 0$

Proof

From the last conditions (4.7) we deduce $\hat{v}_{N-1} = 0$. Now assume $\hat{y}_N > 0$, there exists an index k_0 such that $\hat{v}_{k_0} > 0$. Suppose that k_0 is the last one, hence

$$\hat{v}_{k_0} > 0, \; \hat{v}_{k_0+1} = \ldots = \hat{v}_{N-1} = 0.$$

Since $\hat{y}_N > 0$ then $\hat{y}_{k_0+1} > 0, \ldots, \hat{y}_{N-1} > 0$, hence

$$\sum_{j=k_0+1}^{N-1} f_j'^-(\hat{y}_j) + c_{k_0}'^-(\hat{v}_{k_0}) > 0$$

which contradicts the first condition (4.7). □

---

[1] This assumption is always made and will not be further repeated in the statement of Lemmas and Theorems

we next assume that

(4.15) $c_k'^-(\infty) \leq B$

For any k define H(k) by

(4.16) $H(k) = k$ if $f_{k+1}'^+(0) + c_k'^+(\xi_{k+1}) > B$,

otherwise H(k) is the largest integer strictly bigger than k such that

$$\sum_{j=k+1}^{H(k)} f_j'^+(0) + c_k'^+(\xi_{k+1}) \leq B$$

Similarly define L(ℓ), by

(4.17) $L(\ell) = \ell$ if $c_\ell'^+(\xi_\ell) - f_\ell'^-(0) > B$

otherwise L(ℓ) is the smallest integer, strictly less than ℓ such that

$$- \sum_{j=L(\ell)+1}^{\ell} f_j'^-(0) + c_\ell'^+(\xi_\ell) \leq B$$

Lemma 4.2

Under the assumptions of Lemma 4.1, and (4.15), consider k and N such that $H(k)+1 \leq N$, and assume that $\hat{y}_k \leq 0$ on the optimal trajectory of $J^N(V)$. Then, there exists an additional point k^* between k+1 and H(k)+1 such that $\hat{y}_{k^*} \leq 0$. Similarly consider ℓ and N, with $0 \leq \ell \leq N-1$. Assume that $\hat{y}_{\ell+1} \geq 0$, then there exists an index ℓ^* with $L(\ell) \leq \ell^* \leq \ell$ such that $\hat{y}_{\ell^*} \geq 0$.

Proof

Similar to that of Lemma 3.1 with the use of Theorem 4.1.

(i) If $N = H(k)+1$, since by (4.14) $\hat{y}_N \leq 0$ there is nothing to prove. Assume now $N > H(k)+1$. If the statement is not satisfied then we have

$$\hat{y}_{k+1} > 0, \ldots, \hat{y}_\ell > 0 \text{ with } \ell = H(k)+1.$$

But since $\hat{y}_k \leq 0$, we have $\hat{v}_k > 0$. Therefore from (4.6)

$$\sum_{j=k+1}^{\ell} f_j'^-(\hat{y}_j) + c_k'^-(\hat{v}_k) \leq c_\ell'^+(\hat{v}_\ell) \leq B$$

and since $\hat{y}_j > 0$, $\hat{v}_k > \xi_{k+1}$

$$\sum_{j=k+1}^{\ell} f_j'^+(0) + c_k'^+(\xi_{k+1}) \leq B$$

which contradicts the definition of H(k).

(ii) Next consider the second part of the statement. There is nothing to prove if $L(\ell) = 0$. Suppose $L(\ell) \geq 1$; if the statement is not true then we have

$$\hat{y}_h < 0, \ldots, \hat{y}_\ell < 0$$

where $h = L(\ell)$. Since $\hat{y}_{\ell+1} \geq 0$, we have $\hat{v}_\ell > 0$, and in fact $\hat{v}_\ell > \xi_\ell$. From (4.6) we deduce

$$c'^{+}_{h-1}(\hat{v}_{h-1}) + \sum_{j=h}^{\ell} f'^{+}_j(\hat{y}_j) \geq c'^{-}_\ell(\hat{v}_\ell) \geq c'^{+}_\ell(\xi_\ell)$$

and since $\hat{y}_j < 0$, $f'^{+}_j(\hat{y}_j) \leq f'^{-}_j(0)$

hence

$$B \geq c'^{+}_\ell(\xi_\ell) - \sum_{j=h}^{\ell} f'^{-}_j(0)$$

which contradicts the definition of $L(\ell)$. □

We next prove the analogue of Theorem 3.2. To avoid confusion in notation we write

(4.18) $$\bar{\xi}_{L^*} = \max_{j=1,2,\ldots} \bar{\xi}_j$$

(4.19) $$\bar{\xi}_{L^{**}} = \min_{j=1,2,\ldots} \bar{\xi}_j$$

Assuming of course that these quantities exist (i.e., the max and the min are achieved).

<u>Lemma 4.3</u>

Assume (4.4), (4.5), (4.11), (4.12), (4.18) and (3.8). Then we have for any problem $J^K(V)$ with $K \geq L^*$

(4.20) $$\hat{y}_{L^*} \leq 0$$

Assume (4.4), (4.5), (4.11), (4.19), (4.12) and

(4.21) $$c'^{+}_k(v) \leq c'^{+}_{k+1}(v), \quad \forall v > 0$$

then $\forall K > L^{**}$, if $\hat{y}_{L^{**}} < 0$, we have

(4.22) $$\hat{y}_k < 0, \quad \forall L^{**} \leq k \leq K$$

<u>Proof</u>

(i) Let us prove (4.20). Following the proof of Theorem 3.2, one first checks that there exists $1 \leq s_0 \leq L^*$ such that $\hat{y}_{s_0} \leq 0$. Otherwise we have

$$\hat{y}_1 > 0, \ldots, \hat{y}_{L^*} > 0, \hat{v}_0 > 0$$

and second, by the first part of (4.11) and (3.8), and using (4.6) we get

$$\hat{v}_0 \leq \hat{v}_1 \leq \ldots \leq \hat{v}_{L^*-1}$$

and

$$\hat{v}_{L^*-1} > \bar{\xi}_{L^*}$$

There is a point $r > L^*$ and $r \leq K$ such that $\hat{y}_r \leq 0$ (we choose r to be the first such index).

We have

$$\bar{\xi}_{L*} < \hat{v}_{L*-1} \leq \hat{v}_{L*} \leq \ldots \leq \hat{v}_{r-1}$$

hence $\hat{y}_r > 0$, which contradicts the definition of r.

(ii) Now let us prove (4.22). There is nothing to prove if $L^{**} = K-1$. Assume $L^{**} \leq K-2$, we first show that

(4.23) $\hat{v}_{L**} > 0$

Indeed if $\hat{y}_k < 0$, $\forall k > L^{**}$ (which is actually what we want to prove) then from the last condition (4.7) we obtain

$$c'^{+}_{L**}(\hat{v}_{L**}) \geq - \sum_{j=L**+1}^{K-1} f'^{+}_{j}(\hat{y}_j)$$

$$\geq - \sum_{j=L**+1}^{K-1} f'^{-}_{j}(0) > - f'^{-}_{L**+1}(0)$$

and by (4.12) we deduce (4.23). If all $\hat{y}_k$ with $k > L^{**}$ are not strictly negative, there must be an index h with $L^{**} \leq h < K-1$ such that $\hat{v}_h > 0$. We denote h the first one. Assume $h > L^{**}$. Since $\hat{y}_h < 0$ and $\hat{v}_h > 0$, we deduce from the second condition (4.6) that

$$c'^{+}_{h-1}(\hat{v}_{h-1}) \geq c'^{-}_{h}(\hat{v}_h) - f'^{+}_{h}(\hat{y}_h)$$

$$> c'^{-}_{h}(\hat{v}_h)$$

and by (4.21)

$$c'^{+}_{h}(\hat{v}_{h-1}) > c'^{-}_{h}(\hat{v}_h)$$

which implies $\hat{v}_h \leq \hat{v}_{h-1}$.

Therefore $\hat{v}_{h-1} > 0$, which contradicts the definition of h. Hence (4.23)[1]

Let now k_0 be the last index $0 \leq k_0 < L^{**}$ such that $\hat{y}_{k_0} \geq 0$. Then we have

$$\hat{y}_{k_0+1} < 0, \ \ldots, \ \hat{y}_{L**} < 0$$

hence reasoning as above

----

(1) This is clearly a <u>general property of the optimal policy</u> :
If $\hat{y}_k < 0$ then $\hat{v}_k > 0$, $k = 1, \ldots, N-2$.

(4.24) $\hat{v}_{k_0} \geq \hat{v}_{k_0+1} \geq \hat{v}_{k_0+2} \geq \ldots \geq \hat{v}_{L^{**}-1} \geq \hat{v}_{L^{**}} > 0$

Moreover, since $\hat{y}_{k_0} \geq 0$ we have

(4.25) $\hat{v}_0 + \ldots + \hat{v}_{k_0-1} \geq \xi_1 + \ldots + \xi_{k_0} \geq k_0 \bar{\xi}_{L^{**}}$

Since $\hat{y}_{L^{**}} < 0$, we deduce

$$\hat{v}_0 + \ldots + \hat{v}_{k_0-1} + \hat{v}_{k_0} + \ldots + \hat{v}_{L^{**}-1} - \xi_1 \ldots - \xi_{L^{**}} < 0$$

Hence from (4.24), (4.25) it follows

$$(L^{**} - k_0)\hat{v}_{L^{**}-1} < L^{**}\bar{\xi}_{L^{**}} - k_0 \bar{\xi}_{L^{**}}$$

hence

(4.26) $\hat{v}_{L^{**}-1} < \bar{\xi}_{L^{**}}$

Therefore also

(4.27) $\hat{v}_{L^{**}} < \bar{\xi}_{L^{**}}$

But

$$\begin{aligned} \hat{y}_{L^{**}+1} &= \hat{v}_0 + \ldots + \hat{v}_{L^{**}-1} + \hat{v}_{L^{**}} - (\xi_1 + \ldots + \xi_{L^{**}+1}) \\ &< L^{**} \bar{\xi}_{L^{**}} + \bar{\xi}_{L^{**}} - (L^{**}+1) \bar{\xi}_{L^{**}+1} \\ &\leq 0 \end{aligned}$$

by definition of L^{**}. Hence $\hat{y}_{L^{**}+1} < 0$. Therefore, as above

$$\hat{v}_{L^{**}} \geq \hat{v}_{L^{**}+1}$$

hence $\hat{v}_{L^{**}+1} < \bar{\xi}_{L^{**}}$. Reasoning as above we obtain $\hat{y}_{L^{**}+2}$. By induction we see that

$$\bar{\xi}_{L^{**}} > \hat{v}_{L^{**}-1} \geq \hat{v}_{L^{**}} \geq \ldots \geq \hat{v}_{K-2} > \hat{v}_{K-1} = 0$$

$$\hat{y}_{L^{**}} < 0, \ldots, \hat{y}_K < 0$$

which is (4.22), which thus completes the proof. □

Lemma 4.4

Assume (4.4), (4.5) and (4.11). Then an optimal control satisfies the properties

(4.25) if (4.21) holds then $\hat{v}_{k+1} > \hat{v}_k$ implies $\hat{y}_{k+1} \geq 0$

(4.26) if (3.8) holds then $\hat{v}_{k+1} < \hat{v}_k$ implies $\hat{y}_{k+1} \leq 0$

(4.27) if (3.8) holds then $\hat{y}_{k+1} > 0$ implies $\hat{v}_{k+1} \geq \hat{v}_k$, $k \leq N-2$

(4.28) if (4.21) holds then $\hat{y}_{k+1} < 0$ implies $\hat{v}_{k+1} \leq \hat{v}_k$, $k \leq N-2$

Proof

Let us simply prove the last statement (4.28) to illustrate the idea of the proof. Assume $\hat{y}_{k+1} < 0$ and $\hat{v}_{k+1} > \hat{v}_k$, then from the second condition (4.6) we can write

$$c'^{-}_{k+1}(\hat{v}_{k+1}) \leq c'^{+}_{k}(\hat{v}_k) + f'^{+}_{k+1}(\hat{y}_{k+1})$$

$$\leq c'^{+}_{k}(\hat{v}_k) + f'^{-}_{k+1}(0)$$

$$< c'^{+}_{k}(\hat{v}_k)$$

and by (4.21) :

$$c'^{-}_{k+1}(\hat{v}_{k+1}) < c'^{+}_{k+1}(\hat{v}_k)$$

from which it follows that $\hat{v}_{k+1} \leq \hat{v}_k$. □

Lemma 4.5

Assume (4.4), (4.5), (4.11), (4.12), (4.15), (4.21). For any $k \geq 0$ define $J(k)$ by

(4.29) $J(k) = k$ if $c'^{+}_{k+1}(0) - f'^{-}_{k+1}(0) > c'^{-}_{k}(\infty)$,

otherwise $J(k)$ is the largest integer strictly bigger than k such that

$$c'^{+}_{J(k)}(0) - \sum_{j=k+1}^{J(k)} f'^{-}_{j}(0) \leq c'^{-}_{k}(\infty).$$

Consider k and N such that $k \leq N-3$ and $J(k)+1 \leq N-2$, and assume that $\hat{y}_k \geq 0$ on the optimal trajectory of $J^N(V)$. Then there exists an additional point k^* between $k+1$ and $J(k)+1$ such that $\hat{y}_{k^*} \geq 0$.

Proof

Note first that because of (4.21), the function

$$c'^{+}_{\ell}(0) - \sum_{j=k+1}^{\ell} f'^{-}_{j}(0), \qquad \ell \geq k+1$$

is increasing in ℓ. Therefore $J(k)$ is well defined.

Set $\ell = J(k)+1$. If the satement is not true, then we have

$$\hat{y}_{k+1} < 0, \ \ldots, \ \hat{y}_{\ell} < 0$$

and since $\ell \leq N-2$, we know from in the proof of Lemma 4.3, that (by virtue of (4.21)), $\hat{v}_{k+1} \geq \ldots \geq \hat{v}_{\ell} > 0$. Therefore by applying the second condition (4.6) we get

$$c'^{-}_{\ell}(\hat{v}_{\ell}) \le c'^{+}_{k}(\hat{v}_{k}) + \sum_{j=k+1}^{\ell} f'^{+}_{j}(\hat{y}_{j})$$

$$\le c'^{-}_{k}(\infty) + \sum_{j=k+1}^{\ell} f'^{-}_{j}(0)$$

hence

$$c'^{+}_{\ell}(0) - \sum_{j=k+1}^{\ell} f'^{-}_{j}(0) \le c'^{-}_{k}(\infty)$$

which contradicts the definition of $\ell = J(k)+1$. □

We will now state the main forecast horizon result. However, the following preliminary property concerning functions $J(k)$ and $H(k)$ is needed.

Lemma 4.6

Under the assumptions of Lemma 4.5, $J(k)$ is an increasing function of k. Under the assumptions of Lemma 4.1, and (4.15), (3.8) as well as (4.30)

(4.30) ξ_k decreases with k

then $H(k)$ is an increasing function of k.

Proof

By definition of $J(k)$ (cf. (4.29)) we have

$$c'^{+}_{J(k)+1}(0) - \sum_{j=k+1}^{J(k)+1} f'^{-}_{j}(0) > c'^{-}_{k}(\infty)$$

but then also

$$c'^{+}_{J(k)+1}(0) - \sum_{j=k}^{J(k)+1} f'^{-}_{j}(0) > c'^{-}_{k}(\infty) \ge c'^{-}_{k-1}(\infty)$$

(by (4.21)). Therefore necessarily $J(k)+1 > J(k-1)$, hence $J(k) \ge J(k-1)$.

Similarly, go back to (4.16). Since we assumed (3.8) then $B = c'^{-}_{0}(\infty)$, and we can assert by definition of $H(k)$ that :

$$\sum_{j=k+1}^{H(k)+1} f'^{+}_{j}(0) + c'^{+}_{k}(\xi_{k+1}) > B$$

hence

$$\sum_{j=k}^{H(k)+1} f'^{+}_{j}(0) + c'^{+}_{k-1}(\xi_{k}) > B$$

where we have used (4.30) and (3.8). Therefore $H(k)+1 > H(k-1)$, hence $H(k) \ge H(k-1)$. □

Theorem 4.3.

Assume (4.4), (4.5), (4.11), (4.12), (4.15), (4.21). Set $H = H(0)$ and define

(4.31) $N = J(H) + 3.$

Assume that

(4.32) $\xi_1 \leq \xi_2 \leq \ldots \leq \xi_N$

then N is a forecast horizon.

Set next $J = J(0)$ and define

(4.33) $\tilde{N} = H(J) + 3.$

Assume that instead of (4.21)

(4.34) $c_k'^{+}(v) = c_{k+1}'^{+}(v), \quad \forall v, \forall k$

and that

(4.35) $\xi_1 \geq \xi_2 \geq \ldots \geq \xi_{\tilde{N}}$

then $\tilde{N}$ is a forecast horizon.

Proof

Let $K \geq N$ and consider an optimal control for $J^K(V)$. We will prove that there exists a regeneration point s with $1 \leq s \leq N$. From Lemma 4.2, we know that there exists τ with $1 \leq \tau \leq H+1$, such that $\hat{y}_\tau \leq 0$. We can assume that τ is the first such point. Therefore we have

(4.36) $\hat{y}_1 > 0, \ldots \hat{y}_{\tau-1} > 0, \hat{y}_\tau \leq 0.$

From Lemma 4.5 we know that there exists a point σ with $\tau \leq \sigma \leq J(\tau-1)+1$, such that

(4.37) $\hat{y}_\sigma \geq 0.$

Since J is increasing and $\tau-1 \leq H$, we have

(4.38) $\tau \leq \sigma \leq J(H)+1 \leq N-2$

Let us show that $\hat{y}_\tau = 0$, otherwise we would get a contradiction. Indeed assume $\hat{y}_\tau < 0$. Then by (4.28) we have

$$\hat{y}_{\tau+1} = \hat{y}_\tau + \hat{v}_\tau - \xi_{\tau+1}$$

$$\leq \hat{y}_{\tau-1} + \hat{v}_{\tau-1} - \xi_\tau \leq \hat{y}_\tau$$

where we have used (4.32). Hence we see that $\hat{y}_{\tau+1} < 0$. We can proceed and show that

$$\hat{y}_\tau < 0, \ldots, \hat{y}_K < 0.$$

But this contradicts the existence of σ such that (4.37) holds.

Consider now the situation (4.35). We know that there exists $1 \leq \tau \leq J+1$, such that $\hat{y}_\tau \geq 0$. We can take τ to be the first such point, hence we have

(4.39) $\hat{y}_1 < 0, \ldots, \hat{y}_{\tau-1} < 0, \hat{y}_\tau \geq 0.$

By Lemma 4.2, we know that there exists σ with $\tau \leq \sigma \leq H(\tau-1)+1$, such that

(4.40) $\hat{y}_\sigma \leq 0.$

From (4.34) and (4.35) we can apply the result of Lemma 4.6, hence $H(\tau-1) \le H(J)$, therefore

$$(4.41) \qquad \tau \le \sigma \le H(J)+1 \le \tilde{N}-2$$

Let us show that $\hat{y}_\tau = 0$, otherwise we would get a contradiction. Indeed assume $\hat{y}_\tau > 0$, then by (4.27) we have

$$\hat{y}_{\tau+1} = \hat{y}_\tau + \hat{v}_\tau - \xi_{\tau+1}$$

$$\ge \hat{y}_{\tau-1} + \hat{v}_{\tau-1} - \xi_\tau = \hat{y}_\tau > 0$$

and we can proceed like this, up to $\tilde{N}$-2. Therefore we obtain a contradiction with (4.40). □

Remark 4.1

The proof of Theorem 4.3 shows that the regeneration point will be located before H or J respectively, which is better of course that N or $\tilde{N}$ requested in the definition of the forecast horizon. However we need to know the demands up to N,$\tilde{N}$. Also the result is valid only for $K \ge N$ or $\tilde{N}$. □

Remark 4.2

Assume all costs independent of time. Then, it is easy to check that

$$J(k) = k + J_0$$

where $J_0 \ge 0$ is the largest integer such that

$$J_0 \le \frac{c'^-(\infty) - c'^+(0)}{-f'^-(0)}$$

Going back to the definition (4.17) of $L(\ell)$, we know it is the smallest integer with $L(\ell) \le \ell$ such that

$$\ell - L(\ell) \le \frac{c'^-(\infty) - c'^+(\xi_\ell)}{-f'^-(0)} \le J_0$$

Therefore in Lemma 4.2 we can say that if $\hat{y}_\ell \ge 0$, $\ell \ge 1$, then there exists ℓ^* with $\ell - 1 - J_0 \le \ell^* \le \ell-1$, such that $\hat{y}_{\ell*} \ge 0$.

In other words in blocks of length J_0 we must find non negative inventories.

A similar consideration holds for non positive inventories, with a length of blocks given by

$$H_0 = \frac{c'^-(\infty) - c'^+(0)}{f'^+(0)} . \qquad □$$

V - PRODUCTION SMOOTHING

V - 1. ORIENTATION

The model analyzed so far only includes direct production and inventory cost elements. In practice additional smoothing costs must be explicitly considered.

Changing the production rate between two consecutive periods generates adjustment costs, mostly:hiring and training expenses, set-up charges for additional equipment when production is increased , firing costs and overheads for equipments used below normal capacity when production is decreased. Therefore, there is a natural tendancy to smooth production in order to reach an economic balance between adjustment, production and inventory costs : this is known as the production smoothing problem. For a detailed discussion of employment smoothing costs consult McGarrah [1956], Orr [1962] or Silver [1967].

As an introductory step before presenting our general model, we reconsider the formulation due to Kunreuther and Morton [1973-1] in the framework of optimal control theory (see also section VII).

V - 2. A PRODUCTION SMOOTHING MODEL WITH LINEAR AND STATIONARY COSTS

As in Kunreuther and Morton [1973-1] we consider the cost structure :

h : inventory cost for one unit per period,
c : unit production cost

and the V-shaped smoothing cost function in period j

$$g\cdot(v_j - v_{j-1}) \text{ if } v_j > v_{j-1}$$

$$f\cdot(v_{j-1} - v_j) \text{ if } v_j < v_{j-1}$$

In addition we impose the restrictive conditions :

$$y_0 = y_N = 0$$

$$v_N = 0$$

If, as suggested by Beckmann [1961] (cf. Chapter IV) we pose

$$d = (g + f)/2 \qquad e = (g - f)/2$$

and rewrite the smoothing costs as

$$s(v_j, v_{j-1}) = d\,|v_j - v_{j-1}| + e(v_j - v_{j-1})$$

we obtain the following formulation :

$$\text{(5.1)} \quad \begin{cases} y_{k+1} = y_k + v_k - \xi_{k+1} , & k = 0, \ldots, N-1 \\ y_0 = y_N = 0 \end{cases}$$

$$\text{(5.2)} \quad v_k \geq 0,\ v_N = 0,\ y_k \geq 0$$

where the cost function to be minimized is

$$\text{(5.3)} \quad J(V) = \sum_{j=1}^{N-1} \frac{\alpha}{2}\,|v_j - v_{j-1}| + \sum_{j=1}^{N-1} y_j + \frac{\alpha}{2} v_{N-1} \qquad \text{with } \alpha = 2d/h.$$

Clearly there exists an optimal control. We analyze in the sequel the properties of an optimal production plan.

The following result will be useful in the derivations . The positive solution of the equation :

(5.4) $$x^2 + x - 2\alpha = 0$$

is the number

$$x^* = \frac{-1 + \sqrt{1 + 8\alpha}}{2}$$

and we shall use the integer

(5.5) $$n^* = \begin{cases} x^* & \text{if } x^* \text{ is an integer} \\ [x^*]+1 & \text{if } x^* \text{ is not an integer} \end{cases}$$

where $[x^*]$ denotes the integer part of x^*.

Lemma 5.1

Let $1 \leq k \leq \ell \leq N-1$ with

(5.6) $$\ell - k < n^*$$

Then if $\hat{v}_{k-1} > \hat{v}_k \geq \hat{v}_{k+1} \geq \ldots \geq \hat{v}_{\ell-1}$, necessarily we have :

(5.7) $$\hat{v}_{\ell-1} \geq \hat{v}_\ell$$

Proof

Assume that

$$\hat{v}_{k-1} > \hat{v}_k \geq \hat{v}_{k+1} \geq \ldots \geq \hat{v}_{\ell-1}$$

and

$$\hat{v}_{\ell-1} < \hat{v}_\ell$$

Then transform the control $\hat{V}$ as follows : change $\hat{v}_k$ into $\hat{v}_k + \theta$, $\hat{v}_{k+1}$ into $\hat{v}_{k+1} + \theta$, ..., $\hat{v}_{\ell-1}$ into $\hat{v}_{\ell-1} + \theta$, and $\hat{v}_\ell$ into $\hat{v}_\ell - (\ell-k)\theta$.

The new inventory positions thus become

$$\hat{y}_{k+1} + \theta, \ \hat{y}_{k+2} + 2\theta, \ \ldots, \ \hat{y}_\ell + (\ell-k)\theta$$

and the other values of the control and the state stay unchanged. Call $\tilde{V}$ the new control. It is admissible if θ is sufficiently small. Then we have

$$J(\tilde{V}) - J(\hat{V}) = \theta \sum_{j=1}^{\ell-k} j - \theta \frac{\alpha}{2} - (\ell-k+1)\frac{\alpha}{2}\theta \pm (\ell-k)\frac{\alpha}{2}\theta.$$

The last term is with a plus sign if $\hat{v}_{\ell+1} - \hat{v}_\ell \geq 0$ and with a minus sign if $\hat{v}_{\ell+1} - \hat{v}_\ell < 0$.

But in both cases using (5.6) we have :

$$J(\tilde{V}) - J(\hat{V}) \leq \theta \left[\frac{(\ell-k)(\ell-k+1)}{2} - \alpha\right]$$
$$< 0$$

This contradicts the optimality of $\hat{V}$, which completes the proof of Lemma 5.1. □

As a consequence, we can claim that if $\hat{v}_{k-1} > \hat{v}_k$ then we have $\hat{v}_k \geq \hat{v}_{k+1} \geq \ldots \geq \hat{v}_{k+n^*-1}$ □

Remark 5.1

Clearly the lemma is void if $\alpha \leq 1$.

Lemma 5.2

Let $0 \leq k \leq \ell \leq N-1$ and

(5.8) $\qquad \ell - k < n^*$

Then if

$$\hat{v}_{k+1} \geq \hat{v}_{k+2} \geq \ldots \geq \hat{v}_\ell > \hat{v}_{\ell+1} \quad (\text{where } \hat{v}_{\ell+1} = 0 \text{ if } \ell = N-1)$$

necessarily we have

(5.9) $\qquad \hat{v}_k \geq \hat{v}_{k+1}$

Proof

Assume $\hat{v}_{k+1} > \hat{v}_k$, and make the following transformations :

$$\hat{v}_k \to \hat{v}_k + (\ell-k)\theta$$

$$\hat{v}_{k+1} \to \hat{v}_{k+1} - \theta$$

$$\vdots$$

$$\hat{v}_\ell \to \hat{v}_\ell - \theta$$

then we get

$$J(\tilde{V}) - J(\hat{V}) = \theta \frac{(\ell-k)(\ell-k+1)}{2} \pm (\ell-k)\frac{\alpha}{2}\theta - \theta\frac{\alpha}{2}(\ell-k+1) - \frac{\theta\alpha}{2}$$

$$\leq \theta \left[\frac{(\ell-k)(\ell-k+1)}{2} - \alpha\right] < 0$$

which is a contradiction. □

Lemma 5.3

If $\hat{v}_k > \hat{v}_{k+1}$ then $\hat{y}_{k+1} = 0$, $k \leq N-2$.

Proof

Assume $\hat{y}_{k+1} > 0$. Then we consider the following transformation :

$$\hat{v}_k \to \hat{v}_k - \theta \quad , \quad \hat{v}_{k+1} \to \hat{v}_{k+1} + \theta$$

We get

$$J(\tilde{V}) - J(\hat{V}) = -\theta \pm \frac{\alpha}{2}\theta - \alpha\theta \pm \frac{\alpha\theta}{2}$$

$$\leq -\theta$$

which contradicts the optimality of $\hat{V}$. □

Lemma 5.4.

There exists an optimal control with $\hat{y}_N = 0$.

Proof

Consider an optimal control with $\hat{y}_N > 0$. If $\hat{v}_{N-1} > 0$, then consider the transformation $\hat{v}_{N-1} \to \hat{v}_{N-1} - \theta$ where θ is assumed to be small. We obtain

$$J(\tilde{V}) - J(\hat{V}) = -\frac{\alpha}{2}\theta \pm \alpha\frac{\theta}{2} \leq 0,$$

hence $\tilde{V}$ is also optimal. If $\hat{v}_{N-1} = 0$, then there exists a last integer k_0 such that $\hat{v}_{k_0} > 0$, $k_0 \leq N-2$. Since $\hat{v}_{k_0} > 0$, $\hat{v}_{k_0+1} = 0, \ldots, \hat{v}_{N-1} = 0$, $\hat{y}_N > 0$ we have

$$\hat{y}_{k_0+1} > 0, \ldots, \hat{y}_{N-1} > 0$$

which contradicts Lemma 5.3. □

Lemma 5.5

Let $0 \leq k \leq N-1$. Then there exists ℓ with $k+1 \leq \ell \leq (k + 2n^*) \wedge N$ such that $\hat{y}_\ell = 0$ $\hat{y}_\ell = 0$ ([1]) (at least for some optimal control).

Proof

Let us assume first that $\hat{y}_k = 0$.

If $k + 2n^* \geq N$, there is nothing to prove.

Assume then that $k + 2n^* < N$, together with the following situation :

$$\hat{y}_k = 0, \hat{y}_{k+1} > 0, \ldots, \hat{y}_{k+2n^*} > 0.$$

From Lemma 5.3, we may assert that :

$$\hat{v}_k \leq \hat{v}_{k+1} \leq \ldots \leq \hat{v}_{k+2n^*}$$

and since $\hat{y}_k = 0$, $\hat{y}_{k+1} > 0$, necessarily $\hat{v}_k > 0$.

We may then consider the following transformation of the optimal control :

$$\begin{array}{llll} \hat{v}_k & \to \hat{v}_k - \theta & \hat{v}_{k+n^*+1} & \to \hat{v}_{k+n^*+1} + \theta \\ \hat{v}_{k+1} & \to \hat{v}_{k+1} - \theta & \hat{v}_{k+n^*+2} & \to \hat{v}_{k+n^*+2} + \theta \\ \vdots & & \vdots & \\ \hat{v}_{k+n^*-1} & \to \hat{v}_{k+n^*-1} - \theta & \hat{v}_{k+2n^*} & \to \hat{v}_{k+2n^*} + \theta \\ \hat{v}_{k+n^*} & \to \hat{v}_{k+n^*} & & \end{array}$$

([1]) We note $a \wedge b = \mathrm{Min}\,(a,b)$

The inventory positions thus becomes :

$$\begin{array}{llll} \hat{y}_{k+1} & \to \hat{y}_{k+1} - \theta & \hat{y}_{k+n^*+2} & \to \hat{y}_{k+n^*+2} - (n^*-1)\theta \\ \vdots & & \vdots & \\ \hat{y}_{k+n^*} & \to \hat{y}_{k+n^*} - n^*\theta & \hat{y}_{k+2n^*} & \to \hat{y}_{k+2n^*} - \theta \\ \hat{y}_{k+n^*+1} & \to \hat{y}_{k+n^*+1} - n^*\theta & \hat{y}_{k+2n^*+1} & \to \hat{y}_{k+2n^*+1} \end{array}$$

It then follows :

$$J(\tilde{V}) - J(\hat{V}) = - \theta n^*(n^*+1) \pm \alpha \frac{\theta}{2} + \frac{\alpha}{2}\theta + \frac{\alpha}{2}\theta \pm \frac{\alpha}{2}\theta ,$$

$$\leq 0$$

when the strict inequality holds $\hat{V}$ cannot be optimal. If it is exactly zero, necessarily

$$\hat{v}_k - \hat{v}_{k-1} \leq 0, \; \hat{v}_{k+2n^*+1} - \hat{v}_{k+2n^*} \leq 0.$$

Hence $\hat{v}_k \leq \hat{v}_{k-1}$ and $\hat{v}_k \leq \hat{v}_{k+1} \leq \dots \leq \hat{v}_{k+2n^*}$. But since $\hat{y}_k = 0$, we have $\hat{y}_{k+1} \leq \hat{v}_k$. Hence it is sufficient to choose $\theta \leq \underset{j=k+1,\dots,k+2n^*}{\text{Min}} \hat{y}_j$, to get an admissible θ. Therefore we may select θ such that for $\tilde{V}$, one of the components ℓ of the inventory vanishes with $k+1 \leq \ell \leq k+2n^*$, which proves the desired result.

Since the initial inventory is 0, at most every $2n^*$ periods we must go through a period with zero inventory. Hence the general case. □

Let us introduce the number :

$$(5.10) \qquad E_N = \underset{t=1,\dots,\text{Min}(n^*,N)}{\text{Min}} \frac{\sum_{j=1}^{t} \xi_{N-j+1}}{t}$$

then we have :

<u>Lemma 5.6</u>

There exists an optimal control such that

$$(5.11) \qquad \hat{v}_{N-1} \leq E_N$$

<u>Proof</u>

We already assumed $\hat{y}_N = 0$. If $\hat{v}_{N-1} = 0$, then (5.11) is clearly satisfied. Assume $\hat{v}_{N-1} > 0$, then by Lemma 5.2, we have

$$\hat{v}_{N-1} \leq \hat{v}_{N-2} \leq \dots \leq \hat{v}_{N-\bar{t}} \qquad \text{where } \bar{t} = \text{Min}(n^*,N).$$

Since $\hat{y}_N = 0$, we have :

$$\hat{v}_{N-1} \le \xi_N$$

$$2\hat{v}_{N-1} \le \hat{v}_{N-1} + \hat{v}_{N-2} \le \xi_N + \xi_{N-1}$$

$$\cdots\cdots$$

$$t\,\hat{v}_{N-1} \le \hat{v}_{N-1} + \ldots + \hat{v}_{N-t} \le \xi_N + \ldots + \xi_{N-t+1}$$

for $t \le \bar{t}$, hence the desired result. □

Next let us define for $k \le N$:

$$(5.12)\qquad \begin{cases} D_k^N = 0 \text{ if } k = N \\ \quad = \max\limits_{1\le t\le 2n^*\wedge(N-k)} \dfrac{\sum\limits_{j=1}^{t} \xi_{k+j}}{t} \text{ if } k<N \end{cases}$$

then we have :

Lemma 5.7

Assume $k \le N-1$. Then

$$(5.13)\qquad \hat{v}_k \le D_k^N$$

Proof

From Lemma 5.5, there exists ℓ such that :

$$k+1 \le \ell \le (k+2n^*) \wedge N = k + 2n^* \wedge (N-k)$$

and $\hat{y}_\ell = 0$. We can always assume ℓ to be the smallest such integer. Therefore we have :

$$\hat{y}_{k+1} > 0, \ldots, \hat{y}_{\ell-1} > 0$$

hence

$$\hat{v}_k + \ldots + \hat{v}_{\ell-1} \le \xi_{k+1} + \ldots + \xi_\ell$$

But from Lemma 5.3, we deduce :

$$\hat{v}_k \le \hat{v}_{k+1} \le \ldots \le \hat{v}_{\ell-1}$$

Therefore also

$$\hat{v}_k \le \frac{\xi_{k+1} + \ldots + \xi_\ell}{\ell - k} \le D_k^N . \qquad \square$$

For $1 \le k \le N$, we denote by

$$(5.14)\qquad \begin{cases} \hat{v}_j^k,\ 0 \le j \le k-1, \text{ an optimal control of problem } J^k(V), \text{ i.e., problem} \\ (5.3) \text{ with } N = k. \end{cases}$$

The following key result is now produced :

Lemma 5.8

If $\hat{v}^k_{k-1} > D^N_k$, then

(5.15) $$\hat{v}^k_{k-1} > \hat{v}_k$$

and there exists an optimal control which contains $\hat{v}^k_j$ for $j = 0, \ldots, k-1$.

Proof

If $k = N$, there is nothing to prove since $D^N_k = 0$, $\hat{v}_N = 0$ by convention and the second part of the statement is trivial. We thus assume $1 \leq k < N$. By Lemma 5.7, we have $\hat{v}_k \leq D^N_k$.

Therefore the inequality (5.15) follows immediately from the assumption. Let us prove the second part of the statement. We consider two cases: $\hat{y}_k = 0$ and $\hat{y}_k > 0$.

(i) Assume first that

(5.16) $$\hat{y}_k = 0$$

Then we show that if the optimal control does not satisfy the statement, we can modify it in order to fulfill the requirements.

Consider the functional which is derived from (5.3).

(5.17) $$L^k(V \; ; w) = \sum_{j=1}^{k-1} \frac{\alpha}{2} |v_j - v_{j-1}| + \sum_{j=1}^{k-1} y_j + \frac{\alpha}{2} |w - v_{k-1}|$$

where w is a parameter. Clearly :

(5.18) $$J^k(V) = L^k(V \; ; 0)$$

We note that, by virtue of (5.16), we can write

(5.19) $$J^N(\hat{V}) = L^k(\hat{V} \; ; \hat{v}_k) + J^N_k(\hat{V})$$

Moreover :

(5.20) $\hat{V}$ minimizes $L^k(V \; ; \hat{v}_k)$ among all controls such that $y_k = 0$.

But the control $\hat{V}^k = (\hat{v}^k_0, \ldots, \hat{v}^k_{k-1})$ is admissible for (5.20). Therefore we can write :

(5.21) $$\begin{cases} \displaystyle\sum_{j=1}^{k-1} \frac{\alpha}{2} |\hat{v}_j - \hat{v}_{j-1}| + \frac{\alpha}{2} |\hat{v}_k - \hat{v}_{k-1}| + \sum_{j=1}^{k-1} \hat{y}_j \\ \displaystyle\leq \sum_{j=1}^{k-1} \frac{\alpha}{2} |\hat{v}^k_j - \hat{v}^k_{j-1}| + \frac{\alpha}{2} |\hat{v}_k - \hat{v}^k_{k-1}| + \sum_{j=1}^{k-1} \hat{y}^k_j \end{cases}$$

and by the inequality (5.15) already proved

$$\leq \sum_{j=1}^{k-1} \frac{\alpha}{2} |\hat{v}^k_j - \hat{v}^k_{j-1}| + \frac{\alpha}{2} \hat{v}^k_{k-1} - \frac{\alpha}{2} \hat{v}_k + \sum_{j=1}^{k-1} \hat{y}^k_j$$

Noting that

$$\hat{v}_k + |\hat{v}_k - \hat{v}_{k-1}| \geq \hat{v}_{k-1}$$

we deduce

$$\sum_{j=1}^{k-1} \frac{\alpha}{2} |\hat{v}_j - \hat{v}_{j-1}| + \frac{\alpha}{2} \hat{v}_{k-1} + \sum_{j=1}^{k-1} \hat{y}_j$$
$$\leq \sum_{j=1}^{k-1} \frac{\alpha}{2} |\hat{v}_j^k - \hat{v}_{j-1}^k| + \frac{\alpha}{2} v_{k-1}^k + \sum_{j=1}^{k-1} \hat{y}_j^k.$$

i.e.

$$J^k(\hat{V}) \leq J^k(\hat{V}^k)$$

and by the optimality of $\hat{V}^k$,

$$J^k(\hat{V}) = J^k(\hat{V}^k) \tag{5.22}$$

Taking this into account we can write:

$$\left\{\begin{aligned} J^N(\hat{V}) = &\sum_{j=1}^{k-1} \frac{\alpha}{2} |\hat{v}_j^k - \hat{v}_{j-1}^k| + \sum_{j=1}^{k-1} \hat{y}_j^k + \frac{\alpha}{2} (\hat{v}_{k-1}^k - \hat{v}_{k-1}) \\ &+ \frac{\alpha}{2} |\hat{v}_k - \hat{v}_{k-1}| + J_k^N(\hat{V}) \end{aligned}\right. \tag{5.23}$$

But

$$\hat{v}_k - \hat{v}_{k-1} \leq 0 \tag{5.24}$$

which follows easily from (5.21) and (5.22). Therefore we can write $J^N(\hat{V})$ as

$$J^N(\hat{V}) = L^k(\hat{V}^k \ ; \hat{v}_k) + J_k^N(\hat{V}).$$

Hence we can modify the control by taking the first k-1 components to be those of $\hat{V}^k$, and completing it by the components of $\hat{V}$. The control which is obtained in this manner is still optimal and satisfies the requirement.

(ii) We now assume instead of (5.16) that :

$$\hat{y}_k > 0. \tag{5.25}$$

From Lemma 5.3 we have $\hat{v}_{k-1} \leq \hat{v}_k$, hence by (5.15) :

$$\hat{v}_{k-1} < \hat{v}_{k-1}^k \tag{5.26}$$

By Lemma 5.5 there exists $k+1 \leq \ell \leq (k+2n^*) \wedge N$, such that $\hat{y}_\ell = 0$.

Moreover from the hypothesis $\hat{v}_{k-1}^k > D_k^N$ we obtain :

$$\hat{v}_{k-1}^k > \sum_{j=k+1}^{i} \frac{\xi_j}{i-k}, \ \forall k+1 \leq i \leq (k+2n^*) \wedge N$$

Let then $k+1 \leq \ell^* \leq \ell$ be the smallest index such that

$$\hat{y}_{\ell^*} \leq (\ell^*-k)\ \hat{v}_{k-1}^k - \sum_{j=k+1}^{\ell^*} \xi_j. \tag{5.27}$$

We define a new control as follows :

$$\tilde{v}_j = \hat{v}_j^k \qquad \text{for} \qquad 0 \le j \le k-1$$

$$\tilde{v}_j = \hat{v}_{k-1}^k \qquad \text{for} \qquad k \le j \le \ell^*-2$$

$$\tilde{v}_{\ell^*-1} = \hat{y}_{\ell^*} + \sum_{j=k+1}^{\ell^*} \xi_j - (\ell^*-1-k)\, \hat{v}_{k-1}^k$$

$$\tilde{v}_j = \hat{v}_j \qquad \text{for} \qquad j \ge \ell^*$$

Of course if $\ell^* = N$, we omit the components larger than N.

We note that $\tilde{v}_{\ell^*-1}$ satisfies (when $\ell^* \ge k+2$) :

$$\tilde{v}_{\ell^*-1} = \hat{y}_{\ell^*-1} + \hat{v}_{\ell^*-1} + \sum_{j=k+1}^{\ell^*-1} \xi_j - (\ell^*-1-k)\, \hat{v}_{k-1}^k$$

$$> \hat{v}_{\ell^*-1} \ge 0.$$

We get the following sequence of inventories :

$$\tilde{y}_j = \hat{y}_j^k \qquad \text{for} \qquad 0 \le j \le k$$

$$\tilde{y}_j = (j-k)\, \hat{v}_{k-1}^k - (\xi_{k+1} + \dots + \xi_j), \quad \text{for } k+1 \le j \le \ell^*-1$$

$$\tilde{y}_j = \hat{y}_j \qquad \text{for} \qquad \ell^* \le j \le N$$

Hence $\tilde{V}$ is admissible. Let us compute (assuming $\ell^* \ge k+2$)

$$(5.28) \quad \begin{cases} J(\tilde{V}) - J(\hat{V}) = \displaystyle\sum_{j=1}^{k-1} \frac{\alpha}{2} |\hat{v}_j^k - \hat{v}_{j-1}^k| + \frac{\alpha}{2} |\tilde{v}_{\ell^*-1} - \hat{v}_{k-1}^k| \\ \qquad + \displaystyle\frac{\alpha}{2} |\hat{v}_{\ell^*} - \tilde{v}_{\ell^*-1}| + \sum_{j=1}^{k-1} \hat{y}_j^k + \sum_{j=k+1}^{\ell^*-1} \tilde{y}_j - \sum_{j=1}^{k-1} \hat{y}_j \\ \qquad - \hat{y}_k - \displaystyle\sum_{j=k+1}^{\ell^*-1} \hat{y}_j - \sum_{j=1}^{k-1} \frac{\alpha}{2} |\hat{v}_j - \hat{v}_{j-1}| - \sum_{j=k}^{\ell^*} |\hat{v}_j - \hat{v}_{j-1}|. \end{cases}$$

We first notice that by definition of $\hat{V}^k$:

$$(5.29) \quad \begin{cases} \displaystyle\sum_{j=1}^{k-1} \frac{\alpha}{2} |\hat{v}_j^k - \hat{v}_{j-1}^k| + \sum_{j=1}^{k-1} \hat{y}_j^k \\ \le \displaystyle\sum_{j=1}^{k-1} \frac{\alpha}{2} |\hat{v}_j - \hat{v}_{j-1}| + \sum_{j=1}^{k-1} \hat{y}_j + \frac{\alpha}{2} (\hat{v}_{k-1} - \hat{v}_{k-1}^k) \end{cases}$$

and by definition of ℓ^*

$$(5.30) \qquad \tilde{y}_j \le \hat{y}_j \quad \text{for } j = k+1, \dots, \ell^*-1$$

Since

$$\hat{y}_k > 0, \dots, \hat{y}_{\ell^*-1} > 0$$

from Lemma 5.3 we have

(5.31) $\hat{v}_{k-1} \le \hat{v}_k \le \dots \le \hat{v}_{\ell^*-1} \le \tilde{v}_{\ell^*-1}$

Moreover

(5.32) $$\begin{cases} \tilde{v}_{\ell^*-1} - \hat{v}^k_{k-1} = \hat{y}_{\ell^*} + \sum_{j=k+1}^{\ell^*} \xi_j - (\ell^*-k)\,\hat{v}^k_{k-1} \\ \le 0 \end{cases}$$

Therefore we see that :

$$J(\tilde{V}) - J(\hat{V}) \le \frac{\alpha}{2}(\hat{v}_{k-1} - \hat{v}^k_{k-1}) + \frac{\alpha}{2}(\hat{v}^k_{k-1} - \tilde{v}_{\ell^*-1})$$

$$+ \frac{\alpha}{2}|\hat{v}_{\ell^*} - \tilde{v}_{\ell^*-1}| - \frac{\alpha}{2}|\hat{v}_{\ell^*} - \hat{v}_{\ell^*-1}| - \frac{\alpha}{2}(\hat{v}_{\ell^*-1} - \hat{v}_{k-1}) - \hat{y}_k$$

$$\le \alpha\,\hat{v}_{k-1} - \frac{\alpha}{2}\tilde{v}_{\ell^*-1} - \frac{\alpha}{2}\hat{v}_{\ell^*-1} + \frac{\alpha}{2}|\hat{v}_{\ell^*} - \tilde{v}_{\ell^*-1}|$$

$$- \frac{\alpha}{2}|\hat{v}_{\ell^*} - \hat{v}_{\ell^*-1}| - \hat{y}_k = X - \hat{y}_k.$$

<u>If $\hat{v}_{\ell^*} \le \hat{v}_{\ell^*-1}$,</u> then

$$X = \alpha\hat{v}_{k-1} - \alpha\hat{v}_{\ell^*-1} \le 0.$$

<u>If $\hat{v}_{\ell^*-1} < \hat{v}_{\ell^*}$</u> , then

$$X = \alpha\,\hat{v}_{k-1} - \frac{\alpha}{2}\tilde{v}_{\ell^*-1} - \frac{\alpha}{2}\hat{v}_{\ell^*} + \frac{\alpha}{2}|\hat{v}_{\ell^*} - \tilde{v}_{\ell^*-1}|$$

$$= \alpha\,(\hat{v}_{k-1} - \hat{v}_{\ell^*}) \text{ if } \hat{v}_{\ell^*} \le \tilde{v}_{\ell^*-1}$$

$$= \alpha\,(\hat{v}_{k-1} - \tilde{v}_{\ell^*-1}) \text{ if } \hat{v}_{\ell^*} \ge \tilde{v}_{\ell^*-1}\,.$$

In the first case

$$X \le \alpha\,(\hat{v}_{\ell^*-1} - \hat{v}_{\ell^*}) < 0$$

and in the second case, it is already negative.

Therefore we obtain $\tilde{J}(V) - J(\hat{V}) \le -\hat{y}_k < 0$, which is a contradiction.

If $\ell^* = k+1$, then :

$$J(\tilde{V}) - J(\hat{V}) = \sum_{j=1}^{k-1} \frac{\alpha}{2}|\hat{v}^k_j - \hat{v}^k_{j-1}| + \frac{\alpha}{2}|\tilde{v}_k - \hat{v}^k_{k-1}| + \frac{\alpha}{2}|\hat{v}_{k+1} - \tilde{v}_k|$$
$$+ \sum_{j=1}^{k-1}\hat{y}^k_j - \sum_{j=1}^{k-1}\hat{y}_j - \hat{y}_k - \sum_{j=1}^{k+1}\frac{\alpha}{2}|\hat{v}_j - \hat{v}_{j-1}|$$
$$\le X - \hat{y}_k$$

where :

$$\frac{2}{\alpha}X = 2\,\hat{v}_{k-1} - \tilde{v}_k - \hat{v}_k + |\hat{v}_{k-1} - \tilde{v}_k| - |\hat{v}_{k+1} - \hat{v}_k|.$$

If we take into account that

$$\hat{v}_{k-1}^{k} \geq \tilde{v}_k \geq \hat{v}_k \geq \hat{v}_{k-1}$$

we conclude as above.

Therefore the assumption (5.25) cannot occur for an optimal control, and for the case $\hat{y}_k = 0$, we had already concluded. □

From Lemma 5.8, we can easily produce a planning horizon theorem. Define

$$(5.33) \qquad D_N = \max_{1 \leq t \leq 2n^*} \frac{\sum_{j=1}^{t} \xi_{N+j}}{t}$$

Theorem 5.1

For problem (5.1), (5.2), (5.3), if

$$(5.34) \qquad \hat{v}_{N-1} > D_N$$

then N is a planning horizon.

Proof

Let K > N. Clearly (5.34) can be interpreted as

$$\hat{v}_{N-1}^{N} > D_N^K$$

with the notation of Lemma 5.8. But then we have seen that we can construct an optimal control for $J^K(V)$ which contains $\hat{v}_j^N$ for j = 0, ..., N-1. Hence the desired result. □

Remark 5.2

N is a weak planning horizon, since it requires the knowledge of demand beyond N. Actually it requires the knowledge of 2n* demands beyond N. We may say that N+2n* is a forecast horizon, since the optimal first N decisions will not depend on the knowledge of the demands beyond N+2n* (cf. Remarks 3.1 and 3.2). □

Remark 5.3

One should understand that regeneration points are not necessarily planning horizons. This is due to the fact that the functional is not separable and additive over time, since it contains terms which overlap two consecutive periods. (see also on this matter Lippman et al [1967-1 ; p. 135]. □

V - 3. A GENERAL PRODUCTION SMOOTHING MODEL

The previous formulation is modified as follows :

$$(5.35) \qquad \begin{cases} y_{k+1} = y_k + v_k - \xi_{k+1} \\ y_0 = x \end{cases}$$

$$(5.36) \qquad v_k \geq 0, \; v_N = 0, \; y_k \geq 0$$

(5.37)
$$\begin{cases} J_0(x\ ;\ V) = \sum_{j=0}^{N-1} c_j(v_j) + \sum_{j=1}^{N-1} f_j(y_j) \\ \quad + \sum_{j=1}^{N-1} s_j(v_j - v_{j-1}) + s_N(-\ v_{N-1}) \end{cases}$$

where the production cost function , c_j, and the inventory cost function, f_j, satisfy (1.4) (the standard assumptions of the production planning problem) and where the smoothing cost function

(5.38) $\quad s_j : R \to R^+$ is convex and achieves its minimum at 0.

Clearly the functional (5.3) is a special case of (5.37) for :

$$c_j(v) = 0,\ 1 \leq j \leq N-1$$

$$s_j(z) = \frac{\alpha}{2}\,|z|, \qquad f_j(x) = x, \quad j = 1, \ldots, N-1$$

Because of this convention, it is convenient to add to the relevant components of V (which are $v_0, \ldots, v_{N-1}$), a component v_N which is always 0.

We may also say, in order to let V have an indefinite set of components (which is convenient for notational purposes when the horizon varies), that in (5.36) we add a constraint

(5.36)' $\quad v_N = 0$

when we solve the N horizon problem.

V.3.1 NECESSARY CONDITIONS

These conditions are obtained by combining modifications of policies as in Theorem 1.3 and as in the model of § V.1.

To save notation, it will be convenient to use the following convention

(5.39) functions indexed with integers out of their definition range with respect to a specific control problem are set to be 0.

As a consequence $\quad c_N(v),\ f_N(x),\ s_0(z) \equiv 0$. This convention allows us to write the conditions in a unique way, even for indices including the horizon. For instance, with this convention (1.15) becomes a particular case of (1.14) and can be avoided.

Theorem 5.2

Assume (1.4) and (5.38). An optimal pair $(\hat{v}_0, \ldots, \hat{v}_{N-1}, \hat{v}_N = 0)$, $(\hat{y}_0, \hat{y}_1, \ldots, \hat{y}_N)$ for $J_0(x\ ;\ V)$ satisfies the following conditions :

(5.40)
$$\left\{\begin{array}{l}\text{Let } 0 \le k < \ell \le N. \text{ Suppose that} \\ \hat{v}_k > 0,\ \hat{y}_{k+1} > 0,\ \ldots,\ \hat{y}_\ell > 0. \text{ Then} \\ c_\ell^{\prime +}(\hat{v}_\ell) + s_{k+1}^{\prime +}(\hat{v}_{k+1} - \hat{v}_k) + \chi_{\ell<N}\, s_\ell^{\prime +}(\hat{v}_\ell - \hat{v}_{\ell-1}) - c_k^{\prime -}(\hat{v}_k) \\ - s_k^{\prime -}(\hat{v}_k - \hat{v}_{k-1}) - s_{\ell+1}^{\prime -}(\hat{v}_{\ell+1} - \hat{v}_\ell) - \sum_{j=k+1}^{\ell} f_j^{\prime -}(\hat{y}_j) \ge 0\end{array}\right.$$ (1)

(5.41)
$$\left\{\begin{array}{l}\text{Let } 0 \le k < \ell < N. \text{ Suppose that } \hat{v}_\ell > 0, \text{ then} \\ c_k^{\prime +}(\hat{v}_k) + s_k^{\prime +}(\hat{v}_k - \hat{v}_{k-1}) + s_{\ell+1}^{\prime +}(\hat{v}_{\ell+1} - \hat{v}_\ell) \\ + \sum_{j=k+1}^{\ell} f_j^{\prime +}(\hat{y}_j) - c_\ell^{\prime -}(\hat{v}_\ell) - s_{k+1}^{\prime -}(\hat{v}_{k+1} - \hat{v}_k) - s_\ell^{\prime -}(\hat{v}_\ell - \hat{v}_{\ell-1}) \ge 0\end{array}\right.$$

(5.42)
$$\left\{\begin{array}{l}\text{Let } 0 \le k < \ell < N. \text{ Suppose that } \hat{v}_\ell > 0, \text{ then} \\ \sum_{j=k}^{\ell-1} c_j^{\prime +}(\hat{v}_j) + s_k^{\prime +}(\hat{v}_k - \hat{v}_{k-1}) + s_{\ell+1}^{\prime +}(\hat{v}_{\ell+1} - \hat{v}_\ell)(\ell-k) \\ + \sum_{j=k+1}^{\ell} (j-k)\, f_j^{\prime +}(\hat{y}_j) - (\ell-k)\, c_\ell^{\prime -}(\hat{v}_\ell) - s_\ell^{\prime -}(\hat{v}_\ell - \hat{v}_{\ell-1})(\ell-k+1) \ge 0\end{array}\right.$$

(5.43)
$$\left\{\begin{array}{l}\text{Let } 0 \le k < \ell < N, \text{ and assume that } \hat{v}_{k+1} > 0,\ \ldots,\ \hat{v}_\ell > 0. \\ \text{Then one has :} \\ c_k^{\prime +}(\hat{v}_k)(\ell-k) + s_k^{\prime +}(\hat{v}_k - \hat{v}_{k-1})(\ell-k) \\ + s_{\ell+1}^{\prime +}(\hat{v}_{\ell+1} - \hat{v}_\ell) + \sum_{j=k+1}^{\ell} (\ell-j+1)\, f_j^{\prime +}(\hat{y}_j) \\ - s_{k+1}^{\prime -}(\hat{v}_{k+1} - \hat{v}_k)\,(\ell-k+1) - \sum_{j=k+1}^{\ell} c_j^{\prime -}(\hat{v}_j) \ge 0\end{array}\right.$$

(5.44)
$$\left\{\begin{array}{l}\text{Let } 0 \le k, \text{ and assume that } k + 2m \le N,\ m \ge 1. \text{ Assume that :} \\ \hat{v}_k > 0,\ \hat{v}_{k+1} > 0,\ \ldots,\ \hat{v}_{k+m-1} > 0 \\ \hat{y}_{k+1} > 0,\ \ldots,\ \hat{y}_{k+2m} > 0. \text{ Then one has} \\ \sum_{j=k+m+1} c_j^{\prime +}(\hat{v}_j) + s_{k+m}^{\prime +}(\hat{v}_{k+m} - \hat{v}_{k+m-1}) + s_{k+m+1}^{\prime +}(\hat{v}_{k+m+1} - \hat{v}_{k+m})\end{array}\right.$$

---

(1) $\chi_{\ell<N} = 1$ if $\ell < N$ and 0 otherwise. By our convention if $\ell = N$, $s'_{N+1} = 0$, and $c_N = 0$.

$$
- \sum_{j=k}^{k+m-1} c_j'^{-}(\hat{v}_j) - s_k'^{-}(\hat{v}_k - \hat{v}_{k-1}) - s_{k+2m+1}'^{-}(\hat{v}_{k+2m+1} - \hat{v}_{k+2m})
- \sum_{j=k+1}^{k+m} (j-k)\, f_j'^{-}(\hat{y}_j) - \sum_{j=k+m+1}^{k+2m} (k+2m+1-j)\, f_j'^{-}(\hat{y}_j) \geq 0
$$

(5.45) Let $0 \leq k$ and assume that $k+2m < N$, and that

$\hat{v}_{k+m+1} > 0, \ldots, \hat{v}_{k+2m} > 0$, then one has :

$$
\sum_{j=k}^{k+m-1} c_j'^{+}(\hat{v}_j) + s_k'^{+}(\hat{v}_k - \hat{v}_{k-1}) + s_{k+2m+1}'^{+}(\hat{v}_{k+2m+1} - \hat{v}_{k+2m})
+ \sum_{j=k+1}^{k+m} (j-k)\, f_j'^{+}(\hat{y}_j) + \sum_{j=k+m+1}^{k+2m} (k+2m+1-j)\, f_j'^{+}(\hat{y}_j)
$$
$$
- \sum_{j=k+m+1}^{k+2m} c_j'^{-}(\hat{v}_j) - s_{k+m}'^{-}(\hat{v}_{k+m} - \hat{v}_{k+m-1})
- s_{k+m+1}'^{-}(\hat{v}_{k+m+1} - \hat{v}_{k+m}) \geq 0
$$

The proof is straightforward relying on the comparison of controls. It is therefore omitted. □

One could wonder whether the conditions stated in Theorem 5.2 are not redundant. For instance consider $k \leq j < \ell$. From (5.41), we may write :

$$
c_j'^{+}(\hat{v}_j) + s_j'^{+}(\hat{v}_j - \hat{v}_{j-1}) + s_{\ell+1}'^{+}(\hat{v}_{\ell+1} - \hat{v}_\ell)
+ \sum_{i=j+1}^{\ell} f_i'^{+}(\hat{y}_i) - c_\ell'^{-}(\hat{v}_\ell) - s_{j+1}'^{-}(\hat{v}_{j+1} - \hat{v}_j) - s_\ell'^{-}(\hat{v}_\ell - \hat{v}_{\ell-1}) \geq 0.
$$

We sum up these relations for j equals k to $\ell-1$. We get, after some manipulations :

$$
\sum_{j=k}^{\ell-1} c_j'^{+}(\hat{v}_j) + (\ell-k)\, s_{\ell+1}'^{+}(\hat{v}_{\ell+1} - \hat{v}_\ell) + s_k'^{+}(\hat{v}_k - \hat{v}_{k-1})
+ \sum_{j=k+1}^{\ell} (j-k)\, f_j'^{+}(\hat{y}_j) - (\ell-k)\, c_\ell'^{-}(\hat{v}_\ell) - s_\ell'^{-}(\hat{v}_\ell - \hat{v}_{\ell-1})(\ell-k+1)
+ \sum_{j=k+1}^{\ell-1} [s_j'^{+}(\hat{v}_j - \hat{v}_{j-1}) - s_j'^{-}(\hat{v}_j - \hat{v}_{j-1})] \geq 0
$$

This condition coincides with (5.42) only when

$$
s_j'^{+}(\hat{v}_j - \hat{v}_{j-1}) = s_j'^{-}(\hat{v}_j - \hat{v}_{j-1}), \quad j = k+1, \ldots, \ell-1
$$

or when $\ell = k+1$ (which is trivial). In general, condition (5.42) is better since we can delete a positive additional term.

V.3.2. PROPERTIES OF AN OPTIMAL CONTROL

In the sequel we assume $x = 0$.

Lemma 5.9

Assume that

(5.46) $$c'^{+}_{k}(0) + \sum_{j=k+1}^{N} f'^{+}_{j}(0) - s'^{-}_{k+1}(0) > - s'^{+}_{k}(-\infty), \quad \forall k \leq N-1$$ [1]

then an optimal control satisfies

(5.47) $$\hat{y}_N = 0$$

Proof

Assume $\hat{y}_N > 0$. Let $k_0 \leq N-1$ such that :

$$\hat{v}_{k_0} > 0,\ \hat{y}_{k_0+1} > 0,\ \ldots,\ \hat{y}_N > 0,\ \hat{v}_{k_0+1} = \ldots = \hat{v}_N = 0$$

We apply (5.40) with $k = k_0$, $\ell = N$, and deduce

$$c'^{-}_{k_0}(\hat{v}_{k_0}) + \sum_{j=k_0+1}^{N} f'^{-}_{j}(y_j) \leq s'^{+}_{k_0+1}(\hat{v}_{k_0+1} - \hat{v}_{k_0}) - s'^{-}_{k_0}(\hat{v}_{k_0} - \hat{v}_{k_0-1})$$

hence

$$c'^{+}_{k_0}(0) + \sum_{j=k_0+1}^{N} f'^{+}_{j}(0) \leq s'^{-}_{k_0+1}(0) - s'^{-}_{k_0}(\hat{v}_{k_0} - \hat{v}_{k_0-1})$$
$$\leq s'^{-}_{k_0+1}(0) - s'^{+}_{k_0}(-\infty)$$

hence a contradiction with (5.46). □

Lemma 5.10

Assume that $k \leq N-2$, and

(5.48) $$\begin{cases} c'^{+}_{k}(0) + f'^{+}_{k+1}(0) - 2\, s'^{-}_{k+1}(0) \\ > c'^{-}_{k+1}(\infty) - s'^{+}_{k}(-\infty) - s'^{-}_{k+2}(-\infty), \quad \forall k \leq N-2 \end{cases}$$

then $\hat{v}_k > \hat{v}_{k+1}$ implies $\hat{y}_{k+1} = 0$.

Alternatively if

(5.49) $$\begin{cases} c'^{+}_{k}(\xi_{k+1}) + f'^{+}_{k+1}(0) \\ > c'^{-}_{k+1}(\infty) - s'^{+}_{k}(-\infty) - s'^{-}_{k+2}(-\infty) + 2\, s'^{-}_{k+1}(+\infty) \end{cases}$$

and if $\hat{y}_k = 0$, then $\hat{y}_{k+1} = 0$.

Proof

Left to the reader. This lemma generalizes Lemma 5.3, as well as the case $H(k) = k$ of Lemma 3.1. □

---

[1] Recall that $f_N = 0$, by our convention

For any k define $H^*(k)$ (analogue of n^*) such that $H^*(k) \geq 1$ and, $H^*(k)$ is the first integer larger or equal to 1, such that :

$$(5.50)\quad \begin{cases} \sum_{j=k+1}^{k+H^*(k)} (j-k)\, f_j'^{+}(0) + \sum_{j=k+H^*(k)+1}^{k+2H^*(k)} (k + 2H^* + 1-j)\, f_j'^{+}(0) \\ + \sum_{j=k}^{k+H^*-1} c_j'^{+}(0) > \sum_{j=k+H^*+1}^{k+2H^*} c_j'^{-}(\infty) \\ + s'^{-}_{k+H^*}(+\infty) + s'^{-}_{k+H^*+1}(+\infty) - s_k'^{+}(-\infty) - s'^{+}_{k+2H^*+1}(-\infty) \end{cases}$$

Compared with the definition of n^* (cf. (5.5)), then $H^*(k)$ is equal to $\lceil x^* \rceil+1$, hence $n^* = H^*(k)$ if x^* is not an integer.

Lemma 5.11

Assume (5.46), (5.48). Let $0 \leq k \leq N-1$ and assume that $\hat{y}_k = 0$. Then there exists ℓ with $k+1 \leq \ell \leq [k+2H^*(k)] \wedge N$ such that

$$\hat{y}_\ell = 0.$$

Proof

Analogous to that of Lemma 5.5 □

Remark 5.4

One can also define an integer like H(k) (cf. (3.7)) and obtain a result similar to Lemma 5.11. Details are left to the reader. □

Define

$$(5.51)\qquad D_k^N = \begin{cases} 0 \text{ if } k = N \\ \underset{1 \leq t \leq 2H^*(k) \wedge (N-k)}{\text{Max}} \dfrac{\sum_{j=1}^{t} \xi_{k+j}}{t} \end{cases}$$

Then we obtain :

Lemma 5.12

Assume (5.46), (5.48) and that

(5.52) $H^*(k)$ does not decrease as k increases

Then one has

$$(5.53)\qquad \hat{v}_k \leq D_k^N, \quad \forall k \leq N-1$$

Proof

When condition (5.52) holds, we can assert that $\forall k \leq N-1$, there is an ℓ with $k \leq \ell \leq [k+2H^*(k)] \wedge N$ such that $\hat{y}_\ell = 0$ whether $\hat{y}_k$ vanishes or not. Therefore we can apply the arguments of Lemma 5.7 to conclude. □

We turn now to the generalization of Lemma 5.8, which is the key result to obtain the planning horizon theorem. Unfortunately we need to impose restrictions on the cost functions s_j and c_j, namely :

(5.54) $$\begin{cases} s_j(x) = s_j(0) - \bar{s}_j\, x \text{ for } x \le 0 \qquad (^1), \\ \bar{s}_j \ge 0 \text{ constant} \; ; \; \bar{s}_j \ge \bar{s}_{j+1} \; , \; \forall j \end{cases}$$

(5.55) $$c_j'^{-}(\infty) < f_k'^{+}(0), \quad \forall j \ge k$$

Lemma 5.13.

Assume (5.52), (5.54), (5.55).
If :
(5.56) $$\hat{v}^k_{k-1} > D^N_k$$

then

(5.57) $$\hat{v}^k_{k-1} > \hat{v}_k$$

and there exists an optimal control which contains $\hat{v}^k_j$, j = 0, ..., k-1.

Proof

We assume $1 \le k < N$. Note that (5.54), (5.55) imply (5.46), (5.48). Clearly (5.57) is a consequence of Lemma 5.12 and of (5.56). Let us prove the second part of the statement. We proceed as in Lemma 5.8. Assume first that :

(5.58) $$\hat{y}_k = 0.$$

Consider the functional

(5.59) $$\begin{cases} L^k(V\; ; w) = \sum_{j=1}^{k-1} s_j(v_j - v_{j-1}) + \sum_{j=0}^{k-1} c_j(v_j) \\ \qquad + \sum_{j=1}^{k-1} f_j(y_j) + s_k(w - v_{k-1}). \end{cases}$$

It will be convenient to introduce

(5.60) $$\tilde{J}^k(V) = \sum_{j=1}^{k-1} s_j(v_j - v_{j-1}) + \sum_{j=0}^{k-1} c_j(v_j) + \sum_{j=1}^{k-1} f_j(y_j)$$

Hence we have

(5.61) $$\begin{aligned} L^k(V\; ; w) &= \tilde{J}^k(V) + s_k(w - v_{k-1}) \\ J^k(V) &= \tilde{J}^k(V) + s_k(- v_{k-1}) \\ &= L^k(V\; ; 0). \end{aligned}$$

Because of (5.58), the optimal control $\hat{V}$ minimizes $L^k(V\; ; \hat{v}_k)$ among controls such that $y_k = 0$. Since $\hat{V}_k$ is admissible, we can write :

---

(1) There is no restriction for $x > 0$, provided of course that s_j satisfies (5.38).

$$(5.62)\quad \begin{cases} L^k(\hat{V}\ ;\ \hat{v}_k) = \tilde{J}^k(\hat{V}) + s_k(\hat{v}_k - \hat{v}_{k-1}) \\ \qquad \le \tilde{J}^k(\hat{v}^k) + s_k(\hat{v}_k - \hat{v}^k_{k-1}). \end{cases}$$

On the other hand, since $\hat{V}^k$ minimizes $J^k(V)$ we also have :

$$(5.63)\quad \tilde{J}^k(\hat{V}_k) + s_k(-\hat{v}^k_{k-1}) \le \tilde{J}^k(\hat{V}) + s_k(-\hat{v}_{k-1}).$$

Combining (5.62), (5.63) we see that : :

$$(5.64)\quad s_k(-\hat{v}^k_{k-1}) - s_k(-\hat{v}_{k-1}) \le s_k(\hat{v}_k - \hat{v}^k_{k-1}) - s_k(\hat{v}_k - \hat{v}_{k-1})$$

But now we prove that the converse inequality also holds. Indeed, assume first that

$$\hat{v}^k_{k-1} \ge \hat{v}_{k-1}$$

then by convexity

$$(5.65)\quad s_k(-\hat{v}_{k-1}) - s_k(-\hat{v}^k_{k-1}) \le s_k(\hat{v}_k - \hat{v}_{k-1}) - s_k(\hat{v}_k - \hat{v}^k_{k-1}) \qquad (^1)$$

Then assume that :

$$\hat{v}^k_{k-1} \le \hat{v}_{k-1}$$

thus by (5.58)

$$\hat{v}_k < \hat{v}^k_{k-1} \le \hat{v}_{k-1}$$

By assumption (5.54) we have

$$\begin{aligned} & s_k(-\hat{v}_{k-1}) - s_k(-\hat{v}^k_{k-1}) - s_k(\hat{v}_k - \hat{v}_{k-1}) + s_k(\hat{v}_k - \hat{v}^k_{k-1}) \\ & = \bar{s}^k\,[\hat{v}_{k-1} - \hat{v}^k_{k-1} - (\hat{v}_{k-1} - \hat{v}_k) + \hat{v}^k_{k-1} - \hat{v}_k] \\ & = 0 \end{aligned}$$

Therefore (5.65) holds, which with (5.64) proves that (5.64) is an equality. This and (5.62) prove that :

$$L^k(\hat{V}\ ;\ \hat{v}_k) = L^k(\hat{V}^k\ ;\ \hat{v}_k).$$

This is sufficient to conclude that the reverse inequality in (5.64) is also satisfied. Assume next that :

$$(5.66)\quad \hat{y}_k > 0$$

From Lemma 5.10, we have $\hat{v}_{k-1} \le \hat{v}_k$, hence also

$$(5.67)\quad \hat{v}_{k-1} \le \hat{v}_k < \hat{v}^k_{k-1}.$$

---

(1) If s is convex, non decreasing, and if $x \ge y$ then for $z \ge 0$, $s(x) - s(y) \le s(x+z) - s(y+z)$.

By Lemma 5.11, there exists $k+1 \le \ell \le \lceil k+2H^*(k) \rceil \wedge N$ such that $\hat{y}_\ell = 0$.

We consider the same integer $k+1 \le \ell^* \le \ell$, as in Lemma 5.8 (cf. (5.27)).

We then define the control $\tilde{V}$ as in Lemma 5.8. It remains to compute the difference (for $\ell^* \ge k+2$)

$$(5.68)\quad \begin{cases} J(\tilde{V}) - J(\hat{V}) = \tilde{J}^k(\hat{V}^k) + s_k(\tilde{v}_{\ell^*-1} - \hat{v}^k_{k-1}) \\ + s_{\ell^*}(\hat{v}_{\ell^*} - \tilde{v}_{\ell^*-1}) + f_k(0) + \sum_{j=k+1}^{\ell^*-1} f_j(\tilde{y}_j) + \sum_{j=k}^{\ell^*-2} c_j(\hat{v}^k_{k-1}) \\ + c_{\ell^*-1}(\tilde{v}_{\ell^*-1}) - \tilde{J}^k(\hat{V}) - \sum_{j=k}^{\ell^*} s_j(\hat{v}_j - \hat{v}_{j-1}) \\ - f_k(\hat{y}_k) - \sum_{j=k+1}^{\ell^*-1} f_j(\hat{y}_j) - \sum_{j=k}^{\ell^*-1} c_j(\hat{v}_j) \end{cases}$$

and we have

$$(5.69)\qquad \hat{v}_{k-1} \le \hat{v}_k \le \dots \le \hat{v}_{\ell^*-1} \le \tilde{v}_{\ell^*-1} \le \hat{v}^k_{k-1}$$

Using (5.63) and $\tilde{y}_j \le \hat{y}_j$ for $j = k+1, \dots, \ell^*-1$, we obtain

$$(5.70)\quad \begin{cases} J(\tilde{V}) - J(\hat{V}) \le s_k(-\hat{v}_{k-1}) - s_k(-\hat{v}^k_{k-1}) \\ + s_k(\tilde{v}_{\ell^*-1} - \hat{v}^k_{k-1}) + s_{\ell^*}(\hat{v}_{\ell^*} - \tilde{v}_{\ell^*-1}) - s_{\ell^*}(\hat{v}_{\ell^*} - \hat{v}_{\ell^*-1}) \\ - \sum_{j=k}^{\ell^*-1} s_j(\hat{v}_j - \hat{v}_{j-1}) + \sum_{j=k}^{\ell^*-2} c_j(\hat{v}^k_{k-1}) - c_j(\hat{v}_j) \\ + c_{\ell^*-1}(\tilde{v}_{\ell^*-1}) - c_{\ell^*-1}(\hat{v}_{\ell-1}) + f_k(0) - f_k(\hat{y}_k). \end{cases}$$

Assumptions (5.54) and the set of inequalities (5.69) imply

$$(5.71)\quad \begin{cases} J(\tilde{V}) - J(\hat{V}) \le \bar{s}_k(\hat{v}_{k-1} - \tilde{v}^*_{\ell}{}_{-1}) \\ + s_{\ell^*}(\hat{v}_{\ell^*} - \tilde{v}_{\ell^*-1}) - s_{\ell^*}(\hat{v}_{\ell^*} - \hat{v}_{\ell^*-1}) - \sum_{j=k}^{\ell^*-1} s_j(\hat{v}_j - \hat{v}_{j-1}) \\ + \sum_{j=k}^{\ell^*-2} c_j(\hat{v}^k_{k-1}) - c_j(\hat{v}_j) + c_{\ell^*-1}(\tilde{v}_{\ell^*-1}) - c_{\ell^*-1}(\hat{v}_{\ell^*-1}) \\ + f_k(0) - f_k(\hat{y}_k) \end{cases}$$

But by definition of $\tilde{v}_{\ell^*-1}$ (see Lemma 5.8), we know that

$$\hat{y}_k = \tilde{v}_{\ell^*-1} - \hat{v}_{\ell^*-1} + \sum_{j=k}^{\ell^*-2} (\hat{v}^k_{k-1} - \hat{v}_j).$$

By convexity

(5.72)
$$c_j(\hat{v}^k_{k-1}) - c_j(\hat{v}_j) \le c'_j(\hat{v}^k_{k-1})(\hat{v}^k_{k-1} - \hat{v}_j) \le c'_j(\infty)(\hat{v}^k_{k-1} - \hat{v}_j), \quad j = k, \ldots, \ell^*-2$$

and

(5.73)
$$c_{\ell^*-1}(\tilde{v}_{\ell^*-1}) - c_{\ell^*-1}(\hat{v}_{\ell^*-1}) \le c'_{\ell^*-1}(\infty)(\tilde{v}_{\ell^*-1} - \hat{v}_{\ell^*-1})$$

But

$$f_k(\hat{y}_k) - f_k(0) \ge f'^+_k(0)\,\hat{y}_k = f'^+_k(0)\,[\tilde{v}_{\ell^*-1} - \hat{v}_{\ell^*-1} + \sum_{j=k}^{\ell^*-2} (\hat{v}^k_{k-1} - \hat{v}_j)]$$

hence

$$\sum_{j=k}^{\ell^*-2} [c_j(\hat{v}^k_{k-1}) - c_j(\hat{v}_j)] + c_{\ell^*-1}(\tilde{v}_{\ell^*-1}) - c_{\ell^*-1}(\hat{v}_{\ell^*-1})$$

$$+ f_k(0) - f_k(\hat{y}_k) \le [c'_{\ell^*-1}(\infty) - f'^+_k(0)](\tilde{v}_{\ell^*-1} - \hat{v}_{\ell^*-1})$$

$$+ \sum_{j=k}^{\ell^*-2} [c'_j(\infty) - f'^+_k(0)](\hat{v}^k_{k-1} - \hat{v}_j$$

$$< 0$$

from (5.57) and assumption (5.55).

Therefore it follows from (5.71) that

$$J(\tilde{V}) - J(\hat{V}) < \bar{s}_k(\hat{v}_{k-1} - \tilde{v}_{\ell^*-1})$$

$$+ s_{\ell^*}(\hat{v}_{\ell^*} - \tilde{v}_{\ell^*-1}) - s_{\ell^*}(\hat{v}_{\ell^*} - \hat{v}_{\ell^*-1}) - \sum_{j=k}^{\ell^*-1} s_j(\hat{v}_j - \hat{v}_{j-1})$$

$$= X$$

If $\hat{v}_{\ell^*} \le \hat{v}_{\ell^*-1}$, hence also $\hat{v}_{\ell^*} \le \tilde{v}_{\ell^*-1}$, and we have

$$X = \bar{s}_k(\hat{v}_{k-1} - \tilde{v}_{\ell^*-1}) + \bar{s}_{\ell^*}(\tilde{v}_{\ell^*-1} - \hat{v}_{\ell^*-1}) - \sum_{j=k}^{\ell^*-1} s_j(\hat{v}_j - \hat{v}_{j-1})$$

and by assumption (5.54)

$$\bar{s}_{\ell^*} \le \bar{s}_k$$

hence

$$X \le \bar{s}_k(\hat{v}_{k-1} - \hat{v}_{\ell^*-1}) - \sum_{j=k}^{\ell^*-1} s_j(\hat{v}_j - \hat{v}_{j-1}) \le 0$$

Assume $\hat{v}_{\ell^*} \ge \hat{v}_{\ell^*-1}$, and $\hat{v}_{\ell^*} \ge \tilde{v}_{\ell^*-1}$. Then

$$\hat{v}_{\ell^*} - \hat{v}_{\ell^*-1} \ge \hat{v}_{\ell^*} - \tilde{v}_{\ell^*-1} \ge 0$$

and since s_{ℓ^*} is increasing on R^+, it follows again that $X \le 0$.

The last case is $\hat{v}_{\ell*} \geq \hat{v}_{\ell*-1}$ and $\hat{v}_{\ell*} \leq \tilde{v}_{\ell*-1}$.

$$X \leq \bar{s}_k(\hat{v}_{k-1} - \tilde{v}_{\ell*-1}) + \bar{s}_{\ell*}(\tilde{v}_{\ell*-1} - \hat{v}_{\ell*})$$

$$\leq \bar{s}_k(\hat{v}_{k-1} - \hat{v}_{\ell*}) \leq \bar{s}_k(\hat{v}_{\ell*-1} - \hat{v}_{\ell*}) \leq 0$$

Therefore, we have proven that $J(\tilde{V}) - J(\hat{V}) < 0$, which contradicts the optimality of $\hat{V}$. Hence (5.66) does not hold.

If $\ell^* = k+1$, then :

$$J(\tilde{V}) - J(\hat{V}) = \tilde{J}^k(\hat{V}^k) - s_k(\tilde{v}_k - \hat{v}^k_{k-1})$$

$$+ s_{k+1}(\hat{v}_{k+1} - \tilde{v}_k) + f_k(0) + c_k(\tilde{v}_k) - \tilde{J}^k(\hat{V})$$

$$- s_k(\hat{v}_k - \hat{v}_{k-1}) - s_{k+1}(\hat{v}_{k+1} - \hat{v}_k) - f_k(\hat{y}_k) - c_k(\hat{v}_k)$$

and we have

$$\hat{v}^k_{k-1} \geq \tilde{v}_k \geq \hat{v}_k \geq \hat{v}_{k-1}$$

$$\hat{y}_k = \tilde{v}_k - \hat{v}_k$$

Therefore

$$J(\tilde{V}) - J(\hat{V}) \leq \bar{s}_k(\hat{v}_{k-1} - \tilde{v}_k) + s_{k+1}(\hat{v}_{k+1} - \tilde{v}_k) - s_k(\hat{v}_k - \hat{v}_{k-1})$$

$$- s_{k+1}(\hat{v}_{k+1} - \hat{v}_k) + f_k(0) - f_k(\hat{y}_k) + c_k(\tilde{v}_k) - c_k(\hat{v}_k)$$

and we argue as before. □

We can then produce the following planning horizon theorem.

Theorem 5.2

Assume (1.4), (5.38) and (5.52), (5.54), (5.55). If :

(5.74) $$\hat{v}_{N-1} > D_N$$

where

$$D_N = \underset{1 \leq t \leq 2H^*(N)}{\mathrm{Max}} \frac{\sum_{j=1}^{t} \xi_{N+j}}{t}$$

then N is a planning horizon.

Proof

Same as Theorem 5.1. □

Remark 5.4

In the structure of the cost functional J(V) (cf. (5.37)), instead of considering a final penalty term $s_N(- v_{N-1})$, we could adopt an initial penalty term $s_0(v_0)$. The analysis would lead to similar results. □

VI - MAXIMUM PRINCIPLE IN DISCRETE TIME AND APPLICATIONS TO THE PROBLEM OF PRODUCTION SMOOTHING

VI - 1. INTRODUCTION

As we have seen, production smoothing leads to more elaborate problems for which it is more suitable to use the general framework of optimal control in discrete time. Consider the general production smoothing model (5.35), (5.36), (5.37) and reformulate it as follows. Find

$$y_0, y_1, \ldots, y_N, \quad v_0, \ldots, v_N, \quad w_0, \ldots, w_{N-1}$$

satisfying

$$(6.1) \qquad \begin{cases} v_{k+1} = v_k + w_k \\ y_{k+1} = y_k + v_k - \xi_{k+1}, & k = 0, \ldots, N-1 \\ y_0 = x, \quad v_N = 0 \\ y_k, v_k \geq 0, \quad \forall k = 0, \ldots, N \end{cases}$$

in order to minimize

$$(6.2) \qquad J_0 = \sum_{j=0}^{N-1} c_j(v_j) + \sum_{j=1}^{N-1} f_j(y_j) + \sum_{j=0}^{N-1} s_{j+1}(w_j)$$

where the new variable w_k denotes the change in the production rate between two consecutive periods k and k+1. The introduction of the additional variables, w_k, allows to rewrite the functional (5.37) in a separable form, as a sum of non overlapping terms i.e., indexed by j, involving only variables at time j (see Remark 5.3).

Now the pair v_k, y_k should be considered as a state variable, and w_k is the control. This motivates the following general formulation :

$$(6.3) \qquad \begin{cases} Y_{k+1} = A_k Y_k + B_k V_k - E_{k+1}, & k = 0, \ldots, N-1 \\ C_k Y_k + D_k V_k \leq G_k & , k = 0, \ldots, N \end{cases}$$

$$(6.4) \qquad \operatorname{Min} J_0 = \sum_{j=0}^{N-1} F_j(Y_j) + H_j(V_j)$$

where Y_k, V_k are vectors, A_k, B_k, C_k, D_k are matrix with appropriate sizes and

(6.5) $\qquad F_j$, H_j convex functions of the arguments.

Problem (6.1), (6.2) enters into the general formulation (6.3), (6.4) by setting

$$
(6.6)\quad \left\{
\begin{array}{lll}
Y_k = \begin{pmatrix} y_k \\ v_k \end{pmatrix} , & V_k = w_k , & \\
A_k = \begin{pmatrix} 1 & 1 \\ 0 & 1 \end{pmatrix} , & B_k = \begin{pmatrix} 0 \\ 1 \end{pmatrix} , & E_k = \begin{pmatrix} \xi_k \\ 0 \end{pmatrix} \\
C_k = \begin{pmatrix} -1 & 0 \\ 0 & -1 \end{pmatrix} , & D_k = 0 , & G_k = 0 , \; k=1,\ldots,N-1 \\
C_0 = \begin{pmatrix} 1 & 0 \\ -1 & 0 \\ 0 & -1 \end{pmatrix} , & D_0 = 0 , & G_0 = \begin{pmatrix} x \\ -x \\ 0 \end{pmatrix} \\
C_N = \begin{pmatrix} -1 & 0 \\ 0 & 1 \\ 0 & -1 \end{pmatrix} , & D_N = 0 , & G_N = 0 \qquad (^1) \\
F_j(Y_j) = c_j(v_j) + f_j(y_j) , & j = 0, \ldots, N-1 & \\
H_j(V_j) = s_{j+1}(w_j) , & j = 0, \ldots, N-1 &
\end{array}
\right.
$$

Of course the formulation (6.3), (6.4) can cover a lot of other examples.

Let us, for example, reconsider the production smoothing model proposed by Lippman et al [1967-1], further generalized by Kleindorfer et al [1975].

We set

$$Y_k = \begin{pmatrix} y_k \\ v_k \end{pmatrix}$$

where : y_k = inventory at time k

v_k = work force available at time k

$$V_k = \begin{pmatrix} u_k^1 \\ u_k^2 \\ w_k \end{pmatrix}$$

where :

---

(1) We can add $f_0(y_0) = 0$ in (6.2) without modifying the problem

u_k^1 = production level at time k in regular time

u_k^2 = production level at time k in overtime

w_k = change of the work force level between k and k+1.

The state equations are written in the form (6.3) where

$$A_k = I \text{ (Identity)}$$

$$B_k = \begin{pmatrix} 1 & 1 & 0 \\ 0 & 0 & 1 \end{pmatrix} \qquad E_k = \begin{pmatrix} \xi_k \\ 0 \end{pmatrix}$$

The constraints are the following

$$0 \leq u_k^1 \leq v_k$$
$$0 \leq u_k^2 \leq \alpha\, v_k \quad , \quad \alpha \geq 0 \quad , \quad k = 0, \ldots, N-1$$
$$a_k \leq w_k \leq b_k$$

which can be rewritten under the general form (6.3). There are no restrictive conditions imposed at time N, and the initial states are given. This can also be incorporated into (6.3).

Note that when we impose $u_k^1 = v_k$, $u_k^2 = 0$, and $a_k = -\infty$, $b_k = +\infty$, the model reduces to (6.1).

VI - 2. DISCRETE TIME MAXIMUM PRINCIPLE

For convenience we use lower case to denote vectors in (6.3) in the following derivations. When we interpret the results concerning the model (6.1), (6.2) we turn back to block letters, in order to avoid confusion.

Thus consider

$$(6.7) \quad \begin{cases} y_{k+1} = A_k\, y_k + B_k\, v_k - e_{k+1} & , \ k = 0, \ldots, N-1 \\ C_k\, y_k + D_k\, v_k \leq g_k & , \ k = 0, \ldots, N \end{cases}$$

$$(6.8) \quad J_0 = \sum_{j=0}^{N-1} f_j(y_j) + s_j(v_j)$$

As usual in convex optimization, we introduce the lagrangian

$$(6.9) \quad \begin{cases} L = J_0 + \sum_{k=0}^{N-1} p_k \cdot (y_{k+1} - A_k\, y_k - B_k\, v_k) \\ \quad + \sum_{k=0}^{N} \lambda_k \cdot (c_k\, y_k + D_k\, v_k) \end{cases}$$

We also write

$$\sum_{k=0}^{N-1} p_k \cdot y_{k+1} = \sum_{k=1}^{N} p_{k-1} \cdot y_k$$

hence

$$(6.10)\quad \begin{cases} L = \sum_{k=1}^{N-1} [f_k(y_k) + (p_{k-1} - A_k\, p_k + c_k\, \lambda_k) y_k] \\ \quad + \sum_{k=0}^{N-1} [s_k(v_k) + (- B_k^*\, p_k + D_k^*\, \lambda_k) v_k] \\ \quad + f_0(y_0) + (- A_0^*\, p_0 + C_0^*\, \lambda_0) y_0 + (p_{N-1} + C_N^*\, \lambda_N) y_N + D_N^*\, \lambda_N\, v_N \end{cases}$$

Theorem 6.1

Assume that :

(6.11) f_j, s_j are convex

and that there exists an admissible control such that the subset of inequalities (6.7) which cannot be reduced to equalities, is strictly verified. Then if $\hat{v}_k$ is an optimal control and $\hat{y}_k$ the corresponding state, there exists $p_0, \ldots, p_{N-1}$, $\lambda_0, \ldots, \lambda_N$ such that the following conditions are satisfied

$$(6.12)\quad \begin{cases} \hat{y}_{k+1} = A_k\, \hat{y}_k + B_k\, \hat{v}_k - e_{k+1} , & k = 0, \ldots, N-1 \\ \left.\begin{array}{l} C_k\, \hat{y}_k + D_k\, \hat{v}_k - g_k \le 0 \\ \lambda_k \ge 0 , \quad \lambda_k \,.\, (C_k\, \hat{y}_k + D_k\, \hat{v}_k - g_k) = 0 \end{array}\right\} & k = 0, \ldots, N \end{cases}$$

$$(6.13)\quad \begin{cases} A_k^*\, p_k - p_{k-1} - C_k^*\, \lambda_k \in \partial f_k(\hat{y}_k) , & k = 1, \ldots, N-1 \\ B_k^*\, p_k - D_k^*\, \lambda_k \in \partial s_k(\hat{v}_k) , & k = 0, \ldots, N-1 \end{cases}$$

$$(6.14)\quad A_0^*\, p_0 - C_0^*\, \lambda_0 \in \partial f_0(\hat{y}_0)$$

$$(6.15)\quad p_{N-1} + C_N^*\, \lambda_N = 0, \; D_N^*\, \lambda_N = 0$$

Proof

In (6.13), and (6.14), $\partial f_k(\hat{y}_k)$ means the sub gradient of the convex function f_k at point $\hat{y}_k$. We recall that it is the set of vectors z such that

$$f_k(y) - f_k(\hat{y}_k) \ge z \,.\, (y - \hat{y}_k) \quad , \forall y$$

Then the desired result is a consequence of the classical results on convex optimization (see for instance Rockafellar [1970]).

Now (6.13), (6.14), (6.15) follow from the fact we minimize the Lagrangian in y_k, v_k considered as independent variables. Convexity implies that (6.12),...,(6.15) are also sufficient conditions for optimality. □

Let us apply Theorem 6.1 to model (6.6) (we now return to block letters $\hat{Y}_k$, $\hat{V}_k$).We thus obtain :

$$(6.16)\quad \begin{cases} \lambda_k = \begin{pmatrix}\lambda_k^1\\ \lambda_k^2\end{pmatrix} \text{ for } k = 1, \ldots, N-1, \text{ with} \\ \lambda_k^1 \geq 0,\ \lambda_k^2 \geq 0\ ,\quad \lambda_k^1\,\hat{y}_k = 0,\ \lambda_k^2\hat{v}_k = 0,\quad \hat{y}_k, \hat{v}_k \geq 0 \\ \hat{y}_0 = x,\ \lambda_0^3 \geq 0\ ,\quad \lambda_0^3\hat{v}_0 = 0,\ \hat{v}_N = 0\ ,\ \lambda_N^1 \geq 0\ ,\ \lambda_N^1\hat{y}_N = 0 \\ p_k = \begin{pmatrix}p_k^1\\ p_k^2\end{pmatrix} \text{ for } k = 0, \ldots, N-1 \end{cases}$$

$$(6.17)\qquad p_{N-1}^1 - \lambda_N^1 = 0$$

$$(6.18)\qquad s'^-_{k+1}(\hat{v}_{k+1} - \hat{v}_k) \leq p_k^2 \leq s'^+_{k+1}(\hat{v}_{k+1} - \hat{v}_k)\ ,\quad k = 0, \ldots, N-1$$

$$(6.19)\qquad f'^-_k(\hat{y}_k) \leq p_k^1 - p_{k-1}^1 + \lambda_k^1 \leq f'^+_k(\hat{y}_k)\ ,\qquad k = 1, \ldots, N-1$$

$$(6.20)\qquad c'^-_k(\hat{v}_k) \leq p_k^1 + p_k^2 - p_{k-1}^2 + \lambda_k^2 \leq c'^+_k(\hat{v}_k)\ ,\quad k = 1, \ldots, N-1$$

$$(6.21)\qquad c'^-_0(\hat{v}_0) \leq p_0^1 + p_0^2 + \lambda_0^3 \leq c'^+_0(\hat{v}_0)\qquad (^1)$$

We deduce from (6.18), (6.20) that:

$$(6.22)\quad \begin{cases} c'^-_k(\hat{v}_k) + s'^-_k(\hat{v}_k - \hat{v}_{k-1}) \leq p_k^1 + p_k^2 + \lambda_k^2 \leq c'^+_k(\hat{v}_k) + s'^+_k(\hat{v}_k - \hat{v}_{k-1}), \\ k = 1, \ldots, N-1 \end{cases}$$

Let also $1 \leq k < \ell \leq N-1$, we deduce from (6.19):

$$(6.23)\qquad \sum_{j=k+1}^{\ell} f'^-_j(\hat{y}_j) \leq p_\ell^1 - p_k^1 + \sum_{j=k+1}^{\ell} \lambda_j^1 \leq \sum_{j=k+1}^{\ell} f'^+_j(\hat{y}_j).$$

If $\hat{v}_k > 0,\ \hat{y}_{k+1} > 0, \ldots, \hat{y}_\ell > 0$, then $\lambda_k^2 = 0,\ \lambda_{k+1}^1 = \ldots = \lambda_\ell^1 = 0$, hence

$$\sum_{j=k+1}^{\ell} f'^-_j(\hat{y}_j) \leq p_\ell^1 - p_k^1 \leq c'^+_\ell(\hat{v}_\ell) + s'^+_\ell(\hat{v}_\ell - \hat{v}_{\ell-1}) - p_\ell^2 + p_k^2$$
$$- c'^-_k(\hat{v}_k) - s'^-_k(\hat{v}_k - \hat{v}_{k-1})$$

and from (6.18), it follows (5.40).

----

(1) We have used the fact that for a scalar convex function $\partial f(x) = [f'^-(x), f'^+(x)]$; $c'^-_k(0) = c^+_k(0)$, $f'^-_k(0) = f^+_k(0)$, the functions being continuous in 0 and extended adequately for negative arguments.

Extensions to $k = 0$, or $\ell = N$ are easily made using (6.21) and the conventions adopted in Theorem 5.2. Suppose now $\hat{v}_\ell > 0$, hence $\lambda_\ell^2 = 0$. From (6.23) we have

$$\sum_{j=k+1}^{\ell} f'^{+}_j(\hat{y}_j) \geq p_\ell^1 - p_k^1 \geq c'^{-}_\ell(\hat{v}_\ell) + s'^{-}_\ell(\hat{v}_\ell - \hat{v}_{\ell-1}) - p_\ell^2 + p_k^2$$
$$- c'^{+}_k(\hat{v}_k) - s'^{+}_k(\hat{v}_k - \hat{v}_{k-1})$$

and from (6.18) we deduce (5.41).

Let now $1 \leq k < \ell < N$, $\hat{v}_\ell > 0$, hence $\lambda_\ell^2 = 0$.

From (6.20) we deduce by summation :

$$(6.24) \qquad \sum_{j=k}^{\ell-1} c'^{-}_j(\hat{v}_j) \leq \sum_{j=k}^{\ell-1} p_j^1 + p_{\ell-1}^2 - p_{k-1}^2 + \sum_{j=k}^{\ell-1} \lambda_j^2 \leq \sum_{j=k}^{\ell-1} c'^{+}_j(\hat{v}_j)$$

but

$$(6.25) \qquad \sum_{j=k}^{\ell-1} p_j^1 = (\ell-k)\, p_\ell^1 - \sum_{j=k+1}^{\ell} (j-k)\,(p_j^1 - p_{j-1}^1)$$

hence

$$\sum_{j=k}^{\ell-1} c'^{+}_j(\hat{v}_j) \geq (\ell-k)\, p_\ell^1 - \sum_{j=k+1}^{\ell} (j-k)\,(p_j^1 - p_{j-1}^1) + p_{\ell-1}^2 - p_{k-1}^2$$
$$\geq (\ell-k)\, p_\ell^1 - \sum_{j=k+1}^{\ell} (j-k)\, f'^{+}_j(\hat{y}_j) + p_{\ell-1}^2 - p_{k-1}^2$$
$$\geq (\ell-k)\, c'^{-}_\ell(\hat{v}_\ell) + (\ell-k)\, p_{\ell-1}^2 - (\ell-k)\, p_\ell^2 + p_{\ell-1}^2 - p_{k-1}^2$$

and using again (6.18) we recover (5.42).

Let $1 \leq k < \ell < N$ and $\hat{v}_{k+1} > 0, \ldots, \hat{v}_\ell > 0$, hence $\lambda_{k+1}^2 = \ldots = \lambda_\ell^2 = 0$. The left inequality (6.24), with a shifting of 1, implies that

$$(6.26) \qquad \sum_{j=k+1}^{\ell} c'^{-}_j(\hat{v}_j) \leq \sum_{j=k+1}^{\ell} p_j^1 + p_\ell^2 - p_k^2$$

But we can write

$$(6.27) \qquad \sum_{j=k+1}^{\ell} p_j^1 = (\ell-k)\, p_k^1 + \sum_{j=k+1}^{\ell} (\ell+1-j)\,(p_j^1 - p_{j-1}^1)$$

therefore from (6.19) it follows that :

$$\sum_{j=k+1}^{\ell} c'^{-}_j(\hat{v}_j) \leq p_\ell^2 - p_k^2 + (\ell-k)\, p_k^1 + \sum_{j=k+1}^{\ell} (\ell+1-j)\, f'^{+}_j(\hat{y}_j)$$
$$\leq p_\ell^2 - p_k^2 + (\ell-k)\, c'^{+}_k(\hat{v}_k) - (\ell-k)\, p_k^2 + (\ell-k)\, p_{k-1}^2$$

$$+ \sum_{j=k+1}^{\ell} (\ell+1-j)\ f'^{+}_{j}(\hat{y}_j)$$

and from (6.18) we deduce (5.43).

Similar considerations hold for (5.44), (5.45). Details are left to the reader.

Remark 6.1

Relations (6.12), ..., (6.15) can also be viewied as a generalization of (3.25), with $p_k = c'_k(\hat{v}_k)$. □

VI - 3. QUADRATIC COST SMOOTHING MODELS

Theorem 6.1 can be applied to the following quadratic cost functionals

$$(6.28)\quad \begin{cases} f_j(x) = \frac{1}{2} M_j(x - \bar{y}_j) \, . \, (x - \bar{y}_j) \\ s_j(v) = \frac{1}{2} N_j(v - \bar{v}_j) \, . \, (v - \bar{v}_j) \end{cases}$$

where N_j is a positive definite symetric matrix, and M_j is a symetric non negative definite matrix. Then (6.13) leads to

$$(6.29)\quad \begin{cases} A_k^* p_k - p_{k-1} - C_k^* \lambda_k = M_k(\hat{y}_k - \bar{y}_k) \ , & k = 1, \ldots, N-1 \\ B_k^* p_k - D_k^* \lambda_k = N_k(\hat{v}_k - \bar{v}_k) \ , & k = 0, \ldots, N-1 \end{cases}$$

As a consequence we can write

$$(6.30)\quad \hat{v}_k - \bar{v}_k = N_k^{-1}(B_k^* p_k - D_k^* \lambda_k) \ , \qquad k = 0, \ldots, N-1$$

and p_k, $\hat{y}_k$, λ_k are defined by the following set of inequalities.

$$(6.31)\quad \begin{cases} y_{k+1} = A_k y_k + B_k N_k^{-1}(B_k^* p_k - D_k^* \lambda_k) + B_k \bar{v}_k - e_{k+1}, & k = 0, \ldots, N-1 \\ A_k^* p_k - p_{k-1} - C_k^* \lambda_k = M_k(\hat{y}_k - \bar{y}_k) \ , & k = 1, \ldots, N-1 \\ A_0^* p_0 - C_0^* \lambda_0 = M_0(\hat{y}_0 - \bar{y}_0) \ , \ p_{N-1} + C_N^* \lambda_N = 0 \ , & D_N^* \lambda_N = 0 \\ C_k \hat{y}_k + D_k N_k^{-1}(B_k^* p_k - D_k^* \lambda_k) + D_k \bar{v}_k - g_k \leq 0 \ , & k = 0, \ldots, N \\ \lambda_k \geq 0 \ , \ \lambda_k \, . \, [C_k \hat{y}_k + D_k N_k^{-1}(B_k^* p_k - D_k^* \lambda_k) + D_k \bar{v}_k - g_k] = 0 \ , & \\ & k = 0, \ldots, N \end{cases}$$

One can express all y_k, p_k as affine functions of $\lambda_0, \ldots, \lambda_{N-1}$ and y_0, p_{N-1}. It remains to solve a system of complementary conditions.

VII - SURVEY OF RESEARCH AND RESULTS INTERPRETATION

The convex production planning model corresponds to the case of decreasing returns to scale, which often results from situations where there are multiple limited production (or procurement) sources, at different unit costs, in each period. For example, there might be a linear production cost for production in regular hours, followed by a higher linear production cost for overtime or night-shift production, and a still higher linear cost for subcontracting. When the inventory cost is also linear the production planning model has the structure of the transportation model of linear programming. For this aspect, consult Bowman [1956], Elmaghraby [1957] and Manne [1957] ; these three papers contain also references to earlier works on the subject of production planning. When shortages are not allowed the optimal integer solution can be obtained by a simple forward algorithm :

1 - Satisfy demand in any current period t for t=1,...,N by the least cost sources.

2 - Adjust available capacities to initialize remaining capacities after step 1.

3 - Adjust cost sources by adding the cost of storing one unit during period t, for still available sources from periods t, t-1, t-2, ..., 0.

4 - Repeat steps 1, 2 and 3 for all subsequent periods t+1, ..., N.

However, it should be noted that the procedure must be modified when backorders are allowed. On the other hand, the transportation model does not apply to the production smoothing problem addressed in the last two sections V and VI, i.e. when there is a cost of changing the production rate from one period to the next, even if the adopted formulation allows piecewise linearity of the functionals.

A more general situation was first considered in a published article by Modigliani and Hohn [1955]. They assume a convex production cost function (which obviously implies no setup cost) and a linear unit holding cost, all cost functions being stationary. No backlogging or disposal is permitted, and their model is formulated in discrete time.

In the case of increasing marginal costs,production in anticipation of future peak demand may be economical, depending on inventory costs, especially during periods of slack activity. Modigliani and Hohn are able to develop a nice forward algorithm, together with a <u>weak</u> planning horizon procedure. In contrast to the <u>strong</u> planning horizon results derived for the concave cost models, a weak planning horizon is dependent upon partial knowledge of subsequent demand (cf. definitions given in Chapter I, § IV.4).

However, the Modigliani-Hohn forward procedure may lead to the determination of quasi-strong planning horizon when demand is highly seasonal with : a significant drop in demand immediatly after the peak, a decreasing trend overtime, and damped seasonality. For such a situation the length of the planning horizon is determined by the peak periods, and the forecast horizon generally occurs several periods after the peak period. This statement is not based on a formal proof but rather on computational experiments, and from a graphical exposition (a formal result is given by Kunreuther and Morton [1973]). Modigliani and Hohn proved as a key result, that the optimal cumulative production plan is bounded from above by the upper convex envelope of the cumulative demand schedule (when initial inventory is zero). Since backlogging is not allowed, obviously the optimal cumulative production plan is bounded from below by the cumulative demand itself. The upper convex envelope is the lower concave piecewise linear curve formed by a taut string which links the beginning and the ending points of the cumulative demand curve, and which contains no points below this curve. For a more formal definition consult Lippman et al. [1967-1, pp. 133-134]. The contact points of the upper convex envelope and the cumulative demand occur generally at peak demand periods. They also correspond to optimal cumulative production points, for which inventory is zero. The associated periods are the planning horizons which partitioned the total planning interval into subintervals within which the optimal plan is independent of demand and costs for other periods. For further discussion and controversy see Lee and Orr [1977, pp. 497-498].

Johnson [1955] relaxes the hypothesis of stationarity and is able to extend

Modigliani-Hohn results. The forward algorithm he proposes is very similar to the one derived in the linear case. It performs the same logic, merely by satisfying demand units sequentially in order of exigibility as cheaply as possible. The procedure also applies when there are upper bounds on the production rates and storage limits (see also on this matter Veinott [1964, p. 443] and our section II.3).

Generalization of Johnson's procedure to the case of a firm facing an elastic demand function, for which price and production decisions must be taken simultaneously, are due to Wagner [1960] and Richard [1971].

Alternative approaches for solving the model considered by Johnson are offered by Karush [1958], Klein [1957], and Wagner and Whitin [1958].

Central in the development of a <u>forward algorithm</u> is the production level monotonicity property with respect to demand (see our Lemma 2.1), i.e.

(i) the optimal production level in a given period i, $\hat{v}_i$, is a non-decreasing functions of the demand in any period (i.e. ξ_j for j = 1, ..., N) :

$$\xi_j^* \geq \xi_j, \forall j = 1, \ldots, N \text{ implies } \hat{v}_i^* \geq \hat{v}_i, \forall i = 0, \ldots, N-1$$

On the other hand, <u>weak planning horizon</u> results proceed from a similar monotonicity property which obtains for the cumulative quantities (see also our Lemma 2.1), i.e. :

(ii) the cumulative production is monotonic in the cumulative demand :

$$\underline{\xi_j^*} \geq \underline{\xi_j}, \forall j = 1, \ldots, N \text{ implies } \hat{v}_i^* \geq \hat{v}_i, \quad \forall i = 0, \ldots, N-1$$

Our Lemmas 2.2 and 2.3 propose new monotonicity properties with respect to production and holding costs. If for any period k_0 the production cost increases for all production levels, then the optimal production rate in that period k_0 does not increase, while the quantities produced in any other periods do not decrease . On the other hand, if for any period k_0 the holding cost and its left derivative increase for all quantities, then the optimal production levels for all previous periods to k_0 do not increase, while the optimal quantities produced for all subsequent periods, k_0 included, do not decrease.

Veinott [1964] proves that the two fundamental properties still hold for a quite general version of the production planning model where production and holding costs are convex and non-stationary functions, disposal and backlogging are permitted, and finally upper and lower limits are imposed on the amounts produced and stored. Veinott also extends the first monotonicity property (i) to include the bounds on production and storage (see also Veinott [1971]) :

(i') The optimal production level in a given period i, $\hat{v}_i$, is a non-decreasing function of :

a - the demand in any period, (i.e. ξ_j for j = 1, ..., N) property (i))

b - the upper and lower production capacity limits in the given period, and

c - the upper and lower storage limits in the given and all subsequent periods.

In addition : The optimal production level in a given period, $\hat{v}_i$, is a non-increasing function of :

d - the upper and lower limits in every other period j, $j \neq i$.

e - the upper and lower storage limits in any preceding period j, $j < i$.

Only when no backlogging is allowed Veinott does obtain a generalization of the Johnson's forward algorithm (cf. our section II.3). In order to justify his parametric programming procedure, Veinott makes the two restrictions that cost functions be piecewise linear, and that demands, upper and lower limits on production and storage be all integers. When backlogging is permitted, the possibilities for any period to carry backward production, from any indefinite future, must be considered unless some type of restrictions on the cost functions are made. For examples of such restrictions see Kunreuther [1971] considered thereafter, Lieber [1973] in the continuous convex case (see Chapter III), and conditions (4.21) and (4.34) in our theorem 4.3.

Kunreuther extends the analysis to the backlogging case. Inventory and backlogging costs are linear. The production cost is piecewise linear ; in each period production may be realized in regular time up to a certain limit, and in overtime at a premium beyond this limit. All costs are stationary. Kunreuther develops forecast horizon theorems and forward procedures to determine optimal production in the first period. In this model it is the linear cost structure which limits the number of periods that production needs to be carried forward or backward.

On the other hand Eppen and Gould [1968] consider the possibility of lost sales, with a shortage penalty function which is strictly convex. In this model the ost sales opportunity acts as an alternative source of production to meet future demands. The hypotheses made by Eppen and Gould are similar to those we stated in our section III.5., dealing with smooth cost functions and demands. Only conditions (3.14) is not required in their analysis. It is therefore not surprising that they obtain a quasi-strong planning horizon theorem, since only one strong planning horizon theorem was derived in our Chapter II (Theorem 3.4), and it was precisely for the case of smooth data. However, their planning horizon is not "strong" in the sense of the definition given in Chapter I, section IV.4, since the conditions involved in their result require the existence and knowledge of upper bounds on further demands. The use of Lagrangian techniques allows them to produce a nice foreward algorithm. Their proof shows evidence of the central role played by the complementary slackness conditions, and thus the constraints, in relation to the existence of a planning or a forecast horizon.

This feature is exploited by Lee and Orr [1977] to show that any forecast horizon depends critically on the existence of "bottle-neck" conditions originating either from a limited storage capacity, or the inventory non-negativity constraint (the only one considered by Modigliani-Hohn). Lee and Orr are thus able to extend the Modigliani-Hohn results to the case of a general convex cost structure, but only forecasting horizons obtain. It should be noted that Kuhn and Tucker complementary slackness contitions by themselves, do not allow to locate bottlenecks in advance. Information on demands for the entire problem horizon is thus needed before a bottleneck can be recognized with certainty. This rules out the possibility of finding strong planning horizons.
Other references include Charnes et al. [1955], Charnes and Cooper [1955], and Veinott and Wagner [1962].
The most recent generalizations of the convex cost planning model are due to Kleindorfer and Lieber [1979], Morton [1978] and ourselves.

Kleindorfer and Lieber utilize the extrapolation methodology developed by Lieber [1973] in a continuous time framework. They are thus able to show how to recognize weak planning horizons through computations for the finite horizon problem.

Morton extends the Kleindorfer-Lieber model to its infinite horizon form, and modifies their extrapolation procedure into a true forward algorithm which leads successively to improved bounds for the optimal first period decision. For the no-backlogging case he produces a weak planning horizon theorem when marginal costs of production do not increase with time (see also our Theorem 3.2 whose proof is mainly due to Morton). When backlogging is permitted exact forecast horizons are produced, but only for the special cases of monotonically increasing or decreasing demand, together with restrictive conditions on marginal costs (see our Theorem 4.3 which generalizes Morton result).

Sections III and IV of this chapter are greatly inspired from Morton with only slight generalizations. However, the results obtained for the special case of smooth cost functions and demands are new. In Theorem 3.4, we produce a strong planning horizon theorem provided some conditions on marginal costs.

Production planning models we have considered so far, only include direct production and inventory cost elements. If the models further account for adjustment costs associated with changes in the production levels or the production rates, they are referred to as production smoothing models. Since their cost structure is in general convex, they should be viewed as an extension of the convex production planning models. An exception, however, concerns the paper by Zangwill [1966] which considers a concave cost structure. But standard concave programming techniques do not apply any longer, since the derivative of the cost function is no more concave (it is in fact piecewise concave in Zangwill formulation). Thus ad hoc dynamic programming algorithms must be developed to identify dominant production plans.

Hoffman and Jacobs [1954] were the first to propose an alternative production smoothing model to Modigliani-Hohn formulation. They neglect production costs (or equivalently assume a constant unit production cost), and consider a linear holding cost and a proportional adjustment cost for positive changes in production levels. There is no backlogging and all costs are stationary. Within this framework they derive the same sort of weak planning horizon as in Modigliani-Hohn.

Other references which take only into consideration work force smoothing costs are Antosiewicz and Hoffman [1954], Bellman et al [1954], Karush and Vazsonyi [1957-1] and [1957-2].

Klein [1961] combines the insights of Modigliani-Hohn and Hoffman-Jacobs to produce a full convex production smoothing model. The cost structure includes a strictly convex, non decreasing production cost, a linear holding cost, and a piecewise linear smoothing cost for production rate changes of the form :

$$s(v_j, v_{j-1}) = \begin{cases} g(v_j - v_{j-1}) & \text{if } v_j \geq v_{j-1} \\ f(v_{j-1} - v_j) & \text{if } v_j < v_{j-1} \end{cases}$$

where v_j denotes the production rate in period j for j=1,...,N-1, and g,f are the unit adjustment costs with $g \geq f \geq 0$. Klein imposes rather stringent assumptions on initial and ending production levels (i.e. work force levels) and inventory levels :

$$v_0 = v_N = 0 \quad ,$$

and $$y_0 = y_N = 0$$

where y_j denotes the inventory level in period j. The first constraint supposes the problem starts with no workers in the factory, and in addition that the work force is fired at the end of the problem horizon. Contrary to previous models the minimum cost production plan of a smoothing problem may not imply a zero ending inventory. As a matter of fact, it may be cheaper to carry stocks than to modify substantially the production levels in the last periods.

Essentially Klein extends Modigliani-Hohn key finding concerning the upper bound of the cumulative production plan, and derive the same weak planning horizon results. As a consequence Klein shows that, when cumulative demand is concave, then the optimal production plan consists in producing in each period exactly the quantity demanded for the period. On the other hand, when cumulative demand is convex over the interval between two consecutive planning horizons, then the optimal cumulative production plan is also convex over the same interval. Klein finally extends the Modigliani-Hohn forward algorithm to different cost structures.

Vanthienen [1973] extends the model to the situation where price and production decisions are made simultaneously.

For the other treatments of the production smoothing problem in discrete time see Holt, Modigliani and Simon [1955], Holt, Modigliani and Muth [1956], Holt, Modigliani, Muth and Simon [1960], Hu and Prager [1960]. When the cost functions are strictly convex and quadratic, and when there are no bounds on inventory and production levels, then Holt, Modigliani and Muth show that the optimal production decision in any period is linear and of the form :

$$v_{j+1} = \alpha_j v_j + \beta_j y_j + \gamma_j$$

where α_j, β_j and γ_j are parameters expressed only in terms of the coefficients of the quadratic cost functions and future demand. In this case, the absence of inequality constraints on the variables leads to a simple and attractive decision policy, which allows to solve the production problem in a forward manner.

Application to the problem of batch ordering is addressed by Sobel [1969].

Klein's model is further generalized by Lippman et al [1967-1] for the usual single product situation and Yuan [1967] for a multi-product environment. Yuan's results are similar to those obtained by Lippman et al. when aggregate production is considered.

The most interesting generalization concerns the structure of the problem itself. By relaxing the restrictions imposed by Klein on the initial and ending levels of production and inventory, Lippman et al. can handle the situation where the production capacity (i.e. the work force) is under or over utilized. Indeed, they allow production in overtime up to a fixed proportion of normal capacity, and in some cases the amount of labor productively employed may be smaller than the total labor supply. But adjustment costs only apply to changes in the level of the work force, and are mainly associated with hiring and firing workers. As a consequence there is no smoothing cost incurred by the firm when production changes are met from modifications in the overtime schedule, and/or in the amount of idle capacity, as long as the work force is stable.

Cost functions are quite general, but the adjustment cost function is still piecewise linear and stationary. In addition, they impose that marginal costs of production do not increase from period to period. Furthermore, no backlogging is permitted.

The Modigliani-Hohn upper bound property for the optimal cumulative production plan still holds (adjustment being made for the initial inventory level). However, the planning horizon result is no more valid.

Lippman et al. analyze the properties of the optimal production plan in the two special situations where demand requirements (net of initial inventory) are either monotonic increasing or monotonic decreasing. In the first case they find that the optimal cumulative production schedule is convex, and that the decision variables, i.e. production at regular time, production in overtime, and capacity,are secularly increasing variables. When demand is declining over time, a firm never produces in excess of the current period requirements, and after the inventory level has vanished all the decision variables decrease with time.

Finally, Lippman et al. perform a sensitivity analysis of the optimal decision variables to the problem horizon length. They are thus able to derive some kind of horizon theorems which exhibit monotonic properties of the decision variables for period located far enough in the future.

In a second paper Lippman et al [1967-2] put the emphasis on the model resolution issue. They propose algorithms for finding an optimal production policy under the assumptions that costs are linear and demand requirements are either monotonic increasing or monotonic decreasing. In fact their formulation extends the approach by Johnson and Dantzing [1955].

Planning and forecast horizon results are obtained when it is further assumed that production costs are secularly non increasing (stationarity being a special case), and under various restrictions on the cost and structural parameters.

An other general approach to the production smoothing problem is given by Kunreuther and Morton [1973], [1974], which allows them to extend the model to backlogging and lost sales. Provided some restrictions on the cost functions and the cost parameters they derive "planning horizon for a forecast horizon" results (cf. Chapter I, section IV.4 for the definitions). The proof at this stage become quite involved. Essentially our section V.2 is a restatement of Kunreuther and Morton [1973]. This model is somewhat generalized in section V.3. The proof proceeds by analyzing truncated problems (of horizon smaller than the initial problem horizon), and producing sufficient conditions for a planning horizon to obtain.

Miller [1979] reexamines Kunreuther and Morton's model when the cost structure is linear (piecewise linear). In contrast with Kunreuther and Morton, Miller exploits the duality theory in a linear programming framework. He then extends somewhat Kunreuther and Morton's result,and derive a new planning horizon theorem. Both results are of the "planning horizon for a forecast horizon" type, but they differ concerning the underlying demand structure from which they originate. Kunreuther and Morton planning horizon (like Modigliani-Hohn's) occurs before periods of (seasonaly) low demand, and the forecast horizon conveys the information that demand has become low enough to ensure a reduction in the production rate ; decreasing production causes the problem to decompose. On the contrary, Miller's planning horizon occurs before periods of peak demand, and the associated forecast horizon tells us we have reached periods of high demand which may require an increase in the production rate ; in this case increasing production leads to the problem decomposition.

An alternative formulation is due to Kleindorfer and Lieber [1979] who use the extrapolation procedure developed by Lieber [1971] (see chapter III).

In section V.6 we extend the model by Lippman et al. using the general framework of optimal control theory. We derive the properties of an optimal production policy but no planning horizon theorem obtains. See also Kleindorfer et al. [1975]. The model is further specified for quadratic cost functions. Related works on this specific matter are due to Bergstrom and Smith [1980], Hwang et al. [1967] (see also Haussman et McClain [1971]).

REFERENCES

PRODUCTION PLANNING MODELS

BOWMAN E.H. [1956] , Production scheduling by the transportation method of linear programming, Operations Research, 4(1), pp. 100-103.

CHARNES A. - COOPER W.W. [1955] , Generalizations of the warehousing model , Operations Research Quarterly, 6, pp. 131-172.

CHARNES A. - COOPER W.W. - MELLON B. [1955] , A model for optimizing production by reference to cost surrogates, Econometrica, 23(3), pp. 307-323.

ELMAGHRABY S. [1957] , A note on production scheduling by the use of the transportation method, Operations Research, 16(3), pp. 565-566.

EPPEN G. - GOULD F.J. [1968] , A lagrangian approach to production problems, Operations Research, 16(4), pp. 819-829.

JOHNSON S.M. [1957] , Sequential production planning over time at minimum cost, Management Sciences, 3(4), pp. 435-437.

KARUSH W. [1958] , On a class of minimum cost problems, Management Science, 4(2), pp. 136-155.

KLEIN M. [1957] , Some production planning problems, Naval Research Logistics Quarterly, 4(4), pp. 269-286.

KLEINDORFER P.R. - LIEBER Z. [1979] , Algorithms and planning horizon results for production planning problems with separable costs, Operations Research, 27(5), pp. 874-887.

KUNREUTHER H. [1971] , Production planning algorithms for the inventory-overtime tradeoff, Operations Research, 19(7), pp. 1717-1729.

LEE D.R. - ORR D. [1977] , Further results on planning horizons in the production smoothing problem, Management Science, 23(5), pp. 490-498.

MANNE A.S. [1957] , A note on the Modigliani-Hohn production smoothing model, Management Science, 3(4), pp. 371-379.

MODIGLIANI F. - HOHN F.E. [1955] , Production planning overtime and the nature of the expectation and planning horizon, Econometrica, 23(1), pp. 46-66.

MORTON T.E. [1978] , Universal planning horizons for generalized convex production scheduling, Operations Research, 26(6), pp. 1046-1057.

RICHARD J. , Production planning over time : some further considerations, CORE Discussion paper 6930, Louvain - Belgium.

VEINOTT A.F.Jr. [1964] , Production planning with convex costs : A parametric study, Management Science, 10(3), pp. 441-460.

VEINOTT A.F.Jr. [1971] , Least d-majorized network flows with inventory and statistical application, Management Science, 17(9), pp. 547-567.

VEINOTT A.F.Jr. - WAGNER H.M. [1962] , Optimal capacity scheduling I and II, Operations Research, 10(4), pp. 518-546.

WAGNER H.M. [1960] , A postcript to "dynamic problems in the theory of the firm", Naval Research Logistics Quarterly, 7(1), pp. 7-12.

WAGNER H.M. - WITHIN T.M. [1958] , Dynamic problems in the theory of the firm, Naval Research Logistics Quarterly, 5(1), pp. 53-74.

PRODUCTION SMOOTHING MODELS

ANTOSIEWICZ H. - HOFFMAN A. [1954] , A remark on the smoothing problem, Management Science, 1(1), pp. 92-95.

BELLMAN R.E. - GLICKSBERG I. - GROSS O. [1954] , The theory of dynamic programming as applied to a smoothing problem, J. Soc. Indus. Appl. Math., 2, pp. 82-88.

BERGSTROM G.L. - SMITH B.E. [1970] , Multi-item production planning : an extension of the HMMS rules, Management Science, 16(10), B614-B629.

HAUSMANN F. - HESS S. [1960] , A linear programming approach to production and employment scheduling, Management Technology, 1(1), pp. 46-51.

HAUSMANN F. - McCLAIN J.L. [1971] , A note on the Bergstrom-Smith multi-item production planning model, Management Science, 17(11), pp. 783-785.

HOFFMAN A. - JACOBS W. [1954] , Smooth patterns of production, Management Science, 1(1) pp. 86-91.

HOLT C.C. - MODIGLIANI F. - SIMON H.A. [1955] , A linear decision rule for production and employment scheduling, Management Science, 2(2), pp. 1-30.

HOLT C.C. - MODIGLIANI F. - MUTH J. [1956] , Derivation of a linear decision rule for production and employment, Management Science, 2(3), pp. 159-177.

HOLT C.C. - MODIGLIANI F. - MUTH J. - SIMON M.A. [1960] , Planning production, inventories, and work force, (Prentice Hall, Englewood Cliffs - N.J.).

HU T.C. - PRAGER W. [1959] , Network analysis of production smoothing, Naval Research Logistics Quarterly, 6(1), pp. 17-24.

HWANG C.L. - FAN L.T. - ERICKSON L.E. [1967] , Optimal production planning by the maximum principle, Management Science, 13(9), pp. 751-755.

JOHNSON S. - DANTZIG G. [1955] , A production smoothing problem, Proceedings of the Second Symposium on Linear Programming I, (Washington, D.C.), pp. 151-176.

KARUSH W. - VAZSONYI A. [1957-a] , Mathematical programming and service scheduling, Management Science, 3(2), pp. 140-148.

KARUSH W. - VAZSONYI A. [1957-b] , Mathematical programming and employment scheduling, Naval Research Logistics Quarterly, 4(3), pp. 297-320.

KLEIN M. [1961] , On production smoothing, Management Science, 7(3), pp. 286-293.

KLEINDORFER P.R. - KRIEBEL C.H. - THOMPSON G.L. - KLEINDORFER G.B. [1975] , Discrete optimal control of production plans, Management Science, 22(3), pp. 261-273.

KLEINDORFER P.R.-LIEBER Z. [1979] , Algorithms and planning horizon results for production planning problems with separable costs, Operations Research, 27(5), pp. 874-887.

KUNREUTHER H.C. - MORTON T.E. [1973] , Planning horizons for production smoothing with deterministic demands, I. All demand met from regular production, Management Science, 20(1), pp. 110-125.

KUNREUTHER H.C. - MORTON T.E. [1974] , General planning horizons for production smoothing with deterministic demands, II Extensions to overtime, undertime and backlogging,Management Science, 20(7), pp. 1037-1046.

LIPPMAN S.A. - ROLFE A.J. - WAGNER H.M. - YUAN J.S.C. [1967-1] , Optimal production scheduling and employment smoothing with deterministic demands,Management Science 14(3), pp. 127-158.

LIPPMAN S.A. - ROLFE A.J. - WAGNER H.M. - YUAN J.S.C. [1967-2] , Algorithms for optimal production scheduling and employment smoothing, Operations Research, 15(6), pp.

McGARRAH R.E. [1956] , Production planning, Journal of Industrial Engineering, 7(6), pp. 263-271.

MILLER L.W. [1979] , Using linear programming to derive planning horizons for a production smoothing problem , Management Science, 25(12), pp. 1232-1244.

O'MALLEY R.S. - ELMAGHRABY S.E. - JESKE J.W.Jr. [1966] , An operational system for smoothing batch-type production, Management Science, 12(10), B433-B449.

ORR D. [1962] , A random walk production inventory policy : rationale and implementation, Management Science, 9(1), pp. 108-122.

ROCKAFELLAR R.T. [1970] , Convex analysis (Princeton University Press).

SILVER E.A. [1967] , A tutorial on production smoothing and work force balancing, Operations Research, 15(6), pp. 985-1010.

SOBEL M.J. [1969] , Smoothing start-up and shut-down costs in sequential production, Operations Research, 17(1), pp. 133-144.

VANTHIENEN L.G. [1973] , A simultaneous price-production decision making model with adjustment cost, Center for Mathematical Studies in Business and Economics, Report n° 7307, University of Chicago.

YUAN J.S.C. [1967] , Algorithms and multi-product model in production scheduling and employment smoothing, Technical Report n° 22, Stanford University.

ZANGWILL W.I. [1966] , Production smoothing of economic lot sizes with non-decreasing requirements, Management Science, 13(3), pp. 191-209.

CHAPTER III

PRODUCTION PLANNING MODELS FOR DETERMINISTIC DEMANDS

CONTINUOUS TIME FORMULATIONS

INTRODUCTION

This chapter proposes continuous time formulations of the production planning models for deterministic demands with concave and convex costs, as developed in hapter I and II respectively. While we aim at deriving comparable results to those obtained in the two previous chapters, the transposition is not trivial.

There are two different options in modelling, either the "continuous control" or the "impulse control".

By continuous control we mean that production is continuous. The control is a rate of production, and consequently the inventory level varies continuously. By impulse control we mean that production is run by batches. Orders are placed at a sequence of times (at must countable), which is a decision variable unlike in previous chapters. In this case the trajectory evolves by jumps, and in between two consecutive jumps the level of inventory is depleted according to the rate of demand.

In continuous time this distinction is essential. Chapter II results can only be transposed in the continuous control formulation, while the transposition of Chapter I results is only obtained with the impulse control formulation.

As a matter of fact, in the continuous control formulation we use the necessary conditions for optimality, or the maximum principle of Pontryagin. Although this does not rule out completely concavity assumptions, the most interesting results are derived in the case of convex costs. The derivations are then similar to those developed in Chapter II.

In the impulse control formulation, we use methods similar to those carried in Chapter I, and which rely strongly on concavity arguments and Dynamic Programming.

However, the Dynamic Programming relations are not a straightforward extension of the discrete time case. In continuous time Dynamic Programming does not lead to an equation, but to a system of inequalities with complementary conditions (like in the Kuhn-Tucker theory of mathematical programming). Once this is established we can derive most of the properties which were established in the discrete time case for concave costs.

The theory of impulse control developed in the second part of this chapter is a particular case of a general theory for which we refer to Bensoussan and Lions [1982].

Although limited, some mathematical background is requested for reading this chapter. It concerns more precisely the Lebesgue measure and a sufficiently general form of the maximum principle, as well as some notions of Functional Analysis. The reader will find in the mathematical appendix all what is necessary to follow the derivations of this chapter.

FIRST PART : CONTINUOUS CONTROL FORMULATION

I - THE CONCAVE COST MODEL

Synopsis

This section extends the developements of Chapter I, to a continuous time environment. All cost functions are thus concave and non decreasing. But unlike in Chapter I, for the discrete time formulation, admissible values of the control are bounded from above, except when indicated. This upper bound increases the number of situations where an optimal solution exists. Some of the following results have been presented by Bensoussan and Proth [1983] and Proth [1981].

I - 1. NOTATION AND ASSUMPTIONS

Time is a continuous variable : $t \in [0,T]$ where T denotes the horizon. The demand is defined by :

$$\xi(t) \geq 0, \text{ measurable with } \int_0^T \xi(t)dt < \infty. \tag{1.1}$$

Let v(t) be the production rate with

$$\begin{cases} v(t) \text{ measurable} \\ 0 \leq v(t) \leq M \end{cases} \tag{1.2}$$

In (1.2), M is a given upper bound, and in some cases it will be taken equal to $+\infty$.

The inventory at time t is denoted by y(t) and is defined by :

$$\begin{cases} \dfrac{dy}{dt} = v(t) - \xi(t) \quad , \qquad \forall\ t \in (s,T) \\ y(s) = x \end{cases} \tag{1.3}$$

More precisely y(t) is the following continuous function, conditional on the initial inventory level x and the initial time instant s :

$$y(t) = x + \int_s^t v(\lambda)d\lambda - \int_s^t \xi(\lambda)d\lambda \tag{1.4}$$

To emphasize the dependence of y(t) on the pair (x,s), we write when necessary, $y_{sx}(t)$. A control v(t) at time t satisfying (1.2) is called <u>admissible</u> when the inventory level at the same instant t satisfies the condition :

$$y(t) \geq 0. \tag{1.5}$$

The production cost function is denoted :

$$\begin{cases} c(t;v) : [0,T] \times R^+ \to R^+ \text{ with the following properties :} \\ \quad .\ \text{concave, non decreasing in } v, \\ \quad .\ \int_0^T c(t;v)dt < \infty,\ \forall v \\ \quad .\ \text{a.e.t,} \quad c(t;v) = \tilde{c}(t;v)\ \forall v, \text{ where } \tilde{c} \text{ is a Borel function ,} \\ \quad .\ c(t;v) \neq \text{const. on } \{v > 0\}. \end{cases} \tag{1.6}$$

The inventory cost function is denoted :

$$(1.7)\quad \begin{cases} f(t;x) : [0,T] \times R^{+} \to R^{+} \text{ with the following properties :} \\ .\ \text{concave, non decreasing in } x, \\ .\ \int_0^T f(t;x)dt < \infty, \quad \forall x, \\ .\ \text{a.e. } t\,,\ f(t;x) = \tilde{f}(t;x) \quad \forall x, \text{ where } \tilde{f} \text{ is a Borel function.} \end{cases}$$

From the second conditions in (1.6), (1.7) it follows that $c(t;v(t))$ is a measurable function.

Therefore we may define, for any admissible control, the objective function to minimize :

$$(1.8)\qquad J_{s,x}(v(.)) = \int_s^T [c(t;v(t)) + f(t;z(t))]dt$$

which is well defined, bounded from above if $M < \infty$.

It is then clear that a necessary condition for an optimal control to exist for any initial value x is :

$$(1.9)\qquad M(t - s) - \int_s^t \xi(\lambda)d\lambda \geq 0 \quad, \forall t \in [s,T], \qquad \text{a.e.}$$

In addition if we have

$$(1.10)\qquad x \geq \int_s^T \xi(t)dt$$

then $v(t) = 0$ is an optimal control. This follows from the fact that $J(v(.))$ is a non decreasing function of the control in the following sense :

$$(1.11)\qquad \text{if } v_1(t) \leq v_2(t) \text{ a.e. then } J(v_1(.)) \leq J(v_2(.))$$

The existence proof of optimal controls in the continuous control formulation for the concave cost model is still an open question. In the following we derive properties of the optimal controls, provided they exist.

I - 2. PROPERTIES OF THE OPTIMAL CONTROLS

For simplicity assume in this paragraph that $s = 0$. An optimal control is denoted by $u(.)$ and the corresponding inventory trajectory by $y(.)$.

Lemma 1.1

Assume (1.6), (1.7) and

$$(1.12)\qquad x < \int_0^T \xi(t)dt$$

If there exists an optimal control, then there is one satisfying :

(1.13) $y(T) = 0$

<u>Proof</u>

Assume that (1.13) is not satisfied. Let us consider the function

$$L(t) = y(t) - \int_t^T \xi(\lambda)d\lambda$$

then, given $y(T) > 0$ and assumption (1.12), we obtain respectively :

$$L(T) > 0, \; L(0) = 0$$

Since L is a continuous function, there exists t_0 such that :

$$L(t_0) = 0$$

We then take

$$\tilde{u}(t) = \begin{cases} u(t) \;, & t \in (0, t_0) \\ 0 \;, & t \in (t_0, T). \end{cases}$$

It follows that the inventory trajectory associated to this control is :

$$\tilde{y}(t) = \begin{cases} y(t) \;, & t \in [0, t_0] \\ y(t_0) - \int_{t_0}^{t} \xi(\lambda)d\lambda, & t \in [t_0, T] \end{cases}$$

and

$$y(t_0) - \int_{t_0}^{t} \xi(\lambda)d\lambda = \int_t^T \xi(\lambda)d\lambda \geq 0.$$

This implies that $\tilde{u}$ is admissible. Moreover $\tilde{y}(T) = 0$. Since $\tilde{u} \leq u$, $J(\tilde{u}(.)) \leq J(u(.))$ Hence $\tilde{u}$ is optimal and satisfies (1.13). □

<u>Theorem 1.1</u>

Assume (1.6), (1.7), and

(1.14) $v \to c(t;v)$ or $x \to f(t;x)$ is strictly concave a.e.t

Then an optimal control satisfies the following condition

(1.15) $y(t).u(t)[M - u(t)] = 0$ a.e.t.

<u>Proof</u>

Without loss of generality, we may assume (1.12). Otherwise the optimal control is 0 and (1.15) is satisfied.

It follows from Lemma 1.1 that any optimal policy satisfies (1.13). Indeed, the strict concavity condition in the proof of Lemma 1.1 implies that $J(\tilde{u}(.)) < J(u(.))$ which contradicts the optimality of $u(.)$.

Denote :

(1.16) $\phi(s) = \text{Min}\,[u(s),\ M - u(s)].$

Select :

. t_0 such that $y(t_0) > 0$ ($t_0 < T$), and

. δ such that :

(1.17) $$y(t_0) - \int_{t_0}^{t_0+\delta} \xi(s)ds = 0$$

Such δ, $t_0+\delta \le T$ exists since by (1.13),

$$y(t_0) - \int_{t_0}^{T} \xi(s)ds \le 0$$

and $y(t_0) > 0$. We choose δ such that $t_0+\delta$ is the largest value for which (1.17) is satisfied (if $t_0+\delta < T$, then $y(t_0) - \int_{t_0}^{\theta} \xi(s)ds < 0$ for $\theta \in [t_0+\delta, T]$).

Next, consider δ_0 such that $\delta_0 \le \delta$, and

(1.18) $$\int_{t_0}^{t_0+\delta_0} \phi(s)ds = \frac{1}{2} \int_{t_0}^{t_0+\delta} \phi(s)ds.$$

1) If

(1.19) $$\int_{t_0}^{t_0+\delta} \phi(s)ds > 0$$

then $\delta_0 < \delta$ exists and is unique, provided we choose for δ_0 the largest number such that (1.18) holds. If the integral (1.19) vanishes then we take $\delta_0 = \delta$.

Let us consider the following controls :

(1.20) $$\begin{cases} u_a(t) = \begin{cases} u(t) & \text{on } (0, t_0), (t_0+\delta, T) \\ u(t) + \phi(t) & \text{on } (t_0, t_0+\delta_0) \\ u(t) - \phi(t) & \text{on } (t_0+\delta_0, t_0+\delta) \end{cases} \\ \\ u_b(t) = \begin{cases} u(t) & \text{on } (0, t_0), (t_0+\delta, T) \\ u(t) - \phi(t) & \text{on } (t_0, t_0+\delta_0) \\ u(t) + \phi(t) & \text{on } (t_0+\delta_0, t_o+\delta) \end{cases} \end{cases}$$

Then we have

(1.21) $0 \le u_a(t) \le M, \quad 0 \le u_b(t) \le M.$

Consider next the corresponding inventory trajectories $y_a(t)$, $y_b(t)$.

$$
(1.22)\quad \begin{cases} y_a(t) = y(t) & \text{on } [0,\ t_o] \\ y_a(t) = y(t) + \int_{t_0}^{t} \phi(s)ds & \text{on } [t_0,\ t_o+\delta_o] \\ y_a(t) = y(t) + \int_{t_0}^{t_0+\delta_0} \phi(s)ds - \int_{t_0+\delta_0}^{t} \phi(s)ds & \text{on } [t_0+\delta_0,\ t_o+\delta] \\ y_a(t) = y(t) & \text{on } [t_0+\delta,\ T] \end{cases}
$$

The last property of (1.22) follows from the fact that

$$
\int_{t_0}^{t_0+\delta_0} \phi(s)ds = \int_{t_0+\delta_0}^{t_0+\delta} \phi(s)ds
$$

which is a consequence of (1.18). Clearly $y_a(t) \geq 0$. Consider now $y_b(t)$, defined by

$$
(1.23)\quad \begin{cases} y_b(t) = y(t) & \text{on } [0,\ t_o] \\ y_b(t) = y(t) - \int_{t_0}^{t} \phi(s)ds & \text{on } [t_0,\ t_o+\delta_o] \\ y_b(t) = y(t) - \int_{t_0}^{t_0+\delta_0} \phi(s)ds + \int_{t_0+\delta_0}^{t} \phi(s)ds & \text{on } [t_0+\delta_0,\ t_o+\delta] \\ y_b(t) = y(t) & \text{on } [t_0+\delta,\ T] \end{cases}
$$

Then, for $t \in [t_0,\ t_o+\delta_o]$

$$
\begin{aligned} y_b(t) &= y(t_0) + \int_{t_0}^{t} (u - \phi)(s)ds - \int_{t_0}^{t} \xi(s)ds \\ &\geq y(t_0) - \int_{t_0}^{t} \xi(s)ds \geq y(t_0) - \int_{t_0}^{t_0+\delta} \xi(s)ds = 0 \end{aligned}
$$

Similarly for $t \in [t_0+\delta_0,\ t_o+\delta]$

$$
\begin{aligned} y_b(t) &= y(t_0) + \int_{t_0}^{t_0+\delta_0} (u - \phi)(s)ds - \int_{t_0}^{t} \xi(s)ds + \int_{t_0+\delta_0}^{t} (u + \phi)(s)ds \\ &\geq y(t_0) - \int_{t_0}^{t_0+\delta} \xi(s)ds = 0 \end{aligned}
$$

Hence u_a, u_b, are both admissible controls.

Note that if (1.19) holds, then :

$$(1.24)\quad \begin{cases} u_a, u_b \neq u \text{ on a set of positive measure on } (t_o, t_o+\delta_o) \\ y_a, y_b \neq y \text{ on a set of positive measure on } (t_o, t_o+\delta_o) \end{cases}$$

We obtain next

$$(1.25)\quad \begin{cases} J(u_a(.)) = J(u(.)) + \int_{t_o}^{t_o+\delta_o} [c(t ; u(t) + \phi(t)) - c(t ; u(t)) \\ \quad + f(t ; y(t) + \int_{t_o}^{t} \phi(s)ds) - f(t ; y(t))]dt \\ \quad + \int_{t_o+\delta_o}^{t_o+\delta} [c(t ; u(t) - \phi(t)) - c(t ; u(t)) \\ \quad + f(t ; y(t) + \int_{t_o}^{t_o+\delta_o} \phi(s)ds - \int_{t_o+\delta_o}^{t} \phi(s)ds) - f(t ; y(t))]dt \end{cases}$$

$$(1.26)\quad \begin{cases} J(u_b(.)) = J(u(.)) + \int_{t_o}^{t_o+\delta_o} [c(t ; u(t) - \phi(t)) - c(t ; u(t)) \\ \quad + f(t ; y(t) - \int_{t_o}^{t} \phi(s)ds) - f(t ; y(t))]dt \\ \quad + \int_{t_o+\delta_o}^{t_o+\delta} [c(t ; u(t) + \phi(t)) - c(t ; u(t)) \\ \quad + f(t ; y(t) - \int_{t_o}^{t_o+\delta_o} \phi(s)ds + \int_{t_o+\delta_o}^{t} \phi(s)ds) - f(t ; y(t))]dt \end{cases}$$

Assume that (1.19) holds. By the concavity assumptions we have :

$$(1.27)\quad \begin{cases} c(t ; u(t) + \phi(t)) + c(t ; u(t) - \phi(t)) \leq 2\, c(t ; u(t)) \\ f(t ; y(t) + \int_{t_o}^{t} \phi(s)ds) + f(t ; y(t) - \int_{t_o}^{t} \phi(s)ds) \leq 2\, f(t ; y(t)) \\ f(t ; y(t) + \int_{t_o}^{t_o+\delta_o} \phi(s)ds - \int_{t_o+\delta_o}^{t} \phi(s)ds) \\ \quad + f(t ; y(t) - \int_{t_o}^{t_o+\delta_o} \phi(s)ds + \int_{t_o+\delta_o}^{t} \phi(s)ds) \leq 2f(t;y(t)) \\ \text{a.e. } t. \end{cases}$$

Moreover, one of the first two inequalities is strict on a set of points t on $(t_o, t_o+\delta_o)$ which has a positive Lebesgue measure. Therefore we have :

$$J(u_a(.)) + J(u_b(.)) < 2\, J(u(.))$$

which contradicts the optimality conditions for u(.) :

$$J(u_a(.)) \geq J(u(.)),\ J(u_b(.)) \geq J(u(.))$$

Therefore we have proved that (1.19) does not hold.

2) We can then assert that :

$$(1.28) \qquad \begin{cases} y(t) \int_t^{t+\delta} \phi(s)ds = 0 & \forall\ t \text{ in } [0,T] \text{ , and } \delta \text{ such that} \\ y(t) - \int_t^{t+\delta} \xi(s)ds \geq 0. \end{cases}$$

Hence on the set $I = \{t \mid y(t) > 0\}$, we have

$$\int_t^{t+\delta} \phi(s)ds = 0\ \forall\ \ \delta \leq \delta(t),\ \ \delta(t) > 0\ \ (t+\delta(t) \leq T).$$

Therefore

$$\frac{1}{\delta} \int_t^{t+\delta} \phi(s)ds \to 0 \text{ as } \ \delta \to 0,\ \forall t \in I.$$

However, a.e. in I

$$\frac{1}{\delta} \int_t^{t+\delta} \phi(s)ds \to \phi(t)$$

hence $\phi(t) = 0$ a.e. in I, which completes the proof of the desired result (1.15).□

Remark 1.1

Property (1.15) is better known in the control theory litterature as "bang-bang control". It is the continuous time version of the Wagner-Whithin Theorem (cf. Theorem 3.3, Chapter I). The result holds even when $M = +\infty$. □

Remark 1.2

On the set of points $\bar{I} = \{t \mid y(t) = 0\}$, one has $u(t) = \xi(t)$ a.e. This follows from a result of measure theory, which asserts that on I, one has $\frac{dy}{dt} = 0$ a.e. □

Remark 1.3

The assumption of strict concavity is probably unnecessary in the statement of Theorem 1.1. But, if we had to remove this constraint it would no longer be possible to argue by contradiction. It would also be difficult to develop a proof which suppose to add a regularizing term which is strictly concave, and let it tend to zero. As a matter of fact the cost function being not lower semi-continuous, the convergence of the regularized control could not be proven. □

I - 3. DYNAMIC PROGRAMMING

Let us define for a problem of horizon T :

(1.29) $$\phi(s,x) = \underset{v(.)}{\mathrm{Inf}} \ J_{s,x}(v(.))$$

where $J_{s,x}(v(.))$ was defined in (1.8). Denote by $V_{s,x}$ the set of admissible controls i.e. those controls $v(.) \in V_{s,x}$ satisfying (1.2) and (1.5). This set depends indeed on the pair (s,x).

We remark that :

(1.30) $$z_{s,x}(\theta) = z_{t,z_{s,x}(t)}(\theta), \text{ for } s \le t \le \theta$$

and

(1.31) $$\begin{cases} J_{s,x}(v(.)) = \int_s^t [c(\lambda, v(\lambda)) + f(\lambda \ ; z_{s,x}(\lambda))]d\lambda \\ \\ + \int_t^T [c(\lambda, v(\lambda)) + f(\lambda \ ; z_{t,z_{s,x}(t)}(\lambda))]d\lambda \end{cases}$$

We then decompose $v(.)$ as a pair $(v_1(.), v_2(.))$, where $v_1(.) \in V_{s,x}$ and $v_2(.) \in V_{t,z_{s,x}(t)}$ (this second set depends on $v_1(.)$ through $z_{s,x}(t)$).

We obtain :

$$J_{s,x}(v_1(.), v_2(.)) = \int_s^t [c(\lambda, v_1(\lambda)) + f(\lambda \ ; z_{s,x}(\lambda))]d\lambda + J_{t,z_{s,x}(t)}(v_2(.))$$

Since $v_1(.)$ and $v_2(.)$ can be chosen independently, we infer that $\phi(s,x)$ satisfies the following integral equation

(1.32) $$\begin{cases} \phi(s,x) = \underset{v(.)\in V_{s,x}}{\mathrm{Inf}} \ \{ \int_s^t [c(\lambda, v(\lambda)) + f(\lambda, z_{s,x}(\lambda))]d\lambda + \phi(t,z_{s,x}(t))\}, \\ \\ \forall t \in [s,T] \end{cases}$$

with the initial condition

(1.33) $$\phi(T, x) = 0$$ [1]

Theorem 1.2 specifies regularity properties of ϕ with respect to the parameters s and x.

<u>Theorem 1.2</u>

Assume that :

(1.34)
- . $f(t,x)$ is <u>continuous</u>, $f \ge 0$; $\xi(t)$ is <u>right continuous</u>
- . $c(t,v)$ is <u>continuous</u> in t, <u>uniformly with respect to</u> v, <u>concave in</u> v, <u>non decreasing</u>, $c \ge 0$.

---

[1] Note that $u(s, x)$ is defined on $[0,T] \times R^+$

Assume further that there exists an optimal control u(.) for $J(v(.)) = J_{0,x_0}(v(.))$ with y(.) the corresponding inventory trajectory. [1]

At every instant $t \in (0,T)$, if $\phi(s,x)$ is continuously differentiable in (t, y(t)), then the optimal control u(t) satisfies the condition :

$$(1.35)\quad \begin{cases} \text{if } y(t) > 0, \text{ and } u(.) \text{ is right continuous in } t, \text{ then the concave func-} \\ \text{tion } c(t\ ;\ v) + \frac{\partial\phi}{\partial x}(t, y(t))v \text{ reaches its minimum in } v \text{ over } 0, M \text{ for} \\ u(t). \end{cases}$$

Therefore u(t) = 0 or M.

Proof

(i) Since u(.) is optimal, we have

$$(1.36)\qquad \phi(t, y(t)) = \int_t^{t+\delta} [c(\lambda, u(\lambda)) + f(\lambda, y(\lambda))]d\lambda + \phi(t+\delta, y(t+\delta))$$

Note that

$$\phi(t+\delta, y(t+\delta)) = \phi[t+\delta, y(t) + \delta(u(t) - \xi(t)) + \int_t^{t+\delta} (u(s) - u(t))ds$$
$$- \int_t^{t+\delta} (\xi(s) - \xi(t))ds]$$

But

$$\sup_{t\le s\le t+\delta} |u(s) - u(t)| \to 0 \text{ as } \delta \to 0$$

$$\sup_{t\le s\le t+\delta} |\xi(s) - \xi(t)| \to 0 \text{ as } \delta \to 0$$

It follows that

$$(1.37)\quad \begin{cases} \frac{1}{\delta}\ |\phi(t+\delta, y(t+\delta)) - \phi(t, y(t)) - \delta[\frac{\partial\phi}{\partial s}(t, y(t)) \\ + \frac{\partial\phi}{\partial x}(t, y(t))(u(t) - \xi(t))]| \to 0, \text{ as } \delta \to 0 \end{cases}$$

If u(t) > 0, then $c(\lambda, u(\lambda))$ is continuous at t. From (1.36), by an easy argument using (1.37), and the continuity property of $c(\lambda, v(\lambda))$ at t, we obtain

$$\frac{\partial\phi}{\partial s}(t, y(t)) + \frac{\partial\phi}{\partial x}(t, y(t))(u(t) - \xi(t)) + c(t\ ;\ u(t)) + f(t\ ;\ y(t)) = 0$$

If u(t) = 0 then $c(t\ ;\ u(t)) \le c(t\ ;\ u(\lambda))$ for $\lambda \in [t, t+\delta]$. Hence in all cases we can write :

$$(1.38)\quad \begin{cases} \frac{\partial\phi}{\partial s}(t\ ;\ y(t)) + \frac{\partial\phi}{\partial x}(t\ ;\ y(t))(u(t) - \xi(t)) + c(t\ ;\ u(t)) + \\ \qquad + f(t\ ;\ y(t)) \le 0 \end{cases}$$

---

[1] For simplicity we select as initial conditions : $(0, x_0)$.

(ii) On the other hand, from (1.32) we have :

$$(1.39)\quad \begin{cases} \phi(t\ ;\ y(t)) \leq \int_t^{t+\delta} [c(\lambda\ ;\ v) + f(\lambda\ ;\ y(t) + (\lambda-t)v - \int_t^{\lambda} \xi ds)]d\lambda \\ \qquad + \phi(t+\delta\ ;\ y(t) + \delta v - \int_t^{t+\delta} \xi ds) \end{cases}$$

Reasoning as above we infer that :

$$(1.40)\quad \begin{cases} \frac{\partial\phi}{\partial s}(t\ ;\ y(t)) + \frac{\partial\phi}{\partial x}(t\ ;\ y(t))(v - \xi(t)) + c(t\ ;\ v) \\ \qquad + f(t\ ;\ y(t)) \geq 0\ ,\ \forall v \in [0,M]. \end{cases}$$

The fact that we can take any v in [0,M] in (1.40) is a consequence of $y(t) > 0$.

Indeed $y(t) + \delta v - \int_t^{t+\delta} \xi ds$ is larger than or equal to 0 ; at least for δ small enough, which is sufficient to obtain (1.40). The desired result (1.35) follows from the comparison of (1.38) and (1.40). □

Remark 1.4

From theorem 1.2 we recover (1.15), under different assumptions. Concavity of the inventory cost function f is not necessary, but we need rather stringent regularity assumptions. Moreover, we obtain a feedback rule for the optimal control which is quite precise. □

I - 4. THE CASE OF BACKLOGGING

When backlogging is permitted there is no more constraint on the sign of the inventory level z(t), and the cost function to minimize is :

$$(1.41)\quad J_{s,x}(v(.)) = \int_s^T [c(t\ ;\ v(t)) + f(t\ ;\ z(t))]dt$$

where the production cost function c(t ; v) satisfies the properties (1.6),and f(t ; x) denotes the shortage cost, or the inventory cost, when x is negative or positive respectively: f(t ; x) has the following properties :

(1.42)
- . $f(t\ ;\ x) : [0,T] \times R^- \to R^+$ denotes the shortage cost which is concave and non increasing ;
- . $f(t,x) : [0,T] \times R^+ \to R^+$ denotes the inventory cost which is concave and non decreasing ;
- . a.e.t, $f(t\ ;\ x) = \tilde{f}(t\ ;\ x)$ $\forall x$ positive or negative where $\tilde{f}$ is a Borel function.

It is clear that

$$(1.43)\quad \text{if } x \geq \int_0^T \xi(t)dt, \text{ then 0 is an optimal control.}$$

Lemma 1.2

Assume (1.6), (1.42) and

(1.44) $$x < \int_0^T \xi(t)dt.$$

Then if there exists an optimal control, there exists one satisfying

(1.45) $$y(T) \le 0$$

Proof

If (1.45) is not satisfied then $y(T) > 0$. Then consider

$$L(t) = y(t) - \int_t^T \xi(\lambda)d\lambda$$

which implies

$$L(T) > 0, \; L(0) < 0.$$

Let t_0 such that $L(t_0) = 0$, $L(t) \ge 0$, $t \in [t_0, T]$

Then take

$$\tilde{u}(t) = \begin{cases} u(t), & t \in (0, t_0) \\ 0, & t \in (t_0, T) \end{cases}$$

it follows that

$$\tilde{y}(t) = \begin{cases} y(t) & , t \in [0, t_0] \\ y(t_0) - \int_{t_0}^{t} \xi(\lambda)d\lambda \ge 0, & t \in [t_0, T] \end{cases}$$

$$\tilde{y}(t) = 0$$

We notice that

$$0 \le \tilde{y}(t) \le y(t), \; t \in [t_0, T]$$

hence

$$J(\tilde{u}(.)) \le J(u(.))$$

which proves that $\tilde{u}(.)$ is optimal and satisfies (1.45). □

If c is strictly concave or f is strictly concave on positive x, then any optimal control satisfies necessarily (1.45). This follows from the proof of Lemma 1.2, since then $J(\tilde{u}(.)) < J(u(.))$. □

Theorem 1.3

Assume (1.6), (1.42) and that

(1.46) $$\begin{cases} v \to c(t \,;\, v) \text{ is strictly concave, or} \\ x \to f(t \,;\, x) \text{ is strictly concave for } x \ge 0, \text{ and for } x \le 0. \end{cases}$$

Then an optimal control $u(t)$ is of "bang bang" type, i.e., satisfies

$$(1.47) \qquad y(t)\, u(t)\, [M - u(t)] = 0 \quad \text{a.e.}$$

Proof

Without loss of generality, assume (1.44) and (1.45). (cf. Theorem 1.1). Let us set :

$$(1.48) \qquad \phi(s) = \mathrm{Min}\, [u(s), M - u(s)].$$

Let t_o such that $y(t_o) \neq 0$. Assume for example that $y(t_o) > 0$. Then we construct the controls $u_a(t)$ and $u_b(t)$ as in the proof of Theorem 1.1. As a consequence $y_a(t) = y_b(t) = y(t)$ on $[0, t_o]$ and $[t_o+\delta, T]$, and $y_a(t)$, $y_b(t)$, $y(t) \geq 0$ on $[t_o, t_o+\delta]$.

We can then apply the same concavity arguments as in the proof of Theorem 1.1. When $y(t) < 0$, we deduce through a similar reasoning, that

$$(1.49) \qquad \begin{cases} y(t) \int_t^{t+\delta} \phi(s)ds = 0, \ \forall t \in [0,T) \\ \text{when } \delta \text{ is such that } |y(t)| \geq \int_t^{t+\delta} \xi(s)ds \end{cases}$$

and proceeding as in Theorem 1.1, we conclude (1.47). □

Remark 1.6

It would be interesting to remove the assumption of strict concavity. □

We can write the dynamic programming equation. It is in fact easier now than in (1.3), since here we do not have the state constraint : $y(t) \geq 0$.
We define :

$$(1.50) \qquad U_{ad} = \{v \mid 0 \leq v \leq M\}$$

Setting

$$(1.51) \qquad \phi(s,x) = \operatorname*{Inf}_{v(.)} J_{s,x}(v(.))$$

then ϕ satisfies the relation

$$(1.52) \qquad \begin{cases} \phi(s,x) = \operatorname*{Inf}_{\substack{v(\lambda)\in U_{ad} \\ \text{a.e.}}} \left[\int_s^t [c(\lambda, v(\lambda)) + f(\lambda, z_{s,x}(\lambda))]d\lambda \right. \\ \qquad \left. + \phi(t, z_{s,x}(t))\right] , \ \forall t \in [s, T] \end{cases}$$

with the initial condition

$$(1.53) \qquad \phi(T, x) = 0$$

It is now easy to state conditions under which the function $\phi(s,x)$, defined by (1.51) satisfies the Bellman equation of Dynamic Programming.

Lemma 1.3

Assume that

$$|f(t\ ;\ x_1) - f(t\ ;\ x_2)| \le C_1|x_1 - x_2| \tag{1.54}$$

$$c(t\ ;\ v) \le C_0,\ \forall v \in U_{ad}\ ;\ f(t\ ;\ 0) \le C_o \tag{1.55}$$

then one has

$$|\phi(s_1,x_1) - \phi(s_2,x_2)| \le C_2[(s_1 - s_2)(1 + |x_1| + |x_2|) + |x_1 - x_2|]. \tag{1.56}$$

Proof

Let us write $z(t) = z_{s,x}(t)$, then :

$$z_{s,x}(t) = x + \int_s^t (v(\lambda) - \xi(\lambda))d\lambda$$

$$z_{s_1,x_1}(t) - z_{s_2,x_2}(t) = x_1 - x_2 + \int_{s_1}^{s_2} (v(\lambda) - \xi(\lambda))d\lambda \text{ for } t \ge \text{Max } (s_1, s_2)$$

and recalling that $v(t) \in U_{ad}$, and :

$$0 \le \xi(t) \le M \quad \text{a.e.} \tag{1.57}$$

we deduce

$$\begin{cases} |z_{s_1,x_1}(t) - z_{s_2,x_2}(t)| \le |x_1 - x_2| + 2M\ |s_1 - s_2|, \\ \forall t \in [\text{Max } (s_1, s_2), T] \end{cases} \tag{1.58}$$

Assume to fix the ideas that $s_1 > s_2$ then

$$J_{s_1,x_1}(v(.)) - J_{s_2,x_2}(v(.)) = - \int_{s_2}^{s_1} c(t\ ;\ v(t))dt$$

$$+ \int_{s_1}^{T} [f(t\ ;\ z_{s_1,x_1}(t)) - f(t\ ;\ z_{s_2,x_2}(t))]dt - \int_{s_2}^{s_1} f(t\ ;\ z_{s_2,x_2}(t))dt$$

Hence from (1.54), (1.55) and (1.58) we deduce

$$\begin{cases} |J_{s_1,x_1}(v(.)) - J_{s_2,x_2}(v(.))| \le C_2[|x_1 - x_2| \\ \qquad + |s_1 - s_2|\ (1 + |x_1| + |x_2|)\ ] \end{cases} \tag{1.59}$$

from which (1.56) follows. □

We can then state the following result.

Theorem 1.4

Assume that

(1.60) $f(t, x)$ is continuous, $f \geq 0$ and satisfies (1.54), (1.55)

(1.61) $c(t\ ;\ v)$ is continuous in t, uniformly with respect to v, $c \geq 0$, and satisfies (1.55)

(1.62) $\xi(t)$ is right continuous, has left limits.

Then the function $\phi(s, x)$ defined by (1.51) satisfies (1.56) and is a solution of Bellman equation

$$(1.63)\quad \begin{cases} \dfrac{\partial\phi}{\partial s} + f(s, x) - \xi(s)\dfrac{\partial\phi}{\partial x}(s, x) \\[2ex] \quad + \operatorname*{Inf}_{v\in U_{ad}} [\dfrac{\partial\phi}{\partial x}(s, x)v + c(s\ ;\ v)] = 0, \quad \text{a.e. } s, x \\[2ex] \phi(T, x) = 0 \end{cases}$$

Moreover, it is the maximum element of the set of functions satisfying (1.56) and (1.63).

Proof

The function ϕ satisfies (1.56) from Lemma 1.3. By Rademacher's theorem it follows that ϕ is a.e. differentiable, i.e. a.e. s,x we have

$$(1.64)\quad \frac{|\phi(t,y) - \phi(s,x) - \frac{\partial\phi}{\partial s}(t-s) - \frac{\partial\phi}{\partial x}(y-x)|}{|t-s| + |y-x|} \to 0 \text{ as } |t-s| + |y-x| \to 0.$$

Consider a point s,x where (1.64) holds. Then we show that (1.63) is satisfied, which thus proves that ϕ is a solution of Bellman equation.

Let us set

$$(1.65)\quad H(s, x, p) = \operatorname*{Inf}_{v\in U_{ad}} [pv + c(s\ ;\ v)]$$

We apply (1.52) with $t = s + \delta$ and $v(\lambda) = v \in U_{ad}$, hence

$$\phi(s,x) \leq \int_s^{s+\delta} [c(t;v) + f(t;x+v(t-s)- \int_s^t \xi(\lambda)d\lambda)]dt + \phi(s+\delta,x+v\delta- \int_s^{s+\delta} \xi(\lambda)d\lambda)$$

$$(1.66)\quad \begin{cases} \phi(s,x) \leq \delta[c(s\ ;\ v) + f(s\ ;\ x)] + \phi(s, x) + \delta\dfrac{\partial\phi}{\partial s} + \delta(v-\xi(s))\dfrac{\partial\phi}{\partial x} \\[2ex] + \displaystyle\int_s^{s+\delta} (c(t;v) - c(s;v))dt + \int_s^{s+\delta} [f(t;x+v(t-s) - \int_s^t \xi(\lambda)d\lambda) - f(s,x)]dt \\[2ex] + \phi(s+\delta, x+v\delta - \displaystyle\int_s^{s+\delta} \xi(\lambda)d\lambda) - \phi(s+\delta, x + v\delta - \delta\xi(s)) \\[2ex] +\phi(s+\delta, x+v\delta- \delta\xi(s)) - \phi(s,x) - \delta\dfrac{\partial\phi}{\partial s} - \delta(v - \xi(s))\dfrac{\partial\phi}{\partial x}\ . \end{cases}$$

Dividing by δ and letting δ tend to 0, we deduce from assumptions (1.60), (1.61), (1.62) and lemma 1.3 result (1.56), that :

$$0 \le \frac{\partial \phi}{\partial s} + f(s,x) - \xi(s)\,\frac{\partial \phi}{\partial x} + v\,\frac{\partial \phi}{\partial x} + c(s\ ;\ v)\,, \qquad \forall v$$

hence

$$(1.67) \qquad 0 \le \frac{\partial \phi}{\partial s} + f(s,x) - \xi(s)\,\frac{\partial \phi}{\partial x} + H(s,\ x,\ \frac{\partial \phi}{\partial x}).$$

We go back to (1.52) and write for any v(.),

$$(1.68) \qquad \begin{cases} \phi(s+\delta,\ z_{s,x}(s+\delta)) = \phi(s+\delta,\ x + \int_s^{s+\delta} (v(\lambda) - \xi(\lambda))d\lambda) \\ = \phi(s,\ x) + \frac{\partial \phi}{\partial s}\delta + \frac{\partial \phi}{\partial x} \int_s^{s+\delta} v(\lambda)d\lambda - \delta\xi(s)\,\frac{\partial \phi}{\partial x} \\ - \frac{\partial \phi}{\partial x} \int_s^{s+\delta} (\xi(\lambda) - \xi(s))d\lambda + Z(s,\ x\ ;\ \delta,\ v(.)) \end{cases}$$

where

$$\frac{Z(s,x;\delta;v(.))}{\delta} = \frac{1}{\delta}\,[\phi(s+\delta,x + \int_s^{s+\delta} (v - \xi)d\lambda) - \phi(s,x) - \frac{\partial \phi}{\partial s}\delta - \frac{\partial \phi}{\partial x} \int_s^{s+\delta} (v-\xi)\ d\lambda]$$

From (1.64) and the fact that $0 \le v(t) \le M$, it follows that :

$$(1.69) \qquad \frac{Z(s,\ x\ ;\ \delta,\ v(.))}{\delta} \to 0 \text{ as } \delta \to 0,$$

uniformly with respect to v(.) (for s,x fixed). But from (1.52) and (1.68) we deduce

$$(1.70) \qquad \begin{cases} 0 = f(s,\ x) + \frac{\partial \phi}{\partial s} - \xi(s)\,\frac{\partial \phi}{\partial x} \\ + \operatorname*{Inf}_{v(.)}\ \{\frac{1}{\delta} \int_s^{s+\delta} [v(\lambda)\,\frac{\partial \phi}{\partial x}(s,x) + c(s\ ;\ v(\lambda))]d\lambda + \frac{1}{\delta}\,Z(s,x;\delta;\ v(.)) \\ + \frac{1}{\delta}\,[\int_s^{s+\delta} [c(\lambda;\ v(\lambda)) - c(s;v(\lambda))]\ d\lambda + \frac{1}{\delta} \int_s^{s+\delta} [f(\lambda;z_{s,x}(\lambda)) - f(s,x)]\ d\lambda\} \\ - \frac{1}{\delta}\,\frac{\partial \phi}{\partial x} \int_s^{s+\delta} [\xi(\lambda) - \xi(s)]\,d\lambda \end{cases}$$

Hence

$$0 \ge \frac{\partial \phi}{\partial s} + f(s,\ x) - \xi(s)\,\frac{\partial \phi}{\partial x} + H(s,\ x,\ \frac{\partial \phi}{\partial x})$$

$$+ \operatorname*{Inf}_{v(.)}\ \{\frac{1}{\delta}\,Z(s,x;\delta;v(.)) + \frac{1}{\delta} \int_s^{s+\delta} [c(\lambda;v(\lambda)) - c(s,v(\lambda))]d\lambda$$

$$+ \frac{1}{\delta} \int_s^{s+\delta} [\ f(\lambda;\ z_{s,x}(\lambda)) - f(s;x)]d\lambda\} - \frac{1}{\delta}\,\frac{\partial \phi}{\partial x} \int_s^{s+\delta} [\xi(\lambda) - \xi(s)]d\lambda$$

Letting δ tend to 0, we deduce from (1.69), (1.61), (1.54), that

$$0 \ge \frac{\partial \phi}{\partial s} + f(s,\ x) - \xi(s)\,\frac{\partial \phi}{\partial x} + H(s,\ x,\ \frac{\partial \phi}{\partial x})$$

which together with (1.67) implies (1.63).

Let now ψ be a function satisfying (1.56) and (1.63). For any $v \in U_{ad}$ we have :

$$(1.71) \qquad \frac{\partial \psi}{\partial s} + f(s,x) - \xi(s)\frac{\partial \psi}{\partial x} + \frac{\partial \psi}{\partial x} v + c(s;v) \geq 0 \qquad \text{a.e. } s,x$$

Since ξ is equal a.e. to a continuous function $\xi(s+0)$, we can in (1.71) assume without loss of generality that ξ is continuous. We can also assume that ψ is defined for any s by setting

$$\psi(s, x) = 0 \text{ for } s \geq T$$

and defining conveniently f, c, ξ for $s < 0$, vanishing for $s \leq s_0 < 0$, while extending (1.71) for $s < 0$. We then consider

$$\rho_\varepsilon(s, x) = \frac{1}{\varepsilon^2}\rho\left(\frac{s}{\varepsilon}, \frac{x}{\varepsilon}\right)$$

where

$$\rho(s,x) = \begin{cases} a \exp\left[-\dfrac{1}{1-(|s|^2+|x|^2)}\right] & \text{if } |s|^2 + |x|^2 < 1 \\ 0 & \text{if } |s|^2 + |x|^2 \geq 1 \end{cases}$$

and a being chosen so that

$$\int_{R^2} \rho \, ds\, dx = 1.$$

Consider now the convolution

$$\rho_\varepsilon * f = \int_{R^2} \rho_\varepsilon(s - t, x - y)\, f(t,y)\, dtdy = f_\varepsilon.$$

Note that

$$\frac{\partial f_\varepsilon}{\partial x} = \rho_\varepsilon * \frac{\partial f}{\partial x} \qquad \frac{\partial f_\varepsilon}{\partial s} = \rho_\varepsilon * \frac{\partial f}{\partial s}$$

From (1.71) it then follows that

$$(1.72) \qquad \frac{\partial \psi_\varepsilon}{\partial s} + f_\varepsilon - \xi(s)\frac{\partial \psi_\varepsilon}{\partial x} + v\frac{\partial \psi_\varepsilon}{\partial x} + c_\varepsilon \geq -\theta_\varepsilon$$

where θ_ε is a constant (independant of s,x) which tends to 0 as ε tends to 0. In fact

$$|\xi(s)\frac{\partial \psi_\varepsilon}{\partial x} - \rho_\varepsilon * \xi\frac{\partial \psi}{\partial x}| \leq C_2 \int \rho_\varepsilon(s - t, x - y)\ |\ \xi(s) - \xi(t)| \leq \theta_\varepsilon$$

The function ψ_ε is now a smooth function. Let v(.) be any control, we deduce from (1.72) that :

$$\psi_\varepsilon(t,z_{s,x}(t)) = \psi_\varepsilon(s,x) + \int_s^t \left[\frac{\partial \psi_\varepsilon}{\partial s}(\lambda,z_{s,x}(\lambda)) + \frac{\partial \psi_\varepsilon}{\partial x}(\lambda,z_{s,x}(\lambda))(v(\lambda)-\xi(\lambda))\right]d\lambda$$

$$\geq \psi_\varepsilon(s,x) - \int_s^t [f_\varepsilon(\lambda,z_{s,x}(\lambda)) + c_\varepsilon(\lambda,v(\lambda))]d\lambda - \theta_\varepsilon\,(t-s).$$

We let $\varepsilon \to 0$, and use the pointwise convergence of functions ψ_ε, f_ε, c_ε and the fact that $\theta_\varepsilon \to 0$. From Lebesgue's theorem, we deduce

$$\psi(s,x) \leq \psi(t,z_{s,x}(t)) + \int_s^t [f(\lambda, z_{s,x}(\lambda)) + c(\lambda,v(\lambda))] d\lambda$$

which, applied with $t = T$, implies

$$\psi(s,x) \leq J_{s,x}(v(.))$$

hence $\psi \leq \phi$. This completes the proof of the desired result. □

II - THE CONVEX COST MODEL

Synopsis

In this second section we extend the developments of Chapter II to a continuous time environment. The formulation is quite identical to the one adopted in § I.1. except all cost functions are now convex. Most of the notation is common to both the concave and the convex cost models, except when indicated. Assumptions are specified hereafter.

II - 1. NOTATION AND ASSUMPTIONS

The dynamic system is defined as follows :

$$\text{(2.1)} \qquad \begin{cases} \dfrac{dz}{dt} = v(t) - \xi(t), & t \in (s, T) \\ z(s) = x \end{cases}$$

$$\text{(2.2)} \qquad 0 \leq v(t) \leq M$$

$$\text{(2.3)} \qquad 0 \leq z(t)$$

The production cost function is denoted

$$\text{(2.4)} \qquad \begin{cases} c(t ; v) : [0, T] \times R^+ \to R^+, \text{ with the following properties :} \\ . \text{ convex, non decreasing, } c'^+(t ; 0) > 0 ; \\ . \text{ a.e.t, } \quad c(t ; v) = \tilde{c}(t ; v) \quad \forall v, \text{ where } \tilde{c} \text{ is a Borel function} \end{cases}$$

The inventory cost function is denoted

$$\text{(2.5)} \qquad \begin{cases} f(t ; x) : [0, T] \times R^+ \to R^+, \text{ with the following properties :} \\ . \text{ convex non decreasing in } x ; \\ . \text{ a.e.t } \quad f(t ; x) = \tilde{f}(t ; x) \quad \forall x, \text{ where } \tilde{f} \text{ is a Borel function} \end{cases}$$

We then define the cost function to be minimized :

$$\text{(2.6)} \qquad J_{s,x}(v(.)) = \int_s^T [c(t ; v(t)) + f(t ; z(t))]dt$$

II - 2. EXISTENCE OF AN OPTIMAL CONTROL

Conversely to the concave cost model, it is easy to prove the existence of an optimal control when costs are convex.

We assume that demand is bounded from above.

(2.7) $$0 \leq \xi(t) \leq M$$

M being the same upper bound which applies to the control. Therefore, the set of admissible controls is not empty (i.e., $v(t) = \xi(t)$ is admissible).

Theorem 2.1

Under the assumptions (2.4), (2.5), there exists an optimal control. It is unique if $c(t\ ;\ v)$ is strictly convex in v (a.e. t).

Proof

The function $J(v(.))$ (for simplicity take $s = 0$) is convex and continuous on the subset :

$$K = \{v \in L^2(0,\ T) \mid 0 \leq v(t) \leq M \ \text{ a.e.},\ \int_0^t v\, ds \geq \int_0^t \xi\, ds - x\}$$

of the Hilbert space $L^2(0,\ T)$. Continuity follows from the fact that $c(t\ ;\ v)$ and $f(t\ ;\ x)$ are continuous in v and x respectively. More precisely, let $v_k \to v$ in $L^2(0,\ T)$, hence at least for a subsequence, converging pointwise a.e., we have

$$\int_0^T c(t\ ;\ v_k(t))dt \to \int_0^T c(t\ ;\ v(t))dt.$$

A similar argument applies to f. This completes the proof of the continuity property of $J(v(.))$. On the other hand, K is a convex, bounded, non empty subset of $L^2(0,T)$. The functional $J(v(.))$ is weakly lower semi-continuous, and K weakly compact. Therefore the infimum is attained.

Strict convexity of $J(v(.))$ follows from the strict convexity of c. Hence the minimum of $J(v(.))$ is unique. □

II - 3. THE CASE OF BACKLOGGING

The inventory level is either positive (stock) or negative (shortage) and the functional to be minimized is :

(2.8) $$J_{s,x}(v(.)) = \int_s^T [c(t\ ;\ v(t)) + f(t\ ;\ z(t))]dt$$

where the production cost function $c(t\ ;\ v)$ satisfies (2.4) and $f(t\ ;\ x)$ denotes the inventory and shortage cost function when x is positive and negative respectively: $f(t\ ;\ x)$ has the following properties :

(2.9) $$\begin{cases} f(t\ ;\ x) : [0,\ T] \times R \to R^+ \text{ is convex, achieves its minimum at } 0\ ; \\ \text{a.e. t. } f(t\ ;\ x) = \tilde{f}(t\ ;\ x)\ \forall x, \text{ where } \tilde{f} \text{ is a Borel function} \end{cases}$$

As in theorem 2.1, there exists an optimal control. It is unique if c is strictly convex.

We note that the results of Theorem 1.4 (Bellman equation) apply, since they do not require concavity, but only regularity assumptions.

III - NECESSARY CONDITIONS FOR OPTIMALITY FOR THE CONCAVE AND CONVEX COST MODELS

Synopsis

We derive in this section necessary conditions for optimality, which apply for both the concave and convex cost models. The following common properties of the cost functions will be required :

(3.1) $\begin{cases} f(t\ ;\ x),\ c(t\ ;\ v) \text{ are continuous and have right and left derivati-} \\ \text{ves on } R^+ - \{0\}. \end{cases}$

This follows from the concavity or convexity assumptions.

$$(3.2)\quad \begin{cases} \text{By definition } f'^+(t\ ;\ 0),\ c'^+(t\ ;\ 0) \text{ are respectively the limits of} \\ \dfrac{f(t\ ;\ x) - f(t\ ;\ 0)}{x},\ \dfrac{c(t\ ;\ v) - c(t\ ;\ 0)}{v} \text{ as } x \text{ or } v \to 0. \text{ If } f \text{ is} \\ \text{non decreasing and discontinuous at 0, then this derivative is } +\infty . \end{cases}$$

Note that in the convex (non decreasing) case

$$f(t\ ;\ 0^+) = f(t\ ;\ 0),\ c(t\ ;\ 0^+) = c(t\ ;\ 0)$$

We recall the properties

$$(3.3)\quad \begin{cases} f'^-(t\ ;\ x) \le f'^+(t\ ;\ x),\ \forall x > 0 \text{ (convex cost model)} \\ f'^-(t\ ;\ x) \ge f'^+(t\ ;\ x),\ \forall x > 0 \text{ (concave cost model)} \end{cases}$$

$$(3.4)\quad \begin{cases} x_1 < x_2 \text{ then } f'^+(t\ ;\ x_1) \le f'^-(t\ ;\ x_2) \text{ (convex cost model)} \\ \text{and} \qquad f'^+(t\ ;\ x_1) \ge f'^-(t\ ;\ x_2) \text{ (concave cost model)} \end{cases}$$

Note that (3.4) holds also when $x_1 = 0$.

We will also assume that

(3.5) $\begin{cases} f'^+(t\ ;\ x),\ f'^-(t\ ;\ x),\ c'^+(t\ ;\ v),\ c'^-(t\ ;\ v) \text{ coïncide a.e.t and} \\ \text{any } x \text{ or } v, \text{ with the value taken by a Borel function of both argu-} \\ \text{ments.} \end{cases}$

This assumption is similar to the second property of (1.6), (1.7), (2.4) and (2.5).

III - 1. NECESSARY CONDITIONS

Additional notation is needed : as previously u(.) denotes an optimal control and y(.) the corresponding inventory trajectory. Consider :

$$I = \{t \in (0,\ T)\ |\ u(t) > 0\}$$

$$J = \{t \in (0,\ T)\ |\ u(t) < M\}$$

Since u(t) is not a continuous function, and not even a piecewise continuous function, the sets I and J can be arbitrary Borel sets, up to a set of Lebesgue measure 0. We denote by Meas I and Meas J the Lebesgue measures of the sets I and J (which can be 0) respectively. We now denote

$$I_s^\delta = I \cap (s - \delta,\ s + \delta)$$

$$J_s^\delta = J \cap (s - \delta,\ s + \delta)$$

and define

$$\tilde{I} = \{t \in I \mid \text{Meas } I_t^{\delta} > 0, \forall\delta > 0\}$$

$$\tilde{J} = \{t \in J \mid \text{Meas } J_t^{\delta} > 0, \forall\delta > 0\}$$

Lemma 3.1

If Meas $\tilde{I} = 0$, then Meas $I = 0$, and

(3.6) $\qquad \text{Meas } (I - \tilde{I}) = 0$

Similar results obtain for J and $\tilde{J}$.

Proof

Let us assume that Meas $\tilde{I} = 0$ and Meas $I > 0$. Then there exists $N = \tilde{I}$ such that $N \subset I$, Meas $N = 0$ and such that $\forall t \in I - N$, $\exists\delta_t$ such that Meas $I_t^{\delta_t} = 0$.
Since Meas $I > 0$, we can find K, compact, such that $K \subset I - N$, Meas $K > 0$, and thus: $\forall t \in K$, $\exists\delta_t$ such that Meas $I_t^{\delta_t} = 0$, hence also Meas $K \cap (t - \delta_t, t + \delta_t) = 0$. The balls $(t - \delta_t, t + \delta_t)$ form a covering of the compact set K, from which we can extract a finite covering. Hence

$$K \subset \bigcup_{\text{finite}} (t - \delta_t, t + \delta_t) \text{ , therefore also}$$

$$K \subset \bigcup_{\text{finite}} K \cap (t - \delta_t, t + \delta_t), \text{ which implies Meas } K = 0,$$

hence a contradiction.

A similar reasoning applies to prove (3.6), when K, compact, is included in $I - \tilde{I}$, assuming that lemma (3.1) is false. □

Remark 3.1

We recall that the control $u(.)$ is a (Lebesgue) measurable funciton, which thus coïncides with a Borel function up to a set of Lebesgue measure 0. It is convenient to take a Borel representation of $u(.)$, to characterize I, J, $\tilde{I}$, $\tilde{J}$. Then I,J are Borel sets. □

Next, let us define :

$$I^- = \{t \in \tilde{I} \mid \lim_{\delta\to 0} \frac{1}{\text{Meas } I_t^{\delta}} \int_{t-\delta}^{t+\delta} c'^-(\lambda\ ;\ u(\lambda))\ \chi_I(\lambda)d\lambda = c'^-(t\ ;\ u(t))\}$$

$$J^+ = \{t \in \tilde{J} \mid \lim_{\delta\to 0} \frac{1}{\text{Meas } J_t^{\delta}} \int_{t-\delta}^{t+\delta} c'^+(\lambda\ ;\ u(\lambda))\ \chi_J(\lambda)d\lambda = c'^+(t\ ;\ u(t))\}$$

From the theory of Lebesgue integration, it follows that

(3.7) $\qquad \text{Meas } (\tilde{I} - I^-) = 0, \text{ Meas } (\tilde{J} - J^+) = 0$

Remark 3.2

The sets I^- and J^+ contain all the points of continuity of the functions $c'^-(t\ ;\ u(t))$ and $c'^+(t\ ;\ u(t))$ respectively, but they may also contain many other points. □

We can now state the following

Theorem 3.1

Assume (1.6), (1.7) or (2.4), (2.5). Assume further (3.5). Let u(.) be an optimal control for the problem $J_{0,x}(v(.))$ and y(.) the corresponding trajectory. The following properties hold :

$$(3.8)\quad \begin{cases} \text{Let } s \in I^-,\ t \in J^+ \text{ with } 0 \le s < t < T, \text{ and} \\ y(\lambda) > 0,\ \lambda \in [s, t], \text{ then} \\ c'^-(s\ ;\ u(s)) - c'^+(t\ ;\ u(t)) + \int_s^t f'^-(\lambda\ ;\ y(\lambda))d\lambda \le 0 \end{cases}$$

$$(3.9)\quad \begin{cases} \text{Let } s \in I^-, \text{ and} \\ y(\lambda) > 0,\ \lambda \in [s, T], \text{ then} \\ c'^-(s\ ;\ u(s)) + \int_s^T f'^-(\lambda\ ;\ y(\lambda))d\lambda \le 0 \end{cases}$$

$$(3.10)\quad \begin{cases} \text{Let } s \in J^+,\ t \in I^- \text{ with } 0 \le s < t < T, \text{ then one has} \\ c'^+(s\ ;\ u(s)) - c'^-(t\ ;\ u(t)) + \int_s^t f'^+(\lambda\ ;\ y(\lambda))d\lambda \ge 0 \\ c'^+(s\ ;\ u(s)) + \int_s^T f'^+(\lambda\ ;\ y(\lambda))d\lambda \ge 0 \end{cases}$$

Proof

(i) Let us consider (3.8). Since $s \in I$, $c'^-(s\ ;\ u(s)) > 0$ (cf. (1.6) or (2.4)). Since $s \in \tilde{I}$,

$$\int_{s-\delta}^{s+\delta} c'^-(\lambda\ ;\ u(\lambda))\ \chi_I(\lambda)d\lambda > 0 \text{ for } \delta \text{ small enough and } \delta_0 = \text{Meas } I_s^\delta > 0.$$

Similarly since $t \in J^+$

$$\int_{t-\delta}^{t+\delta} c'^+(\lambda\ ;\ u(\lambda))\ \chi_J(\lambda)d\lambda > 0 \text{ for } \delta \text{ small enough and } \delta_1 = \text{Meas } J_t^\delta > 0.$$

From the theorem of Lusin, we can find a compact subset K_δ^ε of I_s^δ such that

$$\text{Meas } K_\delta^\varepsilon \ge \delta_0 - \varepsilon$$

and u is continuous on K_δ^ε, hence

$$u(\lambda) \ge \underline{u} > 0, \text{ on } K_\delta^\varepsilon.$$

Similarly, we can find a compact subset L_δ^ε of J_t^δ such that

$$\text{Meas } L_\delta^\varepsilon \geq \delta_1 - \varepsilon$$

and u is continuous on L_δ^ε, hence

$$u(\lambda) \leq M - \underline{u}, \quad \lambda \in L_\delta^\varepsilon.$$

We now define a new control as follows

$$\tilde{u}(\lambda) = \begin{cases} u(\lambda) - \dfrac{\theta}{\text{Meas } K_\delta^\varepsilon} & , \lambda \in K_\delta^\varepsilon \\ u(\lambda) + \dfrac{\theta}{\text{Meas } L_\delta^\varepsilon} & , \lambda \in L_\delta^\varepsilon \\ u(\lambda) & , \lambda \notin K_\delta^\varepsilon \cup L_\delta^\varepsilon \end{cases}$$

Note that $s + \delta \leq t - \delta$, and assume that

$$\theta \leq \underline{u} \text{ Min } [\text{Meas } K_\delta^\varepsilon, \text{ Meas } L_\delta^\varepsilon],$$

hence $\qquad 0 \leq \tilde{u}(\lambda) \leq M.$

The corresponding state $\tilde{y}(\lambda)$ satisfies

$$\tilde{y}(\lambda) = \begin{cases} y(\lambda) - \dfrac{\theta}{\text{Meas } K_\delta^\varepsilon} \displaystyle\int_{s-\delta}^{\lambda} \chi_{K_\delta^\varepsilon}(\mu)d\mu & , s - \delta \leq \lambda \leq s + \delta \\ y(\lambda) - \theta & , s + \delta \leq \lambda \leq t - \delta \\ y(\lambda) - \theta + \dfrac{\theta}{\text{Meas } L_\delta^\varepsilon} \displaystyle\int_{t-\delta}^{\lambda} \chi_{L_\delta^\varepsilon}(\mu)d\mu, & t - \delta \leq \lambda \leq t + \delta \\ y(\lambda) & , \lambda \leq s-\delta, \text{ or } \lambda \geq t+\delta \end{cases}$$

θ is also chosen in order that,

$$\theta \leq \underset{s-\delta\leq\lambda\leq t+\delta}{\text{Min}} y(\lambda)$$

and δ is sufficiently small so that $y(\lambda) \geq 0$, $\forall\lambda \in [s-\delta, t+\delta]$, then $\tilde{u}$ is an admissible control. u being optimal, we have

$$J(\tilde{u}) - J(u) \geq 0$$

which implies (noting $\delta_0^\varepsilon = \text{Meas } K_\delta^\varepsilon$, $\delta_1^\varepsilon = \text{Meas } L_\delta^\varepsilon$)

$$\int_{s-\delta}^{s+\delta} [c(\lambda ; u(\lambda) - \frac{\theta}{\delta_0^\varepsilon}) - c(\lambda ; u(\lambda))] \chi_{K_\delta^\varepsilon}(\lambda)d\lambda$$

$$+ \int_{t-\delta}^{t+\delta} [c(\lambda ; u(\lambda) + \frac{\theta}{\delta_1^\varepsilon}) - c(\lambda ; u(\lambda))] \chi_{L_\delta^\varepsilon}(\lambda)d\lambda$$

$$+ \int_{s-\delta}^{s+\delta} [f(\lambda ; \tilde{y}(\lambda)) - f(\lambda ; y(\lambda))]d\lambda + \int_{s+\delta}^{t-\delta} [f(\lambda ; y(\lambda) -\theta) - f(\lambda ; y(\lambda))]d\lambda$$

$$+ \int_{t-\delta}^{t+\delta} [f(\lambda ; \tilde{y}(\lambda)) - f(\lambda ; y(\lambda))]d\lambda \geq 0$$

Since $\tilde{y}(\lambda) \leq y(\lambda)$ and f is increasing, we obtain

$$(3.11) \quad \begin{cases} \int_{s-\delta}^{s+\delta} [c(\lambda ; u(\lambda) - \frac{\theta}{\delta_0^\varepsilon}) - c(\lambda ; u(\lambda))] \chi_{K_\delta^\varepsilon}(\lambda)d\lambda \\ + \int_{t-\delta}^{t+\delta} [c(\lambda ; u(\lambda) + \frac{\theta}{\delta_1^\varepsilon}) - c(\lambda ; u(\lambda))] \chi_{L_\delta^\varepsilon}(\lambda)d\lambda \\ + \int_{s+\delta}^{t-\delta} [f(\lambda ; y(\lambda) - \theta) - f(\lambda ; y(\lambda))]d\lambda \geq 0 \end{cases}$$

Dividing by θ and letting θ tend to 0, we deduce from (3.11) that :

$$(3.12) \quad \begin{cases} - \frac{1}{\delta_0^\varepsilon} \int_{s-\delta}^{s+\delta} c'^-(\lambda ; u(\lambda)) \chi_{K_\delta^\varepsilon}(\lambda)d\lambda + \frac{1}{\delta_1^\varepsilon} \int_{t-\delta}^{t+\delta} c'^+(\lambda ; u(\lambda))\chi_{L_\delta^\varepsilon}(\lambda)d\lambda \\ - \int_{s+\delta}^{t-\delta} f'^-(\lambda ; y(\lambda))d\lambda \geq 0. \end{cases}$$

We let ε tend to 0 in (3.12), then

$$\delta_0^\varepsilon \to \delta_0, \quad \delta_1^\varepsilon \to \delta_1$$

and

$$\int_{s-\delta}^{s+\delta} c'^-(\lambda ; u(\lambda)) \chi_{K_\delta^\varepsilon}(\lambda)d\lambda \uparrow \int_{s-\delta}^{s+\delta} c'^-(\lambda ; u(\lambda)) \chi_I(\lambda)d\lambda$$

$$\int_{t-\delta}^{t+\delta} c'^+(\lambda ; u(\lambda)) \chi_{L_\delta^\varepsilon}(\lambda)d\lambda \uparrow \int_{t-\delta}^{t+\delta} c'^+(\lambda ; u(\lambda)) \chi_J(\lambda)d\lambda$$

since

$$\int_{s-\delta}^{s+\delta} [\chi_I(\lambda) - \chi_{K_\delta^\varepsilon}(\lambda)]d\lambda \downarrow 0$$

$$\int_{t-\delta}^{t+\delta} [\chi_J(\lambda) - \chi_{L_\delta^\varepsilon}(\lambda)]d\lambda \downarrow 0.$$

Therefore it follows from (3.12) that

$$(3.13)\quad \begin{cases} -\dfrac{1}{\delta_0}\displaystyle\int_{s-\delta}^{s+\delta} c'^-(\lambda\ ;\ u(\lambda))\ \chi_I(\lambda)d\lambda + \dfrac{1}{\delta_1}\int_{t-\delta}^{t+\delta} c'^+(\lambda\ ;\ u(\lambda))\chi_J(\lambda)d\lambda \\ -\displaystyle\int_{s+\delta}^{t-\delta} f'^-(\lambda\ ;\ y(\lambda))d\lambda \geq 0 \end{cases}$$

and letting δ tend to 0, we obtain the relation (3.8) since $s \in I^-$, $t \in J^+$.

(ii) The proof of (3.9) follows from similar arguments. Defining K_δ^ε as above, we consider

$$\tilde{u}(\lambda) = \begin{cases} u(\lambda) - \dfrac{\theta}{\text{Meas } K_\delta^\varepsilon} & , \quad \lambda \in K_\delta^\varepsilon \\ u(\lambda) & , \quad \lambda \notin K_\delta^\varepsilon \end{cases}$$

$$\tilde{y}(\lambda) = \begin{cases} y(\lambda) - \dfrac{\theta}{\text{Meas } K_\delta^\varepsilon}\displaystyle\int_{s-\delta}^{\lambda} \chi_{K_\delta^\varepsilon}(\mu)d\mu, & s-\delta \leq \lambda \leq s+\delta \\ y(\lambda) - \theta & , \quad s+\delta \leq \lambda \leq T \\ y(\lambda) & , \quad \lambda \leq s-\delta \end{cases}$$

$\tilde{u}(\lambda)$ is an admissible control for sufficiently small values of θ.

Proceeding as above, we deduce the relation (3.9).

(iii) We turn now to the proof of (3.10).

Consider J_s^δ and I_t^δ, and set

$$\delta_0 = \text{Meas } J_s^\delta, \quad \delta_1 = \text{Meas } I_t^\delta$$

Find K_δ^ε compact subset of J_s^δ, such that

$$\text{Meas } K_\delta^\varepsilon \geq \delta_0 - \varepsilon$$

and u is continuous on K_δ^ε ; hence

$$u(\lambda) \leq M - \underline{u} \quad , \quad \lambda \in K_\delta^\varepsilon$$

Similarly, find L_δ^ε compact subset of I_t^δ such that

$$\text{Meas } L_\delta^\varepsilon \geq \delta_1 - \varepsilon$$

and u is continuous on L_δ^ε, hence

$$u(\lambda) \geq \underline{u}\ ;\quad \lambda \in L_\delta^\varepsilon.$$

We then define a new control as follows

$$\tilde{u}(\lambda) = \begin{cases} u(\lambda) + \dfrac{\theta}{\text{Meas } K_\delta^\varepsilon} & , \quad \lambda \in K_\delta^\varepsilon \\ u(\lambda) - \dfrac{\theta}{\text{Meas } L_\delta^\varepsilon} & , \quad \lambda \in L_\delta^\varepsilon \\ u(\lambda) & , \quad \lambda \notin K_\delta^\varepsilon \cup L_\delta^\varepsilon \end{cases}$$

Choosing θ such chat

$$\theta \leq \underline{u} \text{ Min } [\text{Meas } K_\delta^\varepsilon, \text{ Meas } L_\delta^\varepsilon]$$

we have

$$0 \leq \tilde{u}(\lambda) \leq M.$$

The corresponding state $\tilde{y}$ satisfies

$$\tilde{y}(\lambda) = \begin{cases} y(\lambda) + \dfrac{\theta}{\text{Meas } K_\delta^\varepsilon} \displaystyle\int_{s-\delta}^{\lambda} \chi_{K_\delta^\varepsilon}(\mu)d\mu, & s - \delta \leq \lambda \leq s + \delta \\ y(\lambda) + \theta & , \quad s + \delta \leq \lambda \leq t - \delta \\ y(\lambda) + \theta - \dfrac{\theta}{\text{Meas } L_\delta^\varepsilon} \displaystyle\int_{t-\delta}^{\lambda} \chi_{L_\delta^\varepsilon}(\mu)d\mu, & t - \delta \leq \lambda \leq t + \delta \\ y(\lambda) & , \quad \lambda \leq s - \delta, \quad \lambda \geq t + \delta \end{cases}$$

Hence $\tilde{u}$ is admissible.

Reasoning as above, we easily deduce (3.10). This completes the proof of Theorem 3.1. □

III - 2. SOME CONSEQUENCES OF THE NECESSARY CONDITIONS

Theorem 3.2

Under the assumptions of Theorem 3.1, and (1.12), if u(.) is an optimal control and y(.) the corresponding trajectory

(3.14) $$y(T) = 0$$

Proof

Assume $y(t) > 0$, $\forall t \in [0, T]$, then Meas I = 0. Otherwise Meas $I^- > 0$, and $c'^-(s ; u(s)) > 0$ on I^-, which together with (3.9) yields a contradiction. But if Meas I = 0, we reach a contradiction.

Assume now that there exists a regeneration point, i.e. a point t_o such that $y(t_o) = 0$, hence $t_o < T$. Consider the largest one ; therefore

$$y(t) > 0, \forall t \in [t_o, T].$$

Clearly the set of points $[t_o, T] \cap I$ has a positive measure. But, the set of points $[t_0,T] \cap I^-$ has also a positive measure, which contradicts (3.9). □

Consider the concave case, with $s,t \in I^- \cap J^+$, then both (3.6) and (3.8) hold. On the other hand

$$c'^-(s \; ; u(s)) \geq c'^+(s \; ; u(s))$$

$$- c'^+(t \; ; u(t)) \geq - c'^-(t \; ; u(t))$$

$$f'^-(\lambda \; ; y(\lambda)) \geq f'^+(\lambda \; ; y(\lambda)).$$

Therefore it follows that if $s,t \in I^- \cap J^+$, $s < t$ and $y(\lambda) > 0$, $\forall\lambda \in [s,t]$, then

$$c'^-(s \; ; u(s)) = c'^+(s \; ; u(s))$$

$$c'^-(t \; ; u(t)) = c'^+(t \; ; u(t))$$

$$f'^-(\lambda \; ; y(\lambda)) = f'^+(\lambda \; ; y(\lambda))$$

and

$$c'(s \; ; u(s)) - c'(t \; ; u(t)) + \int_s^t f'(\lambda \; ; y(\lambda))d\lambda = 0. \tag{3.15}$$

This relation also holds, without concavity, when the cost functions $c(s,v)$ and $f(\lambda; x)$ are differentiable with respect to v and x. □

REMARK 3.4

Consider (3.8) in the concave case. Then noting that

$$c'^-(s \; ; M) \leq c'^-(s \; ; u(s))$$

$$c'^+(t \; ; u(t)) \leq c'^+(t \; ; 0)$$

we have

$$c'^-(s \; ; u(s)) - c'^+(t \; ; u(t)) \geq c'^-(s \; ; M) - c'^+(t \; ; 0)$$

which is consistent with the "bang bang" property (at least when there is strict concavity).

III - 3. MAXIMUM PRINCIPLE IN THE CONVEX CASE

The maximum principle of Pontryagin applied to the convex cost model yields necessary but also sufficient conditions for optimality. For simplicity we consider the problem $J_{0,x}(v(.))$.

Assume there exists a control $\bar{v}(s)$ and its corresponding state which satisfy (1.2) and

$$z(t) > 0, \; \forall t \in [0, T] \tag{3.16}$$

From a basic theorem of convex programming in infinite dimensional spaces, we know there exists two adjoint functions $\lambda(t)$, $p(t)$ such that :

. λ , p have bounded variations on [0, T], and are right continuous ;

. λ is non decreasing ;

. $\int_0^T y(t)d\lambda(t) = 0$; and

. the optimal pair (u(.), y(.)) minimizes the Lagrangian

$$\text{(3.17)} \quad \begin{cases} L(v(.), z(.)) = \int_0^T c(t\,;\,v(t))dt + \int_0^T f(t\,;\,z(t))dt - \int_0^T d\lambda z(t) \\ - \int_0^T dp.\ [z(t) - \int_0^t (v(s) - \xi(s))ds - x] \end{cases}$$

on the following set

$$\text{(3.18)} \quad \begin{cases} v(.) \in L^2(0, T),\ 0 \le v(t) \le M \quad \text{a.e.} \\ z(.) \in C(0, T), \end{cases}$$

Using integration by parts formula, we can rewrite the lagrangian as follows :

$$\text{(3.19)} \quad \begin{cases} L(v(.), z(.)) = \int_0^T c(t\,;\,v(t))dt + \int_0^T f(t\,;\,z(t))dt - \int_0^T (d\lambda + dp)z(t) \\ + p(T)\ [\int_0^T (v(s) - \xi(s))ds + x] - p(0)x - \int_0^T p(t)\ [v(t) - \xi(t)]dt. \end{cases}$$

From (3.17) it is clear that p and λ are defined up to an additive constant. As far as p is concerned, we fix it by setting

$$\text{(3.20)} \quad p(T) = 0$$

We can then split the minimization of L into two parts, namely :

$$\text{(3.21)} \quad \begin{cases} \text{Min} \int_0^T [c(t\,;\,v(t)) - p(t)]v(t)\ dt \\ \text{over the constraint set (3.18)} \end{cases}$$

and

$$\text{(3.22)} \quad \begin{cases} \text{Min} \int_0^T f(t\,;\,z(t))dt - \int_0^T z(t)(d\lambda + dp) \\ \text{over all } z \text{ in } C(0, T). \end{cases}$$

Consider $s \in I^-$, and I_s^δ with $s - \delta \ge 0$, $s + \delta \le T$ (cf. Theorem 3.1). Consider further K_δ^ε as in Theorem 3.1 such that u is continuous on K_δ^ε and

$$u(\lambda) \ge \underline{u} > 0 \quad \text{on } K_\delta^\varepsilon.$$

We then take :

$$v(t) = \begin{cases} u(t) - \dfrac{\theta}{\text{Meas } K_\delta^\varepsilon} & , \quad t \in K_\delta^\varepsilon \\ u(t) & , \quad t \notin K_\delta^\varepsilon \end{cases}$$

with

$$\theta \le \underline{u} \text{ Meas } K_\delta^\varepsilon$$

Therefore from (3.21) we obtain

$$\int_{s-\delta}^{s+\delta} [c(t\ ;\ u(t) - \frac{\theta}{\text{Meas } K_\delta^\varepsilon}) - c(t\ ;\ u(t))]\ \chi_{K_\delta^\varepsilon}(t)dt$$

$$+ \int_{s-\delta}^{s+\delta} p(t) \frac{\theta}{\text{Meas } K_\delta^\varepsilon} \chi_{K_\delta^\varepsilon}(t)dt \ge 0$$

Dividing by θ and letting θ tend to 0, we deduce

$$- \frac{1}{\delta_0^\varepsilon} \int_{s-\delta}^{s+\delta} c'^-(t\ ;\ u(t))\ \chi_{K_\delta^\varepsilon}(t)dt + \frac{1}{\delta_0^\varepsilon} \int_{s-\delta}^{s+\delta} p(t)\ \chi_{K_\delta^\varepsilon}(t)dt \ge 0$$

By letting ε tend to 0, it follows that

$$- \frac{1}{\delta_0} \int_{s-\delta}^{s+\delta} c'^-(t\ ;\ u(t))\ \chi_I(t)dt + \frac{1}{\delta_0} \int_{s-\delta}^{s+\delta} p(t)\ \chi_I(t)dt \ge 0$$

from which we may assert that

(3.23) $\quad p(t) - c'^-(t\ ;\ u(t)) \ge 0 \quad$ a.e. t in I

Similarly we can prove that

(3.24) $\quad p(t) - c'^+(t\ ;\ u(t)) \le 0 \quad$ a.e. t in J.

A similar reasoning with (3.22) yields

$$\int_{s-\delta}^{s+\delta} f'^+(t\ ;\ y(t))dt \ge \int_{s-\delta}^{s+\delta} d(\lambda+p) \ge \int_{s-\delta}^{s+\delta} f'^-(t\ ;\ y(t))dt$$

which implies that the measure $d(\lambda+p)$ has a Radon Nikodym derivative with respect to the Lebesgue measure dt, and

(3.25) $\quad f'^-(t\ ;\ y(t)) \le \dfrac{d(\lambda+p)}{dt} \le f'^+(t\ ;\ y(t)) \quad$ a.e.t

We can then state the following

<u>Theorem 3.3</u>

Assume (2.4), (2.5), (3.5) and that there exists an admissible control $\bar{v}(.)$ such that (3.16) holds. Let u(.) be an optimal control for $J_{o,x}(v(.))$ and y(.) the corresponding optimal state. Then, there exists $\lambda(.)$, $p(.)$ functions with bounded variations, right continuous, such that

(3.26) λ is non decreasing

(3.27) $\lambda+p \in H^1(0, T)$ [1]

(3.28) $p(T) = 0$

(3.29) $\int_0^T y(t)d\lambda(t) = 0$

(3.30) $\frac{d}{dt}(\lambda+p) \in \partial f(t ; y(t))$ a.e.

(3.31) $\begin{cases} p(t) \le c'^{+}(t ; u(t)) & \text{a.e. } t \text{ in } J = \{t / u(t) < M\} \\ p(t) \ge c'^{-}(t ; u(t)) & \text{a.e. } t \text{ in } I = \{t / u(t) > 0\} \end{cases}$ □

Remark 3.5

λ is defined up to an additive constant. It is therefore convenient to take

(3.32) $\lambda(0) = 0$

so that $\lambda(t) \ge 0$. □

The function f must be defined for all arguments. We recall that it is a continuous function and that

$$f'^{+}(t ; 0) = f'^{-}(t ; 0)$$ □

We can derive (3.8), (3.9), (3.10) from the results of Theorem 3.3. More precisely let N_I, N_J with measure 0, be subsets of I, J such that (3.31) holds $\forall t \in J - N_J$ and $t \in I - N_I$ respectively. Take $s \in I - N_I$, $t \in J - N_J$ such that $s < t$ and $y(\sigma) = 0$, $\forall \sigma \in [s,t]$.

Then, from (3.29), $\lambda(\sigma)$ is constant on $[s,t]$, and from (3.30)

$$\frac{dp}{dt} \in \partial f(\sigma ; y(\sigma)) \quad \text{a.e. } \sigma \text{ in } (s,t).$$

Therefore

(3.33) $\int_s^t f'^{-}(\lambda ; y(\lambda))d\lambda \le p(t) - p(s) \le \int_s^t f'^{+}(\lambda ; y(\lambda))d\lambda$

But also

----

[1] i.e. $\lambda+p \in L^2(0, T)$, $\frac{d}{dt}(\lambda+p) \in L^2(0, T)$
(cf. the mathematical appendix)

$$p(s) \geq c'^{-}(s\ ;\ u(s))$$

$$p(t) \leq c'^{+}(t\ ;\ u(t))$$

from which we get (3.8).

Property (3.10) is obtained in a similar way.

As to (3.9), it follows from the first inequality (3.33) applied with $t = T$ when (3.28) is taken into account. □

III - 4. THE CASE OF BACKLOGGING

Assume

(3.34) $v \to c(t\ ;\ v)$ is continuous and has right and left derivatives on $R^{+} - \{0\}$

(3.35) $x \to f(t\ ;\ x)$ is continuous and has right and left derivatives.

(3.36) $f'^{+}(t\ ;\ x)$, $f'^{-}(t\ ;\ x)$, $c'^{+}(t\ ;\ v)$, $c'^{-}(t\ ;\ v)$ coincide a.e. t, for any x or v with the value taken by a Borel function of both arguments.

Again (3.34), (3.35) will be satisfied in the convex or concave case.

We now state the result on necessary conditions, which is the analogue of Theorem 3.1.

Theorem 3.4

Assume (1.6), (1.42) or (2.4), (2.9). Moreover assume (3.36). Let u(.), y(.) be an optimal control for $J_{0,x}(v(.))$ and y(.) the corresponding optimal state.

Let I, J, I^{-}, J^{+} as in theorem 3.1, then the following properties hold

(3.37) $$\begin{cases} \text{Let } s \in I^{-},\ t \in J^{+} \text{ with } 0 \leq s < t < T, \text{ then} \\ c'^{-}(s\ ;\ u(s)) - c'^{+}(t\ ;\ u(t)) + \int_s^t f'^{-}(\lambda\ ;\ y(\lambda))d\lambda \leq 0 \\ c'^{-}(s\ ;\ u(s)) + \int_s^T f'^{-}(\lambda\ ;\ y(\lambda))d\lambda \leq 0 \end{cases}$$

(3.38) $$\begin{cases} \text{Let } s \in J^{+},\ t \in I^{-} \text{ with } 0 \leq s < t < T, \text{ then one has} \\ c'^{+}(s\ ;\ u(s)) - c'^{-}(t\ ;\ u(t)) + \int_s^t f'^{+}(\lambda\ ;\ y(\lambda))d\lambda \geq 0 \\ c'^{+}(s\ ;\ u(s)) + \int_s^T f'^{+}(\lambda\ ;\ y(\lambda))d\lambda \geq 0 \end{cases}$$

Proof

Analogue to that of Theorem 3.1. Details are left to the reader. □

Corollary 3.1

Under assumptions of Theorem 3.4, and (1.44) if u(.) is an optimal control and y(.) the corresponding optimal state, then one has :

(3.39) $\quad y(T) \leq 0.$

Proof

We note that $f'^{-}(t\,;\,x) \geq 0$ for $x \geq 0$.

If $y(T) > 0$ we may reason as in Theorem 3.2, using the second necessary condition (3.37) to obtain a contradiction. □

We can finally derive the maximum principle of Pontryagin in the convex case. The situation is easier than in the case of §III.3, since we do not have any state constraints.

Theorem 3.5

Assume (2.4), (2.9), (3.36). Let u(.) be an optimal control for $J_{0,x}(v(.))$ and y(.) be the corresponding trajectory. Then there exists p(t) such that

(3.40) $\quad p \in H^1(0,\,T),\ p(T) = 0$

(3.41) $\quad \frac{dp}{dt} \in \partial f(t\,;\,y(t)) \quad \text{a.e. } t$

(3.42) $$\begin{cases} p(t) \leq c'^{+}(t\,;\,u(t)) & \text{a.e. } t \text{ in } J = \{t \mid u(t) < M\} \\ p(t) \geq c'^{-}(t\,;\,u(t)) & \text{a.e. } t \text{ in } I = \{t \mid u(t) > 0\} \end{cases}$$

Proof

Similar to that of Theorem 3.3.

Remark 3.8

Assume that $f(t\,;\,x)$ is differentiable in x, then we can derive more directly Theorem 3.5. Indeed let v(.) be any admissible control, then $u(.) + \theta[v(.) - u(.)]$ is also admissible ($\theta \in (0,\,1)$). Therefore

$$J(u(.) + \theta[v(.) - u(.)]) - J(u(.)) \geq 0$$

hence

(3.43) $$\begin{cases} \int_0^T [c(t\,;\,u(t) + \theta(v(t) - u(t))) - c(t\,;\,u(t))]dt \\ + \int_0^T [f(t\,;\,y(t) + \theta\tilde{z}(t)) - f(t\,;\,y(t))]dt \geq 0 \end{cases}$$

where

(3.44) $\quad \frac{d\tilde{z}}{dt} = v - u \qquad \tilde{z}(0) = 0$

From the convexity of c we deduce from (3.43) that :

$$\int_0^T (c(t\ ;\ v(t)) - c(t\ ;\ u(t)))dt$$

$$+ \int_0^T \frac{(f(t\ ;\ y(t) + \theta\tilde{z}(t)) - f(t\ ;\ y(t)))dt}{\theta} \geq 0$$

Hence letting θ tend to 0, we obtain

$$(3.45)\qquad \begin{cases} \int_0^T (c(t\ ;\ v(t)) - c(t\ ;\ u(t)))dt \\ \\ + \int_0^T f'(t\ ;\ y(t))\ \tilde{z}(t)dt \geq 0 \end{cases}$$

We then define $p(t)$ by

$$(3.46)\qquad \frac{dp}{dt} = f'(t\ ;\ y(t)),\quad p(T) = 0$$

hence from (3.45)

$$\int_0^T (c(t\ ;\ v(t)) - c(t\ ;\ u(t)))dt + \int_0^T \frac{dp}{dt}\ \tilde{z}(t)dt \geq 0$$

Using integration by parts we deduce

$$\int_0^T (c(t\ ;\ v(t)) - c(t\ ;\ u(t)))\,dt - \int_0^T p(t)\ (v(t) - u(t))dt \geq 0$$

Therefore we are in the situation (3.21) from which we may proceed as in Theorem 3.3. □

IV - PLANNING HORIZONS

Synopsis

In this section we derive Planning horizon theorems which rely on the necessary conditions for optimality of Theorem 3.1. Our approach will be similar to the one followed in the convex-discrete time case (cf. Chapter II), although it will apply to both the concave and convex case, since the validity of Theorem 3.1 is general.

IV - 1. PRELIMINARIES

In this section we impose

$$(4.1)\qquad x = 0$$

and suppose that

$$(4.2)\qquad \int_0^T \xi(t)dt > 0,\quad \forall T > 0.$$

$J_0^T(v(.))$ will denote $J_{0,0}^T(v(.))$. We make the assumptions of Theorem 3.1. By virtue of (4.1), (4.2), theorem 3.2 applies, so that an optimal control satisfies (3.14). We set

(4.3) $$\lambda(T) = \inf J_0^T(v(.))$$

We further assume that :

(4.4) $$\begin{cases} \text{There exists an optimal control } u(.) = u^T(.), \\ y(.) = y^T(.), \text{ i.e., } \lambda(T) = J_0^T(u^T(.)). \end{cases}$$

In the convex case (cf. Theorem 2.1) we know that (4.4) always obtains, provided (2.7) is satisfied, which is the case.

As in the discrete time formulation, we can assert that

(4.5) $$\begin{cases} \text{If } s < T \text{ is a regeneration point of } u^T(.), \text{ then one has} \\ \lambda(s) = J_0^s(u^T(.)) \end{cases}$$

This is a consequence of (3.14) and the general reasoning of Dynamic Programming (cf. Chapter I, lemma 4.1). Again the problem of finding planning horizons amounts to finding regeneration points which do not depend on the horizon.

IV - 2. FORECAST HORIZON

Assumptions specific to the convex and concave cost models are nedded.

(4.6) $$\begin{cases} \text{In the convex case : } \int_0^\infty f'^+(\lambda \; ; \; 0)\, d\lambda = +\infty, \; f'^+(\lambda \; ; \; 0) > 0 \\ \text{In the concave case : } \int_0^\infty f'^-(\lambda \; ; \; M\lambda)\, d\lambda = +\infty \end{cases}$$

(4.7) $$\begin{cases} \text{In the convex case : } c'^-(t \; ; \; M) \text{ is bounded as } t \text{ varies and} \\ c'^+(t \; ; \; \xi(t)) \text{ is lower semi continuous} \\ \text{In the concave case : } c'^+(t \; ; \; 0) \text{ is bounded, and } c'^-(t \; ; \; M) \text{ is lower} \\ \text{semi continuous.} \end{cases}$$

Note that given the second part of (4.7), $c(t \; ; \; v)$ cannot have a discontinuity at $v = 0$.

Let s be fixed $s < t < T$, and consider the function :

(4.8) $$\begin{cases} F(s \; ; \; t) = c'^+(s \; ; \; \xi(s)) + \int_s^t f'^+(\lambda \; ; \; 0)\, d\lambda \quad \text{in the convex case} \\ F(s \; ; \; t) = c'^-(s \; ; \; M) + \int_s^t f'^-(\lambda \; ; \; (\lambda - s)M)\, d\lambda \text{ in the concave case} \end{cases}$$

When s is fixed and t varies, the function $t \to F(s; t)$ is non decreasing and

$$F(s, t) \to +\infty \quad \text{as } t \to +\infty.$$

Consider :

$$(4.9) \qquad B = \begin{cases} \sup_\sigma c'^-(\sigma\ ;\ M) \text{ in the convex case} \\ \sup_\sigma c'^+(\sigma\ ;\ 0) \text{ in the concave case} \end{cases}$$

then we have :

$$F(s,\ s) = c'^+(s\ ;\ \xi(s)) \le c'^+(s\ ;\ M) \le B \quad \text{in the convex case}$$

$$F(s,\ s) = c'^-(s\ ;\ M) \le c'^+(s\ ;\ 0) \le B \quad \text{in the concave case}$$

Therefore we may define

$$(4.10) \qquad H(s) = \inf_{t \ge s} \{F(s,\ t) \ge B\}$$

Lemma 4.1

Under the assumptions of Theorem 3.1 and (4.1), (4.2), (4.4), (4.6), (4.7), let s be a regeneration point of an optimal control for $J_0^T(v(.))$, such that $s < H(s) \le T$. Then, there exists an additional regeneration point in $(s,\ H(s)]$.

Proof

If $H(s) = T$ there is nothing to prove since T is a regeneration point. Therefore assume that : $H(s) < T$, and there is no regeneration point in $(s,\ H(s)]$. Thus we have

$$(4.11) \qquad y(t) > 0,\ \forall t \in (s,\ H(s)]$$

Let

$$I_0 = \{t \mid u(t) > \xi(t)\}$$

then we have

$$(4.12) \qquad \forall \varepsilon > 0,\ s+\varepsilon < T,\ \text{Meas } I_0 \cap (s,\ s+\varepsilon) > 0.$$

Otherwise $\exists \varepsilon$ such that Meas $I_0 \cap (s,\ s+\varepsilon) = 0$. But since $y(s) = 0$, we obtain $y(t) \le 0$, $\forall t \in [s,\ s+\varepsilon]$ which contradicts the property (4.11). Hence (4.12) holds. But, we have also

$$(4.13) \qquad \text{Meas } I_0 \cap I^- \cap (s,\ s+\varepsilon) > 0$$

which follows from a reasoning similar to that of (3.7).

Moreover

$$(4.14) \qquad \text{Meas } J \cap (H(s),\ T) > 0$$

Otherwise, we would have

$$u(t) = M \quad \text{a.e. in } (H(s),\ T)$$

and as a consequence

$$y(T) = y(H(s)) + \int_{H(s)}^{T} (u(t) - \xi(t))dt \geq y(H(s)) > 0$$

which yields a contradiction.

It follows that :

(4.15) $\quad$ Meas $J^+ \cap (H(s), T) > 0.$

Let $\sigma \in (s, s+\varepsilon) \cap I_0 \cap I^-$ and $t \in J^+ \cap (H(s), T)$. We can select ε small enough so that :

$$s+\varepsilon < H(s).$$

Since $y(H(s)) > 0$, we can always choose t so that

(4.16) $\quad y(\lambda) > 0, \forall\lambda \in [\sigma,t]$

Indeed $y(\lambda) > 0, \forall\lambda \in [\sigma, H(s)]$.

Let $T \geq t_1 > H(s)$ such that

$$y(H(s)) - \int_{H(s)}^{t_1} \xi(\lambda)d\lambda = 0$$

Then if Meas $J \cap (H(s), t_1) > 0$, we can choose t in $J^+ \cap (H(s), t_1)$ and (4.16) holds. If Meas $J \cap (H(s), t_1) = 0$, then $y(t_1) \geq y(H(s))$. We can then consider $T \geq t_2 > t_1$ such that

$$y(t_1) - \int_{t_1}^{t_2} \xi(\lambda)d\lambda = 0$$

and proceed as above.

Define a sequence t_n with $t_n < t_{n+1} \leq T$

(4.17) $$\begin{cases} y(t_n) \geq y(t_{n-1}) \\ y(t_n) - \int_{t_n}^{t_{n+1}} \xi(\lambda)d\lambda = 0, \text{ Meas } J \cap (H(s), t_n) = 0 \end{cases}$$

Such a sequence is necessarily finite, otherwise if $\bar{t} = \lim t_n$ then

$$y(\bar{t}) = 0$$

and $\quad y(\bar{t}) \geq y(H(s)) > 0$

which is a contradiction. Therefore there exists an interval (t_n, t_{n+1}), such that (4.17) holds as well as

$$\text{Meas } J \cap (t_n, t_{n+1}) > 0$$

and taking t in $J^+ \cap (t_n, t_{n+1})$ we get (4.16). We may then apply (3.6) so that

$$(4.18) \qquad c'^{-}(\sigma\ ;\ u(\sigma)) - c'^{+}(t\ ;\ u(t)) + \int_\sigma^t f'^{-}(\lambda\ ;\ y(\lambda))d\lambda \leq 0$$

Consider the convex case.

Since $\sigma \in I_0$, $u(\sigma) > \xi(\sigma)$, hence

$$c'^{-}(\sigma\ ;\ u(\sigma)) > c'^{+}(\sigma\ ;\ \xi(\sigma))$$

$$c'^{+}(t\ ;\ u(t)) < c'^{-}(t\ ;\ M)$$

$$f'^{-}(\lambda\ ;\ y(\lambda)) > f'^{+}(\lambda\ ;\ 0)$$

Therefore we deduce from (4.18) that

$$(4.19) \qquad \begin{cases} c'^{+}(\sigma\ ;\ \xi(\sigma)) + \int_\sigma^t f'^{+}(\lambda\ ;\ 0)d\lambda < c'^{-}(t\ ;\ M) \\ \qquad\qquad\qquad\qquad\qquad\qquad < B \end{cases}$$

Let $\varepsilon \downarrow 0$, then $\sigma \downarrow s$, and by the lower semi continuity of $c'^{+}(t\ ;\ \xi(t))$ we deduce

$$c'^{+}(s\ ;\ \xi(s)) + \int_s^t f'^{+}(\lambda\ ;\ 0)d\lambda \leq B$$

But from the definition of H(s), this implies $t \leq H(s)$, which is a contradiction. Hence (4.11) does not hold.

Consider now the concave case.

We have

$$c'^{-}(\sigma\ ;\ u(\sigma)) \geq c'^{-}(\sigma\ ;\ M)$$

$$c'^{+}(t\ ;\ u(t)) \leq c'^{+}(t\ ;\ 0)$$

$$f'^{-}(\lambda\ ;\ y(\lambda)) \geq f'^{-}(\lambda\ ;\ (\lambda-s)M)$$

since

$$y(\lambda) = \int_s^\lambda (u(\mu) - \xi(\mu))d\mu$$

$$\leq M(\lambda-s)$$

Therefore (4.18) implies

$$c'^{-}(\sigma\ ;\ M) + \int_\sigma^t f'^{-}(\lambda\ ;\ (\lambda-s)M)d\lambda \leq c'^{+}(t\ ;\ 0).$$

From the lower semi continuity of $c'^{-}(\sigma\ ;\ M)$ we deduce

$$c'^{-}(s\ ;\ M) + \int_s^t f'^{-}(\lambda\ ;\ (\lambda-s)M)d\lambda \leq B$$

and again $t \leq H(s)$, which yields a contradiction. This completes the proof. □

From Lemma 4.1, it follows

Theorem 4.1

Under the assumptions of Lemma 4.1, let $H = H(0)$ in (4.10). Then H, is a forecast horizon, in the sense that $\forall T > H$ there exists $s = s(T)$ with $0 < s \leq H$ such that an optimal policy for $J_0^T(v(.))$ can be obtained by chosing an optimal policy for J_0^s and completing it adequately on (s, T).

Proof

From Lemma 4.1, an optimal policy for $J_0^T(v(.))$ will necessarily have a regeneration point, s, in (0, H].

Then an optimal policy for $J_0^T(v(.))$ can be obtained by chosing an optimal polify for $J_0^s(v(.))$ and completing it adequately on (s,T]. □

Remark 4.1

Theorem 4.1 tells us that if we know optimal controls for problems $J_0^s(v(.))$, $\forall s \leq H$ then $\forall T > H$, one of these policies will be used as a first part of an optimal control for $J_0^T(v(.))$. Unfortunately, unlike in the discrete time formulation, it is not possible to identify an interval of time, starting at 0, on which the optimal control depends only on the demand up to H.

In the continuous time, as in the discrete time formulation, we can estimate the maximum length of time separating two successive regeneration points. Such properties are sufficient in the discrete time formulation to draw conclusions for the first decision. But unfortunately, there is no analogue of that in the continuous time framework, since the concept of first decision is meaningless. □

IV - 3. WEAK PLANNING HORIZON FOR THE CONVEX COST MODEL

We develop here the continuous time analogue of theorem in Chapter II.

The assumptions of Lemma 4.1, which are relevant for the convex case, are made ; and we further assume that

(4.20) $$c'^{+}(s\ ;\ v) \geq c'^{+}(t\ ;\ v) \text{ if } s \leq t,\ \forall v$$ [1]

We denote the mean demand on the interval (0, t) by

(4.21) $$\bar{\xi}(t) = \frac{1}{t} \int_0^t \xi(s)ds$$

and its maximum value by

(4.22) $$\bar{\xi}(L) = \max_t \bar{\xi}(t).$$

---

[1] For simplicity assume that (4.20) holds for the Borel representation (cf. (3.5))

Theorem 4.2

Under the assumptions of Lemma 4.1, which are relevant for the convex case, and (4.20), (4.22) : L is a planning horizon.

Proof

We need to prove that L is a regeneration point for an optimal control of $J_0^T(v(.))$, $\forall T \geq L$.

Consider an optimal control for $J_0^T(v(.))$, $T > L$, then there exists $s_0 \in (0, L]$ which is a regeneration point. Otherwise we would have

(4.23) $\quad y(t) > 0, \forall t \in (0, L]$

Let r be the first strictly positive regeneration point, then from (4.23) we have

(4.24) $\quad L < r \leq T, \; y(t) > 0, \; \forall t \in (0,r)$

Let us prove that

(4.25) $\quad$ a.e. $s \in (0, L)$, a.e. $t \in (L, r)$, we have $u(s) \leq u(t)$.

Indeed (4.25) is clear if Meas $I \cap (0, L) = 0$, or Meas $J \cap (L, r) = 0$. Thus we may assume that

$$\text{Meas } I \cap (0, L) > 0, \qquad \text{Meas } J \cap (L, r) > 0,$$

and clearly it is sufficient to restrict oneself to

$$s \in I \cap (0, L), \; t \in J \cap (L, r)$$

or

$$s \in I^- \cap (0, L), \; t \in J^+ \cap (L, r).$$

But then we may apply (3.8), which implies

$$c'^-(s \; ; u(s)) - c'^+(t \; ; u(t)) + \int_s^t f'^-(\lambda \; ; y(\lambda))d\lambda \leq 0$$

since

$$f'^-(\lambda \; ; y(\lambda)) \geq f'^+(\lambda \; ; 0) > 0$$

we have

$$\int_s^t f'^-(\lambda \; ; y(\lambda))d\lambda > 0, \text{ hence}$$

$$c'^-(s \; ; u(s)) < c'^+(t \; ; u(t)).$$

From (4.20) it follows that

$$c'^-(s \; ; u(s)) < c'^+(s \; ; u(t))$$

hence

$$u(s) \leq u(t)$$

i.e. (4.25). But then it follows that

$$\frac{1}{r-L}\int_L^r u(t)dt \geq \inf_{t\in(r,L)} u(t) \geq \sup_{s\in(0,L)} u(s) \geq \frac{1}{L}\int_0^L u(s)ds$$

and

$$y(r) = y(L) + \int_L^r u(t)dt - \int_L^r \xi(t)dt$$

$$y(L) = \int_0^L u(s)ds - \int_0^L \xi(s)ds$$

Since $y(L) > 0$, we deduce that

$$\frac{1}{L}\int_0^L u(s)ds > \bar{\xi}(L)$$

hence

$$\int_L^r u(t)dt > (r-L)\,\bar{\xi}(L)$$

and

$$y(r) > (r-L)\,\bar{\xi}(L) - \int_L^r \xi(t)dt$$

$$= (r-L)\,\bar{\xi}(L) + \int_0^L \xi(t)dt - \int_0^r \xi(t)dt$$

$$= r\,\bar{\xi}(L) - r\,\bar{\xi}(r) \geq 0$$

which contradicts the fact that r is a regeneration point. Hence there exists $s_0 \in (0, L]$ which is a regeneration point. Consider the set of points $s \in (0, L]$ which are regeneration points, and

$$\bar{s} = \sup_{s\in(0,L]} \{s \text{ is a regeneration point}\}.$$

By the continuity of y it follows that $\bar{s}$ is also a regeneration point. Necessarily $\bar{s} = L$, otherwise we can reproduce the reasoning applied above, with $\bar{s}$ replacing 0, and find a point strictly larger than $\bar{s}$, which is also a regeneration point. This contradicts the definition of $\bar{s}$.

Therefore we have proved that L is a regeneration point, which completes the proof of the desired result. □

Remark 4.2

L is a weak planning horizon, since its value depends on all demands. (cf. Chapter I, § IV.4). □

Remark 4.3

While the result of theorem 4.2 is a natural extension of the discrete time case, it has not appeared previously in the literature. □

IV - 4. A PARTICULAR OPTIMAL CONTROL

Theorem 3.3 is useful to derive sufficient conditions for $u(t) = \xi(t)$ to be optimal This is analogue to the result of Theorem 3.3 of Chapter 2.

Theorem 4.3

Under the assumptions of Theorem 3.3 and

(4.26) $x = 0$

(4.27) $0 < \xi(t) < M$

(4.28) $$\begin{cases} c'^{+}(t\ ;\ \xi(t)) = c'^{-}(t\ ;\ \xi(t)) = c'(t\ ;\ \xi(t)) \\ \text{right continuous with bounded variations} \end{cases}$$

(4.29) $$\begin{cases} \lambda(t) = \int_0^t f'^{+}(s\ ;\ 0)ds + c'(0\ ;\ \xi(0)) - c'(t\ ;\ \xi(t)) \\ \text{non decreasing.} \end{cases}$$

Then $u(t) = \xi(t)$ is an optimal control.

Proof

We check that the necessary and sufficient conditions for optimality derived in Theorem 3.3 are satisfied with the following specifications :

(4.30) $$\begin{cases} p(t) = c'(t\ ;\ \xi(t)) \quad , \qquad t < T \\ p(T) = 0 \end{cases}$$

(4.31) $$\begin{cases} \lambda(t) = \int_0^t f'^{+}(s\ ;\ 0)ds + c'(0\ ;\ \xi(0)) - c'(t\ ;\ \xi(t)), \quad t < T \\ \lambda(T) = \int_0^T f'^{+}(s\ ;\ 0)ds \end{cases}$$

From the assumption (4.29) $\lambda(t)$ is non decreasing, $\lambda(0) = 0$, and $p(t)$ is right continuous with bounded variations. Moreover

$$\lambda + p = \int_0^t f'^{+}(s\ ;\ 0)ds + c'(0\ ;\ \xi(0))$$

hence

$$\frac{d}{dt}(\lambda+p) = f'^{+}(t\ ;\ 0).$$

Since $u(t) = \xi(t)$ we have $0 < u(t) < M$ and $y(t) = 0$. Therefore all conditions of Theorem 3.3 are satisfied, which completes the proof. □

The following property is helpful in deriving planning horizons for production planning problems where the maximum level of inventory is bounded.

Proposition 4.1

Under the assumptions of Theorem 3.3 and

(4.32) $$\begin{cases} c'^{-}(t\ ;\ v) = c'^{+}(t\ ;\ v) = c'(t\ ;\ v) \\ f'^{-}(t\ ;\ x) = f'^{+}(t\ ;\ x) = f'(t\ ;\ x), \end{cases}$$

consider an S horizon problem $S \geq T$, and let $\tilde{u}$, $\tilde{y}$, $\tilde{p}$, $\tilde{\lambda}$ be an optimal control, trajectory and corresponding adjoint variables for the S horizon problem. Then we have

$$(4.33) \qquad p(0) \leq \tilde{p}(0)$$

Proof

Note that from Theorem 3.2 we have

$$(4.34) \qquad y(T) = 0 \leq \tilde{y}(T)$$

Assume that $\tilde{p}(0) < p(0)$. The right continuity of $\tilde{p}$, p implies there exists an interval $[0,\varepsilon]$ where $\tilde{p}(t) < p(t)$. Then, let us prove that on this interval one has

$$(4.35) \qquad u(t) \geq \tilde{u}(t), \text{ a.e. on } (0,\varepsilon)$$

Indeed it is sufficient to consider points such that $\tilde{u}(t) > 0$ and $u(t) < M$, then,

$$\tilde{p}(t) \geq c'(t\ ;\ u(t)), p(t) \leq c'(t\ ;\ u(t))$$

hence

$$c'(t\ ;\ \tilde{u}(t)) < c'(t\ ;\ u(t))$$

which implies (4.35). But since $y(0) = \tilde{y}(0)$ and from (4.35) we deduce that

$$(4.36) \qquad y(t) \geq \tilde{y}(t)$$

We cannot have

$$(4.37) \qquad u(t) = \tilde{u}(t)$$

except, may be, on a set of Lebesgue measure 0 in $(0,\varepsilon)$. Otherwise if (4.37) holds on $I \cap (0,\varepsilon)$ with Meas $I > 0$, then on $I \cap (0,\varepsilon)$ we have

$$c'(t\ ;\ u(t)) \geq p(t) > \tilde{p}(t) \geq c'(t\ ;\ \tilde{u}(t)) = c'(t\ ;\ u(t))$$

which is a contradiction.

As a consequence

$$(4.38) \qquad y(t) > \tilde{y}(t) \qquad \forall t \in (0,\varepsilon]$$

but then $d\lambda = 0$, and thus

$$dp = f'(t\ ;\ y(t))dt \geq f'(t\ ;\ \tilde{y}(t))dt \geq d\tilde{p}$$

which implies $p(\varepsilon) > \tilde{p}(\varepsilon)$, given that $p(0) > \tilde{p}(0)$. Then we can clearly proceed beyond ε up to time T, and thus $y(T) > 0$, which is a contradiction. Therefore (4.33) holds, which completes the proof. □

Remark 4.4

Proposition 4.1 is inspired from Sethi and Thompson [1981].

These authors consider models with upper and lower constraints on the state variable and deduce planning and forecast horizons results, based on a slightly different concept.

IV - 5. THE CASE OF BACKLOGGING

In addition to the assumptions of Theorem 3.4, (4.1), (4.2), (4.3), (4.4) we also suppose that :

(4.39)
$$\begin{cases} \text{In the convex case } \int_0^\infty f'^{+}(\lambda\ ;\ 0)d\lambda = +\infty,\ f'^{+}(\lambda\ ;\ 0) > 0, \\ \qquad\qquad\qquad\quad \int_0^\infty f'^{-}(\lambda\ ;\ 0)d\lambda = -\infty,\ f'^{-}(\lambda\ ;\ 0) < 0\ ; \\ \text{In the concave case } \int_0^\infty f'^{-}(\lambda\ ;\ M\lambda)d\lambda = +\infty,\ \int_0^\infty f'^{+}(\lambda\ ;\ -M\lambda)d\lambda = -\infty\ ; \end{cases}$$

(4.40)
$$\begin{cases} \text{In the convex case, } c'^{-}(t\ ;\ M) \text{ bounded as } t \text{ varies, } c'^{+}(t\ ;\ \xi(t)) \\ \text{is lower semi continuous ;} \\ \text{In the concave case, } c'^{+}(t\ ;\ 0) \text{ is bounded, } c'^{-}(t\ ;\ M) \text{ is lower semi} \\ \text{continuous ;} \end{cases}$$

Let $s < t < T$, and consider the functions :

(4.41)
$$\begin{cases} F(s\ ;\ t) = c'^{+}(s\ ;\ \xi(s)) + \int_s^t f'^{+}(\lambda\ ;\ 0)d\lambda & \text{in the convex case} \\ \qquad\qquad = c'^{-}(s\ ;\ M) + \int_s^t f'^{-}(\lambda\ ;\ (\lambda-s)M)d\lambda & \text{in the concave case} \end{cases}$$

(4.42)
$$\begin{cases} G(s,\ t) = c'^{+}(t\ ;\ \xi(t)) - \int_s^t f'^{-}(\lambda\ ;\ 0)d\lambda & \text{in the convex case} \\ \qquad\qquad = c'^{-}(t\ ;\ M) - \int_s^t f'^{+}(\lambda\ ;\ (\lambda-t)M)d\lambda & \text{in the concave case} \end{cases}$$

Let also

(4.43)
$$B = \begin{cases} \sup_\sigma c'^{-}(\sigma\ ;\ M) & \text{in the convex case} \\ \sup_\sigma c'^{+}(\sigma\ ;\ 0) & \text{in the concave case} \end{cases}$$

We have

$$F(s,\ t) \to +\infty \qquad \text{as } t \to \infty$$

and

$$F(s,\ s) = c'^{+}(s\ ;\ \xi(s)) \le c'^{+}(s\ ;\ M) \le B \text{ in the convex case}$$

$$F(s,\ s) = c'^{-}(s\ ;\ M) \le c'^{+}(s\ ;\ 0) \le B \quad \text{in the concave case}$$

Therefore we define

(4.44)
$$H(s) = \inf_{t \ge s} \{F(s,\ t) \ge B\}$$

The function $G(s,\ t)$ increases as s decreases for t fixed, and

$$G(t, t) = c'^{+}(t\ ;\ \xi(t)) \leq B \text{ in the convex case}$$

$$G(t, t) = c'^{-}(t\ ;\ M) \leq B \quad \text{in the concave case.}$$

We set

$$L(t) = \inf_{0 \leq s \leq t} \{G(s, t) \leq B\} \tag{4.45}$$

We can then state the following

Lemma 4.2

Under the assumptions of Theorem 3.4 and (4.1), (4.2), (4.3), (4.39), (4.40) and the following condition :

$$\text{there exists an optimal control for the problem } J_0^T(v(.)),\ \forall T > 0.$$

Consider an optimal control for $J_0^T(v(.))$ and let s be a point such that $s < H(s) \leq T$, and $y(s) \leq 0$. Then, there exists an additional point s^* in $(s, H(s)]$ such that $y(s^*) \leq 0$. Similarly, let t be a point such that $L(t) < t \leq T$ and $y(t) \geq 0$. Then, there exists a point t^* in $[L(t), t)$ such that $y(t^*) \geq 0$.

Proof

If $H(s) = T$, there is nothing to prove since $y(T) \leq 0$. Assume $H(s) < T$, and that

$$y(t) > 0 \text{ in } (s, H(s)] \tag{4.46}$$

Necessarily

$$y(s) = 0 \tag{4.47}$$

We are then in a situation similar to that of Lemma 4.1. Therefore for any ε with $s+\varepsilon < H(s)$ we can find σ in $(s, s+\varepsilon)$ and t in $(H(s), T)$ such that $u(\sigma) > \xi(\sigma)$, $y(\lambda) > 0$, $\lambda \in [\sigma,t]$, and $u(t) < M$, σ in I^-, t in J^+ ; applying the first condition (3.37) we obtain

$$c'^{-}(\sigma\ ;\ u(\sigma)) - c'^{+}(t\ ;\ u(t)) + \int_\sigma^t f'^{-}(\lambda\ ;\ y(\lambda))d\lambda \leq 0.$$

We can then follow the same line of argument than in Lemma 4.1 to conclude that $t \leq H(s)$, which is a contradiction.

Let us now prove the second part of the Lemma. If $L(t) = 0$, there is nothing to prove.

Assume therefore that $0 < L(t) < t \leq T$, and that

$$y(s) < 0,\ s \in [L(t),t) \tag{4.48}$$

then necessarily

$$y(t) = 0. \tag{4.49}$$

Recalling the definition of I_0 (cf. Lemma 4.1), we have

$$\forall\varepsilon > 0,\ t-\varepsilon > L(t),\ \text{Meas } I_0 \cap (t-\varepsilon, t) > 0 \tag{4.50}$$

Otherwise $\exists\varepsilon$ such that Meas $I_0 \cap (t-\varepsilon, t) = 0$, then

$$0 = y(t-\varepsilon) + \int_{t-\varepsilon}^{t} (u(s) - \xi(s))ds \leq y(t-\varepsilon) < 0$$

which is a contradiction. Also

(4.51) $$\text{Meas } I_0 \cap I^- \cap (t-\varepsilon, t) = 0$$

Moreover one has

(4.52) $$\text{Meas } J \cap (0, L(t)) > 0$$

Otherwise we have $u(s) = M$ a.e. in $(0, L(t))$ hence

$$y(L(t)) = \int_0^{L(t)} (M - \xi(s))ds \geq 0$$

which is a contradiction.

It follows that

(4.53) $$\text{Meas } J^+ \cap (0, L(t)) > 0$$

We then choose s in $J^+ \cap (0, L(t))$ such that

(4.54) $$y(\lambda) < 0, \lambda \in [s,\theta]$$

where $\theta \in I_0 \cap I^- \cap (t-\varepsilon, t)$. We have already $y(\lambda) < 0$ for $\lambda \in [L(t),\theta]$. Let s_1 in $[0, L(t))$ such that

(4.55) $$y(L(t)) + \int_{s_1}^{L(t)} \xi(\lambda)d\lambda = 0$$

Since

$$0 \leq y(L(t)) + \int_0^{L(t)} \xi(\lambda)d\lambda$$

and $y(L(t)) < 0$, the point s_1 is well defined. If Meas $J \cap (s_1, L(t)) > 0$, we choose s in $J^+ \cap (s_1, L(t))$ and (4.54) holds. Otherwise we have Meas $J \cap (s_1, L(t)) = 0$, which implies

$$y(s_1) = y(L(t)) + \int_{s_1}^{L(t)} (\xi(\lambda) - M)d\lambda \leq y(L(t)) < 0$$

and we define $0 \leq s_2 < s_1$ such that

$$0 = y(s_1) + \int_{s_2}^{s_1} \xi(\lambda)d\lambda.$$

We define a sequence

$$0 \leq s_{n+1} < s_n \dots < L(t)$$

such that

$$y(s_n) \le y(s_{n-1})$$

$$y(s_n) + \int_{s_{n+1}}^{s_n} \xi(\lambda)d\lambda = 0$$

$$\text{Meas } J \cap (s_n, L(t)) = 0.$$

The sequence is necessarily finite. Therefore there exists an interval such that

$$\text{Meas } J^+ \cap (s_{n+1}, s_n) > 0$$

$$\text{Meas } J \cap (s_n, L(t)) = 0$$

and we take s in $J^+ \cap (s_{n+1}, s_n)$, which implies (4.54). From the first condition (3.38) we deduce

$$c'^+(s\ ;\ u(s)) - c'^-(\theta\ ;\ u(\theta)) + \int_s^\theta f'^+(\lambda\ ;\ y(\lambda))d\lambda \ge 0 \tag{4.56}$$

Consider the convex case.

Since $\theta \in I_0$, $u(\theta) > \xi(\theta)$ hence :

$$c'^-(\theta\ ;\ u(\theta)) > c'^+(\theta\ ;\ \xi(\theta)),$$

$$c'^+(s\ ;\ u(s)) < c'^-(s\ ;\ M)$$

and since $y(\lambda) < 0$

$$f'^+(\lambda\ ;\ y(\lambda)) \le f'^-(\lambda\ ;\ 0)$$

therefore we deduce from (4.56)

$$B > c'^+(\theta\ ;\ \xi(\theta)) - \int_s^\theta f'^-(\lambda\ ;\ 0)d\lambda$$

and from the lower semi continuity of $c'^+(t\ ;\ \xi(t))$

$$B \ge G(s, t) \tag{4.57}$$

hence $s \ge L(t)$ which is a contradiction.

In the concave case we have

$$c'^-(\theta\ ;\ u(\theta)) \ge c'^-(\theta\ ;\ M)$$

$$c'^+(s\ ;\ u(s)) \le c'^+(s\ ;\ 0) \le B$$

$$f'^+(\lambda\ ;\ y(\lambda)) \le f'^+(\lambda\ ;\ M(\lambda-t))$$

since

$$y(\lambda) = -\int_\lambda^t (u(\mu) - \xi(\mu))d\mu \ \ge -M(t-\lambda).$$

Therefore from (4.56) it follows that

$$B \geq c'^{-}(t\ ;\ M) - \int_s^t f'^{+}(\lambda\ ;\ M(\lambda - t))d\lambda = G(s,\ t)$$

and again a contradiction. □

Let us now give a result which is the analogue of Theorem 4.2. Considering the average demand function $\bar{\xi}(t)$ (cf. (4.21)) we set

(4.58) $$\bar{\xi}(L^*) = \max_t \bar{\xi}(t)$$

(4.59) $$\bar{\xi}(L^{**}) = \min_t \bar{\xi}(t)$$

As a consequence we assume that both the max and the min are attained. We also assume either (4.20) or

(4.60) $$c'^{+}(s\ ;\ v) \leq c'^{+}(t\ ;\ v) \text{ if } s \leq t,\ \forall v$$

Of course if both (4.20), (4.60) are satisfied, it means that $c'^{+}(s\ ;\ v)$ is independent of s.

Theorem 4.4

Under the assumptions of Lemma 4.2 which are relevant for the convex case, (4.58) and (4.20), let $T \geq L^*$; then we have

(4.61) $$y(L^*) \leq 0.$$

If we assume (4.59) and (4.60) then for $T \geq L^{**}$, the following property holds

(4.62) $$\text{if } y(L^{**}) < 0, \text{ then } y(t) < 0,\ \forall t \in [L^{**},\ T]$$

Proof

Assume $T > L^*$ otherwise (4.61) is clear. We proceed in a way which is quite similar to that of Theorem 4.2. We first prove that there exists $s_0 \in (0,\ L^*]$ such that

(4.63) $$y(s_0) \leq 0$$

Otherwise we have

(4.64) $$y(t) > 0\ ,\ \ \forall t \in (0,\ L^*]$$

Let r be the first strictly positive time such that $y(r) \leq 0$, we necessarily have

(4.65) $$L^* < r \leq T,\ y(r) = 0,\ y(t) > 0;\ \forall t \in (0,\ r)$$

Then we prove that

(4.66) $$\text{a.e. } s \in (0,\ L^*),\ \text{a.e. } t \in (L^*,\ r) \text{ we have } u(s) \leq u(t)$$

The proof of (4.66) is identical to that of Theorem 4.2 ; we also conclude (4.63) as in Theorem 4.2. But then we consider the set of points $s \in (0,\ L^*]$ such that $y(s) \leq 0$ and

$$\bar{s} = \sup_{s \in (0, L^*]} \{\ y(s) \leq 0\}$$

By the continuity of y, it follows that $y(\bar{s}) \leq 0$. Necessarily $\bar{s} = L^*$, otherwise we can follow the same reasoning as above, with $\bar{s}$ replacing 0, and find a point strictly larger of $\bar{s}$ in $(0, L^*]$ for which y is negative. This contradicts the definition of $\bar{s}$.

Let us now prove (4.62). There is nothing to prove if $L^{**} = T$. Assume $L^{**} < T$, and $y(L^{**}) < 0$. If (4.62) does not hold, there exists points t in $(L^{**}, T]$ such that $y(t) \geq 0$, define

(4.67) $$t_0 = \inf_{t \in (L^{**},T]} \{t \mid y(t) \geq 0\}$$

necessarily by the continuity of y

(4.68) $$y(t_0) = 0,\ y(t) < 0,\ t \in [L^{**}, t_0).$$

Let also

(4.69) $$r_0 = \sup_{0 \leq s < L^{**}} \{s \mid y(s) \geq 0\}$$

we also have

(4.70) $$y(r_0) = 0,\ y(t) < 0,\ t \in (r_0, L^{**}]$$

Let us show that

(4.71) a.e.s in (r_0, L^{**}), a.e. t in (L^{**}, t_0), we have $u(s) \geq u(t)$.

There is nothing to prove if

$$\text{Meas } J \cap (r_0, L^{**}) = 0$$

or

$$\text{Meas } I \cap (L^{**}, t_0) = 0$$

Hence we may assume

$$\text{Meas } J \cap (r_0, L^{**}) > 0,\ \text{Meas } I \cap (L^{**}, t_0) > 0$$

and it is enough to prove (4.71) for

$$s \in J \cap (r_0, L^{**}) \text{ and } t \in I \cap (L^{**}, t_0)$$

or

$$s \in J^+ \cap (r_0, L^{**}) \text{ and } t \in I^- \cap (L^{**}, t_0).$$

We can then apply (3.38), which implies

$$c'^+(s\ ;\ u(s)) - c'^-(t\ ;\ u(t)) + \int_s^t f'^+(\lambda\ ;\ y(\lambda))d\lambda \geq 0.$$

Since $y(\lambda) < 0$ for $\lambda \in [s,t]$, we have $f'^+(\lambda\ ;\ y(\lambda)) \leq f'^-(\lambda\ ;\ 0) < 0$

hence

$$c'^{+}(s\ ;\ u(s)) > c'^{-}(t\ ;\ u(t))$$

and from (4.60)

$$c'^{+}(t\ ;\ u(s)) > c'^{-}(t\ ;\ u(t))$$

hence (4.71). Next we have

$$y(L^{**}) = \int_{r_0}^{L^{**}} (u(s) - \xi(s))ds$$

$$0 = \int_{0}^{r_0} (u(s) - \xi(s))ds$$

Therefore

$$(4.72) \qquad y(L^{**}) = \int_{0}^{L^{**}} (u(s) - \xi(s))ds < 0$$

hence

$$(4.73) \qquad \frac{1}{L^{**}} \int_{0}^{L^{**}} u(s)ds < \bar{\xi}(L^{**})$$

Now

$$(4.74) \qquad y(t_0) = y(L^{**}) + \int_{L^{**}}^{t_0} (u(t) - \xi(t))dt$$

and from (4.71)

$$\frac{1}{L^{**}-r_0} \int_{r_0}^{L^{**}} u(s)ds \geq \inf_{s\in(r_0,L^{**})} u(s) \geq \sup_{t\in(L^{**},t_0)} u(t)$$

$$\geq \frac{1}{t_0-L^{**}} \int_{L^{**}}^{t_0} u(t)dt$$

But

$$\int_{r_0}^{L^{**}} u(s)ds = \int_{r_0}^{L^{**}} u(s)ds - \int_{0}^{r_0} \xi(s)ds$$

$$\leq \int_{0}^{L^{**}} u(s)ds - r_0\, \bar{\xi}(L^{**})$$

and from (4.73)

$$< (L^{**} - r_0)\, \bar{\xi}(L^{**})$$

Therefore from (4.75) we deduce

$$\int_{L^{**}}^{t_0} u(t)dt < (t_0 - L^{**})\, \bar{\xi}(L^{**})$$

and (4.74) implies

$$y(t_0) < y(L^{**}) + (t_0 - L^{**})\ \bar{\xi}(L^{**}) + L^{**}\ \bar{\xi}(L^{**}) - \int_0^{t_0} \xi(t)dt$$
$$< y(L^{**}) < 0$$

which contradicts (4.68). This completes the proof of the desired results. □

As in the discrete time case (cf. Lemma 4.5 of Chapter II) we prove the analogue of Lemma 4.2 for positive values of the state. Let us define

$$(4.76)\quad \begin{cases} K(s,t) = c'^{+}(t\ ;\ 0) - \int_s^t f'^{-}(\lambda\ ;\ 0)d\lambda & \text{in the convex case} \\ \quad = c'^{-}(t\ ;\ M) - \int_s^t f'^{+}(\lambda\ ;\ -M(\lambda-s))d\lambda & \text{in the concave case} \end{cases}$$

We assume that

$$(4.77)\quad \begin{cases} c'^{+}(t\ ;\ 0) \text{ is increasing (in the convex case)} \\ c'^{-}(t\ ;\ M) \text{ is increasing (in the concave case)} \end{cases}$$

$$(4.78)\quad \begin{cases} c'^{+}(t\ ;\ \xi(t)) \text{ is upper semi continuous (in the convex case)} \\ c'^{+}(t\ ;\ 0) \text{ is upper semi continuous (in the concave case)} \end{cases}$$

Now from (4.39)

$$K(s,\ t) \uparrow +\infty \quad \text{as } t \uparrow +\infty\ .$$

We set next

$$J(s) = \inf_{t \geq s} K(s,t) \geq \begin{cases} c'^{+}(s\ ;\ \xi(s)) \text{ in the convex case} \\ c'^{+}(s\ ;\ 0) \text{ in the concave case} \end{cases}$$

Note that

$$K(s,\ s) \leq B$$

hence $J(s)$ is well defined.

We have the following

Lemma 4.3.

Under the assumptions of Theorem 1.3, and (4.1), (4.2), (4.3), (4.39), (4.77), (4.78) and assuming that there exists an optimal control for the problem $J_0^T(v(.))$, $\forall T > 0$, consider an optimal control for $J_0^T(v(.))$ and let s be such that

$$(4.79)\quad s < J(s) < T, \quad y(s) \geq 0$$

and

$$(4.80)\quad \begin{cases} c'^{+}(s\ ;\ \xi(s)) + \int_s^T f'^{-}(\lambda\ ;\ 0)d\lambda < 0 \text{ in the convex case} \\ \\ c'^{+}(s\ ;\ 0) + \int_s^T f'^{+}(\lambda\ ;\ -M(\lambda-s))d\lambda < 0 \text{ in the concave case} \end{cases}$$

Then there exists an additional point s^* in $(s, J(s)]$, such that $y(s^*) \geq 0$.

Proof

First remark that (4.80) is satisfied when T-s is large enough (this follows from (4.39), (4.40)).

If the statement is false then we have

$$(4.81)\qquad y(t) < 0,\ \forall t \in (s, J(s)]$$

Necessarily

$$(4.82)\qquad y(s) = 0$$

Let

$$J_0 = \{t \mid u(t) < \xi(t)\}$$

then we have

$$(4.83)\qquad \forall\varepsilon > 0,\ s+\varepsilon < J(s),\ \text{Meas } J_0 \cap (s, s+\varepsilon) > 0.$$

Otherwise, $\exists\,\varepsilon$ such that Meas $J_0 \cap (s, s+\varepsilon) = 0$. But then

$$y(s+\varepsilon) \geq 0$$

which contradicts (4.81). Then also

$$(4.84)\qquad \text{Meas } J_0 \cap J^+ \cap (s, s+\varepsilon) > 0$$

We also have

$$(4.85)\qquad \text{Meas } J \cap (J(s), T) > 0$$

Otherwise $u(t) = 0$ a.e. in $(J(s), T)$, hence

$$y(t) < 0,\ \forall t \in [s, T].$$

Taking σ in $J_0 \cap J^+ \cap (s, s+\varepsilon)$, we have from the second condition (3.38)

$$(4.86)\qquad c'^{+}(\sigma\ ;\ u(\sigma)) + \int_\sigma^T f'^{+}(\lambda\ ;\ y(\lambda))d\lambda \geq 0$$

Consider the convex case. Since $\sigma \in J_0, u(\sigma) < \xi(\sigma)$, hence

$$c'^{+}(\sigma\ ;\ \xi(\sigma)) > c'^{+}(\sigma\ ;\ u(\sigma)).$$

Furthermore, since $y(\lambda) < 0$

$$f'^{+}(\lambda\ ;\ y(\lambda)) \leq f'^{-}(\lambda\ ;\ 0)$$

hence

$$c'^{+}(\sigma \; ; \; \xi(\sigma)) + \int_{\sigma}^{T} f'^{-}(\lambda \; ; \; 0)d\lambda > 0$$

and from (4.78) we deduce, letting ε tend to 0,

$$c'^{+}(s \; ; \; \xi(s)) + \int_{s}^{T} f'^{-}(\lambda \; ; \; 0)d\lambda \geq 0$$

wich contradicts (4.80).

Similarly in the concave case, since

$$u(\sigma) \geq 0, \; y(\lambda) = \int_{s}^{\lambda} (u(\mu) - \xi(\mu))d\mu \geq - M(\lambda-s)$$

$$c'^{+}(\sigma \; ; \; 0) + \int_{\sigma}^{T} f'^{+}(\lambda \; ; \; -M(\lambda-s))ds \geq 0$$

and letting $\varepsilon \to 0$, from (4.78) we obtain

$$c'^{+}(s \; ; \; 0) + \int_{s}^{T} f'^{+}(\lambda \; ; \; -M(\lambda-s))ds \geq 0$$

which contradicts (4.80). Therefore (4.85) is proved. Hence also

(4.87) $\quad \text{Meas } I^{-} \cap (J(s), T) > 0$

We know that there exists t_0 in $(J(s), T]$ such that $y(t_0) \geq 0$, hence there exists $t_1 \leq t_0$ such that

$$y(J(s)) + \int_{J(s)}^{t_1} (M - \xi(\lambda))d\lambda = 0$$

If Meas $I \cap (J(s), t_1) > 0$, then we choose $t \in I^{-} \cap (J(s), t_1)$, hence

(4.88) $\quad y(\lambda) < 0, \; \forall \; \lambda \in (s, t].$

Otherwise we have $y(t_1) \leq y(J(s))$, and we consider t_2 such that $t_1 < t_2 \leq t_0$

$$y(t_1) + \int_{t_1}^{t_2} (M - \xi(\lambda))d\lambda = 0$$

and more generally, for $t_n < t_{n+1} \leq t_0$,

$$y(t_n) \leq y(t_{n-1}) < 0$$

$$y(t_n) + \int_{t_n}^{t_{n+1}} (M - \xi(\lambda))d\lambda = 0.$$

Necessarily we obtain an interval (t_n, t_{n+1}) such that

(4.89) $\quad \text{Meas } I^{-} \cap (t_n, t_{n+1}) > 0, \; y(\lambda) < 0, \; \lambda \in (s, t_{n+1}).$

We then take σ in $J_0 \cap J^+ \cap (s, s+\varepsilon)$ and t in $I^- \cap (t_n, t_{n+1})$. We deduce from the first condition (3.38)

$$(4.90) \qquad c'^+(\sigma ; u(\sigma)) - c'^-(t ; u(t)) + \int_\sigma^t f'^+(\lambda ; y(\lambda))d\lambda \geq 0.$$

<u>Consider the convex case</u>. We deduce from (4.90)

$$c'^+(\sigma ; \xi(\sigma)) + \int_\sigma^t f'^+(\lambda ; 0)d\lambda \geq c'^+(t ; 0)$$

hence from (4.78)

$$c'^+(s ; \xi(s)) \geq K(s,t)$$

therefore $t \leq J(s)$, which is a contradiction.

In <u>the concave case</u>, (4.90) implies

$$c'^+(s ; 0) \geq K(s, t)$$

and we reach the same conclusion. □

<u>Lemma 4.4</u>

Assume that

$$(4.91) \qquad \begin{cases} c'^+(s ; \xi(s)) \text{ is increasing (in the convex case)} \\ c'^+(s ; 0) \text{ is increasing (in the concave case)} \end{cases}$$

then J(s) is an increasing function.

Assume that

$$(4.92) \qquad \begin{cases} c'^+(s ; \xi(s)) \text{ is decreasing (in the convex case)} \\ c'^-(s ; M) \text{ is decreasing (in the concave case)} \end{cases}$$

then H(s) is an increasing function.

<u>Proof</u>

Consider $s_1 < s_2$, we want to prove that

$$(4.93) \qquad J(s_1) \leq J(s_2)$$

We may assume $J(s_1) > s_2$ otherwise we get (4.93) since $J(s_2) \geq s_2$.

In <u>the convex case</u>, consider

$$K(s_2, J(s_1)) = c'^+(J(s_1) ; 0) - \int_{s_2}^{J(s_1)} f'^-(\lambda ; 0)d\lambda$$

$$< c'^+(J(s_1) ; 0) - \int_{s_1}^{J(s_1)} f'^-(\lambda ; 0)d\lambda$$

and from the definition of $J(s_1)$:

$$K(s_2, J(s_1)) < c'^+(s_1 ; \xi(s_1))$$
$$< c'^+(s_2 ; \xi(s_2))$$

therefore (4.93) holds. A similar reasoning holds in the concave case.

Let us prove now the second part of the Lemma, that is :

(4.94) $H(s_1) \le H(s_2)$.

Again we may assume $H(s_1) > s_2$.

In the convex case, we thus have

$$F(s_2, H(s_1)) = c'^+(s_2 ; \xi(s_2)) + \int_{s_2}^{H(s_1)} f'^+(\lambda ; 0)d\lambda$$

and from (4.92)

$$< c'^+(s_1 ; \xi(s_1)) + \int_{s_1}^{H(s_1)} f'^+(\lambda ; 0)d\lambda = B$$

therefore (4.94) holds.

A similar reasoning holds in the concave case. □

A forecast horizon theorem can thus be stated. First , set

(4.95) $\bar{J} = \inf \{t \ge 0 \mid \int_0^t f'^-(\lambda ; 0)d\lambda + c'^+(0 ; \xi(0)) \le 0\}$ in the convex case

$= \inf \{t \ge 0 \mid \int_0^t f'^+(\lambda ; -M(\lambda-s))d\lambda + c'^+(0 ; 0) \le 0\}$ in the concave case.

(4.96) $H = H(0), \ J = J(0)$

Note that $J < \bar{J}$ then, we obtain the following result.

Theorem 4.5

Under the assumptions of Lemma 4.2 and Lemma 4.3, set

$$T = \text{Max } (H, \bar{J}).$$

Then T is a forecast horizon in the sense that $\forall S > T$, there exists an optimal policy for $J_0^S(v(.))$ which has a regeneration point in (0, T].

Proof

Consider an optimal policy for $J_0^S(v(.))$. Since $S > \bar{J}$, there are points r in (0, J] such that $y(r) \ge 0$, by Lemma 4.3.

On the other hand, from Lemma 4.2, we can assert there exists points s in (0, H] such that $y(s) \le 0$. Assume that

$$y(s) < 0, \ s \in (0, H]$$

then $J > H$ and there exists r in $(H, J]$ such that $y(r) \geq 0$. We consider then

$$r_0 = \inf \{r \in (H, J] \mid y(r) \geq 0\}$$

by continuity of y, necessarily $y(r_0) = 0$, hence r_0 is a regeneration point. □

V - PRODUCTION SMOOTHING

Synopsis

In this section we extend the production smoothing model developed in section V of Chapter 2, to a continuous time formulation.

V - 1. NOTATION AND ASSUMPTIONS

The demand function satisfies

$$(5.1) \qquad 0 \leq \xi(t) \text{ for } t \in [0,T] \text{ and } \int_0^T \xi(t)dt < \infty$$

The production and inventory cost functions are denoted

$c(t\ ;\ v)$, $f(t\ ;\ x)$ respectively and satisfy (2.4), (2.5).

There are smoothing cost functions denoted :

$$(5.2) \qquad \begin{cases} h(t\ ;\ w)\ :\ [0,T] \times R \to R^+ \text{ with the following properties :} \\ .\ \text{convex in } w \text{ and its minimum is achieved at } 0, \\ .\ h'^{+}(t\ ;\ -\infty) \text{ and } h'^{-}(t\ ;\ +\infty) \text{ are continuous functions of } t \\ .\ \text{a.e. } t \quad h(t\ ;\ w) = \tilde{h}(t\ ;\ w),\ \forall w, \text{ where } \tilde{h} \text{ is a Borel function} \\ g(T,\ v)\ :\ R \to R^+ \text{ convex, continuous and minimum at } 0 \end{cases}$$

The dynamic system is defined as follows :

$$(5.3) \qquad \begin{cases} \dfrac{dy}{dt} = v(t) - \xi(t) \\ y(0) = x \\ \dfrac{dv}{dt} = w(t) \end{cases}$$

with the constraints

$$(5.4) \qquad y(t) \geq 0,\ v(t) \geq 0$$

The control satisfies

$$(5.5) \qquad w(.) \in L^2(0,T),\ v(0) \geq 0$$

but there are no sign constraints on w. Note that $y(t)$, $v(t)$ are continuous functions, and that (5.4) holds for any t on $[0,T]$.

The functional to be minimized is

$$(5.6) \qquad \begin{cases} J_0(x\ ;\ w(.),\ v(0)) = \int_0^T c(t\ ;\ v(t))dt + \int_0^T f(t\ ;\ y(t))dt \\ \qquad + \int_0^T h(t\ ;\ w(t))dt + g(T\ ;\ v(T)) \end{cases}$$

Now we consider $v(.)$ as a state variable, instead of a control variable, but $v(0)$ remains a control variable.

The functional J_0 is a convex functional.

The above assumptions do not guarantee there exists an optimal control. In the sequel we shall postulate the existence of an optimal control.

V - 2. NECESSARY CONDITIONS FOR OPTIMALITY

We denote by $\hat{w}(.)$ an optimal control an by $\hat{y}(.)$, $\hat{v}(.)$ the corresponding trajectory.

Assume that

$$(5.7)\qquad \begin{cases} \int_0^T |h'^+(t\ ;\ \hat{w}(t))|^2 dt, \int_0^T |h'^-(t\ ;\ \hat{w}(t))|^2 dt \\ \int_0^T |c'^+(t\ ;\ \hat{v}(t))|^2 dt, \int_0^T |c'^-(t\ ;\ \hat{v}(t))|^2 dt \\ \int_0^T |f'^+(t\ ;\ \hat{y}(t))|^2 dt, \int_0^T |f'^-(t\ ;\ \hat{y}(t))|^2 dt \end{cases}$$

are finite. We can then state

Theorem 5.1

Assume (2.4), (2.5), (5.2) and that there exists an optimal control $\hat{w}(.)$ for $J(w(.))$, such that (5.7) holds. Then, there exists adjoint functions $\lambda(.)$, $\mu(.)$, $p_1(.)$, $p_2(.)$ with bounded variations right continuous such that

$$(5.8)\qquad \lambda,\ \mu \text{ are non decreasing},\quad \lambda(0) = \mu(0) = 0$$

$$(5.9)\qquad \begin{cases} \lambda + p_1,\quad \mu + p_2 \in H^1(0, T) \\ \lambda + p_1 \in C([0, T]),\qquad \mu_2 + p_2 \in C(]0,T[) \end{cases}$$

$$(5.10)\qquad p_1(T) = p_2(T) = 0\ ;$$

$$(5.11)\qquad \int_0^T \hat{y}(t)d\mu(t) = 0$$

$$(5.12)\qquad \int_0^T \hat{v}(t)d\lambda(t) = 0$$

$$(5.13)\qquad h'^-(t\ ;\ \hat{w}(t)) \le p_2(t) \le h'^+(t\ ;\ \hat{w}(t)) \quad \text{a.e.}$$

$$(5.14)\qquad \begin{cases} \frac{d}{dt}(\mu(t) + p_2(t)) + p_1(t) \le c'^+(t\ ;\ \hat{v}(t)) \text{ a.e.} \\ \frac{d}{dt}(\mu(t) + p_2(t)) + p_1(t) \ge c'^-(t\ ;\ \hat{v}(t)) \text{ a.e.} \end{cases}$$

$$(5.15)\qquad \begin{cases} \frac{d}{dt}(\lambda(t) + p_1(t)) \le f'^+(t\ ;\ \hat{y}(t)) \text{ a.e.} \\ \frac{d}{dt}(\lambda(t) + p_1(t)) \ge f'^-(t\ ;\ \hat{y}(t)) \text{ a.e.} \end{cases}$$

$$(5.16)\qquad \begin{aligned} &g'^{+}(T,\hat{v}(T)) \geq \mu(T) - (p_2(T^-) + \ (T^-)) \geq g'^{-}(T\ ;\ \hat{v}(T)) \\ &p_2(0^+) + \mu(0^+) = 0 \end{aligned}$$

Proof

We proceed as in the proof of Theorem 3.3. From the theory of convex optimization there exists functions $\lambda(.)$, $\mu(.)$ verifying (5.8), (5.11), (5.12), and functions $p_1(.)$, $p_2(.)$ with bounded variations, right continuous, such that $\hat{v}$, $\hat{y}$, $\hat{w}$ minimizes the Lagrangian

$$(5.17)\qquad \begin{cases} L(w(.),\ v(.),\ y(.)) = \int_0^T c(t\ ;\ v(t))dt + \int_0^T f(t\ ;\ y(t))dt + g(T\ ;\ v(T)) \\ + \int_0^T h(t\ ;\ w(t))dt - \int_0^T d\lambda y(t) - \int_0^T d\mu\ v(t) - \int_0^T dp_1[y(t) \\ - \int_0^t (v(s) - \xi(s))ds - x] - \int_0^T dp_2[v(t) - \int_0^t w(s)ds - v(0)] \end{cases}$$

over the set

$$w(.) \in L^2(0,\ T),\ y(t) \in C(0,T)$$

$$v(.) \in C(0,\ T),$$

We can rewrite the Lagrangian as follows

$$\begin{aligned} L = &\int_0^T c(t\ ;\ v(t))dt + \int_0^T f(t\ ;\ y(t))dt + \int_0^T h(t\ ;\ w(t))dt - \int_0^T d\lambda y(t) \\ &- \int_0^T d\mu v(t) + p_1(T)\ [\int_0^T (v(t) - \xi(t))dt + x] - p_1(0)x \\ &- \int_0^T p_1(t)(v(t) - \xi(t))dt - p_2(0)v(0) + p_2(T)\ [\int_0^T w(t)dt + v(0)] \\ &- \int_0^T p_2(t)\ w(t)dt - \int_0^T y(t)dp_1(t) - \int_0^T v(t)dp_2(t) + g(T\ ;\ v(T)) \end{aligned}$$

Since p_1, p_2 are defined up to an additive constant, we may impose (5.10).

We split the minimization of L in three parts, namely

$$(5.18)\qquad \text{Min} \int_0^T [h(t\ ;\ w(t)) - p_2(t)\ w(t)]dt$$

without constraints

$$(5.19)\qquad \begin{cases} \text{Min} \int_0^T [c(t\ ;\ v(t)) - p_1(t)v(t)]dt - v(t)[dp_2(t) + d\mu(t)] - p_2(0)v(0) \\ + g(T\ ;\ v(T))\ \text{over}\ v(.) \in C(0,\ T) \end{cases}$$

$$(5.20)\qquad \text{Min} \int_0^T f(t\ ;\ y(t))dt - y(t)[d\lambda(t) + dp_1(t)]\ \text{over}\ y(.) \in C(0,\ T)$$

Reasoning as in the proof of Theorem 3.3, we easily deduce the conditions (5.13),

(5.14), (5.15), (5.16). □

Remark 5.1

By virtue of convexity, the conditions stated in Theorem 5.1, are also sufficient conditions for optimality. □

Remark 5.2

We may deduce results analogue to Theorem 5.2 in Chapter II. However due to the regularity problems, we can only write conditions involving integrals. More precisely, let us write the analogue of (5.40) in Chapter II. Consider

$$0 < s < s_1 \leq t_1 < t < T$$

and

$$(5.21) \quad \begin{cases} \hat{v}(\tau) > 0, \; \tau \in [s, s_1] \\ \hat{y}(\tau) > 0, \; \tau \in [s, t] \end{cases}$$

then we have

$$(5.22) \quad \begin{cases} \dfrac{1}{s_1-s} \displaystyle\int_s^{s_1} c'^-(\tau \; ; \hat{v}(\tau))d\tau + \int_{s_1}^{t_1} f'^-(\tau \; ; \hat{y}(\tau))d\tau \\ + \dfrac{[h'^-(t \; ; \hat{w}(t)) - h'^+(t_1 \; ; \hat{w}(t_1))]}{t - t_1} \\ \leq \dfrac{1}{t-t_1} \displaystyle\int_{t_1}^{t} c'^+(\tau \; ; \hat{v}(\tau))d\tau + \dfrac{[h'^+(s_1 \; ; \hat{w}(s_1)) - h'^-(s \; ; \hat{w}(s))]}{t - t_1} \end{cases}$$

Indeed from the second conditions (5.14) and (5.15) we can write

$$c'^-(\tau \; ; \hat{v}(\tau)) \leq p_1(\tau) + \frac{dp_2}{dt}(\tau), \; \tau \in (s, s_1)$$

$$f'^-(\theta \; ; \hat{y}(\theta)) \leq \frac{dp_1}{d\theta} \qquad , \; \theta \in (s, t)$$

It follows that

$$(5.23) \quad \int_s^{s_1} c'^-(\tau \; ; \hat{v}(\tau))d\tau \leq \int_s^{s_1} p_1(\tau)d\tau + p_2(s_1) - p_2(s)$$

But let θ in (t_1, t) and τ in (s, s_1), then we have

$$p_1(\theta) - p_1(\tau) \geq \int_\tau^\theta f'^-(\lambda \; ; \hat{y}(\lambda))d\lambda$$

and thus from (5.23)

$$(5.24) \quad \begin{cases} \displaystyle\int_s^{s_1} c'^-(\tau \; ; \hat{v}(\tau))d\tau \leq (s_1-s)p_1(\theta) - \int_s^{s_1} d\tau \int_\tau^\theta f'^-(\lambda \; ; \hat{y}(\lambda))d\lambda \\ + p_2(s_1) - p_2(s) \end{cases}$$

$$\leq (s_1-s)\, p_1(\theta) - (s_1-s) \int_{s_1}^{\theta} f'^{-}(\tau\, ;\, \hat{y}(\tau))d\tau - \int_{s}^{s_1} (\tau-s)\, f'^{-}(\tau\, ;\, \hat{y}(\tau))d\tau + p_2(s_1) - p_2(s)$$

Now integrate (5.24) for θ varying in (t_1,t), it follows :

$$(5.25)\quad \begin{cases} (t-t_1) \int_{s}^{s_1} c'^{-}(\tau\, ;\, \hat{v}(\tau))d\tau \leq (s_1-s) \int_{t_1}^{t} p_1(\theta)d\theta \\ - (s_1-s) \int_{t_1}^{t} d\theta \int_{s_1}^{\theta} f'^{-}(\tau\, ;\, \hat{y}(\tau))d\tau - (t-t_1) \int_{s}^{s_1} (\tau-s)\, f'^{-}(\tau\, ;\, \hat{y}(\tau))d\tau \\ + (t-t_1)\, (p_2(s_1) - p_2(s)). \end{cases}$$

The first inequality (5.14), allows to assert that

$$\frac{dp_2}{dt} + p_1 \leq c'^{+}(t\, ;\, \hat{v}(t)) \quad \text{a.e.}$$

hence

$$p_2(t) - p_2(t_1) + \int_{t_1}^{t} p_1(\theta)d\theta \leq \int_{t_1}^{t} c'^{+}(\tau\, ;\, \hat{v}(\tau))d\tau$$

We also have

$$\int_{t_1}^{t} d\theta \int_{s_1}^{\theta} f'^{-}(\tau\, ;\, \hat{y}(\tau))d\tau = (t_1-t) \int_{s_1}^{t_1} f'^{-}(\tau\, ;\, \hat{y}(\tau))d\tau + \int_{t_1}^{t} (t-\tau)\, f'^{-}(\tau\, ;\, \hat{y}(\tau))d\tau$$

Collecting results we find :

$$(5.26)\quad \begin{cases} (t-t_1) \int_{s}^{s_1} c'^{-}(\tau\, ;\, \hat{v}(\tau))d\tau \leq (s_1-s) \int_{t_1}^{t} c'^{+}(\tau\, ;\, \hat{v}(\tau))d\tau \\ + [p_2(t_1) - p_2(t)]\, (s_1-s) - (s_1-s)(t_1-t) \int_{s_1}^{t_1} f'^{-}(\tau\, ;\, \hat{y}(\tau))d\tau \\ - (s_1-s) \int_{t_1}^{t} (t-\tau)\, f'^{-}(\tau\, ;\, \hat{y}(\tau))d\tau - (t-t_1) \int_{s}^{s_1} (\tau-s)\, f'^{-}(\tau ;\, \hat{y}(\tau))d\tau \\ + (t-t_1)\, [p_2(s_1) - p_2(s)] \end{cases}$$

and using (5.13) we finally obtain

$$(5.27)\quad \begin{cases} (t-t_1) \int_{s}^{s_1} c'^{-}(\tau\, ;\, \hat{v}(\tau))d\tau + (s_1-s)(t_1-t) \int_{s_1}^{t_1} f'^{-}(\tau\, ;\, \hat{y}(\tau))d\tau \\ + (s_1-s) \int_{t_1}^{t} (t-\tau)\, f'^{-}(\tau\, ;\, \hat{y}(\tau))d\tau + (t-t_1) \int_{s}^{s_1} (\tau-s) f'^{-}(\tau ;\, \hat{y}(\tau))d\tau \end{cases}$$

$$\left\{\begin{array}{l} + (s_1-s)[h'^-(t\ ;\ \hat{w}(t)) - h'^+(t_1\ ;\ \hat{w}(t_1))] \\ \leq (s_1-s) \int_{t_1}^{t} c'^+(\tau\ ;\ \hat{v}(\tau))d\tau + (t-t_1)[h'^+(s_1\ ;\ \hat{w}(s_1)) - h'^-(s\ ;\ \hat{w}(s))]. \end{array}\right.$$

Neglect the 3rd and 4th terms in the left hand side of (5.27), which are positive ; and divide by $(t-t_1)(s_1-s)$. Then we obtain (5.22). Note that when $t-t_1$ and s_1-s are small the 3rd and 4th terms which have been neglected are negligible with respect to the 2nd term

Assume that the function

(5.28) $\quad h'^-(t\ ;\ w) = h'^+(t\ ;\ w) = h'(t\ ;\ w)$ is continuously differentiable in t,w

then we deduce from (5.22) :

(5.29)
$$\left\{\begin{array}{l} c'^-(s\ ;\ \hat{v}(s)) + \int_s^t f'^-(\tau\ ;\ \hat{y}(\tau))d\tau + \frac{d}{dt} h'(t\ ;\ \hat{w}(t)) \\ \leq\ c'^+(t\ ;\ \hat{v}(t)) + \frac{d}{ds} h'(s\ ;\ \hat{w}(s)) \end{array}\right.$$

a.e. $s < t$ which are differentiability points of $\theta \to h'(\theta\ ;\ \hat{w}(\theta))$ and satisfy $\hat{v}(s) > 0$, $\hat{y}(\tau) > 0$, $\forall\tau \in [s, t]$ □

We can give a direct proof to (5.27) as follows. Let δ small such that

$$0 < s-\delta < s+\delta < s_1-\delta < s_1+\delta < t_1-\delta < t_1+\delta < t-\delta < t+\delta < T$$

and θ to be defined later. We consider the modification of the control $\hat{w}$ as follows

$$\tilde{w}(\lambda) = \left\{\begin{array}{ll} \hat{w}(\lambda) & (0,\ s-\delta) \\ \hat{w}(\lambda) - \frac{\theta}{2\delta(s_1-s)} & \text{on } (s-\delta,\ s+\delta) \\ \hat{w}(\lambda) & \text{on } (s+\delta,\ s_1-\delta) \\ \hat{w}(\lambda) + \frac{\theta}{2\delta(s_1-s)} & \text{on } (s_1-\delta,\ s_1+\delta) \\ \hat{w}(\lambda) & \text{on } (s_1+\delta,\ t_1-\delta) \\ \hat{w}(\lambda) + \frac{\theta}{2\delta(t-t_1)} & \text{on } (t_1-\delta,\ t_1+\delta) \\ \hat{w}(\lambda) & \text{on } (t_1+\delta,\ t-\delta) \\ \hat{w}(\lambda) - \frac{\theta}{2\delta(t-t_1)} & \text{on } (t-\delta,\ t+\delta) \\ \hat{w}(\lambda) & \text{on } (t+\delta,\ T) \end{array}\right.$$

Then $\tilde{v}(\lambda)$ becomes

$$\tilde{v}(\lambda) = \begin{cases} \hat{v}(\lambda) & \text{on } (0,\ s-\delta) \\ \hat{v}(\lambda) - \frac{\theta}{2\delta}\frac{(\lambda-s+\delta)}{(s_1-s)} & \text{on } (s-\delta,\ s+\delta) \\ \hat{v}(\lambda) - \frac{\theta}{s_1-s} & \text{on } (s+\delta,\ s_1-\delta) \\ \hat{v}(\lambda) - \frac{\theta}{s_1-s} + \frac{\theta}{2\delta}\frac{(\lambda-s_1+\delta)}{s_1-s} & \text{on } (s_1-\delta,\ s_1+\delta) \\ \hat{v}(\lambda) & \text{on } (s_1+\delta,\ t_1-\delta) \\ \hat{v}(\lambda) + \frac{\theta}{2\delta}\frac{(\lambda-t_1+\delta)}{t-t_1} & \text{on } (t_1-\delta,\ t_1+\delta) \\ \hat{v}(\lambda) + \frac{\theta}{t-t_1} & \text{on } (t_1+\delta,\ t-\delta) \\ \hat{v}(\lambda) + \frac{\theta}{t-t_1} - \frac{\theta}{2\delta}\frac{(\lambda-t+\delta)}{t-t_1} & \text{on } (t-\delta,\ t+\delta) \\ \hat{v}(\lambda) & \text{on } (t+\delta,\ T) \end{cases}$$

and $\tilde{y}(\lambda)$ becomes

$$\tilde{y}(\lambda) = \begin{cases} \hat{y}(\lambda) & \text{on } (0,\ s-\delta) \\ \hat{y}(\lambda) - \frac{\theta}{4\delta}\frac{(\lambda-s+\delta)^2}{s_1-s} & \text{on } (s-\delta,\ s+\delta) \\ \hat{y}(\lambda) - \frac{\theta\delta}{s_1-s} - \frac{\theta(\lambda-s-\delta)}{s_1-s} & \text{on } (s+\delta,\ s_1-\delta) \\ \hat{y}(\lambda) - \theta + \frac{\theta\delta}{s_1-s} - \frac{\theta(\lambda-s_1+\delta)}{s_1-s} + \frac{\theta}{4\delta}\frac{(\lambda-s_1+\delta)^2}{s_1-s} & \text{on } (s_1-\delta,\ s_1+\delta) \\ \hat{y}(\lambda) - \theta & \text{on } (s_1+\delta,\ t_1-\delta) \\ \hat{y}(\lambda) - \theta + \frac{\theta}{4\delta}\frac{(\lambda-t_1+\delta)^2}{t-t_1} & \text{on } (t_1-\delta,\ t_1+\delta) \\ \hat{y}(\lambda) - \theta + \frac{\theta\delta}{t-t_1} + \frac{\theta(\lambda-t_1-\delta)}{t-t_1} & \text{on } (t_1+\delta,\ t-\delta) \\ \hat{y}(\lambda) - \frac{\theta\delta}{t-t_1} + \frac{\theta(\lambda-t+\delta)}{t-t_1} - \frac{\theta}{4\delta}\frac{(\lambda-t+\delta)^2}{t-t_1} & \text{on } (t-\delta,\ t+\delta) \\ \hat{y}(\lambda) & \text{on } (t+\delta,\ T) \end{cases}$$

Since $\hat{v}$, $\hat{y}$ are continuous functions and (5.21) holds, we can choose δ small enough in order that $\hat{v} > 0$ on $[s-\delta,\ s_1+\delta]$ and $\hat{y} > 0$ on $[s-\delta,\ t+\delta]$. We may then choose θ sufficiently small in order that $\tilde{v}$ and $\tilde{y}$ remain positive, and thus $\tilde{v}$ is an admissible control. Comparing costs we obtain :

$$
\begin{aligned}
0 \le J(\tilde{w}) - J(\hat{w}) = & \int_{s-\delta}^{s+\delta} [h(\lambda \; ; \hat{w}(\lambda) - \frac{\theta}{2\delta(s_1-s)}) - h(\lambda \; ; \hat{w}(\lambda))]d\lambda \\
& + \int_{s_1-\delta}^{s_1+\delta} [h(\lambda \; ; \hat{w}(\lambda) + \frac{\theta}{2\delta(s_1-s)}) - h(\lambda \; ; \hat{w}(\lambda))]d\lambda \\
& + \int_{t_1-\delta}^{t_1+\delta} [h(\lambda \; ; \hat{w}(\lambda) + \frac{\theta}{2\delta(t-t_1)}) - h(\lambda \; ; \hat{w}(\lambda))]d\lambda \\
& + \int_{t-\delta}^{t+\delta} [h(\lambda \; ; \hat{w}(\lambda) - \frac{\theta}{2\delta(t-t_1)}) - h(\lambda \; ; \hat{w}(\lambda))]d\lambda \\
& + \int_{s-\delta}^{s+\delta} [c(\lambda \; ; \hat{v}(\lambda) - \frac{\theta}{2\delta} \frac{(\lambda-s+\delta)}{s_1-s}) - c(\lambda \; ; \hat{v}(\lambda))]d\lambda \\
& + \int_{s+\delta}^{s_1-\delta} [c(\lambda \; ; \hat{v}(\lambda) - \frac{\theta}{s_1-s}) - c(\lambda \; ; \hat{v}(\lambda))]d\lambda \\
& + \int_{s_1-\delta}^{s_1+\delta} [c(\lambda \; ; \hat{v}(\lambda) - \frac{\theta}{s_1-s} + \frac{\theta}{2\delta} \frac{(\lambda-s_1+\delta)}{s_1-s}) - c(\lambda \; ; \hat{v}(\lambda))]d\lambda \\
& + \int_{t_1-\delta}^{t_1+\delta} [c(\lambda \; ; \hat{v}(\lambda) + \frac{\theta}{2\delta} \frac{(\lambda-t_1+\delta)}{t-t_1}) - c(\lambda \; ; \hat{v}(\lambda))]d\lambda \\
& + \int_{t_1+\delta}^{t-\delta} [c(\lambda ; \hat{v}(\lambda) + \frac{\theta}{t-t_1}) - c(\lambda \; ; \hat{v}(\lambda))]d\lambda \\
& + \int_{t-\delta}^{t+\delta} [c(\lambda \; ; \hat{v}(\lambda) + \frac{\theta}{t-t_1} - \frac{\theta}{2\delta} \frac{(\lambda-t+\delta)}{t-t_1}) - c(\lambda \; ; \hat{v}(\lambda))]d\lambda \\
& + \int_{s-\delta}^{s+\delta} [f(\lambda \; ; \hat{y}(\lambda) - \frac{\theta}{4\delta} \frac{(\lambda-s+\delta)^2}{s_1-s}) - f(\lambda \; ; \hat{y}(\lambda))]d\lambda \\
& + \int_{s+\delta}^{s_1-\delta} [f(\lambda \; ; \hat{y}(\lambda) - \frac{\theta\delta}{s_1-s} - \frac{\theta(\lambda-s-\delta)}{s_1-s}) - f(\lambda \; ; \hat{y}(\lambda))]d\lambda \\
& + \int_{s_1-\delta}^{s_1+\delta} [f(\lambda \; ; \hat{y}(\lambda) - \theta + \frac{\theta\delta}{s_1-s} - \frac{\theta(\lambda-s_1+\delta)}{s_1-s} + \frac{\theta}{4\delta} \frac{(\lambda-s_1+\delta)^2}{s_1-s}) \\
& - f(\lambda \; ; \hat{y}(\lambda))]d\lambda + \int_{s_1+\delta}^{t_1-\delta} [f(\lambda \; ; \hat{y}(\lambda) - \theta) - f(\lambda \; ; \hat{y}(\lambda))]d\lambda \\
& + \int_{t_1-\delta}^{t_1+\delta} [f(\lambda \; ; \hat{y}(\lambda) - \theta + \frac{\theta}{4\delta} \frac{(\lambda-t_1+\delta)^2}{t-t_1}) - f(\lambda \; ; \hat{y}(\lambda))]d\lambda \\
& + \int_{t_1+\delta}^{t-\delta} [f(\lambda \; ; \hat{y}(\lambda) - \theta + \frac{\theta\delta}{t-t_1} + \frac{\theta(\lambda-t_1-\delta)}{t-t_1}) - f(\lambda \; ; \hat{y}(\lambda))]d\lambda
\end{aligned}
$$

$$+\int_{t-\delta}^{t+\delta}[f(\lambda\ ;\hat{y}(\lambda)-\frac{\theta\delta}{t-t_1}+\frac{\theta(\lambda-t+\delta)}{t-t_1}-\frac{\theta}{4\delta}\frac{(\lambda-t+\delta)^2}{t-t_1})-f(\lambda;\hat{y}(\lambda))]d\lambda$$

Dividing by θ and letting θ tend to 0, we deduce

$$0\le\frac{-1}{2\delta(s_1-s)}\int_{s-\delta}^{s+\delta}h'^-(\lambda\ ;\hat{w}(\lambda))d\lambda+\frac{1}{2\delta(s_1-s)}\int_{s_1-\delta}^{s_1+\delta}h'^+(\lambda\ ;\hat{w}(\lambda))d\lambda$$

$$+\frac{1}{2\delta(t-t_1)}\int_{t_1-\delta}^{t_1+\delta}h'^+(\lambda\ ;\hat{w}(\lambda))d\lambda-\frac{1}{2\delta(t-t_1)}\int_{t-\delta}^{t+\delta}h'^-(\lambda\ ;\hat{w}(\lambda))d\lambda$$

$$-\frac{1}{2\delta(s_1-s)}\int_{s-\delta}^{s+\delta}(\lambda-s+\delta)\ c'^-(\lambda\ ;\hat{v}(\lambda))d\lambda-\frac{1}{s_1-s}\int_{s+\delta}^{s_1-\delta}c'^-(\lambda\ ;\hat{v}(\lambda))d\lambda$$

$$+\frac{1}{2\delta(s_1-s)}\int_{s_1-\delta}^{s_1+\delta}(\lambda-s_1-\delta)\ c'^-(\lambda\ ;\hat{v}(\lambda))d\lambda$$

$$+\frac{1}{2\delta(t-t_1)}\int_{t_1-\delta}^{t_1+\delta}(\lambda-t_1+\delta)\ c'^+(\lambda\ ;\hat{v}(\lambda))d\lambda+\frac{1}{t-t_1}\int_{t_1+\delta}^{t-\delta}c'^+(\lambda\ ;\hat{v}(\lambda))d\lambda$$

$$+\frac{1}{2\delta(t-t_1)}\int_{t-\delta}^{t+\delta}(t+\delta-\lambda)\ c'^+(\lambda\ ;\hat{v}(\lambda))d\lambda$$

$$-\frac{1}{4\delta(s_1-s)}\int_{s-\delta}^{s+\delta}(\lambda-s+\delta)^2\ f'^-(\lambda\ ;\hat{y}(\lambda))d\lambda$$

$$-\frac{1}{s_1-s}\int_{s+\delta}^{s_1-\delta}(\lambda-s)\ f'^-(\lambda\ ;\hat{y}(\lambda))d\lambda$$

$$+\frac{1}{4\delta(s_1-s)}\int_{s_1-\delta}^{s_1+\delta}f'^-(\lambda\ ;\hat{y}(\lambda))\ [(\lambda-s_1-\delta)^2-4\delta(s_1-s)]d\lambda$$

$$-\int_{s_1+\delta}^{t_1-\delta}f'^-(\lambda\ ;\hat{y}(\lambda))d\lambda$$

$$+\frac{1}{4\delta(t-t_1)}\int_{t_1-\delta}^{t_1+\delta}[(\lambda-t_1+\delta)^2-4\delta(t-t_1)]\ f'^-(\lambda\ ;\hat{y}(\lambda))d\lambda$$

$$+\frac{1}{(t-t_1)}\int_{t_1+\delta}^{t-\delta}(\lambda-t)\ f'^-(\lambda\ ;\hat{y}(\lambda))d\lambda$$

$$-\frac{1}{4\delta(t-t_1)}\int_{t-\delta}^{t+\delta}(\lambda-t-\delta)^2\ f'^-(\lambda\ ;\hat{y}(\lambda))d\lambda$$

and letting δ tend to 0 we obtain (5.27). □

V - 3. PROPERTIES OF OPTIMAL CONTROLS

Assume

$$x < \int_0^T \xi(t)dt \tag{5.30}$$

$$\begin{cases} \underline{\forall 0 < s < T}, \ -g'^{+}(T, 0) - h'^{+}(s ; -\infty) < \int_s^T c'^{+}(t ; 0)dt \\ \quad + \int_s^T dt \int_t^T f'^{+}(\lambda ; 0)d\lambda, \\ \\ \underline{\forall 0 < s < s_1 < T}, \ h'^{-}(s_1 ; 0) - h'^{+}(s ; -\infty) < \int_s^{s_1} c'^{+}(t ; 0)dt \\ \quad + \int_s^{s_1} dt \int_t^T f'^{+}(\lambda ; 0)d\lambda \end{cases} \tag{5.31}$$

Theorem 5.2

Under the assumptions of Theorem 5.1 and (5.30), (5.31), an optimal control for $J(w(.), v(0))$ satisfies

$$\hat{y}(T) = 0 \tag{5.32}$$

Proof

Let us assume that (5.32) does not hold, i.e. $\hat{y}(T) > 0$. There are points t such that $\hat{v}(t) > 0$, otherwise we get a contradiction with (5.30). If there are points for which $\hat{y}$ vanishes, we define

$$s = \sup_{0\le t\le T} \{t \mid \hat{y}(t) = 0\}.$$

We have $\hat{y}(s) = 0$, $s < T$ and $\hat{y}(t) > 0$, $t \in (s, T]$. For any $\varepsilon > 0$, $s+\varepsilon < T$, we have

$$\text{Meas } \{t \mid \hat{v}(t) > 0, \ t \in (s, s+\varepsilon)\} > 0$$

otherwise we get a contradiction with the property $\hat{y}(t) > 0$, $t \in (s, T]$. We then take t_1 in $(s, s+\varepsilon)$ such that $\hat{v}(t_1) > 0$. If $\hat{y}(t) > 0$, $\forall t \in [0, T]$, then we take $s = 0$ and t_1 any positive point for which $\hat{v}(t_1) > 0$. We thus have

$$0 \le s < t_1 < T, \ \hat{y}(t) > 0, \ t \in (s, T], \ \hat{v}(t_1) > 0.$$

Assume that $\hat{v}(t) > 0$, $\forall t \in [t_1, T]$, then from the necessary conditions of Theorem 5.1, we have

$$\begin{cases} \dfrac{dp_2}{dt} + p_1 \ge c'^{-}(t ; \hat{v}(t)), \ t \in (t_1, T) \\ \\ \dfrac{dp_1}{dt} \ge f'^{-}(t ; \hat{y}(t)), \ t \in (s, T) \end{cases} \tag{5.33}$$

hence

$$(5.34)\quad \begin{cases} p_1(t) \le -\int_t^T f'^-(\lambda\ ;\ \hat{y}(\lambda))d\lambda,\ t \in (s, T] \\ p_2(T^-) - p_2(t) + \int_t^T p_1(\lambda)d\lambda \ge \int_t^T c'^-(\lambda\ ;\ \hat{v}(\lambda))d\lambda,\ t \in (t_1, T) \end{cases}$$

hence from (5.34)

$$p_2(T^-) - p_2(t) \ge \int_t^T ds \int_s^T f'^-(\lambda\ ;\ \hat{y}(\lambda))d\lambda + \int_t^T c'^-(\lambda\ ;\ \hat{v}(\lambda))d\lambda$$

and from (5.13), (5.16) we deduce

$$-g'^-(T;\hat{v}(T)) - h'^-(t\ ;\ \hat{w}(t)) \ge \int_t^T ds \int_s^T f'^-(\lambda\ ;\ \hat{y}(\lambda))d\lambda + \int_t^T c'^-(\lambda\ ;\ \hat{v}(\lambda))d\lambda$$

Moreover

$$-g'^+(T\ ;\ 0) - h'^+(t\ ;\ -\infty) \ge \int_t^T ds \int_s^T f'^+(\lambda\ ;\ 0)\ d\lambda + \int_t^T c'^+(\lambda\ ;\ 0)d\lambda$$

which contradicts the first assumption (5.31).

Assume then that there are points in $(t_1, T]$ for which $\hat{v}(t)$ vanishes. We may define

$$s_1 = \inf_{t_1 \le t \le T} \{t \mid \hat{v}(t) = 0\}$$

hence $\hat{v}(s_1) = 0$, $t_1 < s_1 < T$. Then we can write

$$(5.35)\quad \begin{cases} \dfrac{dp_2}{dt} + p_1 \ge c'^-(t\ ;\ \hat{v}(t)),\ \text{a.e. in } (t_1, s_1) \\ \dfrac{dp_1}{dt} \ge f'^-(t\ ;\ \hat{y}(t)),\ \text{a.e. in } (s, T) \end{cases}$$

We still have the first part of (5.34). Take ε_1 small such that $t_1 < s_1-\varepsilon_1$ and pick t_2 in $(s_1-\varepsilon, s_1)$. It follows from (5.35)

$$p_2(t_2) - p_2(t_1) + \int_{t_1}^{t_2} p_1(t)dt \ge \int_{t_1}^{t_2} c'^-(t\ ;\ \hat{v}(t))dt$$

and arguing as above we deduce

$$(5.36)\quad \begin{cases} h'^+(t_2\ ;\ \hat{w}(t_2)) - h'^-(t_1\ ;\ \hat{w}(t_1)) \ge \int_{t_1}^{t_2} c'^-(t\ ;\ \hat{v}(t))dt \\ + \int_{t_1}^{t_2} dt \int_t^T f'^-(\lambda\ ;\ \hat{y}(\lambda))d\lambda \ge \int_{t_1}^{t_2} c'^+(t\ ;\ 0)dt + \int_{t_1}^{t_2} dt \int_t^T f'^+(\lambda;0)d\lambda \end{cases}$$

Since $\hat{v}(s_1) = 0$ and $\hat{v}(t) > 0$, on $[t_1, s_1)$, necessarily

$$\text{Meas}\ [(s_1-\varepsilon_1, s_1) \cap \{t \mid \hat{w}(t) < 0\}] > 0$$

hence outside a set of measure 0 we can find points t_2 such that (5.36) holds and $\hat{w}(t_2) < 0$, which implies

$$h'^{+}(t_2 ; \hat{w}(t_2)) \le h'^{-}(t_2 ; 0)$$

and thus we deduce from (5.36) that

$$h'^{-}(t_2 ; 0) - h'^{+}(t_1 ; -\infty) \ge \int_{t_1}^{t_2} c'^{+}(t ; 0)dt + \int_{t_1}^{t_2} dt \int_{t}^{T} f'^{+}(\lambda ; 0)d\lambda$$

which contradicts assumption (5.31). □

Remark 5.5

Assumption (5.31) is restrictive with respect to the derivatives $h'^{-}(t ; x)$, $h'^{+}(t ; x)$ for $x < 0$. It is satisfied when, for instance,

$$h(t ; x) = - \bar{h}(t)x \quad \text{for } x < 0$$

$$g'^{+}(T ; 0) \ge \bar{h}(T)$$

and $\bar{h}(t)$ is a non decreasing function. □

Let us now assume :

$$(5.37) \quad \begin{cases} \forall s < s_1 < t, \\ \dfrac{1}{s_1-s} \displaystyle\int_{s}^{s_1} c'^{+}(\tau ; 0)d\tau + \dfrac{1}{t-s_1} \displaystyle\int_{s_1}^{t} (t-\tau) f'^{+}(\tau ; 0) d\tau \\ + \dfrac{1}{s_1-s} \displaystyle\int_{s}^{s_1} (\tau-s) f'^{+}(\tau ; 0) d\tau > \dfrac{1}{t-s_1} \displaystyle\int_{s_1}^{t} c'^{-}(\tau ; +\infty)d\tau \\ + \dfrac{1}{s_1-s} [h'^{-}(s_1 ; 0) - h'^{+}(s ; -\infty)] + \dfrac{1}{t-s_1} [h'^{-}(s_1 ; 0) - h'^{+}(t ; -\infty)] \end{cases}$$

then we have

Lemma 5.1

Assume that (5.37) holds. If an optimal control satisfies

$$(5.38) \qquad \hat{y}(s) = 0, \ \hat{y}(\lambda) > 0, \ \forall\lambda \in (s, t]$$

then

$$(5.39) \qquad \hat{v}(\lambda) > 0, \ \forall\lambda \in (s, t]$$

Proof

We first notice that

$$(5.40) \qquad \forall\varepsilon > 0, \ s+\varepsilon < t, \text{ there exists } t_1 \text{ in } (s, s+\varepsilon) \text{ such that } \hat{v}(t_1) > 0$$

Assume that the statement is false. Then from (5.40) it follows that

$\exists s_0,\ s < s_0 < t,\ \hat{v}(s_0) > 0$ and

$t_1 = \inf \{\theta \mid s_0 \le \theta \le t,\ \hat{v}(\theta) = 0\}$ satisfies

$s_0 < t_1 \le t,\ \hat{v}(t_1) = 0,\ \hat{v}(\theta) > 0,\quad \theta \in [s_0, t_1).$

It follows also that

(5.41) $\quad \text{Meas } (s_0, t_1) \cap \{\theta \mid \hat{w}(\theta) < 0\} > 0$

Hence we can find s_1 such that

(5.42) $\quad \begin{cases} s_0 < s_1 < t, \\ \hat{w}(s_1) < 0,\ \hat{v}(\theta) > 0,\ \theta \in [s_0, s_1],\ \hat{y}(\theta) > 0,\ \theta \in [s_0, t] \end{cases}$

We can therefore apply the condition (5.27) with s changed in s_0, and $s_1 = t_1$. We obtain

$$\frac{1}{s_1-s}\int_s^{s_1} c'^-(\tau\ ;\ \hat{v}(\tau))d\tau + \frac{1}{t-s_1}\int_{s_1}^{t} (t-\tau)\ f'^-(\tau\ ;\ \hat{y}(\tau))d\tau$$

$$+ \frac{1}{s_1-s}\int_s^{s_1} (\tau-s)\ f'^-(\tau\ ;\ \hat{y}(\tau))d\tau$$

$$+ \frac{1}{t-s_1}(h'\ (t\ ;\ \hat{w}(t)) - h'^+(s_1\ ;\ \hat{w}(s_1)))$$

$$\le \frac{1}{t-s_1}\int_{s_1}^{t} c'^+(\tau\ ;\ \hat{v}(\tau))d\tau + \frac{1}{s_1-s}(h'^+(s_1\ ;\ \hat{w}(s_1)) - h'^-(s\ ;\ \hat{w}(s)))$$

hence also

$$\frac{1}{s_1-s}\int_s^{s_1} c'^+(\tau\ ;\ 0)d\tau + \frac{1}{t-s_1}\int_{s_1}^{t} (t-\tau)\ f'^+(\tau\ ;\ 0)d\tau$$

$$+ \frac{1}{s_1-s}\int_s^{s_1} (\tau-s)\ f'^+(\tau\ ;\ 0)d\tau + \frac{1}{t-s_1}(h'^+(t\ ;\ -\infty) - h'^-(s_1\ ;\ 0))$$

$$\le \frac{1}{t-s_1}\int_{s_1}^{t} c'^+(\tau\ ;\ \infty)\ d\tau + \frac{1}{s_1-s}(h'^-(s_1\ ;\ 0) - h'^+(s\ ;\ -\infty))$$

which is a contradiction to assumption (5.37). □

Assume that

$c(t\ ;\ v) = \bar{c}(t)v \quad , \bar{c}(t)$ decreasing

$h(t\ ;\ x) = -\bar{h}(t)x$, for $x < 0$, $\bar{h}(t)$ concave

then (5.37) is satisfied. □

V - 4. REGENERATION POINTS

We start with a result analogous to Lemma 5.11 of Chapter II. First define for any s, $H^*(s)$ by :

$$(5.43)\quad \begin{cases} H^*(s) = \inf\limits_{\theta>0} \{\theta \mid \int_s^{s+2\theta} f'^{+}(\tau\ ;\ 0)d\tau \\ + \int_s^{s+\theta} (\tau-s)\ f'^{+}(\tau;\ 0)d\tau + \int_{s+\theta}^{s+2\theta} (s+\theta-\tau)\ f'^{+}(\tau\ ;\ 0)d\tau + \int_s^{s+\theta} c'^{+}(\tau;0)d\tau \\ > \int_{s+\theta}^{s+2\theta} c'^{-}(\tau\ ;\ \infty)d\tau + 2h'^{-}(s+\theta\ ;\ +\infty) - h'^{+}(s\ ;\ -\infty) - h'^{+}(s+2\theta\ ;\ -\infty)\} \end{cases}$$

then we have

Theorem 5.3

Given the assumptions of Theorem 5.2 and (5.37), assume that for some s an optimal control satisfies $\hat{y}(s) = 0$. Then, there exists a point s^* in $(s, (s+2\ H^*(s)) \wedge T]$ such that $\hat{y}(s^*) = 0$

Proof

If $s+2\ H^*(s) \geq T$, then the result follows from Theorem 5.2. Thus assume that $s+2\ H^*(s) < T$. If the statement is false then there exists $\theta_0 > H^*(s)$ such that for $\theta \leq \theta_0$, we have

$$\hat{y}(s) = 0,\ \hat{y}(\lambda) > 0,\quad \lambda \in (s,\ s+2\theta].$$

From Lemma 5.1, it follows that

$$\hat{v}(\lambda) > 0,\ \lambda \in (s,\ s+2\theta].$$

From the necessary conditions of Theorem 5.1, we then deduce that

$$(5.44)\quad \begin{cases} \dfrac{dp_1}{dt} \geq f'^{-}(t\ ;\ \hat{y}(t)) \quad ,t \in (s,\ s+2\theta) \\ c'^{-}(t\ ;\ \hat{v}(t)) \leq p_1(t) + \dfrac{dp_2}{dt}(t) \leq c'^{+}(t\ ;\ \hat{v}(t)),\ t \in (s,\ s+2\theta) \end{cases}$$

Let $\lambda \in (s,\ s+\theta)$, we get :

$$p_1(s+\theta) - p_1(\lambda) \geq \int_\lambda^{s+\theta} f'^{-}(t\ ;\ \hat{y}(t))dt$$

Integrating with respect to λ over $(s,\ s+\theta)$, we obtain

$$(5.45)\qquad \theta p_1(s+\theta) - \int_s^{s+\theta} p_1(\lambda)d\lambda \geq \int_s^{s+\theta} d\lambda \int_\lambda^{s+\theta} f'^{-}(t\ ;\ \hat{y}(t))dt.$$

But from the second condition (5.44) we deduce that

$$p_2(s+\theta) - p_2(s) + \int_s^{s+\theta} p_1(t)dt \geq \int_s^{s+\theta} c'^{-}(t\ ;\ \hat{v}(t))dt$$

which combined with (5.45) yields

(5.46)
$$\begin{cases} \theta p_1(s+\theta) + p_2(s+\theta) - p_2(s) - \int_s^{s+\theta} c'^-(t\ ;\ \hat{v}(t))dt \\ \geq \int_s^{s+\theta} d\lambda \int_\lambda^{s+\theta} f'^-(t\ ;\ \hat{y}(t))dt \end{cases}$$

Similarly we take λ in $(s+\theta,\ s+2\theta)$. We have from the first condition (5.44)

$$p_1(\lambda) - p_1(s+\theta) \geq \int_{s+\theta}^{\lambda} f'^-(t\ ;\ \hat{y}(t))dt$$

which we integrate over λ in the interval $(s+\theta,\ s+2\theta)$:

(5.47)
$$\int_{s+\theta}^{s+2\theta} p_1(\lambda)d\lambda - \theta p_1(s+\theta) \geq \int_{s+\theta}^{s+2\theta} d\lambda \int_{s+\theta}^{\lambda} f'^-(t\ ;\ \hat{y}(t))dt\ .$$

Using the last condition (5.44) we have :

$$\int_{s+\theta}^{s+2\theta} p_1(t)dt + p_2(s+2\theta) - p_2(s+\theta) \leq \int_{s+\theta}^{s+2\theta} c'^+(t\ ;\ \hat{v}(t))dt$$

which, combined with (5.47), implies

(5.48)
$$\begin{cases} \int_{s+\theta}^{s+2\theta} c'^+(t\ ;\ \hat{v}(t))dt - p_2(s+2\theta) + p_2(s+\theta) - \theta p_1(s+\theta) \\ \geq \int_{s+\theta}^{s+2\theta} d\lambda \int_{s+\theta}^{\lambda} f'^-(t\ ;\ \hat{y}(t))dt \end{cases}$$

We add (5.46) to (5.48) to obtain

$$\int_s^{s+\theta} d\lambda \int_\lambda^{s+\theta} f'^-(t\ ;\ \hat{y}(t))dt + \int_{s+\theta}^{s+2\theta} d\lambda \int_{s+\theta}^{\lambda} f'^-(t\ ;\ \hat{y}(t))dt$$
$$+ \int_s^{s+\theta} c'^-(t\ ;\ \hat{v}(t))dt \leq \int_{s+\theta}^{s+2\theta} c'^+(t\ ;\ \hat{v}(t))dt + 2p_2(s+\theta)$$
$$- p_2(s) - p_2(s+2\theta).$$

Using (5.13), we deduce that

(5.49)
$$\begin{cases} \int_s^{s+\theta} d\lambda \int_\lambda^{s+\theta} f'^+(t\ ;\ 0)dt + \int_{s+\theta}^{s+2\theta} d\lambda \int_{s+\theta}^{\lambda} f'^+(t\ ;\ 0)dt + \int_s^{s+\theta} c'^+(t;0)dt \\ \leq \int_{s+\theta}^{s+2\theta} c'^-(t\ ;\ \infty)\ dt + 2\ h'^-(s+\theta\ ;\ +\infty\ ) - h'^+(s;\ -\infty) - h'^+(s+2\theta;-\infty) \end{cases}$$

Since (5.49) holds for any $0 \leq \theta \leq \theta_0$, we deduce that $\theta_0 \leq H^*(s)$, which is a contradiction. This completes the proof. □

([1]) We assume that (5.13) holds for any t, after a possible modification of the control over a set of measure 0.

The next result is the analogue of Lemma 5.12 of Chapter II.

Lemma 5.2.

Assume (5.31), (5.37) and that

(5.50) $H^*(s)$ is non decreasing

Then, if $x = 0$, we have

(5.51) $\hat{v}(s) \le D_s^T \quad \forall s < T$

where

(5.52) $$D_s^T = \sup_{0<\theta<2H^*(s)\wedge(T-s)} \frac{1}{\theta} \int_s^{s+\theta} \xi(s)ds$$

Proof

Let us first check that there exists $s^* \in (s, (s+2H^*(s)) \wedge T]$ such that

(5.53) $\hat{y}(s^*) = 0.$

This follows from Theorem 5.3, if $\hat{y}(s) = 0$. Otherwise since $x = 0$, there exists a point s_0 in $(0, 2H^*(0) \wedge T]$ such that $\hat{y}(s_0) = 0$. From (5.50) we have

$$s_0 \le (s+2H^*(s)) \wedge T$$

Let then

$$\bar{s} = \sup \{t \mid 0 < t \le (s+2H^*(s)) \wedge T, \hat{y}(t) = 0\}$$

We have $y(\bar{s}) = 0$. If $s < \bar{s}$ then $s^* = \bar{s}$ is acceptable, otherwise we have

$$\bar{s} \le s$$

and

$$(\bar{s} + 2H^*(\bar{s})) \wedge T \le (s + 2H^*(s)) \wedge T.$$

But there exists a point $\bar{\bar{s}}$ in $(\bar{s}, (\bar{s}+2H^*(\bar{s})) \wedge T]$, hence in $(\bar{s}, (s+2H^*(s)) \wedge T]$, such that $\hat{y}(\bar{\bar{s}}) = 0$. But this contradicts the definition of $\bar{s}$. Let then

$$s^* = \inf\{\lambda \mid s < \lambda \le (s+2H^*(s)) \wedge T, \hat{y}(\lambda) = 0\}$$

it follows that

(5.54) $s < s^*, \ \hat{y}(s^*) = 0, \ \hat{y}(\lambda) > 0, \ \lambda \in (s, s^*).$

We next prove that

(5.55) $\hat{w}(\lambda) \ge 0$, a.e. in (s, s^*)

First notice that if $\hat{v}(\lambda) = 0$ in (s,s^*) then (5.55) is satisfied. Therefore we may assume that there exists t in (s, s^*) such that $\hat{v}(t) > 0$. We assume that (5.55) does not hold, hence

(5.56) $K = \{\lambda \mid \hat{w}(\lambda) < 0\}$, Meas $K \cap (s, s^*) > 0.$

If

$$(5.57) \qquad \hat{v}(t) > 0, \ t \in (s,s^*)$$

we get a contradiction. Indeed we can easily find, outside a set of measure 0, points

$$s < s_0 < s_1 < t < s^*$$

such that (5.42) holds. But as we have seen in the proof of Lemma 5.1, this contradicts assumption (5.37). We may thus assume that

$$(5.58) \qquad \text{there exist points } t_1, t_2 \text{ in } (s,s^*) \text{ such that } \hat{v}(t_1) = 0, \ \hat{v}(t_2) > 0$$

Assume first that

$$(5.59) \qquad \hat{v}(s^*) > 0$$

and let

$$(5.60) \qquad t_0 = \sup \{t \in [s, s^*), \ \hat{v}(t) = 0\}$$

then one has

$$(5.61) \qquad \hat{v}(t_0) = 0, \quad \hat{v}(t) > 0, \ t \in (t_0, s^*]$$

We may assume then that

$$\text{Meas } K \cap (t_0, s^*) = 0$$

otherwise we are in a situation similar to (5.57), which yields a contradiction. Of course it follows from (5.56) that

$$\text{Meas } K \cap (s, t_0) > 0 \quad .$$

This argument shows that we can restrict ourselves to the following situation

$$(5.62) \qquad \begin{cases} (s,s^*), \ \hat{y}(t) > 0, \ t \in (s,s^*) \\ \\ \hat{v}(s^*) = 0, \ \text{Meas } K \cap (s,s^*) > 0 \end{cases}$$

From the last condition, it follows that there are points t in (s,s^*) such that $\hat{v}(t) > 0$, therefore we define

$$(5.63) \qquad s_0 = \sup \{t \mid t \in [s,s^*], \ \hat{v}(t) > 0\}$$

hence

$$(5.64) \qquad \begin{cases} s < s_0 \le s^* \ , \ \hat{v}(s_0) = 0 \\ \forall \varepsilon, \text{ there exist points } t \text{ in } (s_0-\varepsilon, \ s_0) \text{ such that } \hat{v}(t) > 0 \\ \text{Meas } K \cap (s_0-\varepsilon, \ s_0) > 0 \quad . \end{cases}$$

The last condition follows from the fact that,otherwise, $\hat{w}(\lambda) \ge 0$ in $(s_0-\varepsilon, \ s_0)$. Taking t_1 in this interval such that $\hat{v}(t_1) > 0$, then

$$\hat{v}(s_0) = \hat{v}(t_1) + \int_{t_1}^{s_0} \hat{w}(\lambda)d\lambda \ge \hat{v}(t_1) > 0$$

which is a contradiction.

Taking then t_0 such that

$$s < t_0 < s_0 \quad \text{with} \quad \hat{v}(t_0) > 0$$

we define t_1 to be such that

$$t_1 = \inf\{t \in [t_0,s_0] \mid \hat{v}(t) \le \frac{1}{2}\hat{v}(t_0)\}$$

and t_2 in (t_0,t_1) such that $\hat{w}(t_2) < 0$ we get

$$t_0 < t_2 < t_1,\ \hat{w}(t_2) < 0,\ \hat{v}(t) > 0,\ t \in [t_0,t_1],\ \hat{y}(t) > 0,\ t \in [t_0,t_1]$$

which is a situation like (5.42), thus implying a contradiction. Therefore (5.55) holds, which implies

(5.65) $$\hat{v}(s) \le \hat{v}(\lambda),\ \forall\lambda \in [s,s^*]$$

But also from (5.54) it follows that

$$\int_s^{s^*} \xi(\lambda)d\lambda \ge \int_s^{s^*} \hat{v}(\lambda)d\lambda \ge \hat{v}(s)\ (s^* - s)$$

which implies (5.51). □

Remark 5.7

We have been unable to obtain a result which would be the analogue in continuous time of Lemma 5.13 and of the planning horizon Theorem 5.2 of Chapter II. One can conjecture that if $\hat{v}^s(s) \ge D_s^T$, then there is an optimal control which contains $\hat{v}^s(t)$, $t \le s$. We have denoted by $\hat{v}^s(.)$, $\hat{w}^s(.)$, $\hat{y}^s(.)$ the problem for the horizon s. It would be interesting to prove this conjecture. □

SECOND PART : IMPULSE CONTROL FORMULATION FOR THE CONCAVE COST MODEL

Synopsis

In this part a control is no longer continuous but is made of impulses instead. However, this impulse control formulation applies only to the concave cost model. With this formulation we do not impose, a priori, a minimum length between two consecutive decisions, as in the discrete time model.

VI - THE CONCAVE COST MODEL WITH FINITE HORIZON AND NO BACKLOGGING

This section is a direct extension of Chapter I and leads to a natural generalization of the results obtained in the discrete time formulation.

VI - 1. NOTATION AND ASSUMPTIONS

The demand is still defined by an integrable positive function, $\xi(t)$, $t \in (0, T)$ as in § I.1.

The control is specified as follows. There is a sequence

$$s \le \theta_1 \le \theta_2 \le \dots \le \theta_n \le \dots \le T$$

with

$$\theta_i \uparrow T \text{ as } i \to +\infty$$

The sequence θ_i is the sequence of ordering times. Each θ_i is associated to an order $v_i > 0$.

The control is the set

$$V = (\theta_1, v_1 \; ; \; \ldots \; ; \; \theta_i, v_i \; ; \; \ldots)$$

The corresponding trajectory is defined by

$$(6.1) \qquad \begin{cases} dz = -\xi(t)dt + \sum_i v_i \, \delta(t - \theta_i), & t \in (s, T) \\ z(s) = x \end{cases}$$

where $\delta(t)$ denotes the Dirac measure. The interpretation of (6.1) is the following. Knowing $z(\theta_i)$ then one has :

(i) if $\theta_i < \theta_{i+1}$ and $t \in [\theta_i, \theta_{i+1})$:

$$z(t) = z(\theta_i) - \int_{\theta_i}^{t} \xi(s)ds$$

and

$$z(\theta_{i+1}) = z(\theta_{i+1} - 0) + v_{i+1}$$

where

$$z(\theta_{i+1} - 0) = z(\theta_i) - \int_{\theta_i}^{\theta_{i+1}} \xi(s)ds \; ;$$

(ii) if $\theta_i = \theta_{i+1}$,

$$z(\theta_{i+1}) = z(\theta_i) + v_{i+1}.$$

We impose as usual the state constraint

$$(6.2) \qquad z(t) \geq 0$$

The production cost function is denoted as in (1.6) by :

$$(6.3) \qquad \begin{cases} c(t \; ; \; v) : [0,T] \times R^+ \to R^+ \text{ with the following properties :} \\ . \text{ concave non decreasing in } v \; ; \\ . \text{ continuous on } [0,T] \times (0,\infty) \text{ with } c(t;0) = 0, \; c(t;0+) \geq K \; ; \\ . \inf_{t \in [0,T]} c(t \; ; \; v) \to \infty \text{ as } v \to \infty. \end{cases}$$

The inventory cost function is denoted as in (1.7) by :

$$(6.4) \qquad \begin{cases} f(t \; ; \; x) : [0,T] \times R^+ \to R^+ \text{ with the following properties :} \\ . \text{ concave non decreasing in } x \; ; \\ . \text{ a.e. } t \;\; f(t;x) = \tilde{f}(t;x) \; \forall x, \text{ where } \tilde{f} \text{ is a Borel function continuous with respect to } x \; ; \\ . \int_0^T f(t \; ; \; x)dt < \infty \quad \forall x. \end{cases}$$

The cost functional to minimize is

$$J_{s,x}(V) = \int_s^T f(t\ ;\ z(t))dt + \sum_i c(\theta_i,\ v_i)\ \chi_{\theta_i<T} \tag{6.5}$$ [1]

The control V is called an impulse control, by comparison with the continuous control described in section 1.

VI - 2. EXISTENCE OF AN OPTIMAL CONTROL

Theorem 6.1

Assume (6.3), (6.4), then there exists an optimal control.

Proof

First, let us prove that we can restrict the number of impulses to a finite one. Indeed, the following control is admissible (we take s = 0 for simplicity),

$$\theta_1 = 0,\quad \theta_2 = \ldots = T$$

$$v_1 = \int_0^T \xi(t)dt$$

since the corresponding trajectory satisfies

$$z(t) = x + \int_0^T \xi(s)ds - \int_0^t \xi(s)ds,\ 0 < t < T$$
$$\geq 0$$

Therefore we can restrict the set of admissible controls to those satisfying

$$(6.6)\quad \begin{cases} J_{0,x}(V) \leq c(0\ ;\ \int_0^T \xi(t)dt) + \int_0^T f(t\ ;\ x + \int_t^T \xi(s)ds)dt \\ \leq c(0\ ;\ \int_0^T \xi(t)dt) + \int_0^T f(t\ ;\ x + \int_0^T \xi(s)ds)dt \\ = \bar{J}(x) < \infty \end{cases}$$

Now, from assumption (6.3) we have

$$c(\theta_i\ ;\ v_i) \geq K \text{ since } v_i > 0.$$

Therefore

$$J_{0,x}(V) \geq K \sum_i \chi_{\theta_i<T} = KN_i$$

where N_i is the number of orders which are placed strictly before T. Necessarily

$$K\ N_i \leq \bar{J}(x)$$

---

[1] $\chi_{\theta_i<T} = 1$ if $\theta_i < T$ and 0 if $\theta_i \geq T$.

hence we can restrict the impulse controls to those having at most

$$N(x) = \frac{\bar{J}(x)}{K}$$

impulses, strictly before T. Since only the impulses taking place strictly before T can modify the cost functional, and therefore are relevant, we can restrict ourselves to choosing $N(x)$ numbers $0 \le \theta_1 \le \theta_2 \le \dots \le \theta_{N(x)}$.

Note also that we can eliminate controls such that

$$\theta_i = \theta_{i+1} \tag{6.7}$$

Indeed consider a control such that (6.7) holds with corresponding orders v_i and v_{i+1}. Consider a new control where we eliminate the order at θ_{i+1} (i.e. the second order at θ_i) and order at θ_i, $v_i + v_{i+1}$ instead of v_i. Call V the initial impulse control and $\tilde{V}$ the modification as indicated. The trajectory is obviously unchanged, and thus

$$\begin{aligned} J(\tilde{V}) - J(V) &= c(\theta_i \; ; v_i + v_{i+1}) - c(\theta_i \; ; v_i) - c(\theta_i \; ; v_{i+1}) \\ &\le - c(\theta_i \; ; 0+) < 0 \end{aligned}$$

by concavity. Hence the control V is certainly not optimal, and the control $\tilde{V}$ does not satisfy (6.7) (after a relabelling of the orders $\theta_{i+2}, \dots$ provided $\theta_{i+2} > \theta_i$ otherwise the order at θ_{i+2} must also be eliminated).

We now consider N as a parameter with $0 \le N \le N(x)$ and for N fixed, 2N variables $\theta_1, \dots, \theta_N, v_1, \dots, v_N$ with (for $N \ge 1$)

$$\begin{cases} 0 \le \theta_1 < \theta_2 < \dots < \theta_N < T \\ v_1 > 0 \quad \dots \quad v_N > 0 \end{cases} \tag{6.8}$$

Let us assume that

$$x < \int_0^T \xi(t)dt \tag{6.9}$$

otherwise the optimal control is clearly N = 0, and the theorem is proved. If (6.9) holds, then we define for each N fixed

$$\begin{cases} J(N \; ; \theta_1, \dots, \theta_N \; ; v_1, \dots, v_N) = \int_0^{\theta_1} f(t \; ; x - \int_0^t \xi(s)ds)dt \\ + \sum_{i=1}^{N-1} \int_{\theta_i}^{\theta_{i+1}} f(t \; ; x + \sum_{j=1}^{i} v_j - \int_0^t \xi(s)ds)dt \\ + \int_{\theta_N}^{T} f(t \; ; x + \sum_{j=1}^{N} v_j - \int_0^t \xi(s)ds)dt + \sum_{i=1}^{N} c(\theta_i, v_i) \end{cases} \tag{6.10}$$

The parameters $v_1, \dots, v_N$ must also satisfy the constraint

(6.11) $$\begin{cases} x + \sum_{j=1}^{i} v_j \geq \int_0^{\theta_{i+1}} \xi(t)dt, \quad i = 1, \ldots, N \text{ (with } \theta_{N+1} = T) \\ \text{and } x \geq \int_0^{\theta_1} \xi(t)dt \end{cases}$$

It is convenient to consider formula (6.10) on the closure of (6.11), (6.8), which amounts to replacing (6.2) by

(6.12) $$\begin{cases} 0 \leq \theta_1 \leq \theta_2 \leq \ldots \leq \theta_N \leq T \\ v_1 \geq 0, \ldots, v_N \geq 0 \end{cases}$$

and J has to be changed into

(6.13) $$\begin{cases} \tilde{J}(N ; \theta_1, \ldots, \theta_N ; v_1, \ldots, v_N) = \int_0^{\theta_1} f(t ; x - \int_0^t \xi(s)ds)dt \\ + \sum_{i=1}^{N-1} \int_{\theta_i}^{\theta_{i+1}} f(t ; x + \sum_{j=1}^{i} v_j - \int_0^t \xi(s)ds)dt \\ + \int_{\theta_N}^{T} f(t ; x + \sum_{j=1}^{N} v_j - \int_0^t \xi(s)ds)dt + \sum_{i=1}^{N} c(\theta_i, v_i + 0) \end{cases}$$

From the assumptions (6.3), (6.4) the functional $\tilde{J}$ is continuous in $\theta_1, \ldots, \theta_N$, $v_1, \ldots, v_N$. Since each v_i can be restricted to

$$\{v \mid \inf_t c(t ; v) \leq \bar{J}(x)\}$$

which is bounded by virtue of (6.3), it follows that the set of admissible θ_i, v_i is a compact set. Therefore $\forall N \geq 1$, there exist $\theta_1^N, \ldots, \theta_N^N ; v_1^N, \ldots, v_N^N$ realizing the infimum of $\tilde{J}$.

If some $v_i^N = 0$, then we consider the functional for N-1, and keep all controls except the ith. We then have

$$\begin{aligned} &\tilde{J}(N-1 ; \theta_1^N, \ldots, \theta_{i-1}^N, \theta_{i+1}^N, \ldots, \theta_N^N ; v_1^N, \ldots, v_{i-1}^N, v_{i+1}^N, \ldots, v_N^N) \\ &= \tilde{J}(N ; \theta_1^N, \ldots, \theta_N^N ; v_1^N, \ldots, v_N^N) - c(\theta_i^N ; 0+) \\ &< \tilde{J}(N ; \theta_1^N, \ldots, \theta_N^N ; v_1^N, \ldots, v_N^N) \end{aligned}$$

and thus

(6.14) $$\begin{cases} \tilde{J}(N-1 ; \theta_1^{N-1}, \ldots, \theta_{N-1}^{N-1} ; v_1^{N-1}, \ldots, v_{N-1}^{N-1}) < \tilde{J}(N ; \theta_1^N, \ldots, \theta_N^N ; \\ \qquad v_1^N, \ldots, v_N^N) \end{cases}$$

Similarly if $\theta_i^N = \theta_{i+1}^N$, then reasoning as in the case (6.7) , we also get (6.14). Therefore we can eliminate all θ_i^N, v_i^N which do not satisfy (6.8).

Since at least θ_1^1, v_1^1 satisfy (6.8), the set of optima θ_i^N, v_i^N satisfying (6.8) is not empty. Such θ_i^N, v_i^N attain the infimum of (6.10) over the set (6.8), (6.11). From (6.14) it follows that the N for which the infimum of (6.10) over (6.8), (6.11) is not attained can be eliminated. Therefore

$$\inf_{1\le N\le N(x)} \inf_{\substack{\theta_i, v_i \\ \text{satisfying} \\ (6.8),(6.11)}} J(N ; \theta_1, \dots, \theta_N ; v_1, \dots, v_N)$$

is attained. But this quantity coincides with inf J(V). This completes the proof.□

VI - 3. DYNAMIC PROGRAMMING

We derive in this paragraph the properties of the optimal impulse controls :

$$u(s,x) = \operatorname*{Inf}_V J_{s,x}(V). \tag{6.15}$$

When

$$x \ge \int_s^T \xi(\lambda)d\lambda \tag{6.16}$$

we have

$$u(s,x) = \int_s^T f(t ; x - \int_s^t \xi(\lambda)d\lambda)dt \tag{6.17}$$

When $x < \int_s^T \xi(\lambda)d\lambda$, we can write

$$\begin{cases} u(s,x) = \operatorname*{Inf}_N \operatorname*{Inf}_{\substack{\theta_1,\dots,\theta_N \\ v_1,\dots,v_N}} [\int_s^{\theta_1} f(t ; x - \int_s^t \xi(\lambda)d\lambda)dt \\ + \sum_{i=1}^{N-1} \int_{\theta_i}^{\theta_{i+1}} f(t ; x + \sum_{j=1}^{i} v_j - \int_s^t \xi(\lambda)d\lambda)dt \\ + \int_{\theta_N}^T f(t ; x + \sum_{j=1}^{N} v_j - \int_s^t \xi(\lambda)d\lambda)dt + \sum_{i=1}^{N} c(\theta_i ; v_i + 0)] \end{cases} \tag{6.18}$$

The set of admissible θ and v is defined by

$$\begin{cases} s \le \theta_1 \le \dots \le \theta_N \le T \\ v_1 \ge 0 \dots v_N \ge 0 \end{cases} \tag{6.19}$$

$$x + \sum_{j=1}^{i} v_j - \int_s^t \xi(\lambda)d\lambda \ge 0, \ \forall\ \theta_i \le t < \theta_{i+1} \tag{6.20}$$

In (6.18) N can be any integer. We set

$$\begin{cases} u_N(s,x) = \operatorname*{Inf}_{\substack{\theta_1,\dots,\theta_N \\ v_1,\dots,v_N}} [\int_s^{\theta_1} f(t ; x - \int_s^t \xi(\lambda)d\lambda)dt \\ + \sum_{i=1}^{N-1} \int_{\theta_i}^{\theta_{i+1}} f(t ; x + \sum_{j=1}^{i} v_j - \int_s^t \xi(\lambda)d\lambda)dt \end{cases} \tag{6.21}$$

$$\left. + \int_{\theta_N}^{T} f(t\ ;\ x + \sum_{j=1}^{N} v_j - \int_s^t \xi(\lambda)d\lambda)dt + \sum_{i=1}^{N} c_i(\theta_i\ ;\ v_i + 0)\right]$$

where the infimum has to be taken over the set (6.19), (6.20). The function $u_N(s,x)$ is upper semi continuous. Indeed call $U_N(s,x)$ the set (6.19), (6.20). Then the correspondance $U_N(s,x)$ satisfies the two properties :

$$(6.22) \quad \begin{cases} \text{Let } s_n, x_n \to s, x \text{ then } \forall \theta_1, \ldots, \theta_N\ ;\ v_1, \ldots, v_N \\ \text{in } U_N(s,x), \text{ there exists } \theta_1^n, \ldots, \theta_N^n\ ;\ v_1^n, \ldots, v_N^n \\ \text{in } U_N(s_n,x_n) \text{ such that : } \theta_i^n \to \theta_i,\ v_i^n \to v_i \end{cases}$$

$$(6.23) \quad \begin{cases} \text{If } \theta_i^n \to \theta_i,\ v_i^n \to v_i \\ \text{and } (\theta_i^n, v_i^n) \in U_N(s_n,x_n) \text{ then } (\theta_i, v_i) \in U_N(s,x) \end{cases}$$

Property (6.23) follows directly from the definition of $U_N(s,x)$. Let us prove (6.22). Assume

$$\theta_1 > s$$

then take $\theta_i^n = \theta_i$ when $\theta_1 \geq s_n$, and $v_i^n \geq v_i$, $v_i^n \to v_i$, $(v_i^n, \theta_i^n) \in U_N(s_n,x_n)$ which is clearly possible.

If $\theta_1 = s$, and for instance $\theta_2 > s$, then take $\theta_1^n = \theta_1 + (s_n - s)^+$, for $\text{Max}(s_n, s) < \theta_2$, $\theta_2^n = \theta_2$ ...

Other cases are dealt with similarly. Then we have

Lemma 6.1.

The function $u(s,x)$ is upper semi continuous.

Proof

We have

$$u(s,x) = \inf_N u_N(s,x)$$

and

$$(6.24) \qquad u_N(s,x) = \inf_{(\theta_i,v_i)\in U_N(s,x)} \tilde{J}(N\ ;\ \theta_1, \ldots, \theta_N\ ;\ v_1, \ldots, v_N).$$

The function $\tilde{J}$ is continuous for N fixed. Moreover the infimum is actually attained. Let θ_i^n, v_i^n be the minimal point for $u_N(s_n,x_n)$. From the consideration of Theorem 6.1, it follows that θ_i^n, v_i^n remains in a compact set. Consider a converging subsequence

$$\theta_i^n \to \hat{\theta}_i,\ v_i^n \to \hat{v}_i$$

then from (6.23), $\hat{\theta}_i$, $\hat{v}_i$ belongs to $U_N(s,x)$ and

$$u_N(s_n,x_n) = \tilde{J}(N,\ s_n,x_n\ ;\ \theta_i^n,\ v_i^n) \to \tilde{J}(N,\ s,x\ ;\ \hat{\theta}_i,\ \hat{v}_i)$$

therefore

(6.25) $$\underline{\lim}\ u_N(s_n,x_n) \geq u_N(s,x)$$

On the other hand, take any $(\theta_i,\ v_i)$ in $U_N(s,x)$ and $\theta_i^n,\ v_i^n$ in $U_N(s_n,x_n)$ such that

$$\theta_i^n \to \theta_i,\ v_i^n \to v_i,$$

then we have

$$u_N(s_n,x_n) \leq \tilde{J}(N\ ;\ s_n,x_n\ ;\ \theta_i^n,\ v_i^n) \to \tilde{J}(N\ ;\ s,x\ ;\ \theta_i,\ v_i)$$

Therefore

$$\overline{\lim}\ u_N(s_n,x_n) \leq \tilde{J}(N\ ;\ s,x\ ;\ \theta_i,\ v_i)$$

hence

$$\overline{\lim}\ u_N(s_n,x_n) \leq u_N(s,x)$$

We thus have proved that

(6.26) $$u_N(s_n,x_n) \to u_N(s,x)$$

Now

$$\begin{aligned} u_N(s,x) &\geq \overline{\lim}\ u_N(s_n,x_n) \\ &\geq \overline{\lim}\ \inf_N u_N(s_n,x_n) \end{aligned}$$

hence

(6.27) $$\inf_N u_N(s,x) \geq \overline{\lim}\ \inf_N u_N(s_n,x_n).$$

This completes the proof. □

Theorem 6.2.

Assume (6.3), (6.4), then $u(s,x)$ defined by (6.15) satisfies the relations

(6.28) $$\begin{cases} u(T,x) = 0 \\ u(s,x) \leq \int_s^t f(\lambda,\ x - \int_s^\lambda \xi(\mu)d\mu)d\lambda + u(t,x - \int_s^t \xi(\mu)d\mu), \\ \forall t \in [s,T] \text{ such that } x - \int_s^t \xi(\lambda)d\lambda \geq 0 \\ u(s,x) \leq c(s,v\ ) + u(s,x+v),\ \forall v \geq 0,\ \forall s,x. \end{cases}$$

Moreover the set of Borel functions satisfying (6.28) has a maximum element which coincides with the function (6.15).

Proof

First let us prove that $u(s,x)$ defined by (6.15) satisfies (6.28). This is rather straightforward since the right hand side of the inequalities (6.28) corresponds to the cost of constrained policies where no order is placed before t, or an order of size v is placed immediately. Consider now a function which is Borel non negative and belongs to (6.28). Let V be an impulse control as defined in §VI.1. We want to prove

$$u(s,x) \leq \inf_V J_{s,x}(V). \tag{6.29}$$

Actually we may restrict ourselves to impulse controls V satisfying (6.8). Assume $\theta_1 > s$ from (6.28) we have

$$u(s,x) \leq \int_s^{\theta_1} f(\lambda, z(\lambda))d\lambda + u(\theta_1, z(\theta_1 - 0))$$

and

$$u(\theta_1, z(\theta_1 - 0)) \leq c(\theta_1, v_1) + u(\theta_1, z(\theta_1)) \ ;$$

therefore

$$u(s,x) \leq \int_s^{\theta_1} f(\lambda, z(\lambda))d\lambda + c(\theta_1, v_1) + u(\theta_1, z(\theta_1)).$$

If $\theta_1 = s$, this relation is also true. In a similar way we prove that

$$u(s,x) \leq \int_s^{\theta_N} f(\lambda, z(\lambda))d\lambda + \sum_{i=1}^{N} c(\theta_i, v_i) + u(\theta_N, z(\theta_N)) \tag{6.30}$$

Then we have

$$u(\theta_N, z(\theta_N)) \leq \int_{\theta_N}^{T} f(\lambda, z(\lambda))d\lambda \tag{6.31}$$

Since N is the number of impulses of V, taking place strictly before T, it follows from (6.30), (6.31) that

$$u(s,x) \leq J_{s,x}(V).$$

Since V is arbitrary, this completes the proof. □

VI - 4. PROPERTIES OF OPTIMAL IMPULSE CONTROLS

The next result is the continuous time version of Theorem 3.2., Chapter I.

Theorem 6.3.

Assume (6.3), (6.4), then $u(s,x)$ defined by (6.15) is the maximum element of the set

$$u(T,x) = 0$$

$$u(s,x) \leq \int_s^t f(\lambda, x - \int_s^\lambda \xi(\mu)d\mu)d\lambda + u(t, x - \int_s^t \xi(\mu)d\mu),$$

$\forall t \in [s,T]$ such that $x \geq \int_s^t \xi(\lambda)d\lambda$.

If $x < \int_s^T \xi(\lambda)d\lambda$, let θ such that $x = \int_s^\theta \xi(\lambda)d\lambda$, $s \leq \theta < T$, then

$$u(s,x) \leq c(s, \int_s^r \xi(\lambda)d\lambda - x) + \int_s^r f(\lambda, \int_\lambda^r \xi(\mu)d\mu)d\lambda + u(r,0), \forall r \in [\theta,T]$$

Proof

The function u(s,x) defined by (6.15) satisfies the relations (6.32) since the right hand side of the inequalities (6.32) corresponds to some constrained policies which will be identified.

Consider now controls satisfying (6.8), (6.11) which are sufficient to achieve inf J(V), then we shall be able to restrict considerably the set of admissible controls.

Consider the impulse θ_2, v_2 and assume that

$$y(\theta_1 - 0) + v_1 - \int_{\theta_1}^{\theta_2} \xi(\lambda)d\lambda = y(\theta_2 - 0) > 0 \tag{6.33}$$

Set $\Delta = \text{Min}\ (v_1, v_2, y(\theta_2 - 0))$, hence $\Delta > 0$. Consider a control V_a obtained from V by the following modification :

$$v_1 \to v_1 + \Delta = v_{a1}$$

$$v_2 \to v_2 - \Delta = v_{a2}$$

Similarly consider V_b defined as follows from V :

$$v_1 \to v_1 - \Delta = v_{b1}$$

$$v_2 \to v_2 + \Delta = v_{b2}$$

the other impulses being unchanged. The controls V_a, V_b are admissible. Indeed we have

$$y_a(t) = y(t), \qquad t < \theta_1, \qquad t \geq \theta_2$$

$$y_a(t) = y(t) + \Delta, \qquad \theta_1 \leq t < \theta_2$$

$$y_b(t) = y(t), \qquad t < \theta_1, \qquad t \geq \theta_2$$

$$y_b(t) = y(t) - \Delta, \qquad \theta_1 \leq t < \theta_2$$

hence $y_a(t) \geq 0$, $y_b(t) \geq 0$.

Three possibilities have to be considered.

(i) If $\Delta = v_1$ and $\Delta \neq v_2$ or $\Delta \neq y(\theta_2 - 0)$, then :

$v_1 < v_2$, $v_1 < y(\theta_2 - 0)$

necessarily from (6.33) it follows that $y(\theta_1 - 0) > 0$.

In this case $v_{b_1} = 0$.

(ii) $\Delta = v_2$, then $v_{a2} = 0$.

(iii) If $\Delta = y(\theta_2 - 0)$ then $y_b(\theta_2 - 0) = 0$.

Then we define

$$\tilde{V} = \begin{cases} V_a \text{ if } \Delta = v_2 \\ V_b \text{ if } \Delta = v_1 \text{ or } y(\theta_2 - 0) \end{cases}$$

Therefore $\tilde{V}$ has the following properties. Either the impulse at θ_2 is removed, the second one becoming θ_3, or the impulse at θ_1 is removed, the impulse at θ_2 becoming the first one, or both impulses at θ_1, θ_2 remain but then $\tilde{y}(\theta_2 - 0) = 0$.

More generally we consider the first time θ_i, $i \geq 2$ such that $y(\theta_i - 0) > 0$, and we proceed as previously with

$$\Delta = \text{Min}\ (v_{i-1}, v_i, y(\theta_i - 0)).$$

The modification of V into $\tilde{V}$ is such that either the number of impulses has decreased by one, or the first index $i \geq 2$ such that $y(\theta_i - 0) > 0$ has increased by one.

Eventually after a finite number of steps, we construct from the initial control a new one which has the following property : except possibly the first impulse θ_1, all subsequent ones which take place strictly before T, satisfy

$$y(\theta_i - 0) = 0 \qquad i \geq 2 \tag{6.34}$$

The important point is that we can restrict the set of admissible controls to those satisfying the property (6.34). This is proved by showing that if V is an optimal control which does not satisfy the property (6.34), then both controls V_a and V_b constructed from V as indicated above are also optimal. Therefore $\tilde{V}$ constructed from V after a finite number of steps is optimal and satisfies (6.34). The fact that V_a, V_b are also optimal if V is optimal, follows from concavity. Indeed

$$\begin{aligned} J(V_a) + J(V_b) - 2J(V) &= c(\theta_1 ; v_1 + \Delta) + c(\theta_1 ; v_1 - \Delta) \\ &+ c(\theta_2 ; v_2 - \Delta) + c(\theta_2 ; v_2 + \Delta) - 2c(\theta_1 ; v_1) \\ &+ \int_{\theta_1}^{\theta_2} f(t ; y(t) + \Delta)dt + \int_{\theta_1}^{\theta_2} f(t ; y(t) - \Delta)dt \\ &- 2 \int_{\theta_1}^{\theta_2} f(t ; y(t))dt \leq 0 \end{aligned}$$

and since $J(V_a) - J(V) \geq 0$, $J(V_b) - J(V) \geq 0$, we have

$$J(V) = J(V_a) = J(V_b) = \inf J(V).$$

Without loss of generality we can also assume that the optimal control satisfies

$$y(T) = 0 \qquad (\text{if } x < \int_s^T \xi(\lambda)d\lambda), \tag{6.35}$$

which is achieved by diminishing the size of the last order.

We can therefore restrict ourselves to admissible controls which satisfy (6.8), (6.11) and (6.34), (6.35). From (6.34), (6.35) it follows that (for such controls)

$$(6.36)\quad \begin{cases} y(\theta_i - 0) + v_i - \int_{\theta_i}^{\theta_{i+1}} \xi(\lambda)d\lambda = 0 \\ i = 1, \ldots, N \text{ (with } \theta_{N+1} = T, \text{ and } y(\theta_1 - 0) = x \text{ if } \theta_1 = s) \end{cases}$$

Let u be an element of (6.32). Then we have from (6.32)

$$(6.37)\quad u(s,x) \leq \int_s^{\theta_1} f(\lambda ; y(\lambda))d\lambda + u(\theta_1, y(\theta_1 - 0))$$

and from the second inequality (6.32) and (6.36) (with $s = \theta_i$, $r = \theta_{i+1}$)

$$u(\theta_i, y(\theta_i - 0)) \leq c(\theta_i, v_i) + \int_{\theta_i}^{\theta_{i+1}} f(\lambda, y(\lambda))d\lambda + u(\theta_{i+1}, y(\theta_{i+1} - 0)),\ i=1,\ldots,N$$

Adding up we deduce

$$u(s,x) \leq J_{s,x}(V),\ \forall V \text{ satisfying (6.8), (6.11), (6.34), (6.35).}$$

Hence

$$u(s,x) \leq \inf_V J_{s,x}(V).$$

Therefore $\inf_V J_{s,x}(V)$ is indeed the maximum element of the set (6.32). □

The analogue of the Wagner-Within Theorem (cf Chapter I, Theorem 3.3) can be obtained from theorem 6.3.

Theorem 6.4

Assume (6.3), (6.4) and

$$(6.38)\quad x < \int_s^T \xi(\lambda)d\lambda,$$

then, there exists an optimal control for problem (6.5) which has a finite number of impulses taking place strictly before T, satisfying

$$(6.39)\quad \begin{cases} s \leq \theta_1 < \theta_2 < \ldots < \theta_N < T,\ v_1 > 0, \ldots, v_N > 0, \\ y(\theta_i - 0) = 0 \text{ for } i = 2, \ldots, N,\ y(T) = 0, \\ x - \int_s^{\theta_1} \xi(\lambda)d\lambda \geq 0 \\ y(\theta_i - 0) + v_i - \int_{\theta_i}^{\theta_{i+1}} \xi(\lambda)d\lambda = 0,\ i = 1, \ldots, N,\ (\theta_{N+1} = T) \end{cases}$$

Proof

It is a direct consequence of the proof of Theorem 6.3. □

Remark 6.1

If $x = 0$ and $\xi(\lambda) > 0$ a.e. λ then we have $\theta_1 = s$ and $y(\theta_i - 0) = 0 \quad \forall i=1,\dots,N$

Moreover if

$$c(t_1 \,;\, v) \leq c(t_2 \,;\, v) \quad \forall t_1 \geq t_2,\ v > 0 \tag{6.40}$$

then θ_1 is defined by

$$x - \int_s^{\theta_1} \xi(\lambda)d\lambda = 0 \tag{6.41}$$

Indeed let τ such that $s - \int_s^{\tau} \xi(\lambda)d\lambda = 0$, then if $\theta_1 < \tau$, we have $\theta_2 > \tau$, since $y(\tau - 0) = x - \int_s^{\tau} \xi(\lambda)d\lambda + v_1$ hence $y(\tau - 0) > 0$ (as a consequence of (6.39)).

We modify V into $\tilde{V}$ just by shifting the first order from θ_1 to τ. Therefore

$$J(\tilde{V}) - J(V) = \int_{\theta_1}^{\tau} [f(\lambda \,;\, x - \int_s^{\lambda} \xi(\mu)d\mu) - f(\lambda \,;\, x + v_1 - \int_s^{\lambda} \xi(\mu)d\mu)]d\lambda +$$
$$+ c(\tau \,;\, v_1) - c(\theta_1 \,;\, v_1) \leq 0$$

by (6.40), hence $\tilde{V}$ is also optimal if V is optimal and $\tilde{V}$ satisfies (6.41). □

VI - 5. FORWARD DYNAMIC PROGRAMMING AND FORECAST HORIZONS

Consider the notation already introduced with the discrete time formulation in section IV of Chapter I :

$$\lambda(T) = \inf J^T_{0,0}(V) \tag{6.42}$$

where $J^T_{0,0}(V)$ denotes the functional (6.5) with $s = 0$, $x = 0$. We also set

$$\sigma(s,T) = \int_s^T \xi(\lambda)d\lambda. \tag{6.43}$$

Then a functional equation for $\lambda(T)$ (forward Dynamic Programming), can be derived from theorem 6.4, namely,

Theorem 6.5

Assume (6.3), (6.4), then we have

$$\begin{cases} \lambda(T) = \underset{s\in[0,T)}{\text{Min}} \{c(s \,;\, \sigma(s,T)) + \int_s^T f(\lambda \,;\, \sigma(\lambda,T))d\lambda + \lambda(s)\},\ T > 0 \\ \lambda(0) = 0 \end{cases} \tag{6.44}$$

Proof

If $\sigma(0,T) = 0$, then :

$$\lambda(T) = \int_0^T f(\lambda\ ;\ 0)d\lambda$$

and

$$\lambda(T) = \lambda(s) + \int_s^T f(\lambda\ ;\ 0)d\lambda$$

therefore (6.44) is satisfied.

Assume now that $\sigma(0,T) > 0$, then there exists a last set up point $\hat{s}$ of an optimal control of $J^T_{0,0}(V)$, such that $0 \leq \hat{s} < T$. From Theorem 6.4 and Remark 6.1, we have $y(\hat{s} - 0) = 0$.

The size of the order placed at $\hat{s}$ is $\sigma(\hat{s},T) > 0$ since $\hat{s}$ is an impulse time. It follows that

$$\lambda(T) = \lambda(\hat{s}) + c(\hat{s}, \sigma(\hat{s},T)) + \int_{\hat{s}}^T f(\lambda\ ;\ \sigma(\lambda,T))d\lambda$$

hence $\lambda(T)$ is larger or equal to the right hand side of (6.44). On the other hand it is also less than, or equal to the right hand side, since for any $s \in [0,T)$ the cost within brackets in (6.44) corresponds to the cost of a specific policy. Hence the desired result is proved. □

Remark 6.2

In (6.44) the minimum is actually reached in the semi closed interval $[0,T)$. □

We can then derive planning horizon theorems similar to those in the discrete time formulation. Set for $0 \leq s < T$

$$\mu(s,T) = \lambda(s) + c(s, \sigma(s,T)) + \int_s^T f(\lambda\ ;\ \sigma(\lambda,T))d\lambda \tag{6.45}$$

and for $s_1 < S$, $s_2 < T$, $T < S$

$$\phi(s_1, s_2, T, S) = \mu(s_1, S) - \mu(s_1, T) - [\mu(s_2, S) - \mu(s_2, T)]. \tag{6.46}$$

We have for $0 \leq s_1 \leq s_2 < T < S$

$$\left\{\begin{aligned} &\phi(s_1, s_2, T, S) = c(s_1, \sigma(s_1, S)) - c(s_1, \sigma(s_1, T)) \\ &- [c(s_2, \sigma(s_2, S)) - c(s_2, \sigma(s_2, T))] \\ &+ \int_{s_1}^{s_2} [f(\lambda, \sigma(\lambda,S)) - f(\lambda, \sigma(\lambda, T))]d\lambda \end{aligned}\right. \tag{6.47}$$

Assume $\sigma(s_2, T) > 0$, then

$$(6.48)\qquad \begin{cases} \phi(s_1, s_2, T, S) \geq \Big[c'^{+}(s_1, \sigma(s_1, S)) - c'^{-}(s_2, \sigma(s_2, T)) + \\ + \int_{s_1}^{s_2} f'^{+}(\lambda, \sigma(\lambda, S))d\lambda\Big] \sigma(T, S) \end{cases}$$

we deduce

Lemma 6.2

Assume $0 \leq s_1 \leq s_2 < T < S$, $\sigma(s_2, T) > 0$,

$$(6.49)\qquad c'^{+}(s, v) \geq \bar{c}'(s),\ f'^{+}(s\ ;\ x) \geq \bar{f}'(s)$$

and

$$(6.50)\qquad \bar{c}'(s_1) + \int_{s_1}^{s_2} \bar{f}'(\lambda)d\lambda - c'^{-}(s_2, \sigma(s_2, T)) \geq 0$$

then we have

$$(6.51)\qquad \phi(s_1, s_2, T, S) \geq 0$$

Proof

The property (6.51) is an immediate consequence of (6.48) and the assumptions (6.49), (6.50). □

We now define $l(T)$ as the last set up point of the optimal policy specified in the proof of Theorem 6.5. In fact it is the last set up when $\sigma(0, T) > 0$. When $\sigma(0, T) = 0$, we take for $l(T)$ any arbitrary number, strictly less than T. We can then state

Lemma 6.3

Assume (6.49), $\sigma(0, T) > 0$, and

$$(6.52)\qquad \bar{c}'(s) + \int_{s}^{l(T)} \bar{f}'(\lambda)d\lambda - c'^{-}(l(T), \sigma(l(T), T)) \geq 0 \quad \forall s \leq l(T)$$

then we have

$$(6.53)\qquad \mu(s, S) \geq \mu(l(T), S), \quad \forall s \leq l(T),\ T \leq S$$

Proof

We take $s_1 = s$, $s_2 = l(T)$ in (6.51), hence

$$\mu(s, S) - \mu(l(T), S) \geq \mu(s, T) - \mu(l(T), T))$$
$$\geq 0$$

from the definition of $l(T)$. □

Corollary 6.1

Assume that

$$(6.54)\qquad c(s\ ;\ v) = K(s)\,\chi_{v>0} + d(s)v$$

with

(6.55) $\begin{cases} d(s) \text{ decreasing function,} \\ K(s) \text{ decreasing function.} \end{cases}$

Take $l(T) = \frac{T}{2}$ (for simplicity) when $\sigma(0, T) = 0$.

Then $l(T)$ is an increasing function of T.

Proof

For $T \leq S$, we want to prove that

(6.56) $l(T) \leq l(S)$.

If $\sigma(0, S) = 0$ then $\sigma(0, T) = 0$ and (6.56) is a consequence of the definition of $l(T)$.

Assume now that $T < S$; $\sigma(0, S) > 0$ and $\sigma(0, T) = 0$. We have for $s < T$

$$\mu(s, S) - \mu(T, S)$$

$$= c(s ; \sigma(T, S)) - c(T, \sigma(T, S)) + \int_s^T f(\lambda ; \sigma(T, S))d\lambda + \lambda(s) - \lambda(T)$$

$$= c(s, \sigma(T, S)) - c(T ; \sigma(T, S)) + \int_s^T f(\lambda ; \sigma(T, S))d\lambda - \int_s^T f(\lambda;0)d\lambda$$

$$\geq K(s) - K(T) + (d(s) - d(T)) \sigma(T, S)$$

$$\geq 0$$

by (6.55).

Therefore $l(S) \geq T > l(T)$.

Consider finally the case when $\sigma(0, T) > 0$. Then $\sigma(l(T), T) > 0$ and (6.52) is satisfied since

$$\bar{c}'(s) = d(s) \qquad c'^{-}(l(T), \sigma(l(T), T)) = d(l(T)).$$

Therefore (6.53) holds, which implies $l(S) \geq l(T)$, which completes the proof. □

If $\sigma(0, T) > 0$, $\forall T$ then the result of Corollary 6.1 holds even when the second part of assumption (6.55) is not satisfied. This is clear from the proof. □

Corollary 6.2

Under the assumptions of Corollary 6.1, $\forall S \geq T$ there exists an optimal policy for $J^S(V)$ which has a regeneration point between $l(T)$ and T.

Proof

The points $l(S)$, $l(l(S))$, ..., $l^{(k)}(S)$, ... are regeneration points for an optimal policy of $J^S(V)$. But $l^{(k)}(S) \to 0$ as $k \to \infty$, hence there exists k_0 such that

$$(6.57)\qquad l^{(k_0)}(S) \geq T \qquad l^{(k_0+1)}(S) \leq T.$$

But then from the first assertion (6.57) and Corollary 6.1

$$l^{(k_0+1)}(S) \geq l(T)$$

which proves the desired result. □

More generally we can state the following

Theorem 6.6

Assume (6.3), (6.4), (6.49), (6.52) and $\sigma(0, T) > 0$, then T is a forecast horizon in the sense that $\forall S \geq T$, there exists an optimal policy for $J_0^S(V)$ which has a regeneration point between $l(T)$ and T.

Proof

Let $S > T$, then from Lemma 6.3 it follows that

$$l(S) \geq l(T)$$

If $l(S) \leq T$ then the desired result is proved. Otherwise $l(S) > T$, then we can apply (6.53) with S replaced by $l(S)$, from which it follows that

$$l^{(2)}(S) \geq l(T).$$

Therefore as in Corollary 6.2 the sequence $l^{(k)}(S)$ is such that if $l^{(k)}(S) > T$, then $l^{(k+1)}(S) \geq l(T)$. Necessarily there exists an index k_0 such that

$$l^{(k_0)}(S) \geq T \text{ and } l^{(k_0+1)}(S) \leq T$$

hence also

$$l(T) \leq l^{(k_0+1)}(S) \leq T$$

which proves the desired result. □

Remark 6.4

We recover all the properties of regeneration points obtained in the discrete time case. But unlike the discrete time case (cf. Theorem 4.6, Chapter I) we cannot assert that, under the assumptions of Theorem 6.6, $l(T)$ is a planning horizon for the forecast horizon T. This seems to be a serious disadvantage of the continuous time framework with respect to the discrete time one. □

VII - THE CONCAVE COST MODEL WITH INFINITE HORIZON

VII - 1. SETTING OF THE PROBLEM

In this section we extend the impulse control formulation developed in section VI to the case of an infinite horizon. This is the continuous time analogue of section X, Chapter I.

A control is a set

$$V = (\theta_1, v_1 ; \ldots ; \theta_i, v_i ; \ldots)$$

with

$$\theta_i \uparrow \infty \text{ as } i \to +\infty, \ \theta_i = +\infty \text{ is possible.}$$

The trajectory is given by

$$(7.1) \qquad \begin{cases} dz = -\xi(t)dt + \sum_i v_i \, \delta(t - \theta_i), \ t > s \\ z(s) = x \end{cases}$$

We impose the constraint

$$(7.2) \qquad z(t) \geq 0.$$

The production cost function is denoted as in (6.3) by :

$$(7.3) \qquad \begin{cases} c(t\ ;\ v) : [0,\infty) \times R^+ \to R^+ \text{ with the following properties :} \\ .\ \text{concave non decreasing in } v\ ; \\ .\ \text{continuous on } [0,\infty) \times (0,\infty) \text{ with } c(t\ ;\ 0) = 0,\ c(t\ ;\ 0^+) \geq K \\ .\ \inf_{t\in[0,\infty)} c(t\ ;\ v) \to +\infty \quad \text{as } v \to \infty \end{cases}$$

The inventory cost function is denoted as in (6.4) by :

$$(7.4) \qquad \begin{cases} f(t\ ;\ x) : [0,\infty) \times R^+ \to R^+ \text{ with the following properties :} \\ .\ \text{concave non decreasing in } x\ ; \\ .\ \text{a.e. } t \quad f(t,\ x) = \tilde{f}(t\ ;\ x),\ \forall x, \text{ where } \tilde{f} \text{ is a Borel function.} \end{cases}$$

The cost functional to minimize is :

$$(7.5) \qquad J_{s,x}(V) = \int_s^\infty e^{-\alpha(t-s)} f(t\ ;\ z(t))dt + \sum_i c(\theta_i, v_i) e^{-\alpha(\theta_i - s)} \chi_{\theta_i < \infty}$$

We set

$$(7.6) \qquad u(s,\ x) = \inf_V J_{s,x}(V)$$

and assume that

$$(7.7) \qquad u(s,\ x) \leq \bar{u}_0(x).$$

Sufficient conditions for (7.7) to hold may be derived as we consider a given sequence of times

$$\bar{\theta}_1 = s \qquad \bar{\theta}_2 = s+1,\ \ldots$$

and corresponding controls

$$\bar{v}_1 = \int_s^{s+1} \xi(t)dt, \quad \bar{v}_2 = \int_{s+1}^{s+2} \xi(t)dt,\ \ldots$$

In this manner we obtain an impulse control $\bar{V}$, which is clearly admissible. We have

$$\bar{z}(t) = x + \int_t^{s+i} \xi(\lambda)d\lambda , \qquad \bar{\theta}_i \leq t < \bar{\theta}_{i+1}$$

and

$$(7.8) \qquad \begin{cases} J_{s,x}(\bar{V}) = \sum_{i=1}^{\infty} \int_{s+i-1}^{s+i} e^{-\alpha(t-s)} f(t\ ;\ x + \int_t^{s+i} \xi(\lambda)d\lambda)dt \\ + \sum_{i=1}^{\infty} c(s+i-1\ ;\ \int_{s+i-1}^{s+i} \xi(t)dt)e^{-\alpha(i-1)} \end{cases}$$

We may assume that

$$(7.9) \qquad J_{s,x}(\bar{V}) \leq \bar{u}_0(x)$$

which guarantees (7.7).

The stationary case corresponds to :

$$(7.10) \qquad \begin{cases} f(t\ ;\ x) = f(x), \quad c(t\ ;\ v) = c(v), \\ \xi(t) = \xi \end{cases}$$

for which

$$J_{s,x}(\bar{V}) \leq \frac{f(x+\xi)}{\alpha} + \frac{c(\xi)}{1-e^{-\alpha}}$$

VII - 2. APPROXIMATION

Consider the problem, truncated at T :

$$(7.11) \qquad J^T_{s,x}(V) = \int_s^T f(t\ ;\ z(t))e^{-\alpha(t-s)}dt + \sum_i c(\theta_i, v_i)e^{-\alpha(\theta_i - s)} \chi_{\theta_i < T}$$

and set

$$(7.12) \qquad u^T(s,x) = \operatorname*{Inf}_V J^T_{s,x}(V)$$

If $T < T'$, we have

$$J^T_{s,x}(V) \leq J^{T'}_{s,x}(V)$$

hence

$$(7.13) \qquad u^T(s,x) \leq u^{T'}(s,x) \leq u(s,x).$$

To any control V, we associate V^T as follows : we keep all (θ_i, v_i) such that $\theta_i < T$, and we replace the orders placed after T by $\bar{V}$ defined in (7.8) (with s replaced by T).

Note that since $\theta_i \uparrow +\infty$ as $i \uparrow +\infty$, only a finite number of θ_i take place before T, and thus V^T is well defined. Clearly

$$J^T_{s,x}(V) = J^T_{s,x}(V^T).$$

But

$$J_{s,x}(V) = J^T_{s,x}(V^T) + e^{-\alpha(T-s)} J_{T,z(T)}(\bar{V})$$

hence

$$u(s,x) \le J^T_{s,x}(V^T) + e^{-\alpha(T-s)} \bar{u}_0(z(T)) \tag{7.14}$$

Assume that

$$x < \int_s^T \xi(\lambda)d\lambda \tag{7.15}$$

then from Theorem 6.4, we can restrict ourselves to controls V^T such that $z(T) = 0$ The infimum over this restricted class of $J^T_{s,x}(V^T)$ will still be $u^T(s,x)$. Therefore (7.14) implies

$$u(s,x) \le u^T(s,x) + e^{-\alpha(T-s)}\bar{u}_0(0)$$

As a consequence :

Theorem 7.1

Assume (7.3), (7.4), (7.9) and $\int_0^\infty \xi(\lambda)d\lambda = +\infty$, then we have :

$$u^T(s,x) \uparrow u(s,x) \tag{7.16}$$

and ,for T satisfying (7.15) :

$$u(s,x) \le u^T(s,x) + e^{-\alpha(T-s)}\bar{u}_0(0) \tag{7.17}$$ □

Corollary 7.1

The function $u(s,x)$ is upper semi continuous.

Proof

This property follows from the upper semi continuity of $u^T(s,x)$ proved in Lemma 6.1. □

VII - 3. DYNAMIC PROGRAMMING

Theorem 7.2.

Under the assumptions of Theorem 7.1, the function $u(s,x)$ defined by (7.6) satisfies

$$\begin{cases} u(s,x) \le \int_s^t f(\lambda, x - \int_s^\lambda \xi(\mu)d\mu)e^{-\alpha(\lambda-s)}d\lambda + u(t;x - \int_s^t \xi(\mu)d\mu)e^{-\alpha(t-s)}, \\ \forall t \in [s,T] \text{ such that } x - \int_s^t \xi(\lambda)d\lambda \ge 0 \\ u(s,x) \le c(s,v) + u(s,x+v) \quad \forall v \ge 0 \\ u(s,x) \le \bar{u}_0(x) \end{cases} \tag{7.18}$$

Moreover, the set of Borel functions satisfying (7.18) has a maximum element which coincides with the function (7.6).

Proof

The fact that the function u satisfies (7.18) follows easily from the definition of u. Now, consider any function $\tilde{u}$ satisfying (7.18) and a control V such that

$$\theta_i < \theta_{i+1}.$$

The latter may assume without loss of generality following the same arguments as in Theorem 6.1. Reasoning as in Theorem 6.2, we obtain

$$(7.19)\quad \begin{cases} \tilde{u}(s,x) \le \int_s^{\theta_N} e^{-\alpha(t-s)} f(t, z(t))dt + \sum_{i=1}^{N} c(\theta_i,v_i)e^{-\alpha(\theta_i-s)} \\ + \tilde{u}(\theta_N, z(\theta_N))e^{-\alpha(\theta_N-s)} . \end{cases}$$

Let T be fixed. We then select as a control, $\hat{V}^T$, such that

$$u^T(s,x) = J_{s,x}(\hat{V}^T)$$

Taking in (7.19) θ_N for the last set up time of the policy $\hat{V}^T$, and using again the first relation (7.18) with $s = \theta_N$ and $t = T$, we obtain

$$\tilde{u}(s,x) \le u^T(s,x) + \tilde{u}(T, \hat{z}(T))e^{-\alpha(T-s)}$$

and since $\hat{z}(T) = 0$,

$$\tilde{u}(s,x) \le u^T(s,x) + \tilde{u}(T,0)e^{-\alpha(T-s)}$$
$$\le u^T(s,x) + \bar{u}_0(0)e^{-\alpha(T-s)}$$

Letting $T \to \infty$, and using Theorem 9.1., we deduce $\tilde{u} \le u$, which completes the proof of the desired result. □

We next derive the simplified form of the Dynamic Programming relations.

Theorem 7.3

Under the assumptions of Theorem 7.1, the function u(s,x) defined by (7.6) satisfies the relations

$$(7.20)\quad \begin{cases} u(s,x) \le \int_s^t f(\lambda, x - \int_s^\lambda \xi(\mu)d\mu)e^{-\alpha(\lambda-s)}d\lambda + u(t,x - \int_s^t \xi(\lambda)d\lambda)e^{-\alpha(t-s)} \\ \forall t \ge s \text{ such that } x \ge \int_s^t \xi(\lambda)d\lambda. \\ \text{Let } \theta \ge s \text{ such that } x = \int_s^\theta \xi(\lambda)d\lambda, \text{ then one has} \\ u(s,x) \le c(s, \int_s^r \xi(\lambda)d\lambda - x) + \int_s^r f(\lambda, \int_\lambda^r \xi(\mu)d\mu)e^{-\alpha(\lambda-s)}d\lambda \\ + u(r, 0)e^{-\alpha(r-s)} \qquad \forall r \ge \theta \\ u(s,x) \le \bar{u}_0(x). \end{cases}$$

Moreover the set of Borel functions defined by (7.20) has a maximum element which coincides with (7.6).

Proof

Clearly the function u satisfies (7.20). Take now any function $\tilde{u}$ satisfying (7.20). From Theorem 6.3, we can claim that an optimal control for $J^T_{s,x}(V)$ can be taken from the class satisfying (6.8), (6.11). Consider an optimal control $\hat{V}^T$. Reasoning as in Theorem 6.3, we easily obtain

$$\tilde{u}(s,x) \leq u^T(s,x) + e^{-\alpha(T-s)}\,\bar{u}_0(0)$$

and letting T tend to $+\infty$, we deduce $\tilde{u} \leq u$, which corresponds to the desired result. □

VII - 4. THE STATIONARY CASE

We consider in this paragraph the special case already introduced in (7.10) :

$$(7.21) \qquad \begin{cases} \xi(t) = \xi > 0 \\ f(t,x) = f(x), \quad c(t\,;\,v) = c(v) \end{cases}$$

hence

$$(7.22) \qquad J_{s,x}(V) = \int_s^\infty e^{-\alpha(t-s)} f(z(t))dt + \sum_i c(v_i)e^{-\alpha(\theta_i-s)} \chi_{\theta_i<\infty}$$

We know that assumption (7.9) is satisfied in the stationary case.

Lemma 7.1.

The function u(s,x) does not depend on s.

Proof

For any control $V = (\theta_1,v_1, \ldots)$, we have :

$$z(t) = x + \sum_{\{i|\theta_i\leq t\}} v_i - (t-s)\xi$$

Define next

$$\tilde{\theta}_1 = \theta_1-s, \ \ldots, \ \tilde{\theta}_n = \theta_n-s$$

$$\tilde{v}_1 = v_1, \ \ldots, \ \tilde{v}_n = v_n$$

$$\tilde{z}(t) = z(s+t) \qquad \text{for } t \geq 0$$

then

$$\tilde{z}(t) = x + \sum_{\{i|\tilde{\theta}_i\leq t\}} \tilde{v}_i - t\xi, \qquad t \geq 0$$

and

$$J_{s,x}(V) = \int_0^\infty e^{-\alpha t} f(\tilde{z}(t))dt + \sum_i c_i(\tilde{v}_i)e^{-\alpha\tilde{\theta}_i} \chi_{\tilde{\theta}_i<\infty}$$

$$= J_{0,x}(\tilde{V}).$$

Since V is arbitrary, we easily deduce that

$$u(s,x) = u(0,x)$$

hence the desired result. □

It then follows from Theorem 7.3 that u satisfies the relations

$$(7.23) \quad \begin{cases} u(x) \le \int_0^t f(x - \lambda\xi)e^{-\alpha\lambda}\, d\lambda + u(x - t\xi)e^{-\alpha t}, \ \forall t \ge 0 \\ \text{such that } x \ge \xi t \\ \text{If } \theta = \frac{x}{\xi} \text{ then} \\ u(x) \le c(r\xi - x) + \int_0^r f((r-\lambda)\xi)e^{-\alpha\lambda}d\lambda + u(0)e^{-\alpha r}, \ \forall r \ge \theta \\ u(x) \le \bar{u}_0(x) \end{cases}$$

In fact u is the maximum element of the set of functions satisfying (7.23). An explicit formula for u(x) may be given :

$$(7.24) \qquad u(x) = \int_0^\theta f(x - \lambda\xi)e^{-\alpha\lambda}d\lambda + u(0)e^{-\theta\alpha}$$

$$(7.25) \qquad u(0) = \operatorname*{Inf}_{r\ge 0} \{c(r\xi) + \int_0^r f((r-\lambda)\xi)e^{-\alpha\lambda}d\lambda + u(0)e^{-\alpha r}\}$$

Indeed, let us set

$$(7.26) \qquad \phi(r) = \frac{c(r\xi) + \int_0^r f((r-\lambda)\xi)e^{-\alpha\lambda}d\lambda}{1 - e^{-\alpha r}}$$

then we have

$$(7.27) \qquad u(0) = \operatorname*{Inf}_{r\ge 0} \phi(r)$$

Lemma 7.2

Equation (7.25) has a maximum solution given by formula (7.27).

Proof

Denote by ϕ^* the right hand side of (7.27). As a consequence :

(7.28) $$\phi^* \le c(r\xi) + \int_0^r f((r-\lambda)\xi)e^{-\alpha\lambda}d\lambda + e^{-\alpha r}\phi^*$$

But also

$$\phi(r) = c(r\xi) + \int_0^r f((r-\lambda)\xi)e^{-\alpha\lambda}d\lambda + e^{-\alpha r}\phi(r)$$
$$\ge c(r\xi) + \int_0^r f((r-\lambda)\xi)e^{-\alpha\lambda}d\lambda + e^{-\alpha r}\phi^*$$

This last inequality together with (7.28) prove that ϕ^* is a solution of (7.25). Let $\tilde{\phi}$ be any other solution, then clearly

$$\tilde{\phi} \le \phi^*,$$

which completes the proof. □

Finally :

Theorem 7.4

Under the assumptions of Theorem 7.1, and (7.21), defining u(0) by (7.27) and u(x) by (7.24), we thus obtain the maximum solution of (7.23).

Proof

Let us check that proceeding as suggested we obtain an element of (7.23). It is easy to verify that $u(x) \le \bar{u}_0(x)$ follows from

$$u(0) \le c(\xi) + \int_0^1 f((1-\lambda)\xi)e^{-\alpha\lambda}d\lambda + u(0)e^{-\alpha}$$

Let $t \le \frac{x}{\xi} = \theta$, then

(7.29) $$u(x) = \int_0^t f(x-\lambda\xi)e^{-\alpha\lambda}d\lambda + u(0)e^{-\alpha\theta} + \int_t^\theta f(x-\lambda\xi)e^{-\alpha\lambda}d\lambda$$

and

(7.30) $$\begin{cases} u(x - t\xi) = \int_0^{\theta-t} f(x - (\lambda+t)\xi)e^{-\alpha\lambda}d\lambda + u(0)e^{-\alpha(\theta-t)} \\ \qquad = \int_t^\theta f(x - \lambda\xi)e^{-\alpha(\lambda-t)}\,d\lambda + u(0)e^{-\alpha(\theta-t)} \end{cases}$$

Combining (7.29), (7.30) we deduce

$$u(x) = \int_0^t f(x - \lambda\xi)e^{-\alpha\lambda}d\lambda + e^{-\alpha t}\,u(x - t\xi),\ \forall t \ge 0, \text{ such that } x \ge \xi t$$

and thus the first relation (7.23) is satisfied.

We have also

$$u(x) \leq \int_0^\theta f(x - \lambda\xi)e^{-\alpha\lambda}d\lambda + c(\lambda\xi)e^{-\alpha\theta}$$

$$+ \int_0^s f((s-\lambda)\xi)e^{-\alpha(\lambda+\theta)}d\lambda + u(0)e^{-\alpha(s+\theta)}, \ \forall s \geq 0$$

Let us consider $r \geq \theta$, and take $s = r-\theta$, then

$$u(x) \leq \int_0^\theta f((\theta-\lambda)\xi)e^{-\alpha\lambda}d\lambda + c(r\xi-x)e^{-\alpha\theta}$$

$$+ \int_\theta^r f((r-\lambda)\xi)e^{-\alpha\lambda}d\lambda + u(0)e^{-\alpha r}.$$

Since f is non decreasing, then

$$u(x) \leq \int_0^r f((r-\lambda)\xi)e^{-\alpha\lambda}d\lambda + c(r\xi-x) + u(0)e^{-\alpha r}$$

which proves that the second relation (7.23) is satisfied. Now let $\tilde{u}$ be any solution of (7.23). We have

$$\tilde{u}(x) \leq \int_0^\theta f(x - \lambda\xi)e^{-\alpha\lambda}d\lambda + \tilde{u}(0)e^{-\alpha\theta}$$

But from the second relation (7.23) we get

$$\tilde{u}(0) \leq \phi(r)$$

hence

$$\tilde{u}(x) \leq \int_0^\theta f(x - \lambda\xi)e^{-\alpha\lambda}d\lambda + \phi(r)e^{-\alpha\theta}$$

Since r is arbitrary,

$$\tilde{u}(x) \leq \int_0^\theta f(x - \lambda\xi)e^{-\alpha\lambda}d\lambda + u(0)e^{-\alpha\theta}$$

$$= u(x)$$

which completes the proof of the desired result. □

Example

Consider the same example as in the discrete time formulation :

$$c(v) = K\chi_{v>0} + dv$$

$$f(x) = fx$$

Then, we obtain for $r > 0$

$$\phi(r) = \frac{K + d\,r\xi + \frac{f\xi}{\alpha}[r - \frac{1}{\alpha}(1 - e^{-\alpha r})]}{1 - e^{-\alpha r}}$$

and we have

(7.31) $$u(0) = \operatorname*{Inf}_{r \geq 0} \phi(r).$$

Compute $\phi(r)$ for α small. It follows

$$\phi(r) \sim \frac{K + d\, r\xi + f\xi \frac{r^2}{2}}{\alpha r}$$

$$\sim \frac{1}{\alpha}\left[\frac{K}{r} + f\xi \frac{r}{2} + d\xi\right]$$

and we get the same result as in the discrete time formulation (cf. Chapter I) ; ϕ is minimum at the point

$$r^* = \sqrt{\frac{2K}{f\xi}}$$

Remark 7.1

We have not considered the ergodic problem in this section. This would correspond to letting α tend to 1 and would be a very interesting problem to study. Asymptotic expansion with respect to $1-\alpha$ would be very useful for practical purposes.

VIII - THE CONCAVE COST MODEL WITH BACKLOGGING

The model is described in section VI, §VI.1. where the constraint (6.2) is no more imposed. The production cost function $c(t\ ;\ v)$ satisfies (6.3). The backlog-inventory cost function $f(t\ ;\ x)$ has the following properties :

(8.1) $$\begin{cases} f(t\ ;\ x) : [0,T] \times R \to R^+, \text{ concave non decreasing for } x \geq 0, \text{ concave non increasing for } x \leq 0\ ;\ \text{a.e. } t\ \ f(t,x) = \tilde{f}(t\ ;\ x)\ \forall x, \text{ where } \tilde{f} \\ \text{is a Borel function continuous with respect to } x\ ; \\ \int_0^T f(t\ ;\ x)dt < \infty \quad \forall x \end{cases}$$

The cost functional is defined by

(8.2) $$J_{s,x}(V) = \int_s^T f(t\ ;\ z(t))dt + \sum_i c(\theta_i, v_i)\chi_{\theta_i < T}$$

We have the following existence result

Theorem 8.1

Assume (6.3), (8.1), then there exists an optimal impulse control.

Proof

It is very similar to that of Theorem 6.1. Details are left to the reader. □

We next set

(8.3) $$u(s,x) = \operatorname*{Inf}_{V} J_{s,x}(V)$$

and as in § 6.3 we have

$$u(s,x) = \int_s^T f(t\ ;\ x - \int_s^t \xi(\lambda)d\lambda)dt, \text{ if } x \geq \int_s^T \xi(\lambda)d\lambda \tag{8.4}$$

When $x < \int_s^T \xi(\lambda)d\lambda$ we have

$$\begin{cases} u(s,x) = \operatorname{Inf}_N \operatorname{Inf}_{\substack{\theta_1\ldots\theta_N \\ v_1\ldots v_N}} [\int_s^{\theta_1} f(t\ ;\ x - \int_s^t \xi(\lambda)d\lambda)dt \\ + \sum_{i=1}^{N-1} \int_{\theta_i}^{\theta_{i+1}} f(t\ ;\ x + \sum_{j=1}^{i} v_j - \int_s^t \xi(\lambda)d\lambda)dt \\ + \int_{\theta_N}^{T} f(t\ ;\ x + \sum_{j=1}^{N} v_j - \int_s^t \xi(\lambda)d\lambda)dt + \sum_{i=1}^{N} c(\theta_i\ ;\ v_i + 0\ )] \end{cases} \tag{8.5}$$

and the set of admissible θ and v is defined by

$$\begin{cases} s \leq \theta_1 \leq \ldots \leq \theta_N \leq T \\ v_1 \geq 0 \quad \ldots \quad v_N \geq 0 \end{cases} \tag{8.6}$$

We can then state the analogue of Theorem 6.2

Theorem 8.2

Assume (6.3), (8.1), then $u(s,x)$ defined by (8.3) is upper semi continuous and satisfies

$$\begin{cases} u(x,T) = 0 \\ u(s,x) \leq \int_s^t f(\lambda,\ \ x - \int_s^\lambda \xi(\mu)d\mu)d\lambda + u(t,\ x - \int_s^t \xi(\mu)d\mu),\ \forall t \in [s,T] \\ u(s,x) \leq c(s,v) + u(s,x+v),\ \forall v \geq 0,\ \ \forall s,x \end{cases} \tag{8.7}$$

Moreover it is the maximum Borel function in the set (8.7).

Proof

Analogous to Lemma 6.1 and Theorem 6.2. □

We now state the analogue of Theorem 6.3 for the case of backlogging.

Theorem 8.3.

Assume (6.3), (8.1), then $u(s,x)$ defined by (8.3) is the maximum Borel function of the set

$$(8.8)\quad \begin{cases} u(T,x) = 0 \\ u(s,x) \le \int_s^t f(\lambda, x - \int_s^\lambda \xi(\mu)d\mu)d\lambda + u(t, x - \int_s^t \xi(\mu)d\mu) \ \forall t \in [s,T]. \end{cases}$$

If $x < \int_s^T \xi(\lambda)d\lambda$, let $\theta \in [s,T)$ be the first time such that $x \le \int_s^\theta \xi(\lambda)d\lambda$ (i.e. $\theta = s$ if $x \le 0$, and $x = \int_s^\theta \xi(\lambda)d\lambda$ if $x > 0$), then

$$u(s,x) \le c(s, \int_s^r \xi(\lambda)d\lambda - x) + \int_s^r f(\lambda, \int_\lambda^r \xi(\mu)d\mu)d\lambda + u(r,0),\ \forall r \in [\theta,T]$$

Proof

The fact that $u(s,x)$ is an element of the set (8.8) is clear for the same reasons as in Theorem 6.3. We now consider an impulse control V which has a finite number N of impulses taking place strictly before T, and such that

$$(8.9)\quad \begin{cases} s \le \theta_1 < \theta_2 < \dots < \theta_N < T \\ v_1 > 0,\ v_2 > 0,\ \dots,\ v_N > 0 \end{cases}$$

Those controls form a sufficient class to compute the infimum of $J_{s,x}(V)$. We show that we can restrict the class to those impulse controls satisfying :

$$(8.10)\quad \begin{cases} y(\theta_i - 0) \le 0, & i \ge 2, \quad y(T) \le 0 \\ y(\theta_i) \ge 0, & \forall i \end{cases}$$

The method is the same as in Theorem 6.3. From an optimal control $\underset{\sim}{V}$ satisfying (8.9) we construct through a finite number of steps a new control V which is still optimal and satisfies (8.9) (may be with a smaller N) and (8.10).

Note that we may assume that $x < \int_s^T \xi(\lambda)d\lambda$, otherwise any element of the set (8.8) being smaller than $\int_s^T f(\lambda, x - \int_s^\lambda \xi(\mu)d\mu)d\lambda = u(s,x)$ the desired result is proved.

It follows that we may assume $N \ge 1$.

We consider the first index i such that (8.10) does not hold. We have two possibilities either

$$(8.11)\quad y(\theta_i - 0) > 0 \quad , i \ge 2$$

or

$$(8.12)\quad y(\theta_i) < 0$$

Note that (8.11), (8.12) are mutually exclusive since

$$y(\theta_i) = y(\theta_i - 0) + v_i > y(\theta_i - 0)$$

(i) First assume (8.11) and proceed as in the proof of Theorem 6.3. Let :

. $\Delta = \text{Min}\,(v_{i-1}, v_i, y(\theta_i - 0))$;

. V_a obtained from V by the modification

$$v_{i-1} \to v_{i-1} + \Delta$$
$$v_i \to v_i - \Delta \ ;$$

. V_b obtained from V by the modification

$$v_{i-1} \to v_{i-1} - \Delta$$
$$v_i \to v_i + \Delta$$

and we set

$$\tilde{V} = \begin{cases} V_a \text{ if } \Delta = v_i \\ V_b \text{ if } \Delta = v_{i-1} \text{ or } y(\theta_i - 0). \end{cases}$$

Note that if $\Delta = y(\theta_i - 0)$ then the trajectory corresponding to $\tilde{V}$ satisfies $\tilde{y}(\theta_i - 0) = 0$ and $\tilde{y}(\theta_i) > 0$.

Therefore the transformation of V into $\tilde{V}$ is such that either the number of impulses has decreased by one or the first index for which (8.10) is not satisfied has increased by 1.

(ii) If (8.12) holds, then we set

. $\Delta = \text{Min}\,(v_i, v_{i+1}, -y(\theta_i))$ if $i < N$

. $\Delta = \text{Min}\,(v_N, -y(\theta_N))$ if $i = N$

Consider first the case $i < N$, and define

. V_a obtained from V by the modification

$$v_i \to v_i + \Delta$$
$$v_{i+1} \to v_{i+1} - \Delta$$

. V_b obtained from V by the modification

$$v_i \to v_i - \Delta$$
$$v_{i+1} \to v_{i+1} + \Delta.$$

Then we have

$$y_a(t) = y(t) \qquad \text{for } t < \theta_i,\ t \geq \theta_{i+1}$$
$$y_a(t) = y(t) + \Delta \quad \text{for } t \in [\theta_i, \theta_{i+1})$$

and

$$y_b(t) = y(t) \qquad \text{for } t < \theta_i,\ t \geq \theta_{i+1}$$
$$y_b(t) = y(t) - \Delta \quad \text{for } t \in [\theta_i, \theta_{i+1}).$$

Note that $y(t) < 0$ for $t \in [\theta_i, \theta_{i+1})$,

$$y_a(t),\ y_b(t) \le 0 \quad \text{for } t \in [\theta_i, \theta_{i+1}).$$

We can then use a concavity argument to assert that V_a, V_b are both optimal. Setting

$$\tilde{V} = \begin{cases} V_a \text{ if } \Delta = v_{i+1} \text{ or } -y(\theta_i) \\ V_b \text{ if } \Delta = v_i \end{cases}$$

then again we see that the transformation from V into $\tilde{V}$ has either decreased the number of impulses, or has increased the first index for which (8.10) is not satisfied.

Finally if i = N define

. V_a obtained from V by the modification $v_N \to v_N + \Delta$

. V_b obtained from V by the modification $v_N \to v_N - \Delta$.

We have

$$y_a(t) = y_b(t) = y(t)\ , \quad t < \theta_N$$

$$y_a(t) = y(t) + \Delta \quad , \quad t \in [\theta_N, T]$$

$$y_b(t) = y(t) - \Delta \quad , \quad t \in [\theta_N, T]$$

Note that $y(t) < 0$ for $t \in [\theta_N, T]$ and

$$y_a(t) \le 0,\ y_b(t) < 0 \text{ for } t \in [\theta_N, T].$$

Next

$$J(V_a) + J(V_b) - 2J(V) = c(\theta_N, v_N + \Delta) + c(\theta_N, v_N - \Delta) - 2c(\theta_N, v_N)$$
$$+ \int_{\theta_N}^{T} f(\lambda, y(\lambda)+\Delta)d\lambda + \int_{\theta_N}^{T} f(\lambda, y(\lambda) - \Delta)d\lambda - 2\int_{\theta_N}^{T} f(\lambda,y(\lambda))d\lambda \le 0$$

and V_a, V_b are again optimal controls. Choosing

$$\tilde{V} = \begin{cases} V_b \text{ if } \Delta = v_N \\ V_a \text{ if } \Delta = -y(\theta_N) \end{cases}$$

We see that either the number of impulses has decreased by one, or $\tilde{V}$ belongs to the class (8.9), (8.10). At any rate, in a finite number of steps we can obtain an optimal control in the class (8.9), (8.10).

Now for a control satisfying (8.10) we can find times τ_i such that

$$\theta_i \le \tau_i \le \theta_{i+1}, \quad i = 1, \ldots, N \quad (\theta_{N+1} = T)$$

and for which :

$$y(\tau_i) = 0\ ;\ y(t) \ge 0 \text{ for } t \in [\theta_i, \tau_i];\ y(t) \le 0 \text{ for } t \in [\tau_i, \theta_{i+1}).$$

Let u be an element of (8.8), then from the first inequality (8.8) we have

(8.13) $$u(s,x) \le \int_s^{\theta_1} f(\lambda, y(\lambda))d\lambda + u(\theta_1, y(\theta_1 - 0))$$

and from the second inequality (8.8) we deduce

(8.14) $$\begin{cases} u(\theta_i, y(\theta_i - 0)) \le c(\theta_i,v_i) + \int_{\theta_i}^{\tau_i} f(\lambda, y(\lambda))d\lambda + u(\tau_i, y(\tau_i)), \\ i = 1, \dots, N \end{cases}$$

where we have used the fact that

(8.15) $$y(\theta_i - 0) + v_i - \int_{\theta_i}^{\tau_i} \xi(\lambda)d\lambda = y(\tau_i) = 0.$$

Using again the first inequality (8.8) we can write

$$u(\tau_i, y(\tau_i)) \le \int_{\tau_i}^{\theta_{i+1}} f(\lambda, y(\lambda))d\lambda + u(\theta_{i+1}, y(\theta_{i+1} - 0))$$

where $(\theta_{N+1} = T)$

which, combined with (8.14) yields

(8.16) $$\begin{cases} u(\theta_i, y(\theta_i - 0)) \le c(\theta_i, v_i) + \int_{\tau_i}^{\theta_{i+1}} f(\lambda, y(\lambda))d\lambda \\ \qquad + u(\theta_{i+1}, y(\theta_{i+1} - 0)), \ i = 1, \dots, N \end{cases}$$

Adding up and taking (8.13) into account we obtain

$$u(s,x) \le J_{s,x}(V)$$

$\forall V$ in the class (8.9), (8.10). This completes the proof of the desired result. □

Remark 8.1

Property (8.10) for an optimal control is clearly the analogue of Wagner-Within Theorem in the backlogging case (cf. Theorem 7.3 of Chapter I).

IX - FORECAST HORIZONS FOR THE CONCAVE COST MODEL WITH BACKLOGGING

We consider the impulse control problem described in section VIII. To obtain forecast horizons results we impose the final constraints

(9.1) $$z(T) \ge 0$$

Results in this section differ only slightly from those of section VIII. For instance in the statement of Theorem 8.3, the first inequality (8.8) holds for any $t \in [s,T)$ if $x < \int_s^T \xi(\lambda)d\lambda$, and any $t \in [s,T]$ if $x \ge \int_s^T \xi(\lambda)d\lambda$.

Note also that if $\sigma(0,T) > 0$, then there should be at least one impulse, and, if $x = 0$, the optimal impulse control satisfies (compare with (8.10) :

$$(9.2)\qquad \begin{cases} y(\theta_i - 0) \le 0,\ y(\theta_i) \ge 0 \quad \forall i = 1, \ldots, N \\ y(T) = 0 \end{cases}$$

We restrict ourselves from now on to the case $x = 0$. Let

$$(9.3)\qquad \lambda(T) = \inf J^T_{0,0}(V),$$

then a functional equation for $\lambda(T)$ obtains, which is given by theorem 9.1.

Theorem 9.1

Assume (6.3), (8.1), then we have

$$(9.4)\qquad \begin{cases} \lambda(T) = \underset{0\le r\le s<T}{\text{Min}} \{c(s, \sigma(r,T)) + \int_r^s f(\lambda\ ; -\sigma(r,\lambda))d\lambda \\ \qquad + \int_s^T f(\lambda\ ; \sigma(\lambda,T))d\lambda + \lambda(r)\} \end{cases}$$

Proof

Assume first $\sigma(0,T) = 0$, then

$$\lambda(T) = \int_0^T f(\lambda\ ; 0)d\lambda$$
$$= \lambda(r) + \int_r^T f(\lambda\ ; 0)d\lambda, \quad \forall r$$

hence (6.4) is satisfied. Assume next that $\sigma(0,T) > 0$, then there exists at least one impulse $0 < \hat{s} < T$ and from (9.2) $y(\hat{s}) \ge 0$, $y(\hat{s} - 0) \le 0$. If there is only one impulse in the optimal policy, set $\hat{r} = 0$. Otherwise in between the last impulse before $\hat{s}$ and $\hat{s}$, there is a regeneration point which we call $\hat{r}$. The size of the order at $\hat{s}$, is clearly $\sigma(\hat{r},T)$, hence

$$\lambda(T) = c(\hat{s}, \sigma(\hat{r},T)) + \int_{\hat{r}}^{\hat{s}} f(\lambda\ ; -\sigma(\hat{r},\lambda))d\lambda + \int_{\hat{s}}^T f(\lambda\ ; \sigma(\lambda,T))d\lambda + \lambda(\hat{r})$$

Therefore $\lambda(T)$ is larger than the right hand side of (9.4). Since it is clearly less or equal to the right hand side, the result (9.4) is proved. □

We then define for $0 \le r \le s < T$

$$(9.5)\qquad \begin{cases} \mu(r,s,T) = c(s, \sigma(r,T)) + \int_r^s f(\lambda\ ; -\sigma(r,\lambda))d\lambda + \int_s^T f(\lambda\ ; \sigma(\lambda,T))d\lambda \\ \qquad + \lambda(r) \end{cases}$$

If $\sigma(0,T) > 0$, we define $s(T)$ with $r(T) \le s(T) < T$ as being the last regeneration and set up points respectively. More precisely among optimal policies, we take those with the minimum number of impulses, and among them we pick the policy which has the largest last impulse. This is $s(T)$ and the corresponding anterior regeneration point is $r(T)$. We assume (but this can be argumented) that there is at most a finite number of optimal policies.

We next set for $r_1 \le s_1$, $r_2 \le s_2$, $s_1,s_2 < T \le S$

$$(9.6)\quad \begin{cases} \Phi(r_1,s_1\ ;\ r_2,s_2\ ;\ T,S) = \mu(r_1,s_1\ ;\ S) - \mu(r_1,s_1\ ;\ T) \\ - [\mu(r_2,s_2\ ;\ S) - \mu(r_2,s_2\ ;\ T)] \\ = c(s_1,\ \sigma(r_1,S)) - c(s_1,\ \sigma(r_1,T)) - [c(s_2,\ \sigma(r_2,S)) - c(s_2,\ \sigma(r_2,T))] \\ + \int_{s_1}^{T} [f(\lambda\ ;\ \sigma(\lambda,S)) - f(\lambda\ ;\ \sigma(\lambda,T))]d\lambda \\ - \int_{s_2}^{T} [f(\lambda\ ;\ \sigma(\lambda,S)) - f(\lambda\ ;\ \sigma(\lambda,T))]d\lambda. \end{cases}$$

Consider now the special case for which the ordering cost is :

$$(9.7)\quad \begin{cases} c(s\ ;\ v) = K(s)\ \chi_{v>0} + d(s)v \\ d(s) \text{ decreasing} \end{cases}$$

When $\sigma(r_1,S) > 0$, $\sigma(r_2,T) > 0$, then we see that

$$(9.8)\quad \begin{cases} \Phi(r_1,s_1\ ;\ r_2,s_2\ ;\ T,S) \geq [d(s_1) - d(s_2)]\ \sigma(T,S) \\ + \int_{s_1}^{T} [f(\lambda\ ;\ \sigma(\lambda,S)) - f(\lambda\ ;\ \sigma(\lambda,T))]\ d\lambda \\ - \int_{s_2}^{T} [f(\lambda\ ;\ \sigma(\lambda,S)) - f(\lambda\ ;\ \sigma(\lambda,T))]\ d\lambda \end{cases}$$

and if $s_1 \leq s_2$ it follows that

$$(9.9)\quad \Phi(r_1,s_1\ ;\ r_2,s_2\ ;\ T,S) \geq 0$$

Therefore we obtain :

<u>Lemma 9.1</u>

Assume (8.1), (9.7) ; let $T \leq S$, with $\sigma(0,T) > 0$, and $r \leq s \leq s(T)$, such that $\sigma(r,T) > 0$. Then we have

$$(9.10)\quad \mu(r,s\ ;\ S) \geq \mu(r(T),s(T)\ ;\ S).$$

<u>Proof</u>

It is an immediate consequence of (9.9) and the definition (9.6) of Φ . □

It then follows :

<u>Theorem 9.2</u>

Assume (8.1), (9.7), and

$$(9.11)\quad \sigma(s,t) > 0\quad \forall s < t$$

Then

$$(9.12)\quad s(T) \leq s(S) \text{ if } T \leq S$$

If moreover we have

(9.13) $d(s) = d,$

then also

(9.14) $r(T) \le r(S)$ if $T \le S$

Proof

Assumption (9.11) is not essential but simplifies technicalities (cf. Theorem 9.3 of Chapter I). By virtue of (9.11), if we take $r \le s \le s(T)$ then we have (9.10), therefore necessarily (9.12) holds.

Let us now prove property (9.14) under assumption (9.13). Take

$$r_1 \le r_2 \le s_2 \le s_1 \quad , s_2 \le T, \quad s_1 \le S.$$

We have

$$\mu(r_1,s_1 ; S) - \mu(r_2,s_1 ; S) - [\mu(r_1,s_2 ; T) - \mu(r_2,s_2 ; T)]$$
$$= \int_{s_2}^{s_1} [f(\lambda ; -\sigma(r_1,\lambda)) - f(\lambda ; -\sigma(r_2,\lambda))]d\lambda \ge 0$$

Applying with

$$r_1 = r, \ r_2 = r(T), \ s_1 = s(S), \ s_2 = s(T)$$

where $r \le r(T)$, we get

$$\mu(r, s(S), S) - \mu(r(T), s(S), S) \ge \mu(r, s(T), T) - \mu(r(T), s(T), T) \ge 0$$

therefore $r(S) \ge r(T)$. □

We finally obtain the following forecast horizon theorem. In fact any horizon is a forecast horizon

Theorem 9.3

Under the assumptions of Theorem 9.2, $\forall S \ge T$, there exists an optimal policy for $J^S(V)$ which has a regeneration point between $r(T)$ and T.

Proof

The points $r(S)$, $r(r(S))$ ... $r^{(k)}(S)$ are regeneration points for an optimal policy of $J^S(V)$. We argue like in Corollary 6.2 to get the desired result. □

X - SURVEY OF RESEARCH AND RESULTS INTERPRETATION

Contributions which resort to continuous time formulations are much less abundant than for the first two chapters, where only discrete time approaches are reviewed. To our knowledge there is no reference which relates to the production planning problem with concave costs. Except Michel and Vial [1981] who consider a mixed cost structure, only convex cost production planning and production smoothing models have been reconsidered in a continuous time framework.

Some of the continuous time formulations use the calculus of variations, but all others rely on the maximum principle of Pontryagin and Control Theory. This may account for the above observation.

As a matter of fact, discrete optimal control problems require, in general, less mathematical complexity than their continuous time analogues. But, there are also practical motives. Many of the problems relative to cost and parameter estimations are more easily handled in discrete time. Furthermore, following usual practices, production plans are determined on a monthly basis, and the rate of output is not revised continuously. Finally, discretization has also become a common technique to solve dynamic problems on digital computers. Bertsekas [1976] provides an excellent discussion concerning the discretization of continuous problems. He studies the convergence of the optimal solutions of such discretized problems to their continuous analogues, as the discretization interval tends to zero ; he gives also sufficient conditions for convergence.

Some mathematical background may be useful at this stage to fully understand the cited contributions. However, it must be kept in mind that the developments of this book are selfcontent, given the appendix provided at the end. The first three sets of references to chapter III are technical and relate respectively to the areas of the calculus of variations, discrete time optimal control and continuous time optimal control. Some are basic readings, others are more specialized, and address directly the particular structure of production planning and production smoothing problems with convex (or linear) costs,and constraints on the state and the control variables.

For a review of various applications of control theory in Economics (capital theory), consult Arrow [1968], Arrow and Kurz [1970], Burmeister and Dobell [1970] and Shell [1967] ; see also Dorfman [1969]. Applications in Management Science, some concerning Production and Inventory Planning, may be found in Bensoussan, Hurst and Naslund [1974], Bensoussan, Kleindorfer and Tapiero [1978], [1980], Sethi and Thompson [1981] and Tapiero [1978]. See also Tracz [1968] for an anoted list of publications in the period 1964-1967.

Direct extensions of the Modigliani-Hohn model to a continuous time formulation are due to Morin [1955], Arrow and Karlin [1958], Smith [1961 , pp. 306-310] and Anderson [1970]. They all impose the marginal production cost function to be monotone increasing, continuous and differentiable. In addition, they assume constant the marginal cost of holding a unit of the product during a unit of time. All costs are stationary.

They arrive at a quite simple formulation which is a standard problem in the calculus of variations. However, Arrow and Karlin develop their own simplification of variational calculus which is perfectly suitable to problems with convex cost models, and only requires conventional calculus.

They all show that the optimal production plan is made up of two kind of policies which alternate overtime. One is related to the optimality conditions (extremal portions of the optimal path). On the other intervals the production rate is equal to the demand rate, and is said to be "on demand". These bounded portions correspond to time instants where it is less economical to increase production and store it until any subsequent time, than to produce the additional units at a later time.

To find a complete solution it is necessary to identify those intervals on which the production path is extremal, and those on which it is bounded. This is done by expliciting the necessary conditions which must be met at the entering and leaving points of any extremal portion. To be explicit one need to specify the cost function and the demand. When there is zero inventory cost, the optimal policy depends only on the demand and not on the production cost function. The optimal production rate is either constant or on demand. This is the continuous analogue of the solution given by Charnes, Cooper and Mellon [1955] for the discrete case.

Anderson considers a seasonal demand pattern, a quadratic production cost, and is able to retrieve Modigliani-Hohn planning horizon result. The optimal production path v(t) looks like the following graph, where $\xi(t)$ denotes the demand rate. However, the corner conditions impose that the cumulative demand and production schedules be tangent at any common point (this is due to the monotonicity property of the marginal production cost).

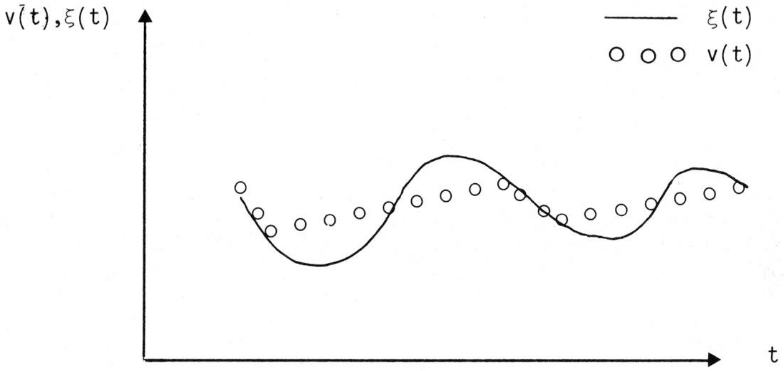

Anderson extends the basic model to a firm producing an intermediate product and a final good, the former being an input of the latter. Smith considers, in addition, the decision concerning the initial stock of capital to be installed by the firm.

Sprzeuzkouski [1967] considers the same basic model but formulated as an optimal control problem. He arrives essentially at the same conclusions, but in addition he proves the existence and the uniqueness of the optimal solution, directly from the maximum principle of Pontryagin and the necessary conditions for optimality.

Pekelman [1974] proposes an alternative formulation for a monopoly which faces the entire market demand for its product, and controls at each instant the price and the production rate. The Modigliani-Hohn planning horizon property still holds in this context.

Lieber [1973] generalizes Sprzeuzkouski's formulation with backlogging being permitted. The production cost function is assumed monotone increasing, strictly convex and twice continuously differentiable. Holding and backlogging costs are linear. The demand rate is a continuously differentiable and strictly positive function of time. When the problem starts there is no inventory and no backlogged demand. Terminal backlogging is required to be zero. All costs are stationary.

Lieber adopts Mangasarian's formulation for optimal control problem [1966], where the state constraints instead of their derivatives, are adjoined directly to construct the Lagrangian.

Lieber is thus able to derive not only necessary, but also sufficient conditions for optimality. The production plans which satisfy all these conditions except the terminal transversality conditions are called "extrapolations", or following Pekelman [1975], "acceptable trajectories". An optimal solution is therefore an extrapolation which satisfies the terminal condition. A major contribution of Lieber's paper is the proof that extrapolations do not intersect. See also Pekelman [1975] who derives the same property for the production smoothing model. Uniqueness of the optimal solution follows directly from this result, but also a weak planning horizon theorem. In an other work Lieber [1971] uses the planning horizon property to construct an algorithm that searches for the optimal production plan, among the extrapolations. From Lieber's developments it becomes clear that what causes planning horizons is the discontinuity in the marginal inventory cost function (rather than the non negativity condition, per se, imposed by others on the inventory level). Finally Lieber addresses the question of how weak is the planning horizon, if it exists ? He shows what are the authorized variations of demand beyond the planning horizon, which do not alter the optimality of the production plan over the period preceding this horizon.

The initial continuous time formulation for the production smoothing problem is due to Arrow and Karlin [1958-1] who extend the work in discrete time by Hoffman and Jacob [1954]. They first introduced the concept of convex envelope to derive the properties of the optimal production policy. This concept was later reformulated in the discrete time framework by Klein [1961] and Lippman et al. [1967-1]. Basically, Klein's results still hold in the continuous case.

In a related contribution Arrow and Karlin [1958-2] consider a formulation where production and smoothing costs are directly related to the labor force size. This is the continuous time analogue of the discrete time formulation treated by Bellman et al [1954] and Karush and Vazsonyi [1957-1][1957-2].

Pekelman [1975] somewhat extends Kunreuther and Morton to a continuous time framework. However, the statement of the problem is slightly different and corresponds to the small firm situation in a competitive market. The exogeneous variable is the price, rather than demand, and price may fluctuate overtime. The firm knows current and future prices and can sell as much as it wishes at the given market price. Therefore the firm never carries inventories. The line of proof follows closely Lieber's contribution. Pekelman derives a "planning horizon for a forecast horizon" theorem which is stronger than Lieber's weak planning horizon, but is similar to Kunreuther and Morton's result. A related work is Pekelman [1971].

Production smoothing models may be transposed to many other industrial or financial situations where adjustment costs are involved. Pekelman [1979] considers the choice between two alternative production processes where one is more economical than the other in some periods, and the shift from one to the other is costly. Planning horizon for a forecast horizon results still obtain.

This chapter extends the work by Lieber [1973] as far as production planning with convex costs is concerned, and generalizes Kunreuther and Morton's production smoothing theory [1973][1974] to a continuous time framework. All the developments concerning the concave cost models, both for the continuous control and impulse control formulations are new, and generalize chapter I results.

REFERENCES

CALCULUS OF VARIATIONS

BOLZA O., [1960] , Lectures on the calculus of variations, Chelsea Publishing Company.

ELSGOLC L.E., [1962] , Calculus of variations, Addison Wesley.

FOX C., [1950] , An introduction to the calculus of variations, Oxford University Press.

GELFAND I.M. - FOMIN S.V., [1963] , Calculus of variations, Prentice Hall.

OPTIMAL CONTROL THEORY

- Discrete time -

BERTSEKAS D.P., [1976] , Dynamic programming and stochastic control, Academic Press.

CANON M.D. - CULLUM C.D.Jr - POLAK E., [1970] , Theory of optimal control and mathematical programming, Mc Graw-Hill.

HOLTZMAN J.M., [1966] , On the maximum principle for non linear discrete time systems, IEEE Transactions on Automatic Control, 4, pp. 528-547.

KLEINDORDER P.R. - KRIEBEL C.H. - THOMPSON G.L. - KLEINDORFER G.B., [1975] , Discrete optimal control of production plans, Management Science, 22(3), pp. 261-273.

- Continuous time -

BELLMAN R., [1957] , Dynamic programming, Princeton University Press.

JACOBSON D.H. - LELE M.M. - SPEYER J.L., [1971] , New necessary conditions of optimality for control problems with state-variable inequality constraint, Journal of Math. Anal. Appl., 35, pp. 255-283.

JOHNSON C.D., [1965] , Singular solutions in problems of optimal control, in C.T. Leondes, ed. Advances in control systems theory and applications, Vol. 2, Academic Press, pp. 209-269.

LEE E.B. - MARKUS L.,[1968] , Foundation of optimal control theory, John Wiley and Sons.

LEITMANN G., [1966] , An introduction to optimal control, Mc Graw-Hill.

MANGASARIAN O.L., [1966] , Sufficient conditions for the optimal control of nonlinear systems, SIAM Journal on Control, 4, pp. 139-152.

McINTYRE J. - PAIEWONSKY B., [1967] , On optimal control with bounded state variables, in C.T. Leondes, ed. Advances in control systems, Vol. 5, Academic Press.

PONTRYAGIN L.S. - BOLTYANSKII V.G. - GRAMKELIDZE R.V. - MISHCHENKO E.F., [1962] , The mathematical theory of optimal processes, John Wiley and Sons.

SPEYER J.L. - BRYSON A., [1968] , Optimal programming problems with a bounded state space, AIAA Journal, 6, pp. 1488-1491.

STRAUSS A., [1968] , An introduction to optimal control theory. Lecture notes in Operations research and mathematical economics, Berlin : Springer Verlag.

APPLICATIONS TO MANAGEMENT SCIENCE AND ECONOMICS

ARROW K.J., [1968] , Applications of control theory to economic growth, American Mathematical Society of the Decision Sciences, Part II, pp. 85-119.

ARROW K.J. - KURZ M., [1970] , Public investment, the rate of return, and optimal fiscal policy, Johns Hopkins Press.

BENSOUSSAN A. - HURST G. - NASLUND B., [1974] , Management applications of modern control theory, North Holland.

BENSOUSSAN A. - KLEINDORFER P. - TAPIERO C.S., [1978] , eds, Applied optimal control, TIMS studies in the management Sciences 9, North Holland.

BENSOUSSAN A. - KLEINDORFER P. - TAPIERO C.S., [1980] , eds, Applied stochastic control in econometrics and management science, North Holland.

BURMEISTER E. - DOBELL A.R., [1970] , Mathematical theories of economic growth, McMillan.

DORFMAN R., [1969] , An economic interpretation of optimal control theory, American Economic Review, 54(5), pp. 817-831.

SETHI S.P. - THOMPSON G.L., [1981] , Optimal control theory : applications to management science, Boston : Martinus Nijhoff.

SHELL K., [1967] , ed., Essays in the theory of optimal economic growth, The MIT Press.

TAPIERO C.S., [1978] , Managerial planning : an optimum and stochastic control approach, Gordon Breach Science Publishers.

TRACZ G.S., [1968] , A selected bibliography on the application of optimal control theory to economic and business systems, management science, and operations research Operations Research, 16(1), pp. 174-186.

PRODUCTION PLANNING MODELS WITH CONCAVE COSTS

BENSOUSSAN A. - PROTH J.M., [1983] , Inventory planning in a deterministic environment. Continuous time model with concave cost, to be published in E.J.O.R.

PROTH J.M., [1981] , Optimisation des decisions dans les problèmes de production à coûts concaves, Thèse d'Etat, Paris IX-Dauphine.

PRODUCTION PLANNING MODELS WITH A MIXED COST STRUCTURE

MICHEL P. - VIAL J.P., An analysis of batch production systems via optimal control theory, Core Discussion Paper n° 8145, Université Catholique de Louvain, Belgium.

PRODUCTION PLANNING MODELS WITH CONVEX COSTS

ANDERSON W.H.L., [1970] , Production scheduling intermediate goods, and labor productivity, American Economic Review, 60(1), pp. 153-162.

ARROW K.J. - KARLIN S., [1958] , Production over time with increasing marginal costs, in K.J. Arrow, S. Karlin and H. Scarf, eds., Studies in the mathematical theory of inventory and production, Stanford University Press, pp. 62-69.

LIEBER Z., [1971] , Production over time with increasing marginal costs, and linear holding and backlogging costs, Center for Mathematical Studies in Business and Economics Report, n° 7124, University of Chicago.

LIEBER Z., [1973] , An extension to Modigliani and Hohn's planning horizons results, Management Science, 20(3), pp. 319-330.

MORIN F., [1955] , Note on an inventory problem discussed by Modigliani and Hohn, Econometrica, 23(4), pp. 447-452.

PEKELMAN D., [1974] , Simultaneous price-production decisions, Operations Research, 22(4), pp. 788-794.

SMITH V.L., [1961] , Investment and production : a study in the theory of the capital using entreprise, Harvard University Press.

SPRZEUZKOUSKI A.Y., [1967] , A problem in optimal stock management, Journal of Optimization Theory and Applications, 1(3), pp. 232-241.

PRODUCTION SMOOTHING MODELS

ARROW K.J. - KARLIN S., [1958-1] , Smoothed production plans, in K.J. Arrow, S. Karlin and H. Scarf, eds., Studies in the mathematical theory of inventory and production, Stanford University Press, pp. 70-85.

ARROW K.J. - KARLIN S., [1958-2] , Production planning without storage, in K.J. Arrow, S. Karlin and H. Scarf, eds., Studies in the mathematical theory of inventory and production, Stanford University Press, pp. 86-91.

PEKELMAN D., [1971] , Optimal production path with adjustment cost and time dependent price, center for Mathematical Studies in Business and Economics Report 7140, University of Chicago.

PEKELMAN D., [1975] , Production smoothing with fluctuating price, Management Science, 21(5), pp. 576-590.

PEKELMAN D., [1979] , On optimal utilization of production processes, Operations Research, 27(2), pp. 260-278.

CHAPTER IV

PRODUCTION PLANNING AND PRODUCTION SMOOTHING MODELS WITH STOCHASTIC DEMAND

DISCRETE TIME FORMULATION

INTRODUCTION

In this chapter we extend the analysis to the situation where demand is stochastic and the system is reviewed periodically. However, the results of Chapter I have no analogue in the stochastic case.

When demand is stochastic it does not make sense, at least in economic terms, to impose zero stockout. In general the nature of uncertainty is such that the possibility of excess demand over the firm total supply cannot be ruled out, except at a prohibitive cost. Thus, excess demand must be either backlogged until further delivery, or is simply lost. Unless it is clearly specified, like in Section IV, we restrict the developments to the backlog case.

In section I, we study the general production planning model with backlogging for the finite and infinite horizon problems. We prove the existence of an optimal control in the form of a feedback. It is important to keep in mind that this is a particular case of much more general results in the theory of stochastic control in discrete time (or the control of Markov chains). At the end of the Chapter the reader will find basic references related to "stochastic optimal control theory". However, because of the simplifications due to the structure of the model, the proofs are simpler than in the general case, and do not require the advanced methods of stochastic control. A minimum probabilistic background is needed, and recalled in the appendix. We also use some concepts of functional analysis and topology, which are useful to obtain rigorous proofs, but they do not play a very essential role. At any rate these concepts are also given in the appendix.

Section II is devoted to the optimality of (S,s) reordering policies. K-convexity will play a key role in the derivations. The finite and infinite horizon problems are studied.

In section III, we analyse the properties of the optimal production policy for the convex cost model. However, we cannot rely as in Chapter II on the theory of necessary conditions. The stochastic nature of demand makes them difficult to use, even in the convex cost case. Moreover, when K-convexity applies the convexity properties are no longer satisfied. For these reasons, our derivations will be based on Dynamic Programming. But we specialize the results of this section to the deterministic case, and compare them with those which were obtained in Chapter II, when using the theory of necessary conditions. A near-forecast horizon result is also derived.

In section IV we consider the production planning problem when excess demand is lost.

In section V we analyze a single period model with recourse which is a generalization of the "newsboy" problem to a multi-echelon production process.

Section VI extends the production smoothing problem addressed in Chapter II.

Finally, section VII presents a survey of research and how our own results relate to the literature.

I - EXISTENCE AND GENERAL PROPERTIES OF AN OPTIMAL PRODUCTION POLICY

I - 1. NOTATION

In the sequel we consider a probability space (Ω,A,P) and a sequence $\xi_1, \ldots, \xi_N$ of real random variables, defined on (Ω,A,P) such that

(1.1) $$\begin{cases} \text{the variables } \xi_1, \ldots, \xi_N \text{ are stochastically independent and} \\ E\ |\xi_i| \leq K < \infty \qquad (^1) \end{cases}$$

where E denotes the expected value operator.

We denote by

(1.2) $$\begin{cases} F_\ell^k \quad \text{the } \sigma\text{-algebra generated by } \xi_n,\ 1 \leq \ell \leq n \leq k \leq N, \text{ and} \\ F^k = F_1^k \end{cases}$$

The control (production decisions) for a problem on the interval [n,N] is noted

(1.3) $$V = (v_n, \ldots, v_{N-1})$$

where v_k, $v_k \geq 0$, is a random variable, and F_{n+1}^k measurable.

Notice that $F_{n+1}^n = (\Omega, \emptyset)$, hence v_n is deterministic.

Production decisions are made at the beginning of each period, and there is a one period delivery lag unless it is specified differently. Demand in each period is supposed to occur at the end of the period, after the order has entered the stock. Unsatisfied demand is carried forward as backlog sales.

The state equations (inventory balance equations) are thus defined by the usual system

(1.4) $$\begin{cases} y_{k+1} = y_k + v_k - \xi_{k+1}, \quad k = n, \ldots, N-1, \qquad \text{with} \\ y_n = x, \quad \text{the initial inventory level.} \end{cases}$$

The cost structure has the following properties, for i = n, ..., N :

----

(1) In fact, in practice the demand remains positive. A negative demand means that the product is returned.

(1.5)

(i) the production cost function :

$c_i(v) : \mathbb{R}^+ \to R^+$ is lower semi continuous, with $c_i(v) \geq \bar{c}_i\ v$, $\forall v \geq 1$;

(ii) the inventory cost function :

$f_i(x) : R \to R^+$ is uniformly continuous, with $f_i(x) \leq \bar{f}_i(1 + |x|)$.

When $x < 0$, $f_i(x)$ is the cost of backlogged sales, x, during the ith period ; and when $x > 0$, $f_i(x)$ is the storage cost of quantity x during that period.

(iii) at the end of the problem horizon we impose a penalty cost, or salvage value function for the terminal net inventory (positive or negative) : [1]

$g_N(x) : R \to R^+$ is uniformly continuous, with $g_N(x) \leq \bar{g}_N(1 + |x|)$.

The objective function to be minimized is the expected value of all the cost incurred over the horizon :

(1.6) $$J_n(x\ ;\ V) = \sum_{i=n}^{N-1} E\,[c_i(v_i) + f_i(y_i)] + E\, g_N(y_N)$$

which is always defined, provided we allow this function to take the value $+\infty$, (E denotes the expected value operator).
For subsequent use, it is convenient at this stage to introduce the following spaces :

(1.7) B_1 = vector space of real Borel functions, with linear growth

If $\phi \in B_1$ then $|\phi(x)| \leq ||\phi||\ (1 + |x|)$ where $||\phi|| = \sup_x \frac{|\phi(x)|}{1 + |x|}$

The space B_1 is a Banach space for the norm $||\ ||$.

(1.8) C_1 = sub space of B_1 of functions ϕ such that $\phi(x)$ is uniformly continuous.

The space C_1 is closed in B_1.

We define on B_1 the operator

----

(1) Instead, terminal conditions of other kinds may be considered as for example "the expected value of terminal net inventory should be positive"; or, like Gonedes and Lieber [1974] we may adopt a chance constraint such as "the probability that ending inventory is non negative should be less than a given constant.

(1.9) $\Phi_n(z)(x) = E\, z(x - \xi_n), \quad \forall z \in B_1$

By (1.1), Φ_n is a linear continuous operator on B_1 and

(1.10) $$|| \Phi_n || = \sup_{z \neq 0} \frac{||\Phi_n(z)||}{||z||} \leq 1 + E|\xi_n|.$$

which follows easily from (1.9).

I - 2. DYNAMIC PROGRAMMING FORMULATION

We introduce the following Dynamic Programming equations :

(1.11) $$\begin{cases} u_n(x) = f_n(x) + \inf\limits_{v \geq 0} \{c_n(v) + \Phi_{n+1}(u_{n+1})(x + v)\} \\ u_N(x) = g_N(x) \end{cases}$$

and we establish the first general existence result :

Theorem 1.1

Assume (1.1) and (1.5), then the relations (1.11) define a sequence of functions in C_1. Moreover, there exists a Borel function $\hat{v}_n(x)$ such that the infimum in (1.11) is attained for any x.

Proof

We proceed by induction. Assume that u_{n+1} belongs to C_1. Consider the points x such that $|x| \leq M$. Set

$$B_n^M = c_n(0) + ||\Phi_{n+1}|| \; ||u_{n+1}|| \; (1 + M)$$

By the assumption (1.5), the set $\{v \mid c_n(v) \leq B_n^M\}$ is bounded, i.e. $0 \leq v \leq \bar{v}_n^M$.

Therefore in (1.11) we can restrict v, $0 \leq v \leq \bar{v}_n^M$, for all the points x satisfying $|x| \leq M$, without loss of generality. Otherwise

$$\begin{aligned} c_n(v) + \Phi_{n+1}(u_{n+1})(x + v) &\geq c_n(v) > B_n^M \\ &\geq c_n(0) + \Phi_{n+1}(u_{n+1})(x) \end{aligned}$$

and v cannot be optimal.

Since the function

(1.12) $\psi_n(x,v) = c_n(v) + \Phi_{n+1}(u_{n+1})(x + v)$

is l.s.i. and bounded from below, the minimum over a compact set is attained. Moreover, from a classical selection theorem we know that (see appendix) there exists a Borel function $\hat{v}_n^M(x)$, such that :

(1.13) $$\psi_n(x\,,\,\hat{v}_n^M(x)) = \operatorname*{Inf}_{0 \leq v \leq \bar{v}_n^M} \psi_n(x,v)\;,\quad \forall x$$

Define next

$$\hat{v}_N(x) = \hat{v}_n^M(x) \text{ for } M-1 < |x| \leq M$$

we obtain a Borel function, such that

$$\psi_n(x, \hat{v}_n(x)) = \underset{v\geq 0}{\text{Inf}} \ \psi_n(x,v) \ , \qquad \forall x$$

Now for $|x_1 - x_2| \leq \delta$

$$|\psi_n(x_1,v) - \psi_n(x_2,v)| = |\Phi_{n+1}(u_{n+1})(x_1+v) - \Phi_{n+1}(u_{n+1})(x_2+v)|$$
$$\leq \sup_{|x_1-x_2|\leq\delta} |u_{n+1}(x_1) - u_{n+1}(x_2)|$$

from which it follows easily that $u_n(x)$ is uniformly continuous. Since

$$\underset{v\geq 0}{\text{Inf}} \ \psi_n(x,v) \leq c_n(0) + ||\Phi_{n+1}|| \ ||u_{n+1}|| \ (1 + |x|)$$

we obtain that u_n belongs to C_1. □

Remark 1.1

The functions $u_n(x)$ are non negative.

I - 3. EXISTENCE OF AN OPTIMAL CONTROL

In the sequel we solve the problem $J_0(x \ ; V)$.

Let us define

$$(1.14) \qquad \begin{cases} \hat{y}_0 = x, \\ \hat{v}_k = \hat{v}_k(\hat{y}_k), & k = 0, \ldots, N-1 \\ \hat{y}_{k+1} = \hat{y}_k + \hat{v}_k - \xi_{k+1}, & k = 0, \ldots, N-1 \end{cases}$$

where $\hat{v}_n(x)$ is a Borel function for which the infimum of (1.11) is attained for any x (see theorem 1.1).

Theorem 1.2

Assume (1.1), (1.5). Set $\hat{V}^0 = (\hat{v}_0, \ldots, \hat{v}_{N-1})$ then $\hat{V}^0$ is an optimal control for the problem $J_0(x \ ; V)$. Moreover

$$(1.15) \qquad u_n(x) = \underset{V}{\text{Min}} \ J_n(x \ ; V)$$

Proof

The proof relies on the following result on conditional expectations stated in Gikhman and Skorokhod [1972] : Let $(Y,\mathcal{Y})$ and $(Z,\mathcal{Z})$ be two measurable spaces and $\eta(\omega)$, $\xi(\omega)$ be two random variables with values in Y, Z respectively. Let H(y,z) be a measurable map from $Y \times Z$ into R, such that

$$E \ |H(\eta,\xi)| < \infty$$

Let $\mathcal{B}$ be a sub σ-algebra of $\mathcal{A}$. Assume that η is $\mathcal{B}$ measurable, then we have :

$$(1.16) \qquad E \ \{H(\eta,\xi) \mid \mathcal{B}\} = E \ \{H(y,\xi) \mid \mathcal{B}\}_{y=\eta}$$

Let V be any admissible control. In fact, without loss of generality we may assume that

(1.17) $\quad E\, c_n(v_n) < \infty \qquad \forall n$

Indeed, if for some n, $E\, c_n(v_n) = \infty$, then clearly $J_n(x\ ;\ V) = +\infty$. Since $J_n(x;0)<\infty$, such a V should be eliminated.

Now from (1.5), if (1.16) holds we also have

$$E\, v_n < \infty,\ \forall n$$

which implies $E\, y_n < \infty$, $\forall n$, as it can be easily shown.

Since $u_n \in C_1$, we can assert that

(1.18) $\quad E\, u_n(y_n) < \infty \qquad \forall n$

Then let us show that

(1.19) $\quad E\, \{u_{n+1}(y_{n+1}) \mid F^n\} = \Phi_{n+1}(u_{n+1})(y_n + v_n) \qquad$ a.s.

Since

$$u_{n+1}(y_{n+1}) = u_{n+1}(y_n + v_n - \xi_{n+1})$$

we can refer to (1.16) with

$$H(y,z) = u_{n+1}(y - z)$$

$$\eta(\omega) = y_n + v_n, \qquad \xi(\omega) = \xi_{n+1}$$

$$\mathcal{B} = F^n.$$

Noting that

$$E\{u_{n+1}(y - \xi_{n+1}) \mid F^n\} = E\, u_{n+1}(y - \xi_{n+1})$$
$$= \Phi_{n+1}(u_{n+1})(y)$$

since ξ_{n+1} is independent of F^n, and applying (1.15), we obtain (1.19).

Now using (1.11) we can assert that

$$u_n(y_n) \leqq f_n(y_n) + c_n(v_n) + \Phi_{n+1}(u_{n+1})(y_n + v_n) \quad \text{a.s.}$$

and from (1.19), we deduce

(1.20) $\quad u_n(y_n) \le f_n(y_n) + c_n(v_n) + \ E\, \{u_{n+1}(y_{n+1}) \mid F^n\}.$

By taking the mathematical expectation of both sides of (1.20) we obtain

$$E\, u_n(y_n) \le E(f_n(y_n) + c_n(v_n)) + E\, u_{n+1}(y_{n+1}).$$

Adding up, for n running from 0 to N-1, we get

(1.21) $\quad u_0(x) \le J_n(x\ ;\ V)$

Consider now the control $\hat{V}^0$. We note from Theorem 1.1 that

$$c_n(\hat{v}_n)) \le c_n(0) + ||\Phi_{n+1}|| \; ||u_{n+1}|| \; (1 + |x|).$$

Therefore

$$c_n(\hat{v}_n) \le \bar{c}_n(1 + \hat{y}_n)$$

hence

$$E\;\hat{v}_n \le \bar{\bar{c}}_n(1 + E\;\hat{y}_n)$$

From (1.1), we deduce by induction that

(1.22) $\quad E\;\hat{v}_n < \infty, \; \forall n$

The control $\hat{V}^0$ is clearly admissible. From the definition of $\hat{v}_n(x)$ and proceeding as above,we obtain

$$E\;u_n(\hat{y}_n) = E(f_n(\hat{y}_n) + c_n(\hat{v}_n)) + E\;u_{n+1}(\hat{y}_{n+1})$$

Adding up for all n, n = 0, ..., N-1, it follows that :

$$u_0(x) = J_n(x\;;\;\hat{V}^0).$$

This and (1.21) complete the proof of Theorem 1.2. □

I - 4. EXTENSION TO THE CASE OF A DELIVERY LAG OF SEVERAL PERIODS

In this model we assume that there is a lag of λ periods, $\lambda \ge 1$, between production decision time and delivery time. Let :

(1.23)
$$\begin{cases} y_n^0 = \text{state of inventory at time } n \\ y_n^1 = \text{quantity to be delivered at } n+1 \\ \vdots \\ y_n^{\lambda-1} = \text{quantity to be delivered at } n+\lambda-1 \\ v_n = \text{quantity ordered at time } n\text{, which is due at time } n+\lambda \end{cases}$$

$y_n^1, \ldots, y_n^{\lambda-1}$ represent the outstanding orders at time n, before the production decision is made.

The following relations are established directly from the previous definitions :

(1.24)
$$\begin{cases} y_{n+1}^0 = y_n^0 + y_n^1 - \xi_{n+1} \\ y_{n+1}^1 = y_n^2 \\ \vdots \\ y_{n+1}^{\lambda-2} = y_n^{\lambda-1} \\ y_{n+1}^{\lambda-1} = v_n \end{cases}$$

The cost functional to be minimized is given by

$$(1.25)\qquad J(V) = E \sum_{n=0}^{N-1} [f_n(y_n^0) + c_n(v_n)]$$

where to simplify we have considered a problem starting at time 0 and a salvage cost equal to 0. The initial inventory level and outstanding orders are :

$$(1.26)\qquad y_0^0 = x^0,\ y_0^1 = x^1,\ \dots,\ y_0^{\lambda-1} = x^{\lambda-1}$$

We want to show that the problem (1.24), (1.25), (1.26) can be reduced to the problem (1.4), (1.6), using suitable transformations.

Let

$$(1.27)\qquad y_n = y_n^0 + y_n^1 + \dots + y_n^{\lambda-1}$$

be the potential inventory at time n, i.e. inventory on hand and on order, hence from (1.24) we deduce

$$(1.28)\qquad \begin{cases} y_{n+1} = y_n + v_n - \xi_{n+1} \\ y_0 = x = x^0 + x^1 + \dots + x^{\lambda-1} \end{cases}$$

Moreover

$$\begin{aligned}
y_0^0 &= x^0 \\
y_1^0 &= x^0 + x^1 - \xi_1 \\
&\vdots \\
y_{\lambda-2}^0 &= x^0 + \dots + x^{\lambda-2} - (\xi_1 + \dots + \xi_{\lambda-2}) \\
y_{\lambda-1}^0 &= y_0 - (\xi_1 + \dots + \xi_{\lambda-1}) \\
y_\lambda^0 &= y_0 + v_0 - (\xi_1 + \dots + \xi_\lambda) = y_1 - (\xi_2 + \dots + \xi_\lambda) \\
&\dots\dots \\
y_n^0 &= y_{n-\lambda+1} - (\xi_{n-\lambda+2} + \dots + \xi_n), \quad n \ge \lambda-1 \\
&\dots\dots
\end{aligned}$$

Therefore we obtain :

$$(1.29)\qquad \begin{cases} \sum_{n=0}^{N-1} f_n(y_n^0) = \sum_{n=0}^{\lambda-2} f_n(x^0 + \dots + x^n - (\xi_1 + \dots + \xi_n)) \\ \quad + \sum_{n=\lambda-1}^{N-1} f_n(y_{n-\lambda+1} - (\xi_{n-\lambda+2} + \dots + \xi_n)) \\ = \sum_{n=0}^{\lambda-2} f_n(x^0 + \dots + x^n - (\xi_1 + \dots + \xi_n)) \\ \quad + \sum_{n=0}^{N-\lambda} f_{n+\lambda-1}(y_n - (\xi_{n+1} + \dots + \xi_{n+\lambda-1})). \end{cases}$$

Now consider :

$$(1.30) \qquad \tilde{f}_n(x) = E\, f_{n+\lambda-1}(x - (\xi_{n+1} + \dots + \xi_{n+\lambda-1})), \; n = 0, \dots, N-\lambda$$

then we have

$$(1.31) \qquad E\, \tilde{f}_n(y_n) = E\, f_{n+\lambda-1}(y_n - (\xi_{n+1} + \dots + \xi_{n+\lambda-1}))$$

which follows from the fact that y_n is F_1^n measurable (see § I.1) and $\xi_{n+1} + \dots + \xi_{n+\lambda-1}$ is independent from F_1^n. Therefore we deduce from (1.25), (1.29) that

$$(1.32) \qquad \begin{cases} J(V) = E \sum_{n=0}^{\lambda-2} f_n(x^0 + \dots + x^n - (\xi_1 + \dots + \xi_n)) \\ + \sum_{n=0}^{N-\lambda} E\,[\tilde{f}_n(y_n) + c_n(v_n)] \end{cases}$$

Consequently the initial problem (1.24), (1.25), (1.26) has been made equivalent to a problem with one period delivery delay and horizon $N-\lambda+1$, where potential inventory plays the role inventory level did previously. The corresponding Dynamic Programming equation is :

$$(1.33) \qquad \begin{cases} w_n(x) = \tilde{f}_n(x) + \inf_{v \geq 0} \{c_n(v) + \Phi_{n+1}(w_{n+1})(x+v)\} \\ w_{N-\lambda+1}(x) = 0, \qquad n = 0, \dots, N-\lambda \end{cases}$$

and we can assert that

$$(1.34) \qquad \operatorname{Min} J(V) = \sum_{n=0}^{\lambda-2} E\, f_n(x^0 + \dots + x^n - (\xi_1 + \dots + \xi_n)) + w_0(x).$$

The result (1.34) can also be obtained analytically considering problem (1.24), (1.25) as of dimension λ. The corresponding Dynamic Programming equation is (by analogy with what has been done before)

$$(1.35) \qquad \begin{cases} u_n(x^0, x^1, \dots, x^{\lambda-1}) = f_n(x^0) \\ + \inf_{v \geq 0} [c_n(v) + E\, u_{n+1}(x^0 + x^1 - \xi_{N-1}, x^2, \dots, x^{\lambda-1}, v)], n=0,\dots,N-1 \\ u_N(x^0, x^1, \dots, x^{\lambda-1}) = 0, \end{cases}$$

We shall show that

$$(1.36) \qquad \begin{cases} u_n(x^0, x^1, \dots, x^{\lambda-1}) = w_n(x) + \sum_{j=0}^{\lambda-2} E\, f_{n+j}\,(x^0 + \dots + x^j - (\xi_{n+1} + \\ \dots + \xi_{n+j})) \end{cases}$$

which is an analytic proof of (1.34), since the left hand sides of both (1.34) and (1.36) are equal.

Property (1.36) is proved by induction. Applying (1.35) with $n = N-1$, we get

$$u_{N-1}(x^0, \dots, x^{\lambda-1}) = f_{N-1}(x^0)$$

$$u_{N-2}(x^0, \dots, x^{\lambda-1}) = f_{N-2}(x^0) + E\, f_{N-1}(x^0 + x^1 - \xi_{N-1})$$

$$u_{N-\lambda}(x^0, \ldots, x^{\lambda-1}) = f_{N-\lambda}(x^0) + E\, f_{N-\lambda+1}(x^0 + x^1 - \xi_{N-\lambda+1}) + \ldots$$

$$\ldots + E\, f_{N-1}(x^0 + x^1 + \ldots + x^{\lambda-1} - (\xi_{N-\lambda+1} + \ldots + \xi_{N-1}))$$

$$= \tilde{f}_{N-\lambda}(x) + \sum_{j=0}^{\lambda-2} E\, f_{N+j-\lambda}(x^0 + \ldots + x^j - (\xi_{N-\lambda+j} + \ldots + \xi_{N-\lambda+1}))$$

$$= w_{N-\lambda}(x) + \sum_{j=0}^{\lambda-2} E\, f_{N+j-\lambda}(x^0 + \ldots + x^j - (\xi_{N-\lambda+j} + \ldots + \xi_{N-\lambda+1}))$$

Assume now that (1.36) is proved for n+1. From (1.35) we deduce

$$u_n(x^0, \ldots, x^{\lambda-1}) = f_n(x^0)$$

$$+ \inf_{v \geq 0} [c_n(v) + E\, w_{n+1}(x + v - \xi_{n+1})$$

$$+ E \sum_{j=0}^{\lambda-2} f_{n+1+j}(x^0 + \ldots + x^{j+1} - (\xi_{n+1} + \ldots + \xi_{n+1+j}))]$$

But the term in the sum corresponding to $j = \lambda-2$ is

$$E\, f_{n+\lambda-1}(x^0 + \ldots + x^{\lambda-1} - (\xi_{n+1} + \ldots + \xi_{n+\lambda-1})) = \tilde{f}_n(x)$$

and

$$E \sum_{j=0}^{\lambda-3} f_{n+1+j}(x^0 + \ldots + x^{j+1} - (\xi_{n+1} + \ldots + \xi_{n+1+j}))$$

$$= E \sum_{j=1}^{\lambda-2} f_{n+j}(x^0 + \ldots + x^j - (\xi_{n+1} + \ldots + \xi_{n+j}))$$

Collecting terms, we obtain

$$u_n(x^0, \ldots, x^{\lambda-1}) = E \sum_{j=0}^{\lambda-2} f_{n+j}(x^0 + \ldots + x^j - (\xi_{n+1} + \ldots + \xi_{n+j}))$$

$$+ \tilde{f}_n(x) + \inf_{v \geq 0} [c_n(v) + E\, w_{n+1}(x + v - \xi_{n+1})]$$

and from (1.33) we deduce that (1.36) holds for n.

Remark 1.2

The results of this paragraph are due to Karlin and Scarf [1958]. □

I - 5. THE INFINITE HORIZON PROBLEM

We now look for the optimal control $V = (v_n, \ldots)$ which minimizes

$$(1.37) \qquad J_n(x\,;\,V) = \sum_{i=n}^{\infty} \alpha^{i-n}\, E[c_i(v_i) + f_i(y_i)]$$

where α is a discount factor, $0 < \alpha \leq 1$. The inventory balance equations are defined for k = n, ... by :

(1.38) $$\begin{cases} y_{k+1} = y_k + v_k - \xi_{k+1}, & k = n, \dots \\ y_n = x \end{cases}$$

In addition to (1.5) we assume

(1.5') $$c_i(0) = 0$$

$$\sup_{|x-x'|\leq\delta} |f_i(x) - f_i(x')| \leq \rho(\delta)$$

$$\rho(\delta) \to 0 \text{ as } \delta \to 0$$

I.5.1. DYNAMIC PROGRAMMING FORMULATION

The dynamic programming equations are written as follows :

(1.39) $$u_n(x) = f_n(x) + \inf_{v\geq 0} \{c_n(v) + \alpha\Phi_{n+1}(u_{n+1})(x + v)\}$$

Our approach here will be different from what we adopted in Chapter I, section X, where we showed that $\inf J_n(x ; V)$ is a solution of (1.39). To obtain an a priori bound on $\inf J_n(x ; V)$ we had to impose a bound on the overall cost function (condition 10.6). This was important to derive an approximation result (Theorem 10.2, Chapter I). However we can prove the existence of the solution of (1.39) in C_1 by different means, and the growth assumption on f_i (condition (1.5)) will actually yield an a priori bound on $\inf J_n(x ; V)$. Consider the linear equation

(1.40) $$w_n(x) = f_n(x) + \alpha\Phi_{n+1}(w_{n+1})(x), \quad w_n \in C_1$$

then the following property is satisfied :

Lemma 1.1

The relations (1.40) define one, and only one, sequence w_n in C_1 with $||w_n||_{C_1} \leq C$. Moreover w_n is explicitly defined

(1.41) $$w_n(x) = f_n(x) + E \sum_{i=n+1}^{\infty} \alpha^{i-n} f_i(x - (\xi_{n+1} + \dots + \xi_i))$$

Proof

Firstly we check that the right hand side of (1.41) is well defined. Indeed we have

$$E \sum_{i=n+1}^{\infty} \alpha^{i-n} f_i(x - (\xi_{n+1} + \dots + \xi_i))$$

$$\leq \sum_{i=n+1}^{\infty} \alpha^{i-n} \bar{f} [1 + |x| + E|\xi_{n+1}| + \dots + E|\xi_i|]$$

$$\leq \bar{f} \sum_{i=n+1}^{\infty} \alpha^{i-n} [1 + |x| + K(i-n)]$$

$$= \bar{f}[\frac{(1+|x|)\alpha}{1 - \alpha} + \frac{K \alpha}{(1-\alpha)^2}] .$$

Let us check that w_n, as defined by (1.41), is a solution of (1.40). We have

$$(1.42)\quad \begin{cases} w_n(x) = f_n(x) + E\,\alpha f_{n+1}(x - \xi_{n+1}) \\ \qquad + \alpha^{i-n} \sum_{i=n+2}^{\infty} E\, f_i(x - (\xi_{n+1} + \dots + \xi_i)) \\ w_{n+1}(x) = f_{n+1}(x) + E \sum_{i=n+2}^{\infty} \alpha^{i-n-1} f_i(x - (\xi_{n+2} + \dots + \xi_i)) \end{cases}$$

Then,

$$\Phi_{n+1}(w_{n+1})(x) = E\, f_{n+1}(x - \xi_{n+1})$$

$$+ E \sum_{i=n+2}^{\infty} \alpha^{i-n-1} f_i(x - (\xi_{n+1} + \dots + \xi_i))$$

which, compared to (1.42), yields (1.40).

The function $w_n(x)$ belongs to C_1. As a matter of fact, we have

$$w_n(x) - w_n(x') = f_n(x) - f_n(x') + E \sum_{i=n+1}^{\infty} \alpha^{i-n} [f_i(x-(\xi_{n+1}+\dots+\xi_i))$$

$$- f_i(x' - (\xi_{n+1} + \dots + \xi_i))]$$

hence

$$|w_n(x) - w_n(x')| \le \rho(\delta) + \sum_{i=n+1}^{\infty} \alpha^{i-n} \rho(\delta)$$

$$= \frac{\rho(\delta)}{1 - \alpha}, \text{ if } |x - x'| \le \delta$$

which implies the desired result.

Let us finally prove the uniqueness of the solution of (1.40). Indeed if $f_n = 0$ then

$$w_n = \alpha^{N-n} \Phi_{n+1} \Phi_{n+2} \dots \Phi_N(w_N)$$

$$w_n(x) = \alpha^{N-n} E\, w_N(x - (\xi_{n+1} + \dots + \xi_N)).$$

Since $||w_n||_{C_1} \le L$ we deduce

$$||w_n||_{C_1} \le \alpha^{N-n} L(1 + |x| + (N-n)K)$$

which tends to 0 as $N \to \infty$. □

Remark 1.3.

We have proved that :

$$(1.43)\qquad ||w_n||_{C_1} \le \frac{\bar{f}(1+|x|)}{1 - \alpha} + \frac{\bar{f}\, K\, \alpha}{(1-\alpha)^2} \qquad \square$$

We now define an approximation of (1.39). First consider :

(1.44)
$$\begin{cases} u_n^0(x) = w_n(x) \\ u_n^{k+1}(x) = f_n(x) + \inf_{v\geq 0} \{c_n(v) + \alpha\Phi_{n+1}(u_{n+1}^k)(x+v)\} \end{cases}$$

then the following result obtains :

Theorem 1.3

Assume (1.5), (1.5'), (1.1), then

(1.45)
$$u_n^0 \geq u_n^1 \geq \ldots \geq u_n^k \geq \ldots \geq 0$$

and

(1.46)
$$u_n^k \downarrow u_n^* \quad , u_n \in B_1 \text{ solution of } (1.39)$$

If $\tilde{u}_n$ is a solution of (1.39) such that $\tilde{u}_n \leq w_n$, then $\tilde{u}_n \geq u_n^*$.

Proof

We have

$$0 \leq u_n^1(x) \leq f_n(x) + \alpha\Phi_{n+1}(w_{n+1})(x) = w_n(x) = u_n^0(x).$$

Assume that

$$u_n^{k-1}(x) \geq u_n^k(x)$$

then we have

$$\begin{aligned} u_n^{k+1}(x) &\leq f_n(x) + \inf_{v\geq 0} \{c_n(v) + \alpha\Phi_{n+1}(u_{n+1}^{k-1})(x+v)\} \\ &= u_n^k(x) \end{aligned}$$

hence (1.45) is proved. The functions u_n^k belong to C_1. Therefore $u_n^k \downarrow u_n^*$, u_n^* u.s.c, hence $u_n^* \in B_1$. We have

$$u_n^{k+1}(x) \geq f_n(x) + \inf_{v\geq 0} \{c_n(v) + \alpha\Phi_{n+1}(u_{n+1}^*)(x+v)\}$$

hence

(1.47)
$$u_n^*(x) \geq f_n(x) + \inf_{v\geq 0} \{c_n(v) + \alpha\Phi_{n+1}(u_{n+1}^*)(x+v)\}.$$

On the other hand let v be arbitrary. We have

$$u_n^{k+1}(x) \leq f_n(x) + [c_n(v) + \alpha\Phi_{n+1}(u_{n+1}^k)(x+v)].$$

Noting that

$$\Phi_{n+1}(u_{n+1}^k)(x) = E\, u_{n+1}^k(x - \xi_{n+1}) \downarrow E\, u_{n+1}(x - \xi_{n+1})$$

we deduce

$$u_n^*(x) \leq f_n(x) + c_n(v) + \alpha\Phi_{n+1}(u_{n+1}^*)(x+v)$$

and since v is arbitrary, the converse of (1.47) holds, hence the existence of a solution for (1.39).

Let $\tilde{u}_n$ be any solution of (1.39) such that $\tilde{u}_n \le w_n \le u_n^0$. Then one has

$$\tilde{u}_n(x) \le f_n(x) + \inf_{v \ge 0} \{c_n(v) + \alpha\Phi_{n+1}(u_{n+1}^0)(x + v)\}$$
$$= u_n^1(x)$$

and by induction it follows that $\tilde{u}_n(x) \le u_n^k(x)$.

Therefore $\tilde{u}_n(x) \le u_n^*(x)$. This completes the proof of the desired result. □

I.5.2. SOLUTION OF THE STOCHASTIC CONTROL PROBLEM

We say that V is an admissible control if the following condition holds

$$(1.48) \qquad \begin{cases} \forall x,\ n,\ \alpha^{N-n}\ E\ w_N(x + v_n + \dots + v_{N-1} - (\xi_{n+1} + \dots + \xi_N)) \to 0, \\ \text{as } N \to \infty\ . \\ v_k \text{ is } F_{n+1}^k \text{ measurable, } k \ge n. \end{cases}$$

We call $\mathcal{V}$ the set of admissible controls.

Theorem 1.4

Assume (1.5), (1.5'), (1.1), then the maximum solution u_n^* of (1.39) is given explicitly by

$$(1.49) \qquad u_n^*(x) = \inf_{V \in \mathcal{V}} J_n(x\ ;\ V)$$

Proof

The set $\mathcal{V}$ is not empty. Indeed it contains the control (0, 0, ...) since backlogging is permitted. Let us call $z_n(x)$ the right hand side of (1.49). We first show that

$$(1.50) \qquad u_n^*(x) \ge z_n(x)$$

Indeed, we have

$$u_n^0(x) = w_n(x) \ge z_n(x)$$

then we shall show that

$$(1.51) \qquad u_n^k(x) \ge z_n(x),\ \forall k$$

which implies (1.50).

Let us introduce the subset of admissible controls

$$(1.52) \qquad \mathcal{V}_n^k = \{V \in \mathcal{V} \mid v_\ell = 0, \text{ for } \ell \ge n+k\}$$

and we show that

$$(1.53) \qquad u_n^k(x) = \inf_{V \in \mathcal{V}_n^k} J_n(x\ ;\ V)$$

which would imply (1.51) since $\mathcal{V} = \mathcal{V}_n^\infty \supset \mathcal{V}_n^k$. The proof of (1.53) is similar to that of Theorem 1.2. Let $V \in \mathcal{V}_n^k$, we have from (1.44)

$$u_n^k(x) \le f_n(x) + c_n(v_n) + \alpha\, E\, u_{n+1}^{k-1}(y_{n+1})$$

$$E\, u_{n+1}^{k-1}(y_{n+1}) \le E[f_{n+1}(y_{n+1}) + c_{n+1}(v_{n+1}) + \alpha\, u_{n+2}^{k-2}(y_{n+2})]$$

- - - - - - - - -

$$E\, u_{n+k-1}^{1}(y_{n+k-1}) \le E[f_{n+k-1}(y_{n+k-1}) + c_{n+k-1}(v_{n+k-1}) + \alpha\, w_{n+k}(y_{n+k})]$$

and

$$E\, w_{n+k}(y_{n+k}) = E \sum_{\ell=n+k}^{\infty} \alpha^{\ell-n-k} f_\ell(y_\ell)$$

Adding up we obtain

$$u_n^k(x) \le \inf_{V \in \mathcal{V}_n^k} J_n(x\, ;\, V) \tag{1.54}$$

since V is arbitrary in $\mathcal{V}_n^k$.

On the other hand the functions u_n^k being in C_1. Reasoning as in Theorem 1.1, we see that there exist feedback controls $\hat{v}_n^k(x)$ which are Borel functions and satisfy

$$c_n(\hat{v}_n^k(x)) + \alpha\Phi_{n+1}(u_{n+1}^k)(x + \hat{v}_n^k(x)) = \inf_{v \ge 0} \{c_n(v) + \alpha\Phi_{n+1}(u_{n+1}^k)(x+v)\}. \tag{1.55}$$

Then by induction we define the control denoted by $\hat{V}_n^k$:

$$\hat{v}_n = \hat{v}_n^{k-1}(x), \quad \hat{y}_{n+1} = x + \hat{v}_n - \xi_{n+1}$$

$$\hat{v}_{n+1} = \hat{v}_{n+1}^{k-2}(\hat{y}_{n+1}) \quad \ldots.$$

$$\ldots\ldots$$

$$\hat{v}_{n+j} = \hat{v}_{n+j}^{k-j-1}(\hat{y}_{n+j}), \qquad 0 \le j \le k-1$$

$$\hat{v}_{n+j} = 0 \qquad \text{for } j \ge n+k$$

and the next equalities are satisfied :

$$u_n^k(x) = f_n(x) + c_n(\hat{v}_n) + \alpha\, E\, u_{n+1}^{k-1}(\hat{y}_{n+1})$$

$$E\, u_{n+1}^{k-1}(\hat{y}_{n+1}) = E[f_{n+1}(\hat{y}_{n+1}) + c_{n+1}(\hat{v}_{n+1}) + \alpha\, u_{n+2}^{k-2}(\hat{y}_{n+2})]$$

$$\ldots\ldots$$

$$E\, u_{n+k-1}^{1}(\hat{y}_{n+k-1}) = E[f_{n+k-1}(\hat{y}_{n+k-1}) + c_{n+k-1}(\hat{v}_{n+k-1}) + \alpha w_{n+k}(\hat{y}_{n+k})]$$

Moreover :

$$E\, w_{n+k}(\hat{y}_{n+k}) = E \sum_{i=n+k}^{\infty} \alpha^{i-(n+k)} f_i(\hat{y}_i)$$

Therefore we can deduce from the definition of $\hat{V}_n^k$ that :

$$u_n^k(x) = J_n(x \; ; \hat{V}_n^k)$$

and since $\hat{V}_n^k$ belongs to $\mathcal{V}_n^k$ the result (1.53) has been proved and therefore (1.51) also.

On the other hand let u_n be any solution in B_1 of (1.39) such that $u_n \leq w_n$. Let also V be any element of $\mathcal{V}$,

$$V = (v_n, v_{n+1}, \ldots)$$

and let $y_n = x, y_{n+1}, \ldots$

be the corresponding trajectory. We have, for $j \geq 0$

$$u^*_{n+j}(y_{n+j}) \leq f_{n+j}(y_{n+j}) + c_{n+j}(v_{n+j}) + \alpha\Phi_{n+j+1}(u^*_{n+j+1})$$

and

$$\Phi_{n+j+1}(u^*_{n+j+1})(y_{n+j} + v_{n+j}) = E\,[u^*_{n+j+1}(y_{n+j+1}) \mid F^{n+j}_{n+1}]$$

hence

$$E\, u^*_{n+j}(y_{n+j}) \leq E[f_{n+j}(y_{n+j}) + c_{n+j}(v_{n+j}) + \alpha u^*_{n+j+1}(y_{n+j+1})]$$

Summing up for j running from 0 to N-n-1 we obtain

$$u_n^*(x) \leq E \sum_{j=0}^{N-n-1} [f_{n+j}(y_{n+j}) + c_{n+j}(v_{n+j})]\; \alpha^j + E\, \alpha^{N-n}\, w_N(y_N)$$

hence

$$u_n^*(x) \leq J_n(x \; ; V) + \alpha^{N-n}\, E\, w_N(y_N)$$

But using definition (1.48) we deduce

$$u_n^*(x) \leq J_n(x \; ; V)$$

and since V is arbitrary in $\mathcal{V}$, we have proved that

$$u_n^*(x) \leq z_n(x)$$

which together with (1.50) proves (1.49) and completes the proof of theorem 1.4. □

Corollary 1.1

The maximum solution u_n^* of (1.39) belongs to C_1.

Proof

This follows from the interpretation of (1.49). Indeed using the definition (1.37) we have

$$J_n(x' ; V) - J_n(x ; V) = \sum_{i=n}^{\infty} \alpha^{i-n} E[f_i(x' + \sum_{j=n}^{i-1} v_j - \sum_{j=n+1}^{i} \xi_j)$$
$$- f_i(x + \sum_{j=n}^{i-1} v_j - \sum_{j=n+1}^{i} \xi_j)]$$

and from the assumptions (1.5) and (1.5')

$$|J_n(x' ; V) - J_n(x ; V)| \leq \sum_{i=n}^{\infty} \alpha^{i-n} \rho(|x' - x|)$$
$$= \frac{\rho(|x'-x|)}{1 - \alpha}$$

from which it follows that

$$|u_n^*(x') - u_n^*(x)| \leq \frac{\rho(|x'-x|)}{1 - \alpha}$$

which leads to the desired result. □

From the regularity property which has just been proved we can deduce the existence of an optimal control for the problem (1.37), (1.38). Indeed since u_n^* belongs to C_1 there exists a Borel map $\hat{v}_n(x)$ such that

$$c_n(\hat{v}_n(x)) + \alpha\Phi_{n+1}(u_{n+1}^*)(x + \hat{v}_n(x))$$
$$= \inf_{v \geq 0} \{c_n(v) + \alpha\Phi_{n+1}(u_{n+1}^*)(x + v)\}$$

We can then define inductively

$$(1.56) \qquad \begin{cases} \hat{y}_n = x, \quad \hat{v}_n = \hat{v}_n(x), \quad \hat{y}_{n+1} = \hat{y}_n + \hat{v}_n - \xi_{n+1} \\ \hat{v}_{n+1} = \hat{v}_{n+1}(\hat{y}_{n+1}) \ \ldots \end{cases}$$

from which we can assert the next result.

Corollary 1.2

Assume that the control defined by (1.56) belongs to $\mathcal{V}$ then this control is optimal.

Proof

First check the relation

$$u_n^*(x) = E \sum_{i=n}^{N-1} \alpha^{i-n}[f_i(\hat{y}_i) + c_i(\hat{v}_i)] + \alpha^{N-n} E\, u_N^*(\hat{y}_N)$$

and since $u_N^* \leq w_N$ and $\hat{V} \in \mathcal{V}$, we have $\alpha^{N-n} E\, u_N^*(\hat{y}_N) \to 0$ as $N \to \infty$. Therefore

$$u_n^*(x) = E \sum_{i=n}^{\infty} \alpha^{i-n}[f_i(\hat{y}_i) + c_i(\hat{v}_i)]$$
$$= J_n(x ; \hat{V})$$

which with (1.49) completes the proof of the desired result. □

Let us now define the sequence $u_{n,k}$ as follows

$$(1.57) \qquad \begin{cases} u_{n,0}(x) = 0 \\ u_{n,k+1}(x) = f_n(x) + \inf_{v\geq 0} \{c_n(v) + \alpha\Phi_{n+1}(u_{n+1,k})(x + v)\} \end{cases}$$

The following properties can then be deduced.

Theorem 1.5

Assume (1.5), (1.5'), (1.1), then we have

$$(1.58) \qquad u_{n,0} \leq u_{n,1} \leq \ldots \leq u_{n,k} \leq w_n$$

and

$$(1.59) \qquad u_{n,k} \uparrow u_n, \text{ solution of (1.39) (in } B_1).$$

If $\tilde{u}_n$ is any positive solution of (1.39), then one has $u_n \leq \tilde{u}_n$.

Proof

The property (1.58) is proved as in Theorem 1.3 for (1.45). Note that if $u_{n+1,k} \leq w_{n+1}$, then

$$u_{n,k+1}(x) \leq f_n(x) + \alpha\Phi_{n+1}(w_{n+1})(x) = w_n(x)$$

Therefore $u_{n,k} \uparrow u_n$, which is l.s.c.

We easily check that

$$(1.60) \qquad u_n(x) \leq f_n(x) + \inf_{v\geq 0} \{c_n(v) + \alpha\Phi_{n+1}(u_{n+1})(x + v)\} \cdot$$

To prove the reverse inequality, first let us obtain a bound on $\hat{v}_{n,k}$ which attains the infimum on the right hand side of (1.57). We have from the assumptions (1.5), (1.5') that :

$$\bar{c}_n \hat{v}_{n,k} \leq \alpha\Phi_{n+1}(u_{n+1,k})(x)$$
$$\leq \alpha(1+K) ||w_n|| (1 + |x|)$$

hence

$$(1.61) \qquad 0 \leq \hat{v}_{n,k}(x) \leq M_n(1 + |x|)$$

where M_n is a constant, which does not depend on k. Let $k < \ell$, we deduce from (1.57) :

$$(1.62) \qquad \begin{cases} u_{n,\ell+1}(x) = f_n(x) + c_n(\hat{v}_{n,\ell}(x)) + \alpha\Phi_{n+1}(u_{n+1,\ell})(x + \hat{v}_{n,\ell}(x)) \\ \qquad\qquad \geq f_n(x) + c_n(\hat{v}_{n,\ell}(x)) + \alpha\Phi_{n+1}(u_{n+1,k})(x + \hat{v}_{n,\ell}(x)) \end{cases}$$

Let $\ell \to \infty$, with k fixed. From (1.61) we can extract a subsequence $\hat{v}_{n,\ell'}(x)$ (which depends on n,x) such that

$$\hat{v}_{n,\ell'}(x) \to \bar{v}_n(x).$$

Recalling that $u_{n+1,k}$ is uniformly continuous and c_n l.s.c., we can pass to the limit in the right hand side of (1.62). We obtain (noting that the left side converges as well)

$$u_n(x) \geq f_n(x) + c_n(\bar{v}_n(x)) + \alpha\Phi_{n+1}(u_{n+1,k})(x + \bar{v}_n(x))$$
$$\geq f_n(x) + \operatorname*{Inf}_{v\geq 0} \{c_n(v) + \alpha\Phi_{n+1}(u_{n+1,k})(x + v)\}$$

which, with (1.60) proves that u_n is a solution of (1.39). If $\tilde{u}_n$ is a positive solution of (1.39), we have

$$\tilde{u}_n \geq u_{n,0}$$

and if $\tilde{u}_n \geq u_{n,k}$, then by (1.57)

$$u_{n,k+1}(x) \leq f_n(x) + \inf_{v\geq 0} \{c_n(v) + \alpha\Phi_{n+1}(\tilde{u}_{n+1})(x + v)\}$$
$$= \tilde{u}_n(x)$$

hence letting k tend to $+\infty$, $u_n(x) \leq \tilde{u}_n(x)$. □

From Theorems 1.3 and 1.4 it follows that $u_n(x) \leq u_n^*(x)$, which can also be derived from the interpretation of the next property.

Theorem 1.6

Assume (1.5), (1.5'), (1.1), then the minimum solution u_n of (1.39) is given explicitly by

$$u_n(x) = \operatorname*{Min}_{V} \; J_n(x \; ; V) \tag{1.63}$$

Moreover u_n belongs to C_1.

Proof

An important step is to give an interpretation of the increasing scheme $u_{n,k}(x)$. In fact we have

$$u_{n,k}(x) = \inf_{V} \; J_{n,k}(x \; ; V) \tag{1.64}$$

where we have set

$$J_{n,k}(x \; ; V) = \sum_{i=n}^{n+k-1} E[c_i(v_i) + f_i(y_i)]\alpha^{i-n} \tag{1.65}$$

The proof is similar to (1.53). Let V be any control, then we have

$$u_{n,k}(x) \leq f_n(x) + c_n(v_n) + \alpha E\, u_{n+1,k-1}(y_{n+1})$$
$$E\, u_{n+1,k-1}(y_{n+1}) \leq E[f_{n+1}(y_{n+1}) + c_{n+1}(v_{n+1}) + \alpha u_{n+2,k-2}(y_{n+2})]$$
$$\cdots\cdots\cdots\cdots$$
$$E\, u_{n+k-1,1}(y_{n+k-1}) \leq E[f_{n+k-1}(y_{n+k-1}) + c_{n+k-1}(v_{n+k-1})].$$

Adding up we deduce (since V is arbitrary)

(1.66) $$u_{n,k}(x) \le \inf_V J_{n,k}(x\ ;\ V)$$

On the other hand using the feedback controls $\hat{v}_{n,k}(x)$ defined in the proof of Theorem 1.5, in the same way as in Theorem 1.4, we can show that there exists a control $\hat{V}_{n,k}$ such that

$$u_{n,k}(x) = J_{n,k}(x\ ;\ \hat{V}_{n,k})$$

which proves (1.64). Now considering the proof of Corollary 1.1 we see that

$$|J_{n,k}(x'\ ;\ V) - J_{n,k}(x\ ;\ V)| \le \frac{\rho(|x'-x|)}{1-\alpha}$$

hence

$$|u_{n,k}(x') - u_{n,k}(x)| \le \frac{\rho(|x'-x|)}{1-\alpha}$$

and therefore also

$$|u_n(x') - u_n(x)| \le \frac{\rho(|x'-x|)}{1-\alpha}$$

from which it follows that u_n belongs to C_1.

Therefore there exists a Borel map $\hat{v}_n(x)$ (different of course from that defined in (1.56) which corresponds to u_n^*) such that

$$c_n(\hat{v}_n(x)) + \alpha\Phi_{n+1}(u_{n+1})(x + \hat{v}_n(x)) = \inf_{v\ge 0} \{c_n(v) + \alpha\Phi_{n+1}(u_{n+1})(x + v)\}.$$

As in Corollary 1.2 it then follows that

$$u_n(x) = E \sum_{i=n}^{N-1} \alpha^{i-n}[f_i(\hat{y}_i) + c_i(\hat{v}_i)] + \alpha^{N-n} E\, u_N(\hat{y}_N)$$

hence in particular

(1.67) $$u_n(x) \ge J_n(x\ ;\ \hat{V}) \ge \inf_V J_n(x\ ;\ V)$$

On the other hand from (1.66) we deduce clearly

$$u_{n,k}(x) \le J_{n,k}(x\ ;\ V) \le J_n(x\ ;\ V)$$

hence letting k tend to $+\infty$, it follows that

$$u_n(x) \le J_n(x\ ;\ V) \qquad \forall V$$

which combined with (1.67) clearly proves that

$$u_n(x) = J_n(x\ ;\ \hat{V}) = \inf_V J_n(x\ ;\ V)$$

which completes the proof of Theorem 1.6. □

I.5.3. THE STATIONARY CASE

We can now specialize the previous results for the infinite horizon problem to the stationary case. Namely we assume

$$(1.68)\qquad \begin{cases} c(v) : R^+ \to R^+ \quad \text{l.s.c.} \\ c(v) \geq \bar{c}\, v, \ \forall v \geq 1,\ c(0) = 0 \\ f(x) : R \to R^+ \quad ,\ f(x) \leq \bar{f}(1 + |x|) \\ \sup\limits_{|x'-x|\leq\delta} |f(x) - f(x')| \leq \rho(\delta) \quad ,\ \rho(\delta) \to 0 \text{ as } \delta \to 0 \end{cases}$$

(1.69) The variables ξ_i are independent and identically distributed, $E|\xi| \leq K$

The dynamic programming equation is now written as follows

$$(1.70)\qquad u(x) = f(x) + \inf_{v\geq 0} \{c(v) + \alpha\Phi(u)(x + v)\}$$

where Φ denotes the operator

$$(1.71)\qquad \Phi(u)(x) = E\, u(x-\xi)$$

We define w by the equation

$$(1.72)\qquad w(x) = f(x) + \alpha\Phi(w)(x)$$

which has a unique solution in C_1, given by

$$(1.73)\qquad w(x) = f(x) + E \sum_{i=1}^{\infty} \alpha^i f[x - (\xi_1 + \dots + \xi_i)].$$

We next introduce the following control problem

$$(1.74)\qquad \begin{cases} y_{k+1} = y_k + v_k - \xi_{k+1},\ k = 0, 1, \dots \\ y_0 = x \end{cases}$$

$$(1.75)\qquad J(x\,;V) = \sum_{i=0}^{\infty} \alpha^i \ E[c(v_i) + f(y_i)]$$

Write F^k for $F_1^k = \sigma(\xi_1, \dots, \xi_k)$, $k \geq 0$. We define the class of controls

$$(1.76)\qquad \begin{cases} \mathcal{V} = \{V \mid \forall x,\ \alpha^N E\, w_N[x + v_0 + \dots + v_{N-1} - (\xi_1 + \dots + \xi_N)] \to 0 \text{ as} \\ \qquad N \to \infty\} \end{cases}$$

Then as a consequence of Theorems 1.3 to 1.6 we can state the following

Theorem 1.7

Assume (1.68), (1.69), then there exists a minimum solution u and a maximum solution u^* of (1.70). They are both in C_1 and are explicitly given by

$$(1.77)\qquad u(x) = \text{Min}\ J(x\,;V)$$

$$(1.78)\qquad u^*(x) = \inf_{V\in\mathcal{V}} J(x\,;V) \qquad \square$$

Remark 1.4

One can show that the functions $u_n(x)$ and $u_n^*(x)$ (respectively the minimum and the maximum solution of (1.39)) do not depend on n. Moreover

$$\inf_{V} J_n(x\ ;\ V) \quad \text{or} \quad \inf_{V\in\mathcal{V}} J_n(x\ ;\ V)$$

do not depend on n either, from which (1.77) , (1.78) follow immediately. It is also possible to proceed directly, without referring to the non stationary case first. □

I.5.4. MODEL WITH NO DELIVERY DELAY

I.5.4.1. THE PROBLEM

In all the previous models that we have considered we have assumed that there exists a lag of one period between the time a production decision is made and its effective materialization in the stock. We shall relax this assumption here, in the sense that we shall assume that the production is instantaneous. Very little changes if we assume that between two decisions there is a delay of one period (this is automatic if there is a production lag of one period). However, when production is instantaneous, nothing prevents in theory to consider successive decisions taking place at the same time. This brings a priori more flexibility and thus may improve the cost function. Such a gain may be effective when there are diseconomies of scales (strict convexity of the variable production cost). When this is not the case it is reasonable to expect that grouping decisions taking place at the same time is preferable, since there is a saving arising from the fixed costs. Our objective in this section is to derive such a property. At the same time we shall shed some light of the dynamic programming relations when one allows successive decisions at the same time. For simplicity, we shall restrict ourselves to the stationary case. We thus consider the framework of §1.5.3. The equations describing the evolution of the stocks are still (1.74) but the functional becomes :

$$J(x\ ;\ V) = E \sum_{i=0}^{\infty} \alpha^i [c(v_i) + f(y_i+v_i)] \tag{1.79}$$

and the corresponding dynamic programming equation reads

$$u(x) = \operatorname*{Inf}_{v\geq 0} [f(x+v) + c(v) + \alpha\Phi(u)(x+v)] \tag{1.80}$$

It will be convenient in the following to introduce explicitly the discontinuity at 0 of the function c(v). We shall more precisely assume that

$$\begin{cases} c(v) = K\,\chi_{v>0} + c_0(v) \\ c_0 \text{ is continuous and } c_0(0) = 0, \\ c_0(v) \geq \bar{c}v, \quad \forall v \geq 1 \end{cases} \tag{1.81}$$

I.5.4.2. A SYSTEM OF COMPLEMENTARY CONDITIONS

We shall now introduce the following analytic problem, whose solution is still denoted by u to save notation. Its relation with (1.80) will be analyzed later.

The problem is the following :

$$(1.82)\qquad \begin{cases} u(x) \le f(x) + \alpha\Phi(u)(x) \\ u(x) \le K + \inf\limits_{v\ge 0} \{c_0(v) + u(x+v)\} \\ [u(x) - f(x) - \alpha\Phi(u)(x)]\,[u(x) - K - \inf\limits_{v\ge 0} (c_0(v) + u(x+v))] = 0. \end{cases}$$

The regularity of u that we are looking for will be analyzed later on. We shall also use the notation

$$(1.83)\qquad Mu(x) = K + \inf_{v\ge 0} \{c_0(v) + u(x+v)\}.$$

It will be useful to introduce an intermediary problem as follows. Let

$$(1.84)\qquad g \in B_1$$

we consider the problem

$$(1.85)\qquad u(x) = \text{Min}\,[f(x) + \alpha\Phi(u)(x),\, g(x)]\ ,\ u \in B_1$$

We have the following

Theorem 1.8

Assume that $f,g \in B_1$, $f,g \ge 0$, and (1.69). Then there exists one and only one solution of (1.85), and $u \ge 0$.

Proof

Let us prove uniqueness. Let us notice first that

$$(1.86)\qquad |\text{Min}\,(z_1(x), g(x)) - \text{Min}\,(z_2(x), g(x))| \le |z_1(x) - z_2(x)|$$

If u_1, u_2 are two solutions of (1.85), then from (1.86) it follows that

$$|u_1(x) - u_2(x)| \le \alpha|\Phi(u_1)(x) - \Phi(u_2)(x)|$$

therefore also setting $\tilde{u} = u_1 - u_2$:

$$|\tilde{u}(x)| \le \alpha|\Phi(\tilde{u})(x)|$$

Iterating we get

$$|\tilde{u}(x)| \le \alpha^N|\Phi^N(\tilde{u})(x)|$$

But

$$\Phi^N(\tilde{u})(x) = E\,\tilde{u}(x - \xi_1 \dots - \xi_N)$$

hence

$$|\Phi^N(\tilde{u})(x)| \le ||\tilde{u}||\ (1 + |x| + N\,E\,|\xi|).$$

Therefore we deduce

$$|\tilde{u}(x)| \le \alpha^N\ ||\tilde{u}||\ (1 + |x| + N\,E\,|\xi|)$$

Letting N tend to $+\infty$, we obtain $\tilde{u}(x) = 0$.

To prove the existence, we consider an iterative scheme as follows

$$u^0(x) = g(x)$$

$$u^{n+1}(x) = \text{Min}\,[f + \alpha\Phi(u^n),\, g]$$

One then checks by induction that

$$u^0 \geq u^1 \geq \ldots \geq u^n \geq \ldots \geq 0$$

Hence $u^n(x) \downarrow u(x)$, $u \in B_1$. Going to the limit, we obtain that u is solution of (1.85). □

Let us now prove a useful regularity result on the solution of (1.85), namely

Theorem 1.9

If $f,g \in C_1$, then the solution of (1.85) belongs to C_1.

Proof

Let

$$\rho_f(\delta) = \sup_{|x'-x|\leq\delta} |f(x) - f(x')|$$

and let ρ_g be defined in the same way. Let us notice that

(1.87) $$\begin{cases} |\text{Min}\,[z(x),\, g(x)] - \text{Min}\,[z(x'),\, g(x')]| \leq \text{Max}\,(\rho_z(\delta),\, \rho_g(\delta)) \\ \text{if } |x - x'| \leq \delta \end{cases}$$

It follows that the functions $u^n(x)$ are uniformly continuous and if one sets

$$\rho^n(\delta) = \sup_{|x-x'|\leq\delta} |u^n(x) - u^n(x')|$$

from (1.87) the following recursion can be deduced

(1.88) $$\rho^{n+1}(\delta) \leq \text{Max}\,[\rho_g(\delta),\, \rho_f(\delta) + \alpha\rho^n(\delta)]$$

Clearly

$$\rho^0(\delta) = \rho_g(\delta) \leq \text{Max}\,[\rho_g(\delta),\, \rho_f(\delta)] = X$$

$$\rho^1(\delta) \leq X(1+\alpha)$$

$$\rho^2(\delta) \leq X + X\,\alpha(1+\alpha) = X(1+\alpha+\alpha^2)$$

Iterating we get

$$\rho^n(\delta) \leq \frac{X}{1-\alpha}$$

From the pointwise convergence of $u^n(x)$ to $u(x)$, it follows that

(1.89) $$|u(x) - u(x')| \leq \frac{\text{Max}[\rho_g(\delta),\rho_f(\delta)]}{1 - \alpha}, \quad \forall x,x' \text{ with } |x-x'| \leq \delta$$

which proves that u belongs to C_1. □

Clearly we can write the problem (1.82) as follows

(1.90) $$u(x) = \text{Min}\,[f(x) + \alpha\Phi(u)(x),\ Mu(x)]$$

Then we have the following

Theorem 1.10

Assume f in C_1 and (1.81). Then the set of positive solutions of (1.90) in B_1 is not empty and has a minimum element u and a maximum element u^*.

Proof

Let us consider the increasing scheme

(1.91) $$\begin{cases} u_{n+1} = \text{Min}\,[f + \alpha\Phi(u_{n+1}),\ Mu_n] \\ u_0 = 0 \end{cases}$$

The fact that (1.91) is an increasing scheme follows from a monotonicity property of the solution of (1.85) with respect to the function g. It can be deduced using an induction argument from the iterative scheme defined in the proof of Theorem 1.8.

Note also that

$$u_{n+1} \leq f + \alpha\Phi(u_{n+1})$$

and

$$u_{n+1} - w \leq \alpha\Phi(u_{n+1} - w)$$

Iterating we deduce

$$u_{n+1} - w \leq \alpha^N \Phi^N(u_{n+1} - w)$$

and letting N tend to 0 we get $u_{n+1} \leq w$. Therefore we have

(1.92) $$u_n \uparrow u \quad , \quad 0 \leq u \leq w$$

Moreover from Theorem 1.9, we deduce that $u_n \in C_1$. Therefore there exists $\hat{v}_n(x)$ such that

$$Mu_n(x) = K + c_0(\hat{v}_n(x)) + u_n(x + \hat{v}_n(x))$$

Moreover from the last assumption (1.81) it follows that

(1.93) $$\bar{c}\,\hat{v}_n(x) \leq K + u_n(x) \leq K + w(x).$$

Take m > n, we can write

$$u(x) \geq u_{m+1}(x) = \text{Min}[f(x) + \alpha\Phi(u_{m+1})(x),\ K + c_0(\hat{v}_m(x)) + u_m(x+\hat{v}_m(x))]$$

$$\geq \text{Min}[f(x) + \alpha\Phi(u_{n+1})(x),\ K + c_0(\hat{v}_m(x)) + u_n(x+\hat{v}_m(x))]$$

Letting m tend to $+\infty$, we can extract a subsequence from $\hat{v}_m(x)$, still denoted by

$\hat{v}_m(x)$ which converges to $v^*(x)$. By the continuity of c_0 and u_n we deduce

$$u(x) \geq \mathrm{Min}[f(x) + \alpha\Phi(u_{n+1})(x),\ K + c_0(\hat{v}^*(x)) + u_n(x + \hat{v}^*(x))]$$

Letting next n tend to $+\infty$, we obtain

$$(1.94)\quad \begin{cases} u(x) \geq \mathrm{Min}[f(x) + \alpha\Phi(u)(x),\ K + c_0(\hat{v}^*(x)) + u(x + \hat{v}^*(x))] \\ \qquad \geq \mathrm{Min}[f(x) + \alpha\Phi(u)(x),\ K + Mu(x)] \end{cases}$$

On the other hand from (1.91) we have

$$u_{n+1} \leq \mathrm{Min}[f + \alpha\Phi(u),\ Mu]$$

hence

$$u \leq \mathrm{Min}[f + \alpha\Phi(u),\ Mu]$$

which with (1.94) proves that u is a solution of (1.90). It is the minimum non negative solution since if $\tilde{u}$ is an other non negative solution, then one has by induction if $u_n \leq \tilde{u}$,

$$u_{n+1} \leq \mathrm{Min}[f + \alpha\Phi(\tilde{u}),\ M\tilde{u}] = \tilde{u}$$

and thus

$$u \leq \tilde{u}$$

If we start now with

$$u^0 = w$$

and define the iterative scheme

$$u^{n+1} = \mathrm{Min}[f + \alpha\Phi(u^{n+1}),\ Mu^n]$$

then we prove by similar methods that

$$u^0 \geq u^1 \geq \ldots \geq u^n \geq \ldots \geq 0$$

and $u^n \downarrow u^*$ which is the maximum solution of (1.91). □

I.5.4.3. EQUIVALENCE OF THE TWO PROBLEMS

We can now establish the following

Theorem 1.11

We make the assumptions of Theorem 1.10 with c_0 sublinear. Then the set of solutions of (1.80) and (1.90) coincide.

Proof

Let u be a solution of (1.80) and let x be fixed. Assume first that

$$u(x) = f(x) + \alpha\Phi(u)(x)$$

we shall prove that

$$(1.95)\qquad u(x) \leq K + c_0(v) + u(x+v)\ ,\ \forall v > 0$$

which will imply that the relation (1.90) holds for that x.

Assume that (1.95) is false. Then there exists v_0 such that

$$u(x) > K + c_0(v_0) + u(x + v_0) \tag{1.96}$$

We have either

$$u(x + v_0) = f(x + v_0) + \alpha\Phi(u)(x + v_0)$$

or

$$u(x + v_0) = K + \operatorname*{Inf}_{v>0} [f(x + v_0 + v) + c_0(v) + \alpha\Phi(u)(x + v_0 + v)]$$

The first possibility does not hold. Indeed if it does, then

$$u(x) > K + c_0(v_0) + f(x + v_0) + \alpha\Phi(u)(x + v_0)$$

which is a contradiction. If the second possibility holds, then one has

$$u(x) > 2K + c_0(v_0) + \operatorname*{Inf}_{v>0} [f(x+v) + c_0(v) + \alpha\Phi(u)(x + v_0 + v)]$$

and by the sublinearity of c_0, it follows that

$$u(x) > 2K + \operatorname*{Inf}_{v>0} [f(x + v_0 + v) + c_0(v_0 + v) + \alpha\Phi(u)(x + v_0 + v)]$$

which also yields a contradiction.

Assume next that

$$u(x) < f(x) + \alpha\Phi(u)(x)$$

and

$$u(x) = K + \operatorname*{Inf}_{v>0} [f(x+v) + c_0(v) + \alpha\Phi(u)(x+v)] \tag{1.97}$$

Let us show that

$$u(x) = M(x) \tag{1.98}$$

Assume that there exists $\tilde{v}$ such that

$$u(x) > K + c_0(\tilde{v}) + u(x+\tilde{v})$$

it follows from (1.97) that

$$K + c_0(\tilde{v}) + u(x+\tilde{v}) < K + c_0(\tilde{v}) + f(x+\tilde{v}) + \alpha\Phi(u)(x+\tilde{v})$$

hence

$$u(x+\tilde{v}) < f(x+\tilde{v}) + \alpha\Phi(u)(x+\tilde{v})$$

but then we deduce necessarily

$$u(x+\tilde{v}) = K + \operatorname*{inf}_{v>0} [f(x + \tilde{v} + v) + c_0(v) + \alpha\Phi(u)(x + \tilde{v} + v)]$$

and thus

$$u(x) > 2K + c_0(\tilde{v}) + \inf_{v>0}[f(x + \tilde{v} + v) + c_0(v) + \alpha\Phi(u)(x + \tilde{v} + v)]$$
$$> 2K + \inf_{v>0}[f(x + \tilde{v} + v) + c_0(v + \tilde{v}) + \alpha\Phi(u)(x + \tilde{v} + v)]$$

which is a contradiction. This shows that

$$(1.99) \qquad u(x) \le Mu(x)$$

There cannot be a strict inequality. Indeed, otherwise, there exists a fixed number $a(x)$ such that

$$u(x) < K + c_0(v) + u(x+v) - a(x), \qquad \forall v > 0$$

Since

$$u(x+v) \le f(x+v) + \alpha\Phi(u)(x+v)$$

it follows that

$$u(x) < K + c_0(v) + f(x+v) + \alpha\Phi(u)(x+v) - a(x), \quad \forall v > 0$$

which contradicts (1.97). Therefore we have proved that (1.98) holds, hence also (1.90). This completes the proof that any solution of (1.80) (in B_1) is also a solution of (1.90). The reverse is also proved by similar arguments. □

Remark 1.5

In particular the minimum solutions as well as the maximum solutions of problems (1.80) and (1.90) coincide (if c_0 is sublinear). In fact (1.90) corresponds to the dynamic programming equation of a problem where we allow successive decisions to take place at the same time (see § I.5.4.1). We have not given the details of that theory to avoid lengthy developments. The result of Theorem 1.11 shows that when c_0 is sublinear this additional flexibility is not really of any use. We can without loss of generality impose a delay of one period between two successive decisions. This is due to the fact that, since the large orders are not penalized with respect to the small ones, a grouping is possible which avoids paying several times the set up cost.

II - THE OPTIMALITY OF (S,s) REORDERING POLICIES

A reordering policy is of the (S,s) type if for any period n, there exist two critical numbers s_n and S_n, with $s_n \le S_n$, such that in the event the level of stock on hand and on order falls below s_n, an order is placed to replenish the stock to the level S_n ; when at the time the system is rewieved the stock level exceeds s_n, then no order is placed.

This fundamental result has been established for various conditions on demand and cost functions. Still, Scarf [1960] has provided the less restrictive sufficient conditions for optimality of this policy, and the most elegant proof based on the concept of K-convexity. Adopting Scarf's line of proof this section considers sufficient conditions which imply the existence of a feedback $\hat{v}_n(x)$ of the type (S_n, s_n).

Remark 2.1

The existence of the function $\hat{v}_n(x)$ was proved in Theorem 1.1. Following Chapter I, §II.2, it is called a feedback.

II - 1. DEFINITION, STATEMENT OF RESULTS

The key concept in the proof is K-convexity of a function as introduced by Scarf [1960].

A function $g(x) : R \to R$ is said to be K convex, $K \geq 0$ if it satisfies the property

$$(2.1)\qquad \begin{cases} K + g(z+y) \geq g(y) + z \dfrac{g(y) - g(y-b)}{b} \\ \forall z \geq 0, \quad b > 0, \ y \end{cases}$$

the study of the properties of K convex functions is delayed until §II.2. First, we state the main results.

Assume for $n = 0, \ldots, N-1$ that

$$(2.2)\qquad f_n(x) \text{ and } g_N(x) \text{ are convex,}$$

$$(2.3)\qquad c_n(v) = K_n \chi_{v>0} + c_n v$$

where $K_n \geq 0$, K_n decreasing with n, $c_n \geq 0$, $\chi_{v>0}$ denotes the characteristic function of the set $v > 0$.

$$(2.4)\qquad c_n x + \Phi_{n+1}(f_{n+1})(x) \to +\infty \quad \text{as } x \to -\infty$$

Then the following result obtains :

Theorem 2.1

Assume (1.1), (1.5), (2.2), (2.3), (2.4). Then there exists a sequence of numbers s_n, S_n, $n = 0, \ldots, N-1$, with $s_n \leq S_n$ such that the feedback

$$(2.5)\qquad \hat{v}_n(x) = \begin{cases} S_n - x & \text{for} \quad x \leq s_n \\ 0 & \text{for} \quad x > s_n \end{cases}$$

is optimal. In addition we have $s_{N-1} = -\infty$ if g_N is increasing. □

II - 2. PROPERTIES OF K CONVEX FUNCTIONS

The following properties are easily deduced as immediate consequences of the definition (cf. Bertsekas [1976, p. 85])

(2.6) If g is K convex, it is L convex for any $L \geq K$. In particular if g is convex, i.e. 0 convex, it is also K convex for any $K \geq 0$.

(2.7) If g_1 is K convex and g_2 is L convex, then for $\alpha, \beta \geq 0$, $\alpha g_1 + \beta g_2$ is $\alpha K + \beta L$ convex.

(2.8) If g is K convex, and ξ is a random variable such that $E|g(x-\xi)| < \infty$, then $x \to E\, g(x-\xi)$ is also K convex.

The main resuls on K-convex functions are collected in the following proposition :

Proposition 2.1

Let g be a K convex continuous function such that $g(x) \to +\infty$ as $|x| \to \infty$. Then there exist numbers s,S, $s \le S$ such that

(2.9) $g(S) = \inf f(x)$

(2.10) $g(s) = K + g(S)$

(2.11) g is strictly decreasing on $(-\infty, s]$

(2.12) $g(x) \le K + g(y)$, $\forall x,y$ such that $s \le x \le y$

Proof

Since g is continuous and $g(x) \to +\infty$ as $|x| \to \infty$, there exists a point S such that (2.9) holds. Next consider the set

$$z \le S \text{ and } g(z) = K + g(S)$$

which is not empty and bounded. It has a minimum (smallest) element that we call s, hence (2.10) holds.

Let $x < s$, from the definition of K-convexity we have

$$K + g(S) \ge g(s) + \frac{S-s}{s-x} [g(s) - g(x)]$$

hence $g(s) \le g(x)$. Since $x < s$ and s is the smallest number such that (2.10) holds, necessarily

(2.13) $g(s) < g(x)$ if $x < s$

Now, consider $x_1 < x_2 < s$; K-convexity implies

$$K + g(S) \ge g(x_2) + \frac{S-x_2}{x_2-x_1} [g(x_2) - g(x_1)]$$

and (2.13) leads to $g(x_2) > K + g(S)$,

hence

$$g(x_2) < g(x_1)$$

which proves (2.11).

As a final step, let us prove (2.12). It holds when $x = y$, or $x = s$, or $x = S$. It remains to consider two cases $S < x < y$, or $s < x < S$.

If $S < x < y$, by K convexity we have :

$$K + g(y) \ge g(x) + \frac{y-x}{x-S} [g(x) - g(S)]$$

$$\ge g(x)$$

hence (2.12) holds.

In the second case, for $s < x < S$, using again K convexity we obtain :

$$g(s) = K + g(S) \geq g(x) + \frac{S-x}{x-s}[g(x) - g(s)]$$

hence

$$g(s)(1 + \frac{S-x}{x-s}) \geq g(x)(1 + \frac{S-x}{x-s})$$

which implies

$$g(s) \geq g(x).$$

Therefore

$$g(x) \leq g(S) + K \leq g(y) + K$$

which completes the proof. □

Remark 2.2

When $K = 0$, s will be the smallest minimum of g. In this case it is convenient to choose $S = s$. □

Proposition 2.2

If g is a continuous K-convex function such that $g(x) \to +\infty$ as $|x| \to +\infty$, then we have

$$h(x) = \inf_{y \geq x} [K\chi_{y>x} + g(y)] = \begin{cases} K + g(S) & \text{for } x \leq s \\ g(x) & \text{for } x > s \end{cases} \tag{2.14}$$

and $h(x)$ is K-convex.

Proof

If $x < s$, we have $g(x) > K + g(S)$. But $y = S$ is admissible, therefore we can eliminate the choice $y = x$. If the set of constraints is reduced to $y > x$, then the problem amounts to minimizing $g(y)$ over this set. Since $y = S$ is admissible, it is certainly the best choice.

Now if $x > s$, it clearly follows from (2.12) that $y = x$ realizes the infimum in (2.14). Now let us show that $h(x)$ is K-convex, i.e.

$$\begin{cases} K + h(y+z) \geq h(y) + z\,\dfrac{h(y) - h(y-b)}{b} \\ \forall z \geq 0,\ y,\ b > 0. \end{cases} \tag{2.15}$$

Three cases must be considered :

CASE 1 : $y \geq s$

If $y-b \geq s$, then $h(y) = g(y)$, $h(y+z) = g(y+z)$, $h(y-b) = g(y-b)$, and (2.15) follows from the K-convexity of g.

If $y-b < s$, then (2.15) amounts to :

$$K + g(y+z) \geq g(y) + z\,\frac{g(y) - g(s)}{b} \tag{2.16}$$

Since $y \geq s$, by the K-convexity of g we have

$$(2.17)\qquad \begin{cases} K + g(y+z) \geq g(y) + z\,\dfrac{g(y) - g(s)}{y - s} \\ K + g(y+z) \geq g(y) \end{cases}$$

Therefore if $g(y) \geq g(s)$, using the first relation (2.17) and noting that $y-s < b$ we deduce (2.16).

If $g(y) \geq g(s)$ we use the second relation (2.17) to obtain again (2.16).

CASE 2 : $y+z \geq s \geq y$

The relation (2.15) becomes in this case

$$(2.18)\qquad K + g(y+z) \geq g(s)$$

which is true since

$$K + g(y+z) \geq K + g(S) = g(s).$$

CASE 3 : $y+z \leq s$

then (2.15) becomes

$$K + g(s) \geq g(s)$$

which is trivially true. □

II - 3. PROOF OF THE MAIN RESULT

We can now proceed with the proof of Theorem 2.1.

The Dynamic Programming equations (1.11) can be written as follows

$$(2.19)\qquad \begin{cases} u_n(x) = f_n(x) - c_n.x + \operatorname*{Inf}_{y\geq x} [K_n \chi_{y>x} + c_n y + \Phi_{n+1}(u_{n+1})(y)] \\ u_N(x) = g_N(x). \end{cases}$$

Setting for $0 \leq n \leq N-1$

$$(2.20)\qquad \begin{cases} z_n(x) = c_n x + \Phi_{n+1}(u_{n+1})(x) \\ h_n(x) = \operatorname*{Inf}_{y\geq x} [K_n \chi_{y>x} + z_n(y)] \end{cases}$$

then

$$(2.21)\qquad u_n(x) = f_n(x) - c_n.x + h_n(x).$$

Moreover for $n \leq N-1$, $z_n(x) \geq c_n x$, $h_n(x) \geq c_n x$, hence $u_n(x) \geq f_n(x)$.

From (2.4) it follows that

$$(2.22)\qquad z_n(x) \to +\infty \text{ as } |x| \to \infty\,, \text{ for } n \leq N-2$$

and z_n are uniformly continuous.

Now, let us prove that

$$(2.23)\qquad u_{N-1}(x) \text{ is } K_{N-1} \text{ convex}$$

We have

$$z_{N-1}(x) = c_{N-1}x + \Phi_N(g_N)(x),$$

and z_{N-1} is convex. If z_{N-1} is increasing then clearly $h_{N-1}(x) = z_{N-1}(x)$, and from (2.21) u_{N-1} is convex which proves (2.23). If z_{N-1} attains its minimum then necessarily $z_{N-1}(x) \to +\infty$ as $|x| \to \infty$. Applying proposition 2.2, we deduce that $h_{N-1}(x)$ is K_{N-1} convex and from (2.21) we derive (2.23).

We can then proceed by induction using proposition 2.2. Firstly, z_{N-2} is K_{N-1}-convex, hence also K_{N-2}-convex and proposition 2.2 implies that h_{N-2} is K_{N-2}-convex. Therefore u_{N-2} is K_{N-2}-convex. We have so far proved that

u_n is K_n-convex

z_n is K_{n+1}-convex

h_n is K_n-convex,

for $n \leq N-1$. Using (2.22), the first part of proposition (2.2) yields the desired result (2.5) at least for $n \leq N-2$. For $n = N-1$, we have two cases :

either z_{N-1} achieves its minimum in which situation proposition 2.2 can be applied to yield (2.5) even when $n = N-2$; or, z_{N-1} is increasing, in which case

$$\hat{v}_{N-1}(x) = 0.$$

We may consider then that (2.5) holds with $s_{N-1} = -\infty$ and S_{N-1} arbitrary. This completes the proof of Theorem 2.1. □

II - 4. THE INFINITE HORIZON PROBLEM

Let us now consider the situation where (2.2), (2.3), (2.4) hold for $n = 0, 1, \ldots$ We then have the analogue of Theorem 2.1, namely

Theorem 2.2

Assume (1.5), (1.5'), (1.1), and (2.2), (2.3), (2.4). Then, there exists a sequence of numbers s_n, S_n, $n = 0, 1, \ldots$ with $s_n \leq S_n$ such that the feedback

$$\text{(2.24)} \qquad \hat{v}_n(x) = \begin{cases} S_n - x & \text{for} \quad x \leq s_n \\ 0 & \text{for} \quad x > s_n \end{cases}$$

is optimal.

Proof

Let us define the functions z_n and h_n as in § II.3. Again we have $z_n(x) \to \infty$ as $|x| \to +\infty$ and z_n belongs to C_1. If we prove that u_n is K_n-convex, then as in § II.3 it will follow that z_n is K_{n+1}-convex and h_n is K_n-convex, and from proposition 2.2 the desired result will follow.

To prove that u_n is K_n-convex, one first shows that $u_{n,k}$ is K_n-convex, whose proof is by induction as in § II.3. Now it is clear from the definition of K-convexity, that going to the limit with k, the function $u_n(x)$ will also be K_n-convex. □

Corollary 2.1

Assume (1.5), (1.5'), (1.1) with the restriction that

(2.25) $\bar{c}_i = \bar{c}$ independant of i.

Assume (2.2), (2.3), (2.4) and moreover that :

(2.26) $\operatorname{Inf}_n[c_n x + \alpha\Phi_{n+1}(f_{n+1})(x)] \to +\infty$ as $x \to -\infty$.

Then the solution of (1.39) is unique.

Proof

To prove the desired result, it is sufficient to show that the control defined by the feedback (2.24) belongs to V (see (1.48)).

Let us first show that we have

(2.27) $|S_n| \leq \bar{S}$

Indeed we first note that since S_n realizes the infimum of $z_n(x)$ (cf. § II.3) then one has

$$\begin{aligned} c_n S_n + \alpha\Phi_{n+1}(u_{n+1})(S_n) &\leq \alpha\Phi_{n+1}(u_{n+1})(0) \\ &\leq C \end{aligned}$$

and since $u_{n+1} \geq 0$, we deduce that $c_n S_n \leq C$.

Therefore if $S_n \geq 0$, it follows from the assumption $\bar{c}_i = \bar{c}$ and (1.5), (1.5') that

(2.28) $S_n \leq \bar{S}$

where $\bar{S}$ is some constant.

On the other hand since $u_n \geq f_n$ we have

$$C \geq c_n S_n + \alpha\Phi_{n+1}(u_{n+1})(S_n) \geq c_n S_n + \alpha\Phi_{n+1}(f_{n+1})(S_n)$$

and (2.26) implies that S_n is necessarily bounded from below which completes the proof of (2.27).

Now from the construction of the optimal feedback (2.24), we have

$$\hat{y}_{j+1} = \begin{cases} S_j - \xi_{j+1} & \text{if} \quad \hat{y}_j \leq s_j \\ \hat{y}_j - \xi_{j+1} & \text{if} \quad \hat{y}_j > s_j \end{cases}$$

hence

$$|\hat{y}_{j+1}| \leq |\hat{y}_j| + |S_j| + |\xi_{j+1}| \leq |\hat{y}_j| + \bar{S} + |\xi_{j+1}|$$

Therefore

$$|\hat{y}_N| \leq |x| + (N-n)\bar{S} + |\xi_{n+1}| + \dots + |\xi_N|$$

hence

$$E|\hat{y}_N| \leq |x| + (N-n)\bar{S} + (N-n)K$$

(by assumption (1.1)). Now using (1.43) we easily check that the condition (1.48) is satisfied and thus V belongs to $\mathcal{V}$. □

Considering the increasing scheme $u_{n,k}(x)$ defined by (1.57) we also define $s_{n,k} \leq S_{n,k}$, such that the feedback

$$\hat{v}_{n,k}(x) = \begin{cases} S_{n,k} - x & \text{if} \quad x \leq s_{n,k} \\ 0 & \text{if} \quad x > s_{n,k} \end{cases}$$

realizes the infimum at the right hand side of (1.57).

We now prove the following results.

Theorem 2.3

Under the assumptions of Corollary 2.1, we have

(2.29) $\qquad s_{n,k}, S_{n,k}$ remain bounded in k (for fixed n)

(2.30) $\qquad$ If $s_{n,k}, S_{n,k}$ is a converging subsequence to s_n, S_n as $k \to +\infty$, for any n, then the pair s_n, S_n satisfy the properties of Theorem 2.2.

Proof

By definition of $s_{n,k}, S_{n,k}$ we have the relation

$$c_n s_{n,k} + \alpha\Phi_{n+1}(u_{n+1,k})(s_{n,k}) = K_n + c_n S_{n,k} + \alpha\Phi_{n+1}(u_{n+1,k})(S_{n,k})$$

from which we deduce

$$\begin{cases} c_n s_{n,k} + \alpha\Phi_{n+1}(f_{n+1})(s_{n,k}) \leq K_n + c_n S_{n,k} + \alpha\Phi_{n+1}(u_{n+1,k})(S_{n,k}) \\ \qquad\qquad \leq K_n + \alpha\Phi_{n+1}(u_{n+1})(0) \\ \qquad\qquad \leq K_n + \alpha\Phi_{n+1}(w_{n+1})(0) \leq C \end{cases} \tag{2.31}$$

Therefore using (2.26) we see that $s_{n,k}$ is bounded from below by a constant independent of n,k. Using also (2.5), we deduce that $S_{n,k}$ remains bounded above by a constant independent of n,k.

We can define subsequences $s_{n,k(n,p)}$ and $S_{n,k(n,p)}$ which converge to s_n, S_n as $p \to \infty$. We will still denote them $s_{n,k}, S_{n,k}$ to simplify the notation. We associate to the pair (s_n, S_n) the feedback $\hat{v}_n(x)$ as in (2.24). Let us show that

$$f_n(x) + c_n(\hat{v}_n(x)) + \alpha\Phi_{n+1}(u_{n+1})(x + \hat{v}_n(x)) \leq u_n(x). \tag{2.32}$$

Indeed we have for $k_0 \leq k$

$$(2.33)\qquad \begin{cases} f_n(x) + c_n(\hat{v}_{n,k}(x)) + \alpha\Phi_{n+1}(u_{n+1,k_0})(x + \hat{v}_{n,k}) \\ \leq f_n(x) + c_n(\hat{v}_{n,k}(x)) + \alpha\Phi_{n+1}(u_{n+1,k})(x + \hat{v}_{n,k}) = u_{n,k+1}(x) \\ \leq u_n(x) \end{cases}$$

Let $x > s_n$, then for k large enough $x > s_{n,k}$ and $\hat{v}_{n,k}(x) = 0 = \hat{v}_n(x)$, hence

$$(2.34)\qquad f_n(x) + c_n(\hat{v}_n(x)) + \alpha\Phi_{n+1}(u_{n+1,k_0})(x + \hat{v}_n(x)) \leq u_n(x).$$

Letting k_0 tend to $+\infty$, we recover (2.32).

Let $x < s_n$ then for k large enough $x < s_{n,k}$ and $\hat{v}_{n,k}(x) = S_{n,k} - x$.

Therefore $\hat{v}_{n,k}(x) \to \hat{v}_n(x)$ as $k \to +\infty$.

Noting in this case that

$$c_n(\hat{v}_{n,k}(x)) = K_n + c_n\, \hat{v}_{n,k}(x) \to c_n(\hat{v}_n(x))$$

and using the continuity of u_{n+1,k_0}, we still deduce (2.34), hence again (2.32).

We have thus proved (2.32) for any $x \neq s_n$.

We now apply (2.32) with $x = s_n - \varepsilon$, hence $\hat{v}_n(x) = S_n - s_n + \varepsilon$, from which it follows that

$$f_n(s_n-\varepsilon) + K_n + c_n(S_n-s_n+\varepsilon) + \alpha\Phi_{n+1}(u_{n+1})(S_n) \leq u_n(s_n-\varepsilon)$$

Letting $\varepsilon \to 0$, we deduce, using the continuity of f_n and u_n, that (2.32) holds also for s_n. However, $u_n(x)$ is clearly less or equal to the left hand side of (2.32), therefore the equality holds in (2.32) and $\hat{v}_n(x)$ is an optimal feedback. □

If we now make the stationarity assumption of § I.5.3., and if, in addition,

$$(2.35)\qquad \begin{cases} f(x) \text{ is convex} \\ c(v) = K\chi_{v>0} + c\, v \end{cases}$$

$$(2.36)\qquad cx + \alpha\Phi(f)(x) \to +\infty \text{ as } x \to -\infty$$

then we can assert from Theorems 1.7, 2.2 and 2.3 that the solution of the dynamic programming equation (1.70) is unique, that u is K convex, and that there is an optimal feedback defined by a (s,S) policy.

III - PRODUCTION PLANNING MODELS WITH CONVEX COSTS

III - 1. PRELIMINARIES

We now return to the general problem (1.4), (1.6) and make the following additional assumptions

(3.1) $f_n(x)$ and $c_n(v)$ are convex for $n = 0, \ldots, N-1$, and $g_N(x)$ is convex.

In this section we analyze in detail the properties of the Dynamic Programming equations when costs are convex, and study the implications in terms of the optimal production policy. A few intermediate steps are inescapable.

Proposition 3.1

Let $\phi(v) : R^+ \to R^+$, $\psi(x) : R \to R^+$ be convex functions. Consider

$$L(x) = \operatorname*{Inf}_{v \geq 0} [\phi(v) + \psi(x+v)] \tag{3.2}$$

Then $L(x)$ is convex. Assume that $\phi(v) \to +\infty$ as $v \to +\infty$, then setting

$$\hat{v}(x) = \sup \{v \geq 0 \mid \phi'^{-}(v) + \psi'^{-}(x+v) \leq 0 \} \tag{3.3}$$

$\hat{v}(x)$ realizes the infimum in (3.2), and it is the largest point realizing the infimum. It is a monotone decreasing function of x.

Proof

Consider

$$\begin{cases} L(\theta x_1 + (1-\theta)x_2) = \operatorname*{Inf}_{v \geq 0} [\phi(v) + \psi(\theta x_1 + (1-\theta)x_2 + v)] \\ \qquad = \operatorname*{Inf}_{\substack{v_1 \geq 0 \\ v_2 \geq 0}} [\phi(\theta v_1 + (1-\theta)v_2) + \psi(\theta(x_1 + v_1) + (1-\theta)(x_2+v_2)] \end{cases} \tag{3.4}$$

Let us check this last equality. Call X the infimum relative to the second equality

For any $v_1 \geq 0$, $v_2 \geq 0$ set $v = \theta v_1 + (1-\theta)v_2$ then

$$\begin{cases} \phi(v) + \psi(\theta x_1 + (1-\theta)x_2 + v) \\ = \phi(\theta v_1 + (1-\theta)v_2) + \psi(\theta(x_1 + v_1) + (1-\theta)(x_2 + v_2)). \end{cases} \tag{3.5}$$

hence

$$L(\theta x_1 + (1-\theta)x_2) \leq \phi(\theta v_1 + (1-\theta)v_2) + \psi(\theta(x_1 + v_1) + (1-\theta)(x_2 + v_2))$$

and since v_1, v_2 are arbitrary

$$L(\theta x_1 + (1-\theta)x_2) \leq X$$

Next for any $v \geq 0$, assuming $\theta \neq 0$, we take $v_1 = \frac{v}{\theta}$, $v_2 = 0$. Again we have (3.5), hence

$$\phi(v) + \psi(\theta x_1 + (1-\theta)x_2 + v) \geq X$$

and since v is arbitrary

$$L(\theta x_1 + (1-\theta)x_2) \geq X$$

and therefore (3.4) holds true. Now, by convexity of ϕ, ψ, it follows that

$$L(\theta x_1 + (1-\theta)x_2) \le \operatorname*{Inf}_{\substack{v_1\ge 0\\ v_2\ge 0}} [\theta(\phi(v_1) + \psi(x_1+v_1)) + (1-\theta)(\phi(v_2) + \psi(x_2+v_2))]$$

$$= \theta L(x_1) + (1-\theta)\, L(x_2)$$

which implies the convexity of L.

Note that ψ is continuous and the only possible discontinuity of ϕ is at 0 ($\phi(0^+) \le \phi(0)$). Therefore the infimum is also that of $\phi(v+0) + \psi(x+v)$ which is continuous bounded below (by 0) and tend to $+\infty$ as $v \to +\infty$. Therefore the infimum is achieved.

Let $\hat{v}$ be a minimum point. We have

$$(3.6) \qquad \begin{cases} \phi'^{+}(\hat{v}) + \psi'^{+}(x+\hat{v}) \ge 0 \\ \phi'^{-}(\hat{v}) + \psi'^{-}(x+\hat{v}) \le 0 \text{ if } \hat{v} > 0 \end{cases}$$

If $\hat{v}(x)$ (defined by (3.3)) is 0, then

$$\forall v > 0,\ \phi'^{-}(v) + \psi'^{-}(x+v) > 0$$

necessarily $\hat{v} = 0$ is the unique minimum.

Assume in the following that $\hat{v}(x) > 0$. First, note that $\hat{v}(x) < +\infty$.

Otherwise, if $\hat{v}(x) = +\infty$, we have

$$\phi'^{-}(v) + \psi'^{-}(x+v) \le 0\ , \quad \forall v.$$

But then if $\hat{v}$ is a minimum point, for any $v_2 > v_1 > \hat{v}$, we have, by convexity

$$0 \le \phi'^{+}(\hat{v}) + \psi'^{+}(x+\hat{v}) \le \phi'^{-}(v_1) + \psi'^{-}(x+v_1)$$

$$\le \phi'^{+}(v_1) + \psi'^{+}(x+v_1) \le \phi'^{-}(v_2) + \psi'^{-}(x+v_2) \le 0$$

hence

$$\phi'(v) + \psi'(x+v) = 0 \qquad \forall v > \hat{v}$$

which contradicts the fact that $\phi(v) + \psi(x+v) \to +\infty$ as $v \to \infty$.

Since $\hat{v}(x) < \infty$, it is an element of the set (3.3) (the function $\phi'^{-}(v) + \psi'^{-}(x+v)$ being left continuous). Necessarily $\hat{v}(x)$ realizes the infimum since otherwise by (3.6)

$$\phi'^{+}(\hat{v}(x)) + \psi'^{+}(x+\hat{v}(x)) < 0$$

and there would exist $v > \hat{v}(x)$ such that

$$\phi'^{-}(v) + \psi'^{-}(x+v) \le 0$$

(since $\phi'^{-}(v) + \psi'^{-}(x+v) \downarrow \phi'^{+}(\hat{v}(x)) + \psi'^{+}(x+\hat{v}(x))$ as $v \downarrow \hat{v}(x)$), contradicting the definition of $\hat{v}(x)$.

Clearly $\hat{v}(x)$ is the largest point realizing the infimum.

Let now $x_1 \geq x_2$, then assuming $\hat{v}(x_1) > 0$

$$0 \geq \phi'^{-}(\hat{v}(x_1)) + \psi'^{-}(x_1 + \hat{v}(x_1))$$
$$\geq \phi'^{-}(\hat{v}(x_1)) + \psi'^{-}(x_2 + \hat{v}(x_1))$$

therefore $\hat{v}(x_1) \leq \hat{v}(x_2)$ (if $\hat{v}(x_1) = 0$, this is trivial). This completes the proof of the desired result . □

Corollary 3.1

Let χ be a convex function from $R \to R^+$. Define

$$M(x) = \operatorname*{Inf}_{v \geq 0} \; [\phi(v) + \chi(x+v)] \tag{3.7}$$

Let $\hat{w}(x)$ be the largest infimum, defined as for $\hat{v}(x)$. Assume that

$$\chi'^{-}(x) \geq \psi'^{-}(x) \qquad \forall x \tag{3.8}$$

then

$$\hat{w}(x) \leq \hat{v}(x) \qquad \forall x \tag{3.9}$$

Proof

Indeed if $\hat{w}(x) > 0$, we have

$$\phi'^{-}(\hat{w}(x)) + \chi'^{-}(x+\hat{w}(x)) \leq 0$$

hence by (3.8)

$$\phi'^{-}(\hat{w}(x)) + \psi'^{-}(x + \hat{w}(x)) \leq 0$$

which implies (3.9), by definition of $\hat{v}(x)$. If $\hat{w}(x) = 0$, then (3.9) is trivially satisfied. □

We can give an explicit form for the function $\hat{v}(x)$ when $\phi(v)$ is convex piecewise linear. More precisely, let us now assume that

$$\phi(v) = \phi_0 v + (\phi_1 - \phi_0)(v - v_0)^+ + \dots + (\phi_N - \phi_{N-1})(v - v_{N-1})^+ \tag{3.10}$$

where

$$0 < \phi_0 \leq \phi_1 \leq \dots \leq \phi_N$$
$$0 < v_0 < v_1 < \dots < v_{N-1}$$

i.e.

$$\phi(v) = \begin{cases} \phi_0 v & , \; 0 \leq v \leq v_0 \\ \phi_1 v - (\phi_1 - \phi_0) v_0 & , \; v_0 \leq v \leq v_1 \\ \vdots & \\ \phi_k v - (\phi_1 - \phi_0) v_0 - \dots - (\phi_k - \phi_{k-1}) v_{k-1}, & v_{k-1} \leq v \leq v_k \\ \dots\dots & \end{cases}$$

$$\left| \phi_N v - (\phi_1 - \phi_0) v_0 - \dots - (\phi_N - \phi_{N-1}) v_{N-1}, \quad v_{N-1} \le v \right.$$

We thus have

(3.11) $\phi'^-(v) = \phi_k, \ v_{k-1} < v \le v_k$.

It is convenient to set

$$v_N = +\infty \quad , \ v_{-1} = 0$$

so that (3.11) holds for $k = 0, \dots, N$

Next let us define

(3.12) $y_k = \sup \{y \mid \psi'^-(y) \le - \phi_k\}$, $k = 0, \dots, N$

and we have

(3.13) $y_{-1} = \infty \ge y_0 \ge y_1 \ge \dots \ge y_N$.

We can then assert the following result.

Proposition 3.2

If we assume (3.10), then the function $\hat{v}(x)$ defined by (3.3) is given by

(3.14)
$$\begin{cases} \hat{v}(x) = \begin{cases} y_k - x & \text{for} \quad y_k - v_k \le x \le y_k - v_{k-1} \\ v_{k-1} & \text{for} \quad y_k - v_{k-1} \le x \le y_{k-1} - v_{k-1} \end{cases} \\ k = N, \dots, 0 \end{cases}$$

Moreover

(3.15)
$$L(x) = \begin{cases} \phi(y_k - x) + \psi(y_k) & \text{for } y_k - v_k \le x \le y_k - v_{k-1} \\ \phi(v_{k-1}) + \psi(x + v_{k-1}) & \text{for } y_k - v_{k-1} \le x \le y_{k-1} - v_{k-1} \end{cases}$$

(3.16)
$$L'^-(x) = \begin{cases} - \phi_k & \text{for } x \in (y_k - v_k, y_k - v_{k-1}] \\ \psi'^-(x + v_{k-1}) & \text{for } x \in (y_k - v_{k-1}, y_{k-1} - v_{k-1}\,] \end{cases}$$

Considering χ satisfying (3.8), and defining

(3.17) $\bar{z}_k = \sup \{y \mid \chi'^-(y) \le - \phi_k\}$

then we have

(3.18) $z_k \le y_k$

and

(3.19) $M'^-(x) \ge L'^-(x)$

Proof

Assume that

$$y_k - v_k < x \le y_k - v_{k-1}$$

Let v be such that $v_{h-1} < v \le v_k$, with $h \le k-1$, then

$$\phi'^-(v) + \psi'^-(x+v) = \phi_h + \psi'^-(x+v) \le \phi_k + \psi'^-(x+v)$$

and

$$x+v \le x+v_h \le x+v_{k-1} \le y_k$$

Therefore

$$\phi'^-(v) + \psi'^-(x+v) \le \phi_k + \psi'^-(x+v_{k-1}) \le 0.$$

Hence

(3.20) $$\phi'^-(v) + \psi'^-(x+v) \le 0, \ \forall v \le v_{k-1}$$

On the other hand $x + v_k > y_k$ implies

(3.21) $$\phi_k + \psi'^-(x + v_k) > 0$$

and $x + v_{k-1} \le y_k$ yields

(3.22) $$\phi_k + \psi'^-(x + v_{k-1}) \le 0.$$

Let $v_{k-1} < v \le v_k$, we have

$$\phi'^-(v) + \psi'^-(x+v) = \phi_k + \psi'^-(x+v)$$

which increases from $\phi_k + \psi'^-(x+v_{k-1})$ to $\phi_k + \psi'^-(x+v_k)$. At point y_k-x it changes signs, hence (3.14) for $y_k - v_k < x \le y_k - v_{k-1}$.

Consider now the situation

(3.23) $$y_k - v_{k-1} < x \le y_{k-1} - v_{k-1}$$

Let v such that $v_{h-1} < v \le v_h$, with $h \le k-1$ then

$$\begin{aligned} \phi'^-(v) + \psi'^-(x+v) &= \phi_h + \psi'^-(x+v) \\ &\le \phi_{k-1} + \psi'^-(x+v_{k-1}) \\ &\le \phi_{k-1} + \psi'^-(y_{k-1}) \le 0 \end{aligned}$$

Now for $v_k \ge v > v_{k-1}$, $x+v > x + v_{k-1} > y_k$

and

$$\phi'^-(v) + \psi'^-(x+v) = \phi_k + \psi'^-(x+v) > 0$$

since $x+v > y_k$. This completes the proof of (3.14). Note that $\hat{v}(x)$ is a continuous function. Formulas (3.15) and (3.16) are easy verified, as well as property (3.18).

Let us check (3.19). Consider $(y_k - v_k, y_k - v_{k-1}]$. We have two possibilities

(3.24) $$z_h-v_h \le y_k-v_k < z_h-v_{h-1}$$

or

(3.25) $$z_h-v_{h-1} \le y_k-v_k < z_{h-1}-v_{h-1}$$

In both cases, necessarily $h \le k$, since if $h > k$, then $h-1 \ge k$, hence

$$y_k \ge y_{h-1} \ge z_{h-1} \ge z_h$$

and $v_k \le v_{h-1}$ hence $y_k-v_k \ge z_{h-1}-v_{h-1} \ge z_h-v_{h-1}$ which contradicts both assumptions (3.24), (3.25).

On $(y_k-v_k, y_k-v_{k-1}]$, $L'^-(x) = -\phi_k$ and since $x > y_k-v_k \ge z_h-v_h$, $M'^-(x)$ (which is increasing) is larger than $-\phi_h \ge -\phi_k$ since $h \le k$.

Therefore (3.19) holds on $(y_k-v_k, y_k-v_{k-1}]$.

Consider now the interval $(y_k-v_{k-1}, y_{k-1}-v_{k-1}]$. Again two possibilities must be considered : either

(3.26) $$z_h-v_h \le y_k-v_{k-1} < z_h-v_{h-1}$$

or

(3.27) $$z_h-v_{h-1} \le y_k-v_{k-1} < z_{h-1}-v_{h-1}$$

In the first case necessarily $h < k$. Indeed if $h \ge k$, then $y_k \ge y_h \ge z_h$, $v_{k-1} \le v_{h-1}$ hence a contradiction. Now $L'^-(x) = \psi'^-(x+v_{k-1})$ and since $x+v_{k-1} \le y_{k-1}$

$$\psi'^-(x+v_{k-1}) \le \psi'^-(y_{k-1}) \le -\phi_{k-1} \le -\phi_h$$

But since $x > z_h-v_h$, $M'^-(x) \ge -\phi_h$, hence (3.19) holds on $(y_k-v_k, y_k-v_{k-1}]$, if we assume (3.26).

Consider finally the situation (3.27). Necessarily we have $h \le k$. Otherwise $h > k$, implies $h-1 \ge k$, $y_k \ge y_{h-1} \ge z_{h-1}$ and $v_{k-1} < v_{h-1}$, which yields a contradiction to (3.27).

We have

$$L'^-(x) = \psi'^-(x+v_{k-1}) \le \psi'^-(y_{k-1}) \le -\phi_{k-1}.$$

Therefore if $h < k$, the analysis is the same as before. Assume $h = k$, hence

$$z_k-v_{k-1} \le y_k-v_{k-1} < z_{k-1}-v_{k-1} \le y_{k-1}-v_{k-1}.$$

For points $x > z_{k-1}-v_{k-1}$, $M'^-(x) \ge -\phi_{k-1} \ge L'^-(x)$.

For points $x \in (y_k-v_{k-1}, z_{k-1}-v_{k-1}]$, we have

$$L'^-(x) = \psi'^-(x+v_{k-1})$$

$$M'^-(x) = \chi'^-(x+v_{k-1})$$

and (3.8) implies again (3.19).

This completes the proof of proposition 3.2. □

III - 2. APPLICATION TO DYNAMIC PROGRAMMING

We will now use the previous results of § III.1. to obtain additional properties for the solution of the dynamic programming equations (1.11). We first obtain the following result.

Theorem 3.1

Assume (1.1), (1.5) and (3.1), then the solution $u_n(x)$ of (1.11) is convex. The feedback $\hat{v}_n(x)$ can be characterized by

$$\hat{v}_n(x) = \sup_{v\geq 0} \{c'^{-}_n(v) + \Phi_{n+1}(u'^{-}_{n+1})(x+v) \leq 0\} \tag{3.28}$$

and is a monotone decreasing function of x. □

As an intermediary step in the proof of Theorem 3.1. we need the subsequent Lemma.

Lemma 3.1

Let $z \in C_1$, z convex. Let ξ be a random variable with $E|\xi| < \infty$. Then $x \to E\, z(x-\xi) = \Phi(z)(x)$ is convex in C_1 and

$$\begin{cases} \Phi(z)'^{+}(x) = \Phi(z'^{+})(x) \\ \Phi(z)'^{-}(x) = \Phi(z'^{-})(x) \end{cases} \tag{3.29}$$

Proof

We know that Φ maps C_1 into itself. Convexity is straightforward. To prove (3.29) we notice that

$$\begin{cases} \dfrac{z(x-y) - z(x-h-y)}{h} \leq z'^{-}(x-y) \leq z'^{+}(x-y) \leq \dfrac{z(x+k-y) - z(x-y)}{k} \\ \forall h,k > 0 \end{cases} \tag{3.30}$$

and

$$z'^{-}(x-y) = \lim_{h\downarrow 0} \frac{z(x-y) - z(x-h-y)}{h}$$

$$z'^{+}(x-y) = \lim_{k\downarrow 0} \frac{z(x+k-y) - z(x-y)}{k}$$

Since for h,k fixed the two extreme functions in (3.30) are integrable in y with respect to the probability μ of ξ, and since the limits are respectively monotone increasing and monotone decreasing, by applying Lebesgue's Theorem, we deduce (3.29). □

Proof of Theorem 3.1

It is a direct consequence of Proposition 3.1. As a matter of fact, consider u_{N-1} and the function

$$L_{N-1}(x) = \inf_{v\geq 0} \{c_{N-1}(v) + \Phi_N(g_N)(x+v)\}$$

We can refer to equation 3.2 with

$$\phi(v) = c_{N-1}(v),\ \psi(x) = \Phi_N(g_N)(x)$$

hence

$L_{N-1}(x)$ is convex, therefore u_{N-1} also.

By induction $u_n(x)$ is convex for any n. The property (3.28) follows immediately from (3.3) and application of Lemma 3.1. □

Proposition 3.2 implies additional properties for the optimal feedback, provided we further assume the production cost function is convex piecewise linear (property (3.10)) :

$$c_n(v) = c_n^0 v + (c_n^1 - c_n^0)(v - v_n^0)^+ + \dots + (c_n^K - c_n^{K-1})(v - v_n^{K-1})^+ \tag{3.31}$$

where $0 < c_n^0 \leq c_n^1 \leq \dots \leq c_n^K$

$$v_n^{-1} = 0 < v_n^0 < v_n^1 < \dots < v_n^{K-1} < v_n^K = +\infty$$

Without loss of generality we use the same index K for all functions $c_n(v)$, since we allow the coefficients c_n^j to be equal.

Next, we define the quantities (see 3.12 and 3.13)

$$y_n^k = \sup \{y \mid \Phi_{n+1}(u'^-_{n+1})(y) \leq - c_n^k\}, \quad k = 0, \dots, N \tag{3.32}$$

and

$$y_n^{-1} = +\infty \geq y_n^0 \geq y_n^1 \geq \dots \geq y_n^K. \tag{3.33}$$

We can then state as an immediate consequence of Proposition 3.2 :

Theorem 3.2

Assume (1.1), (1.5), (3.1), (3.31), then the optimal feedback $\hat{v}_n(x)$ is given by

$$\hat{v}_n(x) = \begin{cases} y_n^k - x & \text{for } y_n^k - v_n^k \leq x \leq y_n^k - v_n^{k-1} \\ v_n^{k-1} & \text{for } y_n^k - v_n^{k-1} \leq x \leq y_n^{k-1} - v_n^{k-1} \end{cases} \quad k = 0,\dots,K \tag{3.34}$$

and we have (for n = 0, ..., N-1)

$$u'^-_n(x) = f'^-_n(x) + \begin{cases} - c_n^k & \text{for } x \in (y_n^k - v_n^k,\ y_n^k - v_n^{k-1}) \\ \Phi_{n+1}(u'^-_{n+1})(x + v_n^{k-1}) & \text{for } x \in (y_n^k - v_n^{k-1}, y_n^{k-1} - v_n^{k-1}] \end{cases} \tag{3.35}$$

To proceed with the derivation of a monotonicity property for the optimal feedback with respect to demand, we need to introduce the concept of stochastic dominance.

(3.36) Let ξ_1 and ξ_2 be two random variables with probability distributions Φ_1 and Φ_2 and cumulative distributions $F_1(.)$ and $F_2(.)$. We will say that ξ_2 dominates ξ_1, write $\xi_2 \gtrsim \xi_1$ or indifferently, that the density Φ_1 is stochastically smaller than the density Φ_2, write $\Phi_1 \subset \Phi_2$, if :

(i) $E\,\Psi(\xi_1) \le E\,\Psi(\xi_2)$
for any Ψ non decreasing real valued function such that $\psi(\xi_1)$ and $\Psi(\xi_2)$ are integrable, or equivalently,
(ii) $F_1(x) \ge F_2(x)$ for all x.

Conditions (i) and (ii) were shown to be equivalent by Veinott [1965-2, theorem 3] and Lehmann [1955]. This concept of stochastic dominance was first introduced by Karlin [1960]. For further discussion on the properties of stochastic dominance and related issues consult Veinott [1965-2] and Hammond [1974]. See also Bawa [1982]

From condition (ii) ξ_2 dominates ξ_1 when demands based on Φ_1 have a larger probability of taking smaller values than those based on the density Φ_2.

Then we can state the following monotonicity property.

Theorem 3.3

Under the assumptions of Theorem 3.2, and given two sequences of demand functions : $\xi_1, \ldots, \xi_N$ and $\xi_1^*, \ldots, \xi_N^*$ such that :

(3.37) $$\xi_i \lesssim \xi_i^*, \ \forall i = 1, \ldots, N,$$

the optimal feedbacks $v_n(x)$ and $v_n^*(x)$ satisfy the relation

(3.38) $$v_n(x) \le v_n^*(x), \ \forall x, \ \forall n = 0, \ldots, N-1$$

Proof

It is a consequence of Corollary 3.1, provided the following inequality is satisfied :

(3.39) $$\Phi_{n+1}(u_{n+1}^{*,'-})(x) \le \Phi_{n+1}(u_{n+1}^{'-})(x), \ \forall x, \ n = 0, \ldots, N-1$$

We have

$$u_N^{*,'-} = u_N^{'-} = g_N^{'-}$$

The function $g \to g_N^{'-}(x-y)$ (where x is fixed) is monotone decreasing hence by (3.37) for i = N,

$$E\, g_N^{'-}(x - \xi_N) \ge E\, g_N^{'-}(x - \xi_N^*)$$

and thus (3.39) is satisfied for n = N-1.

Assume that (3.39) holds for n and let us prove it for n-1. Applying property (3.19) we have

(3.40) $$u_n^{*,'-}(x) \le u_n^{'-}(x).$$

Since $u_n^{*,'-}(x)$ is increasing

$$E\, u_n^{*,'-}(x - \xi_n^*) \le E\, u_n^{*,'-}(x - \xi_n)$$
$$\le E\, u_n^{'-}(x - \xi_n)$$

which proves (3.39) at n-1, and completes the proof of Theorem 3.3. □

Remark 3.1

Convex piecewise linearity of $c_n(v)$, property (3.31), is required only to apply (3.19). □

Remark 3.2

The result of Theorem 3.3 bears similarities with that of Lemma 2.1 in Chapter II. □

III - 3. DETERMINISTIC CASE

It is interesting at this stage to drop uncertainty in order to compare the approach of dynamic programming developed in this chapter, with the approach relying on the necessary conditions for optimality adopted in Chapter II.

The next result completes Proposition 3.1.

Lemma 3.2

The left and right derivatives of L(x), as defined in (3.2), satisfy the properties

(3.41) $$L'^-(x) \geq \psi'^-(x + \hat{v}(x))$$

(3.42) $$L'^+(x) \leq \psi'^+(x + \hat{v}(x))$$

Proof

Indeed, we have

$$\frac{L(x) - L(x-h)}{h} \geq \frac{\phi(\hat{v}(x)) + \psi(x+\hat{v}(x)) - \phi(\hat{v}(x)) - \psi(x-h+\hat{v}(x))}{h}$$

from which (3.41) follows immediately. A similar approach leads to (3.42). □

Remark 3.3

If ψ is differentiable, then L is differentiable with

(3.43) $$L'(x) = \psi'(x + \hat{v}(x)).$$

This property holds even if $\hat{v}(x)$ is not unique (any point of minimum is admissible), but of course the expression to the right hand side of (3.43) is uniquely defined.□

Remark 3.4

In the special case of Proposition 3.2, where we were able to explicit $L'^-(x)$ (cf. (3.16), we note that :

$$L'^-(x) = \psi'^-(x+\hat{v}(x)) \text{ on } (y_k - v_{k-1}, y_{k-1}-v_{k-1}]$$

However, on $(y_k - v_k, y_k - v_{k-1}]$ we have

$$\psi'^-(x+\hat{v}(x)) = \psi'^-(y_k) \leq - \phi_k = L'^-(x)$$

and strict inequality may obtain if $\psi'^-(y_k) < \psi'^+(y_k)$. □

The dynamic programming approach applied to the general convex cost case, leads to the result of Theorem 3.1. If there is no more uncertainty on demand, then

(3.44) $\Phi_{n+1}(z)(x) = z(x-\xi_{n+1}),\ n = 0, \ldots, N-1.$

where $\xi_1, \ldots, \xi_N$ is a given sequence of positive numbers (demand) and, the terminal value function for inventory may be set to zero :

(3.45) $g_N(x) = 0$

We show now that we can retrieve the results of theorem 4.1 in Chapter II from theorem 3.1 of this chapter and related lemmas.

The feedback $\hat{v}_n(x)$ satisfies the relations

(3.46) $c_n'^{+}(\hat{v}_n(x)) + u_{n+1}'^{+}(x + \hat{v}_n(x) - \xi_{n+1}) \geq 0$

(3.47) $c_n'^{-}(\hat{v}_n(x)) + u_{n+1}'^{-}(x + \hat{v}_n(x) - \xi_{n+1}) \leq 0$ if $\hat{v}_n(x) > 0.$

Moreover by the equation of dynamic programming and Lemma 3.2, we get

(3.48) $u_n'^{-}(x) \geq f_n'^{-}(x) + u_{n+1}'^{-}(x + \hat{v}_n(x) - \xi_{n+1})$

(3.49) $u_n'^{+}(x) \leq f_n'^{+}(x) + u_{n+1}'^{+}(x + \hat{v}_n(x) - \xi_{n+1})$

Applying these relations for $x = \hat{y}_n$, $\hat{v}_n(x) = \hat{v}_n$, $x + \hat{v}_n(x) - \xi_{n+1} = \hat{y}_{n+1}$, we obtain

(3.50) $$\begin{cases} c_n'^{+}(\hat{v}_n) + u_{n+1}'^{+}(\hat{y}_{n+1}) \geq 0 \\ c_n'^{-}(\hat{v}_n) + u_{n+1}'^{-}(\hat{y}_{n+1}) \leq 0 \text{ if } \hat{v}_n > 0 \end{cases}$$

(3.51) $$\begin{cases} u_n'^{-}(\hat{y}_n) \geq f_n'^{-}(\hat{y}_n) + u_{n+1}'^{-}(\hat{y}_{n+1}) \\ u_n'^{+}(\hat{y}_n) \leq f_n'^{+}(\hat{y}_n) + u_{n+1}'^{+}(\hat{y}_{n+1}) \end{cases}$$

Adding up relations (3.51) for n running from k+1 to ℓ , $k < \ell < N$, we deduce :

(3.52) $$u_{k+1}'^{-}(\hat{y}_{k+1}) \geq \sum_{j=k+1}^{\ell} f_j'^{-}(\hat{y}_j) + u_{\ell+1}'^{-}(\hat{y}_{\ell+1})$$

(3.53) $$u_{k+1}'^{+}(\hat{y}_{k+1}) \leq \sum_{j=k+1}^{\ell} f_j'^{+}(\hat{y}_j) + u_{\ell+1}'^{+}(\hat{y}_{\ell+1})$$

and using relations (3.50) it follows :

(3.54) $$\begin{cases} \text{if } \hat{v}_k > 0,\ 0 \leq k < \ell < N, \text{ then} \\ c_k'^{-}(\hat{v}_k) + \sum_{j=k+1}^{\ell} f_j'^{-}(\hat{y}_j) \leq - u_{\ell+1}'^{-}(\hat{y}_{\ell+1}) \\ \qquad \leq c_\ell'^{+}(\hat{v}_\ell) + u_{\ell+1}'^{+}(\hat{y}_{\ell+1}) - u_{\ell+1}'^{-}(\hat{y}_{\ell+1}) \end{cases}$$

This relation does not compare exactly with relation (4.6) in Chapter II, where the term $[u_{\ell+1}'^{+}(\hat{y}_{\ell+1}) - u_{\ell+1}'^{-}(\hat{y}_{\ell+1})]$ in the right hand side is absent.

Note that when applying the first inequality in (3.54) for $\ell = N-1$, and using $u_N = 0$, we obtain the first inequality of (4.7) in Chapter II.

However, the term $[u'^{+}_{\ell+1}(\hat{y}_{\ell+1}) - u'^{-}_{\ell+1}(\hat{y}_{\ell+1})]$ can be removed from (3.54) once we notice that : $\hat{v}_0, \ldots, \hat{v}_\ell$ is optimal for the control problem

$$(3.55) \quad \begin{cases} \sum_{j=0}^{\ell} c_j(v_j) + f_j(y_j) \\ y_{j+1} = y_j + v_j - \xi_{j+1}, \; v_j \geq 0 \\ y_0 = x \end{cases}$$

and provided we impose the final constraint $y_{\ell+1} = \hat{y}_{\ell+1}$.

Since we are in the framework of convex optimization, we can take care of this additional constraint by introducing a Lagrange multiplier. Therefore, there exists a convenient scalar μ such that $\hat{v}_0, \ldots \hat{v}_\ell$ is optimal for the control problem

$$(3.56) \qquad \sum_{j=0}^{\ell} c_j(v_j) + f_j(y_j) + \mu y_{\ell+1}$$

If we treat that problem through dynamic programming we obtain the usual relations with the final function

$$u_{\ell+1}(x) = \mu x$$

for which $u'^{+}_{\ell+1} = u'^{-}_{\ell+1}$, hence the desired result.

Similarly we have

$$- u'^{+}_{\ell+1}(\hat{y}_{\ell+1}) \leq c'^{+}_k(\hat{v}_k) + \sum_{j=k+1}^{\ell} f'^{+}_j(\hat{y}_j)$$

and if $\hat{v}_\ell > 0$

$$c'^{-}_\ell(\hat{v}_\ell) \leq - u'^{-}_{\ell+1}(\hat{y}_{\ell+1})$$

$$\leq c'^{+}_k(\hat{v}_k) + \sum_{j=k+1}^{\ell} f'^{+}_j(\hat{y}_j) + u'^{+}_{\ell+1}(\hat{y}_{\ell+1}) - u'^{-}_{\ell+1}(\hat{y}_{\ell+1})$$

and we proceed as above to derive the second inequality (4.7) in Chapter II.

Remark 3.5

The preceding reasoning is of course limited to the deterministic situation. No extension is possible to the stochastic case. □

Remark 3.6

If f_n for $n = 0, \ldots, N-1$ and g_N are differentiable, then u_n is also differentiable. This follows by induction from the relations (3.48), (3.49). This property carries over to the stochastic case. Note that in the deterministic case when there is differentiability, by setting

$$(3.57) \qquad p_n = - u'_{n+1}(\hat{y}_{n+1})$$

we retrieve the maximum principle derived in § VI.2 of Chapter II, for this problem. □

III - 4. DETERMINING BOUNDS UNDER STATIONARITY ASSUMPTIONS

Under stationarity assumptions, it is possible to determine upper and lower bounds on the first period production decision and the cost function. We suppose the conditions of Theorem 3.2 are met, together with the following stationarity hypotheses :

$$(3.58)\quad \begin{cases} f_n(x) = f(x) \text{ belongs to } C_1, \text{ convex, minimum at } 0,\ f(x) = f^+x,\ x \geq 0, \\ c_n(v) = c(v) = c^0 v + (c^1-c^0)(v-v^0)^+ + \dots + (c^K-c^{K-1})(v-v^{K-1})^+ \\ 0 < c^0 \leq c^1 \leq \dots \leq c^K \\ v^{-1} = 0 < v^0 < \dots < v^{K-1} < v^K = +\infty \end{cases}$$

$$(3.59)\quad \begin{cases} \xi_1, \dots, \xi_N \text{ are identically distributed} \\ \Phi(z)(x) = E\, z(x-\xi)\ ,\ E\,\xi^2 < \infty\ ,\quad \xi \geq 0 \end{cases}$$

We start with some preliminary results for the one period problem.

First, consider the operator :

$$(3.60)\qquad T(z)(x) = f(x) + \operatorname*{Inf}_{v\geq 0} \{c(v) + \Phi(z)(x+v)\}.$$

Since we may have to consider functions with quadratic growth, we introduce more notation :

$$C_2 = \{z \mid z \text{ continuous},\ \sup \frac{|z(x)|}{1+|x|^2} = ||z|| < \infty\}$$

$$C_2^+ = \{z \in C_2,\ z \geq 0\}$$

Lemma 3.3

The operator T maps C_2^+ into itself.

Proof

Clearly the infimum is attained at a point $\hat{v}(x)$ such that

$$(3.61)\qquad c^0\hat{v}(x) \leq ||z||\ (1 + 2|x|^2 + 2\,E\,\xi^2)$$

Let us check that T(z) is continuous. Denoting $\hat{v}_n = \hat{v}(x_n)$, $\hat{v} = \hat{v}(x)$, if $x_n \to x$, it follows from (3.61) that $\hat{v}_n$ remains bounded. Extracting a subsequence converging to v^* , we have

$$T(z)(x_n) \to f(x) + c(v^*) + \Phi(z)(x+v^*)$$

and since

$$T(z)(x_n) \leq f(x) + c(v) + \Phi(z)(x_n+v) \qquad \forall v \geq 0$$

it follows that

$$f(x) + c(v^*) + \Phi(z)(x+v^*) = T(z)(x).$$

The fact that T(z) has quadratic growth and is positive is clear form the formula (3.60). □

If z is convex then the results of Proposition 3.1 apply, taking into account Lemma 3.1.

Lemma 3.4

Let z be the function

$$(3.62) \qquad z = \begin{cases} - c_0 x & x \leq 0 \\ \dfrac{f^+ x^2}{2q} & x \geq 0 \end{cases}$$

where $q = E\,\xi$, then we have :

$$(3.63) \qquad T(z)'^-(x) \leq z'^-(x)$$

Proof

We have

$$z'^-(x) = \begin{cases} - c_0 & \text{for } x \leq 0 \\ \dfrac{f^+ x}{q} & \text{for } x > 0 \end{cases}$$

and

$$E\, z'^-(x-\xi) = - c_0\, E\chi_{\xi \geq x} + \frac{f^+}{q} E(x-\xi)\chi_{\xi < x}$$

where χ_A denotes the characteristic function of the set A. Since $\xi \geq 0$, it follows that

$$(3.64) \qquad E\, z'^-(x-\xi) = \begin{cases} -c_0 \ , & x \leq 0 \\ -c_0\, E\chi_{\xi \geq x} + \dfrac{f^+}{q} E(x-\xi)\chi_{\xi < x} & , x > 0 \end{cases}$$

Considering the notation of Proposition 3.1, we obtain

$$\psi(x) = Ez(x-\xi)$$

Since $\psi'^-(x) = - c_0$ for $x \leq 0$ and $\psi'^-(x) > - c_0$ for $x > 0$, it follows from the definition (3.11) that $y_0 = 0$.

Applying (3.16) we have

$$(T(z))'^-(x) = f'^-(x) - c_0 \text{ for } (-v_0, 0]$$

and by monotonicity of f'^-

$$(T(z))'^-(x) \leq f'^-(-v_0) - c_0 \text{ for } x < - v_0$$

Therefore (3.63) holds for $x \leq 0$, since $f'^-(x) \leq 0$ for $x \leq 0$. For $x > 0$, we deduce from (3.64) that

$$Ez'^-(x-\xi) \le \frac{f^+}{q} E(x-\xi)$$
$$= \frac{f^+}{q} x - f^+$$

Noting that $v_{-1} = 0$, $y_{-1} = \infty$, (3.16) implies that :

$$T(z)'^-(x) = f'^-(x) + \psi'^-(x) \quad \text{for } x > 0$$
$$= \frac{f^+}{q} x$$

and (3.63) holds for $x > 0$. □

III.4.1. BOUNDS FROM BELOW

We shall use the preceding results to derive an estimate from below for the first feedback $\hat{v}_0(x)$. In fact, since we shall only consider a rolling horizon, it is convenient to use the notation $\hat{v}_0(x\ ;\ N)$.

Subsequently we shall need to refer to the truncated control problem with horizon $K \le N$, and the final salvage cost $z(x)$, defined by (3.62) with the restriction that

(3.65) $$g_N'^-(x) \le z'^-(x).$$

Considering the control problem with horizon K and final cost $z(x)$, the corresponding dynamic programming relations are defined as follows :

(3.66) $$\begin{cases} \tilde{u}_K(x) = z(x) \\ \tilde{u}_n(x) = f(x) + \inf\limits_{v\ge 0} \{c(v) + \Phi(\tilde{u}_{n+1})(x+v)\} \\ n = 0, \ldots, K-1 \end{cases}$$

We shall denote by $\tilde{v}_0(x\ ;\ K)$ the corresponding first feedback.

Theorem 3.4

Assume (3.58), (3.59), (3.65). Then the following property holds

(3.67) $$\hat{v}_0(x\ ;\ N) \ge \tilde{v}_0(x\ ;\ N) \ge \tilde{v}_0(x\ ;\ N-1) \ldots \ge \tilde{v}_0(x\ ;\ 1)$$

Proof

We notice first that

(3.68) $$z'^-(x) \ge u_n'^-(x), \quad \forall n = 0, \ldots, N$$

Indeed (3.68) is satisfied for $n = N$, by the assumption (3.65). Assume that :

$$z'^-(x) \ge u_{n+1}'^-(x)$$

and note that

$$u_n(x) = T(u_{n+1})(x)$$

Since also

$$\Phi(z'^-)(x) \ge \Phi(u_{n+1}'^-)(x)$$

it follows from Proposition 3.2 (see (3.19)) that

$$(T(z))'^{-}(x) \geq (T(u_{n+1}))'^{-}(x) = u_n'^{-}(x)$$

and by (3.63) we deduce (3.68).

Therefore, by (3.66)

$$z'^{-}(x) = \tilde{u}_K'^{-}(x) \geq u_K'^{-}(x)$$

$$\tilde{u}_{K-1}'^{-}(x) = (T(\tilde{u}_K))'^{-}(x) \geq (T(u_K))'^{-}(x) = u_{K-1}'^{-}(x)$$

and also

$$\tilde{u}_{K-1}'^{-}(x) \leq \tilde{u}_K'^{-}(x)$$

Similarly

$$\tilde{u}_{K-2}'^{-}(x) = (T\ \tilde{u}_{K-1})'^{-}(x) \leq (T\ \tilde{u}_K)'^{-}(x) = \tilde{u}_{K-1}'^{-}(x)$$

$$\tilde{u}_{K-2}'^{-}(x) = (T\ \tilde{u}_{K-1})'^{-}(x) \geq (T\ u_{K-1})'^{-}(x) = u_{K-2}'^{-}(x).$$

Collecting results we can write

$$(3.69)\qquad \begin{cases} u_0'^{-}(x) \leq \tilde{u}_0'^{-}(x) \leq \tilde{u}_1'^{-}(x) \ \dots \leq \tilde{u}_K'^{-}(x). \\ \qquad u_n'^{-}(x) \leq \tilde{u}_n'^{-}(x), \quad n = 0, \dots, K \end{cases}$$

We notice that

$$(3.70)\qquad \begin{cases} \tilde{v}_0(x\ ;\ K-1) = \tilde{v}_1(x\ ;\ K) \\ \vdots \\ \tilde{v}_0(x\ ;\ 1) = \tilde{v}_{K-1}(x\ ;\ K) \end{cases}$$

Since

$$\tilde{u}_1'^{-}(x) \leq \tilde{u}_2'^{-}(x)$$

and

$$\tilde{u}_0 = T(\tilde{u}_1), \quad \tilde{u}_1 = T(\tilde{u}_2)$$

it follows from Corollary 3.1 that

$$\tilde{v}_0(x\ ;\ K) \geq \tilde{v}_1(x\ ;\ K)$$

hence by (3.70)

$$\tilde{v}_0(x\ ;\ K) \geq \tilde{v}_0(x\ ;\ K-1)$$

By induction we check that

$$(3.71)\qquad \tilde{v}_0(x\ ;\ K) \geq \tilde{v}_0(x\ ;\ K-1) \ \dots \geq \tilde{v}_0(x\ ;\ 1)$$

Now since, $u_1'^{-}(x) \leq \tilde{u}_1'^{-}(x)$, it also implies that $\hat{v}_0(x\ ;\ N) \geq \tilde{v}_0(x\ ;\ K)$.

Given that $K \leq N$ and the monotonicity property (3.71), then (3.66) follows. □

Remark 3.7

The main thrust of Theorem 3.4 is to provide bounds from below for the first decision $\hat{v}_0(x\ ;\ N)$. These bounds can be sharpened while increasing the complexity of the problem to solve. □

III.4.2. BOUNDS FROM ABOVE

It is much easier to obtain bounds from above on the first feedback $\hat{v}_0(x\ ;\ N)$. Indeed we have

(3.72) $$\hat{v}_0(x\ ;\ N) \leq \frac{1}{c_0}\ \Phi(u_1)(x)$$

and

(3.73) $$u_1 = T^{N-1}(g_N)$$

Now from (3.60) we also have

(3.74) $$\begin{cases} T(z)(x) \leq f(x) + \Phi(z)(x) \\ \qquad\qquad = \tilde{T}(z)(x) \end{cases}$$

therefore

$$T^{N-1}(g_N) \leq T^{N-2}\ \tilde{T}(g_N) \leq T^{N-3}\ \tilde{T}^2(g_N) \leq \ldots \leq \tilde{T}^{N-1}(g_N)$$

hence setting

(3.75) $$\frac{1}{c_0}\ \Phi\ T^{N-k}\ \tilde{T}^{k-1}(g_N)(x) = v_0^*(x\ ;\ N-k+1) \quad , \quad k = 1, \ldots, N$$

we obtain

(3.76) $$\hat{v}_0(x\ ;\ N) \leq v_0^*(x\ ;\ N) \leq v_0^*(x\ ;\ N-1) \leq\ \ldots \leq v_0^*(x\ ;\ 1)$$

which complements the result (3.67).

We can use the bounds (3.67) and (3.76) to derive a bound on the cost function .

Let us set

(3.77) $$\begin{cases} \tilde{u}_0(x\ ;\ L) = \text{best expected cost taking into account that we force the} \\ \text{first decision to be } \tilde{v}_0(x\ ;\ L). \end{cases}$$

Analytically $\tilde{u}_0$ is characterized by

(3.78) $$\tilde{u}_0(x\ ;\ L) = c(\tilde{v}_0(x\ ;\ L)) + f(x) + \Phi(u_1)(x + \tilde{v}_0(x\ ;\ L)).$$

Consider now the optimal control

$$\hat{V} = \hat{v}_0(x),\ \hat{v}_1\ \ldots\ \hat{v}_{N-1} \quad (\text{cf. § 1.3})$$

and $\tilde{V}$ which differs from $\hat{V}$ only by the first element :

$$\tilde{V} = \tilde{v}_0(x\ ;\ L)\ \ ;\hat{v}_1 + \hat{v}_0 - \tilde{v}_0,\ \hat{v}_2,\ \ldots,\ \hat{v}_{N-1}.$$

$\tilde{V}$ is admissible since $\hat{v}_0 - \tilde{v}_0$ is positive and deterministic. Clearly the corresponding trajectory is

$$\tilde{y}_0 = x,\ \tilde{y}_1 = \hat{y}_1 - (\hat{v}_0 - \tilde{v}_0),\ \tilde{y}_2 = \hat{y}_2, \dots,\ \tilde{y}_N = \hat{y}_N.$$

We can assert that

$$\begin{aligned}\tilde{u}_0(x\ ;\ L) &\le J_0(x\ ;\ \tilde{V})\\ &= J_0(x\ ;\ \hat{V}) + c(\tilde{v}_0) - c(\hat{v}_0)\\ &+ E(c(\hat{v}_1 + \hat{v}_0 - \tilde{v}_0) - c(\hat{v}_1)) + E(f(\hat{y}_1 - (\hat{v}_0 - \tilde{v}_0)) - f(\hat{y}_1))\\ &= u_0(x) + (\hat{v}_0 - \tilde{v}_0)\ E(c'^-(\hat{v}_1 + \hat{v}_0 - \tilde{v}_0) - c'^+(\tilde{v}_0))\\ &+ E(f(x + \tilde{v}_0 - \xi) - f(x + \hat{v}_0 - \xi)).\end{aligned}$$

Noting that

$$c'^-(v) \le c^K \qquad c'^+(v) \ge c^0$$

we deduce

$$(3.79)\quad \left\{\begin{aligned}\tilde{u}_0(x\ ;\ L) - u_0(x) &\le (c^K - c^0)(\hat{v}_0 - \tilde{v}_0) + E(f(x + \tilde{v}_0 - \xi) - f(x + \hat{v}_0 - \xi))\\ &\le \operatorname*{Sup}_{\tilde{v}_0(x;L) \le v \le v_0^*(x;L)} [(c^K - c^0)(v - \tilde{v}_0(x\ ;\ L))\\ &\qquad + \Phi(f)(x + \tilde{v}_0(x\ ;\ L))\\ &\qquad - \Phi(f)(x+v)]\\ &= B_L\end{aligned}\right.$$

Let $L_1 < L_2$, note that

$$\tilde{v}_0(x\ ;\ L_1) \le \tilde{v}_0(x\ ;\ L_2)$$
$$v_0^*(x\ ;\ L_1) \ge v_0^*(x\ ;\ L_2)$$

hence

$$\begin{aligned}&B_{L_1} - B_{L_2} \ge (c^K - c^0)(\tilde{v}_0(x\ ;\ L_2) - \tilde{v}_0(x\ ;\ L_1))\\ &+ \Phi(f)(x + \tilde{v}_0(x\ ;\ L_1)) - \Phi(f)(x + \tilde{v}_0(x\ ;\ L_2))\\ &\ge (\tilde{v}_0(x\ ;\ L_2) - \tilde{v}_0(x\ ;\ L_1))\ \ [c^K - c^0 - E\ f'^+(x + \tilde{v}_0(L_2) - \xi)]\\ &\ge (\tilde{v}_0(x\ ;\ L_2) - \tilde{v}_0(x\ ;\ L_1))\ \ [c^K - c^0 - f^+]\\ &\ge 0 \text{ if } c^K - c^0 - f^+ \ge 0.\end{aligned}$$

We can summarize the above results in the following theorem.

Theorem 3.5

Assume (3.58), (3.59), (3.65). The first optimal decision $\hat{v}_0(x\ ;\ N)$ satisfies the inequalities (3.76). Moreover, if we define $\tilde{u}_0(x\ ;\ L)$ by (3.77) , then we have the inequality

(3.80) $$0 \le \tilde{u}_0(x\ ;\ L) - u_0(x) \le B_L(x)$$

where $B_L(x)$ has been defined in (3.79). If we assume that

(3.81) $$c^K - c^0 - f^+ \ge 0$$

then B_L decreases as L increases.

The interpretation of this result is given in Section VII. □

IV - PRODUCTION PLANNING MODELS WITH LOST SALES

IV - 1. SETTING OF THE PROBLEM

Several formulations may be adopted depending on the delivery delay of an order and the time of occurence of the demand in any period (beginning or end of any period).
Two models are subsequently considered.

In model A, we assume as usual that the order v_k is placed at time k, and that the quantity v_k will be delivered at time k+1 (one period delivery lag). The demand ξ_{k+1} materializes at k+1. Therefore during the period (k,k+1) the inventory level is y_k. At time k+1, just before demand occurs, the total supply of the firm is y_k+v_k. If $y_k+v_k \ge \xi_{k+1}$ the firm can meet the demand, and the remaining inventory is $y_{k+1}+v_k-\xi_{k+1}$. If $y_k+v_k < \xi_{k+1}$, part of the demand, $\xi_{k+1}-y_k-v_k$, cannot be satisfied immediatly and is completely lost. Then, the firm will start the next period with zero inventory.

MODEL A

(4.1) $$\begin{cases} y_{k+1} = (y_k + v_k - \xi_{k+1})^+, & k = n\ ,\ \dots,\ N-1 \\ y_n = x \end{cases}$$

(4.2) $$J_n(x\ ;\ V) = E \sum_{k=n}^{N-1} [c_k(v_k) + f_k(y_k) + h_k((y_k + v_k - \xi_{k+1})^-)]$$

In model B, we still assume that there is a delivery delay of one period, but the demand ξ_{k+1} materializes at time k instead of k+1 (i.e. at the beginning of the period). When demand occurs the firm supply is y_k and the same rationing scheme as in model A applies. In other words, model A corresponds to model B with immediate delivery.

MODEL B

(4.3) $$\begin{cases} y_{k+1} = v_k + (y_k - \xi_{k+1})^+, & k = n,\ \dots,\ N-1 \\ y_n = x \end{cases}$$

(4.4) $$J_n(x\ ;\ V) = E \sum_{k=n}^{N-1} [c_k(v_k) + f_k((y_k + \xi_{k+1})^+) + h_k((y_k - \xi_{k+1})^-)]$$

For both models the cost structure has the following properties, for $k = 0, \ldots, N-1$

(4.5)

(i) the production cost function :

$c_k(v) : R^+ \to R^+$ is lower semi continuous, with

$c_k(v) \geq \bar{c}_k\ v \quad \forall v \geq 1$

(ii) the storage cost function, $f_k(x)$, and the shortage cost function, $h_k(x)$:

$f_k(x),\ h_k(x) : R^+ \to R^+$ are uniformly continuous, with

$f_k(x) \leq \bar{f}_k(1+x)$, and

$h_k(x) \leq \bar{h}_k(1+x)$

Moreover we assume

(4.6) $\xi_1, \ldots, \xi_N$ are independent random variables and $\xi_k \geq 0$, $E\xi_k < \infty$.

The dynamic programming equations for both models are :

MODEL A

(4.7)
$$\begin{cases} u_n(x) = f_n(x) + \operatorname*{Inf}_{v \leq 0} [c_n(v) + E\, h_n((x + v - \xi_{n+1})^-) + \\ \qquad + E\, u_{n+1}((x + v - \xi_{n+1})^+)] \\ u_N(x) = 0 \end{cases}$$

MODEL B

(4.8)
$$\begin{cases} u_n(x) = E[f_n((x - \xi_{n+1})^+) + h_n((x - \xi_{n+1})^-)] + \\ \qquad + \operatorname*{Inf}_{v \geq 0} [c_n(v) + E\, u_{n+1}(v + (x - \xi_{n+1})^+)] \\ u_N(x) = 0 \end{cases}$$

These equations can be studied as in § I.2, and we obtain existence results which are similar to those of Theorem 1.1.

However, the interesting questions arise when we want to derive explicit forms for the feedbacks. This is the topic of the next two sections.

IV - 2. OPTIMAL PRODUCTION POLICY FOR MODEL A

Let us assume that :

(4.9) $c_n(v) = K_n\, \chi_{v>0} + c_n\, v$ where $K_n \geq 0$, K_n decreasing, $c_n \geq 0$

(4.10) $$f_n(x),\ h_n(x) \text{ are convex, non decreasing}$$

(4.11) $$\begin{cases} c_n < E\, h_n'^{+}(\xi_{n+1}),\ n = 0, \ldots, N-1 \\ c_{n+1} \le f_{n+1}'^{+}(0) + h_n'^{+}(0) \end{cases}$$

Then the optimal feedback is of the (S,s) type policy : (see SHREVE mentioned in Bertsekas [1976, p. 105]).

Theorem 4.1

Assume (4.5), (4.6) and (4.9), (4.10), (4.11), then there exists a sequence s_n, S_n $n = 0, \ldots, N-1$, with $s_n \le S_n$ such that the feedback

(4.12) $$\hat{v}_n(x) = \begin{cases} S_n - x & \text{for } x \le s_n \\ 0 & \text{for } x > s_n \end{cases}$$

is an optimal feedback.

Proof

We write (4.7) as follows

(4.13) $$\begin{cases} u_n(x) = f_n(x) - c_n x + \operatorname*{Inf}_{y \ge x} [K_n \chi_{y>x} + c_n y + E\, h_n((y - \xi_{n+1})^-) \\ \qquad + E\, u_{n+1}((y - \xi_{n+1})^+)]. \end{cases}$$

and define the functions

(4.14) $$H_n(x) = h_n(x^-) + u_{n+1}(x^+)$$

(4.15) $$Z_n(x) = c_n x + \Phi_{n+1}(H_n)(x)$$

(4.16) $$G_n(x) = \operatorname*{Inf}_{y \ge x} [K_n \chi_{y>x} + Z_n(y)]$$

According to Proposition 2.2 everything amounts to proving that

(4.17) $$\begin{cases} Z_n(x) \text{ continuous } K_n\text{-convex,} \\ Z_n(x) \to +\infty \text{ as } |x| \to \infty. \end{cases}$$

Continuity follows from the general theory which tells that $u_n \in C_1$, hence H_n and Z_n also by formulas (4.14) and (4.15). Next we have

$$H_n(x) \ge h_n(x^-)$$

hence

$$Z_n(x) \ge c_n x + E\, h_n((x - \xi_{n+1})^-).$$

Consider $x \le 0$, and note that

$$h_n((x - \xi_{n+1})^-) - h_n(\xi_{n+1}) \ge - h_n'^{+}(\xi_{n+1}) x$$

hence

$$Z_n(x) \geq - E\, h_n(\xi_{n+1}) - x[E\, h_n'^{+}(\xi_{n+1}) - c_n] \to \infty$$

as $x \to -\infty$, by (4.11).

It remains to prove the K_n-convexity of Z_n.

Suppose we know that u_{n+1} is K_{n+1}-convex (hence K_n-convex), it does not follow that

(4.18) $H_n(x)$ is K_n-convex

from which it will follow that Z_n is K_n-convex, hence also G_n by Proposition 2.2. From (4.13) it will then follow that u_n is K_n-convex and the induction can proceed. Therefore everything amounts to proving (4.18). We shall prove that

$$(4.19)\quad \begin{cases} K_{n+1} + H_n(y+z) \geq H_n(y) + z \dfrac{H_n(y) - H_n(y-b)}{b} \\ \forall z \geq 0,\ b > 0, z \end{cases}$$

We consider four different cases

Case a : $0 \leq y-b < y \leq y+z$

then one has

$$H_n(y+z) = h_n(0) + u_{n+1}(y+z)$$

$$H_n(y) = h_n(0) + u_{n+1}(y)$$

$$H_n(y-b) = h_n(0) + u_{n+1}(y-b)$$

and (4.19) is a consequence of the K_{n+1}-convexity of u_{n+1}.

Case b : $y-b < y \leq y+z \leq 0$

then

$$H_n(y+z) = h_n(-y-z) + u_{n+1}(0)$$

$$H_n(y) = h_n(-y) + u_{n+1}(0)$$

$$H_n(y-b) = h_n(-(y-b)) + u_{n+1}(0)$$

and (4.19) follows from the convexity of $h_n(x^-)$ ([1])

Case c : $y-b < y \leq 0 \leq y+z$

We have

$$H_n(y+z) = h_n(0) + u_{n+1}(y+z)$$

$$H_n(y) = h_n(-y) + u_{n+1}(0)$$

$$H_n(y-b) = h_n(-(y-b)) + u_{n+1}(0)$$

([1]) if g is convex and h is convex non decreasing, then h(g(x)) is convex.

and (4.19) amounts to

$$(4.20)\qquad \begin{cases} K_{n+1} + h_n(0) + u_{n+1}(y+z) \geq h_n(-y) + u_{n+1}(0) \\ \qquad + z\,\dfrac{h_n(-y) - h_n(-(y-b))}{b} \end{cases}$$

We use the following inequalities

$$h_n(0) - h_n(-y) \geq h_n'^{+}(-y)y$$

$$h_n(-y) - h_n(-(y-b)) \leq - h_n'^{+}(-y)b$$

therefore to prove (4.20) it is sufficient to prove that

$$(4.21)\qquad K_{n+1} + u_{n+1}(y+z) \geq u_{n+1}(0) - h_n'^{+}(-y)(y+z).$$

But from (4.13)

$$u_{n+1}(x) = f_{n+1}(x) - c_{n+1}\, x + G_{n+1}(x)$$

$$= f_{n+1}(x) - c_{n+1}\, x + \begin{cases} Z_{n+1}(s_{n+1}) & , \text{ if } x \leq s_{n+1} \\ Z_{n+1}(x) & , \text{ if } x > s_{n+1} \end{cases}$$

Therefore if $\text{Max}(0, s_{n+1}) \leq y+z$, we have to check that

$$K_{n+1} + f_{n+1}(y+z) - c_{n+1}(y+z) + Z_{n+1}(y+z)$$
$$\geq f_{n+1}(0) + Z_{n+1}(s_{n+1}) - h_n'^{+}(-y)(z+y)$$

Noting that

$$Z_{n+1}(s_{n+1}) = K_{n+1} + Z_{n+1}(S_{n+1})$$

and

$$Z_{n+1}(y+z) \geq Z_{n+1}(S_{n+1})$$

$$f_{n+1}(y+z) - f_{n+1}(0) + h_n'^{+}(-y)(z+y) - c_{n+1}(y+z)$$
$$\geq (f_{n+1}'^{+}(0) + h_n'^{+}(0) \; - c_{n+1})(y+z)$$

the desired result follows from (4.11).

If instead $0 \leq y+z \leq s_{n+1}$, we have to check that

$$K_{n+1} + f_{n+1}(y+z) - c_{n+1}(y+z) + Z_{n+1}(s_{n+1})$$
$$\geq f_{n+1}(0) + Z_{n+1}(s_{n+1}) - h_n'^{+}(z+y)$$

and the result again follows from (4.11).

<u>Case d</u> : $y-b < 0 < y \leq y+z$

We obtain

$$H_n(y+z) = h_n(0) + u_{n+1}(y+z)$$

$$H_n(y) = h_n(0) + u_{n+1}(y)$$

$$H_n(y-b) = h_n(-(y-b)) + u_{n+1}(0)$$

We have to check that

$$K_{n+1} + u_{n+1}(y+z) \geq u_{n+1}(y) + z\,\frac{u_{n+1}(y) - u_{n+1}(0) + h_n(0) - h_n(b-y)}{b} \tag{4.22}$$

We consider the two opposite situations (4.23) and (4.24).

$$\frac{u_{n+1}(y) - u_{n+1}(0)}{y} \geq \frac{u_{n+1}(y) - u_{n+1}(0) + h_n(0) - h_n(b-y)}{b} \tag{4.23}$$

Then it is sufficient to check

$$K_{n+1} + u_{n+1}(y+z) \geq u_{n+1}(y) + z\,\frac{u_{n+1}(y) - u_{n+1}(0)}{y}$$

which is a consequence of the K_{n+1} convexity of u_{n+1}.

If we now assume that :

$$\frac{u_{n+1}(y) - u_{n+1}(0)}{y} < \frac{u_{n+1}(y) - u_{n+1}(0) + h_n(0) - h_n(b-y)}{b} \tag{4.24}$$

which amounts to :

$$\frac{u_{n+1}(y) - u_{n+1}(0)}{y} < \frac{h_n(0) - h_n(b-y)}{b-y} \tag{4.25}$$

We deduce that

$$\left\{\begin{aligned} & u_{n+1}(y) + z\,\frac{u_{n+1}(y) - u_{n+1}(0) + h_n(0) - h_n(y-b)}{b} \\ & < u_{n+1}(0) + y\,\frac{h_n(0) - h_n(b-y)}{b-y} \\ & \qquad + \frac{z}{b}\,[h_n(0) - h_n(y-b) + \frac{y}{b-y}\,(h_n(0) - h_n(b-y))] \\ & < u_{n+1}(0) + (y+z)\,\frac{h_n(0) - h_n(b-y)}{b-y} \\ & < u_{n+1}(0) - (y+z)\,h_n'^{+}(0) \\ & \leq K_{n+1} + u_{n+1}(y+z) \end{aligned}\right. \tag{4.26}$$

which has been proved to check (4.21), by virtue of (4.11). This completes the proof of the desired result (4.18), hence also (4.12). □

IV - 3. OPTIMAL PRODUCTION POLICY FOR MODEL B

We do not know for model B if a feedback of the (S,s) type is optimal. In fact, it is much likely that it is not. We shall restrict here to the convex case.

Let us assume that :

(4.27) $c_n(v) = c_n\, v,\ c_n \geq 0$, which is equivalent to (4.9) with $K_n = 0$;

(4.28) $\begin{cases} f_n(x),\ h_n(x) \text{ convex, continuously differentiable ; } f_n'(0) > 0, \\ h_n'(0) > 0,\ f_n'(+\infty),\ h_n'(+\infty) < \infty. \end{cases}$

(4.29) The distribution law of ξ_n has a density $p_n(y)$ defined on $[0,\infty)$, which is a continuous function, $p_n(y) > 0,\ \forall y$, $\int_0^\infty y\, p_n(y)\, dy < \infty$.

then the optimal policy has the following properties (see Karlin and Scarf [1958])

Theorem 4.2

Assume (4.27), (4.28), (4.29), then for $n = 0, \ldots, N-1$, the functions u_n defined by (4.8) are continuously differentiable, strictly convex, such that

(4.30) $- h_n'(\infty) < u_n'(x) < \lim_{x\to\infty} u_n'(x) < \infty$ and positive.

Moreover there exists a unique minimum $\hat{v}_n(x)$ realizing the infimum at the right hand side of (4.8). The function $\hat{v}_n(x)$ is continuous, decreasing and

(4.31) $\hat{v}_n(x) = 0$ for $x \geq \Sigma_n$

The function $x + \hat{v}_n(x)$ is strictly increasing.

Proof

We proceed by induction. We have

(4.32) $u_{N-1}(x) = L_{N-1}(x)$

where we have set

(4.33) $$\begin{cases} L_n(x) = E\,[f_n((x - \xi_{n+1})^+) + h_n((x - \xi_{n+1})^-)] \\ \quad = \int_0^{x\vee 0} [f_n(x-y) + h_n(0)]\, p_{n+1}(y)dy \\ \qquad + \int_{x\vee 0}^{+\infty} [f_n(0) + h_n(y-x)]\, p_{n+1}(y)dy. \end{cases}$$

Thus :

(4.34) $$L_n'(x) = \begin{cases} -\int_0^\infty h_n'(y-x)\, p_{n+1}(y)dy & \text{for } x \leq 0 \\ \int_0^x f_n'(x-y)\, p_{n+1}(y)dy - \int_x^\infty h_n'(y-x)\, p_{n+1}(y)dy & \text{for } x \geq 0 \end{cases}$$

The function $L_n'(x)$ is continuous and strictly increasing. Indeed if $x_1 < x_2$

$$- h_n'(y - x_1) < - h_n'(y - x_2)$$

$$- \int_{x_1}^{\infty} h_n'(y - x_1)p_{n+1}(y)dy = - \int_{x_1}^{x_2} h_n'(y - x_1)p_{n+1}(y)dy$$

$$- \int_{x_2}^{\infty} h_n'(y - x_1)p_{n+1}(y)dy$$

$$< - \int_{x_2}^{\infty} h_n'(y - x_2)p_{n+1}(y)dy$$

and similar considerations obtain for $\int_0^x f_n'(x-y)p_{n+1}(y)dy$.

Therefore

$$L_n'(x_1) < L_n'(x_2)$$

hence L_n is strictly convex. Moreover

(4.35) $$- h_n'(0) < L_n'(x) < f_n'(+\infty)$$

(4.36) $$L_n'(x) \to f_n'(+\infty) \text{ as } x \to \infty$$

Since

$$\hat{v}_{N-1}(x) = 0,$$

we can take

(4.37) $$\Sigma_{N-1} = - \infty$$

and all the assertions of the theorem are satisfied for $n = N-1$. We assume that all the properties hold for $n+1$, and we shall prove them for n.

We define

(4.38) $$\begin{cases} \psi_n(x,v) = c_n\, v + u_{n+1}(v) \int_{x\vee 0}^{\infty} p_{n+1}(y)dy \\ \qquad + \int_0^{x\vee 0} u_{n+1}(x - v - y)p_{n+1}(y)dy \end{cases}$$

(4.39) $$\begin{cases} \theta_n(x,v) = \dfrac{\partial\psi_n}{\partial v} = c_n + u_{n+1}'(v) \int_{x\vee 0}^{\infty} p_{n+1}(y)dy \\ \qquad + \int_0^{x\vee 0} u_{n+1}'(x + v - y)p_{n+1}(y)dy. \end{cases}$$

It is clear that $\theta_n(x,v)$ is strictly increasing with respect to v, hence $\psi_n(x,v)$ is strictly convex with respect to v and $\psi_n(x,v) \to +\infty$ as $v \to \infty$. Therefore $\psi_n(x,v)$ has a unique minimum in v (for $v \geq 0$) denoted by $\hat{v}_n(x)$.

The function $\hat{v}_n(x)$ is continuous.

Let us next show that $\theta_n(x,v)$ is increasing with respect to x. Indeed let $x_1 < x_2$, then

$$\theta_n(x_2,v) - \theta_n(x_1,v) = - u'_{n+1}(v) \int_{x_1 \vee 0}^{x_2 \vee 0} p_{n+1}(y)dy$$

$$+ \int_0^{x_2 \vee 0} u'_{n+1}(x_2+v-y)p_{n+1}(y)dy - \int_0^{x_1 \vee 0} u'_{n+1}(x_1+v-y)p_{n+1}(y)dy$$

$$= \int_0^{x_1 \vee 0} (u'_{n+2}(x_2+v-y) - u'_{n+1}(x_1+v-y))p_{n+1}(y)dy$$

$$+ \int_{x_1 \vee 0}^{x_2 \vee 0} (u'_{n+1}(x_2+v-y) - u'_{n+1}(v))p_{n+1}(y)dy \geq 0.$$

The strict inequality holds if $x_2 > 0$. This implies that :

(4.40) $$\hat{v}_n(x_1) \geq \hat{v}_n(x_2)$$

As a matter of fact, if $\hat{v}_n(x_2) = 0$, there is nothing to prove. Let us assume that $\hat{v}_n(x_2) > 0$. Then $\hat{v}_n(x_2)$ satisfies

(4.41) $$\theta_n(x_2, \hat{v}_n(x_2)) = 0$$

But, necessarily $x_2 > 0$ (otherwise from (4.38), $\hat{v}_n(x_2) = 0$), and therefore, from the above derivations, we have

(4.42) $$\theta_n(x_1, \hat{v}_n(x_2)) < 0$$

But from (4.39) we check that

(4.43) $\theta_n(x_1,v) \to c_n + u'_{n+1}(+\infty)$ as $v \to \infty$, which is strictly > 0.

Therefore $\theta_n(x_1,v)$ vanishes between $\hat{v}_n(x_2)$ and $+\infty$, at a point which is necessarily $\hat{v}_n(x_1)$, hence (4.40). Since

$$\theta_n(x,v) \geq c_n + \int_0^{+\infty} u'_{n+1}(x-y)p_{n+1}(y)dy$$

which is strictly positive for x sufficiently large, we can assert that for x large enough $\hat{v}_n(x) = 0$. Since $\hat{v}_n(x)$ is a continuous non increasing, non negative function, which vanishes for x sufficiently large, there exists Σ_n such that

(4.44) $$\begin{cases} \hat{v}_n(x) > 0 & \text{for } x < \Sigma_n \\ \hat{v}_n(x) = 0 & \text{for } x \geq \Sigma_n \end{cases}$$

Let us now show that the function $x + \hat{v}_n(x) = w_n(x)$ is strictly increasing.

For $x < \Sigma_n$, $w_n(x)$ satisfies

(4.45) $$\chi_n(x, w_n(x)) = 0$$

where we have set

$$(4.46)\quad \begin{cases} \chi_n(x,w) = c_n + u'_{n+1}(w-x)\int_{x\vee 0}^{\infty} p_{n+1}(y)dy \\ \qquad + \int_0^{x\vee 0} u'_{n+1}(w-y)p_{n+1}(y)dy \end{cases}$$

For $x_1 < x_2$, we obtain :

$$(4.47)\quad \begin{cases} \chi_n(x_1,w) - \chi_n(x_2,w) = u'_{n+1}(w-x_1)\int_{x_1\vee 0}^{\infty} p_{n+1}(y)dy \\ \qquad - u'_{n+1}(w-x_2)\int_{x_2\vee 0}^{\infty} p_{n+1}(y)dy - \int_{x_1\vee 0}^{x_2\vee 0} u'_{n+1}(w-y)p_{n+1}(y)dy \\ \qquad = [u'_{n+1}(w-x_1) - u'_{n+1}(w-x_2)]\int_{x_2\vee 0}^{\infty} p_{n+1}(y)dy \\ \qquad + \int_{x_1\vee 0}^{x_2\vee 0} [u'_{n+1}(w-x_1) - u'_{n+1}(w-y)]p_{n+1}(y)dy > 0 \end{cases}$$

and $\chi_n(x,w)$ is also strictly increasing with respect to w.

If $x_1 < x_2 < \Sigma_n$, we have by (4.45)

$$\chi_n(x_1, w_n(x_1)) = 0$$

$$\chi_n(x_2, w_n(x_2)) = 0$$

$$\chi_n(x_2, w_n(x_1)) < 0.$$

Therefore necessarily

$$w_n(x_2) > w_n(x_1).$$

Next, if $x_1 < \Sigma_n \le x_2$, then we have

$$(4.48)\quad \chi_n(x_1, w_n(x_1)) = 0,\ \chi_n(x_2, w_n(x_1)) < 0$$

Moreover, $\hat{v}_n(x_2) = 0$. Then let us show that

$$(4.49)\quad w_n(x_1) < x_2$$

which will prove that

$$(4.50)\quad x_1 + \hat{v}_n(x_1) < x_2 + \hat{v}_n(x_2)$$

But

$$\chi_n(x_2,x_2) = c_n + u'_{n+1}(0)\int_{x_2\vee 0}^{\infty} p_{n+1}(y)dy + \int_0^{x_2\vee 0} u'_{n+1}(x_2-y)p_{n+1}(y)dy$$

However necessarily

$$\theta_n(x_2,0) = \theta_n(x_2, \hat{v}_n(x_2)) \ge 0$$

and using (4.39) we see that $\chi_n(x_2,x_2) \ge 0$, therefore from (4.48) we deduce (4.49).

If $\Sigma_n \le x_1 < x_2$, then $\hat{v}_n(x_1) = \hat{v}_n(x_2) = 0$ and (4.50) is obvious.

Let us finally compute

$$u_n(x) = L_n(x) + \psi_n(x, \hat{v}_n(x))$$

For $x \ge \Sigma_n$ we have

$$u_n(x) = L_n(x) + u_{n+1}(0) \int_{x\vee 0}^{\infty} p_{n+1}(y)dy + \int_0^{x\vee 0} u_{n+1}(x-y)p_{n+1}(y)dy$$

hence

$$u_n'(x) = L_n'(x) + \int_0^{x\vee 0} u_{n+1}'(x-y)p_{n+1}(y)dy$$

For $x < \Sigma_n$, since $\hat{v}_n(x) > 0$, we have

$$u_n'(x) = L_n'(x) + \int_0^{x\vee 0} u_{n+1}'(x + \hat{v}_n(x) - y)p_{n+1}(y)dy \tag{4.51}$$

Since $x + \hat{v}_n(x)$ is strictly increasing, it easily follows that $u_n'(x)$ is strictly increasing and continuous. Moreover

$$u_n'(x) \ge L_n'(-\infty) \ge - h_n'(+\infty),$$

and

$$u_n'(x) \to L_n'(+\infty) + u_{n+1}'(+\infty) \quad \text{as } x \to \infty ,$$

hence

$$u_n'(+\infty) = u_{n+1}'(+\infty) + f_n'(+\infty).$$

Therefore, in fact

$$u_n'(+\infty) = \sum_{j=1}^{N-1} f_j'(+\infty)$$

and the proof of the desired results is then completed. □

<u>Remark 4.2</u>

If we impose $K_n = 0$ in Theorem 4.1, the cost structures become identical in both models A and B. However, results of theorem 4.1 and 4.2 differ in some respect.

When $K_n = 0$ in model A, $s_n = S_n$, and the optimal feedback (4.12) is of the "base stock" type :

$$\hat{v}_n(x) = \begin{cases} S_n - x & \text{for } x \le S_n \\ 0 & \text{for } x > S_n \end{cases}$$

But the function $x + \hat{v}_n(x)$ is not strictly increasing, at least for $x < S_n$.

For model B, we cannot derive a formal optimal production policy.

V - SINGLE PERIOD MODEL WITH RECOURSE

This model concerns industries which must deal with fashion goods, like cloths,.. ; or, short life goods because either they become rapidly obsolete, like news-papers, magazines, ..., or they spoil after a relatively small time interval, like some chemical products, ..., or they must be kept in stock until the next season if not sold, like antifreeze, Christmas cards, ...

This problem may also concern the production decision of spare parts which require special and expensive tools for each batch.

The model encompasses all manufacturing situations where the production decision must be made "once for all" to meet some future stochastic demand. The one-stage model corresponds to the well known "newsboy" problem which will not be reviewed here.

In this Section we address a more intricated problem where not only the final product to be sold can be held in stock, but also semi-finished products and raw materials. In addition, we assume that once a stockout for the final product has been identified, it is still possible to meet further demand by launching production from either the semi-finished product stage or the raw material one. A production lag is however inevitable, and leads to demand attribution before the order is received. On the other hand, this setting presents the advantage for the firm to reduce its financial risk due to excess inventory, since it carries a stock which has a lower cost than if it were a one stage inventory, constitued of final products only.
This multi-echelon production process requires to take an initial once for all ordering decision for each stage, i.e. x_1 for the final stage, x_2 for the intermediate level, and x_3 for the raw material echelon. Demand for the final product occurs after the production decision is made. It is a random variable denoted by ξ such that

(5.1) $$E|\xi| < \infty$$

When excess demand must be met from recourse to upper inventory levels, β percents of the sales are lost when production is started from the semi-finished product level, and γ percents when it is from the raw material level with $0 < \beta < \gamma < 1$. As a consequence we can compute the volume of lost sales when demand is in excess of x_1 :

(5.2) $$\begin{cases} \text{Volume of lost sales} = \beta(x_1-\xi)^- + \gamma(x_2-(1-\beta)(x_1-\xi)^-)^- \\ \qquad + (x_3-(1-\gamma)(x_2-(1-\beta)(x_1-\xi)^-)^-)^- \end{cases}$$

where we use the usual notation

$$u^+ = \text{Max}(u,0) \text{ and } \bar{u} = -\text{Min}(u,0).$$

On the other hand, the levels of activities derived from each inventory level are respectively

(5.3) $(x_1-\xi)^+$ for the finished product level

(5.4) $(x_2-(1-\beta)(x_1-\xi)^-)^+$ for the intermediate level

(5.5) $(x_3-(1-\gamma)(x_2-(1-\beta)(x_1-\xi)^-)^-)^+$ for the raw material level

If f_0, g_0 and h_0 denote the corresponding contribution functions and if f_1 is the shortage cost function, then the firm valuation function to be minimized is :

$$(5.6)\quad \begin{cases} J(x_1,x_2,x_3) = E\, f_1[\beta(x_1-\xi)^- + \gamma(x_2-(1-\beta)(x_1-\xi)^-)^- \\ \quad + (x_3-(1-\gamma)(x_2-(1-\beta)(x_1-\xi)^-)^-)^-] + E f_0[(x_1-\xi)^+] \\ \quad + E\, g_0[(x_2-(1-\beta)(x_1-\xi)^-)^+] \\ \quad + E\, h_0[(x_3-(1-\gamma)(x_2-(1-\beta)(x_1-\xi)^-)^-)^+] \end{cases}$$

We will assume in the sequel that the functions f_0, g_0, h_0 and f_1 are linear. In this case we obtain :

$$(5.7)\quad \begin{cases} J(x_1,x_2,x_3) = f_1\Big[\beta \int_{x_1}^{\infty} (\xi-x_1)\mu(\xi)d\xi + \gamma \int_{x_1+\frac{x_2}{1-\beta}}^{+\infty} ((1-\beta)(\xi-x_1)-x_2)\mu(\xi)d\xi \\ \quad + \int_{x_1+\frac{x_2}{1-\beta}+\frac{x_3}{(1-\beta)(1-\gamma)}}^{+\infty} ((1-\gamma)((1-\beta)(\xi-x_1)-x_2)-x_3)\, \mu(\xi)d\xi\Big] \\ \quad + f_0 \int_{-\infty}^{x_1} (x_1-\xi)\, \mu(\xi)d\xi \\ \quad + g_0\Big[\int_{-\infty}^{x_1} x_2\, \mu(\xi)d\xi + \int_{x_1}^{x_1+\frac{x_2}{1-\beta}} (x_2-(1-\beta)(\xi-x_1))\mu(\xi)d\xi\Big] \\ \quad + h_0\Big[\int_{-\infty}^{x_1+\frac{x_2}{1-\beta}} x_3\mu(\xi)d\xi \\ \quad + \int_{x_1+\frac{x_2}{1-\beta}}^{x_1+\frac{x_2}{1-\beta}+\frac{x_3}{(1-\beta)(1-\gamma)}} (x_3-(1-\gamma)((1-\beta)(\xi-x_1)-x_2))\mu(\xi)d\xi\Big] \end{cases}$$

We can next compute the partial derivatives of J, using the distribution function

$$(5.8)\qquad F(x) = \text{Prob}\,[\xi < x].$$

We get the following relations :

$$(5.9)\qquad \frac{\partial J}{\partial x_3} = (h_0 + f_1)\, F(x_1 + \frac{x_2}{1-\beta} + \frac{x_3}{(1-\beta)(1-\gamma)}) - f_1$$

(5.10)
$$\left\{\begin{aligned} \frac{\partial J}{\partial x_2} &= (g_0 + f_1\gamma - h_0(1-\gamma))\, F(x_1 + \frac{x_2}{1-\beta}) - f_1 \\ &+ (f_1 + h_0)(1-\gamma)\, F(x_1 + \frac{x_2}{1-\beta} + \frac{x_3}{(1-\beta)(1-\gamma)}) \end{aligned}\right.$$

(5.11)
$$\left\{\begin{aligned} \frac{\partial J}{\partial x_1} &= (f_0 + f_1\beta - g_0(1-\beta))\, F(x_1) \\ &+ (1-\beta)(g_0 + f_1\gamma - h_0(1-\gamma))\, F(x_1 + \frac{x_2}{1-\beta}) \\ &+ (1-\beta)(1-\gamma)(f_1 + h_0)\, F(x_1 + \frac{x_2}{1-\beta} + \frac{x_3}{(1-\beta)(1-\gamma)}) - f_1 \end{aligned}\right.$$

Then the following result obtains :

Theorem 5.1

Assume that

(5.12) $$0 < h_0 < g_0 < \frac{\gamma f_0 + (1-\gamma)\,\beta h_0}{\beta + \gamma - \beta\gamma}$$

(5.13) $$F(0) < \frac{\beta f_1}{\beta(f_1 + g_0) + f_0 - g_0}$$

then there exists a unique non negative solution $\hat{x}_1$, $\hat{x}_2$, $\hat{x}_3$ for the system

(5.14) $$\frac{\partial J}{\partial x_1} = \frac{\partial J}{\partial x_2} = \frac{\partial J}{\partial x_3} = 0 \cdot$$

It is given by the relations

(5.15) $$F(\hat{x}_1 + \frac{\hat{x}_2}{1-\beta} + \frac{\hat{x}_3}{(1-\beta)(1-\gamma)}) = \frac{f_1}{h_0 + f_1}$$

(5.16) $$F(\hat{x}_1 + \frac{\hat{x}_2}{1-\beta}) = \frac{\gamma f_1}{\gamma(f_1 + h_0) + g_0 - h_0}$$

(5.17) $$F(\hat{x}_1) = \frac{\beta f_1}{\beta(f_1 + g_0) + f_0 - g_0}$$

and $\hat{x}_1$, $\hat{x}_2$, $\hat{x}_3$ realize the minimum of J.

Proof

By setting $x = (x_1, x_2, x_3)$ we can compute :

$$(5.18)\quad \begin{cases} (\frac{\partial J}{\partial x}(x) - \frac{\partial J}{\partial x}(y)).(x-y) = (f_0 + f_1\beta - g_0(1-\beta))(F(x_1) - F(y_1))(x_1 - y_1) \\ + (g_0 + f_1\gamma - h_0(1-\gamma))(1-\beta)(F(x_1 + \frac{x_2}{1-\beta}) - F(y_1 + \frac{y_2}{1-\beta}))(x_1-y_1+\frac{x_2-y_2}{1-\beta}) \\ + (h_0 + f_1)(1-\beta)(1-\gamma)\ [F(x_1 + \frac{x_2}{1-\beta} + \frac{x_3}{(1-\beta)(1-\gamma)}) \\ - F(y_1 + \frac{y_2}{1-\beta} + \frac{y_3}{(1-\beta)(1-\gamma)})]\ (x_1 - y_1 + \frac{x_2-y_2}{1-\beta} + \frac{x_3-y_3}{(1-\beta)(1-\gamma)}) \geq 0 \end{cases}$$

since F is non decreasing. It follows that J is a convex function of x (at least if $f_0 > g_0$ and $g_0 > h_0$). The remainder of the proof follows from simple computations. The last condition (5.12) is obtained by expressing that the right hand side of (5.17) is smaller than the right hand side of (5.16). □

V - 1. A MULTI PERIOD MODEL WITH FAST DELIVERY

We consider now a model in which production can originate from two sources : a normal one and a fast one.

For the normal one there is a delivery lag of one period after the production has been decided.

In the fast one the delivery is instantaneous. Of course the fast delivery is more costly than the normal one. We shall denote by v_k the fast order and by m_k the normal order at time k. Then the inventory balance equations are :

$$(5.19)\quad \begin{cases} y_{k+1} = y_k + v_k + m_k - \xi_{k+1}, \quad k = 0, \dots \\ y_0 = x \end{cases}$$

and we want to minimise the payoff function

$$(5.20)\quad \begin{cases} J(V,M) = E \sum_{k=0}^{\infty} \alpha^k(f(y_k + c(v_{k+1}) + \tilde{c}(m_k)), \\ \text{where } V = (v_0, v_1, \dots) \text{ and } M = (m_0, m_1, \dots) \end{cases}$$

The equation of dynamic programming is

$$(5.21)\quad u(x) = \operatorname*{Inf}_{v\geq 0, m\geq 0} [f(x+v) + c(v) + \tilde{c}(m) + \alpha\Phi(u)(x+v+m)]$$

The general theory extends easily. We shall now concentrate on (s,S) policies. We assume that

$$(5.22)\quad f \text{ convex, } f \in B_1,\ f \geq 0,\ f \to +\infty \text{ as } |x| \to +\infty$$

$$(5.23)\quad E|\xi| < \infty$$

$$(5.24)\quad c(v) = K\,\chi_{v>0} + c_0 v, \quad c_0 > 0$$

$$(5.25)\quad f(x) + c_0 x \to +\infty \text{ as } |x| \to \infty$$

$$(5.26)\qquad \begin{cases} \tilde{c}(m) = K\,\chi_{m>0} + c_1 m \\ c_1 < \alpha c_0 \end{cases}$$

To simplify slightly the discussion, we shall consider a finite horizon problem, which yields the following induction

$$(5.27)\qquad \begin{cases} u^n(x) = -c_0 x + \inf\limits_{z\geq x} \{f(z) + K\,\chi_{z>x} + (c_0 - c_1)z \\ \qquad\qquad + \inf\limits_{y\geq z} (K\,\chi_{y>z} + c_1 y + \alpha\Phi\,(u^{n+1})(y))\} \\ u^N(x) = 0 \end{cases}$$

Let us define also the functions

$$(5.28)\qquad h^n(y) = c_1 y + \alpha\Phi(u^{n+1})(y)$$

$$(5.29)\qquad g^n(z) = f(z) + (c_0 - c_1)z + \inf_{y\geq z}.\ (K\,\chi_{y>z} + h^n(y))$$

We shall show by induction that the functions $u^n(x)$, $h^n(y)$, $g^n(z)$ are K-convex, and h^n, g^n are continuous and tend to $+\infty$ when the norm of the argument tends to $+\infty$. More precisely we will prove the following

<u>Theorem 5.2</u>

We assume (5.22), ..., (5.26). Then there exists numbers s_n, S_n, σ_n, Σ_n with $s_n \leq S_n$, $\sigma_n \leq \Sigma_n$ such that the following feedback is optimal

$$(5.30)\qquad \hat{m}_n(x) = \begin{cases} \Sigma_n - x & \text{if } x \leq \sigma_n \\ 0 & \text{if } x > \sigma_n \end{cases}$$

$$(5.31)\qquad \hat{v}_n(x) = \begin{cases} S_n - (x+\hat{m}_n(x)) & \text{if } x + \hat{m}_n(x) \leq s_n \\ 0 & \text{if } x + \hat{m}_n(x) > s_n \end{cases}$$

<u>Proof</u>

We have

$$u^{N-1}(x) = -c_0 x + \inf_{z\geq x} \{f(z) + c_0 z + K\,\chi_{z>x}\}$$

and thus u^{N-1} is K-convex, continuous and $u^{N-1}(x) \geq 0$, $u^{N-1}(x) \geq -c_0 x + c_0\sigma$, where σ is such that $\inf\limits_{z\geq x} \{f(z) + c_0 z + K\,\chi_{z>x}\} = f(\sigma) + c_0\sigma$ for $x \leq \sigma$.

It follows that $h^{N-2}(y)$ is K-convex, continuous and

$$h^{N-2}(y) \geq c_1 y$$

$$h^{N-2}(y) \geq c_1 y + \alpha\Phi(-c_0 y + c_0\sigma) = (c_1 - \alpha c_0)y + \alpha c_0\sigma + \alpha c_0\,E\xi\ ,\ \forall y.$$

Hence $h^{N-2} \to +\infty$ as $|y| \to \infty$. It follows that there exist s_{N-2}, S_{N-2} such that

$$g^{N-2}(z) = f(z) + (c_0-c_1)z + \begin{cases} h^{N-2}(s_{N-2}) = K + h^{N-2}(S_{N-2}) & \text{for } z \le s_{N-2} \\ h^{N-2}(z) & \text{for } z \ge s_{N-2} \end{cases}$$

Hence $g^{N-2}(z)$ is K-convex, continuous and

$$g^{N-2}(z) \ge f(z) + c_0 z$$

therefore $g^{N-2}(z) \to +\infty$ as $|z| \to +\infty$.

But then there exist σ_{N-2}, Σ_{N-2} such that

$$u^{N-2}(x) = - c_0 x + \begin{cases} g^{N-2}(\sigma_{N-2}) & \text{for } x \le \sigma_{N-2} \\ g^{N-2}(x) & \text{for } x \ge \sigma_{N-2} \end{cases}$$

and

$$g^{N-2}(\sigma_{N-2}) = K + g^{N-2}(\Sigma_{N-2})$$

It follows that $u^{N-2}(x)$ is K-convex, continuous and $u^{N-2} \ge 0$, $u^{N-2}(x) \ge -c_0 x + c_0 \sigma_{N-2}$.

More generally one can prove the existence of numbers s_n, S_n, σ_n, Σ_n, $0 \le n \le N-2$ such that

(5.32) $$g^{n}(z) = f(z) + (c_0-c_1)z + \begin{cases} h^{n}(s_n) = K + h^{n}(S_n) & \text{if } z \le s_n \\ h^{n}(z) & \text{if } z \ge s_n \end{cases}$$

(5.33) $$u^{n}(x) = - c_0 x + \begin{cases} g^{n}(\sigma_n) = K + g^{n}(\Sigma_n) & \text{for } x \le \sigma_n \\ g^{n}(x) & \text{for } x \ge \sigma_n \end{cases}$$

and the desired result follows. □

VI - PRODUCTION SMOOTHING MODELS

VI - 1. SETTING OF THE PROBLEM

In this section we extend the model developed in § V.3 of Chapter II to the case of random demands. The model has the following structure :

(i) Inventory balance equations :

(6.1) $$\begin{cases} y_{k+1} = y_k + v_k - \xi_{k+1}, \ k = n, \dots, N-1 \\ y_n = x, \text{ where } x \text{ is the initial inventory level.} \end{cases}$$

(ii) demands :

(6.2) $$\begin{cases} \xi_1, \ldots, \xi_N \quad \text{independent random variables,} \\ \xi_i \geq 0 \text{ and } E\,\xi_i < \infty \end{cases}$$

(iii) production decisions :

(6.3) $v_k \geq 0$ adapted to the σ-algebra generated by : $\xi_1, \ldots, \xi_k$, $\forall k = 1, \ldots, N-1$, v_0 deterministic, and delivery takes place in the same period the decision is made, before demand occurs.

(iv) cost function, for $j = n, \ldots, N-1$:

c_j : production cost function
f_j : inventory cost function
g_N : penalty cost function applying to the terminal inventory level

c_j, f_j, g_N satisfy conditions (1.5).
h_j : adjustment cost function

(6.4) $$\begin{cases} h_j : R \to R^+, \text{ uniformly continuous} \\ h_j(x) \leq \overline{h_j}(1 + |x|) \end{cases}$$

(6.5) All cost functions c_j, f_j, h_j and g_N are convex.

(v) the problem valuation function to be minimized is :

(6.6) $$J_n(x;V) = E\,\{ \sum_{j=n}^{N-1} c_j(v_j) + \sum_{j=n}^{N-1} f_j(y_j) + \sum_{j=n}^{N-1} h_j(v_j - v_{j-1}) + g_N(y_N) + h_N(-v_{N-1}) \}$$

where it is assumed that

(6.7) $$v_{n-1} = 0$$

VI - 2. DYNAMIC PROGRAMMING

We shall refer to the following dynamic programming equations :

(6.8) $$\begin{cases} u_n(x,z) = f_n(x) + \operatorname*{Inf}_{v\geq 0} \{c_n(v) + h_n(v-z) + E\, u_{n+1}(x+v-\xi_{n+1}, v)\} \\ u_N(x,z) = g_N(x) + h_N(-z) \end{cases}$$

The functions u_n are defined on the set $x \in R$, $z \in R^+$.

We can adapt the techniques of the proof of Theorem 1.1 and 1.2 to obtain that :

$$(6.9)\qquad \begin{cases} u_n \text{ is uniformly continuous} \\ \dfrac{|u_n(x,z)|}{1+|x|+|z|} \le ||u_n|| < \infty \end{cases}$$

and to show that there exists :

(6.10) $\hat{v}_n(x,z)$ Borel map which realizes the infimum in (5.7) for any x,z

Moreover, there exists an optimal control for $J_0(x ; V)$ obtained as follows :

$$(6.11)\qquad \begin{cases} \hat{v}_0 = \hat{v}_0(x,0),\ \hat{y}_1 = x + \hat{v}_0 - \xi_1 \\ \hat{v}_1 = \hat{v}_1(\hat{y}_1,\hat{v}_0),\ \hat{y}_2 = \hat{y}_1 + \hat{v}_1 - \xi_2 \\ \cdot\ \cdot\ \cdot\ \cdot\ \cdot \\ \hat{v}_{N-1} = \hat{v}_{N-1}(\hat{y}_{N-1},\ \hat{v}_{N-2}),\ \hat{y}_N = \hat{y}_{N-1} + \hat{v}_{N-1} - \xi_N\ . \end{cases}$$

In this section we derive additional properties of the optimal feedback when costs are convex. Some preliminary results are however unavoidable.

VI - 3. PRELIMINARY RESULTS

We start with additional notation :

Let $\psi(x,z)$ be a convex function defined on $R \to R^+$, then the function

$$\lambda \to \psi(x + \lambda,\ z + \lambda) = \tilde{\psi}(\lambda)$$

is also convex. We shall write $\psi'^+(x,z) = \tilde{\psi}'^+(\lambda)|_{\lambda=0}$ and $\psi'^-(x,z) = \tilde{\psi}'^-(\lambda)|_{\lambda=0}$ (defined if $z > 0$).

The analogue of Proposition 3.1 obtains for the production smoothing problem :

Proposition 6.1

Let $\phi(v) : R^+ \to R^+$, $\beta(z) : R \to R^+$, $\psi(x ; v) : R \times R^+ \to R^+$ be convex functions, ψ continuous. The function

$$(6.12)\qquad L(x,z) = \operatorname*{Inf}_{v\ge 0} [\phi(v) + \beta(v-z) + \psi(x+v,v)]$$

is convex. Assume that $\phi(v) \to +\infty$ as $v \to +\infty$, then setting

$$(6.13)\qquad \hat{v}(x,z) = \sup \{v \ge 0 \mid \phi'^-(v) + \beta'^-(v-z) + \psi'^-(x+v,\ v) \le 0\}$$

the function $\hat{v}(x,z)$ realizes the infimum in (6.12). It is the largest point realizing the infimum. It is monotone increasing in z.

Proof

Convexity is proved as in Proposition 3.1. Similarly we check that the infimum is attained, that $\hat{v}(x,z)$ defined by (6.13) is increasing in z.

If $z_1 \ge z_2$ and $\hat{v}(x,z_2) > 0$, then we have

$$\phi'^-(\hat{v}(x,z_2)) + \beta'^-(\hat{v}(x,z_2)-z_2) + \psi'^-(x+\hat{v}(x,z_2),\hat{v}(x,z_2)) \le 0$$

hence

$$\phi'^{-}(\hat{v}(x,z_2)) + \beta'^{-}(\hat{v}(x,z_2)-z_1) + \psi'^{-}(x+\hat{v}(x,z_2),\ \hat{v}(x,z_2)) \leq 0$$

which implies $\hat{v}(x,z_2) \leq \hat{v}(x,z_1)$. □

We can derive a more explicit form of the feedback, in the case where ϕ,β are convex piecewise linear. To simplify the analysis, we restrict ourselves to the following case :

$$\text{(6.14)} \qquad \begin{cases} \phi(v) = \phi\ v \\ \beta(z) = \beta|z| \end{cases}$$

We have

$$\text{(6.15)} \qquad \beta'^{-}(z) = \begin{cases} -\beta & z \leq 0 \\ \beta & z > 0 \end{cases}$$

We define

$$\text{(6.16)} \qquad \begin{cases} \bar{v}(x) = \sup\ \{v \geq 0 \mid \psi'^{-}(x+v,\ v) \leq -\phi - \beta\} \\ \bar{\bar{v}}(x) = \sup\ \{v \geq 0 \mid \psi'^{-}(x+v,\ v) \leq -\phi + \beta\} \end{cases}$$

Clearly we have

$$\text{(6.17)} \qquad 0 \leq \bar{v}(x) \leq \bar{\bar{v}}(x)$$

and

$$\text{(6.18)} \qquad \bar{v}(x) = 0 \text{ if and only if } \psi'^{-}(x+v,\ v) + \phi + \beta > 0, \quad \forall v > 0$$

We then obtain the following form for the optimal feedback.

Proposition 6.2

If we assume (6.14), then the function $\hat{v}(x,z)$ defined by (6.13) satisfies

$$\text{(6.19)} \qquad \hat{v}(x,z) = \begin{cases} \bar{v}(x) & \text{if} \quad 0 \leq z \leq \bar{v}(x) \\ z & \text{if} \quad \bar{v}(x) \leq z \leq \bar{\bar{v}}(x) \\ \bar{\bar{v}}(x) & \text{if} \quad z \geq \bar{\bar{v}}(x) \end{cases}$$

Proof

Let us define

$$M(x,z\ ;\ v) = \phi'^{-}(v) + \beta'^{-}(v-z) + \psi'^{-}(x+v,\ v)$$

$$= \phi + \psi'^{-}(x+v,\ v) + \begin{cases} -\beta, & \text{if } v \leq z \\ \beta, & \text{if } v > z \end{cases}$$

(i) If $0 \leq z \leq \bar{v}(x)$,

$$M(x,z\ ;\ v) \leq 0 \text{ for } v \leq \bar{v}(x),$$

and $\qquad M(x,z\ ;\ v) > 0$ for $v > \bar{v}(x)$

which implies the first case of (5.19).

(ii) If $\bar{v}(x) < z \le \bar{\bar{v}}(x)$

$$M(x,z\ ;\ v) \le 0 \text{ for } v \le z$$

$$M(x,z\ ;\ v) > 0 \text{ for } v > z$$

hence the second case of (5.19).

(iii) Finally, if $z > \bar{\bar{v}}(x)$,

$$M(x,z\ ;\ v) \le 0 \text{ for } v \le \bar{\bar{v}}(x)$$

and

$$M(x,z\ ;\ v) > 0 \text{ for } v > \bar{\bar{v}}(x)$$

which completes the proof of (5.19). □

Proposition 6.3

Assume that

(6.20) $\qquad \psi'^{-}(x+v,\ v)$ is monotone increasing in x, for any v

then

(6.21) $\qquad \bar{v}(x)\ ,\ \bar{\bar{v}}(x)$ are decreasing.

On the other hand, if we assume that

(6.22) $\qquad \psi'^{-}(y,y-x)$ is monotone decreasing in x, for any y $(x \le y)$

then

(6.23) $\qquad x + \bar{v}(x),\ x + \bar{\bar{v}}(x)$ are increasing.

Proof

We only prove (6.23). Suppose $x_1 > x_2$, we want to show that

(6.24) $\qquad x_1 + \bar{v}(x_1) \ge x_2 + \bar{v}(x_2).$

There is nothing to prove if $x_1 \ge x_2 + \bar{v}(x_2)$. Assume $x_2 + \bar{v}(x_2) > x_1$, then by (6.16), we get:

$$\psi'^{-}(x_2 + \bar{v}(x_2),\ \bar{v}(x_2)) \le -\ \phi\ -\ \beta$$

hence, by the assumption (6.22) :

$$\psi'^{-}(x_2 + \bar{v}(x_2),\ \bar{v}(x_2) - (x_1 - x_2)) \le -\ \phi\ -\ \beta$$

or

$$\psi'^{-}(x_1 + x_2 - x_1 + \bar{v}(x_2),\ x_2 - x_1 + \bar{v}(x_2)) \le -\ \phi\ -\ \beta$$

hence

$$x_2 - x_1 + \bar{v}(x_2) \le \bar{v}(x_1)$$

i.e. (6.24). □

Remark 6.1

If (6.21) and (6.23) are satisfied, then v, $\bar{\bar{v}}$ are Lipschitz continuous and

$$|\bar{v}(x_1) - \bar{v}(x_2)| \le |x_1 - x_2|$$

$$|\bar{\bar{v}}(x_1) - \bar{\bar{v}}(x_2)| \le |x_1 - x_2| \qquad \square$$

Remark 6.2

Properties (6.20), (6.22) would follow from

(6.25) $\psi_v'^-(x,v)$ is monotone increasing in x, $\forall v > 0$

(6.26) $\psi_x'^-(x,v)$ is monotone increasing in v, $\forall x$

Indeed, note that the quantities (6.25), (6.26) are well defined since $v \to \psi(x,v)$, $x \to \psi(x,v)$ are convex functions. Next, consider

$$\psi(x+v,\ v) - \psi(x+v-h,\ v-h) = \psi(x+v,\ v) - \psi(x+v-h,\ v) + \psi(x+v-h,\ v)$$
$$- \psi(x+v-h,\ v-h) = \int_{v-h}^{v} \psi_x'^-(x+\lambda,\ v)d\lambda + \int_{v-h}^{v} \psi_v'^-(x+v-h,\ \lambda)d\lambda$$

If $x_1 > x_2$, then by convexity

$$\psi_x'^-(x_1+\lambda,\ v) \ge \psi_x'^-(x_2+\lambda,\ v)$$

and from (6.25)

$$\psi_v'^-(x_1+v-h,\ \lambda) \ge \psi_v'^-(x_2+v-h,\ \lambda)$$

therefore

$$\psi(x_1+v,\ v) - \psi(x_1+v-h,\ v-h) \ge \psi(x_2+v,\ v) - \psi(x_2+v-h,\ v-h)$$

from which we obtain (6.20).

Similarly, consider

$$\psi(y,\ y-x) - \psi(y-h,\ y-h-x) = \psi(y,\ y-x) - \psi(y-h,\ y-x) + \psi(y-h),\ y-x)$$
$$- \psi(y-h,\ y-h-x) = \int_{y-h}^{y} \psi_x'^-(\lambda,\ y-x)d\lambda + \int_{y-h}^{y} \psi_v'^-(y-h,\ \lambda-x)d\lambda.$$

If $x_1 > x_2$, then by convexity

$$\psi_v'^-(y-h,\ \lambda-x_1) \le \psi_v'^-(y-h,\ \lambda-x_2)$$

and from (6.26)

$$\psi_x'^-(\lambda,\ y-x_1) \le \psi_x'^-(\lambda,\ y-x_2)$$

from which we easily deduce (6.22). □

Proposition 6.4

Assume (6.14), (6.25), (6.26), then $L(x,z)$ defined by (6.12) satisfies (6.25), (6.26).

Proof

From Proposition 6.2, it follows that

$$(6.27)\qquad L(x,z) = \begin{cases} \phi\bar{v}(x) + \beta(\bar{v}(x)-z) + \psi(x+\bar{v}(x),\bar{v}(x)), & \text{if } 0 \le z \le \bar{v}(x) \\ \phi z + \psi'(x+z, z) & , \text{ if } \bar{v}(x) \le z \le \bar{\bar{v}}(x) \\ \phi\bar{\bar{v}}(x) + \beta(z-\bar{\bar{v}}(x)) + \psi(x+\bar{\bar{v}}(x),\bar{\bar{v}}(x)), & \text{if } z \ge \bar{\bar{v}}(x) \end{cases}$$

We can also deduce that :

$$(6.28)\qquad \begin{cases} L(x,z) - L(x,z-h) = -\beta h, \text{ if } 0 < z \le \bar{v}(x),\ 0 \le h \le z \\ \qquad = \phi h + \psi(x+z,z) - \psi(x+z-h,z-h), \\ \qquad\qquad \text{if } \bar{v}(x) < z \le \bar{\bar{v}}(x),\ 0 \le h \le \dfrac{z-\bar{v}(x)}{2} \\ \qquad = \beta h \quad , \text{ if } z > \bar{\bar{v}}(x),\ 0 \le h \le \dfrac{z-\bar{\bar{v}}(x)}{2} \end{cases}$$

To establish (6.28), we use the fact that

$$\bar{v}(x) \le \bar{v}(x-h) \le \bar{v}(x)+h.$$

Let $x_1 > x_2$. Recalling that

$$\bar{v}(x_1) \le \bar{v}(x_2),\ \bar{\bar{v}}(x_1) \le \bar{\bar{v}}(x_2)$$

We must consider two possibilities

$$(6.29)\qquad 0 \le \bar{v}(x_1) \le \bar{v}(x_2) \le \bar{\bar{v}}(x_1) \le \bar{\bar{v}}(x_2)$$

or

$$(6.30)\qquad 0 \le \bar{v}(x_1) \le \bar{\bar{v}}(x_2) \le \bar{v}(x_2) \le \bar{\bar{v}}(x_1)$$

We denote

$$X_h = \frac{1}{h}\,[L(x_1,z) - L(x_1,z-h) - (L(x_2,z) - L(x_2,z-h))].$$

We then have

$$(6.31)\qquad X_h \to L_z'^{-}(x_1,z) - L_z'^{-}(x_2,z), \text{ as } h \to 0$$

A - Consider first the case (6.29)

(i) Assume $0 < z \le \bar{v}(x_1)$, $h \le z$, then from (6.28), $X_h = 0$. Assume next that

$$0 \le \bar{v}(x_1) < z \le \bar{v}(x_2)$$

and take $h \le \dfrac{z-\bar{v}(x_1)}{2} \le z$.

We deduce

$$X_h = \frac{1}{h}[\phi h + \psi(x_1+z,z) - \psi(x_1+z-h,z-h) + \beta h]$$

$$= \frac{1}{h}\int_{z-h}^{z} [\psi'^{-}(x_1+\lambda,\lambda) + \phi + \beta]\, d\lambda$$

Since $z-h \geq h+\bar{v}(x_1)$, it follows from the definition (6.16) of $\bar{v}(x_1)$, that $X_h > 0$.

(ii) Assume next that

$$0 \leq \bar{v}(x_1) \leq \bar{v}(x_2) < z \leq \bar{\bar{v}}(x_1) \leq \bar{\bar{v}}(x_2)$$

and

$$h \leq \frac{z-\bar{v}(x_2)}{2} \leq \frac{z-\bar{v}(x_1)}{2}$$

then

$$X_h = \frac{1}{h}[\psi(x_1+z,z) - \psi(x_1+z-h,z-h) - (\psi(x_2+z,z) - \psi(x_2+z-h,z-h))]$$

$$= \frac{1}{h}\int_{z-h}^{z} [\psi'^{-}(x_1+\lambda,\lambda) - \psi'^{-}(x_2+\lambda,\lambda)]\, d\lambda \geq 0$$

by the property (6.20) (which follows from (6.25)).

(iii) Assume now that

$$0 \leq \bar{v}(x_1) \leq \bar{v}(x_2) \leq \bar{\bar{v}}(x_1) < z \leq \bar{\bar{v}}(x_2)$$

and

$$h \leq \frac{z-\bar{\bar{v}}(x_1)}{2} \leq \frac{z-\bar{v}(x_2)}{2}$$

then by (6.28),

$$X_h = \frac{1}{h}[\beta h - (\phi h + \psi(x_2+z,z) - \psi(x_2+z-h,z-h))]$$

$$= \frac{1}{h}\left[\int_{z-h}^{z} (-\psi'^{-}(x_2+\lambda,\lambda) - \phi + \beta)\, d\lambda\right]$$

Since $z \leq \bar{\bar{v}}(x_2)$, we have for $\lambda \lneq z$

$$\psi'^{-}(x_2+\lambda,\lambda) + \phi - \beta \leq 0$$

hence $X_h \geq 0$.

(iv) Finally assume that

$$0 \leq \bar{v}(x_1) \leq \bar{v}(x_2) \leq \bar{\bar{v}}(x_1) \leq \bar{\bar{v}}(x_2) < z$$

and

$$h \leq \frac{z-\bar{\bar{v}}(x_2)}{2} \leq \frac{z-\bar{\bar{v}}(x_1)}{2}$$

then $X_h = 0$. We thus have proved that in case (6.29), $X_h \geq 0$, for h sufficiently small. Therefore from (6.31) we deduce

$$(6.32) \qquad L_z'^{-}(x_1,z) - L_z'^{-}(x_2,z) \geq 0$$

B - We now consider the situation (6.30)

The only additional case to check is the following

$$(v) \qquad 0 \leq \bar{v}(x_1) \leq \bar{\bar{v}}(x_1) < z \leq \bar{v}(x_2) \leq \bar{\bar{v}}(x_2)$$

For $h \leq \frac{z-\bar{\bar{v}}(x_1)}{2} \leq z$ we have

$$X_h = \frac{1}{h}[\beta h - (-\beta h)] = 2\beta$$

hence again (6.32).

Consider now

$$(6.33) \quad \begin{cases} L(x,z) - L(x-h,z) = (\phi+\beta)(\bar{v}(x) - \bar{v}(x-h)) + \psi(x+\bar{v}(x),\bar{v}(x)) \\ \qquad - \psi(x-h+\bar{v}(x-h),\bar{v}(x-h)) \\ \qquad \text{if } 0 < z \leq \bar{v}(x), \\ = \psi(x+z,z) - \psi(x-h+z,z) \\ \qquad \text{if } \bar{v}(x) < z \leq \bar{\bar{v}}(x),\ h \leq z - \bar{v}(x) \\ = (\phi-\beta)(\bar{\bar{v}}(x) - \bar{\bar{v}}(x-h)) + \psi(x+\bar{\bar{v}}(x), \bar{\bar{v}}(x)) \\ \qquad - \psi(x-h+\bar{\bar{v}}(x-h),\bar{\bar{v}}(x-h)) \\ \qquad \text{if } z > \bar{\bar{v}}(x),\ h \leq z-\bar{\bar{v}}(x) \end{cases}$$

In (6.33) we have used the fact that

$$h \leq z-\bar{\bar{v}}(x) \text{ implies } \bar{\bar{v}}(x-h) \leq z.$$

Let $z_1 > z_2$. We set

$$Y_h = \frac{1}{h}[L(x,z_1) - L(x-h,z_1) - (L(x,z_2) - L(x-h,z_2))] .$$

We have

$$(6.34) \qquad Y_h \to L_x'^{-}(x,z_1) - L_x'^{-}(x,z_2), \text{ as } h \to 0$$

(i) If $z_1 \leq \bar{v}(x)$, then $Y_h = 0$

(ii) If $z_2 \leq \bar{v}(x) < z_1 \leq \bar{\bar{v}}(x)$, $h < z_1 - \bar{v}(x)$

then

$$Y_h = \frac{1}{h}[\psi(x+z_1,z_1) - \psi(x-h+z_1,z_1) - (\phi+\beta)(\bar{v}(x)-\bar{v}(x-h))$$
$$- \psi(x+\bar{v}(x),\bar{v}(x)) + \psi(x-h+\bar{v}(x-h),\bar{v}(x-h))]$$
$$= \frac{1}{h}[\psi(x+z_1,z_1) - \psi(x-h+z_1,z_1) - (\psi(x+\bar{v}(x-h),\bar{v}(x-h))$$
$$- \psi(x-h+\bar{v}(x-h),\bar{v}(x-h))) + (\phi+\beta)(\bar{v}(x-h)-\bar{v}(x))$$
$$+ \psi(x+\bar{v}(x-h),\bar{v}(x-h)) - \psi(x+\bar{v}(x),\bar{v}(x))]$$
$$= \frac{1}{h}\int_{z_1-h}^{z_1} \psi'^{-}_x(x+\lambda,z_1)d\lambda - \int_{\bar{v}(x-h)-h}^{\bar{v}(x-h)} \psi'^{-}_x(x+\lambda,\bar{v}(x-h))d\lambda$$
$$+ \int_{\bar{v}(x)}^{\bar{v}(x-h)} [\phi + \beta + \psi'^{-}(x+\lambda,\lambda)]d\lambda$$

The last integral is positive, since the integrand $\lambda > \bar{v}(x)$ (using the definition of $\bar{v}(x)$). Now we have

$$\bar{v}(x-h) \le \bar{v}(x)+h < z_1$$

hence from the assumption (6.26),

$$\psi'^{-}_x(x+\lambda,\bar{v}(x-h)) \le \psi'^{-}_x(x+\lambda,z_1)$$

Therefore we deduce

$$Y_h \ge \frac{1}{h}\left[\int_{z_1-h}^{z_1} \psi'^{-}_x(x+\lambda,z_1)d\lambda - \int_{\bar{v}(x-h)-h}^{\bar{v}(x-h)} \psi'^{-}_x(x+\lambda,z_1)d\lambda\right]$$
$$= \frac{1}{h}\left[\int_{(z_1-h)\vee\bar{v}(x-h)}^{z_1} \psi'^{-}_x(x+\lambda,z_1)d\lambda - \int_{\bar{v}(x-h)-h}^{(z_1-h)\wedge\bar{v}(x-h)} \psi'^{-}_x(x+\lambda,z_1)d\lambda\right] \ge 0$$

from the convexity of the map $x \to \psi(x,z)$. [1]

(iii) Assume next that $z_2 \le \bar{v}(x) \le \bar{\bar{v}}(x) < z_1$, $h < z_1 - \bar{\bar{v}}(x)$, then we have

$$Y_h = \frac{1}{h}[(\phi-\beta)(\bar{\bar{v}}(x)-\bar{\bar{v}}(x+h)) + \psi(x+\bar{\bar{v}}(x),\bar{\bar{v}}(x)) - \psi(x-h+\bar{\bar{v}}(x-h),\bar{\bar{v}}(x-h))$$
$$- (\phi+\beta)(\bar{v}(x)-\bar{v}(x-h)) - \psi(x+\bar{v}(x),\bar{v}(x))$$
$$+ \psi(x-h+\bar{v}(x-h),\bar{v}(x-h))]$$
$$= \frac{1}{h}[(\phi-\beta)(\bar{\bar{v}}(x)-\bar{\bar{v}}(x-h)) + \psi(x-h+\bar{\bar{v}}(x),\bar{\bar{v}}(x)) - \psi(x-h+\bar{\bar{v}}(x-h),\bar{\bar{v}}(x-h))$$
$$+ \psi(x+\bar{\bar{v}}(x),\bar{\bar{v}}(x)) - \psi(x-h+\bar{\bar{v}}(x),\bar{\bar{v}}(x))$$
$$+ (\phi+\beta)(\bar{v}(x-h)-\bar{v}(x)) + \psi(x+\bar{v}(x-h),\bar{v}(x-h))$$
$$- \psi(x+\bar{v}(x),\bar{v}(x)) - (\psi(x+\bar{v}(x-h),\bar{v}(x-h))$$
$$- \psi(x-h+\bar{v}(x-h),\bar{v}(x-h)))]$$

[1] $a \vee b = \mathrm{Max}(a,b)$ $\quad a \wedge b = \mathrm{Min}(a,b)$

$$= \frac{1}{h}\Bigg[- \int_{\bar{\bar{v}}(x)}^{\bar{\bar{v}}(x-h)} (\phi-\beta+ \psi'^{-}(x-h+\lambda,\lambda))d\lambda + \int_{\bar{v}(x)}^{\bar{v}(x-h)} (\phi+\beta+ \psi'^{-}(x+\lambda,\lambda))d\lambda$$

$$+ \int_{\bar{\bar{v}}(x)-h}^{\bar{\bar{v}}(x)} \psi_x'^{-}(x+\lambda,\bar{\bar{v}}(x))d\lambda$$

$$- \int_{\bar{v}(x-h)-h}^{\bar{v}(x-h)} \psi_x'^{-}(x+\lambda,\bar{v}(x-h))d\lambda \Bigg]$$

and if $\bar{\bar{v}}(x) \geq \bar{v}(x-h)$, we conclude that $Y_h \geq 0$.

If $\bar{v}(x) < \bar{\bar{v}}(x)$, then for $h \leq \bar{\bar{v}}(x) - \bar{v}(x)$ we have indeed $\bar{v}(x-h) \leq \bar{\bar{v}}(x)$. On the other hand if $\bar{v}(x) = \bar{\bar{v}}(x)$, then

$$Y_h = \frac{1}{h}[\ \phi(\bar{v}(x-h)-\bar{\bar{v}}(x-h)) - \beta(2\bar{v}(x)-\bar{\bar{v}}(x-h)-\bar{v}(x-h))$$

$$+ \psi(x-h+\bar{v}(x-h),\bar{v}(x-h)) - \psi(x-h+\bar{\bar{v}}(x-h),\bar{\bar{v}}(x-h))]$$

$$= \frac{1}{h}[\phi(\bar{v}(x-h)-\bar{\bar{v}}(x-h)) - \beta(2\bar{v}(x)-\bar{\bar{v}}(x-h)-\bar{v}(x-h))$$

$$- \int_{\bar{v}(x-h)}^{\bar{\bar{v}}(x-h)} \psi'^{-}(x-h+\lambda,\lambda)d\lambda]$$

$$\geq \frac{1}{h}[\phi(\bar{v}(x-h)-\bar{\bar{v}}(x-h)) - \beta(2\bar{v}(x)-\bar{\bar{v}}(x-h)-\bar{v}(x-h))$$

$$- (-\phi+\beta)(\bar{\bar{v}}(x-h)-\bar{v}(x-h))]$$

$$= \frac{1}{h}[-2\beta(\bar{v}(x)-\bar{v}(x-h))] \geq 0$$

(iv) Consider now the case $\bar{v}(x) < z_2 < z_1 \leq \bar{\bar{v}}(x)$, and $h \leq z_2-\bar{v}(x) < z_1-\bar{v}(x)$. We have

$$Y_h = \frac{1}{h}[\psi(x+z_1,z_1) - \psi(x-h+z_1,z_1) - (\psi(x+z_2,z_2) - \psi(x-h+z_2,z_2))]$$

$$= \frac{1}{h}\left[\int_{z_1-h}^{z_1} \psi_x'^{-}(x+\lambda,z_1)d\lambda - \int_{z_2-h}^{z_2} \psi_x'^{-}(x+\lambda,z_2)d\lambda\right]$$

$$\geq \frac{1}{h}\left[\int_{z_1-h}^{z_1} \psi_x'^{-}(x+\lambda,z_1)d\lambda - \int_{z_2-h}^{z_2} \psi_x'^{-}(x+\lambda,z_1)d\lambda\right]$$

from (6.26). It follows that $Y_h \geq 0$, since $z_1 > z_2$, by the convexity of the map $x \to \psi(x,z)$.

(v) The next case is $\bar{v}(x) < z_2 \leq \bar{\bar{v}}(x) < z_1$ and $h \leq z_2-\bar{v}(x)$, $h \leq z_1-\bar{\bar{v}}(x)$. We have

$$Y_h = \frac{1}{h}[(\phi-\beta)(\bar{\bar{v}}(x)-\bar{\bar{v}}(x-h)) + \psi(x+\bar{\bar{v}}(x),\bar{\bar{v}}(x)) - \psi(x-h+\bar{\bar{v}}(x-h),\bar{\bar{v}}(x-h))$$

$$- \psi(x+z_2,z_2) + \psi(x-h+z_2, z_2)]$$

$$= \frac{1}{h}\left[-\int_{\bar{\bar{v}}(x)}^{\bar{\bar{v}}(x-h)} (\psi'^{-}(x-h+\lambda,\lambda)+\phi-\beta)d\lambda + \int_{\bar{\bar{v}}(x)-h}^{\bar{\bar{v}}(x)} \psi'^{-}_x(x+\lambda,\bar{\bar{v}}(x))d\lambda \right.$$

$$\left. -\int_{z_2-h}^{z_2} \psi'^{-}_x(x+\lambda,z_2)d\lambda \right] \geq 0$$

(vi) Finally we have the case $\bar{v}(x) \leq \bar{\bar{v}}(x) < z_2 < z_1$ and $h \leq z_2-\bar{\bar{v}}(x) < z_1-\bar{\bar{v}}(x)$. We obtain $Y_h = 0$.

In all cases we have proved that $Y_h \geq 0$ for h sufficiently small. By (6.34) this implies

$$L'^{-}_x(x,z_1) - L'^{-}_x(x,z_2) \geq 0.$$

which completes the proof of the proposition. □

Proposition 6.5

Assume (6.14), (6.25), (6.26), then L(x,z) defined by (6.12) satisfies

(6.35) $$-\beta \leq L'^{-}_z(x,z) \leq \beta \quad , \quad \forall x,\ \forall z > 0$$

(6.36) $$\psi'^{-}_x(x+\bar{v}(x),\bar{v}(x)) \leq L'^{-}_x(x,z) \leq \lim_{h\downarrow 0} \psi'^{-}_x(x+\bar{\bar{v}}(x)+h,\bar{\bar{v}}(x)+h)$$

Proof

The property (6.35) follows immediately from (6.25). Let us prove (6.36). The left inequality follows from (see Lemma 3.2) :

$$L'^{-}_x(x,z) \geq \psi'^{-}_x(x+\hat{v}(x,z),\hat{v}(x,z))$$

But from (6.19), $\hat{v}(x,z) \geq \bar{v}(x)$.

From this, (6.26) and convexity, we deduce

$$\psi'^{-}_x(x+\hat{v}(x,z),\hat{v}(x,z)) \geq \psi'^{-}_x(x+\bar{v}(x),\bar{v}(x)).$$

Let us next prove the right inequality (6.36). We have from (6.33)

(6.37)
$$\begin{cases} L(x,z) - L(x-h,z) = -\displaystyle\int_{\bar{v}(x)}^{\bar{v}(x-h)} [\phi+\beta+\psi'^{-}(x+\lambda,\lambda)]d\lambda \\ \qquad + \psi(x+\bar{v}(x-h),\bar{v}(x-h)) - \psi(x-h+\bar{v}(x-h),\bar{v}(x-h)) \\ \qquad \leq \psi(x+\bar{v}(x-h),\bar{v}(x-h)) - \psi(x-h+\bar{v}(x-h),\bar{v}(x-h)) \\ \qquad \text{if } 0 \leq z \leq \bar{v}(x). \end{cases}$$

It follows that

$$L(x,z) - L(x-h,z) \le \int_{\bar{v}(x-h)-h}^{\bar{v}(x-h)} \psi_x'^{-}(x+\lambda,\bar{v}(x-h))d\lambda$$

$$\le h\, \psi_x'^{-}(x+\bar{v}(x-h),\bar{v}(x-h))$$

$$\le h\, \psi_x'^{-}(x+\bar{v}(x)+h,\bar{v}(x)+h)$$

$$\le h\, \psi_x'^{-}(x+\bar{\bar{v}}(x)+h,\bar{\bar{v}}(x)+h))$$

hence the second inequality (6.36) holds if $0 \le z \le \bar{v}(x)$. Assume next that $\bar{v}(x) < z \le \bar{\bar{v}}(x)$, $h \le z-\bar{v}(x)$, then from (6.33) we deduce that

$$L(x,z) - L(x-h,z) = \psi(x+z,z) - \psi(x-h+z,z)$$

$$= \int_{z-h}^{z} \psi_x'^{-}(x+\lambda,z)d\lambda$$

$$\le h\, \psi_x'^{-}(x+z,z) \le h\, \psi_x'^{-}(x+\bar{\bar{v}}(x),\bar{\bar{v}}(x))$$

$$\le h\, \psi_x'^{-}(x+\bar{\bar{v}}(x)+h,\bar{\bar{v}}(x)+h)$$

hence again the second inequality (6.36). Finally for $z > \bar{\bar{v}}(x)$, $h \le z-\bar{\bar{v}}(x)$, we have from (6.33)

$$L(x,z) - L(x-h,z) = -\int_{\bar{\bar{v}}(x)}^{\bar{\bar{v}}(x-h)} [\psi-\beta+ \psi'^{-}(x+\lambda,\lambda)]d\lambda$$

$$+ \int_{\bar{\bar{v}}(x-h)-h}^{\bar{\bar{v}}(x-h)} \psi_x'^{-}(x+\lambda,\bar{\bar{v}}(x-h))d\lambda$$

$$\le h\, \psi_x'^{-}(x+\bar{\bar{v}}(x-h),\bar{\bar{v}}(x-h)) \le h\, \psi_x'^{-}(x+\bar{\bar{v}}(x)+h,\bar{\bar{v}}(x)+h)$$

which completes the proof of (6.36). Note that $\psi_x'^{-}(x+\bar{\bar{v}}(x)+h,\bar{\bar{v}}(x)+h)$ decreases as h decreases to 0. □

VI - 4. PROPERTIES OF THE OPTIMAL PRODUCTION POLICY

We now apply the results of the preceding paragraph to the production smoothing problem, governed by equation (6.8).

In order to satisfy conditions (6.14), we need to assume that the production cost is linear and the adjustment cost is piecewise linear :

$$\text{(6.38)} \qquad \begin{cases} c_n(v) = c_n\, v \\ h_n(z) = h_n|z| \end{cases}$$

then the optimal feedback has the following properties (see Sobel [1969]).

Theorem 6.1

Assume (1.5), (6.5), (6.38), then there exists sequences $\bar{v}_n(x)$, $\bar{\bar{v}}_n(x)$, $n = 0,\dots,N-1$

such that $0 \leq \bar{v}_n(x) \leq \bar{\bar{v}}_n(x)$, and the feedback $\hat{v}_n(x,z)$ defined in (6.10) is given by

$$\hat{v}_n(x,z) = \begin{cases} \bar{v}_n(x) & \text{if } 0 \leq z \leq \bar{v}_n(x) \\ z & \text{if } \bar{v}_n(x) \leq z \leq \bar{\bar{v}}_n(x) \\ \bar{\bar{v}}_n(x) & \text{if } z \geq \bar{\bar{v}}_n(x) \end{cases} \tag{6.39}$$

Moreover the following properties hold

(6.40) $\bar{v}_n(x)$, $\bar{\bar{v}}_n(x)$ are monotone decreasing

(6.41) $x+\bar{v}_n(x)$, $x+\bar{\bar{v}}_n(x)$ are monotone increasing

Proof

We use a backward induction. Let $n = N-1$, and set

$$\psi(x,z) = E \; g_N(x-\xi_N) - h_N z$$

which is a convex continuous function. Moreover one has

$$\psi'^{-}_x(x,z) = E \; g'^{-}_N(x-\xi_N)$$

$$\psi'^{-}_x(x,z) = - h_N$$

and assumptions (6.25), (6.26) are trivially satisfied. Writing

$$u_n(x,z) = f_n(x) + L_n(x,z), \; n = 0, \ldots, N-1 \tag{6.42}$$

we first see from Proposition 6.2 and 6.3 that there exists functions $\bar{v}_{N-1}(x)$, $\bar{\bar{v}}_{N-1}(x)$ which satisfy (6.40), (6.41) such that the feedback $\hat{v}_{N-1}(x,z)$ is given by (6.39). Moreover from Proposition 6.4, we deduce that $L_{N-1}(x,z)$ satisfies also (6.25), (6.26). Noting that

$$u'^{-}_{N-1,x}(x,z) = f'^{-}_{N-1}(x) + L'^{-}_{N-1,x}(x,z)$$

$$u'^{-}_{N-1,z}(x,z) = L'^{-}_{N-1,z}(x,z)$$

it clearly follows that $u_{N-1}(x,z)$ satisfies (6.25), (6.26). But then also the map

$$x,z \to E \; u_{N-1}(x-\xi_{N-1},z)$$

satisfies the same properties, from which the induction can proceed. □

Theorem 6.2

Under the assumptions of Theorem 6.1, there exists a sequence of independent bounds $\bar{y}_n$, $\bar{\bar{y}}_n$ with $\bar{y}_n \leq \bar{\bar{y}}_n$, and such that

$$\bar{y}_n \leq x+\bar{v}_n(x) \leq x+\bar{\bar{v}}_n(x) \leq \bar{\bar{y}}_n, \; \forall x, \; n = 0, \ldots, N-1 \tag{6.43}$$

Proof

We first notice that

$$u'^{-}_N(x,z) = g'^{-}_N(x) - h_N$$

and setting

$$\psi_n(x,z) = E\, u_{n+1}(x-\xi_{n+1},z),\ n = 0, \ldots, N-1$$

we deduce

$$\psi'^{-}_{N-1}(x,z) = E\, g'^{-}_N(x-\xi_N) - h_N = \bar{\psi}_{N-1}(x). \tag{6.44}$$

Define

$$\begin{cases} \bar{y}_{N-1} = \sup \{y \mid \bar{\psi}_{N-1}(y) \le - c_{N-1} - h_{N-1}\} \\ \bar{\bar{y}}_{N-1} = \sup \{y \mid \bar{\psi}_{N-1}(y) \le - c_{N-1} + h_{N-1}\} \end{cases} \tag{6.45}$$

we deduce

$$\begin{cases} \bar{v}_{N-1}(x) + x = \bar{y}_{N-1} \text{ if } x \le \bar{y}_{N-1},\ \bar{v}_{N-1}(x) = 0 \text{ if } x > \bar{y}_{N-1} \\ \bar{\bar{v}}_{N-1}(x) + x = \bar{\bar{y}}_{N-1} \text{ if } x \le \bar{\bar{y}}_{N-1},\ \bar{\bar{v}}_{N-1}(x) = 0 \text{ if } x > \bar{\bar{y}}_{N-1} \end{cases} \tag{6.46}$$

As a consequence (6.43) holds from $n = N-1$.

Using (6.36) we assert that

$$E\, g'^{-}_N(\bar{y}_{N-1}-\xi_N) \le L'^{-}_{N-1,x}(x,z) \le E\, g'^{+}_N(\bar{\bar{y}}_{N-1} \vee x-\xi_N)$$

hence

$$\begin{cases} f'^{-}_{N-1}(x) + E\, g'^{-}_N(\bar{y}_{N-1}-\xi_N)-h_{N-1} \le u'^{-}_{N-1}(x,z) \le f'^{-}_{N-1}(x) \\ \qquad + E\, g'^{+}_N(\bar{\bar{y}}_{N-1} \vee x-\xi_N)+h_{N-1} \end{cases} \tag{6.47}$$

$$\bar{\psi}_{N-2}(x) \le \psi'^{-}_{N-2}(x,z) \le \bar{\bar{\psi}}_{N-2}(x) \tag{6.48}$$

where we have set

$$\bar{\psi}_{N-2}(x) = E\, f'^{-}_{N-1}(x-\xi_{N-1}) + E\, g'^{-}_N(\bar{y}_{N-1}-\xi_N)-h_{N-1} \tag{6.49}$$

$$\bar{\bar{\psi}}_{N-2}(x) = E\, f'^{-}_{N-1}(x-\xi_{N-1}) + E\, g'^{+}_N(\bar{\bar{y}}_{N-1} \vee (x-\xi_{N-1})-\xi_N)+h_{N-1} \tag{6.50}$$

Then we define

$$\bar{y}_{N-2} = \sup \{y \mid \bar{\bar{\psi}}_{N-2}(y) \le - c_{N-2} - h_{N-2}\} \tag{6.51}$$

$$\bar{\bar{y}}_{N-2} = \sup \{y \mid \bar{\psi}_{N-2}(y) \le - c_{N-2} + h_{N-2}\} \tag{6.52}$$

Clearly $\bar{y}_{N-2} \le \bar{\bar{y}}_{N-2}$. Moreover (6.48) implies that if $x < \bar{y}_{N-2}$ then

$$\begin{aligned} \psi'^{-}_{N-2}(\bar{y}_{N-2}-\varepsilon, \bar{y}_{N-2}-x-\varepsilon) &\le \bar{\bar{\psi}}_{N-2}(\bar{y}_{N-2}-\varepsilon) \\ &\le - c_{N-2}-h_{N-2} \end{aligned}$$

hence

$$\bar{y}_{N-2}-x-\varepsilon \leq \bar{v}_{N-2}(x).$$

Similarly

$$\psi'^{-}_{N-2}(\bar{\bar{y}}_{N-2}\vee x+\varepsilon,\bar{\bar{y}}_{N-2}\vee x-x+\varepsilon) \geq \bar{\psi}_{N-2}(\bar{\bar{y}}_{N-2}\vee x+\varepsilon) > -c_{N-2}+h_{N-2}$$

hence

$$\bar{\bar{y}}_{N-2}\vee x-x+\varepsilon \geq \bar{\bar{v}}_{N-2}(x)$$

and since ε is arbitrary (6.43) holds for $n = N-2$.

It follows that (from (6.36))

$$\begin{aligned} L'^{-}_{N-2,x}(x,z) &\geq \psi'^{-}_{N-2,x}(x+\bar{v}_{N-2}(x),\bar{v}_{N-2}(x)) \\ &\geq \bar{\psi}_{N-2}(x+\bar{v}_{N-2}(x))+h_{N-1} \\ &\geq \bar{\psi}_{N-2}(\bar{y}_{N-2})+h_{N-1} \end{aligned}$$

and

$$\begin{aligned} L'^{-}_{N-2,x}(x,z) &\leq \lim \psi'^{-}_{N-2,x}(x+\bar{\bar{v}}_{N-2}(x)+h,\bar{\bar{v}}_{N-2}(x)+h) \\ &\leq \lim_{h\downarrow 0} (\bar{\bar{\psi}}_{N-2}(x+\bar{\bar{v}}_{N-2}(x)+h)-h_{N-1}) \\ &\leq \bar{\bar{\psi}}_{N-2}(\bar{\bar{y}}_{N-2}\vee x+0)-h_{N-1} \end{aligned}$$

hence

$$f'^{-}_{N-2}(x) + \bar{\psi}_{N-2}(\bar{y}_{N-2})+h_{N-1}-h_{N-2} \leq u'^{-}_{N-2}(x,z) \leq f'^{-}_{N-2}(x) + \bar{\bar{\psi}}_{N-2}(\bar{\bar{y}}_{N-2}\vee x+0)-h_{N-1}+h_{N-2}$$

and therefore we deduce the induction

$$\bar{\psi}_{N-3}(x) = E\ f'^{-}_{N-2}(x-\xi_{N-2}) + \bar{\psi}_{N-2}(\bar{y}_{N-2})+h_{N-1}-h_{N-2}$$

$$\bar{\bar{\psi}}_{N-3}(x) = E\ f'^{-}_{N-2}(x-\xi_{N-2}) + E\ \bar{\bar{\psi}}_{N-2}(\bar{\bar{y}}_{N-2}\vee(x-\xi_{N-2})+0)-h_{N-1}+h_{N-2}$$

More generally we obtain the formulas

$$(6.53)\quad \begin{cases} \bar{\psi}_n(x) = E\ f'^{-}_{n+1}(x-\xi_{n+1}) + \bar{\psi}_{n+1}(\bar{y}_{n+1})+h_{n+2}-h_{n+1} \\ \bar{\bar{\psi}}_n(x) = E\ f'^{-}_{n+1}(x-\xi_{n+1}) + E\ \bar{\bar{\psi}}_{n+1}(\bar{\bar{y}}_{n+1}\vee(x-\xi_{n+1})+0)-h_{n+2}+h_{n+1}, \\ n = 0, \ldots, N-2 \end{cases}$$

where we have set

$$(6.54)\quad \bar{\psi}_{N-1}(x) = \bar{\bar{\psi}}_{N-2}(x) = E\ g'^{-}_{N}(x-\xi_N)-h_N$$

and we obtain the desired result (6.43) with

$$(6.55)\quad \begin{cases} \bar{y}_n = \sup\ \{y \mid \bar{\bar{\psi}}_n(y) \leq -\ c_n-h_n\} \\ \bar{\bar{y}}_n = \sup\ \{y \mid \bar{\psi}_n(y) \leq -\ c_n+h_n\} \end{cases}$$

□

VII - SURVEY OF RESEARCH AND RESULTS INTERPRETATION

Efficient forward algorithms and planning horizon results are inherently more difficult to obtain when the firm faces a stochastic demand pattern. This has induced a wide concern in the search for optimal myopic ordering policy. For such policy the decision process at each period consists in solving the current one period problem, provided a suitable terminal value function for inventory is adopted. The one period decision rule is myopic if it is also N-optimal. A number of production planning models for which myopic policies are optimal have been studied by Veinott [1965-1], [1965-2],[1966-1], Karlin [1960], Ignall and Veinott [1969] and Morton [1971], [1973]. See also Kleindorfer and Kunreuther [1978]. A related contribution concerning a multi-echelon model is Bessler and Veinott [1966].

Forecast horizon results are obtained by Kleindorfer and Kunreuther [1978], Morton [1973], Charnes and al. [1966] and ourselves.

We shall comment on these major contributions later on, in this section.

The usual distinction between production planning and production smoothing problems still will structure our presentation. However, it is no more appropriate to distinguish between concave and convex cost models since all the cost structures considered are either convex (eventually linear), or mixed with a concave production cost (usually linear with a set up) and convex inventory and adjustment costs.

The stochastic nature of the problem requires to be very specific about the decision process itself, since decisions are taken once only part of the uncertainty has been resolved. Several formulations are then possible.

Time is divided in periods of equal length. Demand usually occurs at the end of each period, but it may also take place at the beginning (cf. model B for the lost sales model in our Section IV). The problem horizon is N, possibly infinite. Demands $\xi_1, \ldots, \xi_N$ are non negative random variables which are usually postulated stochastically independent, but not necessarily identically distributed.

We assume the firm adopts a rolling horizon planning procedure. More precisely, at the beginning of each period, say n, the system is reviewed once the last demand ξ_n is known and inventory has adjusted to its new level, y_n, given by

$$y_n = y_{n-1} + v_{n-1} - \xi_n$$

where y_n is the sum of inventory on hand and outstanding orders (there are outstanding orders only when the delivery lag is greater than one period). The review of the system consists in forecasting demand for the next N periods, then to solve the N-period problem on the basis of currently available data, precisely the history $H_n = (x, v_0, \ldots, v_{n-1}, y_1, \ldots, y_n, \xi_1, \ldots, \xi_n)$. An order may be placed for any positive quantity, $v_n \geq 0$, which will be delivered at the beginning of period $n+\lambda$, where the delivery lag λ is either a positive integer or zero. When λ is greater than one period we need to make the distinction between "inventory on hand" and "potential inventory", i.e., inventory on hand and on order. Only potential inventory triggers a replenishment decision. See our Section I, § 4 and Karlin and Scarf [1958].

The usual decision process corresponds to the following scheme :

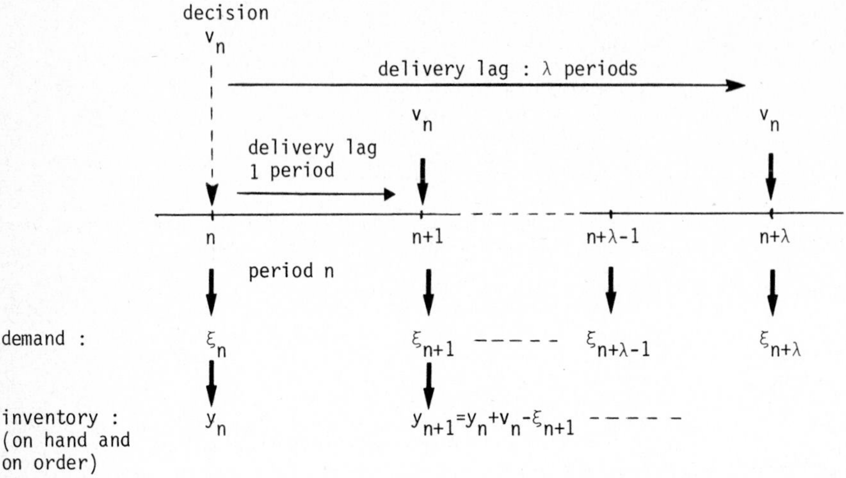

Except for cases of trivial uncertainty the firm cannot avoid the possibility of running out of stock. Excess demand in each period can be either backlogged and satisfied by subsequent deliveries, or it can simply be lost. In the first case inventory is allowed to become negative by the amount of backlogged sales : in the other, the stock level at the start of the next period is zero where there is excess demand.

When demand is stochastic,clearly we cannot omit the information cost associated with forecasting the demand distribution. Under such circumstances we do not need exact forecast-horizons. Near forecast horizons are practically adequate,provided the maximal benefit for the firm adopting a longer horizon is more than offset by the corresponding increase in data processing costs. See Kleindorfer and Kunreuther [1978] on this issue.

Production Planning Models

An extensive literature has built on the pionnering contributions of Arrow, Harris and Marschak [1951], Dvoretzky, Kiefer and Wolfowitz [1952-1], [1952-2],[1953], and Bellman, Glicksberg and Gross [1955].

The main concern has been with the determination of the characteristics of the optimal reordering policy, for various cost assumptions. Roughly, the (S,s) policy is optimal when the ordering cost is concave (usually composed of a set up cost and a proportional ordering cost), and holding and shortage costs are convex. On the other hand, the base stock policy is optimal for proportional ordering cost and convex inventory costs.

(i) concave production cost

The fundamental result for this problem is due to Scarf [1960] who generalizes previous work by Karlin [1958-1], [1958-2]. See also Zabel [1962]. Scarf shows for the stationary backlog case, that if

- the production cost is linear with a fixed set-up cost,
- the expected holding and shortage cost is convex (which is ensured if holding and shortage costs are convex),

then, the optimal ordering policy in the current period, n, is characterized by two critical numbers S_n and s_n, with $S_n \geq s_n$, and works as follows :

$$\begin{cases} \text{if } y_n < s_n, \text{ order } S_n - y_n \text{ ;} \\ \text{if } y_n \geq s_n, \text{ do not order ;} \end{cases}$$

where y_n denotes inventory on hand and on order at time n.

This result is still valid when demands in successive periods are dependent, but in this instance s_n and S_n depend on the past history of demand.

The proof crucially depends on the property that

$$u_n(x) = \underset{V}{\text{Min}}\ J_n(x \ ; V)$$

is K_n-convex. (see Section II, § 2 for definitions).

Section II of this chapter slightly generalizes Scarf's presentation to the non-stationary case. Veinott [1966-1] proposes different sufficient conditions for optimality of the (S,s) policy.

In section IV, we extend the analysis to the lost sales case (model A) and find that the (S,s) policy is still optimal under additional minor restrictions on the cost structure, especially on the growth rate of the cost function (Theorem 4.1). This result is similar to Shreve mentioned in Bertsekas [1976, p. 105].

For practical purposes this rather simple and intuitive decision rule has less appeal than it just appeared, since there is no known way of computing the exact values of the critical numbers. However, several authors have developed methods to approximate the optimal values of the reorder point s_n and the minimum order quantity $\Delta_n = S_n - s_n$, under different assumptions concerning costs and demand. See on this matter Veinott [1966-2] and Snyder [1974].

Concerning our introductory concern about finding myopic decision rules, Iglehart [1963-1], [1963-2] has shown for the infinite horizon problem with a discount factor α, $0 \leq \alpha \leq 1$, and Scarf's hypotheses, that there exists an optimal (S,s) policy which is stationary, i.e., $(S_n, s_n) = (S,s)$ for all n, and independent of the initial inventory on hand and on order. Iglehart also obtains bounds on these two critical numbers. Veinott and Wagner [1965] and Veinott [1966-2] have further tightened these bounds.

A continuous review version of the discrete stochastic production model is produced by Gonedes and Lieber [1974] where demand is treated as a stochastic process. See also Veinott [1966-2, p. 761].

(ii) <u>proportional production cost</u>

The situation where production cost is linear relates to the previous models by imposing the set up cost K_n to be zero. As a consequence $s_n = S_n = \bar{S}_n$ and the optimal reordering policy is of the <u>base stock</u> type, i.e. :

If the stock level on hand and on order, y_n, at time n, before ordering, is less than the base stock level $\bar{S}_n$, then order $\bar{S}_n - y_n$; otherwise, do not order at time n.

In addition this reordering policy is <u>myopic</u> in the sense that the base stock level

$\bar{S}_n(x)$ is computed at each period as the solution of the minimum one period expected cost, in period n considered independently from all other periods, and subject to $\bar{S}_n(x) \geq x$, x being the initial stock level in period n.

As opposed to the concave production cost situation, the critical parameter $\bar{S}_n(x)$ can easily be computed either as the unique positive solution of a transcendental equation (as for example in the stationary case), or by ad hoc algorithms. Moreover it is shown than the quantity ordered $v_k = \bar{S}_n(x) - x$ is a non increasing function of the initial inventory x (see Veinott [1965-2]).

Nonetheless,some minimal conditions are required to ensure that this policy is optimal. The analysis of these sufficient conditions for optimality, and the study of the monotonicity property of the base stock level may be found in numerous papers (see Veinott [1966-2] for references). However, the most important contributions on this question are Bellman et al [1955] for the stationary case and Karlin [1960], Veinot [1963], [1965-1], [1965-2] for the non stationary environment.

A sufficient condition for the base stock policy to be optimal, in the stationary case, is that the expected holding and shortage costs to be incurred in the current period be convex. This condition obviously obtains when the holding and shortage cost functions are both convex increasing functions, which vanish at the origin. Other sufficient conditions are given in Karlin [1958-1],[1958-2].

For the non stationary case Veinott [1965-1] shows that optimality of the base stock policy is ensured provided the stock on hand and on order at the end of the current period n, say y_{n+1}, will not exceed the base stock level $\bar{S}_{n+1}$, whatever is the demand ξ_{n+1} in period n, i.e.

$$y_{n+1} = y_n + v_n - \xi_{n+1} \leq \bar{S}_{n+1}$$

Clearly this condition is satisfied if $\bar{S}_n \leq \bar{S}_{n+1}$ since the reordering policy implies $y_{n+1} \leq y_n + v_n = \bar{S}_n$.

Consequently sufficient conditions have been established to ensure that the base stock levels do not decrease over time. Stochastic dominance, as defined in Section III, § 2, plays a crucial role in the results produced by Karlin [1960] and Veinott [1965-2] . Roughly speaking, given some minor restrictions on the cost structure, the optimality of the base stock policy is shown provided the demand distribution increases stochastically over time.

Other planning production models for which a myopic reordering policy is optimal are produced by Ignall and Veinott [1969], which is an outgrowth of Veinott [1965-1]. See also Bessler and Veinott [1966].

So far we have only considered the backlog case with proportional production cost. When excess demand is lost (instead of being deferred until further delivery) and delivery is not immediate, the reordering policy and critical parameters can no longer be expressed functionally in terms of the potential inventory (on hand and on order). See Karlin and Scarf [1958] and our generalization in section IV, § 3. When delivery is immediate, i.e. takes place in the current period before demand occurs, the lost sales model has been shown to be equivalent to a model with backlogging. See Veinott and Wagner [1965 , p. 528], Veinott [1963, section 5] and Wagner [1962, p. 113].

Morton [1971] has shown that the optimal policy for the lagged lost sales model with linear production, holding and storage costs, and the stationarity assumption is near-myopic ; but the myopic policy is not of the base stock type. Morton [1973] has further shown that the same property applies to the non stationary case, and has derived forecast horizon results. Morton adopts a bounding procedure for the first period decision which consists, for an N-period problem, in setting all demands beyond period N to very large values to obtain the upper bounds, and to zero to obtain the lower bounds. In fact, these bounds are special cases of the more general monotonicity properties derived, for the convex piecewise linear production cost case, by Kleindorfer and Kunreuther [1978] and ourselves in Section III, §2.

Lundin [1974] has extended Morton's analysis to the stochastic cash balance problem with proportional costs.

Application to the stochastic warehousing problem, where uncertainty bears on fufure selling prices and buying costs, is due to Charnes, Dreze and Miller [1966] who derive forecast horizon results and produce a forward algorithm. The main feature of this algorithm consists in placing upper and lower bounds on an implicit valuation function for the terminal inventory in the current period. Then these bounds are tightened on the basis of new forecasts for additional periods, until unambiguous first period decision emerges. This procedure is very much in the spirit of the developments by Kleindorfer and Kunreuther [1978] and ourselves.

(iii) <u>convex piecewise linear production cost</u>

Sobel [1970] and Kleindorfer and Kunreuther [1978] consider the situation where production is conducted in regular time up to normal capacity, say $\bar{v}_n^0$, and in overtime beyond this limit. Production cost is composed of a base cost independent of the production level v, say $c_n^0.v$, and of a premium for utilizing capacity overtime, $(c_n^{11} - c_n^0)(v - v_n^0)^+$ where c_n^{11} is the unit cost of production in overtime with $c_n^{11} > c_n^0$. In addition Sobel considers a penalty cost for idle capacity, $(c_n^{12} - c_n^0)(v - v_n^0)^-$ with $c_n^{12} > c_n^0$.

Sobel shows for the non stationary backlog and lost sales models that the optimal production policy depends on two parameters y_n^0 and y_n^1 with $y_n^0 > y_n^1$, and is given by :

$$\hat{v}_n(x) = \begin{cases} y_n^1 - x & \text{if } x < y_n^1 - \bar{v}_n^0 \\ \bar{v}_n^0 & \text{if } y_n^1 - \bar{v}_n^0 \leq x \leq y_n^0 - \bar{v}_n^0 \\ \max(y_n^0 - x, 0) & \text{if } x > y_n^0 - \bar{v}_n^0 \end{cases}$$

where x is the initial inventory level in period n. This reordering rule is derived for the terminal inventory value function $g_N(x) = - c_N^0\, x$; this means that when x is positive excess inventory is redeemed at its lowest per unit production cost, and when x is negative then backordered demand is satisfied at the regular time production cost. In addition Sobel shows that y_n^0 and y_n^1 are bounded from above and below.

The contribution of Kleindorfer and Kunreuther builds on Sobel's formulation to produce a near forecast horizon result. First, they show that the optimal production level in any period does not decrease as demand distribution increases stochastically. This monotonicity property is then used to derive :

- upper and lower bounds on the first production decision,
- a maximum deviation of the problem valuation function from its optimal value, say $B_L(x)$, when solving an L-horizon problem.

Section III generalizes the previous results to the case of a general convex piecewise linear function. Following Kleindorfer and Kunreuther Theorem 3.5 can be interpreted as a near-forecast horizon result. Indeed B_L represents the potential benefit for solving a problem of horizon N, $N \geq L$, provided g_N defined by (3.65) is used as a terminal inventory valuation function. If the cost associated with forecasting demand beyond L and solving a N-horizon problem ($N \geq L$) is greater than B_L, then the firm is better off implementing the decision $\tilde{v}_0(x\ ;\ L)$ for the first period, than any other decision based on a longer horizon.

The property that the production and cumulative production levels in any period are monotonic non decreasing in the demand sequence, was already shown for the deterministic case by Veinott [1965-1] (see references to Chapter II) and ourselves in Chapter II. At this stage it is interesting to show how this result for the deterministic case relates to the uncertainty issue. Although future demand cannot be perfectly forecasted, assume it is however possible to approach the unknown actual future demands $\xi_1, \ldots, \xi_N$ through maximal and minimal forecasts of the cumulative requirements : $\underline{\xi}_1^u, \ldots, \underline{\xi}_N^u$ and $\underline{\xi}_1^d, \ldots, \underline{\xi}_N^d$ respectively, with assurance that

$$\underline{\xi}_i^d \leq \underline{\xi}_i \leq \underline{\xi}_i^u \text{ for all } i = 1, \ldots, N$$

where $\underline{\xi}_i$ denotes the cumulative demand up to period i. The corresponding optimal maximal and minimal cumulative production levels $\underline{\hat{v}}_0^u, \ldots, \underline{\hat{v}}_{N-1}^u$ and $\underline{\hat{v}}_0^d, \ldots, \underline{\hat{v}}_{N-1}^d$ respectively, can then be computed. From the monotonicity property it follows that the cumulative production levels : $\underline{\hat{v}}_0, \ldots, \underline{\hat{v}}_{N-1}$ which are optimal for the unknown actual demands : $\xi_1, \ldots, \xi_N$, are such that :

$$\underline{\hat{v}}_i^d \leq \underline{\hat{v}}_i \leq \underline{\hat{v}}_i^u \text{ for all } i = 0, \ldots, N-1$$

It is happens that :

$$\underline{\hat{v}}_0^d = \underline{\hat{v}}_0^u \ ; \ \ldots \ ; \ \underline{\hat{v}}_h^d = \underline{\hat{v}}_h^u$$

for the first h consecutive periods, then these values are the optimal quantities to produce in periods 0 to h without perfect knowledge of the actual demands. In such instance h is a planning horizon for the forecast horizon N.

Otherwise the forecast accuracy must be improved in order to narrow the width of the interval $[\underline{\hat{v}}_i^d\ ,\ \underline{\hat{v}}_i^u]$, at least for the first periods.

Production Smoothing Models

The basic contribution on stochastic production smoothing is due to Beckmann [1961] who considers a stochastic stationary version of the model analyzed in Chapter II. Delivery is immediate (which corresponds to one period delivery lag in our formulation), excess demand is backlogged and the cost structure is linear. The production, inventory and smoothing cost functions are respectively :

$$c_n(v) = c \cdot v$$

$$f_n(y_n) = \begin{cases} f^h . y_n & \text{if} \quad y_n \geq 0 \\ -f^s . y_n & \text{if} \quad y_n < 0 \end{cases}$$

$$\text{with } 0 < f^h < f^s$$

$$g_n(v_n - v_{n-1}) = \begin{cases} d.(v_n - v_{n-1}) & \text{if} \quad v_n \geq v_{n-1} \\ e.(v_{n-1} - v_n) & \text{if} \quad v_n < v_{n-1} \end{cases}$$

with $d,e > 0$.

The optimal production policy is a function of the initial inventory on hand x, before the production decision is made, and of the last production rate v_{n-1}. In addition it is shown to depend on two critical functions $\bar{v}(x)$ and $\bar{\bar{v}}(x)$, such that $0 \leq \bar{v}(x) \leq \bar{\bar{v}}(x)$, which are non increasing in x. The reordering rule works as follows (see also figure below) :

- if for a given initial stock level x, the last rate of production v_{n-1} falls in the shaded area delimited by $\bar{v}(x)$ and $\bar{\bar{v}}(x)$: $\bar{v}(x) \leq x \leq \bar{\bar{v}}(x)$, then the rate of production should not be changed

$$\hat{v}_n(x, v_{n-1}) = v_{n-1} \ ;$$

- if $x > \bar{\bar{v}}(x)$, the production rate should be reduced to $\bar{\bar{v}}(x)$;
- if $x < \bar{v}(x)$, the production rate sould be increased to $\bar{v}(x)$.

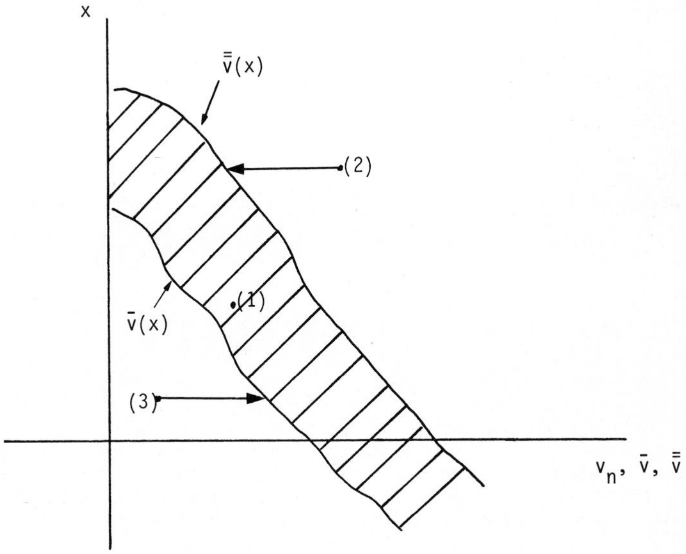

In schematic form :

$$\hat{v}_n(x, v_{n-1}) = \begin{cases} \bar{v}(x) & \text{if} \quad 0 \leq v_{n-1} < \bar{v}(x) \\ v_{n-1} & \text{if} \quad \bar{v}(x) \leq v_{n-1} \leq \bar{\bar{v}}(x) \\ \bar{\bar{v}}(x) & \text{if} \quad v_{n-1} > \bar{\bar{v}}(x) \end{cases}$$

The shaded area between $\bar{v}$ and $\bar{\bar{v}}$ corresponds to the combinations of initial stock level x, and last production rate v_{n-1}, for which the production system is "in control". Outside these limits the system is "out of control", and the reordering policy calls for an adjustment of the production rate on the frontier. In other words, the existence of adjustment costs restrict the number of changes in the production rates, by postponing any change as long as the production system stays in control, i.e., stays in a tolerance zone.

The same formulation applied to the dynamic cash balance problem by Eppen and Fama [1969], leads to the same type of optimal decision rule.

Kunreuther [1966] in a paper related to Beckmann's formulation proposes suboptimal policies based on the concept of deviation from long-run equilibrium values for production and inventory levels.

On the other hand, Mills [1957] considers a variant of Beckmann's formulation where excess demand is lost instead of backlogged. He then shows that the optimal policy is :

$$\hat{v}_n(x,v_{n-1}) = \begin{cases} y_n^1 - x & \text{if} \quad v_{n-1} < y_n^1 - x \\ v_{n-1} & \text{if} \quad y_n^1 - x \le v_{n-1} \le y_n^0 - x \\ y_n^0 - x & \text{if} \quad y_n^0 - x < v_{n-1} \end{cases}$$

where $y_n^0 > y_n^1$. This reordering rule corresponds exactly to Beckmann's policy when we set

$$\bar{v}_n(x) = y_n^1 - x \text{ and } \bar{\bar{v}}_n(x) = y_n^0 - x$$

but for the stationary case Mills [1957, p. 228] proves that the critical parameters y_n^1 and y_n^0 are constant.

However, Sobel [1969] challenges Mill's proof and extends the backlog model to allow non stationary costs and demands, and convex expected inventory costs. Sobel [1971] further considers the infinite horizon problem under stationarity assumptions.

Section VI mainly reformulates Sobel [1969] in the framework of optimal control theory and we obtain the same basic results (Theorems 5.1 and 5.2). It is shown that the reordering policy is of the form given above with :

- $\bar{v}_n(x)$ and $\bar{\bar{v}}_n(x)$ monotonic decreasing functions in x,
- $y_n^1(x) = \bar{v}_n(x) + x$ and $y_n^0(x) = \bar{\bar{v}}_n(x) + x$ monotonic increasing functions in x.

Moreover, $y_n^1(x)$ and $y_n^0(x)$ are uniformly bounded, i.e. there exists a sequence $\bar{y}_n$ and $\bar{\bar{y}}_n$, $\bar{y}_n < \bar{\bar{y}}_n$ such that

$$\bar{y}_n \le y_n^1(x) \le y_n^0(x) \le \bar{\bar{y}}_n$$

for any initial inventory x.

Kleindorfer and Glover [1973] propose a generalization of Sobel's formulation using the framework of stochastic optimal control theory.

A related issue is when adjustment costs are tied to the employment level of direct labor, instead of production level, per se. This problem is often called work force balancing, employment smoothing, or also capital accumulation. In this instance the size of the available work force acts as a capacity limit, which can be adjusted over time at a smoothing cost. Two decisions must be made simultaneously at each period on employment and production levels in anticipation of stochastic demand. This problem has been addressed by Iglehart [1965], Sobel [1970] and Holt et al. [1960].

Sobel extends the above analysis to this problem and find that a similar reordering policy holds for production, but which is slightly weaker in the sense that there is no uniform bounds on y_n^1 and y_n^0. While Sobel analysis applies to the reversible capital accumulation problem with constant returns to scale, Iglehart considers the irreversible model with increasing returns to scale. Iglehart then shows that the optimal policy concerning capital investment and production is completely described by several monotonic functions.

The joint problem of capacity regulation and production under demand uncertainty has also been treated by Holt et al. who assume that all costs can be approximated by quadratic functions. They solve a certainty equivalent for the stochastic problem which is known to exist for problems involving quadratic functions (see Holt et al., Chapter VI). This leads to optimal decisions for the current period concerning production and employment levels which are linear functions of initial work force and inventory, and demand forecast for future periods. The simplicity of the solution is partly due to the fact there are no constraints on the control and state variables. Computations show that practically a finite forecast horizon, H, leads to an optimal first period decision for any N horizon problem with $N > H$.

REFERENCES

STOCHASTIC OPTIMAL CONTROL THEORY

BAUM R.F. , [1972] , Optimal control systems with stochastic boundary conditions and state equations, Operations Research, 20, pp. 875-887.

BERTSEKAS D. , [1976] , Dynamic programming and stochastic control, Academic Press.

BERTSEKAS D. - SHREVE S. , [1978] , Stochastic optimal control : the discrete time case, Academic Press.

BENSOUSSAN A. - LIONS J.L. , [1982] , Contrôle impulsionnel et inéquations quasi-variationnelles, Paris, Dunod.

GIKHMAN I.I. - SKOROKHOD A.V., [1972] , Stochastic differential equations, Springer Verlag, Berlin.

KLEINDORFER P.R. - GLOVER , [1973] , Linear convex stochastic optimal control with applications in production planning, IEEE Transactions on Optimal Control,AC-18(1) pp. 56-59.

KUSHNER H.J. , [1965] , On the stochastic maximum principle : fixed time of control, Journal of Math. Anal. Appl., 11, pp. 78-92.

KUSHNER H.J. , [1968] , On the existence of optimal stochastic controls, SIAM Journal Control, Ser. A., 3, pp. 463-474.

KUSHNER H.J. - SCHWEPPE F.C. , [1964] , A maximum principle for stochastic control systems, Journal of Math. Anal. Appl., 8, pp. 287-302.

PRODUCTION PLANNING MODELS

ARROW K.J. - HARRIS T. - MARSCHAK J., [1951] , Optimal inventory policy, Econometrica, 19(3), pp. 250-272.

BAWA V.S., [1982] , Stochastic dominance : a research bibliography. Management Science, 28(6), pp. 698-712.

BELLMAN R. - GLICKSBERG I. - GROSS O., [1955] , On the optimal inventory equation, Management science, 2(1), pp. 83-104.

BESSLER S. - VEINOTT A.F. Jr., [1966] , Optimal policy for a dynamic multi-echelon inventory model, Naval Research Logistics Quarterly, 13(4), pp. 355-389.

CHARNES A. - DREZE J. - MILLER M., [1966] , Decision and horizon rules for stochastic planning problems : A linear example, Econometrica, 34(2), pp. 307-330.

DVORETZKY A. - KIEFER J. - WOLFOWITZ J., [1952-1], The inventory problem : I. Case of known distributions of demand, Econometrica, 20(2), pp. 187-222.

DVORETZKY A. - KIEFER J. - WOLFOWITZ J., [1952-2], The inventory problem : II. Case of known distributions of demand, Econometrica, 20(3), pp. 451-466.

DVORETZKY A. - KIEFER J. - WOLFOWITZ J., [1953] , On the optimal character of the (s,S) policy in inventory theory, Econometrica, 21(4), pp. 586-596.

EPPEN G. - FAMA E., [1969] , Cash balance and simple dynamic portfolio problems with proportional costs, INternational Economic Review, 10(2), pp. 119-133.

GONEDES N.J. - LIEBER Z., [1974] , Production planning for a stochastic demand process, Operations Research, 22(4), pp. 771-787.

HAMMOND III J.S., [1974] , Simplifying the choice between uncertain projects where preference is nonlinear, Management Science, 20(7), pp. 1047-1072.

IGLEHART D.L., [1963-1] , Optimality of (S,s) policies in the infinite horizon dynamic inventory problem, Management Science, 9(2), pp. 259-267.

IGLEHART D.L., [1963-2] , Dynamic programming and stationary analysis of inventory problems, in H. Scarf, D. Gilford, M. Shelly,eds.,Multistage inventory models and techniques, Stanford University Press, Chapter 1.

IGNALL E. - VEINOTT A.F. Jr., [1969] , Optimality of myopic inventory policies for several substitute products, Management Science, 15(5), pp. 284-304.

KARLIN S., [1958-1] , One stage inventory models with uncertainty, in S. Karlin and H. Scarf, eds.,Studies in the mathematical theory of inventory and production, Stanford University Press, Chapter 8.

KARLIN S., [1958-2] , Optimal inventory policy for the Arrow-Harris-Marschak dynamic model, in K.J Arrow, S. Karlin and H. Scarf, eds, Studies in the mathematical theory of inventory and production, Stanford University Press, Chapter 9.

KARLIN S., [1960] , Dynamic inventory policy with varying stochastic demand, Management Science, 6(3), pp. 231-258.

KARLIN S. - SCARF H. , [1958] , Inventory models of the Arrow-Haaris-Marschak type with time lag, in K.J Arrow, S. Karlin and H. Scarf, eds. Studies in the mathematical theory of inventory and production, Stanford University Press, Chapter 10.

KLEINDORFER P. - KUNREUTHER H., [1978] , Stochastic horizons for the aggregate planning problem, Management Science, 24(5), pp. 485-497.

LEHMANN E., [1955] , Ordered families of distributions, Annals of Mathematical Statistics, 26(3), pp. 399-419.

LUNDIN R.A., [1974] , Planning horizon type theorems for the discrete time, non stationary cash balance problem with proportional costs, Working Paper n° 26, Goteborg University, Sweden.

MILLS E.S., [1957] , The theory of inventory decisions, Econometrica 25(2), pp. 222-238.

MORTON T.E., [1971] , The near myopic nature of the lagged proportional cost inventory problem with lost sales, Operations Research, 19(7), pp. 1708-1716.

MORTON T.E., [1973] , The non stationarity infinite horizon periodic review inventory problem : I and II, Center for Mathematical Studies in Business and Economics Reports 7332 and 7333, University of Chicago.

SCARF H., [1960] , The optimality of (S,s) policies in the dynamic inventory problem, in K.J Arrow, S. Karlin and P. Suppes, eds., Mathematical Methods in the Social Sciences, Stanford University Press, Chapter 13.

SNYDER R.D., [1974] , Computation of (S,s) ordering policy parameters, Management Science, 21(2), pp. 223-229.

SOBEL M.J., [1970] , Making short-run changes in production when the employment level is fixed, Operations Research, 18(1), pp. 35-51.

VEINOTT A.F.Jr. , [1963] , Optimal stockage policies with non stationarity stochastic demands, in H. Scarf, D. Gilford and M. Shelly, eds., Multistage inventory models and techniques, Stanford University Press, Chapter 4.

VEINOTT, A.F.Jr., [1965-1] , Optimal policy for a multi-product dynamic non-stationary inventory problem, Management Science, 12(3), pp. 206-222.

VEINOTT A.F.Jr., [1965-2] , Optimal policy in a dynamic, single product, non stationary inventory model with several demand classes, Operations Research, 13(5), pp. 761-778.

VEINOTT A.F.Jr., [1966-1] , On the optimality of (S,s) policies : New conditions and a new proof, SIAM Journal of Applied Mathematics, 14, pp. 1067-1083.

VEINOTT A.F.Jr., [1966-2] , The status of mathematical inventory theory, Management Science, 12(11), pp. 745-777.

VEINOTT A.F.Jr. - WAGNER H.M., [1965] , Computing optimal (s,S) inventory policies, Management Science, 11(5), pp. 525-552.

WAGNER H.M., [1962] , Statistical management of inventory systems, John Wiley and Sons, Chapter 2.

ZABEL E. [1962] , A note on the optimality of (S,s) policies in inventory theory, Management Science, 9(1), pp. 123-125.

PRODUCTION SMOOTHING MODELS

BECKMANN M.J., [1961] , Production smoothing and inventory control, Operations Research, 9(4), pp. 456-467.

HOLT C.C. - MODIGLIANI F. - MUTH J. - SIMON H., [1960] , Planning production, inventories, and work force, Prentice Hall.

IGLEHART D.L., [1965] , Capital accumulation and production for the firm : optimal dynamic policies, Management Science, 12(3), pp. 193-205.

KUNREUTHER H., [1966] , Scheduling short-run changes in production to minimize long run expected costs, Management Science, 12(7), pp. 541-554.

SOBEL M.J., [1969] , Production smoothing with stochastic demand I : finite horizon case, Management Science, 16(3), pp. 195-207.

SOBEL M.J., [1970] , Employment smoothing (capital accumulation) with production for stochastic demand, Management Science, 16(5), pp. 340-349.

SOBEL M.J., [1971] , Production smoothing with stochastic demand II : infinite horizon case, Management Science, 17(11), pp. 724-735.

CHAPTER V

SOFTWARE FOR PRODUCTION PLANNING MODELS WITH CONCAVE COSTS AND DETERMINISTIC DEMAND

DISCRETE TIME FORMULATION

INTRODUCTION

A general software is proposed which allows to compute the optimal production plan (i.e. optimal control) at time 0,1, ..., n-1, for a large class of production planning models with concave costs and deterministic demand.

The following assumptions are made :

1 - Demand at discrete times 1,2, ..., n-1,n is known ;
2 - The initial inventory level at time 0 is known and not necessarily zero ;
3 - No backlogging is permitted, i.e. inventory levels are required to stay positive ;
4 - Inventory and production costs are both concave, not necessarily stationary, but piecewise linear.

Piecewise linearity of the cost functions proceeds from the mere observation that, in practice, it would be hard to expect a production manager to provide the analyst with analytical estimations of the cost functions. At best the production manager will be able to approximate these cost functions by a few points, and we shall assume linearity between these points.

The chapter is structured as follows. We begin with the "MAIN PROGRAM" which provides the user with parametered Input/Output instructions (READ and WRITE). Then the three subprograms "CCONC", "VERI" and "COUT" are presented.

CCONC is divided into two parts. It starts by verifying whether the inputs are coherent with the constraints of the problem. The second part of CCONC consists in computing the optimal total production and inventory cost and the optimal control.

The subprogram VERI tests the cost functions.

The last subprogram COUT computes the production and inventory costs given the cost functions and the production schedule.

Figure 1 summarizes the structure of the software.

MAIN PROGRAM

1. The user gives the inputs (initial stock level, demand, sets of points which define the cost functions, ...)
2. CCONC is called

   CCONC

   2.1. Test of the inputs (using the subprogram VERI)
   2.2. Computation of the optimal control and the corresponding costs :

   2.2.1. Case where the total demand between 0 and n is not greater than the initial stock level
   2.2.2. Case where the total demand between 0 and n is greater than the initial stock level.

   2.2.2.1. First step

   It uses the backward dynamic programming equations. This step needs the subprogram COUT

   2.2.2.2. Second step

   Computation of the optimal control and of the corresponding overall cost, given the results obtained at the previous step. The subprogram COUT is also used.

3. Printing of the results.

FIGURE 1

We now detail the main program and the subprograms, and we give technical informations about their inputs and outputs.

I - THE MAIN PROGRAM

The following arrays are used and their dimensions can be modified, according to the constraints :

1 - the dimension of either d, v, w, z, il, is, kt must be at least equal to the number of periods of the problem.
2 - the dimension of y is at least equal to the number of periods of the problem plus one.
3 - the dimension of al and bl is at least equal to the number of points used in order to define the set of production costs.
4 - the dimension of as and bs is at least equal to the number of points used in order to define the set of inventory costs.
5 - the dimension of ml is at least equal to the number of production cost functions used.
6 - the dimension of ms is at least equal to the number of inventory cost functions considered.

The program refers to two I/O devices :

1 - A screen, which :

- . displays the questions in order to guide the user in the introduction of the inputs.
  Ex : write (0,X) (list or nothing)
- . introduced the data
  Ex : read (0,X) (list)

2 - a printer, which prints the result
   Ex : write (21,X) (list)

Two files are associated with these devices (0=screen, 21=printer). They are opened at the beginning of the program, and the file 21 (printer) is closed at the end.

The instructions corresponding to the I/O devices may be modified according to the type of computer used. The program listed thereafter is written for the system MULTICS .

The main program allows to enter the inputs, to call the subprogram CCONC and to write the results.

We now present the listing of the main program.

```
      dimension d(50),v(50),y(51),w(50),z(50)
      dimension al(100),bl(100),il(50),ml(20)
      dimension as(100),bs(100),is(50),ms(20)
      dimension kt(50)
      open(0)
      open(21,form="formatted")
c
c     Number of periods
c
      write(0,1)
1     format(3x,"Number of periods?-i3")
      read(0,2)n
2     format(i3)
      eps=1.e-5
c
c     Demand
c
      write(0,3)
3     format(8x,"Input of the demand",/,8x,19("+"),/)
      do 4 i=1,n
      write(0,5)i
5     format(2x,"Demand at the end of the",i3,"-th period ?")
4     read(0,6)d(i)
6     format(f8.2)
c
c     Initial stock level
c
      write(0,7)
7     format(/,12x,"Stock level at the beginning of the first period ?")
      read(0,6)y0
      iu=0
c
c     Input of the production cost fonctions
c
      do 200 i=1,n
200   il(i)=0
      write(0,8)
8     format(/,12x,"Production cost fonctions ?",/,12x,27("+"),/)
      nl=0
      iml=0
17    write(0,9)
9     format(/,2x,"Type 1 in order to introduce another production
     & cost function",/,2x,"and 0 if the input of the production cost
```

```
      & functions is terminated.")
       read(0,10)k
10     format(i1)
       if(k.eq.0) go to 20
       nl=nl+1
       if(nl.gt.1) iu=1
       write(0,11)nl
11     format(/,12x,"Input of the ",i2,"-th production cost function",
      &/,12x,43("-"),/)
       write(0,12)
12     format(/,2x,"The points which define the function must be
      & introduced in the",/,2x,"increasing order of the x-axis va
      &lues.",/,2x,"In the case two x-axis values are equal,the
      & corresponding y-axis",/,2x,"values must be introduced in
      & the increasing order.")
       ml(nl)=0
14     write(0,13)
13     format(/,2x,"Type successively the x-axis and the y-axis values
      &(real values),",/,2x,"or -1. to stop the input.")
       read(0,6)x
       if(x.lt.0.) go to 18
       ml(nl)=ml(nl)+1
       iml=iml+1
       al(iml)=x
       read(0,6)bl(iml)
       go to 14
18     write(0,15)
15     format(3x,"Applicable to periods: (I3) or -10 (to stop)")
19     read(0,2)i
       if(i.lt.0)go to 17
       il(i)=nl
       go to 19
20     js=0
       do 201 i=1,n
       if(il(i).gt.0)go to 201
       write(0,202)i
202    format(2x,"Give the production cost function for period",1x,i3)
       js=1
201    continue
       if(js.eq.1)go to 17
c
c      Input of the inventory cost functions
c
       do 400 i=1,n
400    is(i)=0
       write(0,28)
28     format(/,12x,"Inventory cost functions ?",/,12x,26("+"),/)
       ns=0
       ims=0
37     write(0,29)
29     format(/,2x,"Type 1 in order to introduce another inventory
      & cost function",/,2x,"and 0 if the inputs end")
       read(0,10)k
       if(k.eq.0)go to 40
       ns=ns+1
       if(ns.gt.1) iu=1
       write(0,31)ns
31     format(12x,"Input of the",1x,i2,"-th inventory cost function ",
      &/,12x,42("-"),/)
       write(0,12)
```

```
      ms(ns)=0
34    write(0,13)
      read(0,6)x
      if(x.lt.0)go to 38
      ms(ns)=ms(ns)+1
      ims=ims+1
      as(ims)=x
      read(0,6)bs(ims)
      go to 34
38    write(0,15)
39    read(0,2)i
      if(i.lt.0)go to 37
      is(i)=ns
      go to 39
40    js=0
      do401 i=1,n
      if(is(i).gt.0)go to 401
      write(0,402)i
402   format(2x,"Give the inventory cost function for period",i3)
      js=1
401   continue
      if(js.eq.1)go to 37
      nl=n+1
      call cconc(y0,d,v,y,cl,cs,cc,itma,itic,w,z,iu,nl,kk,n,al,bl,il,
     &ml,nl,as,bs,is,ms,ns,iml,ims,eps,iwd)
      write(21,6666)iwd
6666  format(2x,"Code=",i4)
      write(21,600)n
600   format(12x,"Number of periods:",2x,i4,/,12x,17("*"),//)
      write(21,601)y0
601   format(5x,"Initial stock level:",2x,e14.7,/,5x,19("*"),//)
      write(21,602)
602   format(22x,"Demand",/,22x,6("*"),//)
      do 603 i=1,n
603   write(21,604)i,d(i)
604   format(2x,"End of the",1x,i4,"-th period:",2x,e14.7)
      write(21,605)
605   format(2x///)
      write(21,606)
606   format(12x,"Production cost function",/,12x,24("+"))
      ml=0
      do 650 i=1,nl
      write(21,607)i
607   format(//,2x,i4,"-th production cost function:",/)
      kz=ml(i)
      m2=ml+kz
      ml=ml+1
      write(21,608)(al(j),bl(j),j=ml,m2)
608   format(2x,3("x=",f8.2,2x,"y=",f8.2,4x))
      iw=0
      do 609 j=1,n
      if(il(j).ne.i)go to 609
      iw=iw+1
      kt(iw)=j
609   continue
      if(iw.eq.0)go to 650
      write(21,610)(kt(j),j=1,iw)
610   format(/,2x,"Applicable to periods:",/,2x,18i4)
650   ml=m2
      write(21,605)
```

```
164          write(21,616)
165 616      format(12x,"Inventory cost functions",/,12x,24("+"))
166          ml=0
167          do 660 i=1,ns
168          write(21,617)i
169 617      format(//,2x,i4,"-th inventory cost function:",/)
170          kz=ms(i)
171          m2=ml+kz
172          ml=ml+1
173          write(21,608)(as(j),bs(j),j=ml,m2)
174          iw=0
175          do 619 j=1,n
176          if(is(j).ne.i)go to 619
177          iw=iw+1
178          kt(iw)=j
179 619      continue
180          if(iw.eq.0)go to 660
181          write(21,610)(kt(j),j=1,iw)
182 660      ml=m2
183          if(iwd.ne.0) go to 6667
184          write(21,605)
185          write(21,661)
186 661      format(1x,78("*"))
187          write(21,662)n,cl
188 662      format(2x,"Total production cost during the",1x,i2,1x,"periods:",
189         &2x,e14.7,/,2x,43("-"),//)
190          write(21,663)n,cs
191 663      format(2x,"Total inventory cost during the",1x,i2,1x,"periods:",
192         &2x,e14.7,/,2x,42("-"),//)
193          write(21,664)cc
194 664      format(9x,"Optimal cost:",2x,e14.7,/,9x,12("-"),//)
195          write(21,665)(i,v(i),i=1,n)
196 665      format(12x,"Optimal control",/,12x,15("-"),//,(2x,"At the end of the",
197         &i4,1x,"-th period:",e14.7))
198          write(21,666)y0
199 666      format(2x//2x,"Stock level during the   1-th period",2x,e14.7)
200          n2=n-1
201          do 667 i=1,n2
202          jl=i+1
203 667      write(21,668)jl,y(i)
204 668      format(2x,"Stock level during the",i4,"-th period",2x,e14.7)
205          write(21,669)kk
206 669      format(//2x,"Number of set up points:",i4,/,2x,23("-"))
207          write(21,670)itma,itic
208 670      format(//,2x,"Maximum values of the stock level to be considered:",
209         &i4,/,2x,50("-"),//,2x,"Values of the stock level which have been",
210         &" considered:",i4,/,2x,52("-"),///)
211 6667     close(21)
212          stop
213          end
```

II - THE SUBROUTINE "CCONC"

CCONC is divided into two main parts. It begins by verifying whether the inputs are coherent with the constraints of the problem. For instance, the following questions are investigated : Is the final time greater then zero ? Is the initial stock level non-negative ? Are the demands non-negative ? Are the cost functions concave ? (the answer to the last question requires in addition the subprogram VERI (see below)). If at least one of these tests is negative, the program stops, and the integer parameter ICOD, takes a strictly positive value, according to the first negative test which has been found (see below in II.2. the different possible values of ICOD and their meaning).

The second part of CCONC consists in computing the optimal cost and the optimal control. The case where cumulative demand is not greater than the initial stock level is first investigated (in that situation, we know that a nul replenishment at each time is optimal). The remaining case is then processed. It requires two computation steps. The first one uses the backward linear programming equations (see Chapter I) in order to obtain, at each time, the optimal production if the stock level is the smallest which can appear at this time (taking into account the initial stock level), and the optimal cost for each stock level which can be reached in the optimal situation.

The second computation step starts considering time 0 and the initial stock level.

Then, for each time 0, 1, ..., n-1 :

1. if the stock level is the smallest which can appear at this time, taking into account the initial stock level, then the optimal production is the one which has been computed in the first step.

2. if not, the optimal production is null. The next stock level can be computed, and so on.

We then obtain the string of optimal productions and the string of corresponding.

II - 1. INPUTS

n	: number of periods
y_0	: stock level at time 0 (i.e. initial stock level)
d(i),i=2,...,n	: demand at time i
i u =	1 if at least one of the cost functions is non-stationary 0 if both cost functions are stationary.
eps	: precision limit which is a real number. Each real x with absolute value $\|x\|$ less than eps will be considered equal to zero. Of course, eps must not be less tant the precision of the computer being used. For instance, we set eps = 10^{-5} for the examples we consider in this chapter.

II.1.1. INPUTS RELATIVE TO THE PRODUCTION COST FUNCTIONS

As we already mentioned, any cost function is defined by a string of points and is suppposed to be linear between two successive points.

Let us consider the following cost functions :

(x_1,y_1), (x_2,y_2), ..., (x_i,y_i), ..., (x_r,y_r), where x_i and y_i are respectively the x-axis and the y-axis values of the i-th point which defines this function.

The following constraints must be satisfied :

1. $\underline{r \geq 2}$
2. $x_1 = 0$
3. $\underline{\text{if } r = 2}$, $0 = x_1 < x_2$
4. $\underline{\text{if } r > 2}$:
   4.1. $x_2 < x_3 < \ldots < x_r$

   4.2. $0 = x_1 \leq x_2$ and, if $x_1 = x_2$, $y_1 < y_2$

The linear function is the same between x_{r-1} and x_r, and after x_r.

The x-axis and y-axis values of the points which define the production cost functions are stored in the arrays al and bl respectively.

The points are input in the increasing order of their x-axis values. If two different points have the same x-axis null value, we first introduce the one with the smallest y-axis value.

In the case of non-stationarity, we have to consider several production cost functions. They are stored sequentially in al and bl, in order to spare memory size (the dimension of these arrays is iml)

nl is the number of production cost functions considered.
ml(i), for i = 1,2,...,nl, is the number of points which define the i-th production cost function.
il(j), for j = 1,2,...,n, is the index of the production cost function applicable at time j-1. (Production at time j-1 is available at time j).

As an illustration consider the following non-stationary problem :
n = 5.

The production cost function applicable at times 0,2 and 3 is linear and fined by the two points : (0,0), (10,2).
The production cost function applicable at times 1 and 4 is defined by : (0,0), (0,5), (15,15) and (30,20).

We can introduce the linear production cost function first, which gives :

al(1) = 0	al(2) = 10	al(3) = 0	al(4) = 0	al(5) = 15	al(6) = 30
bl(1) = 0	bl(2) = 2	bl(3) = 0	bl(4) = 5	bl(5) = 15	bl(6) = 20
ml(1) = 2	ml(2) = 4				
il(1) = 1	il(2) = 2	il(3) = 1	il(4) = 1	il(5) = 2	

If we reverse the order of entry we obtain :

al(1) = 0	al(2) = 0	al(3) = 15	al(4) = 30	al(5) = 0	al(6) = 10
bl(1) = 0	bl(2) = 5	bl(3) = 15	bl(4) = 20	bl(5) = 0	bl(6) = 2
ml(1) = 4	ml(2) = 2				
il(1) = 2	il(2) = 1	il(3) = 2	il(4) = 2	il(5) = 1	

II.1.2. INPUTS RELATIVE TO THE STORAGE COST FUNCTIONS

The comments made for the production cost function (s) also apply to the storage cost functions. We just need to replace :

al	by	as
bl	by	bs
iml	by	ims
il	by	is
ml	by	ms
nl	by	ns

where is(j), for j=1,...,n, denotes the storage order of the storage cost function applicable on the period [j-1,j[.

II - 2. OUTPUTS

The results of the computations can be retrieved in the following variables :

y(j), j = 2, ..., n+1 denotes the optimal stock level on [j-1,j[and y(1) = y_0

If the total amount demand over the problem horizon is not less than the initial stock level y_0, we know that y(n+1) = 0.

v(j), j = 1, 2, ..., n is the optimal production level decided at time j-1 and available at time j.

cl is the optimal total cost of producing for the n period problem.

cs is the optimal total inventory cost for the n period problem.

cc = cl + cs is the optimal total cost on [0,n]

The user will also find two integer values which give some information about the amount of computations which lead to the optimal control :

itma : maximal number of values of the stock level to be considered for computations

itic : effective number of values of the stock level that have been considered for computations.

The higher the inventory costs relative to the production costs, the greater is itma relative to itic.

kk is the number of set up points.

Finally, icod denotes a control variable which indicates the outcome of the various validity test runs in the subroutine VERI. It may take the following values :

icod = 0 : the validity tests were all positive and the results can be found in y,v and cc.

The program stops in the cases :

icod = 1 : $n \leq 0$

icod = 2 : $y_0 < 0$

icod = 3 : demand in at least one period is strictly negative

icod = 11 : at least a production cost function is only defined by one point icod = 12 : for at least one of the production cost functions, the x-axis values are not ranked by increasing values

icod = 13 : at least one production cost function is not increasing

icod = 14 : for at least one of the production cost functions, two x-axis values are different from zero and equal

icod = 15 : at least one of the production cost functions is not concave

icod = 16 : at least one of the production cost functions is only defined by two points, with their x-axis values equal to zero

icod = 17 : for at least one of the production cost functions, two successive points are the same

The values icod = 21, 22, 23, 24, 25, 26 and 27 have the same meaning as icod = 11, 12, 13, 14, 15, 16 and 17, respectively, but for the storage cost functions instead

At the end of CCONC the user first has to check the value of icod. If icod = 0, the output gives the optimal control, otherwise some inputs must be modified.

II - 3. WORKING VARIABLES

When the backward linear programming equations are applied, two arrays, denoted w and z, are used in order to store the optimal costs compiled for two consecutive points in time.

The dimensions of w and z must at least be equal to the number of periods.

II - 4. LIST OF CCONC

Note that some computers allow the use of the dimension 1 in the subprograms if the actual dimension is provided in the main program.

Subroutine cconc

```
      subroutine cconc(y0,d,v,y,cl,cs,cc,itma,itic,w,z,iu,nl,kk,
     &n,al,bl,il,ml,nl,as,bs,is,ms,ns,iml,ims,eps,icod)
      dimension d(nl),v(nl),w(nl),z(nl),y(nl)
      dimension al(iml),bl(iml),il(n),ml(nl)
      dimension as(ims),bs(ims),is(n),ms(ns)
      open(0)
c+++++++++++++++++++++++++++++++++++++++++++++++++++++++++++++++
c
c          PRODUCTION PLANNING MODELS WITH CONCAVE COSTS
c                    AND DETERMINISTIC DEMAND
c                   DISCRETE TIME FORMULATION
c
c+++++++++++++++++++++++++++++++++++++++++++++++++++++++++++++++
c
c************************ Inputs ********************************
c
c          y0: Initial stock level
c
c          n:Number of periods
c
c          d(i),i=1,...,n: Demand at the end of the i-th period
c
c          iu=0 if the production cost and inventory cost functions do
```

```
c              not depend on time (stationary) and iu=1 otherwise.
c
c          eps:Positive real value.Each value x which
c              verifies |x| < eps is supposed to be null.
c
c      PRODUCTION COST FUNCTIONS:
c
c          nl:Number of production cost functions used.
c
c          ml(i),i=1,2,...,nl:Number of points which define
c               the production cost function indexed by i.
c
c          il(j),j=1,2,...,n:Index of the production cost function
c               associated to production in period j.
c
c          iml:Greater than or equal to the total number of points
c              which define the set of production cost functions
c
c          al(i) and bl(i),i=1,2,...,iml:X-axis values (quantity) and
c               corresponding Y-axis values($) of the points which
c               define the production cost functions.
c
c      INVENTORY COST FUNCTIONS
c
c          ns:Number of functions used.
c
c          ms(i),i=1,2,...,ns:Number of points which define
c               the function indexed by i.
c
c          is(j),j=1,...,n:Index of the inventory cost
c               function associated to the j-th period.
c
c          ims:Greater than the total number of points used which
c              define the set of the inventory cost functions.
c
c          as(i) and bs(i),i=1,2,...,ims:X-axis values (quantity) and
c               corresponding Y-axis values($) of the points which
c               define the inventory cost functions.
c
c*************************************************************
c
c
c*********************** Outputs *****************************
c
c          v(i),i=1,...,n: Optimal control
c                          v(i) is the order quantity which enters the
c                          inventory at the end of the i-th period.
c
c          y(i),i=1,...,n: Stock levels corresponding to the optimal control
c                          y(i) is the stock level in the i-th period.
c
c          cl: Total optimal production cost for the n-period problem.
c
c          cs: Total optimal holding cost for the n-period problem.
c
c          cc: Optimal total cost (=cl+cs).
c
c          itma: Maximal number of values of the stock level
c               to be considered for computations.
c
```

```
c                  that have been considered for computations.
c
c            kk:Number of set up points
c
c            icod:if icod=0,then the inputs are consistent
c                           with the model assumptions.
c                 if icod<>0,one input at least is not consistent,
c                            and the program stops.
c
c*************************************************************
c
c*********************** Remarks *****************************
c
c            w and z : internal variables to the program
c*************************************************************
c*************************************************************
c
c
c          TEST OF THE INPUTS
c
       if(n)950,950,941
 950   icod=1
       go to 1000
 941   if(y0)942,943,943
 942   icod=2
       go to 1000
 943   do 944 i=1,n
       if(d(i))945,944,944
 945   icod=3
       go to 1000
 944   continue
       it=10
       call veri(al,bl,il,ml,iml,n,nl,eps,icod,it)
       if(icod)1000,947,1000
 947   it=20
       call veri(as,bs,is,ms,ims,n,ns,eps,icod,it)
       if(icod)1000,948,1000
 948   itma=1
       itic=1
       s=0.
       do 1 i=1,n
       s=s+d(i)
       if(s.lt.y0) go to 1
       k=i
       go to 2
 1     continue
c+++++++++++++++++++++++++++++++++++++++++++++++++++++++++++++
c+++++++++++++++++++++++++++++++++++++++++++++++++++++++++++++
c
c
c          COMPUTATION OF THE SOLUTION
c
c*******CASE WHERE THE TOTAL DEMAND IS LESS
c          THAN THE INITIAL STOCK LEVEL
c
       a=y0
       cc=0.
       cs=0.
       cl=0.
       do 3 i=1,n
```

```
      do 3 i=1,n
      cs=cs+cout(as,bs,is,ms,ims,n,ns,eps,a,i)
      cl=cl+cout(al,bl,il,ml,iml,n,nl,eps,0.,i)
      v(i)=0.
      y(i)=a-d(i)
3     a=y(i)
      cc=cs+cl
      itma=n
      itic=n
      go to 1000
c+++++++++++++++++++++++++++++++++++++++++++++++++++++++++++++++++++++
c+++++++++++++++++++++++++++++++++++++++++++++++++++++++++++++++++++++
c
c********GENERAL CASE: TOTAL DEMAND
c           IS GREATER THAN THE INITIAL STOCK LEVEL
c
c
c  +++FIRST STEP: BACKWARD DYNAMIC PROGRAMMING EQUATIONS
c
2     z(1)=0.
      iz=1
      do 101 i=n-1,1,-1
      il=i+1
      xm=y0
      do 4 j=1,i
4     xm=xm-d(j)
      if(xm.le.0.) xm=0.
      iw=2
      if((xm.eq.0.).and.(d(il).eq.0.)) go to 6
      if(xm.ge.d(il)) iw=1
      if(iw.eq.2) go to 6
c
c------stock level >= next demand
c
      if(iu.ne.0) go to 7
c
c         stationary case
c
      cl=cout(as,bs,is,ms,ims,n,ns,eps,xm,il)
      c2=cout(al,bl,il,ml,iml,n,nl,eps,0.,il)
      w(1)=cl+c2+z(1)
      v(il)=0.
      itma=itma+1
      itic=itic+1
      iz=1
8     z(1)=w(1)
      go to 101
c
c        non stationary case
c
7     v(il)=0.
      c2=cout(al,bl,il,ml,iml,n,nl,eps,0.,il)
      u=c2+z(1)
      if(iz.eq.1) go to 1023
      sl=0.
      do 9 j=il,k-1
9     sl=sl+d(j)
      kww=k
      if(xm.eq.d(il)) kww=k+1
      do 10 j=2,iz
```

```
204            s1=s1+d(j1)
205            r=s1-xm
206            c2=cout(al,bl,il,ml,iml,n,nl,eps,r,il)
207            p=c2+z(j)
208            if(p.ge.u) go to 11
209            u=p
210            v(il)=r
211 11         c1=cout(as,bs,is,ms,ims,n,ns,eps,s1,il)
212            c2=cout(al,bl,il,ml,iml,n,nl,eps,0.,il)
213            w(j)=c1+c2+z(j)
214 10         continue
215 1023       c1=cout(as,bs,is,ms,ims,n,ns,eps,xm,il)
216            w(1)=c1+u
217            itma=itma+n-k+2
218            itic=itic+iz
219            if(iz.eq.1) go to 8
220 40         iz1=1
221            u=w(1)
222            z(1)=w(1)
223            do 12 j=2,iz
224            if(w(j).ge.u) go to 12
225            u=w(j)
226            iz1=j
227 12         z(j)=w(j)
228            iz=iz1
229            go to 101
230 c
231 c------stock level < next demand
232 c
233 6          itma=itma+n-i+1
234 c
235 c          Stationary or non stationary case and next demand > 0
236 c
237 20         s=d(il)
238            s1=s-xm
239            v(il)=s1
240            c2=cout(al,bl,il,ml,iml,n,nl,eps,s1,il)
241            c3=cout(al,bl,il,ml,iml,n,nl,eps,0.,il)
242            c1=cout(as,bs,is,ms,ims,n,ns,eps,s,il)
243            ss=c2+z(1)
244            w(2)=c1+c3+z(1)
245            if(iz.eq.1) go to 23
246            do 25 j=2,iz
247            i2=i+j
248            s=s+d(i2)
249            s1=s-xm
250            c2=cout(al,bl,il,ml,iml,ik1,nl,eps,s1,il)
251            u=c2+z(j)
252            if(u.ge.ss) go to 24
253            ss=u
254            v(il)=s1
255 24         c1=cout(as,bs,is,ms,ims,n,ns,eps,s,il)
256            w(j+1)=c1+c3+z(j)
257 25         continue
258 23         c1=cout(as,bs,is,ms,ims,n,ns,eps,xm,il)
259            w(1)=c1+ss
260            iz=iz+1
261            itic=itic+iz
262            go to 40
263 101        continue
```

```
      itma=itma+1
      itic=itic+1
c***********************************************************************
c
c     +++ SECOND STEP
c
      if(y0.lt.d(1)) go to 30
c
c------Initial stock level >= first demand
c
      if(iu.eq.0) go to 31
c
c      non stationary case
c
      v(1)=0.
      cl=cout(al,bl,il,ml,iml,n,nl,eps,0.,1)
      ss=cl+z(1)
      if(iz.eq.1) go to 32
      sl=y0
      do 37 j=1,n
      sl=sl-d(j)
      if(sl.ge.0.)go to 37
      jj=j
      go to 38
37    continue
38    sl=sl+d(jj)
      jj=jj-1
      do 33 j=2,iz
      jj=jj+1
      sl=sl-d(jj)
      s2=-sl
      cl=cout(al,bl,il,ml,iml,n,nl,eps,s2,1)
      u=cl+z(j)
      if(u.ge.ss) go to 33
      ss=u
      v(1)=s2
33    continue
32    c2=cout(as,bs,is,ms,ims,n,ns,eps,y0,1)
      cc=c2+ss
      go to 50
c
c      stationary case
c
31    c2=cout(as,bs,is,ms,ims,n,ns,eps,y0,1)
      cl=cout(al,bl,il,ml,iml,n,nl,eps,0.,1)
      cc=cl+c2+z(1)
      v(1)=0.
      go to 50
c
c------Initial stock level < first demand
c
30    s=d(1)-y0
      v(1)=s
      cl=cout(al,bl,il,ml,iml,n,nl,eps,s,1)
      ss=cl+z(1)
      if(iz.eq.1) go to 3555
      do 35 j=2,iz
      s=s+d(j)
      cl=cout(al,bl,il,ml,iml,n,nl,eps,s,1)
      u=cl+z(j)
```

```
324          if(u.ge.ss ) go to 35
325          ss=u
326          v(1)=s
327 35       continue
328 3555     c2=cout(as,bs,is,ms,ims,n,ns,eps,y0,1)
329          cc=c2+ss
330 c
331 c*****************************************************************
332 c*****************************************************************
333 c
334 c********FORWARD COMPUTATIONS
335 c
336 50       c1=0.
337          cs=0.
338          xm=y0
339          yl=y0
340          y(1)=y0
341          kk=0
342          do 70 i=1,n
343          u=0.
344          tt=xm+d(i )/10.
345          if(yl.gt.tt ) go to 99
346          u=v(i )
347          if(v(i ).ne.0. ) kk=kk+1
348 99       c1=cout(al,bl,il,ml,iml,n,nl,eps,u,i )
349          c2=cout(as,bs,is,ms,ims,n,ns,eps,yl,i )
350          c1=c1+c1
351          cs=cs+c2
352          v(i )=u
353          y(i )=yl-d(i )+v(i )
354          yl=y(i )
355          xm=xm-d(i )
356          if(xm.lt.0. ) xm=0.
357 70       continue
358 1000     return
359          end
```

III - THE SUBROUTINE "VERI"

This subroutine is called by CCONC in order to test the validity of the cost functions.

III - 1. INPUTS

a and b are either al and bl respectively, when the production cost functions are tested,or as and bs when the storage cost functions are tested. The dimension of a and b is denoted i5.

Accordingly, i is either il or is and of dimension n.

m contains either the same values as ml (if the production cost functions are tested) or the same values as ms (if the storage cost functions are tested). Its dimension is denoted i6 which is equal either to nl or ns.

eps was defined in CCONC

$$it = \begin{cases} 10 \text{ when the production cost functions are tested} \\ 20 \text{ when the storage cost functions are tested.} \end{cases}$$

II - 2. INPUT - OUTPUT VARIABLE

ikl is set to zero in CCONC before the subroutine VERI is called, and it keeps this value when VERI starts.

Only if an error is detected ikl takes one of the values : 11 to 17, or 21 to 27 different from zero (section II).

III - 3. LIST OF VERI

Note that, with many computers, it is possible to give the dimension 1 to a, b, i and m (idem CCONC).

Subroutine veri

```
 1              subroutine veri(a,b,i,m,i5,n,i6,eps,ikl,it)
 2              dimension a(i5),b(i5),i(n),m(i6)
 3              k=0
 4              do 1  j=1,i6
 5              jj=0
 6              kl=k+m(j)
 7              mm=m(j)-2
 8              if(mm)3,2,2
 9   3          ikl=it+1
10              go to 1000
11   2          k=k+2
12              do 4  l=k,kl
13              u=b(l)-b(l-1)
14              if(l.eq.k) go to 18
15              w=u+(a(l)-a(l-1))
16              w=abs(w)
17              if(w.gt.eps) go to 18
18              ikl=it+7
19              go to 1000
20  18          if(u)5,6,6
21   5          ikl=it+3
22              go to 1000
23   6          u=a(l)-a(l-1)
24              if(u)7,8,8
25   7          ikl=it+2
26              go to 1000
27   8          ul=abs(u)-eps
28              if(ul)9,10,10
29   9          k2=l-k
30              if(k2)11,16,11
31  16          ll=m(j)-3
32              if(ll)17,4,4
33  17          ikl=it+6
34              go to 1000
35  11          ikl=it+4
36              go to 1000
37  10          xx=(b(l)-b(l-1))/(a(l)-a(l-1))
38              if(jj)13,12,13
```

```
12      jj=1
        go to 15
13      u=xy-xx
        if(u)14,15,15
14      ikl=it+5
        go to 1000
15      xy=xx
4       continue
1       k=kl
1000    return
        end
```

IV - THE SUBROUTINE "COUT"

This subroutine allows to compute the cost (production cost or inventory cost) given the cost function defined by a set of points in CCONC and a production schedule denoted by w.

The inputs a, b, isl, msl, imsl, nsl, n respectively are the same as a, b, i, m, i5, i6, n in VERI.

eps has the same meaning as in CCONC.

i is the period index.

Function cout

```
        realfunction cout(a,b,isl,msl,imsl,n,nsl,eps,w,i)
        dimension a(imsl),b(imsl),isl(n),msl(nsl)
        nn2=isl(i)
        nn2=nn2-1
        if(nn2)1,1,2
1       nn1=0
        go to 3
2       nn1=0
        do 4 l=1,nn2
4       nn1=nn1+msl(l)
3       nn2=nn1+msl(nn2+1)
        u=w-eps
        if(u)5,6,6
5       cout=b(nn1+1)
        go to 1000
6       nn1=nn1+2
        do 7 l=nn1,nn2
        u=a(l)-w
        if(u)7,8,8
8       nn2=l
        go to 9
7       continue
9       u=(b(nn2)-b(nn2-1))/(a(nn2)-a(nn2-1))
        cout=b(nn2)+(w-a(nn2))*u
1000    return
        end
```

V - EXAMPLES OF APPLICATION OF THE SOFTWARE

V -1. EXAMPLE 1 (NON STATIONARITY)

We notice that no error has been found in the inputs (ikl = 0).

```
Code=    0
          Number of periods:     10
          *****************

   Initial stock level:    0.8000000E+01
   *******************

                    Demand
                    ******

End of the     1-th period:    0.2000000E+01
End of the     2-th period:    0.7000000E+01
End of the     3-th period:    0.4000000E+01
End of the     4-th period:    0.1200000E+02
End of the     5-th period:    0.1700000E+02
End of the     6-th period:    0.4000000E+01
End of the     7-th period:    0.8000000E+01
End of the     8-th period:    0.2000000E+01
End of the     9-th period:    0.0000000E+00
End of the    10-th period:    0.1400000E+02


          Production cost functions
          ++++++++++++++++++++++++


   1-th production cost function:

x=    0.00  y=    0.00    x=    5.00  y=   10.00    x=   10.00  y=   15.00

Applicable to periods:
   1   2   3   7   8   9  10


   2-th production cost function:

x=    0.00  y=    0.00    x=    0.00  y=    5.00    x=   10.00  y=    7.00

Applicable to periods:
   4   5   6
```

Inventory cost functions
++++++++++++++++++++++++

1-th inventory cost function:

x= 0.00 y= 0.00 x= 2000.00 y= 130.80 x= 4000.00 y= 206.00

Applicable to periods:
1 2 3 4 5 6 7 8 9 10 11 12

****

Total production cost for the 12 period problem: 0.1679600E+05

Total inventory cost for the 12 period problem: 0.2616000E+03

Optimal cost: 0.1705760E+05

Optimal control

At the end of the 1 -th period: 0.2000000E+04
At the end of the 2 -th period: 0.2000000E+04
At the end of the 3 -th period: 0.4000000E+04
At the end of the 4 -th period: 0.0000000E+00
At the end of the 5 -th period: 0.2000000E+04
At the end of the 6 -th period: 0.2000000E+04
At the end of the 7 -th period: 0.2000000E+04
At the end of the 8 -th period: 0.2000000E+04
At the end of the 9 -th period: 0.4000000E+04
At the end of the 10 -th period: 0.0000000E+00
At the end of the 11 -th period: 0.2000000E+04
At the end of the 12 -th period: 0.2000000E+04

Stock level during the 1-th period: 0.0000000E+00
Stock level during the 2-th period: 0.0000000E+00
Stock level during the 3-th period: 0.0000000E+00
Stock level during the 4-th period: 0.2000000E+04
Stock level during the 5-th period: 0.0000000E+00
Stock level during the 6-th period: 0.0000000E+00
Stock level during the 7-th period: 0.0000000E+00
Stock level during the 8-th period: 0.0000000E+00
Stock level during the 9-th period: 0.0000000E+00
Stock level during the 10-th period: 0.2000000E+04
Stock level during the 11-th period: 0.0000000E+00
Stock level during the 12-th period: 0.0000000E+00

```
Number of set up points:   7
------------------------

Maximum values of the stock level to be considered:  56
------------------------------------------------

Values of the stock level which have been considered:  26
---------------------------------------------------
```

V - 2. EXAMPLE 2

The second inventory cost function was defined as a decreasing function, then icod takes the value 23, and no computation is made.

```
Code=  23
        Number of periods:     10
        *****************


   Initial stock level:    0.2800000E+02
   ******************


                  Demand
                  ******


End of the    1-th period:   0.1500000E+02
End of the    2-th period:   0.1200000E+02
End of the    3-th period:   0.3000000E+01
End of the    4-th period:   0.0000000E+00
End of the    5-th period:   0.1400000E+02
End of the    6-th period:   0.1200000E+02
End of the    7-th period:   0.0000000E+00
End of the    8-th period:   0.7000000E+01
End of the    9-th period:   0.9000000E+01
End of the   10-th period:   0.5000000E+01


        Production cost functions
        ++++++++++++++++++++++++


   1-th production cost function:

x=    0.00  y=    0.00    x=   10.00  y=    2.00

Applicable to periods:
   1   2   3   4   5   6   7


   2-th production cost function:

x=    0.00  y=    0.00    x=   10.00  y=   10.00    x=   20.00  y=   15.00

Applicable to periods:
   8   9  10
```

Inventory cost functions
+++++++++++++++++++++++++

1-th inventory cost function:

x= 0.00 y= 0.00 x= 2.00 y= 10.00

Applicable to periods:
1 2 3 4

2-th inventory cost function:

x= 0.00 y= 0.00 x= 10.00 y= 5.00 x= 20.00 y= 3.00

Applicable to periods:
5 6 7 8 9 10

V - 3. EXAMPLE 3 (NON STATIONARY)

Code= 0
Number of periods: 10
****

Initial stock level: 0.1400000E+02
****

Demand
******

End of the	1-th period:	0.5000000E+01
End of the	2-th period:	0.7000000E+01
End of the	3-th period:	0.5000000E+01
End of the	4-th period:	0.0000000E+00
End of the	5-th period:	0.1400000E+02
End of the	6-th period:	0.1200000E+02
End of the	7-th period:	0.6000000E+01
End of the	8-th period:	0.1000000E+01
End of the	9-th period:	0.9000000E+01
End of the	10-th period:	0.1300000E+02

```
          Production cost function
          ++++++++++++++++++++++++

   1-th production cost function:

x=     0.00  y=     0.00    x=   10.00  y=     2.00

Applicable to periods:
   1   2   3   4   5   6   7

   2-th production cost function:

x=     0.00  y=     0.00    x=   10.00  y=    10.00    x=   20.00  y=    15.00

Applicable to periods:
   8   9  10


          Inventory cost functions
          ++++++++++++++++++++++++

   1-th inventory cost function:

x=     0.00  y=     0.00    x=    0.00  y=     8.00    x=   10.00  y=     9.00

Applicable to periods:
   1   2   3   4   5

   2-th inventory cost function:

x=     0.00  y=     0.00    x=   10.00  y=     2.00    x=   20.00  y=     3.00

Applicable to periods:
   6   7   8   9  10
```

```
*******************************************************************************
Total production cost during the 10 periods:    0.1160000E+02
-------------------------------------------


Total inventory cost during the 10 periods:    0.3530000E+02
-------------------------------------------


        Optimal cost:    0.4690000E+02
        ------------


           Optimal control
           ---------------

At the end of the   1 -th period: 0.0000000E+00
At the end of the   2 -th period: 0.0000000E+00
At the end of the   3 -th period: 0.3000000E+01
At the end of the   4 -th period: 0.0000000E+00
At the end of the   5 -th period: 0.1400000E+02
At the end of the   6 -th period: 0.1200000E+02
At the end of the   7 -th period: 0.2900000E+02
At the end of the   8 -th period: 0.0000000E+00
At the end of the   9 -th period: 0.0000000E+00
At the end of the  10 -th period: 0.0000000E+00


Stock level during the   1-th period    0.1400000E+02
Stock level during the   2-th period    0.9000000E+01
Stock level during the   3-th period    0.2000000E+01
Stock level during the   4-th period    0.0000000E+00
Stock level during the   5-th period    0.0000000E+00
Stock level during the   6-th period    0.0000000E+00
Stock level during the   7-th period    0.0000000E+00
Stock level during the   8-th period    0.2300000E+02
Stock level during the   9-th period    0.2200000E+02
Stock level during the  10-th period    0.1300000E+02


Number of set up points:   4
-----------------------


Maximum values of the stock level to be considered:   55
----------------------------------------------------


Values of the stock level which have been considered:   31
----------------------------------------------------
```

V - 4. EXAMPLE 4

The initial inventory level is greater than the total demand. The optimal control is thus a null replenishment for each decision instant.

```
Code=   0
          Number of periods:      5
          *****************


   Initial stock level:   0.2000000E+02
   *******************


                     Demand
                     ******


End of the     1-th period:    0.1000000E+01
End of the     2-th period:    0.4000000E+01
End of the     3-th period:    0.2000000E+01
End of the     4-th period:    0.3000000E+01
End of the     5-th period:    0.6000000E+01


          Production cost functions
          +++++++++++++++++++++++++


   1-th production cost function:

x=    0.00  y=     0.00     x=     0.00  y=     5.00     x=   10.00  y=     6.00

Applicable to periods:
   1    2    3    4    5


          Inventory cost functions
          +++++++++++++++++++++++++


   1-th inventory cost function:

x=    0.00  y=     0.00     x=    10.00  y=     1.00

Applicable to periods:
   1    2    3    4    5
```

```
*******************************************************************************
Total production cost during the  5 periods:   0.0000000E+00
--------------------------------------------

Total inventory cost during the  5 periods:   0.7700000E+01
--------------------------------------------

        Optimal cost:   0.7700000E+01
        ------------

          Optimal control
          ---------------

At the end of the   1 -th period: 0.0000000E+00
At the end of the   2 -th period: 0.0000000E+00
At the end of the   3 -th period: 0.0000000E+00
At the end of the   4 -th period: 0.0000000E+00
At the end of the   5 -th period: 0.0000000E+00

Stock level during the   1-th period   0.2000000E+02
Stock level during the   2-th period   0.1900000E+02
Stock level during the   3-th period   0.1500000E+02
Stock level during the   4-th period   0.1300000E+02
Stock level during the   5-th period   0.1000000E+02

Number of set up points:   0
------------------------

Maximum values of the stock level to be considered:   5
---------------------------------------------------

Values of the stock level which have been considered:   5
-----------------------------------------------------
```

VI - REAL WORLD APPLICATION

This software has been applied in a factory which manufactures transformers where two thousand switches of a given type need to be produced every month.

Both stationary and non stationary situations are considered. The latter is refering to the months of march, april, september and october where production needs overtime.

VI - 1. THE STATIONARY CASE

Note that the optimal solution consists of producing every four months a lot of size 8000 units.

```
Code=    0
            Number of periods:     12
            *****************


    Initial stock level:    0.0000000E+00
    ******************


                         Demand
                         ******


End of the      1-th period:    0.2000000E+04
End of the      2-th period:    0.2000000E+04
End of the      3-th period:    0.2000000E+04
End of the      4-th period:    0.2000000E+04
End of the      5-th period:    0.2000000E+04
End of the      6-th period:    0.2000000E+04
End of the      7-th period:    0.2000000E+04
End of the      8-th period:    0.2000000E+04
End of the      9-th period:    0.2000000E+04
End of the     10-th period:    0.2000000E+04
End of the     11-th period:    0.2000000E+04
End of the     12-th period:    0.2000000E+04


              Production cost functions
              +++++++++++++++++++++++++


    1-th production cost function:

  x=     0.00  y=     0.00     x=     0.00  y=   142.00     x= 2000.00  y= 1450.00
x= 4000.00  y= 2202.00

  Applicable to periods:
    1   2   3   4   5   6   7   8   9  10  11  12


              Inventory cost functions
              ++++++++++++++++++++++++


    1-th inventory cost function:

  x=     0.00  y=     0.00     x= 2000.00  y=   130.80     x= 4000.00  y=   206.00

  Applicable to periods:
    1   2   3   4   5   6   7   8   9  10  11  12
```

****

Total production cost during the 12 periods: 0.1111800E+05

Total inventory cost during the 12 periods: 0.1854000E+04

Optimal cost: 0.1297200E+05

Optimal control

At the end of the 1 -th period: 0.8000000E+04
At the end of the 2 -th period: 0.0000000E+00
At the end of the 3 -th period: 0.0000000E+00
At the end of the 4 -th period: 0.0000000E+00
At the end of the 5 -th period: 0.8000000E+04
At the end of the 6 -th period: 0.0000000E+00
At the end of the 7 -th period: 0.0000000E+00
At the end of the 8 -th period: 0.0000000E+00
At the end of the 9 -th period: 0.8000000E+04
At the end of the 10 -th period: 0.0000000E+00
At the end of the 11 -th period: 0.0000000E+00
At the end of the 12 -th period: 0.0000000E+00

Stock level during the 1-th period 0.0000000E+00
Stock level during the 2-th period 0.6000000E+04
Stock level during the 3-th period 0.4000000E+04
Stock level during the 4-th period 0.2000000E+04
Stock level during the 5-th period 0.0000000E+00
Stock level during the 6-th period 0.6000000E+04
Stock level during the 7-th period 0.4000000E+04
Stock level during the 8-th period 0.2000000E+04
Stock level during the 9-th period 0.0000000E+00
Stock level during the 10-th period 0.6000000E+04
Stock level during the 11-th period 0.4000000E+04
Stock level during the 12-th period 0.2000000E+04

Number of set up points: 3

Maximum values of the stock level to be considered: 79

Values of the stock level which have been considered: 79

VI - 2. THE NON STATIONARY CASE

Only the production cost is non stationary. We obtain an optimal control which is quite different from the previous one.

```
Code=   0
          Number of periods:     12
          *****************


   Initial stock level:    0.0000000E+00
   ******************


                   Demand
                   ******


End of the    1-th period:   0.2000000E+04
End of the    2-th period:   0.2000000E+04
End of the    3-th period:   0.2000000E+04
End of the    4-th period:   0.2000000E+04
End of the    5-th period:   0.2000000E+04
End of the    6-th period:   0.2000000E+04
End of the    7-th period:   0.2000000E+04
End of the    8-th period:   0.2000000E+04
End of the    9-th period:   0.2000000E+04
End of the   10-th period:   0.2000000E+04
End of the   11-th period:   0.2000000E+04
End of the   12-th period:   0.2000000E+04


          Production cost functions
          ++++++++++++++++++++++++


   1-th production cost function:

  x=    0.00  y=    0.00    x=    0.00  y=  150.00    x= 2000.00  y= 1458.00
x= 4000.00  y= 2210.00

  Applicable to periods:
     3   4   9  10


   2-th production cost function:

  x=    0.00  y=    0.00    x=    0.00  y=  100.00    x= 2000.00  y= 1408.00
x= 4000.00  y= 2160.00

  Applicable to periods:
     1   2   5   6   7   8  11  12
```

Inventory cost functions
++++++++++++++++++++++++

1-th inventory cost function:

x= 0.00 y= 0.00 x= 2000.00 y= 130.80 x= 4000.00 y= 206.00

Applicable to periods:
1 2 3 4 5 6 7 8 9 10 11 12

** --

Total production cost for the 12 period problem: 0.1654800E+05

Total inventory cost for the 12 period problem: 0.7848000E+03

Optimal cost: 0.1733280E+05

Optimal control

At the end of the 1 -th period: 0.4000000E+04
At the end of the 2 -th period: 0.0000000E+00
At the end of the 3 -th period: 0.4000000E+04
At the end of the 4 -th period: 0.0000000E+00
At the end of the 5 -th period: 0.4000000E+04
At the end of the 6 -th period: 0.0000000E+00
At the end of the 7 -th period: 0.4000000E+04
At the end of the 8 -th period: 0.0000000E+00
At the end of the 9 -th period: 0.4000000E+04
At the end of the 10 -th period: 0.0000000E+00
At the end of the 11 -th period: 0.4000000E+04
At the end of the 12 -th period: 0.0000000E+00

Stock level during the 1-th period: 0.0000000E+00
Stock level during the 2-th period: 0.2000000E+04
Stock level during the 3-th period: 0.0000000E+00
Stock level during the 4-th period: 0.2000000E+04
Stock level during the 5-th period: 0.0000000E+00
Stock level during the 6-th period: 0.2000000E+04
Stock level during the 7-th period: 0.0000000E+00
Stock level during the 8-th period: 0.2000000E+04
Stock level during the 9-th period: 0.0000000E+00
Stock level during the 10-th period: 0.2000000E+04
Stock level during the 11-th period: 0.0000000E+00
Stock level during the 12-th period: 0.2000000E+04

Number of set up points: 6

Maximum values of the stock level to be considered: 79

Values of the stock level which have been considered: 79

Before using the software, two thousand switches were produced every month.

CHAPTER VI

SOFTWARE FOR PRODUCTION PLANNING MODELS WITH CONCAVE COSTS AND DETERMINISTIC DEMAND

CONTINUOUS TIME CASE

INTRODUCTION

We propose a software which leads to an optimal piecewise, continuous production policy under the following hypotheses :

1 - the instantaneous demand is piecewise continuous, and given over a period $[t_1,t_2]$;

2 - the initial inventory level at time t_1 is given, and may be different from zero ;

3 - the inventory level must never become negative over $[t_1,t_2]$;

4 - instantaneous inventory and production costs are concave and piecewise continuous functions of the inventory level and of the production rate, respectively, and piecewise continuous functions of time ;

5 - the optimal production policy belongs to the set of piecewise continuous functions which lie between two piecewise continuous functions called the upper and the lower bounds of the control.

We know from Chapter III that such an optimal control exists and is of the "bang-bang" type (see theorem 1.1) : if the inventory level is strictly positive, then it is equal either to the lower bound or to the upper bound of the admissible production rates ; if the inventory level is equal to zero, the optimal control is equal either to the lower bound, the upper bound of the admissible production rates, or the demand if it lies between these bounds.

At each point in time, we then have to select an optimal control among at most three possibilities. The following software is based on this result and rests on the backward dynamic programming equations. Of course, we have to discretize time and the inventory level variable. This leads to a systematic error, and we shall comment on this problem.

This chapter details the presentation of inputs, outputs, the structure of the algorithm, the main program and subprograms together with their listings.

The main program depends strongly on the computer used since it contains many I/O instructions which can be made on or from a disk, a screen or a printer. The same problem arises for two subprograms, ph1 and ph2. We give some clues to modify accordingly these instructions. Note that this software runs on MULTICS.

We finally develop two examples, the second one being a real world industrial application to a rolling-mill for a 24 hour period.

I - LIST OF INPUTS

The algorithm we present requires the following inputs :

1 - starting and ending times of the problem, t_1 and t_2 respectively ;

2 - the initial inventory level, y_0, at time t_1 ;

3 - instantaneous demand d(t), which is a piecewise continuous function of time ;

4 - lower and upper bounds of the instantaneous production rates m(t) and M(t) respectively, which are piecewise continuous : $m(t) \leq v(t) \leq M(t)$;

5 - the instantaneous inventory cost f(t,y), which is a piecewise continuous functions of time t, $t \in [t_1,t_2]$, concave and non decreasing function of the stock level, y, for $y \geq 0$;

6 - the instantaneous production cost c(t,v), which is a piecewise continuous function of time t, $t \in [t_1,t_2]$, concave and non decreasing function of the instantaneous production rate v, for $v \geq 0$.

In addition, we need to specify the following technical inputs :

7 - the number of computation steps m, between the starting and the ending times. The user chooses this integer. If this number is large enough, the computations are more precise, but at the expense of a higher number of calculations, and consequently of "truncating" and "systematic" errors. The optimal value of this integer cannot be found "a priori" and the second best solution consists in trying several values and retain the one which leads to the minimum cost ;

8 - the precision limit which is a real number denoted eps. Each real x, with value $|x|$ less than eps will be considered equal to zero ;

9 - the maximum number of values for the inventory level, which can be used at any time. This number, denoted mm, must be equal to, or less than, the dimensions of p1, p2, x1 and id (see the subroutines below). In fact the number of values of y which will appear at a given time cannot be anticipated, and mm is used to assess it.

II - LIST OF OUTPUTS

The following outputs are provided :

1 - the optimal cost ;

2 - for each computation time, the optimal production rate between this time and the next computation time, and the value of the inventory level

III - STRUCTURE OF THE ALGORITHM

This algorithm proceeds in three main steps.

STEP 1 : Verification of the inputs (subroutine verto)

We check that :

. the cost functions are non negative and concave ;

. the demand, the lower and upper bounds of the production rates are non negative ;

. etc ... (cf. Section V).

The subroutine verto performs this series of verifications and the outcome is a number, icod :

- if icod = 0, no error has been detected in the inputs, and we can proceed to the next steps ;
- if icod ≠ 0, at least one error has been found and the value of icod gives the type of the first detected error (see Section V).

STEP 2 : Use of the backward dynamic programming equation (ph1 subroutine)

Given the number of computation steps, the demand, the lower and upper bounds of the production rates and the starting and ending points of the problem, we compute the time step and the inventory level step, denoted dax and day respectively.

Let us consider :

$I_i = [t_1 + i\ dax,\ t_1 + (i+1)dax]$ for $i = 0, 1, \ldots, m-1$, where m is the number of steps in time.

For every I_i, we compute Δy_i and δy_i defininied as follows :

Δy_i = |inventory level at time t_1+i dax - inventory level at time t_1 + (i+1)dax| when the production rate is equal to the upper bound of the production on I_i.

δy_i = the same value when the production rate is equal to the lower bound of the production on I_i.

We then choose :

$$day = \min_{i=0,\ldots,m-1} (\delta y_i, \Delta y_i).$$

We then use the backward dynamic programming equations.

Given the notation already introduced in Section I, the problem is to find the optimal control v(t) which minimizes the functional :

$$J_{\theta_n}(v, y_n) = \int_{\theta_n}^{t_2} [c(t, v(t)) + f(t, y(t))]dt \tag{1}$$

where :

(2) . y(t) is solution of $\frac{dy}{dt}(t) = v(t) - d(t)$

. d is the instantaneous demand,

. $y_n = y(\theta_n)$,

. $\theta_n = t_1 + n.dax < t_2$.

Of course, at each discontinuity point of v and d, (2) will be replaced by :

(3) $$\frac{dy}{dt}(t-0) = v(t^-) - f(t^-), \text{ and}$$
$$\frac{dy}{dt}(t+0) = v(t^+) - d(t^+).$$

We suppose that $y(t) \geq 0$ and $m(t) \leq v(t) \leq M(t)$ for each $t \in [t_1,t_2]$ (i.e. v is an admissible control).

The theoretical aspects of this problem have already been addressed in Chapter III. In the sequel we need only the following result :

there exists a piecewise continuous control v^* which is :

1 - admissible

2 - equal either to $m(t)$ or $M(t)$ for each $t \in [t_1,t_2]$ if $y(t) > 0$,

3 - equal either to $m(t)$, $M(t)$ or $d(t)$ at each $t \in [t_1,t_2]$ if $y(t) = 0$,

4 - "as close as we want" from the optimal control.

Property 4 needs to be further specified.

4' - if D is the set of admissible controls and v^* the optimal control then, whatever $\varepsilon > 0$, we can find v, such that

$$\operatorname*{Min}_{v \in D} J_{t_1}(v, y_0) \leq J_{t_1}(v^*, y_0) < \operatorname*{Min}_{v \in D} J_{t_1}(v, y_0) + \varepsilon.$$

In order to be able to derive an efficient solution to Problem 1, we make a stronger hypothesis and suppose that v^* is :

a - equal, either to m or M on the whole interval (θ_n, θ_{n+1}) if $y(\theta_n) > 0$

b - equal, either to m or M or d on the whole interval (θ_n, θ_{n+1}) if $y(\theta_n) = 0$.

Indeed, it is easy to see that a - and b - lead to a computational error which increases with dax.

We can rewrite the backward dynamic programming equations as follows :

(4) $$J^*_{\theta_n}(y_n) = \operatorname*{Min}_{v \in D(y_n,\theta_n,\theta_{n+1})} \{\int_{\theta_n}^{\theta_{n+1}} [c(t,v(t)) + f(t,y(t))]dt + J^*_{\theta_{n+1}}(y(\theta_{n+1}))\}$$

where

$$D(y_n,\theta_n,\theta_{n+1}) = \{m,M\} \text{ if } y_n > 0$$

$$D(y_n,\theta_n,\theta_{n+1}) = \{m,M,d\} \text{ if } y_n = 0$$

$y(t)$ is defined by (2) and (3), and $J^*_{\theta_n}(y_n)$ is a "good approximation" to the optimal cost between θ_n and t_2 if the state at time θ_n is y_n.

Of course :

(5) $J^*_{t_2}(y) = 0$ whatever $y \geq 0$

We can then sketch STEP 2 of the algorithm.

0. Initialization : $J^*_{t_2}(y) = 0$ whatever $y \geq 0$
1. Computation of day
2. Computation of $J^*_{\theta_n}(y_n)$, using (4), for :

   $\theta_n := t_2 - dax, t_2 - 2\,dax, \ldots, t_1$

   and $y_n := 0, day, 2\,day, \ldots, Y_n$

   where Y_n is the minimal stock level at time θ_n which admits m as an admissible control between θ_n and t_2.

Phase 2 starts from (5) and uses (4) taking into account (2) and (3). For each (θ_n, y_n), the computation leads to two values :

1 - the optimal control between θ_n and θ_{n+1}, when the state of the system is y_n at time θ_n. This control is, as we know, either M or m or d.

2 - the good approximation of the maximum cost, $J^*_{\theta_n}(y_n)$.

Furthermore, for each time θ_n, we obtain two important values :

1 - Y_n (see above) which is the minimal value of y_n so that m is optimal between θ_n and t_2.

2 - Z_n which is the value of y_n so that M is an optimal control between θ_n and t_2.

These values are stored on a computer disc. This part of the program may be modified, because read from, or write on, a disc instructions may differ from one computer to the other. This is the reason why in the program we just outline the instructions which relate to disc storage.

STEP 3 : Derivation of the "optimal" cost and the "optimal" control (subroutine ph2)

The derivation of the optimal cost is straightforward. Given the initial stock, y_0 :

- if $y_0 \geq Y_0$, we compute the optimal cost with m(t) as an optimal control on $[t_1, t_2]$. In this instance the computation stops here ;

- if $y_0 < Z_0$, there does not exist an admissible control, and the computation ends here too ;

- if $Y_0 \leq m\ day \leq y_0 \leq (m+1)day \leq Z_0$, we make the additional hypothesis that the cost function is linear between m.day and (m+1).day. Then :

$$J^*_{t_1}(y_0) = J^*_{t_1}(m.day) + (y_0-m)\ \frac{J^*_{t_1}((m+1).day) - J^*_{t_1}(m.day)}{day}$$

The optimal control at time t_1 is obtained as follows :

a - either, the optimal control is the same for m.day and (m+1).day, and this control is also optimal for the state y_0.

b - or, it is not, and

if $(m+1).day - y_0 < y_0 - m.day$, we choose the control obtained for m.day.

This control leads to the state y_1 at time $\theta_1 = t_1 + dax$ and so on for $\theta_2 = t_2 + 2\ dax$, θ_3 ...

At each step θ_i, we load on the computer disc :

1 - the "optimal" state y_i

2 - the "optimal" control v_i

These loading statements are outlined in the subroutine ph2.

Figure 1 summarizes the structure of the algorithm.

STEP 1

STEP 2

STEP 3

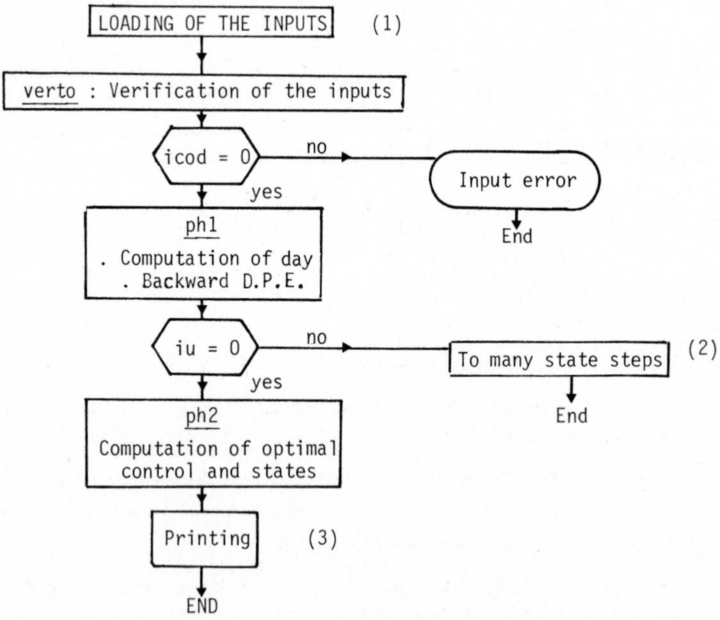

FIGURE 1 : Structure of the algorithm.

Remark 1

Phases denoted (1) and (3) on Figure 1 are highly dependent on users's data loading system, on the desired formats for the outputs, and on the computer disc directory.

Remark 2

If phase (2), on Figure 1, occurs, then the number of required values for the state y at a certain time $\theta_n \in [t_1,t_2]$ is greater than mm (see Section I, §9). In that case, the user must increase the dimension of p1, p2, x1 and id and start again with the value of this dimension for mm.

IV - THE MAIN PROGRAM

Some arrays are used and their dimensions are defined as follows (see also Section V, §1) :

. the dimensions of dx and d are equal to or greater than the number of points which define the demand.

. the dimensions of cx1 and c1 must be equal to or greater than the number of points which define the lower bound of the demand.

. the dimensions of cx2 and c2 must be equal to or greater than the number of points which define the upper bound of the demand.

. the dimensions of xc and yc must be equal to, or greater thant, the number of points which define the set of the instantaneous production cost function.

. the dimensions of xl and yl must be equal to, or greater than, the number of points which define the set of the instantaneous inventory cost function.

. the dimensions of tc and mc must be equal to, or greater than, the number of points in time for which an instantaneous production cost function is known.

. the dimensions of tl and ml must be equal to, or greater than, the number of points in time for which an instantaneous inventory cost function is known.

. the dimension of nic is equal to, or greater than, the number of points which define the instantaneous production cost functions.

. the dimension of nil is equal to, or greater thant, the number of points which define the instantaneous inventory cost function.

. the dimensions of p1, p2, x1, id are equal to, or greater than, the maximum number of stock levels to be considered. This number is an input of the program.

. the dimension of a is equal to, or greater than, the sum of the dimensions of dx, cx1 and cx2.

In this program, we use for interface devices :

1 - A screen, as I/O device. This screen is defined like a disc-file (file 0) with sequential access. It has to be opened, but not closed.

2 - A disc file, called 40, as an output device with sequential access. This file contains the outputs of the software. We can replace this file by a printer.

3 - A disc-file, called 4, as an I/O device with direct access. This working file contains m+1 records, where m is the number of computation steps. The size of

each records is $127 \times 2 = 254$ bytes.

4 - A disc-file called 7, as an I/O device with sequential access. This working file, like the previous one, contains m+1 records. The size of each record is $58 \times 2 = 116$ bytes.

The listing of the main program follows.

When the program runs, it provides enough information on the inputs formats. More details can be found in §5.

```
 1          dimension dx(20),d(20),cx1(20),c1(20),cx2(20),c2(20)
 2          dimension p1(200),id(200),xc(100),yc(100),tc(15)
 3          dimension mc(15),nic(50),x1(100),y1(100),t1(15),m1(15)
 4          dimension nil(50),x1(200),a(80),p2(200)
 5          open(0)
 6          open(40,form="formatted",mode="inout")
 7          open(4,access="direct",mode="inout",form="formatted",recl=127)
 8          open(7,form="formatted",mode="inout")
 9 c
10 c   INPUTS
11 c
12          write(0,1)
13 1        format(5x,"Starting time ?")
14          read(0,2)t1
15 2        format(f6.3)
16          write(0,3)
17 3        format(5x,"Ending time ?")
18          read(0,2)t2
19          eps=1.e-6
20          write(0,4)
21 4        format(5x,"Initial stock level?")
22          read(0,2)y0
23 5        format(2x,//)
24 c
25 c   Input of the demand.
26 c
27          write(0,6)
28 6        format(10x,"Demand",/,10x,6("*"),/)
29          write(0,7)
30 7        format(1x,"The demand must be a piecewise linear func",
31         &"tion.",/,2x,"Thus give a string of points ranked in ",
32         &"the increasing order of",/," the x-values.",/,2x,"If two ",
33         &"x-values are equal (discontinuity point),give first the point",
34         &/," for which the y-value is the left limit of the demand.",/)
35          write(0,8)
36 8        format(5x,"Type successively the x-axis and the y-axis values",
37         &" for each point",/,5x,"or -1. to stop the input.",/)
38          i=0
39 9        read(0,2)ww
40          if(ww.lt.0.)go to 10
41          i=i+1
42          dx(i)=ww
43          read(0,2)d(i)
44          go to 9
45 10       nd=i
46          write(0,5)
47 c
48 c   Input of the lower bound of the production rate.
49 c
```

```
      write(0,11)
 11   format(10x,"Lower bound of the instanteneous production rate",/,
     &10x,48("*"),/)
      write(0,12)
 12   format(2x,"This function is also piecewise linear.",/,2x,
     &"Follow the same injunctions as for the demand.",//)
      write(0,8)
      i=0
 13   read(0,2)ww
      if(ww.lt.0.)go to 20
      i=i+1
      cx1(i)=ww
      read(0,2)c1(i)
      go to 13
 20   nc1=i
      write(0,5)
c
c  Input of the upper bound of the production rate.
c
      write(0,21)
 21   format(10x,"Upper bound of the instantaneous production rate",/,
     &10x,48("*"),/)
      write(0,12)
      write(0,8)
      i=0
 23   read(0,2)ww
      if(ww.lt.0.)go to 30
      i=i+1
      cx2(i)=ww
      read(0,2)c2(i)
      go to 23
 30   nc2=i
      write(0,5)
c
c  Input of the production costs.
c
 56   write(0,31)
 31   format(10x,"Input of the production costs",/,10x,29("*"),//)
      write(0,32)
 32   format(12x,"Definition times",/,12x,16("-"),//)
      write(0,33)
 33   format(2x,"If two different functions are known at the same ",
     &"time (left and right limits)",/,2x,"then this time must be ",
     &"given two times successively.",2x,"The times must be given",/,
     &"  in the non decreasing order.",//)
      write(0,34)
 34   format(2x,"Give the definition time or -1. to stop the input.")
      i=0
 41   read(0,2)ww
      if(ww.lt.0.)go to 40
      i=i+1
      tc(i)=ww
      go to 41
 40   nc=i
      write(0,5)
      do 49 i=1,nc
 49   mc(i)=0
      ndc=0
      ij=0
 47   write(0,42)
```

```
 42    format(/,2x,"Type 1 in order to introduce another production",
      &" cost function",/,2x,"and 0 if the input is finished.")
       read(0,43)j
 43    format(i1)
       if(j.eq.0)go to 70
       ndc=ndc+1
       write(0,5)
       write(0,44)ndc
 44    format(8x,"Input of the ",i2,"-th production cost function",
      &/,8x,43("-"),//)
       write(0,8)
 46    read(0,2)ww
       if(ww.lt.0.)go to 45
       ij=ij+1
       xc(ij)=ww
       read(0,2)yc(ij)
       go to 46
 45    nic(ndc)=ij
       write(0,50)
 50    format(/,12x,"Definition times concerned",/,12x,26("-"),/)
       write(0,51)
 51    format(2x,"Type 0 for no and 1 for yes",/)
       do 52 i=1,nc
       write(0,53)tc(i)
 53    format(2x,"time:",2x,f8.2,"?")
       read(0,43)k
       if(k.eq.0)go to 52
       mc(i)=ndc
 52    continue
       go to 47
 70    write(0,5)
       k=0
       do 54 i=1,nc
       if(mc(i).gt.0)go to 54
       k=k+1
       write(0,55)tc(i)
 55    format(4x,"Missing:which production cost function at time",
      &2x,f8.2,1x,"?")
 54    continue
       if(k.gt.0)go to 56
c
c  Input of the inventory costs.
c
 156   write(0,131)
 131   format(10x,"Input of the inventory cost functions",/,10x,37("*"),/
      &/)
       write(0,32)
       write(0,33)
       write(0,34)
       i=0
 141   read(0,2)ww
       if(ww.lt.0.)go to 140
       i=i+1
       tl(i)=ww
       go to 141
 140   nl=i
       write(0,5)
       do 149 i=1,nl
 149   ml(i)=0
       ndl=0
```

```
170        ij=0
171 147    write(0,142)
172 142    format(2x,"Type 1 in order to introduce another inventory ",
173        &"cost function",/,2x,"and 0 if the input is finished")
174        read(0,43)j
175        if(j.eq.0)go to 170
176        nd1=nd1+1
177        write(0,5)
178        write(0,144)nd1
179 144    format(8x,"Input of the ",i2,"-th inventory cost function",/,
180        &8x,42("-"),//)
181        write(0,8)
182 146    read(0,2)ww
183        if(ww.lt.0.)go to 145
184        ij=ij+1
185        xl(ij)=ww
186        read(0,2)yl(ij)
187        go to 146
188 145    nil(nd1)=ij
189        write(0,50)
190        write(0,51)
191        do 152 i=1,nl
192        write(0,53)tl(i)
193        read(0,43)k
194        if(k.eq.0)go to 152
195        ml(i)=nd1
196 152    continue
197        go to 147
198 170    write(0,5)
199        k=0
200        do 154 i=1,nl
201        if(ml(i).gt.0)go to 154
202        k=k+1
203        write(0,155)tl(i)
204 155    format(4x,"Missing:which inventory cost function at time",
205        &2x,f8.2,1x,"?")
206 154    continue
207        if(k.gt.0)go to 156
208 c
209 c  TEST OF THE INPUTS
210 c
211        call verto(nd,nc1,nc2,tl,t2,eps,nl,nd1,nc,ndc,icod,y0,dx,d,
212        &cxl,cl,cx2,c2,xc,yc,tc,nic,xl,yl,tl,nil)
213        if(icod.eq.0)go to 200
214        write(40,201)icod
215 201    format(2x,///,4x,"Input error:icod=",1x,i3)
216        go to 505
217 c
218 c  Number of steps in time
219 c  and maximum number of stock levels to be considered
220 c
221 200    write(40,700)tl,t2
222 700    format(12x,"Period:",2x,"[",1x,f9.3,1x,",",f9.3,1x,"]",/,
223        &12x,6("*"),//)
224        write(40,701)y0
225 701    format(12x,"Initial stock level:",f9.3,/,12x,19("*"),//)
226        write(40,702)
227 702    format(24x,"Instantaneous demand",/,24x,20("*"),//)
228        write(40,703)(dx(i),d(i),i=1,nd)
229 703    format(4(2x,"x=",1x,f8.3,2x,"y=",1x,f8.3))
```

```
      write(40,704)
704   format(1x,//)
      write(40,705)
705   format(20x,"Lower bound of the instantanous production rate",/,
     &20x,48("*"),/)
      write(40,703)(cx1(i),c1(i),i=1,nc1)
      write(40,5)
      write(40,706)
706   format(20x,"Upper bound of the instantaneous production rate",/,
     &20x,48("*"),/)
      write(40,703)(cx2(i),c2(i),i=1,nc2)
      write(40,5)
      write(40,707)
707   format(24x,"Instantaneous production cost function",/,24x,38("*")
     &,/)
      do 708 i=1,nc
      t=tc(i)
      write(40,804)t
804   format(/,6x,"Time:",1x,e14.7,/,6x,5("-"))
      k=mc(i)
      m2=nic(k)
      m1=1
      if(k.ne.1)m1=nic(k-1)+1
      write(40,703)(xc(j),yc(j),j=m1,m2)
708   continue
      write(40,1707)
1707  format(//,24x,"Instantaneous inventory cost function",/,24x,37("*"
     &),/)
      do 1708 i=1,nl
      t=tl(i)
      write(40,804)t
      k=ml(i)
      m2=nil(k)
      m1=1
      if(k.ne.1)m1=nil(k-1)+1
      write(40,703)(xl(j),yl(j),j=m1,m2)
1708  continue
      write(0,80)
80    format(1x,//,2x,"Give the  number of steps in time",/,2x,
     &"and the maximum number of stock levels to be considered",
     &" in i4")
      read(0,81)m,mm
81    format(i4)
c
c  COMPUTATION OF THE BACKWARD STEPS
c
      call phl(m,t1,t2,nd,nc1,nc2,nc,nl,eps,mm,iu,c,dax,day,y0,dx,d,
     &cx1,c1,cx2,c2,xc,yc,tc,mc,nic,xl,yl,tl,ml,nil,p1,id,x1,a,p2)
      write(40,202)dax
      write(40,5)
202   format(//,5x,"Calculation step on [t1,t2]:",1x,e14.7)
      write(40,203)day
      write(40,5)
203   format(5x,"Calculation step on the stock level:",1x,e14.7)
      if(iu.eq.0)go to 300
      if(iu.eq.2001)go to 301
      write(40,302)
302   format(4x,"The maximum number of allowed values for the stock leve
     &l is too small",/,4x,"Please try again with a bigger number")
      go to 505
301   write(40,303)
```

```
 303   format(4x,"There is no solution to the problem")
       go to 505
c
c       COMPUTATION OF THE FORWARD STEPS
c
 300   call ph2(m,t1,nd,nc1,nc2,nc,n1,eps,mm,iu,c,dax,day,y0,dx,d,
      &cx1,c1,cx2,c2,xc,yc,tc,mc,nic,x1,y1,t1,m1,ni1,p1,id,x1,a)
1296   format(1x,4e14.7,i1)
       write(40,500) c
 500   format(12x,"OPTIMAL COST :",1x,e14.7,/,12x,13("+"),//)
       write(40,501)
 501   format(25x,"OPTIMAL CONTROL",/,25x,15("*"))
       write(40,502)
 502   format(/,8x,"PERIOD",10x,"STOCK LEVEL",10x,"CONTROL",/,
      &8x,6("-"),10x,11("-"),10x,7("-"),//)
       rewind 7
       mss=m
 504   read(7,1296)yt,bma,bmi,tt1,jc
       tt2=tt1+dax
       write(40,503)tt1,tt2,yt,jc
 503   format(2x,"[",f8.3,",",f8.3,"]",3x,f12.5,12x,i2)
       if(mss.eq.1)goto 505
       mss=mss-1
       go to 504
 505   close(40)
       close(4)
       close(7)
       stop
       end
```

V - SURBROUTINE verto

As we mentioned earlier in Section III, subroutine verto checks the validity of the inputs. We give here a precise description of these inputs and the type of error corresponding to each value of icod, when icod $\neq 0$.

V - 1. INPUTS

These inputs appear as parameters of verto

a - Basic inputs

t_1 : Starting time of the problem.

t_2 : Ending time of the problem.

eps : Precision parameter whose value can be set as small as the user wishes, but greater than the computation precision. For instance if computation is made with 8 digits, we can take eps = 10^{-7} but not 10^{-9}.

y_0 : Initial stock level at time t_1.

b - Demand : d(t)

Demand is a piecewise continuous function given by a string of points. These points are ranked in increasing order of the x-values. A point of discontinuity corresponds to two x-values which are equal. In that case, we enter first the y-value corresponding to the left limit of the function.

nd : Total number of points.
dx(i), i = 1, ..., nd : x-values of the points.
d(i), i = 1, ..., nd : Corresponding y-values.

c - Lower bound of the replenishment : m(t)

This function has the same properties as the demand. The corresponding inputs follow :

nc1	:	Total number of points
cx1(i), i=1, ..., nc1	:	x-values of the points
c1(i), i=1, ..., nc1	:	Corresponding y-values

d - Upper bound of the replenishment : M(t)

M is defined as above :

nc2	:	Total number of points
cx2(i), i=1, ..., nc2	:	x-values of the points
c2(i), i=1, ..., nc2	:	Corresponding y-values

For instance, if demand is the function defined by Figure 2, the inputs will be :

nd = 7

dx(1) = 8   dx(2) = 4   dx(3) = 4   dx(4) = 7   dx(5) = 8,5   dx(6) = 8,5
dx(7) = 12

d(1) = 7   d(2) = 8   d(3) = 13   d(4) = 10   d(5) = 15   d(6) = 10   d(7) = 12

FIGURE 2

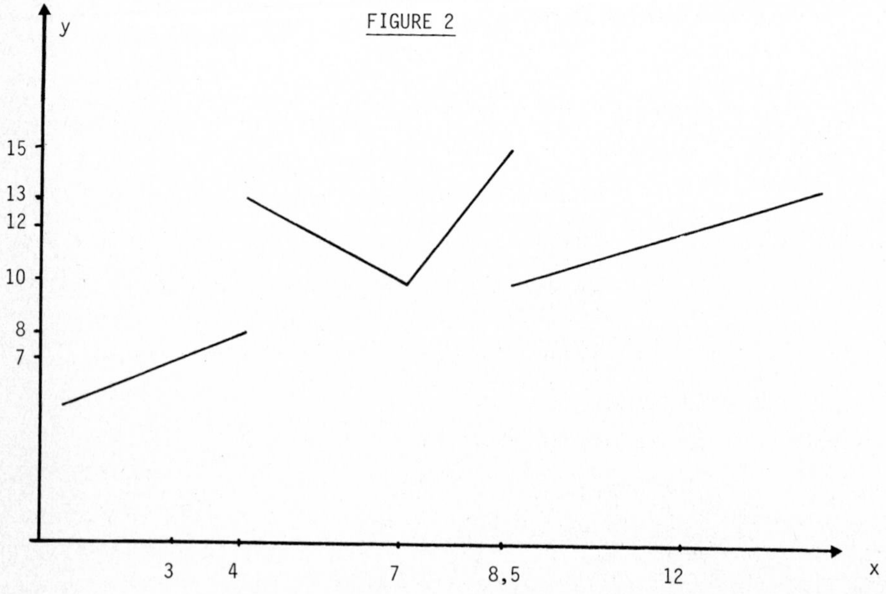

e - Production cost function : $c(t,v)$

We suppose that c is known for some instants $\theta_0=t_1 < \theta_1 < \theta_2 < \dots < \theta_n = t_2$, and that it is a linear function of time (for any given value of the production rate) over (θ_i, θ_{i+1}) $(i = 0, \dots, n-1)$.

For instance, if the cost function doesn't depend on time on (θ_i, θ_{i+1}), we have to enter the same functions at times θ_i and θ_{i+1}.

Furthermore, each function is supposed piecewise linear in v, for $v > 0$.

If two functions are entered at time θ_i $(i=1, \dots, n-1)$, the first one holds for $[\theta_{i-1}, \theta_i]$ and the second one for $[\theta_i, \theta_{i+1}]$. Of course, we must have only one definition of c at time $\theta_0 = t_1$ and $\theta_n = t_2$.

In order to gain storage space, we keep only the different definitions of c, and these functions are stored in the same arrays, and defined as follows :

nc	:	Total number of functions.
tc(i), i=1, ..., nc	:	Definition times. If two different functions are known at the same time t, then tc(i) = tc(i+1) = t for a i. Furthermore, tc(i) ≤ tc(i+1) for i = 1, ..., nc-1
xc(i), yc(i) } i = 1,2, ...	:	xc and yc contain respectively the x-value and y-value of the points which define the production cost functions.

Remark 1

The different functions are stored in any order.

Remark 2

A given function is stored in increasing order of its x-axis values. It may be that there exist two different points for the first x-axis value. In that case, the second y-axis value stored is the right limit of the function.

ndc	:	Number of different functions for the production cost
nic(i), i=1,...,ndc	:	Rank in xc and yc of the last point of the i'th stored definition of the production cost function. Of course, the dimension of xc (yc) must be greater than -or equal to- nic(ndc).
mc(i), i=1,..., nc	:	Storage rank of the function which holds at time tc(i).

f - Inventory cost function : $f(t,y)$

This function is defined like the production cost function with :

nl	instead of	nc
tl	instead of	tc
xl and yl	instead of	xc and yc
ndl	instead of	ndc
nil	instead of	nic
ml	instead of	mc

For instance, suppose that there are four production cost functions at time t_1, $\theta_1 = [\frac{1}{2}(t_1 + t_2)]^-$, $\theta_2 = [\frac{1}{2}(t_1 + t_2)]^+$ and t_2, respectively

first definition : (0,0), (0,1), (1,2), (10.2) at time t_1

second definition : (0,0), (5,5), (15,6) at times θ_1 and θ_2

third definition : (0,1), (7,5) at time t_2

In that case, one can store these inputs as follows :

nc = 4

tc(1) = t_1, tc(2) = $[\frac{1}{2}(t_1+t_2)]$, tc(3) = $[\frac{1}{2}(t_1+t_2)]$, tc(4) = t_2

xc(1) = 0 , xc(2) = 2, xc(3) = 1, xc(4) = 10, xc(5) = 0, xc(6) = 5

yc(1) = 0, yc(2) = 1, yc(3) = 2, yc(4) = 2, yc(5) = 0, yc(6) = 5

xc(7) = 15, xc(8) = 0, xc(9) = 7

yc(7) = 6, yc(8) = 1, yc(9) = 5

ndc = 3

nic(1) = 4, nic(2) = 7, nic(3) = 9

mc(1) = 1, mc(2) = 2, mc(3) = 2, mc(4) = 3

V - 2. OUTPUTS

verto has only one output, the integer icod, which can take the following values :

icod = 0 : the inputs are all correct. The computations can carry on.

In all other cases, an error has been detected, and the program stops.

icod = 1 : $t_1 \geq t_2$

icod = 2 : The initial stock level is negative.

a - Errors in the definition of demand : d(t)

icod = 11 : Demand is defined by less than two points.

icod = 12 : Demand is not stored in the increasing order of the x-axis values.

icod = 13 : The first y-axis value is negative.

icod = 14 : There exist two points which have the smallest or the largest x-axis value.

icod = 15 : The value of demand at time t_1 is negative.

icod = 16 : The value of demand at time t_2 is negative.

b - Errors in the definition of the lower bound of the production rate : m(t)

icod can take one of the values 21, 22, 23, 24, 25 or 26 which have the same meaning as for the demand i.e. 11, 12, 13, 14, 15 and 16 respectively.

c - Errors in the definition of the upper bound of the production rate : M(t)

In the case of an error in the definition of the upper bound of the production rate, the value of icod will be either 31, 32, 33, 34, 35 or 36 which must be interpreted as 11, 12, 13, 14, 15 or 16 respectively.

d - Error in the definition of the storage cost function : f(t,y)

icod = 100 : Less than two definitions for f are given.

icod = 101 : No definition for f is given at time t_1.

icod = 102 : No definition for f is given at time t_2.

icod = 103 : One of the definitions for f is given with less than two points.

icod = 104 : For a given definition of f, two different points have the smallest x-axis value and, among the two corresponding y-axis values, the smaller is given first.

icod = 105 : The x-axis values are not given in the increasing order (for a given definition of f).

icod = 106 : There exists a definition for f which is non-increasing.

icod = 107 : There exists a definition for f which is not concave.

e - Error in the definition of the production cost function : c(t,v)

In the case of an error in the definition of c, icod takes one of the values 200 to 207 which must be interpreted accordingly as 100 to 107.

V - 3. FUNCTIONS AND SUBROUTINES USED

verto needs two "FUNCTION" programs called ivr1 and ivr2

ivr1 is called to verify the demand inputs and the lower and the upper bounds of the control.

ivr2 is called to verify the cost inputs.

The "FUNCTION" ivr1 calls the SUBROUTINE enca. Figure 3 summarizes this structure.

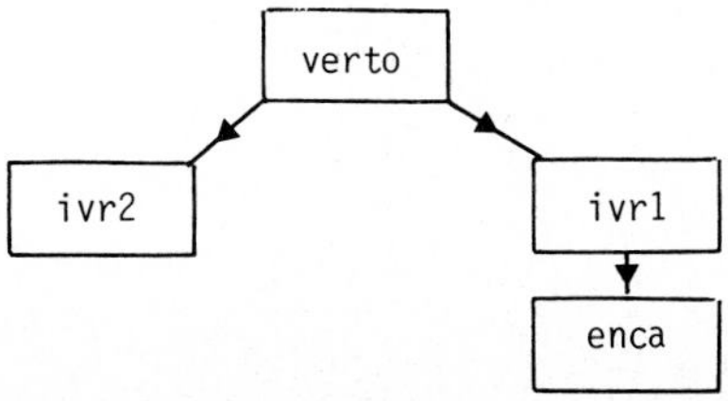

Figure 3 : Structure of the subroutines associated to verto

V - 4. ARRAY DIMENSIONS

It is crucial to give the appropriate dimensions to the different arrays. If an array belongs to the set of a subprogram parameters, its dimension can be set equal to 1 ; in that case, this dimension will be automatically set equal to the dimension of the corresponding array in the program (or subprogram) which calls the initial subprogram.

We recall the minimum dimensions of the arrays used in verto.

Array	Minimum dimension
xc	Total number of points used to define all the different instantaneous production cost functions
yc	The same as the dimension of xc
tc	Number of points belonging to $[t_1,t_2]$ for which an instantaneous production cost function is defined.
mc	The same as the dimension of tc
nic	Number of different functions for the instantaneous inventory cost functions
xl	Total number of points used to define all the different instantaneous inventory cost functions
yl	The same as the dimension of xl
tl	Number of points belonging to $[t_1,t_2]$ for which an instantaneous inventory cost function is defined.
ml	The same as the dimension of tl
nil	Number of different functions for the instantaneous inventory cost

Array	Minimum dimension
dx	Number of points used to define the demand
d	The same as the dimension of dx
cx1	Number of points used to define the lower bound of the instantaneous production rates
c1	The same as dimension of cx1
cx2	Number of points used to define the upper bound of the instantaneous production rates
c2	The same as the dimension of cx2

V - 5. LISTING OF SUBPROGRAMS

a) Listing of subroutine <u>verto</u>

```
 1          subroutine verto(nd,ncl,nc2,t1,t2,eps,n1,nd1,nc,ndc,icod,y0,
 2         &dx,d,cx1,c1,cx2,c2,xc,yc,tc,nic,x1,y1,t1,nil)
 3          dimension xc(1),yc(1),tc(1),nic(1)
 4          dimension x1(1),y1(1),t1(1),nil(1)
 5          dimension dx(1),d(1),cx1(1),c1(1),cx2(1),c2(1)
 6          icod=0
 7          u=t1-t2
 8          if(u)2,1,1
 9 1        icod=1
10          go to 100
11 2        if(y0)7,8,8
12 7        icod=2
13          go to 100
14 8        icod=ivrl(nd,1,t1,t2,d,dx)
15          if(icod)100,3,100
16 3        icod=ivrl(ncl,2,t1,t2,c1,cx1)
17          if (icod)100,4,100
18 4        icod=ivrl(nc2,3,t1,t2,c2,cx2)
19          if(icod)100,5,100
20 5        icod=ivr2(t1,t2,1,eps,t1,n1,x1,y1,nil,nd1)
21          if(icod)100,6,100
22 6        icod=ivr2(t1,t2,2,eps,tc,nc,xc,yc,nic,ndc)
23 100      return
24          end
```

b) Listing of function ivr2

```
      function ivr2(t1,t2,j,eps,tt,nt,xt,yt,nit,ndt)
      dimension xt(1),yt(1),tt(1),nit(1)
      icod=0
      nn=nt-2
      if(nn)2,1,1
2     icod=100*j
      go to 500
1     u=abs(t1)
      v=u-1
      if(v)3,3,4
3     u=1
4     v=tt(1)
      v=v-t1
      v=abs(v)/u-eps
      if(v)6,6,5
5     icod=100*j+1
      go to 500
6     u=abs(t2)
      v=u-1
      if(v)7,7,8
7     u=1.
8     v=tt(nt)
      v=v-t2
      v=abs(v)/u-eps
      if(v)10,10,9
9     icod=100*j+2
      go to 500
10    n1=1
      do 11 i=1,ndt
      ii1=0
      n2=nit(i)
      nn=n2-n1
      if(nn)12,12,13
12    icod=100*j+3
      go to 500
13    v=xt(n1+1)-xt(n1)
      u=abs(v)-eps
      if(u)21,16,16
21    u=yt(n1+1)-yt(n1)
      if(u)22,20,20
22    icod=100*j+4
      go to 500
16    if(v)17,17,18
17    icod=100*j+5
      go to 500
18    p1=(yt(n1+1)-yt(n1))/v
      ii1=ii1+1
      if(p1)19,20,20
19    icod=100*j+6
      go to 500
20    nn=nn-1
      if(nn)111,111,23
23    nn=n1+2
      do 24 k=nn,n2
      v=xt(k)-xt(k-1)
      u=v-eps
```

```
      if(u)17,26,26
26    v=(yt(k)-yt(k-1))/v
      if(v)19,27,27
27    if(iil)29,28,29
28    p1=v
      ii1=1
      go to 24
29    p2=v
      u=p1-p2
      if(u)30,31,31
30    icod=100*j+7
      go to 500
31    p1=p2
24    continue
111   n1=n2+1
11    continue
500   ivr2=icod
      return
      end
```

c) Listing of function ivrl

```
      function ivrl(n,j,t1,t2,y,x)
      dimension x(1),y(1)
      icod=0
      nn=2-n
      if(nn)1,1,2
2     icod=1+10*j
      go to 100
1     u=y(1)
      if(u)3,4,4
3     icod=3+10*j
      go to 100
4     u=x(1)
      ii=0
      do 5 i=2,n
      z=x(i)-u
      if(z)8,7,6
8     icod=2+10*j
      go to 100
6     ii=1
      go to 11
7     if(ii)10,9,10
10    ii=0
11    z=y(i)
      if(z)3,5,5
5     u=x(i)
      if(ii)12,9,12
9     icod=4+10*j
      go to 100
12    call enca(n,t1,i1,i2,yy,y,x)
      if(yy)13,14,14
13    icod=5+10*j
      go to 100
14    call enca(n,t2,i1,i2,yy,y,x)
      if(yy)15,100,100
15    icod=6+10*j
100   ivrl=icod
      return
      end
```

d) Listing of subroutine <u>enca</u>

```
 1              subroutine enca(n,xx,i1,i2,yy,y,x)
 2              dimension x(1),y(1)
 3              i1=0
 4              do 1 i=1,n
 5              u=xx-x(i)
 6              if(u)2,1,1
 7  2           i2=i
 8              i1=i-1
 9              go to 3
10  1           continue
11              i1=n
12              i2=n+1
13  3           if(i1)4,5,4
14  5           j1=1
15              j2=2
16              go to 8
17  4           i=i1-n
18              if(i)6,7,6
19  7           j1=n-1
20              j2=n
21              if(j1.ne.0) go to 8
22              yy=y(1)
23              go to 1000
24  6           j1=i1
25              j2=i2
26  8           v=(y(j2)-y(j1))/(x(j2)-x(j1))
27              yy=y(j1)+(xx-x(j1))*v
28  1000        return
29              end
```

VI - SUBROUTINE ph1

This SUBROUTINE is activated after verto,only if icod = 0.

VI - 1. INPUTS

The inputs are those of verto and, in addition two parameters associated with the discretization procedure :

m   :   Number of calculation steps on $[t_1,t_2]$, i.e. number of time intervals on $[t_1,t_2]$.

mm   :   Maximum number of values of the stock level which can be used on any time.

VI - 2. WORKING ARRAYS

We need the arrays p1, id, x1 and p2 whose dimensions are given below.

VI - 3. OUTPUTS

We distinguish between the parameters and the outputs stored in a file :

c   :   Total optimal cost-or partial optimal cost.

dax :   Calculation step on $[t_1,t_2]$.

day : Calculation step on the stock level.

iu : iu = 0 : the subroutine ph1 has run correctly. Computations can be completed through ph2.

iu = 2001 : there is no solution to the problem.

iu = 2000 : the value of mm is too small. We must run the program again with a greater value for mm. We should not forget to verify that the dimensions of p1, p2, id, x1 are still greater than mm. If not, they must be adjusted accordingly and the whole program must be run again.

b) Stored parameters

At each computation time, some parameters will be stored on file 4 :

iil : (iil-1).day is the minimum value of the stock level for which an optimal control has been computed.

jjl : (jjl-1).day is the maximum value of the stock level for which an optimal control has been computed.

bma : The value of Y_n defined in Section III;

bmi : The value of Z_n defined in Section III;

tom : The minimal value in $[t_1,t_2]$ so that m, the minimal production rate is admissible on $[tom,t_2]$ with a zero stock level at time tom ;

id(j),j=1,mm : Contains the optimal controls. Only the values stored in id(j), j=iil,jjl hold.

If id(j) = 2 : Minimal production rate for the stock level (j-1).day.

id(j) = 3 : Maximal production rate for the stock level (j-1).day.

id(j) = 1 : Production rate equal to the demand. This situation can only occur if j = 1.

Note

The instructions which permit the storage in a file are enclosed between two lines of stars, one at the top of the sequence of instructions, the other at the bottom. Of course, these sequences may change with the computer used. Note that, for the computer we used and in the case of sequential access the file index is increased automatically by one unit after each writing or reading.

VI - 4. SUBROUTINES AND FUNCTIONS USED

The subroutine ph1 calls four other subroutines :

class, enca, sint1 and xlin.

Furthermore, xlin calls divi, sint1, class and ical.

Figure 4 summarizes the structure of ph1.

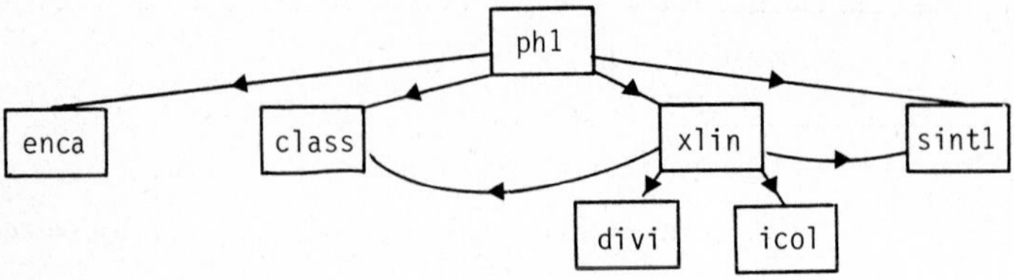

Figure 4 : Structure of ph1

VI - 5. DIMENSIONS

The dimensions of the arrays used in these subroutines are the following.

a) SUBROUTINE ph1

See verto (section V, § 4a) for the arrays which are still used in this subprogram. We use in verto and ph1 the same names for arrays of same dimension. In addition, we need four working arrays

Arrays	Minimum dimension
p1,p2,id,x1	mm
a	Sum of the dimensions of dx, cx1 and cx2

b) SUBROUTINE enca

See Section V, § 4d.

c) SUBROUTINE class

This subroutine uses only one array, a which is the same as a contained in ph1 (see Section VI, § 5a).

d) SUBROUTINE xlin

The dimensions of a, xc, yc, tc, mc, nic, x, y, dx and d are set equal to the dimensions of the corresponding arrays in the list of the parameters if xlin is called in ph1. In other words, the dimensions of each of these arrays in xlin are automatically set equal to the dimensions of the array of the same rank in the program which called xlin.

The other arrays are presented in the following table.

Arrays	Dimensions
co	Always 5
a	The same as in ph1
x5	The dimension of x5 must always be equal to, or greater than, the maximum of the dimensions of dx, cx1 and cx2
y5	The same as the dimension of x5
tu	Always 5
vu	Always 5

e) SUBROUTINES sint1, divi and icol

The dimensions of the arrays used are set equal to the dimensions of the corresponding arrays in the list of the parameters when the subroutine is called. (i.e. the dimension of a given array in a subroutine is set equal to the dimension of the array of the same rank in the list of the parameters in the program which called the subroutine).

VI - 6. LISTING OF SUBPROGRAMS

a) Listing of subroutine ph1

```
      subroutine ph1(m,t1,t2,nd,nc1,nc2,nc,n1,eps,mm,iu,c,dax,day,yt,
     &dx,d,cx1,c1,cx2,c2,xc,yc,tc,mc,nic,x1,y1,t1,m1,ni1,p1,id,x1,a,
     &p2)
      dimension a(1),dx(1),d(1),cx1(1),c1(1),cx2(1),c2(1)
      dimension p1(1),p2(1),id(1),xc(1),yc(1),tc(1)
      dimension mc(1),nic(1),x1(1),y1(1),t1(1),m1(1)
      dimension ni1(1),x1(1)
      tom=t2
      dax=(t2-t1)/m
      iu=0
      i=0
      do 1 j=1,nd
      i=i+1
    1 a(i)=dx(j)
      do 2 j=1,nc1
      i=i+1
    2 a(i)=cx1(j)
```

```
      do 3 j=1,nc2
      i=i+1
3     a(i)=cx2(j)
      call class(a,i,eps)
      do 4 j=1,i
      u=a(j)
      call enca(nd,u,i1,i2,yy1,d,dx)
      call enca(nc1,u,i1,i2,yy2,c1,cx1)
      call enca(nc2,u,i1,i2,yy3,c2,cx2)
      z1=yy2-yy1
      z2=yy3-yy1
      jj=j-1
      if(jj)6,5,6
5     xam=z2
      xim=z1
      go to 4
6     u=xim-z1
      if(u)8,8,7
7     xim=z1
8     u=z2-xam
      if(u)4,4,9
9     xam=z2
4     continue
      xim=abs(xim)
      u=xam-xim
      if(u)11,11,10
10    day=xam*dax
      go to 12
11    day=xim*dax
12    u=day-eps
      if(u)13,14,14
13    day=dax
14    do 15 i=1,mm
      p1(i)=0.
      ii=i-1
15    x1(i)=ii*day
      bmi=0.
      bma=0.
      tt2=t2
      jj1=1
      ii1=1
      do 16 i=1,m
      i9=i+1
      ii2=0
      jj2=0
      tt1=tt2-dax
      call sint1(dx,d,nd,tt1,tt2,eps,s1)
      call sint1(cx1,c1,nc1,tt1,tt2,eps,s2)
      call sint1(cx2,c2,nc2,tt1,tt2,eps,s3)
      ss1=0.
      ss2=s1-s2
      ss3=s1-s3
      bma1=bma+ss2
      bmi1=bmi+ss3
      if(bma1)17,18,18
17    tom=tt1
      ii1=1
      jj1=1
      bma=0
```

```
         bmi=0.
         do 727 i99=1,mm
    727  id(i99)=2
c****************************************************************
         write(4'i,1295,err=1000)iil,jjl,bma,bmi,tom,(id(j),j=1,mm)
c****************************************************************
         tt2=ttl
         go to 16
    18   if(bmil)19,20,20
    19   bmil=0.
    20   u=bmal/day
         m2=int(u)+2
         m3=m2-mm
         if(m3)22,22,21
    21   iu=2000
         go to 1000
    22   ir=0
         h=0.
         call xlin(ttl,dax,tc,mc,xc,yc,nic,nc,dx,d,nd,
        &dx,d,nd,h,eps,0,tual,a)
         call xlin(ttl,dax,tc,mc,xc,yc,nic,nc,cxl,cl,ncl,
        &dx,d,nd,h,eps,0,tua2,a)
         call xlin(ttl,dax,tc,mc,xc,yc,nic,nc,cx2,c2,nc2,
        &dx,d,nd,h,eps,0,tua3,a)
         do 23 j=1,m2
         u=bmil-h
         if(u)24,24,47
    24   if(ii2)75,76,75
    76   ii2=j
    75   u=h-bmal
         if(u)27,27,25
    25   if(jj2)47,49,47
    49   jj2=j-1
         if(ir)77,26,77
    26   jj2=ii2
         bmal=h
         id(ii2)=2
         tu=tua2
         call xlin(ttl,dax,tl,ml,xl,yl,nil,nl,cxl,cl,ncl,
        &dx,d,nd,h,eps,1,tul,a)
         p2(j)=pl(iil)+tu+tul
         go to 77
    27   ir=1
         u=h-eps
         if(u)29,28,28
    29   u=ss2-ssl
         if(u)28,28,30
    30   u=ssl-ss3
         if(u)31,32,32
    31   p2(j)=1.E10
         go to 47
    32   il=1
         i2=3
         go to 33
    28   il=2
         i2=3
    33   ii=il-1
         if(ii)35,34,35
    34   yb=h
```

```
      tu=tual
      call xlin(ttl,dax,tl,ml,xl,yl,nil,nl,dx,d,nd,
     &dx,d,nd,h,eps,l,tul,a)
      go to 36
35    yb=h-ss2
      tu=tua2
      call xlin(ttl,dax,tl,ml,xl,yl,nil,nl,cxl,cl,ncl,
     &dx,d,nd,h,eps,l,tul,a)
36    yh=h-ss3
      tw=tua3
      call xlin(ttl,dax,tl,ml,xl,yl,nil,nl,cx2,c2,nc2,
     &dx,d,nd,h,eps,l,twl,a)
      jul=j-ii2
      if(jul)521,521,522
521   ii=jj2-1
      if(ii)522,522,40
522   ii=iil-jjl
      u=bmi-yb
      if(u)37,37,38
38    u=yh-bma
      if(u)39,39,40
40    p2(j)=pl(iil)+tw+twl
42    id(j)=3
      go to 47
39    if(ii)41,85,41
85    yy=pl(iil)
      go to 86
41    call enca(jjl,yh,ikl,ik2,yy,pl,xl)
86    p2(j)=yy+tw+twl
      go to 42
37    u=yh-bma
      if(u)43,43,44
44    id(j)=il
      if(ii)87,88,87
88    yy=pl(iil)
      go to 89
87    call enca(jjl,yb,ikl,ik2,yy,pl,xl)
89    p2(j)=yy+tu+tul
      go to 47
43    if(ii)90,91,90
91    yy=pl(iil)
      go to 92
90    call enca(jjl,yb,ikl,ik2,yy,pl,xl)
92    zl=yy+tu+tul
      if(ii)94,93,94
94    call enca(jjl,yh,ikl,ik2,yy,pl,xl)
93    z2=yy+tw+twl
      u=z2-zl
      if(u)45,45,46
45    id(j)=i2
      p2(j)=z2
      go to 47
46    id(j)=il
      p2(j)=zl
47    h=h+day
23    continue
77    iil=ii2
      jjl=jj2
      bma=bmal
```

```
      bmi=bmil
      tt2=ttl
c***************************************************************
      write(4'i,1295,err=1000)iil,jjl,bma,bmi,tom,(id(j),j=1,mm)
c***************************************************************
1295  format(1x,2i2,3E14.7,80il)
      do 50 j=1,mm
      pl(j)=p2(j)
      id(j)=0
50    p2(j)=0.
16    continue
c***************************************************************
      write(4'i9,1295,err=1000)iil,jjl,bma,bmi,tom,(id(j),j=1,mm)
c***************************************************************
      i9=i9+1
      u=bmi-yt-eps
      if(u)71,70,70
70    iu=2001
      go to 1000
71    u=yt-bma
      if(u)72,73,73
72    call enca(jjl,yt,ikl,ik2,c,pl,xl)
      go to 1000
c***************************************************************
73    rewind 4
      write(4'i,1295,err=1000)iil,jjl,bma,bmi,tl,(id(j),j=1,mm)
c***************************************************************
      c=0.
1000  return
      end
```

b) Listing of subroutine class

```
      subroutine class(a,n,eps)
      dimension a(1)
      nl=n-1
      do 1 k=1,nl
      kl=k+1
      do 1 l=kl,n
      u=a(l)-a(k)
      if(u)10,1,1
10    u=a(k)
      a(k)=a(l)
      a(l)=u
1     continue
      k=1
      v=a(k)
      v=abs(v)
      u=v-1.
      if(u)2,3,3
2     u=1.
      go to 4
3     u=v
4     l=1
5     u=(a(k)-a(l))/u
```

```
      u=abs(u)-eps
      if(u)6,7,7
7     k=k+1
      a(k)=a(1)
      v=a(k)
      v=abs(v)
      u=v-1.
      if(u)8,9,9
8     u=1.
      go to 6
9     u=v
6     l=l+1
      nl=n-1
      if(nl)11,5,5
11    n=k
      return
      end
```

c) Listing of subroutine xlin

```
       subroutine xlin(til,dax,tc,mc,xc,yc,nic,nc,x,y,n,
      &dx,d,nd,yt,eps,jl,wu,a)
       dimension co(5),a(1),xc(1),yc(1),tc(1),mc(1),nic(1)
       dimension x(1),x5(20),y5(20),y(1),dx(1),d(1),tu(5),vu(5)
       s=0.
       do 1 i=1,n
       x5(i)=x(i)
1      y5(i)=y(i)
       n5=n
       co(1)=14.
       co(2)=64.
       co(3)=24.
       co(4)=64.
       co(5)=14.
       ti2=til+dax
       i=1
       call divi(tc,nc,til,ti2,a,mi,ma,i)
       if(jl)12,11,12
12     call sintl(x,y,n,til,ti2,eps,sl)
       call sintl(dx,d,nd,til,ti2,eps,s2)
       n=2
       x(1)=til
       x(2)=ti2
       y(1)=yt
       y(2)=yt+sl-s2
11     call divi(x,n,til,ti2,a,mil,mal,i)
       i=i+1
       a(i)=ti2
       call class(a,i,eps)
       nl=i
       icl=mi
       ivl=mil
       wu=0.
       do 27 i=2,nl
       ss=0.
       ic2=icl+1
```

```
      iv2=iv1+1
      u=(a(i)-a(i-1))/4.
      ss1=u
      tu(1)=a(i-1)
      do 34 k=2,5
34    tu(k)=tu(k-1)+u
      if(iv1)29,28,29
28    i1=1
      i2=2
      go to 32
29    k=n+1-iv2
      if(k)31,30,31
31    i1=iv1
      i2=iv2
      go to 32
30    i1=n-1
      i2=n
32    u=(y(i2)-y(i1))/(x(i2)-x(i1))
      do 33 k=1,5
33    vu(k)=y(i1)+(tu(k)-x(i1))*u
      if(ic1)36,35,36
35    j1=1
      j2=2
      go to 39
36    k=nc+1-ic2
      if(k)38,37,38
38    j1=ic1
      j2=ic2
      go to 39
37    j1=nc-1
      j2=nc
39    na2=mc(j1)
      nb2=mc(j2)
      k=na2-1
      if(k)41,40,41
40    na1=1
      go to 42
41    na1=nic(na2-1)+1
42    na2=nic(na2)
      k=nb2-1
      if(k)44,43,44
43    nb1=1
      go to 45
44    nb1=nic(nb2-1)+1
45    nb2=nic(nb2)
      do 46 k=1,5
      u=vu(k)
      v=abs(u)-eps
      if(v)47,48,48
47    v1=yc(na1)
      v2=yc(nb1)
      go to 52
48    call icol(xc,yc,na1,na2,u,v1,eps)
      call icol(xc,yc,nb1,nb2,u,v2,eps)
52    v=(tc(j2)-tu(k))/(tc(j2)-tc(j1))
      v=v2-(v2-v1)*v
      ss=ss+co(k)*v
46    continue
      ss=ss1*ss/45.
```

```
      wu=wu+ss
      k=nc+1-ic2
      if(k)56,55,56
   56 u=tc(ic2)-a(i)
      u=abs(u)-eps
      if(u)57,55,55
   57 k=ic2-nc
      if(k)59,58,59
   58 ic1=ic2
      go to 55
   59 u=tc(ic2+1)-tc(ic2)
      u=abs(u)-eps
      if(u)60,60,61
   60 ic1=ic2+1
      go to 55
   61 ic1=ic2
   55 k=iv2-n-1
      if(k)62,27,62
   62 u=x(iv2)-a(i)
      u=abs(u)-eps
      if(u)63,27,27
   63 k=iv2-n
      if(k)65,64,65
   64 ic1=ic2
      go to 27
   65 u=x(iv2+1)-x(iv2)
      u=abs(u)-eps
      if(u)66,66,67
   66 iv1=iv2+1
      go to 27
   67 iv1=iv2
   27 continue
      n=n5
      do 2 i=1,n
      x(i)=x5(i)
    2 y(i)=y5(i)
      return
      end
```

d) <u>Listing of subroutine sint1</u>

```
      subroutine sint1(x,y,n,a1,b1,eps,s)
      dimension x(1),y(1)
      s=0.
      icod=0
      a=a1
      b=b1
      u=a-1.
      d=a
      if(u)1,1,2
    1 d=1.
    2 t=b-a
      u=abs(t)/d-eps
      if(u)500,4,4
    4 if(t)6,6,5
    5 si=1.
      go to 7
    6 u=b
```

```
18            b=a
19            a=u
20            si=-1.
21  7         do 8 i=1,n
22            u=x(i)-a
23            if(u)8,8,9
24  9         il=i
25            go to 10
26  8         continue
27            il=n+1
28            jl=n
29            go to 11
30 10         do 12 i=1,n
31  ·         u=x(i)-b
32            if(u)12,12,13
33 13         jl=i-1
34            go to 11
35 12         continue
36            jl=n
37 11         i=jl-il
38            if(i)14,15,16
39 14         if(jl)18,17,18
40 17         u=(y(2)-y(1))/(x(2)-x(1))
41            za=y(1)-u*(x(1)-a)
42            zb=y(1)-u*(x(1)-b)
43 21         s=s+(za+zb)*(b-a)/2.
44 42         s=s*si
45            go to 500
46 18         i=n-jl
47            if(i)19,20,19
48 20         u=(y(n)-y(n-1))/(x(n)-x(n-1))
49            za=y(n)+u*(a-x(n))
50            zb=y(n)+u*(b-x(n))
51            go to 21
52 19         u=(y(il)-y(jl))/(x(il)-x(jl))
53            za=y(jl)+(a-x(jl))*u
54            zb=y(jl)+(b-x(jl))*u
55            go to 21
56 15         i=il-1
57            if(i)23,17,23
58 23         i=il-n
59            if(i)24,20,24
60 24         u=(y(il)-y(il-1))/(x(il)-x(il-1))
61            za=y(il-1)+(a-x(il-1))*u
62            s=s+(za+y(il))*(x(il)-a)/2
63 25         u=(y(jl+1)-y(jl))/(x(jl+1)-x(jl))
64            zb=y(jl)+(b-x(jl))*u
65            s=s+(zb+y(jl))*(b-x(jl))/2.
66            go to 42
67 16         j2=jl-1
68            do 26 i=il,j2
69 26         s=s+(y(i+1)+y(i))*(x(i+1)-x(i))/2.
70            i=il-1
71            if(i)28,27,28
72 27         u=(y(2)-y(1))/(x(2)-x(1))
73            za=y(1)-u*(x(1)-a)
74 29         s=s+(za+y(il))*(x(il)-a)/2.
75            i=jl-n
76            if(i)25,30,25
```

```
30     u=(y(n)-y(n-1))/(x(n)-x(n-1))
       zb=y(n)+u*(b-x(n))
       s=s+(zb+y(j1))*(b-x(j1))/2.
       go to 42
28     u=(y(i1)-y(i1-1))/(x(i1)-x(i1-1))
       za=y(i1-1)+(a-x(i1-1))*u
       go to 29
500    return
       end
```

e) Listing of subroutine divi

```
       subroutine divi(tt,n,ti1,ti2,a,mi,ma,i)
       dimension a(1),tt(1)
       a(i)=ti1
       mi=0
       do 1 k=1,n
       u=tt(k)
       v=u-ti1
       if(v)3,3,2
3      mi=k
       go to 1
2      v=u-ti2
       if(v)4,5,5
5      ma=k
       go to 100
4      i=i+1
       a(i)=u
1      continue
       ma=n+1
100    return
       end
```

f) Listing of subroutine icol

```
       subroutine icol(x,y,n1,n2,u,v1,eps)
       dimension x(1),y(1)
       v=x(n1)-u
       v=abs(v)
       v1=v-1.
       if(v1)4,4,5
4      v1=1.
       go to 6
5      v1=v
6      v=v/v1-eps
       if(v)8,7,7
8      v1=y(n1)
       go to 3
7      do 1 l=n1,n2
       v=x(l)-u
       if(v)1,2,2
2      v=(y(l)-y(l-1))/(x(l)-x(l-1))
       v1=y(l-1)+(u-x(l-1))*v
       go to 3
1      continue
       v=(y(n2)-y(n2-1))/(x(n2)-x(n2-1))
       v1=y(n2-1)+(u-x(n2-1))*v
3      return
       end
```

VII - SUBROUTINE ph2

This subroutine is activated after ph1 only if iu = 0.

VII - 1. INPUTS

They are the same as those in ph1. In addition we need :

a - c, dax and day, which are output parameters from ph1

b - ii1, jj1, bma, bmi, tom, id(j), j=1, mm which were stored in file 4 by ph1. These values are read in ph2, starting at the end of the file.

VII - 2. WORKING ARRAYS

p1, id and x1 are used as working arrays.

VII - 3. OUTPUTS

The outputs are stored in file 7.

For each computation time t_1, t_1+dax, ..., t_2, we store a statement which contains

yt : Optimal stock level

bma : } See Section VI, § 3b.
bmi : }

tt1 : Time

jc : Control between tt1 and tt1+dax

jc = 1 : Control = demand.
jc = 2 : Control = minimum instantaneous production rate
jc = 3 : Control = maximum instantaneous production rate

At the end of ph2, the user will reread these values in order to print them.

VII - 4. SUBROUTINES USED

ph2 calls enca, sint1 and xlin. Furthermore, xlin calls divi, sint1, class and icol.

Figure 5 summarizes the stucture of ph2.

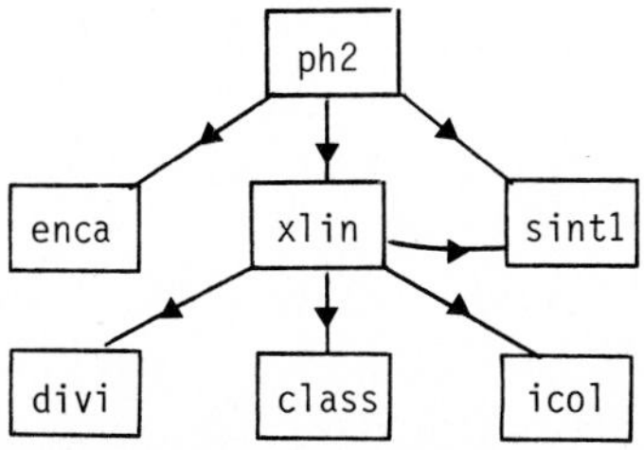

Figure 5 : Structure of ph2

The dimensions of the arrays used in these subroutines are the same as those of
the corresponding arrays in the list of the parameters, when these subroutines are
called.

VII - 5. LISTING OF SUBROUTINE ph2

```
 1          subroutine ph2(m,tl,nd,ncl,nc2,nc,nl,eps,mm,iu,c,dax,day,yt,
 2         &dx,d,cxl,cl,cx2,c2,xc,yc,tc,mc,nic,xl,yl,tl,ml,nil,pl,id,xl,a)
 3          dimension xl(1),pl(1),dx(1),cxl(1),cl(1),cx2(1),c2(1)
 4          dimension id(1),xc(1),yc(1),tc(1),mc(1),nic(1)
 5          dimension d(1),xl(1),yl(1),tl(1),ml(1),nil(1)
 6          if(iu)500,1,500
 7 1        a=0.
 8          do 2 j=1,mm
 9          xl(j)=a
10          a=a+day
11 2        pl(j)=0.
12          ttl=tl
13          do 3 i=1,m
14          tt2=ttl+dax
15 c*********************************************************************
16          i8=m-i+1
17          read(4´i8,1295,err=500)iil,jjl,bma,bmi,tom,(id(j),j=1,mm)
18 1295     format(1x,2i2,3E14.7,80il)
19 c*********************************************************************
20          u=tom-ttl
21          if(u)17,17,5
22 17       il=i
23          go to 4
24 5        if(yt)30,30,31
25 30       yt=bmi
26          ikl=1
27          ik2=2
28          go to 33
29 31       call enca(jjl,yt,ikl,ik2,yy,pl,xl)
30 33       ii=iil-ikl
31          if(ii)21,21,20
32 20       ii=iil-1
33          u=yt-ii*day
34          if(u)26,25,25
35 26       jc=3
36          if(yt)501,8,8
37 501      yt=bmi
38          go to 8
39 25       jc=id(iil)
40          go to 8
41 21       ii=ik2-jjl
42          if(ii)23,23,22
43 22       u=bma-yt
44          if(u)27,27,28
45 27       jc=2
46          go to 8
47 28       jc=id(jjl)
48          go to 8
49 23       ul=xl(ik2)-yt
50          u2=yt-xl(ikl)
51          u=u2-ul
52          if(u)7,7,6
```

```
53 6       jc=id(ik2)
54         go to 8
55 7       jc=id(ik1)
56 c**************************************************************
57 8       write(7,1296)yt,bma,bmi,ttl,jc
58 1296    format(1x,4E14.7,i1)
59 c**************************************************************
60         ii=jc-2
61         call sintl(dx,d,n,ttl,tt2,eps,s2)
62         if(ii)11,10,9
63 10      call sintl(cxl,cl,ncl,ttl,tt2,eps,s1)
64         yt=yt+s1
65         go to 12
66 11.     yt=yt+s2
67         go to 12
68 9       call sintl(cx2,c2,nc2,ttl,tt2,eps,s3)
69         yt=yt+s3
70 12      yt=yt-s2
71 3       ttl=tt2
72         bma=0.
73         bmi=0.
74         jc=0
75 c**************************************************************
76         write(7,1296)yt,bma,bmi,ttl,jc
77 c**************************************************************
78         go to 500
79 4       do 13 i=il,m
80         jc=2
81 c**************************************************************
82         write(7,1296)yt,bma,bmi,ttl,jc
83 c**************************************************************
84         call sintl(dx,d,nd,ttl,tt2,eps,s2)
85         call sintl(cxl,cl,ncl,ttl,tt2,eps,s1)
86         call xlin(ttl,dax,tc,mc,xc,yc,nic,nc,cxl,cl,ncl,
87        &dx,d,nd,yt,eps,0,tu,a)
88         call xlin(ttl,dax,tl,ml,xl,yl,nil,nl,cxl,cl,ncl,
89        &dx,d,nd,yt,eps,1,tul,a)
90         c=c+tu+tul
91         yt=yt-s2+sl
92         ttl=tt2
93         tt2=tt2+dax
94 13      continue
95 500     return
96         end
```

VIII - TWO EXAMPLES

VIII - 1. Example 1

(i) Inputs

```
Period: [    0.000 ,    4.000 ]
*****


Initial stock level:    2.000
*******************
```

Instantaneous demand
****

x= 0.000 y= 0.000 x= 2.000 y= 3.000 x= 4.000 y= 1.000

Lower bound of the instantanous production rate
****

x= 0.000 y= 1.000 x= 4.000 y= 1.000

Upper bound of the instantaneous production rate
****

x= 0.000 y= 2.000 x= 4.000 y= 2.000

Instantaneous production cost function
****

Time: 0.0000000E+00
-----
x= 1.000 y= 0.000 x= 10.000 y= 1.000

Time: 0.3000000E+01
-----
x= 1.000 y= 0.000 x= 10.000 y= 1.000

Time: 0.3000000E+01
-----
x= 1.000 y= 0.000 x= 1.000 y= 2.000 x= 10.000 y= 3.000

Time: 0.4000000E+01
-----
x= 1.000 y= 0.000 x= 1.000 y= 2.000 x= 10.000 y= 3.000

Instantaneous inventory cost function
****

Time: 0.0000000E+00
-----
x= 0.000 y= 0.000 x= 0.000 y= 1.000 x= 10.000 y= 5.000

Time: 0.2000000E+01
-----
x= 0.000 y= 0.000 x= 0.000 y= 1.000 x= 10.000 y= 5.000

Time: 0.2000000E+01
-----
x= 0.000 y= 0.000 x= 20.000 y= 1.000

Time: 0.4000000E+01

x= 0.000 y= 0.000 x= 20.000 y= 1.000

Calculation step on [t1,t2]: 0.1000000E+00
Calculation step on the stock level: 0.2000000E+00

(ii) Outputs

OPTIMAL COST : 0.3811605E+01

OPTIMAL CONTROL

PERIOD		STOCK LEVEL	CONTROL
[0.000,	0.100]	2.00000	2
[0.100,	0.200]	2.09250	2
[0.200,	0.300]	2.17000	2
[0.300,	0.400]	2.23250	2
[0.400,	0.500]	2.28000	2
[0.500,	0.600]	2.31250	2
[0.600,	0.700]	2.33000	2
[0.700,	0.800]	2.33250	2
[0.800,	0.900]	2.32000	2
[0.900,	1.000]	2.29250	2
[1.000,	1.100]	2.25000	2
[1.100,	1.200]	2.19250	2
[1.200,	1.300]	2.12000	2
[1.300,	1.400]	2.03250	2
[1.400,	1.500]	1.93000	2
[1.500,	1.600]	1.81250	2
[1.600,	1.700]	1.68000	2
[1.700,	1.800]	1.53250	2
[1.800,	1.900]	1.37000	2
[1.900,	2.000]	1.19250	2
[2.000,	2.100]	1.00000	2
[2.100,	2.200]	0.79250	2
[2.200,	2.300]	0.57000	2
[2.300,	2.400]	0.33250	3
[2.400,	2.500]	0.18000	3
[2.500,	2.600]	0.01250	3
[2.600,	2.700]	0.08000	3
[2.700,	2.800]	0.04500	3
[2.800,	2.900]	0.02000	3
[2.900,	3.000]	0.00500	3
[3.000,	3.100]	0.00000	3
[3.100,	3.200]	0.00000	3
[3.200,	3.300]	0.00000	3
[3.300,	3.400]	0.00000	1
[3.400,	3.500]	0.00000	1
[3.500,	3.600]	0.00000	1
[3.600,	3.700]	0.00000	1
[3.700,	3.800]	0.00000	1
[3.800,	3.900]	0.00000	1
[3.900,	4.000]	0.00000	1

Finally, figure 6 shows the optimal trajectory for the stock level and the functions $Y_n = Y_n(t)$ and $Z_n = Z_n(t)$.

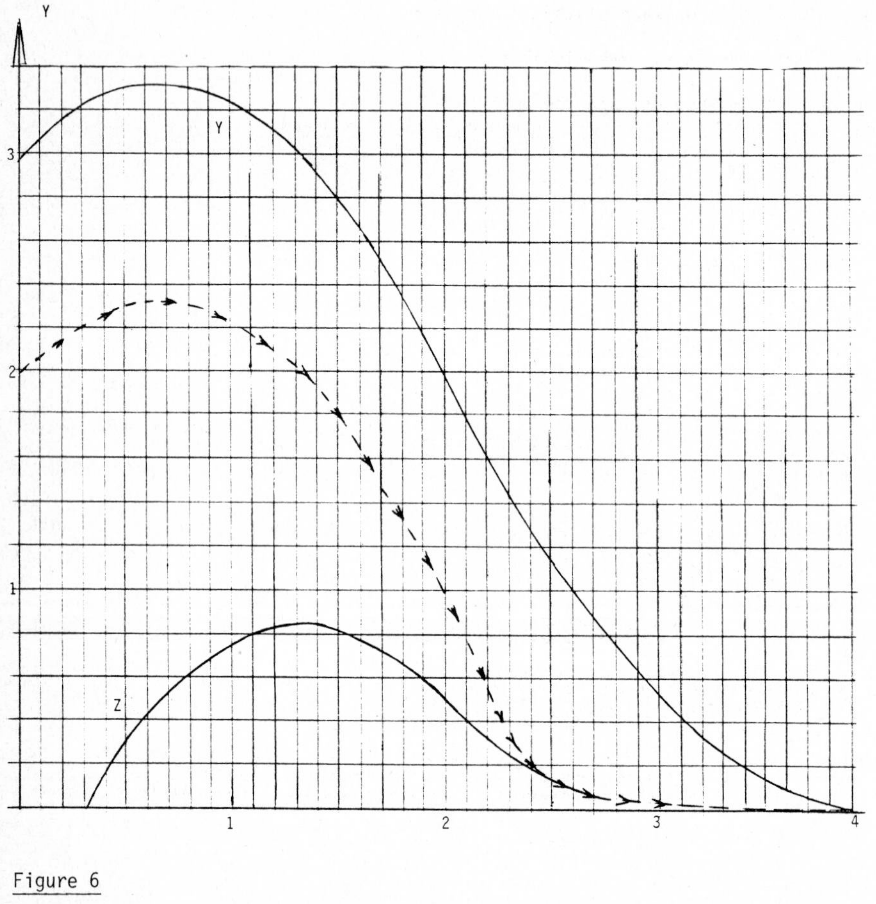

Figure 6

VIII - 2. EXAMPLE 2 : CONTROL OF A ROLLING MILL

We give the optimal production rate for a rolling-mill over a 24 hour period, with several values for the computation step Δt.

VIII.2.1. INPUTS

t_1 and t_2 are respectively the beginning and the ending times of the period i.e., $t_1 = 0$ and $t_2 = 24$.

m is the number of elementary intervals :

$\Delta t = (t_2 - t_1) / m$

mm is the maximum number of values for the stock level which can be used for any $t_1 + n\Delta t \in [t_1, t_2]$.

We set mm = 100 for each of the following runs.

The initial inventory level is always 1.

The demand, its bounds, and the costs are given below.

```
Period:  [      0.000 ,    24.000 ]
******

Initial stock level:     1.000
*******************

                 Instantaneous demand
                 ********************

x=    0.000  y=    0.800  x=   17.000  y=    1.800  x=   24.000  y=    0.600

            Lower bound of the instantanous production rate
            ***********************************************

x=    0.000  y=    1.000  x=   24.000  y=    1.000

            Upper bound of the instantaneous production rate
            ************************************************

x=    0.000  y=    1.500  x=   24.000  y=    1.500

                 Instantaneous production cost function
                 **************************************

   Time:  0.0000000E+00
   -----
x=    0.000  y=    0.000  x=    1.000  y=    2.500

   Time:  0.2400000E+02
   -----
x=    0.000  y=    0.000  x=    1.000  y=    2.500
```

```
                 Instantaneous inventory cost function
                 ************************************

      Time:   0.0000000E+00
      -----
 x=    1.000  y=    8.000  x=    1.200  y=    8.500  x=    1.500  y=    8.600

      Time:   0.2400000E+02
      -----
 x=    1.000  y=    8.000  x=    1.200  y=    8.500  x=    1.500  y=    8.600

     Calculation step on [t1,t2]:  0.6666667E+00


     Calculation step on the stock level:  0.6000000E+00
```

VIII 2.2. OUTPUTS

Successive runs are conducted for m = 24, m = 36, and m = 50.

The smallest cost is obtained for m = 50.

The results follows.

OPTIMAL COST : 0.1124475E+03
++++++++++++

OPTIMAL CONTROL
****

PERIOD	STOCK LEVEL	CONTROL
[0.000, 0.667]	1.00000	2
[0.667, 1.333]	1.12026	2
[1.333, 2.000]	1.21438	2
[2.000, 2.667]	1.28235	2
[2.667, 3.333]	1.32418	2
[3.333, 4.000]	1.33987	2
[4.000, 4.667]	1.32941	2
[4.667, 5.333]	1.29281	2
[5.333, 6.000]	1.23007	2
[6.000, 6.667]	1.14118	2
[6.667, 7.333]	1.02614	2
[7.333, 8.000]	0.88497	3
[8.000, 8.667]	1.05098	2
[8.667, 9.333]	0.85752	3
[9.333, 10.000]	0.97124	3
[10.000, 10.667]	1.05882	3
[10.667, 11.333]	1.12026	3
[11.333, 12.000]	1.15556	3
[12.000, 12.667]	1.16471	3
[12.667, 13.333]	1.14771	3
[13.333, 14.000]	1.10457	3
[14.000, 14.667]	1.03529	3
[14.667, 15.333]	0.93987	3
[15.333, 16.000]	0.81830	3
[16.000, 16.667]	0.67059	3
[16.667, 17.333]	0.49673	3
[17.333, 18.000]	0.29673	3
[18.000, 18.667]	0.07059	3
[18.667, 19.333]	0.00000	3
[19.333, 20.000]	0.00000	3
[20.000, 20.667]	0.00000	1
[20.667, 21.333]	0.00000	1
[21.333, 22.000]	0.00000	1
[22.000, 22.667]	0.00000	2
[22.667, 23.333]	0.07619	2
[23.333, 24.000]	0.22857	2

Case m = 36

Control : 1 if the control is equal to the demand

2 if the control is equal to its lower bound

3 if the control is equal to its upper bound

OPTIMAL COST : 0.1011926E+03
++++++++++++

OPTIMAL CONTROL
****

PERIOD	STOCK LEVEL	CONTROL
[0.000, 0.480]	1.00000	2
[0.480, 0.960]	1.08922	2
[0.960, 1.440]	1.16489	2
[1.440, 1.920]	1.22701	2
[1.920, 2.400]	1.27558	2
[2.400, 2.880]	1.31059	2
[2.880, 3.360]	1.33205	2
[3.360, 3.840]	1.33995	2
[3.840, 4.320]	1.33431	2
[4.320, 4.800]	1.31511	2
[4.800, 5.280]	1.28235	2
[5.280, 5.760]	1.23605	2
[5.760, 6.240]	1.17619	2
[6.240, 6.720]	1.10278	2
[6.720, 7.200]	1.01581	2
[7.200, 7.680]	0.91529	2
[7.680, 8.160]	0.80122	3
[8.160, 8.640]	0.91360	2
[8.640, 9.120]	0.77242	3
[9.120, 9.600]	0.85769	3
[9.600, 10.080]	0.92941	3
[10.080, 10.560]	0.98758	3
[10.560, 11.040]	1.03219	3
[11.040, 11.520]	1.06325	3
[11.520, 12.000]	1.08075	3
[12.000, 12.480]	1.08471	3
[12.480, 12.960]	1.07511	3
[12.960, 13.440]	1.05195	3
[13.440, 13.920]	1.01525	3
[13.920, 14.400]	0.96499	3
[14.400, 14.880]	0.90118	3
[14.880, 15.360]	0.82381	3
[15.360, 15.840]	0.73289	3
[15.840, 16.320]	0.62842	3
[16.320, 16.800]	0.51040	3
[16.800, 17.280]	0.37882	3
[17.280, 17.760]	0.23369	3
[17.760, 18.240]	0.07501	3
[18.240, 18.720]	0.02222	3
[18.720, 19.200]	0.00000	3
[19.200, 19.680]	0.00000	3
[19.680, 20.160]	0.00000	3
[20.160, 20.640]	0.00000	1
[20.640, 21.120]	0.00000	1
[21.120, 21.600]	0.00000	1
[21.600, 22.080]	0.00000	2
[22.080, 22.560]	0.01426	2
[22.560, 23.040]	0.06802	2
[23.040, 23.520]	0.16128	2
[23.520, 24.000]	0.29403	2

Case m = 50

Control :

1 if equal to the demand

2 if equal to the lower bound

3 if equal to the upper bound

OPTIMAL COST : 0.1092018E+03
+++++++++++++

OPTIMAL CONTROL
****

PERIOD	STOCK LEVEL	CONTROL
[0.000, 1.000]	1.00000	2
[1.000, 2.000]	1.17059	2
[2.000, 3.000]	1.28235	2
[3.000, 4.000]	1.33529	2
[4.000, 5.000]	1.32941	2
[5.000, 6.000]	1.26471	2
[6.000, 7.000]	1.14118	2
[7.000, 8.000]	0.95882	2
[8.000, 9.000]	0.71765	3
[9.000, 10.000]	0.91765	3
[10.000, 11.000]	1.05882	3
[11.000, 12.000]	1.14118	3
[12.000, 13.000]	1.16471	3
[13.000, 14.000]	1.12941	3
[14.000, 15.000]	1.03529	3
[15.000, 16.000]	0.88235	3
[16.000, 17.000]	0.67059	3
[17.000, 18.000]	0.40000	3
[18.000, 19.000]	0.07059	3
[19.000, 20.000]	0.00000	3
[20.000, 21.000]	0.00000	1
[21.000, 22.000]	0.00000	1
[22.000, 23.000]	0.00000	2
[23.000, 24.000]	0.14286	2

Case m = 24

Control : 1 if equal to the demand

2 if equal to the lower bound

3 if equal to the upper bound

CHAPTER VII

SOFTWARE FOR PRODUCTION PLANNING MODELS WITH CONVEX COSTS AND DETERMINISTIC DEMAND

DISCRETE TIME FORMULATION

INTRODUCTION

In this chapter we develop a software to find the optimal production policy $V = (v_0, \dots, v_{n-1})$ for production planning models with convex piecewise linear costs and deterministic demand. The formulation is in discrete time and allows for non stationary cost functions.

The following basic assumptions are made :

1 - Demand at times 1, ..., n is known ;

2 - The initial inventory level x, at time 0, is given and may be different from zero ;

3 - No-backlog is permitted, i.e. the inventory level must never become negative ;

4 - The production and inventory cost functions are convex piecewise linear, and may vary over time ;

5 - There is a one period delivery lag in production.

The algorithm is based on the result that at the optimum, the total cost J(V) is a convex and increasing function in the controls $v_1, \dots, v_{n-1}$, (see Theorem 1, Chapter III). The algorithm proceeds by first computing an admissible control, i.e. for which the corresponding inventory levels $y_1, \dots, y_n$ are non negative. Then it searches for a couple of controls v_i, v_j such that :

(i) It is possible to obtain a new admissible production policy from reducing the first control v_i by a given amount Δ and increasing the second one v_j by the same quantity Δ ;

(ii) The transformation described by (i) leads to an improved total cost value.

We start with notation and some generalities in section I, then proceed with the description of the algorithm in section II. In section III, the main program and the subroutines are presented. The listings of the programs follow in section IV and we end this chapter with an example in section V.

I - NOTATION AND GENERALITIES

I - 1. For i = 0, 1, ..., N-1

The inventory cost function f_i is given by the set of m_i points (s_k^i, f_k^i) for $k = 1, \ldots, m_i$ $(m_i > 1)$, with:

1 - $s_1^i = 0$

2 - $s_1^i < s_2^i < \ldots < s_{k-1}^i < s_k^i < \ldots < s_{m_i}^i$

3 - $\alpha_{k-1}^i \leq \alpha_k^i$ $(k = 3, \ldots, m_i)$ where :

$$\alpha_k^i = \frac{f_k^i - f_{k-1}^i}{s_k^i - s_{k-1}^i} \quad \text{for } k = 2, 3, \ldots, m_i$$

We do not take into account this property if $m_i = 2$.

4 - f_i is linear between (s_{k-1}^i, f_{k-1}^i) and (s_k^i, f_k^i) $(k = 2, \ldots, m_i)$

5 - f_i is linear after the last point $(s_{m_i}^i, f_{m_i}^i)$ and is obtained by extension of the straight line drawn between $(s_{m_i-1}^i, f_{m_i-1}^i)$ and $(s_{m_i}^i, f_{m_i}^i)$.

Figure 1 shows an example of such a function for $m_i = 4$.

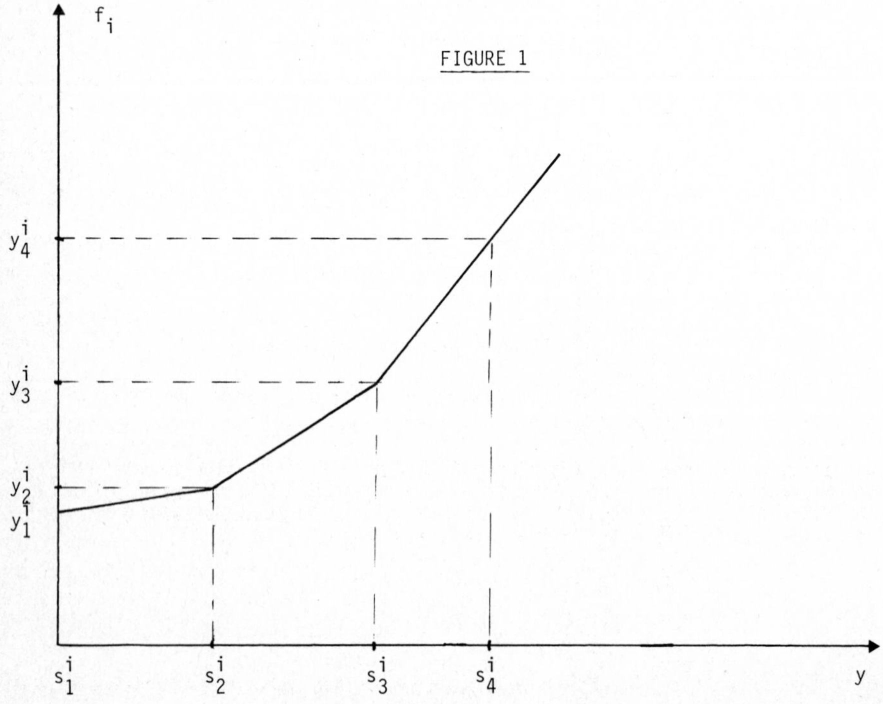

FIGURE 1

I - 2. IN THE SAME WAY, FOR $i = 0, 1, \ldots, N-1$

The production cost function c_i is given by the set of n_i points $(x_k^i, c_k^i)_{k=1,..,n_i}$ $(n_i > 1)$.

Properties 1 to 5 hold for functions c_i as well, and we write :

$$\beta_k^i = \frac{c_k^i - c_{k-1}^i}{x_k^i - x_{k-1}^i} \quad (k = 2, \ldots, n_i)$$

Let us denote by v_i $(i = 0, \ldots, n-1)$ an admissible control (production levels), and y_i $(i = 0, \ldots, N)$ the corresponding set of states (inventory levels).

I - 3. AT EACH v_i $(i = 0, \ldots, n-1)$,

we associate four quantities, r_i, R_i, g_i and G_i defined as follows :

a) If $x_1^i \leq x_{k-1}^i < v_i < x_k^i \leq x_{n_i}^i$, then

$$r_i = v_i - x_{k-1}^i$$
$$R_i = x_k^i - v_i$$
$$g_i = G_i = \beta_k^i$$

b) If $v_i > x_{n_i}^i$, then

$$r_i = v_i - x_{n_i}^i$$
$$R_i = +\infty$$
$$g_i = G_i = \beta_{n_i}^i$$

c) If $v_i = x_k^i$ for $k \in \{2, \ldots, n_i-1\}$, then

$$r_i = x_k^i - x_{k-1}^i$$
$$R_i = x_{k+1}^i - x_k^i$$
$$g_i = \beta_k^i$$
$$G_i = \beta_{k+1}^i$$

d) If $v_i = x_1^i$, then

$$r_i = 0$$
$$R_i = x_2^i - x_1^i$$
$$g_i = 0$$
$$G_i = \beta_2^i$$

e) If $v_i = x^2_{n_i}$, then

$$r_i = x^i_{n_i} - x^i_{n_i-1}$$
$$R_i = +\infty$$
$$g_i = G_i = \beta^i_{n_i}$$

I - 4. AT EACH y_i ($i = 0, 1, \ldots, n-1$),

we also associate four quantities denoted p_i, P_i, h_i and H_i, defined in the same way as r_i, R_i, g_i and G_i respectively, when using f_i instead of c_i, y_i instead of v_i and α^i_k instead of β^i_k.

II - THE ALGORITHM

Let $0 \le i_1 < j_1 \le N-1$.

We first consider :

(1) $$\Delta_1 = \text{Min } \{r_{i_1}, R_{j_1}, p_{i_1+1}, \ldots, p_{j_1}\}$$

V being an admissible control, we define the control $V^* = (v^*_0, v^*_1, \ldots, v^*_{n-1})$ by the following modification :

1 - $v^*_i = v_i$ if $i \ne i_1$ and $i \ne j_1$

2 - $v^*_{i_1} = v_{i_1} - \Delta_1$

3 - $v^*_{j_1} = v_{j_1} + \Delta_1$

It is easy to verify that V^* is admissible.

If $J(V)$ and $J(V^*)$ are the total costs corresponding to V and V^* respectively, we note that :

$$J(V^*) = J(V) - g_{i_1}\,\Delta_1 + G_{j_1}\,\Delta_1 - \sum_{i=i_1+1}^{j_1} h_i\,\Delta_1$$

or :

(2) $$J(V^*) = J(V) + A_1 \cdot \Delta_1$$

with

(3) $$A_1 = - g_{i_1} + G_{j_1} - \sum_{i=i_1+1}^{j_1} h_i$$

We then consider

(4) $$\Delta_2 = \text{Min } \{R_{i_1}, r_{j_1}, p_{i_1+1}, \ldots, p_{j_1}\}$$

and we construct the control $V^{**} = (v^{**}_0, v^{**}_1, \ldots, v^{**}_{n-1})$ as follows :

1 - $v_i^{**} = v_i$ if $i \neq i_1$ and $i \neq i_2$

2 - $v_{i_1}^{**} = v_i + \Delta_2$

3 - $v_{j_1}^{**} = v_{j_1} - \Delta_2$.

V^{**} is also admissible and if $J(V^{**})$ is the cost corresponding to V^{**}, we obtain :

$$J(V^{**}) = J(V) + G_{i_1}.\Delta_2 - g_{j_1}.\Delta_2 + \sum_{i=i_1+1}^{j_1} H_i.\Delta_2$$

or :

(5) $$J(V^{**}) = J(V) + A_2 \, . \, \Delta_2$$

with

(6) $$A_2 = G_{i_1} - g_{j_1} + \sum_{i=i_1+1}^{j_1} H_i$$

Starting from these results, we can proceed with the following algorithm :

If $y_0 > \sum_{i=1}^{N} d_i$ (where d_i is the demand at time i), the control $v_0 = v_1 = \ldots = v_{n-1} = 0$ is optimal.

Otherwise, we use the following initial control V :

for i = 0, 1, ..., n-1

- $v_i = 0$ if $y_i \geq d_{i+1}$
- $v_i = d_{i+1} - y_i$ otherwise

Then starting from V, we have to complete the following calculation steps :

```
1. For i1 = 0 to n-2
   For j1 = i1+1 to n-1
       1.1. Compute A1 and A2 (see (2), (3), (5) and (6))
       1.2. Consider A1
            1.2.1. If A1 ≥ 0, go to 1.3.
            1.2.2. If A1 < 0 :
                   1.2.2.1. Compute Δ1 (see(1))
                   1.2.2.2. Consider Δ1
                            1.2.2.2.1. If Δ1 = 0, go to 1.3.
                            1.2.2.2.2. If Δ1 > 0 :
                                       . Compute V*
                                       . V ← V*
                                       . go to 1
       1.3. Consider A2
            1.3.1. If A2 ≥ 0, go to 2
            1.3.2. If A2 < 0 :
                   1.3.2.1. Compute Δ2 (see (4))
                   1.3.2.2. Consider Δ2
                            1.3.2.2.1. If Δ2 = 0, go to 2
                            1.3.2.2.2. If Δ2 > 0 :
                                       . Compute V**
                                       . V ← V**
                                       . go to 1
2. End of loops j1 and i1
3. End of the computations (i.e. V is optimal)
```

III - PRESENTATION OF THE PROGRAMS

We now turn to the presentation of the main program colosi and the three subroutines conco, solo and cost.

The main program colosi allows to enter the inputs and to display the results. It calls the surbroutine conco. Then, conco calls successively solo and cost.

III - 1. SUBROUTINE conco

conco is the control subroutine of the algorithm :

- . it tests the validity of the inputs, i.e. checks that the initial inventory level is non negative, and the cost functions are monotonic increasing and convex piecewise linear ;
- . it then computes the initial admissible control ;
- . it tries to find a new admissible control which improves the total cost function, using the outputs of solo after it has been called by conco. This step is repeted until the optimum is reached.

III.1.1. INPUTS

a) Functions f_i $(i = 0, 1, \ldots, n-1)$

In order to save space, all the points which define the functions f_i are stored in only two arrays called csx (x-axis values) and csy (corresponding y-axis values).

If $f_{i_1} \equiv f_{i_2}$ for $i_1 \neq i_2$, this function is only stored once. Then, the dimension of csx and csy is equal to the total number of points used in order to define, among the functions f_i, those that are different.

If ks is the number of input inventory cost functions (of course $ks \leq n$), we use the array ns whose elements are the positions of the last points of dissimilar functions stored in csx and csy.

Of course, the dimension of ns is equal to ks.

Finally, we use the array ms of dimension n. The i-th element of ms gives the storage rank of f_i in csx and csy.

Let us present an example with n = 4.

We consider two different functions g and h (see Figures 2 and 3) and we suppose that :

$$f_0 = f_2 = f_3 = h$$

and

$$f_1 = g.$$

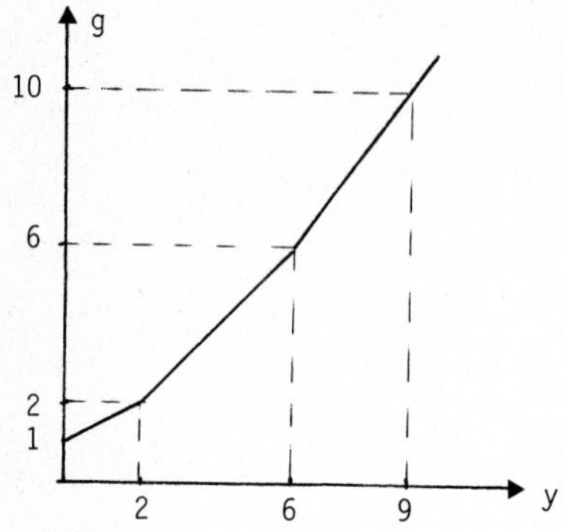

FIGURE 2

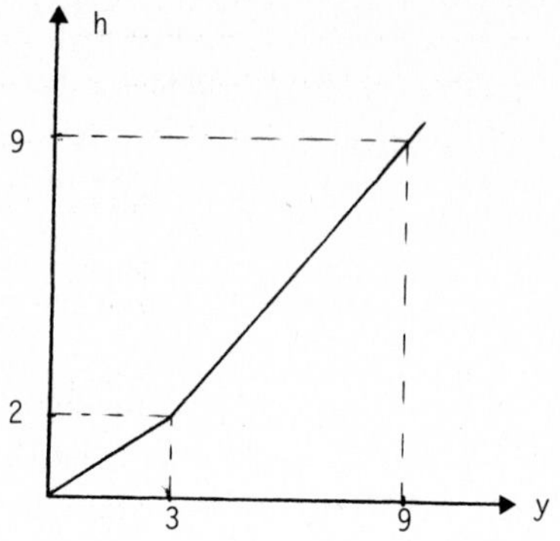

FIGURE 3

If h is stored before g, the values of the inputs are :

csx(1) = 0, csx(2) = 3, csx(3) = 9, csx(4) = 0, csx(5) = 2, csx(6) = 6, csx(7) = 9
csy(1) = 0, csy(2) = 2, csy(3) = 9, csy(4) = 1, csy(5) = 2, csy(6) = 6, csy(7) = 10
ks = 2
ns(1) = 3, ns(2) = 7
ms(1) = 1, ms(2) = 2, ms(3) = 1, ms(4) = 1

On the contrary, if g is stored before h, then the inputs are :

csx(1) = 0, csx(2) = 2, csx(3) = 6, csx(4) = 9, csx(5) = 0, csx(6) = 3, csx(7) = 9
csy(1) = 1, csy(2) = 2, csy(3) = 6, csy(4) = 10, csy(5) = 0, csy(6) = 2, csy(7) = 9
ks = 2
ns(1) = 4, ns(2) = 7
ms(1) = 2, ms(2) = 1, ms(3) = 2, ms(4) = 2

To sum up, the inputs used to define the inventory cost functions are :

n	: Number of periods
ks	: Number of different functions used
ns(i), i=1,...,ks	: Rank, in csx and csy, of the last point of the i-th stored function
csx(i), csy(i) } i=1,...,ns(ks)	: x-axis and y-axis values of the i-th point used to define the inventory cost functions.
ms(i), i=1,...,n	: Storage rank of function f_{i-1}.

Furthermore, the points which define a given function are entered in the order of increasing x-axis values.

b) Functions c_i (i = 0,1, ..., n-1)

The production cost functions c_i are defined in the same way as the f_i's. The parameters used to define the c_i's are :

kl	: Number of different production cost functions used.
nl(i), i=1,...,kl	: Rank, in cls and cly, of the last point of the i-th stored function
clx(i), cly(i) } i=1,...,nl(kl)	: x-axis value and y-axis value of the i-th point used to define the production cost function
ml(i), i=1,...,n	: Storage rank of the function c_{i-1}

As above, the points which define a given function are entered in the order of increasing x-axis values.

c) Other inputs

d(i), i=1,...,n	: Represents the demand at time i
eps	: Precision parameter which can be set at a value as small as the user wants, but greater than the computer computation precision. For instance, for a computer which has a word of eight bites, we can take eps = 10^{-7} (but not 10^{-9}).
y(1)	: Initial stock level.

III.1.2. OUTPUTS

The subroutine conco produces the following outputs :

v(i), i=1,..., n	: Optimal control. v(i) is the optimal production batch decided at time i-1 and delivered at time i.
y(i), i=1,...,n,n+1	: Inventory level carried during period i.
c	: Optimal total cost
icod	: Indicator concerning the validity of the inputs.

icod may take several values depending of the type of error detected in the inputs :

icod = 0	: Inputs are correct and outputs describe an optimal solution
icod = 1	: One of the production cost functions is defined by less than two points.
icod = 2	: One of the definition points of a production cost function has a negative x-axis value.
icod = 3	: One of the definition points of a production cost function has a negative y-axis value.

icod = 4 : The slope between two successive points is negative.

icod = 5 : The consecutive values of the segment slopes are not in increasing order.

icod = 11,12,13,14,15 : Same meaning as icod = 1,2,3,4,5, but considering the inventory cost functions instead of the production cost functions.

icod = 20 : n is less than 1.

When using conco, icod must be tested. If icod = 0, v, y and c contain respectively an optimal control (production policy) and the corresponding states (inventory levels) and total cost. If icod ≠ 0, the value of icod indicates the first error which has been detected when checking the inputs, and the program must be rerun with modified values for the inputs.

III.1.3. WORKING VARIABLES

The following arrays are used as working variables :

as1 and as2 contain respectively the values h_i and H_i (see I - 4) ;

dimis and dimas contain respectively p_i and P_i (see I - 4) ;

al1 and al2 contain respectively g_i and G_i (see I - 3) ;

dimil and dimial contain respectively r_i and R_i (see I - 3).

The dimensions of these arrays must not be less than N.

III - 2. SUBROUTINE solo

The subroutine solo is called by conco and searches for the values of the parameters (G_i, g_i, $\overline{H_i, h_i}$, r_i, R_i, p_i, $\overline{P_i}$ introduced in section II) which allow to obtain the couple of controls which must be modified in the optimization procedure.

Inputs are an admissible control with the corresponding state vector, and either the inventory or the production cost functions.

Outputs are either r_i, R_i, g_i and G_i for i = 0, ..., n-1 when they relate to the producing cost functions (cf. I - 3) or p_i, P_i, h_i and H_i for i = 0, ..., n-1 otherwise (cf. I - 4).

III.2.1. INPUTS

eps : see (III.1.1.c)

t : control (case 1) or state (case 2)

s : cumulative production (sum of the components of the control)

nt, ctx, cty, mt : These parameters are either nl, clx, cly, ml respectively (case 1) or ns, csx, csy, ms respectively (case 2) (see (III.1.1.a) and (III.1.1.b))

n : Number of periods.

III.2.2. OUTPUTS

$\left.\begin{array}{l} \text{atl(i)} \\ \text{al2(i)} \end{array}\right\} i=1,\ldots,n$: are g_i and G_i ($i = 0, \ldots, n-1$) respectively in case 1 and h_i and H_i ($i = 0, \ldots, n-1$) respectively in case 2 (see I - 3).

$\left.\begin{array}{l} \text{dimit(i)} \\ \text{dimat(i)} \end{array}\right\} i=1,\ldots,n$: are r_i and R_i ($i = 0, \ldots, n-1$) respectively in case 1 and p_i and P_i ($i = 0, \ldots, n-1$) respectively in case 2 (see I - 3).

III - 3. FUNCTION cost

Finally, the function <u>cost</u> computes the total cost corresponding to a given control and an initial inventory level.

Inputs are the cost functions, a control with its corresponding states, and n (see III - 1).

Then, <u>cost</u> takes the value of the total cost associated to the input data.

IV - LISTINGS OF THE PROGRAMS

IV - 1. THE MAIN PROGRAM colosi

```
    1         dimension d(50),v(50),y(51),kt(50)
    2         dimension clx(100),cly(100),ml(50),nl(20)
    3         dimension csx(100),csy(100),ms(50),ns(20)
    4         dimension all(21),al2(21),dimil(21),dimal(21)
    5         dimension asl(21),as2(21),dimis(21),dimas(21)
    6         open(0)
    7         open(21,form="formatted")
    8  c
    9  c      Number of periods
   10  c
   11         write(0,1)
   12  1       format(3x,"Number of periods?-i3")
   13         read(0,2)n
   14  2       format(i3)
   15         eps=1.e-5
   16  c
   17  c      Demand
   18  c
   19         write(0,3)
   20  3       format(8x,"Input of the demand",/,8x,19("+"),/)
   21         do 4 i=1,n
   22         write(0,5)i
   23  5       format(2x,"Demand at the end of the",i3,"-th period ?")
   24  4       read(0,6)d(i)
   25  6       format(f8.2)
   26  c
   27  c      Initial inventory level
   28  c
   29         write(0,7)
   30  7       format(/,12x,"Inventory level at the beginning of the first",
   31        &" period ?")
   32         read(0,6)y(1)
   33  c
```

```
c       Input of the production cost functions
c
        do 200 i=1,n
200     ml(i)=0
        write(0,8)
8       format(/,12x,"Production cost functions ?",/,12x,27("+"),/)
        kl=0
        iml=0
17      write(0,9)
9       format(/,2x,"Type 1 in order to introduce another production
       & cost function",/,2x,"and 0 if the input of the production cost
       & functions is finished.")
        read(0,10)k
10      format(i1)
        if(k.eq.0) go to 20
        kl=kl+1
        write(0,11)kl
11      format(/,12x,"Input of the ",i2,"-th production cost function",
       &/,12x,43("-"),/)
        write(0,12)
12      format(/,2x,"The points which define the function must be
       & introduced in the",/,2x,"increasing order of the x-axis va
       &lues.",/,2x,"Two x-axis values cannot be equal.")
        nl(kl)=0
        if(kl.gt.1) nl(kl)=nl(kl-1)
14      write(0,13)
13      format(/,2x,"Type successively the x-axis and the y-axis values
       &(real values),",/,2x,"or -1. to stop the input.")
        read(0,6)x
        if(x.lt.0.) go to 18
        nl(kl)=nl(kl)+1
        iml=iml+1
        clx(iml)=x
        read(0,6)cly(iml)
        go to 14
18      write(0,15)
15      format(3x,"Applicable to periods: (I3) or -10 (to stop)")
19      read(0,2)i
        if(i.lt.0)go to 17
        ml(i)=kl
        go to 19
20      js=0
        do 201 i=1,n
        if(ml(i).gt.0)go to 201
        write(0,202)i
202     format(2x,"Give the production cost function for period",1x,i3)
        js=1
201     continue
        if(js.eq.1)go to 17
c
c       Input of the inventory cost functions
c
        do 400 i=1,n
400     ms(i)=0
        write(0,28)
28      format(/,12x,"Inventory cost functions ?",/,12x,26("+"),/)
        ks=0
        ims=0
37      write(0,29)
29      format(/,2x,"Type 1 in order to introduce another inventory
```

```
     & cost function",/,2x,"and 0 otherwise.")
      read(0,10)k
      if(k.eq.0)go to 40
      ks=ks+1
      write(0,31)ks
31    format(12x,"Input of the",1x,i2,"-th inventory cost function ",
     &/,12x,42("-"),/)
      write(0,12)
      ns(ks)=0
      if(ks.gt.1) ns(ks)=ns(ks-1)
34    write(0,13)
      read(0,6)x
      if(x.lt.0)go to 38
      ns(ks)=ns(ks)+1
      ims=ims+1
      csx(ims)=x
      read(0,6)csy(ims)
      go to 34
38    write(0,15)
39    read(0,2)i
      if(i.lt.0)go to 37
      ms(i)=ks
      go to 39
40    js=0
      do 401 i=1,n
      if(ms(i).gt.0)go to 401
      write(0,402)i
402   format(2x,"Give the inventory cost function for period",i3)
      js=1
401   continue
      if(js.eq.1)go to 37
      call conco(ks,ms,ns,csx,csy,k1,m1,n1,c1x,c1y,y,v,
     &as1,as2,dimis,dimas,al1,al2,dimil,dimal,eps,c,icod,n,d)
      write(21,6666)icod
6666  format(2x,"Code=",i4)
      write(21,600)n
600   format(12x,"Number of periods:",2x,i4,/,12x,17("*"),//)
      write(21,601)y(1)
601   format(5x,"Initial inventory level:",2x,e14.7,/,5x,19("*"),//)
      write(21,602)
602   format(22x,"Demand",/,22x,6("*"),//)
      do 603 i=1,n
603   write(21,604)i,d(i)
604   format(2x,"End of the",1x,i4,"-th period:",2x,e14.7)
      write(21,605)
605   format(2x///)
      write(21,606)
606   format(12x,"Production cost function",/,12x,24("+"))
      m1=0
      do 650 i=1,k1
      write(21,607)i
607   format(//,2x,i4,"-th production cost function:",/)
      m2=n1(i)
      m1=m1+1
      write(21,608)(c1x(j),c1y(j),j=m1,m2)
608   format(3(2x,"x=",f8.2,2x,"y=",f8.2,2x))
      iw=0
      do 609 j=1,n
      if(m1(j).ne.i)go to 609
      iw=iw+1
```

```
      kt(iw)=j
 609  continue
      if(iw.eq.0)go to 650
      write(21,610)(kt(j),j=1,iw)
 610  format(/,2x,"Applicable to periods:",/,2x,18i4)
 650  m1=m2
      write(21,605)
      write(21,616)
 616  format(12x,"Inventory cost functions",/,12x,24("+"))
      m1=0
      do 660 i=1,ks
      write(21,617)i
 617  format(//,2x,i4,"-th inventory cost function:",/)
      m2=ns(i)
      m1=m1+1
      write(21,608)(csx(j),csy(j),j=m1,m2)
      iw=0
      do 619 j=1,n
      if(ms(j).ne.i)go to 619
      iw=iw+1
      kt(iw)=j
 619  continue
      if(iw.eq.0)go to 660
      write(21,610)(kt(j),j=1,iw)
 660  m1=m2
      if(icod.ne.0) go to 6667
      write(21,605)
      write(21,661)
 661  format(1x,78("*"))
      write(21,664)c
 664  format(9x,"Optimal total cost:",2x,e14.7,/,9x,12("-"),//)
      write(21,665)(i,v(i),i=1,n)
 665  format(12x,"Optimal control",/,12x,15("-"),//,(2x,"At the end",
     &" of the",i4,1x,"-th period:",e14.7))
      n2=n+1
      write(21,6678)
 6678 format(//,12x,"Optimal inventory levels",/,12x,20("-"),//)
      do 667 i=1,n2
 667  write(21,668)i,y(i)
 668  format(2x,"Inventory level during the",i4,"-th period:",2x,e14.7)
 6667 close(21)
      stop
      end
```

IV - 2. SUBROUTINE conco

```
      subroutine conco(ks,ms,ns,csx,csy,kl,ml,nl,clx,cly,y,v,
     &as1,as2,dimis,dimas,al1,al2,dimil,dimal,eps,c,icod,n,d)
      dimension ms(1),ns(1),csx(1),csy(1),ml(1),nl(1),clx(1)
      dimension cly(1),y(1),v(1),as1(1),as2(1),dimis(1),dimas(1)
      dimension al1(1),d(1),al2(1),dimil(1),dimal(1)
      icod=0
c
c+++++++++++++++++++++++++++++++++++++++++++++++++++++++++++++++++++
c+++++++++++++++++++++++COMMENTS++++++++++++++++++++++++++++++++++++
c+++++++++++++++++++++++++++++++++++++++++++++++++++++++++++++++++++
c
c-------------------------------------------------------------------
c                         INPUTS
c-------------------------------------------------------------------
c
c
c       n              :Number of periods
c
c       d              :Demand.The dimension of d must not be
c                       less than n
c
c       eps            :Every x which verifies |x|<eps is
c                       considered to be equal to zero
c
c       y(1)           :Initial stock level
c
c
c
c                          INVENTORY COST FUNCTIONS
c
c
c       ks             :Number of various inventory cost func-
c                       tions
c                                 1<=ks<=n
c
c       csx and csy    :Contain respectively the x-axis values
c                       and the corresponding y-axis values of
c                       the ks inventory cost functions,ranked
c                       in the increasing order of the x-axis
c                       values for every function.
c                       Dimension of csx and csy must not be less
c                       than the total number of points used in
c                       order to define all the inventory cost
c                       functions.
c
c       ns             :ns(i) contains the rank of the last point
c                       which defines the i-th function stored in
c                       csx and csy.
c                       Dimension of ns >= ks
c
c       ms             :ms(i) is the storage rank of the function
c                       used during the i-th period.
c                       Dimension of ms = n
c
```

```
55 c                    PRODUCTION COST FUNCTIONS
56 c
57 c        The variables which define the production cost functions
58 c        can be deduced from those which define the inventory cost
59 c        functions,replacing ks,csx,csy,ns,ms respectively by
60 c        kl,clx,cly,nl,ml.
61 c
62 c
63 c------------------------------------------------------------------
64 c                    WORKING VARIABLES
65 c------------------------------------------------------------------
66 c
67 c        The following arrays,whose dimensions must not
68 c        be less than n,are used as working variables:
69 c             as1,as2,dimis,dimas
70 c             al1,al2,dimil,dimal
71 c
72 c------------------------------------------------------------------
73 c                    OUTPUTS
74 c------------------------------------------------------------------
75 c
76 c        v          :This array contains the optimal control.
77 c                    Dimension of v >= n
78 c
79 c        y          :This array contains the optimal stock
80 c                    level.
81 c                    Dimension of y >= n+1
82 c
83 c        c          :Optimal cost
84 c
85 c        icod       :Indicator
86 c                    If icod=0,the optimal control can be com-
87 c                    puted.
88 c                    If icod<>0,there is at least one error
89 c                    in the inputs.
90 c
91 c------------------------------------------------------------------
92 c
93 c+++++++++++++++++++++++++++++++++++++++++++++++++++++++++++++++++++
94 c+++++++++++++++++++++++++++++++++++++++++++++++++++++++++++++++++++
95 c
96 c   TEST OF N
97 c
98         if(n)15,15,17
99 15      icod=20
100        go to1000
101 c
102 c   TEST OF PIECEWISE CONVEXITY AND MONOTONICITY OF THE PRODUCTION COST
103 c   FUNCTIONS
104 c
105 17      nl=1
106        do 1 i=1,kl
107        n2=nl(i)
108        nn=n2-n1
109        if(nn)2,2,3
110 2      icod=1
111        go to 1000
112 3      do 4 j=n1,n2
113        x2=clx(j)
114        y2=cly(j)
115        if(x2)5,6,6
```

```
5     icod=2
      go to 1000
6     if(y2)7,8,8
7     icod=3
      go to 1000
8     jj=j-n1
      if(jj)13,13,10
10    xx=x2-x1
      if(xx)11,11,12
11    icod=4
      go to 1000
12    s2=(y2-y1)/xx
      jj=jj-1
      if(jj)13,13,14
14    xx=s2-s1+eps
      if(xx)16,13,13
16    icod=5
      go to 1000
13    s1=s2
      x1=x2
      y1=y2
4     continue
      n1=n2+1
1     continue
c
c     TEST OF PIECEWISE CONVEXITY AND MONOTONICITY OF THE STORAGE COST
c     FUNCTION.
c
      n1=1
      do 21 i=1,ks
      n2=ns(i)
      nn=n2-n1
      if(nn)22,22,23
22    icod=11
      go to 1000
23    do 24 j=n1,n2
      x2=csx(j)
      y2=csy(j)
      if(x2)25,26,26
25    icod=12
      go to 1000
26    if(y2)27,28,28
27    icod=13
      go to 1000
28    jj=j-n1
      if(jj)33,33,30
30    xx=x2-x1
      if(xx)31,31,32
31    icod=14
      go to 1000
32    s2=(y2-y1)/xx
      jj=jj-1
      if(jj)33,33,34
34    xx=s2-s1+eps
      if(xx)36,33,33
36    icod=15
      go to 1000
```

```
 33   s1=s2
      x1=x2
      y1=y2
 24   continue
      n1=n2+1
 21   continue
c
c   INITIAL VALUES OF THE CONTROL
c
      z=y(1)
      do 50 i=1,n
      z=z-d(i)
      if(z)51,52,52
 52   v(i)=0.
      go to 50
 51   v(i)=-z
      z=0.
 50   continue
      n1=n+1
c
c   COMPUTATION OF THE CORRESPONDING STATES
c
 53   do 54 i=2,n1
 54   y(i)=y(i-1)+v(i-1)-d(i-1)
c
c   CUMULATIVE PRODUCTION BETWEEN 0 AND N
c
      nn=n-2
      if(nn)56,57,56
 56   s=0.
      do 55 i=1,n
 55   s=s+v(i)
c
c   COMPUTATION OF THE SIGNIFICANT COEFFICIENTS
c
      call solo(eps,v,s,n1,c1x,c1y,n,a11,a12,dimi1,dima1,m1)
      call solo(eps,y,s,ns,csx,csy,n,as1,as2,dimis,dimas,ms)
      nn=n-1
      do 60 i1=1,nn
      m1=i1+1
      do 60 j1=m1,n
      a1=-a11(i1)+a12(j1)
      a2=-a11(j1)+a12(i1)
      i2=i1+1
      do 61 k=i2,j1
      a1=a1-as1(k)
 61   a2=a2+as2(k)
      iv=-1
      u=a1+eps
      if(u)63,64,64
 63   x=dimi1(i1)
      z=dima1(j1)
      u=x-z
      if(u)65,66,66
 65   del=x
      go to 67
 66   del=z
 67   do 68 k=i2,j1
      x=dimis(k)
      u=x-del
```

```
      if(u)69,68,68
69    del=x
68    continue
      u=del-eps
      if(u)64,64,70
70    v(il)=v(il)-del
      v(jl)=v(jl)+del
      go to 53
64    u=a2+eps
      if(u)80,60,60
80    x=dimil(jl)
      z=dimal(il)
      u=x-z
      if(u)82,81,81
82    de2=x
      go to 83
81    de2=z
83    do 84 k=i2,jl
      x=dimas(k)
      u=x-de2
      if(u)85,84,84
85    de2=x
84    continue
      u=de2-eps
      if(u)60,60,90
90    v(il)=v(il)+de2
      v(jl)=v(jl)-de2
      go to 53
60    continue
57    c=cost(ms,ns,csx,csy,ml,nl,clx,cly,y,v,n)
1000  return
      end
```

IV - 3. SUBROUTINE solo

```
      subroutine solo(eps,t,s,nt,ctx,cty,n,at1,at2,dimit,dimat,mt)
      dimension t(1),nt(1),ctx(1),cty(1)
      dimension mt(1),at1(1),at2(1),dimit(1),dimat(1)
      do 110 i=1,n
      k=mt(i)
      nn=k-1
      if(nn)25,26,25
26    n1=1
      go to 27
25    n1=nt(k-1)+1
27    n2=nt(k)-1
      nn=n2-n1
      if(nn)3,2,3
2     at2(i)=(cty(n1+1)-cty(n1))/(ctx(n1+1)-ctx(n1))
      dimat(i)=s+eps
      u=ctx(n1)-t(i)
      u=abs(u)-eps
      if(u)5,4,4
5     at1(i)=0.
      dimit(i)=0.
      go to 110
4     at1(i)=at2(i)
      dimit(i)=t(i)-ctx(n1)
      go to 110
3     do 6 j=n1,n2
      u=ctx(j)-t(i)
      u=abs(u)-eps
      at2(i)=(cty(j+1)-cty(j))/(ctx(j+1)-ctx(j))
      if(u)8,7,7
7     u=ctx(j+1)-t(i)-eps/2.
      if(u)30,30,9
30    nn=n2-j
      if(nn)6,31,6
31    at1(i)=at2(i)
      dimit(i)=t(i)-ctx(j)
      go to 12
9     at1(i)=at2(i)
      dimit(i)=t(i)-ctx(j)
      dimat(i)=ctx(j+1)-t(i)
      go to 110
8     nn=n1-j
      if(nn)11,10,11
10    at1(i)=0.
      dimit(i)=0.
      dimat(i)=ctx(j+1)-t(i)
      go to 110
11    at1(i)=(cty(j)-cty(j-1))/(ctx(j)-ctx(j-1))
      dimit(i)=t(i)-ctx(j-1)
      nn=n2-j
      if(nn)13,12,13
12    dimat(i)=s+eps
      goto 110
13    dimat(i)=ctx(j+1)-t(i)
      go to 110
6     continue
110   continue
      return
      end
```

IV - 4. FUNCTION cost

```
      function cost(ms,ns,csx,csy,ml,nl,clx,cly,y,v,n)
      dimension ms(1),ns(1),csx(1),csy(1),ml(1),nl(1),clx(1)
      dimension cly(1),y(1),v(1)
      s=0.
      do 1 i=1,n
      k=ms(i)
      nn=k-1
      if(nn)2,8,2
 2    n1=ns(nn)+1
      go to 3
 8    n1=1
 3    n2=ns(k)-1
      do 4 j=n1,n2
      u1=y(i)-csx(j)
      u2=csx(j+1)-y(i)
      w=u1*u2
      if(w)5,6,6
 6    c=u1*csy(j+1)
      c=c+u2*csy(j)
      c=c/(u1+u2)
      s=s+c
      go to 7
 5    ii=n2-j
      if(ii)4,6,4
 4    continue
 7    k=ml(i)
      nn=k-1
      if(nn)11,15,11
 11   n1=nl(nn)+1
      go to 10
 15   n1=1
 10   n2=nl(k)-1
      do 12 j=n1,n2
      u1=v(i)-clx(j)
      u2=clx(j+1)-v(i)
      w=u1*u2
      if(w)13,14,14
 14   c=u1*cly(j+1)
      c=c+u2*cly(j)
      c=c/(u1+u2)
      s=s+c
      go to 1
 13   ii=n2-j
      if(ii)12,14,12
 12   continue
 1    continue
      cost=s
      return
      end
```

Remark 7.1

The programs presented here can be run on a micro-computer. Unfortunatly, the number of computations depends on the number of definition points for the cost functions, and therefore can be very large in some cases. In order to deal with such situations, the reader may modify conco in the following way :

1 - add a parameter, say MZ, to the string of the existing parameters

2 - initialize mzi = 0 after the last dimension of conco

3 - replace in conco :

```
53 do 54 i = 2, nl
```

by

```
53 mzi = mzi + 1
   if (mzi.gt.mz) go to 57
   do 54 i = 2, nl
```

The computation will then stop after mz loops, if the optimal solution is not obtained before. Of course, the outputs of the software may be different from the optimal solution in that case.

V - EXAMPLE

```
Code=   0
            Number of periods:      8
            *****************


      Initial inventory level:   0.1500000E+02
      *******************


                   Demand
                   ******


End of the    1-th period:    0.8000000E+01
End of the    2-th period:    0.5000000E+01
End of the    3-th period:    0.1600000E+02
End of the    4-th period:    0.2000000E+01
End of the    5-th period:    0.8000000E+01
End of the    6-th period:    0.1100000E+02
End of the    7-th period:    0.3000000E+01
End of the    8-th period:    0.5000000E+01
```

```
          Production cost functions
          ++++++++++++++++++++++++++


   1-th production cost function:

x=     0.00  y=     1.00     x=     5.00  y=     2.00     x=    12.00  y=     8.00
x=    13.00  y=    18.00

Applicable to periods:
   1    2    3    4    5


   2-th production cost function:

x=     0.00  y=     0.00     x=     2.00  y=     2.00

Applicable to periods:
   6    7    8



          Inventory cost functions
          ++++++++++++++++++++++++


   1-th inventory cost function:

x=     0.00  y=     0.00     x=     2.00  y=     2.00     x=     6.00  y=    16.00

Applicable to periods:
   1    2    3


   2-th inventory cost function:

x=     0.00  y=     0.00     x=    12.00  y=     1.00

Applicable to periods:
   4    5    6    7    8



********************************************************************************
        Optimal total cost:    0.1092333E+03
        ------------


          Optimal control
          ---------------


At the end of the   1 -th period: 0.0000000E+00
At the end of the   2 -th period: 0.2000000E+01
At the end of the   3 -th period: 0.1200000E+02
At the end of the   4 -th period: 0.5000000E+01
At the end of the   5 -th period: 0.1200000E+02
At the end of the   6 -th period: 0.4000000E+01
At the end of the   7 -th period: 0.3000000E+01
At the end of the   8 -th period: 0.5000000E+01
```

Optimal inventory levels

```
Inventory level during the   1-th period:    0.1500000E+02
Inventory level during the   2-th period:    0.7000000E+01
Inventory level during the   3-th period:    0.4000000E+01
Inventory level during the   4-th period:    0.0000000E+00
Inventory level during the   5-th period:    0.3000000E+01
Inventory level during the   6-th period:    0.7000000E+01
Inventory level during the   7-th period:    0.0000000E+00
Inventory level during the   8-th period:    0.0000000E+00
Inventory level during the   9-th period:    0.0000000E+00
```

MATHEMATICAL APPENDIX

INTRODUCTION

We review in this appendix the mathematical concepts which are used in the book, mostly in Chapters III and IV, and which may not be familiar to the readers.

Some notions of measure theory, functional analysis, as well as probability theory are necessary, especially for continuous time models.

It must be clear that this appendix is not sufficient by itself. In particular, no proofs are included. But given all the results stated in this appendix, the chapters of the text become self contained. The reader interested in the proofs or developments of the mathematical results stated in this review, will find easily extended material in the classical text books mentioned in the bibliography.
On the other hand this appendix may be used as a guide for those who desire to strenghten their mathematical expertise in areas related to production management, in order to go further into current research.

I - MEASURE THEORY

I - 1. MEASURABLE SPACES

Let E be a set. A σ-algebra A on E is a set of subsets of E satisfying the following properties :

a) $E \in A$

b) if $A \in A$ then A^c (complement of A in E) $\in A$

c) if $A_i \in A$, where $i \in I$ (countable set of indices) then $\bigcap_i A_i$ and $\bigcup_i A_i$ belong to A.

The pair (E,A) is called a measurable space. The elements of A are called the measurable sets.

Note that $P(E)$ the set of all subsets of E and $(E,\emptyset)$ are σ-algebras.

Any intersection of σ-algebras on E is also a σ-algebra on E.

If C is a set of subsets of E (not necessarily a σ-algebra) we can define the smallest σ-algebra on E which contains C. It is denoted by $\tau(C)$ and called the σ-algebra generated by C.

I - 2. BOREL σ-algebra

If E is a topological space, i.e., a set where the concepts of open and closed sets are defined, then the σ-algebra generated by the open sets plays a fundamental role and is called the Borel σ-algebra on E. The elements of the Borel σ-algebra are called the Borel sets.

If $E = R^n$, the Borel σ-algebra denoted by R^n is also generated by the following class

$$C = \{ \prod_{i=1}^{n} (a_i, b_i), \quad -\infty < a_i < b_i < \infty\}$$

I - 3. MEASURABLE FUNCTIONS. BOREL FUNCTIONS

Let E, E' be two sets and suppose that (E', A') is a measurable space. Let g be a map from E into E'. The set

$$g^{-1}(A') = \{g^{-1}(A') \ ; \ A' \in A'\}$$

is a σ-algebra on E.

If (E,A), (E',A') are two measurable spaces, a map $g : E \to E'$ is measurable if

$$g^{-1}(A') \subset A.$$

If A, A' are Borel σ-algebras, then g is said Borel, instead of measurable.

In practice it may be difficult to check whether a map is measurable or not. However, the following key result is the main tool in that respect. The map $g : E \to E'$ is measurable if there exists a class C' of subsets of E', which generates A', whose reciprocal image

$$g^{-1}(C') = \{g^{-1}(C') \ : \ C' \in C'\}$$

is contained in A.

For instance, if $f : (E,A) \to R$, then it is measurable provided that $\{f < a\} \in A$, $\forall a \in R$.

The measurability is a transitive property : the composition of two measurable maps is also measurable (like the composition of continuous functions is continuous).

If E, E' are topological spaces and A, A' are the corresponding Borel σ-algebras, then continuous functions from E into E' are Borel. But the class of Borel functions is much larger.

Let E be a set and E_i, A_i, $i \in I$ an arbitrary family of measurable spaces. Let f_i, $i \in I$ be maps from E into E_i.

The σ-algebra on E generated by $\bigcup_i f_i^{-1}(A_i)$ is the smallest σ-algebra on E for which all maps f_i are measurable. It is called the σ-algebra generated by the family f_i, and noted $\sigma(f_i, i \in I)$.

I - 4. PRODUCT OF MEASURABLE SPACES

Let (E_m, A_m), $m = 1, \ldots, n$ be n measurable spaces. We define the product σ-algebra $\bigotimes_1^n A_m$ on $\prod_1^n E_m$ as the σ-algebra generated by the class

$$\prod_1^n \mathcal{A}_m = \{\prod_1^n A_m \; ; \; A_m \in \mathcal{A}_m\}.$$

If C_m generates $\mathcal{A}_m$, then $\bigotimes_1^n \mathcal{A}_m$ is also generated by

$$\prod_1^n C_m = \{\prod_1^n C_m \; ; \; C_m \in C_m\}.$$

We can prove that $\bigotimes_1^n \mathcal{A}_m$ is also the smallest σ-algebra on $\prod_1^n E_m$ generated by the coordinate maps $X_i : \prod_1^n E_m \to E_i$.

I - 5. POSITIVE MEASURES

Let $(E,\mathcal{A})$ be a measurable space. A positive measure m on $(E,\mathcal{A})$ is a map from $\mathcal{A}$ into $[0,\infty)$, which satisfies the property of σ-additivity

$$m(\bigcup_i A_i) = \sum_i m(A_i)$$

for any countable family of measurable sets A_i, such that $A_i \cap A_j = \emptyset$ if $i \neq j$.

The Lebesgue measure on $(R^n, \mathcal{R}^n)$ is probably the most important positive measure, since it is the (unique) positive measure on $(R^n, \mathcal{R}^n)$, such that :

$$m_o(\prod_1^n |a_i,b_i|) = \prod_1^n (b_i-a_i) \tag{1.1}$$

where $|a_i,b_i|$ denotes a bounded interval, $a_i < b_i$, which can be open, closed, or semi-open.

Let us give some elementary properties of positive measures. We have :

$$\begin{cases} m(B) \leq m(A) \text{ if } B \subset A \\ m(\emptyset) = 0 \\ m(\bigcup_i A_i) \leq \sum_i m(A_i) \end{cases} \tag{1.2}$$

for any countable family of measurable sets.

$$\begin{cases} \text{If } A_1 \subset A_2 \subset \ldots \text{ is an increasing family of measurable sets, then :} \\ m(\bigcup_n A_n) = \lim_{n\to\infty} m(A_n) \end{cases} \tag{1.3}$$

The introduction of a measure on a measurable space permits to extend the concept of measurable sets and measurable functions. Let $(E,\mathcal{A},m)$ where m is a positive measure. We define $\mathcal{A}_m$, called the σ-algebra of m measurable sets as follows

$$\begin{cases} B \subset E \text{ is an element of } \mathcal{A}_m \text{ if there exist } A_1, A_2 \in \mathcal{A} \text{ such that} \\ A_1 \subset B \subset A_2 \text{ and } m(A_2 - A_1) = 0. \end{cases} \tag{1.4}$$

Consider $(E,\mathcal{A},m)$ and $(E',\mathcal{A}')$, then a map $g : E \to E'$ is $(m, \mathcal{A}')$ measurable, (or simply m-measurable if E' is a topological space and $\mathcal{A}'$ is the Borel σ-algebra), if g is measurable in the sense of $(E,\mathcal{A}_m)$, $(E', \mathcal{A}')$. In particular $f : (E,\mathcal{A},m) \to R$ is m-measurable if and only if there exist f_1, f_2 measurable (i.e. $\mathcal{A}$ measurable) such that

$$(1.5)\qquad \begin{cases} f_1 \le f \le f_2 \\ f_1 = f_2 \text{ except on a set of m measure 0.} \end{cases}$$

A subset of E is negligeable if it is contained in a measurable set of m measure 0.

Clearly, the σ-algebra A_m is generated by A and the negligeable sets.

We say that a property holds almost everywhere (in short a.e. or more precisely m a.e) if it holds except on a negligeable set.

The measure m extends from A to A_m, by setting (cf. (1.4))

$$m(B) = m(A_1) = m(A_2), \quad \forall B \in A_m.$$

In the case where $E = R^n$, $A = R^n$ and m_o = Lebesgue measure, then the m_o-measurable functions are called (Lebesgue) measurable functions.

I - 6. PROPERTIES OF REAL MEASURABLE FUNCTIONS

Let (E,A) be a measurable space, and let f_n be a sequence of real measurable functions, then $\underline{\lim}\, f_n(x)$, $\overline{\lim}\, f_n(x)$ are measurable. In particular, if $f(x) = \lim f_n(x)$ then f(x) is measurable.

The concept of a.e. convergence becomes very important when there is a measure m on (E,A). The sequence f_n is said to converge a.e. if the set of points where f_n does not converge is negligeable. We define a.e. lim f_n as any m measurable function f such that

$$f_n(x) \to f(x) \quad \text{a.e.}$$

In fact, a.e. convergence is an equivalence class concept, since we do not distinguish between the limit functions (they may differ on negligeable sets).

Let us consider a Lebesgue measurable real function f(x) on R^n. Then it satisfies the property of Lusin, namely for any compact K of R^n and any $\varepsilon > 0$, there exists a compact $K_\varepsilon \subset K$ such that $m_o(K-K_\varepsilon) \le \varepsilon$ and the restriction of f to K_ε is continuous.

By this property a Lebesgue measurable function is not too far from being continuous. Nevertheless, this property is extremely general and satisfied by most functions in practice. For a general measurable function, a piecewise constant function is a good approximation. A piecewise constant function $f : E \to R$ is a function which takes only a finite number of values. If (E,A) is a measurable space, a piecewise constant function is measurable if and only if $\{f = a\} \in A$, where a spans the set of values of f.

Any measurable positive function on (E,A) is the limit of (at least) one increasing sequence of positive measurable piecewise constant functions.

II - INTEGRATION - LEBESGUE INTEGRAL

II - 1. INTEGRATION WITH RESPECT TO A MEASURE

Let (E,A,m) be a measurable space where m is a positive measure. Let f be a positive measurable piecewise constant function. Now, define the integral :

$$\int f\, dm = \sum_{a \in f(E)} a\, m(\{f = a\}) \qquad (^1)$$

If $E = R^n$, $A = \mathcal{R}^n$, $m = m_0$ the Lebesgue measure, we use the notation $\int f(x)dx$.

If f is any positive measurable function, then we can consider increasing sequences of positive measurable piecewise constant functions f_n converging to f. The sequence $\int f_n\, dm$ converges to a limit which does not depend on the particular sequence. This limit is called the integral of f with respect to the measure m, and is denoted $\int f\, dm$. The main properties of this integral are the following :

(2.1) $\begin{cases} \text{if } f \le g, \text{ then } \int f\, dm \le \int g\, dm \;; \\ \text{if } f_n \text{ is an increasing family of positive measure functions, then} \\ \int (\lim \uparrow f_n) dm = \lim \uparrow \int f_n\, dm. \end{cases}$

(2.2) $\int \sum_n f_n\, dm = \sum_n \int f_n\, dm.$

(2.3) $\int (\underline{\lim}_{n\to\infty} f_n) dm \le \underline{\lim}_{n\to\infty} \int f_n\, dm$ for any sequence of positive measurable functions.

This last property is known as the Fatou's inequality.

II - 2. INTEGRABLE FUNCTIONS

A positive measurable function on (E,A,m) is integrable if the integral $\int f\, dm$ is finite.

A real measurable function is integrable if $|f|$ is integrable. We define :

$$\int f\, dm = \int f^+\, dm - \int f^-\, dm.$$

The following property is satisfied :

(2.4) $\int |f|\, dm = 0$ if and only if $f = 0$ a.e.

Therefore the integral extends to m-measurable functions.

Lebesgue's theorem constitutes the most useful result of the integrable functions theory : if f_n is a sequence of real measurable functions such that

$$|f_n| \le g \quad \text{a.e.} \quad \text{with } \int g\, dm < \infty$$

then, the functions f_n and a.e. lim f_n are integrable and we have :

(2.5) $\int \text{a.e.} \lim f_n\, dm = \lim \int f_n\, dm.$

Since the integrals of two functions which are almost everywhere equal are the same, the left hand side of (2.5) is uniquely defined.

----

(1) This integral may take the value $+\infty$.

Lebesgue's Theorem is, in practice, a very powerful tool which does not hold for the classical Riemann integral. Note that the integral considered above (called the Lebesgue's integral) is more general than the Riemann's integral. Each time the latter is defined, the former is also defined and the values coïncide.

II - 3. RADON MEASURES ON R^n

Let m be a positive measure on $(R^n, \mathcal{R}^n)$. It is easy to check that the space of real functions which are m integrable, is a vector space, denoted by $L^1(R^n\,;\,m)$. The integral defines a linear positive form on this vector space.

If m is finite on bounded Borel sets, then the continuous functions on R^n which vanish outside a compact set, belong to $L^1(R^n\,;\,m)$. Let us denote by $C_K(R^n)$ this set. Hence, the integral also defines a linear positive form on $C_K(R^n)$. Therefore we see that it corresponds a linear positive form on $C_K(R^n)$ (through the integral), to any positive measure on $(R^n, \mathcal{R}^n)$ which is finite on bounded Borel sets. The reverse property, due to F. Riesz, is true. Namely, to any positive linear form μ on $C_K(R^n)$ corresponds a unique positive measure m on $(R^n, \mathcal{R}^n)$ which is finite on bounded Borel sets, and such that

$$\mu(f) = \int f\, dm\,,\ \forall f \in C_K(R^n). \tag{2.6}$$

The linear positive forms on $C_K(R^n)$ are called Radon measures. Therefore Riesz' Theorem asserts there is a one to one correspondance between Radon measures and positive measures on $(R^n, \mathcal{R}^n)$ which are finite on bounded Borel sets.

This result is fundamental. As a matter of fact it is easy to construct linear positive forms on $C_K(R^n)$. For instance, the Riemann integral defines a linear positive form on $C_K(R^n)$. It can be shown that the corresponding positive measure on $(R^n, \mathcal{R}^n)$ is Lebesgue measure.

By extension any positive measure on $(R^n, \mathcal{R}^n)$ which is finite on bounded Borel sets is called a Radon measure.

In the case of functions on $(R, \mathcal{R})$, Radon measures can be characterized in a unique way by the concept of primitive.

If m is a Radon measure on $(R, \mathcal{R})$ a primitive of m is any function F such that

$$m((x,y]) = F(y) - F(x).$$

A possible primitive is

$$F_0(z) = \begin{cases} m((0,z\,)\ \text{if}\ z > 0 \\ -\ m\ ((z,0])\ \text{if}\ z \le 0 \end{cases}$$

and all primitives differ just by additive constants. Then, the following result can be shown : the primitives of a positive Radon measure on R are increasing, right continuous functions with left limits. Conversely, any increasing right continuous function (with left limits) is the primitive of a positive Radon measure which is uniquely defined.

II - 4. RADON NOKODYM DERIVATIVES

Let (E,A,m) be a measurable space provided with a positive measure m. We assume that m is σ-finite, i.e. there exists an increasing sequence A_n, $n \in N$, in A such that $E = \bigcup_n A_n$, and $m(A_n) < \infty$, $\forall n$. The measure m is finite if $m(E) < \infty$.

For instance the Lebesgue measure on (R^n, R^n) is σ-finite, but the Lebesgue measure on R^n is not.

Let f be a positive m-measurable function, and define the new measure denoted by fm :

$$fm(A) = \int_A f \, dm = \int f\chi_A \, dm \tag{2.7}$$

where χ_A is the characteristic function of the set A.

We say that f is the Radon Nikodym derivative of fm with respect to the measure m. This concept, again, is more that of an equivalence class, since f can be replaced by any function which is a.e. equal to it.

Generalizing slightly the concept of integrable function, we say that f is locally integrable, if fm is σ-finite. For instance, bounded (Lebesgue) measurable functions on R^n are locally integrable. Note the formula :

$$\int g \, d(fm) = \int g \, f \, dm$$

Let μ and ν be two positive σ-finite measures on (E,A). Then, there exists a function $f \geq 0$ locally μ integrable, such that

$$\nu = f\mu$$

if and only if a negligeable set with respect to μ is also negligeable with respect to ν.

II - 5. LEBESGUE POINTS. LEBESGUE SETS

Consider a space (E,A,m) where m is a positive σ-finite measure. Let f be a m locally integrable function. The Lebesgue points of f satisfy

$$\frac{1}{m(A)} \int_A |f(y) - f(x)| \, dm(y) \to 0$$

as m(A) tends to 0.

The Lebesgue set is the set of Lebesgue points. Clearly continuity points are Lebesgue points. But the Lebesgue set contains many other points ; as a matter of fact the set of non Lebesgue points is of measure 0.

II - 6. PRODUCT MEASURES. FUBINI'S THEOREM

Let (E_1,A_1,m_1), (E_2,A_2,m_2) be two measurable spaces provided with σ-finite measures. We can define in a unique way a measure on $E_1 \times E_2$, $A_1 \otimes A_2$, denoted $m_1 \otimes m_2$ and called the product measure, such that

$$m_1 \otimes m_2 \, (A_1 \times A_2) = m_1(A_1) \, m_2(A_2), \ \forall A_1 \in A_1, \ A_2 \in A_2.$$

Consider a function $f(x_1,x_2)$ which is positive and measurable with respect to the product measure. Let us set

$$F_1(x_1) = \int_{E_2} f(x_1,x_2)\, dm_2(x_2)$$

$$F_2(x_2) = \int_{E_1} f(x_1,x_2)\, dm_1(x_1).$$

These functions are respectively m_1 and m_2 measurable.

Moreover the following property (Fubini's Theorem) holds :

$$\int_{E_1 \times E_2} f\, d(m_1 \otimes m_2) = \int_{E_1} F_1(x_1)\, dm_1(x_1) = \int_{E_2} F_2(x_2)\, dm_2(x_2).$$

Let g be a real $m_1 \otimes m_2$ measurable function. The function g is $m_1 \otimes m_2$ integrable if and only if the function $\int_{E_2} |g(x_1,x_2)|\, dm_2(x_2)$ is m_1 integrable, or the function $\int_{E_1} |g(x_1,x_2)|\, dm_1(x_1)$ is m_2 integrable. Then $g(x_1,.)$ is m_2 integrable, for m_1 a.e. point x_1, and $g(.,x_2)$ is m_1 integrable for m_2 a.e. point x_2. In addition $\int_{E_2} g(.,x_2)\, dm_2(x_2)$ is m_1 integrable. The symetrical property holds when x_2 is changed in x_1, and the above Fubini relations are satisfied.

III - TOPOLOGICAL SPACES

III - 1. METRIC SPACES - FRECHET SPACES

Let E be a set. A map $d : E \times E \to R^+$ is called a distance on E if the following properties hold

$$d(x,x) = 0 , \qquad d(x_1,x_2) = 0 \Longrightarrow x_1 = x_2$$

$$d(x_1,x_3) \leq d(x_1,x_2) + d(x_2,x_3)$$

A set where a distance is defined, is called a metric space. A Cauchy sequence is a sequence $x_n \in E$ such that :

$$d(x_n,x_m) \to 0, \; n,m \to \infty.$$

Clearly, any converging sequence is a Cauchy sequence. When the converse is true for any Cauchy sequence, the space is called a complete metric space.

A vector space which is a complete metric space is called a Frechet space.

III - 2. BANACH AND HILBERT SPACES

Let E be a vector space. A norm on E is a mapping from $E \to R^+$, $x \to ||x||$ such that

$$||x|| = 0 \quad \Longrightarrow \quad x = 0$$

$$||x_1 + x_2|| \leq ||x_1|| + ||x_2||$$

$$||\lambda x|| = |\lambda| \; ||x||$$

A vector space for which there exists a norm is called a normed vector space. It is a metric space with the distance

$$d(x_1,x_2) = ||x_1 - x_2||$$

A normed vector space which is complete is called a Banach space.

A scalar product on E is a mapping from $E \times E \to R$ denoted (x_1,x_2) (or $((x_1,x_2))$) such that

$$(x_1,x_2+x_3) = (x_1,x_2) + (x_1,x_3)$$

$$(x_1,x_2) = (x_2,x_1)$$

$$(\lambda x_1,x_2) = \lambda(x_1,x_2)$$

$$(x,x) \geq 0, \; (x,x) = 0 \Longrightarrow x = 0$$

A scalar product defines a norm on E by setting

$$||x|| = (x,x)^{1/2}.$$

A Banach space whose norm is defined by a scalar product is called a Hilbert space.

III - 3. FUNCTIONAL SPACES

The most important examples of Banach and Hilbert spaces are functional spaces.

Let (E,A,m) be a measurable space with a positive measure. Consider the equivalence classes of functions which are m integrable (two functions are equivalent when they are equal a.e. for the measure m). Then the quantity

$$||f||_1 = \int |f| \; dm \tag{3.1}$$

depends only of the equivalence class. It defines a norm on the vector space of the equivalence classes which is denoted by $L^1(E,A,m)$.

The space L^1 provided with the norm (3.1) is a Banach space.

More generally consider the vector space of equivalence classes, such that

$$||f||_p = (\int |f|^p \; dm)^{1/p} \quad , \infty > p \geq 1 \tag{3.2}$$

is finite. The quantity (3.2) is a norm on this vector space, and the latter is a Banach space for the norm (3.2). It is denoted by $L^p(E,A,m)$.

The case where $p = 2$ is particularly interesting since the norm $|| \; ||_2$ is derived from the scalar product :

$$(f,g) = \int f \; g \; dm.$$

Let E be a metric space (or more generally a topological space). The set of continuous bounded functions on E, is a Banach space for the norm

$$||f|| = \sup_x |f(x)|.$$

It is denoted by C(E).

Consider (E, A, m) a measurable space with a positive measure m ; then the space $L^{\infty}(E,A,m)$ of m measurable functions which are bounded, except on a negligeable set, is a Banach space for the norm

$$||f||_{L^{\infty}} = \text{ess.sup}\ |f(x)|$$

where ess.sup means all points except the set (of measure 0) where f is unbounded.

If (E,A) is a measurable space (without measure), the vector space of bounded measurable functions is a Banach space for the norm

$$||f|| = \sup_{x} |f(x)|$$

This space is denoted by B(E).

In a similar way, we can define functional spaces of functions which are unbounded, but with a prescribed growth. For instance we shall use the spaces B_1, C_1.

Suppose that E is a normed vector space, let us consider the functions f such that

$$||f||_1 = \sup \frac{|f(x)|}{1+|x|}$$

is finite. The corresponding vector space is a Banach space for the norm $||f||_1$.

The subspace of continuous (or uniformly continuous) functions is also a Banach space for the same norm.

IV - SPACES IN DUALITY

IV - 1. DUAL OF BANACH AND HILBERT SPACES

Let E be a Banach space and E^* the set of linear continuous functions on E. Denote

(4.1) $$e_*(e) = \langle e_*, e\rangle ,$$

if $e_* \in E^*$, where the symbol < , > is called a duality product.

The space E^* is also a Banach space for the norm

$$||e_*|| = \sup_{e \neq 0} \frac{|\langle e_*, e\rangle|}{||e||}$$

More generally, let E,F be two Banach spaces, and denote by $L(E\ ;\ F)$ the space of linear continuous maps from E to F. $L(E\ ;\ F)$ is a Banach space for the norm

$$||L|| = \sup_{e \neq 0} \frac{||L(e)||_F}{||e||_E}$$

If E is a Hilbert space, then E^* is also a Hilbert space. This follows from a theorem due to Riesz : To any $e_* \in E^*$ corresponds in a unique way an element $\bar{e}$ in E such that

$$\langle e_*, e \rangle = (\bar{e}, e).$$

The map $e_* \to \bar{e}$ is an isomorphism from which E^* can be identified to E.

IV - 2. DUAL OF FUNCTIONAL SPACES

The dual of $L^p(E,A,m)$ is $L^q(E,A,m)$ where $1 \le p,q < \infty$, and

$$\frac{1}{p} + \frac{1}{q} = 1.$$

Note that the dual of L^1 is L^∞, but the dual of L^∞ is larger than L^1.

Consider the space $C([0,T])$. We note that linear positive forms (i.e. Radon measures on $[0,T]$) are necessarily continuous functions on $C([0,T])$ (considered as a Banach space). Therefore Radon measures on $C([0,T])$ are elements of the dual of $C([0,T])$. Moreover as mentionned in § 2.3 the Radon measures are also defined uniquely by their primitives, which are increasing right continuous functions with left limits (defined up to an additive constant).

Therefore, if f_* is a positive element of the dual of $C([0,T])$ (i.e. $\langle f_*,f\rangle \ge 0$ wherever $f \ge 0$), then there exists a unique function $f_*(t)$, increasing, continuous to the right, with left limits, defined up to an additive constant such that

$$\begin{aligned}\langle f_*,f\rangle &= \int_0^T f\, df_* \\ &= \lim \sum_{i=0}^{N-1} f(t_i)[f_*(t_{i+1}) - f_*(t_i)]\end{aligned}$$

where $t_0 = 0 < t_1 < \dots < t_N = T$ is a splitting of $[0,T]$ such that

$$\max(t_{i+1} - t_i) \to 0.$$

Since f_* is defined up to an additive constant, we can <u>standardize</u> f_* by setting $f_*(0) = 0$, in which case $f_* \ge 0$.

This result can be generalized, as follows, to represent all elements of the dual of $C([0,T])$ (non necessarily ≥ 0). If f_* belongs to the dual of $C([0,T])$, there exists a function $f_*(t)$ with bounded variations, right continuous, with left limits, such that $f_*(0) = 0$, and

$$\begin{aligned}\langle f_* , f \rangle &= \int_0^T f\, df_* \\ &= \lim \sum_{i=0}^{N-1} f(t_i)\, [f_*(t_{i+1}) - f_*(t_i)]\end{aligned}$$

Note that a function with bounded variations, is represented in a unique way as the difference of two increasing functions.

Hence f_* is the difference of two Radon measures.

IV - 3. STRONG AND WEAK CONVERGENCE IN BANACH SPACES

Let E be a Banach space and e_n a sequence in E. We say that $e_n \to e$ <u>strongly</u> if

$$||e_n - e|| \to 0 \quad \text{as } n \to \infty.$$

We say that $e_n \to e$ <u>weakly</u> if

$$\langle e_*, e_n\rangle \to \langle e_*, e\rangle\ , \quad \forall e_* \in E^*.$$

Let now e_*^n be a sequence in E^*(which is also a Banach space). Besides the concept of weak convergence in E^*(defined as above) one can define the concept of weak star convergence as follows. We say that

$$e_*^n \to e_* \quad \text{weakly star}$$

if

$$\langle e_*^n, e\rangle \to \langle e_*, e\rangle\ , \quad \forall e \in E.$$

Note that E^{**} (dual of E^* = bidual of E) contains E but, generally, is different from E. Therefore the weak star convergence is different from the weak convergence. It is a weaker concept in the sense that if a sequence e_*^n converges to e_* weakly star, it also converges weakly. If $E^{**} = E$, we say that E is a reflexive Banach space. Then weak and weak star convergences coïncide.

In particular a Hilbert space is reflexive. The spaces $L^p(E,A,m)$, $1 < p < \infty$ are reflexive, whereas L^1 is not.

V - DISTRIBUTIONS AND WEAK DERIVATIVES

V - 1. DISTRIBUTION

Consider the open interval (0,T). We denote by D((0,T)) the vector space of functions $\phi(t)$ which are infinitely differentiable with compact support on (0,T) (ϕ and all derivatives vanish outside a compact interval included in (0,T)). Let ϕ_n be a sequence of elements of D((0,T)). We say that

$$\phi_n \to \phi \quad \text{in} \quad D((0,T))$$

if the following condition holds :

$$\begin{cases} \text{all } \phi_n \text{ have the same compact support K on (0,T) and} \\ \sup\limits_{t \in K} \left|\dfrac{d^m}{dt^m}(\phi_n - \phi)\right| \to 0,\ \forall m = 0, 1, \ldots \end{cases}$$

A linear functional $T(\phi)$ on D((0,T)) is said to be continuous if $T(\phi_n) \to T(\phi)$ whenever $\phi_n \to \phi$ in the above sense.

A linear continuous functional on D((0,T)) is called a distribution. To illustrate, consider a real function f which is integrable with respect to the Lebesgue measure on (0,T), then

$$T_f(\phi) = \int_0^T f(t)\ \phi(t)dt$$

defines a distribution (in a unique way). It is convenient to identify T_f to f. Distributions appear as generalized functions. Clearly a Radon measure on (0,T) defines a distribution by the formula

$$T_m(\phi) = \int_0^T \phi(t)\ dm(t).$$

Since ϕ vanishes at 0 and T , the Radon measures on (0,T) or [0,T] define the same distribution.

V - 2. DERIVATIVE OF A DISTRIBUTION

Let T be a distribution. The derivative of T is the distribution denoted T' and defined as follows :

$$T'(\phi) = - T(\phi'), \quad \forall\phi \in D((0,T)).$$

As a consequence, any function f which may not be differentiable in the usual sense, can have a distribution derivative.

V - 3. SOBOLEV SPACES

Let $f \in L^2(0,T)$. Consider its distribution derivative f', which is generally not a function. Nethertheless, if there exists $g \in L^2(0,T)$ such that

$$\int_0^T g(t)\ \phi(t)dt = - \int_0^T f(t)\ \phi'(t)dt$$

then we have

$$g = f'$$

and we say that the distribution derivative of f is an element of $L^2(0,T)$. Define

$$H^1(0,T) = \{f \in L^2(0,T)\ |\ f' \in L^2(0,T)\}.$$

The space H^1 is a Sobolev space. It is a Hilbert space for the scalar product

$$||f||^2_{H^1} = |f|^2_{L^2} + |f'|^2_{L^2}.$$

Note that f is a.e. differentiable in the usual sense and its derivative coincides with f' up to a negligeable set.

Rademacher's theorem asserts that a Lipschitz function, i.e. a function f on R^n such that :

$$|f(x_1) - f(x_2)| \leq C|x_1 - x_2|$$

$\forall x_1, x_2 \in R$, where C is a constant, is a.e. differentiable in the usual sense. This is equivalent to saying that its distribution derivative belongs to L^∞.

VI - CONVEXITY

VI - 1. CONVEX FUNCTIONALS

First recall that if α_n is a sequence of real numbers, then :

$$\left\{ \underline{\lim}\ \alpha_n = \text{largest number such that there exists at most a finite number of elements } \alpha_n \text{ at its left.} \right.$$

A symmetric definition holds for $\overline{\lim}\ \alpha_n$. Let J be a functional on a reflexive Banach space E. We say that J is lower semi continuous l.s.c. if

$$e_n \to e \implies J(e) \leq \underline{\lim}\ J(e_n).$$

The functional J is weakly l.s.c. if

$$e_n \to e \text{ (weakly)} \implies J(e) \le \underline{\lim}\, J(e_n).$$

If J is weakly l.s.c., obviously it is also l.s.c. But the converse is not true in general. It is however true for <u>convex</u> functionals J, which satisfy the convexity property :

$$J(\theta e_1 + (1-\theta)e_2) \le \theta J(e_1) + (1-\theta)\, J(e_2) \;,$$

$$\forall e_1, e_2 \in B, \qquad \theta \in (0,1)$$

VI - 2. CONVEX SETS

A set A in a reflexive Banach space E is convex if

$$e_1, e_2 \in A \implies \theta e_1 + (1-\theta)\, e_2 \in A, \;\; \forall\theta \in (0,1)$$

The set A is <u>closed</u> if for any sequence $e_n \in A$ which converges towards e in E, then $e \in A$. The set A is <u>weakly closed</u> if for any sequence $e_n \in A$, which is weakly convergent towards e, than $e \in A$. A weakly closed set is obviously closed, but the reverse is not true in general, except for closed convex sets.

VI - 3. WEAK COMPACTNESS

In R^n the unit ball is a compact set. Therefore from any sequence in the unit ball we can extract a converging subsequence. This is no more true in Hilbert or Banach spaces.

However the following result is used frequently.

Let E^* be the dual of a Banach space E. Let e_*^n be a sequence in E^* such that $||e_*^n||_{E^*} \le 1$, then there exists a subsequence which is weakly star convergent, i.e. there exists e_* in E^* such that

$$\langle e_*^n, e\rangle \to \langle e_*, e\rangle \;\;, \forall e \in E.$$

In particular if E is a Hilbert space and if e_n is a sequence in the unit ball, there exists a weakly convergent subsequence.

VII - OPTIMIZATION

VII - 1. BASIC EXISTENCE THEOREM

Consider a functional J on a Hilbert space E, which is convex, l.s.c. and bounded from below. Then it attains its minimum over a convex closed bounded subset of E.

A l.s.c. function on R^n which is bounded below, attains its minimum on a bounded closed subset.

VII - 2. SELECTION THEOREMS

Let $J(x,v)$ be a function on $R^n \times R^m$, l.s.c., and bounded from below. Consider $\operatorname{Inf}_{v \in K} J(x,v)$, where K is a compact set, then from VII.1. the minimum is attained on a bounded subset of points, which depends on x.

The following important <u>selection theorem</u> holds, namely there exists a <u>Borel</u> map $\hat{v}(x)$ such that :

$$J(x, \hat{v}(x)) = \operatorname*{Inf}_{v \in K} J(x,v).$$

One can weaken the condition of lower semi continuity of both variables, by imposing Lebesgue measurability.

We assume that

- a.e. x, $J(x,.)$ is l.s.c. on K
- there exists a function $\tilde{J}$ which is globally Borel and such that a.e. x, $\tilde{J}(x,.) = J(x,.)$.

Then there exists a Lebesgue measurable function $\hat{v}(x)$ such that

$$\text{a.e. } x,\ J(x,\hat{v}(x)) = \operatorname*{Inf}_{v \in K} J(x,v)$$

VII - 3. LAGRANGE MULTIPLIERS

Derivations in optimal control theory require a sufficiently general result on optimization and Lagrange multipliers.

Let $J : \Phi \to R$ be a convex functional defined on a Hilbert space. Let now $B : \Phi \to \Psi$, where Ψ is a Banach space, on which is defined a cone of positive elements P. Let Φ_{ad} be a convex subset of Φ. Consider the following minimization problem :

$$(7.1) \qquad \begin{cases} \operatorname{Inf} J(g) \\ g \in \Phi_{ad},\ B(g) \le 0. \end{cases}$$

It is further assumed that the cone P has a non empty interior, denoted by $\{\psi \mid \psi > 0\}$, and that there exists $\bar{g} \in \Phi_{ad}$ such that

$$B(\bar{g}) < 0.$$

In addition B is supposed to be convex :

$$B(\theta g_1 + (1-\theta)g_2) \le \theta B(g_1) + (1-\theta)\, B(g_2).$$

Then, if $\hat{g}$ is a solution of (7.1), there exists $\hat{\psi}_*$ in Ψ^* (the dual of Ψ), such that

$$\hat{\psi}_* \ge 0$$

$$J(g) + \langle \hat{\psi}_*, B(g) \rangle \ge J(\hat{g}),\ \forall g \in \Phi_{ad}$$

We shall apply this result in Chapter III for the case $\Psi = C(0,T)$.

VIII - PROBABILITY

VIII - 1. PROBABILITY SPACE

Let (Ω,A,P) be a measurable space with a positive finite measure P. It is a probability when

$$P(\Omega) = 1$$

and (Ω,A,P) is called a probability space.

In the language of probability theory, the points of Ω are called the <u>elementary events</u>, and the elements of A the <u>events.</u>

A measurable mapping with values in R^n is called a <u>random variable</u>.

VIII - 2. CONDITIONAL EXPECTATION

Let $\xi = \xi(\omega)$ be a random variable, such that $\xi \in L^1(\Omega,A,P)$, then :

$$E\xi = \int \xi dP$$

is called the expectation of ξ. Let $\mathcal{B}$ be a sub σ-algebra of A(i.e. a set of subsets of Ω which belong to A and form a σ-algebra).

The conditional expectation $E^{\mathcal{B}}\xi$ is the unique element of $L^1(\Omega,\mathcal{B},P)$ such that :

$$E\, E^{\mathcal{B}}\xi\eta = E\xi\eta \quad , \quad \forall\eta \text{ bounded and } \mathcal{B} \text{ measurable.} \tag{8.1}$$

An important rule for computing conditional expectations is given in Chapter III, § 1.3.

REFERENCES

DIEUDONNE J., [1963] , Fondements de l'Analyse Moderne, Gauthier Villars.

DUNFORD N. - SCHWARTZ J.T., [1958] , Linear Operators, Interscience.

EKELAND I. - TEMAN R., [1974] , Analyse convexe et problèmes variationnels, Dunod, Paris.

LOEVE M., [1961] , Probability Theory. Van Nostrand.

NEVEU J., [1964] , Calcul des probabilités, Masson.

SCHWARTZ L., [1973] , Théorie des distributions, Hermann.

YOSIDA K., [1965] , Functional analysis, Springer Verlag.